Indian Administration

Indian Administration

Evolution and Practice

Bidyut Chakrabarty

Faculty, Department of Political Science, University of Delhi

and

Prakash Chand

Faculty, Department of Political Science, Dyal Singh (E) College, University of Delhi

SAGE | TEXTS

www.sagepublishing.com

Los Angeles | London | New Delhi | Singapore | Washington DC | Melbourne

First published in 2016 by

SAGE | TEXTS

SAGE Publications India Pvt Ltd
B1/I-1 Mohan Cooperative Industrial Area
Mathura Road, New Delhi 110 044, India
www.sagepub.in

SAGE Publications Inc
2455 Teller Road
Thousand Oaks, California 91320, USA

SAGE Publications Ltd
1 Oliver 's Yard, 55 City Road
London EC1Y 1SP, United Kingdom

SAGE Publications Asia-Pacific Pte Ltd
3 Church Street
#10-04 Samsung Hub
Singapore 049483

Published by Vivek Mehra for SAGE Publications India Pvt Ltd, typeset in ITC Stone Serif 9.5/11 pts by Diligent Typesetter India Pvt Ltd, Delhi and printed at Saurabh Printers Pvt Ltd, Greater Noida.

Library of Congress Cataloging-in-Publication Data Available

ISBN: 978-93-515-0733-8 (PB)

The SAGE Team: Amit Kumar, Indrani Dutta, Vandana Gupta and Rajinder Kaur

Dedicated to
our parents and teachers

BRIEF CONTENTS

LIST OF ILLUSTRATIONS xvii
PREFACE xix
ABOUT THE AUTHORS xxi

Introduction 1
1. Evolution of Indian Administration 17
2. Philosophical and Constitutional Framework of Indian Administration 40
3. Structure of Central Administration 63
4. State Administration 81
5. District Administration 95
6. Local Governance in India: Rural and Urban 108
7. Civil Services in India 131
8. Administrative Reforms in India 148
9. Public Policy in India 163
10. Planning and Economic Development in India 183
11. Financial Management in India 200
12. Citizens and Administration in India 224
13. Social Welfare Administration in India 243
14. Environmental Administration in India 265
15. Major Issues in Indian Administration 285
Part I – Conceptual Issues 285
Part II – Empirical Issues 314
Conclusion 337

BIBLIOGRAPHY B–1
INDEX I–1

DETAILED CONTENTS

LIST OF ILLUSTRATIONS xvii
PREFACE xix
ABOUT THE AUTHORS xxi

Introduction **1**

Chapter 1: Evolution of Indian Administration **17**
Kautilya (c. 350–283 BC) 18
Ziauddin Barani (1285–1357) 19
The Mughal Administration 20
  Conceptual Points 20
  Administrative Structure in the Mughal Era 21
The British Legacy in Indian Administration 24
  The Regulating Act, 1773 24
  The Charter Act, 1833 26
  The Act for the Good Government of India, 1858 27
  The Government of India Act, 1935 30
All India Civil Services and Public Administration 32
Concluding Observations 35

Chapter 2: Philosophical and Constitutional Framework of Indian Administration **40**
The Founding Principles of the Constitution 41
The Preamble 44
Fundamental Rights 46
Fundamental Duties 49
The Directive Principles of State Policy 49
Federalism 52
Parliamentary System 54
Amending Procedures 57
Concluding Observations 59

Chapter 3: Structure of Central Administration **63**
The Central Secretariat 63
  Evolution of the Central Secretariat 64
  The Role and Functions of the Central Secretariat 64
  Organizational Structure of the Secretariat 65
  Staffing Pattern at the Secretariat 67
  Sources of Placement 69
  The Central Secretariat Service (CSS) 69
  Expansion of the Secretariat 70
The Cabinet Secretariat 70
  Organization of the Cabinet Secretariat 72
  The Cabinet Secretary 72
  The Cabinet Committees 74

The Prime Minister's Office 75
The Attached and Subordinate Offices 76
The Boards and Commissions 77
Concluding Observations 79

Chapter 4: State Administration **81**
The Secretariat 81
The Chief Secretary 82
The Directorate as an Executive Agency 84
Pattern of Relationship between the Secretariat and the Directorates 85
The State Finance Commissions 86
The Fourth Finance Commission—Rajasthan (2010–15) 87
Recommendations 88
State Control over Local Governments 90
Institutional Control 91
Administrative Control 91
Financial Control 91
Judicial Control 91
Supervisory Control 92
Problem of Excessive Control and Issues of Conflict between State and Local Governments 92
Concluding Observations 93

Chapter 5: District Administration **95**
District Administration: Historical Continuity 95
British Intervention 96
District Administration in Post-independent India 96
Organization of the District Administration 97
District Collector: The Kingpin of District Administration 98
Changing Role of the District Collector 98
Role of the Collector in Independent India 99
Development Imperatives and Role of the District Administration 100
Democratic Decentralization and the Role of the Collector 101
The 73rd Amendment Act, 1992, and the Role of the Collector 102
New Patterns of Relationship between the Collector and the Panchayati Raj Institutions 102
The District Collector: Power and Functions 104
Revenue Administrator 104
Ensuring Law and Order 105
Chief Coordinator 105
Development Administrator 105
Crisis Administrator 105
Connecting Link between the State Government and PRIs 106
Concluding Observations 106

Chapter 6: Local Governance in India: Rural and Urban **108**
From Government to Local Governance 108
Decentralization: A Vehicle for Local Self-governance 110
The Concept 110
Main Characteristics of Decentralization 111
Significance of Decentralization 111
Democratic Decentralization 112

India's Journey to Local Governance 112
Local Governance: Post-independence Initiatives 113
  Balwantrai Mehta Committee (1957) 114
  Ashok Mehta Committee (1978) 115
Rural Local Governance 115
  Panchayati Raj Institutions (PRIs) 115
  The Seventy-third (73rd) Constitutional Amendment Act, 1992 115
  The Context 116
  Main Features of the 73rd Amendment Act 116
  Working of the Panchayati Raj System 117
  Weaknesses of the Panchayati Raj System 118
Urban Local Governance 119
  Structure 119
  Functions 120
  The 74th Amendment Act, 1992: Main Provisions 120
  Major Challenges for Urban Local Governance 121
Implications of the 73rd and 74th Amendment Acts 122
  Constitutional Status 122
  Administrative Powers 122
  Financial Autonomy 122
  Transparency in Governance 123
  Accountability in Governance 123
  Deepening of Democracy 123
  Gender Empowerment 123
  Empowerment of the Disadvantaged 124
  Popular Participation 124
  Decentralized Planning 124
Civil Society: Facilitating People's Participation in Local Governance 125
  Role of Civil Society in Rural Development 125
  Role of Civil Society in Urban Development 125
New Dimensions of Local Governance 126
  The Global–Local Debate 126
  New Localism 127
  Urban Development Dynamics 128
Concluding Observations 128

Chapter 7: Civil Services in India **131**
Civil Service, Public Service and Bureaucracy: Different Connotations 131
Civil Services in India: An Evolutionary Perspective 132
Civil Services under the British Crown 132
Civil Services in Independent India 133
All India Services: The Steel Frame of Indian Administration 134
  Recruitment and Placement 134
  The Central Civil Services 135
  A New Pattern of the Civil Services Examination 135
The Union Public Service Commission (UPSC): Recruitment Body 137
  Historical Background 137
  Constitutional Provisions 137
  Training of Civil Services 138
  Managing Personnel Issues 139

Promotions 139
Civil Service Code of Conduct 139
Political Rights of Civil Servants 140
Civil Service Neutrality 140
Civil Service Activism 140
Civil Service Reforms 141
Concluding Observations 146

Chapter 8: Administrative Reforms in India **148**
Administrative Reforms in India 149
National Police Commission Report 153
Recent Trends in Administrative Reforms in India 156
Concluding Observations 160

Chapter 9: Public Policy in India **163**
Growing Importance of Public Policy As a Field of Study 163
What Is Public Policy? 164
The Significance of Public Policy 165
Types of Public Policy 166
The Policy Environment 166
The Official Policy-makers 167
Unofficial Participants 168
Political Parties 168
Pressure Groups 168
Individual Citizens 169
Who Implements Policy? 169
Politico-ideological and Institutional Settings 170
Socialistic Pattern of Society 172
Neoliberal Economic Reforms in India 173
Changing Economic Horizons 174
Contingent Circumstances and Policy-making 176
Public Policy Process in India 178
Concluding Observations 179

Chapter 10: Planning and Economic Development in India **183**
Planning and Economic Development 184
The Concept of Planned Development 185
The Genesis and Development of Planning in India 186
Role of the Planning Commission 187
Planning in the Era of Economic Liberalization 190
A Shift of Focus: From the Planning Commission to the NITI Aayog 192
Concluding Observations 196

Chapter 11: Financial Management in India **200**
Budget Policy Orientations over the Years 201
Major Actors in the Budgetary Process 202
The Budget System in India 204
The Budget Process 206
Budget Planning 206
Budget Scrutiny 207

Budget Implementation 207
Budget Accounting 208
Budget Audit 208
Finance Management in India 208
Finance Revenues and Expenditures 209
Funds and Government Bonds 210
Budget System Reforms in India 211
Finance System Reforms in India 212
Evaluative Remarks 213
The Comptroller and Auditor General of India (CAG) 214
A Brief History 214
Position in the Indian Constitution 215
Independent CAG in Independent India 216
Powers and Duties of the CAG 216
Major Changes in CAG's Organization During the 1990s 218
Evaluative Remarks 220
Concluding Observations 221

Chapter 12: Citizens and Administration in India 224
The Citizen–Administration Interface 225
Citizen's Perceptions about the Administration 226
Barriers in Citizen-centric Administration in India 227
Ensuring Citizen-friendly Administration 227
People's Participation in Administration 229
Ensuring Good Governance 229
Administrative Accountability 230
Administrative Accountability in India 231
Redressal of Public Grievances 231
The Central Vigilance Commission 232
Organizational Set-up 232
Functions and Powers of the CVC 233
The Lokpal and Lokayukta: Combating Corruption 233
The Lokayukta in the States 234
The Lokpal: The National Ombudsman 234
Salient Features of the Lokpal and Lokayuktas Act, 2013 234
E-Governance 235
Bringing People Closer to the Administration 236
The Citizens' Charter 237
Right to Information (RTI) 238
Voluntary Agencies: New Players of Grievance Redressal 239
Civil Society: Articulating Citizens' Interests in a Market Economy 240
The Governance Discourse and the Changing Role of Citizens 240
Concluding Observations 241

Chapter 13: Social Welfare Administration in India 243
The Concept of Social Welfare 243
Social Welfare: An Evolutionary Perspective 244
Social Welfare Administration 245
Education and Training in Social Welfare Administration 246
Principles of Social Welfare Administration 247

Social Welfare Administration and Protection of the Weaker Sections in India 247
Social Welfare: The Indian Perspective 248
Constitutional Provisions 248
Legislative Measures 249
Social Welfare Ministry in India 249
Welfare Provisions for the SCs 250
National Commission for Scheduled Castes 251
National Commission for *Safai Karamchari* 251
Welfare Schemes for the SCs 251
Welfare of the Scheduled Tribes (STs) 252
Welfare of Other Backward Classes (OBCs) 253
Welfare of Persons with Disabilities 254
Gender Equality and Female Empowerment in India 254
Female Empowerment in India 255
The Protection and Welfare of Children 259
Social Welfare Policies in India 259
Mahatma Gandhi National Rural Employment Guarantee Act (MGNREGA) 259
Sarva Shiksha Abhiyan (Education for All) 261
National Rural Health Mission 262
Concluding Observations 263

Chapter 14: Environmental Administration in India 265
Environmental Issues in India 265
Environmental Pollution 266
Air Pollution 266
Water Pollution 267
Noise Pollution 268
Land Degradation 269
Solid and Hazardous Waste 269
Threats to Biodiversity 271
Deforestation 271
Constitutional and Legal Provisions for Environmental Protection in India 272
Judicial Response to Environmental Issues in India 276
Public Interest Litigation in Environmental Cases 277
Civil Society and Environmental Governance in India 280
Chipko Movement 280
Silent Valley Movement 281
Narmada Bachao Andolan 281
Appiko Movement 282
Concluding Observations 282

Chapter 15: Major Issues in Indian Administration 285

Part I Conceptual Issues 285
Generalist versus Specialist Debate 285
Conceptual and Empirical Roots 286
Concluding Observations 287
Political and Permanent Executive 289
Roots of the Debate 289
Decoding the Debate 290

History of the Friction between Political and Permanent Executives 291
Concluding Observations 292
Ethics in Governance 293
Stating the Issue 293
How Was the Issue Addressed? 294
The Second Administrative Reforms Commission, 2005 295
Concluding Observations 296
Corruption and Administration 297
Statement of the Problem 297
How to Combat Corruption? 298
Concluding Observations 299
Challenges of Good Governance in India 299
Addressing the Challenges of Good Governance in India 301
Concluding Observations 302
Non-governmental Organizations, Civil Society Organizations and Development 303
The Indian Reality 304
Concluding Observations 306
The Public Sector in India in the Pre- and Post-liberalization Era 306
The Indian Scene 307
Changes since the Industrial Policy Resolution 1977 307
Concluding Observations 310
Human Rights Administration in India 310
Achievements of the Commission 311
Limitations of the Commission 312
Concluding Observations 313

Part II Empirical Issues **314**
Disaster Management in India 314
Types of Disaster 314
Disasters in India 315
Disaster Management 315
Mitigating Measures to Disaster Management 316
Disaster Management in India 316
Emergence of an Institutional Arrangement in India 316
Organization and Structure of Disaster Management 317
The Disaster Management Act, 2005 317
The Role of Civil Society 318
Future Challenges 318
Land Acquisition for Development 318
The Land Acquisition Rehabilitation and Resettlement Act, 2014 320
Issue of Contention 320
Women in Administration 321
Feminist Assertion 321
The Public–Private Division 322
Gender's Dilemma 323
Gender Imbalance in Public Organizations 323
Accountability in Administration 324
Administrative Accountability in India 325
Challenges of Bringing Accountability in the Public Services 325
Information Technology and Its Impact on Administration 326

Bringing People Closer to the Administration 326
Transparency and the Right to Information 328
The Right to Information: Ensuring Transparency in Administration 328
Liberal Economic Reforms and the Role of the Bureaucracy 330

Conclusion 337

BIBLIOGRAPHY B–1
INDEX I–1

LIST OF ILLUSTRATIONS

TABLES

3.1 Cabinet Secretaries since 1950 73

4.1 Devolution of Funds to Local Bodies in Rajasthan for the Period 2010–15 88

4.2 States Having Devolution as a Percentage of State Revenues, 2010 89

7.1 Papers to Be Counted for Merit 136

13.1 Constitution of India Guarantees 248

14.1 Ambient Air Quality Standards in Respect of Noise 268

14.2 Forestland Diversions in India (1990–2001) 272

FIGURES

4.1 Administrative Structure in India 90

14.1 Forest Cover in India (Total Forest Cover 21.09%) 271

PREFACE

Writing a book on Indian administration is always challenging. It is challenging because the field is almost saturated with texts seeking to unravel the dynamics of Indian administration. These efforts are useful though may not be intellectually satisfying or stimulating because of their focus merely on the structure of administration, generally ignoring the processes shaping the structure in a particular fashion. Hence one is unable to comprehend the peculiar dynamics in which administration evolves. Given the organic connect of administration with the prevalent socio-economic and political processes, it would be difficult, if not impossible, to conceptualize its functioning without any reference to the context. This book is a serious endeavour towards capturing the complex dynamics of Indian administration in a historical perspective. It is argued here that a fair understanding of the nature of administration also involves a critical scanning of the milieu in which it is based. In other words, it is believed that in view of its clear contextual roots, Indian administration cannot be conceptualized independently of the socio-economic and political circumstances in which it is located.

There is another significant point that cannot be undermined, that is, while conceptualizing Indian administration it is incumbent on the analyst to pay adequate attention to its historical roots for two important reasons. First, given the fact that Indian administration in post-Independence India is a continuity of the past, one has to be sensitive to the factors that contributed to its peculiar nature despite India being decolonized. It was not merely a structural continuity; it also represented some of the fundamental values that informed colonial administration. For instance, liberalism of the British variety remained a persuasive ideology for those who presided over India's destiny immediately after its political freedom. Second, it will also be misleading if we confine ourselves to the structural continuity of colonial administration since the founding fathers also drew on several other competing ideological impulses while setting in motion a new system of administration. There is no denying the fact that Jawaharlal Nehru, India's first Prime Minister, was appreciative of the Leninist New Economic Programme which remained critical in his conceptualization of the 'socialistic pattern of society'. Furthermore, the paradigm of state-led-planned-economic-development that India endorsed with the formation of the Planning Commission in 1950 was also the result of Nehru's unwavering faith in the socialist system. Drawn on this, not only was the Indian administration conceptualized accordingly, but it was also structured to give primacy to the state which was considered to be a perfect instrument to bring about inclusive growth.

The scene however changes with the onset of globalization and India's acceptance of the neoliberal economic design in the wake of the severe financial crisis in the early 1990s. Arguments for state-led development lost their appeal and the state became one of the many instruments involved in socio-economic growth and change. Besides the state, market and civil society gradually become critical in public administration. As an actor in growth and development, the state has now to coordinate with the market and civil society while fulfilling its traditional responsibilities. The state has not declined, but has refashioned its role in the changed environment where the forces of globalization seem to have dwarfed the distinct nationalist voice. This is evident globally and Indian administration appears to have adapted to the socio-economic transformation, following the acceptance of the New Economic Policy in 1991. Not only has its structure undergone a metamorphosis, but the philosophy that so far has remained integral to Indian administration seems also to have phased out.

The book thus provides two major and two supplementary arguments. The first *argument* is about the nature of Indian administration which is hinted at by its subtitle: this is an analytical account of Indian administration with reference to its *evolutionary perspective*. Given the critical importance of the dialectics between text and context, the book argues that Indian administration is being constantly reinvented. Linked with the first argument that Indian administration is in flux is the second *argument* which draws upon the critical importance of the connect between structures and processes. The second argument, by underlining 'the structure-process dialectics', emphasizes that a fair understanding of Indian administration is simply impossible without comprehending the intricate relationship between the structure and processes of administration in a historical perspective. Of the two supplementary arguments, the first one is a claim that the book is unique in character and analysis. This is not a conventional study, but an attempt to refashion our approach to Indian administration by unearthing subtle processes which usually escape our notice. The second *supplementary argument* reinforces the point that this study will surely contribute to further research in this complex but volatile area of human endeavour and Indian administration shall thus become a vantage entry point for those seeking to unravel contemporary Indian politics in its most complex manifestation.

Book writing is a collaborative project. Besides the author, one needs a good and sensitive publishing house to provide a safe home for the text. We are fortunate to have SAGE as our publisher. This book is a sequel to the ones that we have already published with SAGE. This would not have been possible without the support of our colleagues at SAGE. We would like to particularly thank Mr Amit Kumar, Ms Indrani Dutta, and Ms Vandana Gupta for their unflinching support during the preparation of the book. As teachers, we are also fortunate to have been benefitted intellectually by the searching questions of our students. We express our gratitude to them; if the book serves them well, we will have reasons to feel contended. We take this occasion to convey heartfelt gratitude to our teachers; without their blessing and intellectual backing, we would not have succeeded in the academia. We are also grateful to faculty members across the country who have provided their review comments, which have helped us improve the text to a considerable extent, especially Dr Imankalyan Lahiri, Department of International Relations, Jadavpur University; Dr Kannamma Raman, Department of Civics and Politics, University of Mumbai and Dr Md Ayub Mallick, Department of Political Science, Kalyani University. Our successful academic engagement would not have been possible without the support that we have received from our parents, brothers and sisters. Last, but not the least, by allowing us to concentrate on our academic feats, our respective spouses have played a role which is not only appreciative, but it also deserves a 'Big Thank You'. We cannot thank them enough for their contribution in sustaining our academic zeal and productivity. By being creatively destructive, our kids always remain sources of joy and happiness. In a nutshell, we would not have had what we have so far without our families being so supportive and indulgent of our whims and idiosyncrasies.

ABOUT THE AUTHORS

Bidyut Chakrabarty is a faculty at the Department of Political Science, University of Delhi, India. He has also been Dean of the Faculty of Social Sciences and Head of the Department of Political Science, University of Delhi. He earned his PhD from the London School of Economics and has been associated with teaching and research for more than three decades. He has taught in some of the most prestigious educational institutions such as the London School of Economics; Indian Institute of Management (IIM) Calcutta, India; Monash University, Australia; National University of Singapore and Hamburg University, Germany.

Dr Chakrabarty has authored three books for SAGE India: *Indian Government and Politics* (with Rajendra Kumar Pandey, 2008); *Modern Indian Political Thought* (with Rajendra Kumar Pandey, 2009) and *Public Administration in a Globalizing World* (with Prakash Chand, 2012).

Prakash Chand is a faculty of Political Science at Dyal Singh (E) College, University of Delhi, India. He was awarded a Doctoral Fellowship by ICSSR and a Postdoctoral Research Award by University Grants Commission (UGC). Dr Chand has rich teaching experience of over 14 years and his research papers have appeared in various journals including *Indian Social Science Review, Gandhi Marg, Indian Journal of Public Administration,* and *Urban India* and *Social Change.*

His areas of interest and research include public administration and environmental governance in India. He has co-authored a book titled *Public Administration in a Globalizing World* (with Bidyut Chakrabarty, 2012), published by SAGE.

INTRODUCTION

I

Indian administration in an evolutionary perspective is a conceptual formulation. Implicit here is the theoretical assumption that public administration is in a constant flux. Given its organic nature, public administration is contingent on the prevalent socio-economic and political circumstances, which means that there can never be a universal model to adequately capture its complexities. This is contrary to not only the Weberian conceptualization but also the governance model seeking to comprehend public administration in a one-size-fits-all formula. Theoretically unsound and conceptually problematic, this formulation while defending 'neo-Taylorism' does not seem to be satisfactory at all for two fundamental reasons: First, being mechanical the assumption glossing over the societal features of public administration has inherent theoretical limitations. Second, there is a serious lacuna in this assumption because it is distinctly ethnocentric given its roots in the western context. The fundamental point is that in view of its society-dependent nature, public administration can never properly be understood in a derivative format. In other words, as public administration is situation-specific, there is no way that one can comprehend its nature by ignoring the socio-economic and political milieu in which it organically evolves.

In the light of the fundamental theoretical proposition that public administration is context dependent, a study with analytical depth can be pursued by being sensitive to the contextual peculiarities of public administration. This is more so in those countries with a long colonial past. Despite being politically independent, post-colonial nations continue to be guided by past administrative laws and ethos which remain, more or less, undisturbed even after the end of colonialism. This is the case in most of the former British colonies. India is no exception. Indian administration, even after more than six decades of political freedom, carries the imprint of colonial administration. One of the reasons that explains such a continuity is definitely the acceptance of the Westminster form of governance which was introduced in India over the course of 200 years of colonial rule. This was reinforced with the increasing popularity of political liberalism complementary to the British administration which addressed the nationalist campaign by being accommodative of dissent and opposition. The two instruments of persuasion and coercion thus remained integral to Indian administration even in the colonial context presumably because of the distinctive nature of British colonialism.

Philosophically, the Indian administration drew upon the British Enlightenment tradition that always privileged dialogue and discussion as the best means to resolve differences and defuse crises. Appreciative benevolence, compassion and tolerance, the British Enlightenment contributed to the consolidation of those social virtues which significantly influenced the ruler–ruled interactions. By being open to dialogue even in the midst of no-win situations, the colonial administration in India set in motion the processes which gradually became critical in articulating democracy as a mechanism for governance. Institutions also developed accordingly. Historically ordained, the Indian administration, while being conditioned by the Enlightenment philosophy, led to the consolidation of the exalted values of Enlightenment in the course of time and they became so well-entrenched that the Indian nationalist leadership was instinctively drawn to them. Not only did these ideas lay the foundation of democratic administration in post-independent India, but they also sustained the structure of the administration that helped build a democratic India. The argument is simple: as colonialism had immensely contributed to the shaping of Indian administration, its influence was most intimately felt. It is true that the main aim of the British administration was to consolidate, for obvious reasons, colonialism but, by being accommodative of democratic protests, it also sparked off movements fulfilling the nationalist aspirations. Colonialism despite being devastating economically and politically, had a benign presence in India simply because it let lose forces which, in fact, consolidated, if not strengthened, political liberalism as a persuasive ideology capable of ventilating mass grievances most effectively. What is fundamental here is the fact that the Indian administration, despite having sustained colonialism in its spirit and tone, created an environment in which forces opposed to the British rule evolved. One thus cannot gloss over this aspect of British colonialism which also accommodated the opposition, perhaps as a well thought out strategy to defuse nationalist attacks on its supremacy. In the process, the Indian administration acquired certain distinctive characteristics which were relative to the historical circumstances in which it had emerged. It will not be an exaggeration to suggest that though India became free in 1947, the administrative system which was meant to execute the policies of the new government, was not a new design, but inherited from the erstwhile British rule.

Indian administration is thus context-driven. As it has a clear legacy of the past, it has those characteristics which are contrary to the fundamental ethos of a free democratic country. By imbibing the tendencies towards centralization of authority, the Indian administration seems to have encouraged the iron fist rule at one level, while at another, there are new initiatives to articulate the goals of democratic India. Given its complex evolution in an equally peculiar historical context, Indian administration represents a creative blending of the past with the present in which the former creates the foundation while the latter reinvents its nature in the changed social, economic and political environment. What is most fundamental in this study is the conceptualization of the metamorphosis in Indian administration with reference to the rapidly changing historical circumstances. Change is inherent in administration as circumstances in which it is grounded do not remain static. The rigid colonial administration which also released democratic forces by choking nationalist aspirations was replaced following decolonization in 1947. In view of the bloodbath that accompanied the 1947 transfer of power, it was found necessary to retain the colonial structure of administration which was, of course, imbued with the nationalist spirit. What is most striking is the continuity of the steel frame of the All India Services which acted ruthlessly to contain the nationalist movement presumably because of their utility in governance even today. So, it was a mere structural continuity since the spirit in which the steel frame services were to discharge their responsibilities was radically different. Clearly, Weberian in its manifestation and functions, the contemporary Indian administration, by being responsive to the changing mass mood, is a unique example in which the past is creatively blended with the present in order to become meaningful in independent India. An analytical probe into its nature would be of great academic and practical utility in order to clearly understand the dialectics between the administration and its context in a historical perspective. By seeking to fulfil a distinctly nationalist role, the Indian administration, by being receptive to different kinds of historical responsibilities, gradually became a powerful instrument of social, economic and political transformation.

II

Administration is inherently contextual. What governed the nationalist choice in favour of the instrument of colonial administration were surely the unique circumstances of communal riots becoming useful to the Indian rulers who had hardly any experience of managing the state. In view of the well-entrenched legacy of the British Raj, the post-colonial administration in India bore an uncanny similarity with its past incarnation. Three major ideological influences seem to have been critical in Indian administration: colonialism, nationalism and democracy. Two points need to be kept in mind: First, although colonialism and nationalism are surely antagonistic to each other there is no doubt that the former provoked circumstances in which nationalism emerged as a powerful ideology to articulate the voices of the colonized. Second, colonialism also led to a slow process of democratization by gradually involving people, favourably disposed towards the alien administration. The colonial state had permitted some measures of representation to carefully selected Indian interests. But it had also ensured that 'the state had always operated at a level removed from the society which it governed'. Appropriating 'the executive privilege' for itself, the colonial state appeared to 'stand outside the realm of and therefore free to arbiter over, social conflict and political competition [and its relationship with the subject] continued to be conducted in the language of supplication and concession, grants and demands, charters and petition, grievances and repression' (Chandravarkar 2007). The British were admittedly influenced by their own 'theories of liberalism and self-government'. Through a mixture of motives that ranged from 'self-interests and ideological commitments', the colonial government introduced principles of representation, appropriate for its rule, into the colonial legislature (Chakrabarty 2007, 36). The British imperial attitudes in India seem to be 'highly ambiguous' resulting from their efforts to negotiate their liberal regard for self-rule as the best form of government and their vested interests in being imperial masters (Low 1997).

Modelled on the *British North America Act, 1867,* which established the Canadian federation, the Government of India Act 1935 is certainly a powerful constitutional intervention that the colonial rulers seriously made to accommodate the nationalist zeal within the colonial administrative format. This is also illustrative of efforts legitimizing the growing democratic aspirations of the ruled in India through a constitutional intervention. Interestingly, the 1935 Act remained the strongest influence during the making of the 1950 Constitution for free India. Some 250 clauses of the present Constitution were, in fact, lifted from the Government of India Act. Although the political system of independent India draws its sustenance from universal adult franchise and political sovereignty, the governing rules are undoubtedly derived from its colonial past. The most striking provisions that the Constitution of India derived from its 1935 counterpart are the 'emergency provisions' that enable the President to suspend democratically elected governments and fundamental rights of the citizens. Furthermore, colonial provisions for 'preventive detention' of the so-called 'politically subversive individuals' remain in force in independent India in different forms. The infamous Maintenance of Internal Security Act (MISA), 1972, the Terrorist and Disruptive Activities (Prevention) Act (TADA) of the early 1980s and the Prevention of Terrorist Act (POTA) in recent times are examples of some legislations drawn on the colonial and authoritarian legislation of the colonial past. Nonetheless, the Government of India Act 1935 is undoubtedly a very significant concession that the colonial government was forced to concede to because of the rising tide of nationalism and democratization.

There is no doubt that the post-colonial state in India inherited its habits of governance from colonial practices. And, its *weltanschauung* (world view) is based on 'the mixed legacies of colonial rule' that also upheld rule of law, bureaucracy, citizenship, parasitic landlords, modern political institutions and 'two-track tradition' of protest and participation (Mitra 2004, 29–34). What accounted for the relative stability of colonialism in India was its ability to adapt to changed socio-political circumstances and also the gradual but steady 'internalization' of domination by the subjects of colonial rule which led Ashis Nandy to characterize colonialism as 'an intimate enemy' because the dominated saw 'the virtues of being dominated' for their own betterment (Nandy 1989). Colonialism was not seen as an absolute evil. For the subjects, as Nandy argues,

> [I]t was a product of one's own emasculation and defeat in legitimate power politics. For the rulers, colonial exploitation was an incidental and regrettable by-product of a philosophy of

> life that was in harmony with superior forms of political and economic organization. This was the consensus that rulers of India sought, consciously or unconsciously... [while] the subjects collaborated on a long-term basis [because] they seemed to have accepted the ideology of the system, either as players or as counter-players. This is the only way they could preserve a minimum of self-esteem in a situation of unavoidable injustice. (pp. 10–11)

Colonialism drew on such a cultural consensus that was further strengthened through the evolution of mechanisms to defuse threats and also nationalist ire as and when required. For instance, when the British model of unitary governance proved relatively ineffective for a diverse country like India, the colonial rulers began introducing, by degrees, doses of 'decentralization' and 'federalism' starting in the 1920s, in which the Government of India Act 1935 was the most significant institutional step (Morris-Jones 1974, 15–48). Although the colonial state was hardly federal in the classical sense, the federal arrangement that the Act stipulated seemed to have provided critical inputs to the founding fathers while deliberating on federalism in the Constituent Assembly.

These selective examples are illustrative of the argument underlining the critical importance of the three ideological forces of colonialism, nationalism and democratization in charting out a distinctive path for India. The argument that this study seeks to draw on the dialectical interaction between colonialism, nationalism and democratization over a historical time period leading to India's independence and its aftermath. Hence, it is neither intended to suggest that political freedom from colonial rule wrought no changes to the Indian polity nor to argue that post-colonial India is just a continuity of her colonial past. Major political institutions, despite their clear colonial roots, have undergone dramatic metamorphosis in independent India. A careful look at the evolution of institutions in India clearly shows that they evolved creatively to adjust to changing circumstances. The Westminster model of parliamentary democracy that India adopted was for instance not a clone, but was responsive to the situation-specific ethos and the existent socio-cultural milieu. Similarly, there is no other persuasive example of 'deepening of democracy' than the 1977 and 2004 national polls which were announced by the incumbent ruling authority, allegedly not favourably disposed towards 'democratic values and procedures'. Political parties in India cannot afford to ignore the importance of election which is a testimony to the deep-rootedness of democracy in India. This is true across the ideological spectrum, as is evident in India's political history since inauguration of constitutional democracy in India (Guha 2007, 756). Furthermore, the changing socio-economic profile of the Legislative Assemblies and national Parliament is also indicative of a trend towards a genuinely inclusive democracy. Given the growing politicization of the peripheral sections of society, elite-centric governance is fading away with the consolidation of people-centric governance. The change of political authority at regular intervals through elections is an eloquent testimony to the depth of democratic processes that are not merely articulated in periodic elections.[1] The introduction of adult suffrage transformed India's politics beyond recognition. Democracy is, therefore, no longer confined to electoral participation of the voters, but also articulates the 'every day struggle' in which people are involved while exercising their rights as citizens.

There is however a note of caution. Colonialism contributed to nationalism, but not to a nation-state in India for a variety of reasons connected with India's socio-cultural diversity. Post-colonial India was therefore hardly a nation-state, but a state-nation simply because the institutions of governance, very much a part of British legacy, were already in place when the 1947 transfer of power took place. The nationalist leaders, except M. A. Jinnah, deliberately avoided the nationalist language that could be devastating in view of the absence of cultural and moral unity in India that characterized the rise of nations in the west. The nation, as a conscious political articulation, hardly figured in the political discourse of the day. Indian nationalism was not based on a shared language, religion or ethnic identity. Perhaps the presence of a common enemy, namely, British colonialism, 'united men and women from different parts of the subcontinent in a common and shared endeavour' (Guha 2007, 757).

A nation was consolidated, but followed a completely different path that was not in the least a derivative of European sources. The nation that India is, does not privilege a single language or a religious faith. Although a majority of its citizens are Hindus, India is not 'a Hindu–Pakistan'. Its Constitution does not discriminate between people on the basis of faith, nor did the nationalist movement that resulted in decolonization. Although the joy of freedom was marred by the partition on the basis of a religious chasm between Hindus and Muslims, the failure to avoid the division made Gandhi's political successors determined to construct independent India as a secular republic.

III

The Constitution governs the administration by linking it with the fundamental ethos of the democratic aspirations of the people. In that sense, the role of the Constitution can never be ignored. Besides laying out the principles of governance, it is also responsible for safeguarding India's democratic fabric by appropriately guiding the rulers. Faced with the complex conundrum of meeting out scores of seemingly mutually competing and sometimes contradictory claims on the Constitution of independent India, the Constitution makers had to adopt a policy of drafting a lengthy and all-encompassing document which contained not only the classical tenets of a Constitution like the provisions defining the powers and functions of the various organs of government at both the union and the state levels, the fundamental rights guaranteed to the people, etc., but also a number of unconventional provisions like the Directive Principles of State Policy to make the Constitution an instrument of socio-economic change in the country. The Constitution makers, therefore, had to draw on all the available Constitutions and other legislative documents to provide the building blocks to erect the edifice called the Constitution of India. To be precise, the framers banked heavily upon colonial construction, that is, the Government of India Act, 1935, to get the foundational base of the Constitution of India, an ironic epitome of the fact that the framers could not move much away from the system of governance devised by the British for India.

Thus, keeping the core drawn from the Act of 1935, the framers looked upon other Constitutions like the American and the Irish Constitutions to provide for the operational dynamics of the democratic system of government in the country through the provisions of fundamental rights and the visions of a new India, marching on the path of rapid socio-economic transformation through the guiding force of the Directive Principles of State Policy. However, the physical structure of the Constitution of India, as drawn from the above-mentioned sources, would have remained hollow and infertile, had the breathing spirit to it not been provided by the Objectives Resolution, drafted by Nehru himself and approved by the Constituent Assembly on 22 January 1947. Besides laying down 'only certain fundamentals', including the system of government that must 'fit in with the temper of our people and be acceptable to them', Nehru (2003, 60, 62), the Resolution, also known as the Declaration, exhorts,

> [W]e should ... rise above our ordinary selves and party disputes [and undertake the task] in the widest and most tolerant and most effective manner so that, whatever we may produce, should be worthy of India as a whole and should be such that the world should recognise that we have functioned as we should have ... in this high adventure.

Finding its manifestation through the Preamble of the Constitution, which declared the pious goals of the Constitution to secure to all its citizens; justice, social, economic and political; liberty of thought, expression, belief, faith and worship; equality of status and of opportunity and to promote among them all fraternity, assuring the dignity of the individual; this resolution put into black and white the very raison d'être for which the Constitution of India was supposed to come into existence.

With the broad structure and essence of the future polity of the country as obvious, the Constituent Assembly arrived at seven basic decisions on the nature of the new state, namely, a written Constitution, federal structure of the polity, republic form of state, Parliamentary democracy, membership of the Commonwealth of Nations, secular nature of state and welfare character of the state. These decisions were, in fact, cherished dreams of the leadership of the national movement whose fulfilment was sought to be attained through the new Constitution. The various provisions of the Constitution of India appear, in a way, nothing more than the bricks and mortar to facilitate the construction of the structure of a constitutional polity in the country.

Analyzing the inherent philosophical moorings of the Indian Constitution, Austin discerns a 'seamless web', consisting of three strands namely, protecting and enhancing national unity and integrity; establishing the institutions and spirit of democracy and fostering a social revolution to better the lot of the mass of Indians (Austin 1999, 6). Bestowing equal weightage and significance to all the three strands in time and space, Austin asserts the mutual dependence and inextricable intertwinedness of these strands and warns that any undue strain on, and slackness in, any one strand would distort the web and risk its destruction and, with it, the destruction of the nation. The Constitution of India is thus not just a document, but a living organism, meant to sustain equilibrium and also bring about changes relative to the circumstances. Hence, Austin argues,

> [T]he essence of democracy and social reform strands is to be found throughout the Constitution: in the democratic political institutions and processes of the parliamentary system, in adult suffrage, and in the independent judiciary; and in Parts III and IV of the Constitution, which lay down the 'Fundamental Rights' and the 'Directive Principles of State Policy'. (1999, 7)

The ideas were in place and the Constitution acquired a shape in accordance with the mandate that the Constituent Assembly had for the newly emerged nation following the British withdrawal from India in 1947. Besides providing the fundamental guiding principles of governance, the Constitution of India also set in motion a philosophical tradition which the founding fathers had derived from their engagement with the Gandhi-led nationalist movement in the context of the British administration.

However, despite the mutual dependence and mutual compatibility of the three strands, as stressed by Austin, it may be argued that there appeared a certain degree of prioritization amongst the three strands and the framers seemed to be fairly clear on first things first in the Indian Constitution. Framed with much painstaking perseverance and imbued with the long cherished dreams of national leaders, the Constitution of India reflected the wisdom of the framers in not only meeting out the challenges at hand like preserving the unity and integrity of the nation, threatened by communal violence, but also a prophetic vision of heralding in an era of what Gandhi called 'Ramrajya'. To put it differently, the first and foremost priority of the framers at the time of independence, and probably afterwards, appeared to be of jealously guarding the unity and integrity of the county, for which they were willing to afford so much of unfettered powers to the Central government even at the risk of rendering the federal set-up of the polity meaningless. Apparently, it appears paradoxical that though very few mentions have been made in the Constitution with regard to the unity and integrity of the country, sweeping powers and unwritten discretion was provided, in addition to the retention of the colonial constructions like the All India Services like the Indian Administrative Service (formerly the Indian Civil Service) and the Indian Police Service (formerly Indian Police), to the Central government that it would not be impertinent to argue that the preservation of the unity and integrity of country was the running consideration pervading from the first to the last word of the Constitution.

Having been reassured of the indestructibility of India as a nation, the framers set on to infuse the ethos and spirit of democratic governance in the country, within the broad spectrum of the Parliamentary system, based on the sanctities of universal adult franchise. Banking heavily, if not exclusively, on periodic elections, to be conducted by an independent constitutional body, the framers' trump card, with regard to democracy, turned out to be the classical negative rights of the western mould, ensuring the common people the basic minimum constitutional guarantees through which they could feel as being citizens of an independent country enjoying the freedom of not only choosing their rulers but also living a life of their volition, notwithstanding, the traditional character of Indian society and the socio-economic backwardness of the masses of people. Thus, unlike the absolute value of unity and integrity, democracy did not become an absolute value for the framers who, nonetheless, wished it to underpin the Indian polity and evolve in the course of time. The value of social revolution, as referred to by Austin, appears only at the last stage of contemplation by the framers, after ingraining fully the values of unity and integrity as well as democracy in the Constitution. Though fully aware of the indispensability and unavoidability of a subtle social revolution in the country in order to make democracy meaningful and sustainable, the framers seemed to be convinced of the primacy and pivotal position of the other two values, which were bound to become the substructure over which the superstructure of social revolution could be erected.

In sum, undoubtedly, the Indian Constitution appears to be a seamless web characterized by the three strands of the unity and integrity of the country, institutions and spirit of democracy and social revolutionary fervour, yet, the shape of the web does not appear to be circular and it is not possible to figure out the sequence and placing of the particular value. Rather, it may be argued that the shape of the web would probably be pyramidal in which the three values are arranged in ascending order with the base position occupied by the value of unity and integrity of the nation, the next position accorded to the value of democracy and finally the value of social revolution, in order of their dispensability from top to bottom. In other words, it demonstrates a Venn diagrammatic nature of the Indian Constitution where by one value resides in the hard shell of the other, paving the way for the realization of the other value only once assured of its own durable existence.[2]

IV

Democracy is a guarantee of adult suffrage in India. This has unleashed a process that has gone beyond mere voting by empowering people in a manner which has radically changed the contour of Indian politics. The process is getting translated into rage and revolt, making India 'a country of a million little mutinies' (Naipaul 1991, 106). But these mutinies have created a tangible space for democratic aspirations to flourish. And also, they have made the state available for those who hitherto remain peripheral from any political transactions (Mitra 1991, 567–68). The process is significant for another related reason, namely, democratic empowerment of the lower strata of society and formerly excluded groups leading to the articulation of voices that have always remained 'feeble' in the past. These groups have interpreted 'their disadvantage and dignity in caste terms, social antagonism and competition for state benefits expressed themselves increasingly in the form of intense caste rivalries' (Kaviraj 2000, 156–57). So the growing importance of caste in contemporary Indian politics is essentially a modern phenomenon and not 'a throwback traditional behaviour'. This is theoretically puzzling since caste action in India, articulated in modern political vocabulary, cannot be comprehended within the available liberal democratic parameters unless one is drawn to the empirical context that radically differs from the typical liberal society in the West.

Politicization and democratization seem to be dialectically interlinked. As a result, the outcome of such intermingling may not be predictable. In a typical Western liberal context, the deepening of democracy invariably leads to a consolidation of 'liberal values'. In the Indian context, democratization is translated into the greater involvement of people not as 'individuals' which is a staple to the liberal discourse, but as communities or groups. Individuals are getting involved in the public sphere not as 'atomized' individuals but as 'members of primordial communities' drawn on religious, caste or *jati* identities. Similarly, a large section of women is being drawn to the political processes not as 'women' or individuals, but as members of a community holding a sectoral identity. Community-identity seems to be the governing force. It is therefore not surprising that the so-called peripheral groups continue to maintain their identities with reference to the social groups (caste, religion or sect) to which they belong while getting involved in political processes despite the fact that their political goals remain more or less identical. Nonetheless, the processes of steady democratization have contributed to the articulation of a political voice, hitherto unheard of, which is reflective of radical changes in India's political texture. The expanding circle of democratic participation since independence has thus transformed 'the character of politics as previously subordinate groups have gained a voice' (Adeney and Wyatt, 1). By helping to articulate the political voice of the marginalized, democracy in India has led to 'a loosing of social strictures' and empowered the peripherals to be confident of their ability to improve the socio-economic conditions in which they are placed.[3] This is a significant political process that has led to what Christophe Jaffrelot describes as 'a silent revolution' (Jaffrelot 2005) through a meaningful transfer of power from the upper caste elites to various subaltern groups within the democratic framework of public governance. At the national level, this occurred in the early 1990s with the acceptance of the Mandal Commission Report which recommended reservations for the Other Backward Classes in proportion to their share in the demography. Rajni Kothari (2002, 200) captures this change by saying that 'a new democratic process' seems to have begun 'at a time when the old democracy is failing to deliver the goods [leading to] a new revolution representing new social churnings that are already under way … in the electoral and party processes, as also within the deeper arenas of the non-party political processes'.

V

Unlike her South Asian neighbours, political institutions have developed organic roots in India. There has been however a clear deterioration of the Indian Parliament in its role in view of the decline of 'the moral credibility' of the elected representatives. Not only has the quality of the debate on policy issues gone down, but the Parliamentarians also tend to lose their dignity on the floor of Parliament once they are challenged by their colleagues. While attributing the steady decline of the Parliament in India to the general moral decadence and the growing importance of extra-constitutional factors in elections, Sumanta Banerjee explains this phenomenon by underlining the lack (a) of common adherence to the basic norms of Parliamentary democracy and (b) a sense of awareness of the line between the responsible exercise of the Right to freedom of speech and unrestricted license of speech within the walls of the Parliament (Banerjee 2006, 3838). The Parliamentary decline seems to be matched by the ascendancy of other political institutions of Indian democracy. For instance, the President, Supreme Court of India and the Election Commission have, among others, shown a remarkable resilience in upholding some of the intrinsic liberal values.

India's President no longer remains an ornamental head of the state. In the context of the decline of the single-party rule, the first citizen of the country seems to have redefined his/her constitutional role by being more 'proactive' than before. Article 53 of the Constitution vests 'the executive power of the Union … in the President', as the Constitutional head of state he/she is expected to act as an agent of the political executive, namely the council of ministers or cabinet. The rise of a coalition government and the spread of corruption—in the political executive, legislatures and civil services—have created a legitimate space for other constitutional functionaries, including the presidency, 'to act as guardians of fairness and constitutional balance' (Rudolph and Rudolph 2002, 141). That the President was not a mere 'rubber stamp' was evident when the late K. R. Narayanan prevented the Uttar Pradesh Governor, Ramesh Bhandari from arbitrarily dismissing the Kalyan Singh-led BJP government and replacing it with Jagdambika Pal's Congress–Samajwadi coalition. Bhandari dismissed the Singh government without giving the Chief Minister an opportunity to prove his majority on the floor of the Assembly, which Narayanan thought, was both 'unconstitutional' and also 'partisan', designed to help the ruling United Front-Congress in the forthcoming elections.[4] A landmark Supreme Court judgement 'reinstalled' the BJP government justifying K. R. Narayanan's intervention for constitutional propriety since there was 'widespread disenchantment ... with the excessive use of President's rule for partisan purposes' (Manor 2005, 116). Similarly, Narayanan's reluctance to endorse the decision of V. C. Pande, the Bihar Governor to appoint the Nitish Kumar-led minority government immediately after the 2000 state assembly elections would have led to a serious constitutional crisis had Nitish Kumar not resigned. The fact that the Rabri Devi-led RJD coalition won the vote of confidence 'intensified the clamour against the governor's precipitous and apparently partisan action' (Rudolph and Rudolph 2002, 150). Recently, President A. P. J. Abdul Kalam's refusal to approve the 2006 office of Profit Bill when it was sent to him after its endorsement by both the houses of Parliament redefined the role of this institution in the changed socio-political environment. Although the President had no alternative but to grant assent once the Bill was approved by the Parliament a second time, the episode was nonetheless reflective of the growing independence of India's highest constitutional authority. Three important principles were consolidated in the wake of this controversial office of profit episode: First, the underlying principle debarring the holder of an office of profit under the government from being a member of Parliament is drawn on a foundational principle of the doctrine of separation of powers, namely, there should be a demarcation of authority and power between the executive and the legislature to avoid 'misappropriation of authority and power' by these two wings of government. The famous Kesavananda Bharati judgement (1973) of the Supreme Court endorses this principle as part of the basic structure of the Constitution of India. Second, the President's reluctance to approve the Bill was also suggestive of the fact that there needed to be uniformity in interpreting the law as regards the office of profit. In fact, given the Supreme Court ruling on this, there is no scope of different interpretations and as an apex judicial institution in the country, the Supreme Court is constitutionally authorized to enforce uniformity in this regard. Finally, by sending the Bill back to the Parliament for reconsideration, the President also upheld the judicial sanctity of the criteria that the Supreme Court devised to settle the controversy. These criteria are: (a) it must be a post, created by and under the control of the government, (b) the appointee of the post should also be under governmental control, (c) the holder of the post must be entitled to some profit or benefit other than compensatory allowance, whether he/she takes it or not and (d) their power/authority attached to that position that can be exercised by the holder.[5] It is true that the controversy was finally resolved not by following judicial wisdom, but by political considerations. Nonetheless, this episode established beyond doubt a healthy trend, which was constitutionally creative and politically challenging in so far as the institutions of governance were concerned. The Bill was therefore a significant intervention in redefining the institutions' politico-ideological tilt that had also creatively responded to the issues by catapulting 'people' onto the centre stage of India's political processes.

Similarly, Supreme Court in the famous Bommai judgement of 1994 also radically altered the complexion of the debate on the basic structure of the Constitution. Critical of the indiscriminate application of Article 356 to dismiss duly elected state governments, the Supreme Court came out heavily against the Union government. B. R. Ambedkar was confident, as his statements in the Constituent Assembly endorse, that Emergency provisions in the

Constitution of India would rarely be invoked and as the Indian democracy matured, the need to do so would be less compelling, reducing Article 356 to 'a dead letter'. However, by 1994, this provision was applied more than 90 times, the Supreme Court noted and thus made this Article 'a death letter', rather than 'a dead letter', as the founding fathers foresaw. The judgement put to rest all speculations regarding the 'delicate balance of powers in a federal polity' by saying that 'federalism envisaged in the Constitution is a basic structure. ... The state *qua* the Constitution is federal and independent in its exercise of legislative and executive power'. It is true that the Constitution prefers an arrangement which is tilted in favour of the centre. But that does not mean that 'the States are mere appendages of the Centre. Within the sphere allotted to them, States are supreme. The Centre cannot temper with their powers'. Simultaneously by clarifying the constitutional status of the states, the judgement also redefined the role of the president who is not a mere stooge of the Union Government by underlining,

> [T]he provision requires that the material before the President must be sufficient to indicate that unless a proclamation (under article 356) is issued, it is not possible to carry on the affairs of the state as per the provisions of the Constitution. It is not every situation arising in the State but a situation which shows that constitutional government has become an impossibility, which alone will entitle the President to issue the proclamation.[6]

B. R. Ambedkar was right when he suggested that growing democratization will make the Emergency Provision redundant. The Supreme Court is certainly an important component in this process. By creatively interpreting the constitutional provisions, the apex court contributed to the redrawing of the basic contours of Indian federalism having its roots in the 1935 constitutional structure, evolving organically out of an engagement with the constantly changing social, economic and cultural milieu. The Bommai judgement is a watershed, perhaps most significant, in the evolution of organic federalism in India which is surely a break with the past.

The revival of the Election Commission as a political watchdog is a remarkable development supporting the growing democratization of Indian politics. Established in 1950, the Election Commission was set up as a constitutional agency and entrusted, according to Article 324 of the Constitution, with the task of superintendence, direction and control of all national and state level elections. The Commission holds substantial powers in so far as the procedural aspects of the elections are concerned. In fact, it derives its strength from the code of conduct, formulated by the political parties participating in the elections generally by consensus. There is no doubt that by its sincere involvement in the processes of elections, starting from the preparation of the voters' roll to the declaration of the poll outcomes, the Commission has played a critical role in redefining India's democracy. The role of the Commission in the state election in West Bengal in 2006 is illustrative here: with the announcement of the dates of elections, the Commission took control of the election machinery of the state in an unprecedented manner. First, it took ample care to revise the voter's roll since the incumbent Left Front government was charged with manipulating the voters' list. The Election Commission found a large number of them in various districts. During the clean-up operation, the observer found 1,300,000 false names[7] in the list of voters, and struck them off. Hence, the charge seemed authenticated and the media thus attributed the sustained electoral victory of the Left Front to 'the bogus voters'. Second, following its success in Bihar in holding a free and fair election under the strict surveillance of the state-controlled coercive forces, the Commission decided to conduct the poll on five fairly dispersed dates stretching almost two months. The Commission requisitioned police and paramilitary forces from outside the state simply because the state police did not appear to be reliable. Because the dates were dispersed, it was possible to get an adequate number of them to supervise the voting on the day of the election. It was a remarkable election in West Bengal which was held under the strict control of the Election Commission that implemented its authority strictly in accordance with its constitutional obligations to Indian democracy. Although the electoral outcome brought back the incumbent Left Front government to power, unlike in Bihar where a new government was installed replacing the government that held power for more than 15 years, the Commission provided critical inputs to the processes of democratization by empowering the ordinary voters who now became part of 'the movers and shakers' of Indian democracy and could be ignored only at the cost of the political parties seeking political power. In other words, the voters were not merely seasonal participants had also been made to feel their importance in the political processes that hardly mattered so far in their everyday lives.

VI

No study on Indian administration can be conclusive without reference to the context. In other words, a history-specific understanding of administration is the only way of conceptualizing its nature in the rapidly changing socio-economic and political milieu. There cannot be an exception to this formulation. However, there do exist some common conceptual parameters which are useful to initiate probing into the specificities of governance. For instance, the Weberian 'laboratory-version of ideal form of organization' is such a parameter that provides an explanatory model which purports to be universal! Similarly, the Marxist conceptualization of bureaucracy being 'state-formalism' is theoretically immensely significant while critiquing Max Weber's ideal form of organization. Likewise, the non-Western tradition in public administration, articulated by Gandhi, Julius Nyerere, Mao-Zedong, among other, is another powerful endeavour at theory-building by being sensitive to the structure of administration in different historical-contextual milieu. Despite being situation-specific, this alternative outlook seems to have given adequate space as a well-defined structure to the Weberian idea of bureaucracy while seeking to understand the specific socio-economic roots of public administration that had evolved in different contexts. So, conceptually, the well-established theoretical parameters of the Western variety cannot be abandoned so easily because of their intellectual viability, although not in grasping specific public administration in its entirety, but in at least, getting into the problem. A comprehensive study of a specific administration can thus be initiated only when one, despite being faithful to classical theoretical parameters, is equally sensitive of the historical context in which it has its organic roots; only then, is a fair understanding of public administration possible.

In light of the above conceptual clarifications, one is now well-equipped to pursue a meaningful study of Indian administration in historical contexts which also act as the determinants of its nature. There are three basic questions that the present study seeks to address for an appropriate understanding of India's governance which bears a clear imprint of colonialism as well.

The first question is conceptual and relates to the nature of Indian public administration that has evolved in the contrasting socio-economic contexts of colonialism and its aftermath. How does one conceptualize Indian administration as a historical category? A plausible answer to this question involves a threadbare discussion of the historical reality, beginning with the British rule till the adoption of the New Economic Policy 1991 of globalization, liberalization and privatization, which always creates new priorities for the administration. There are clearly three different historical contexts with completely contrasting kinds of demands: colonialism had its preferences which were not, for obvious reasons, appealing to the nation after decolonization; with the endorsement of the socialistic pattern of society model during the phase before liberalization, Indian administration had to adapt to the new circumstances while seeking to execute the political belief of the government in terms of specific administrative feats; while endeavouring to articulate neoliberal policy decisions, the New Economic Policy 1991 put new demands on the administration which was expected to change gear accordingly. These roughly divided phases are a testimony of how Indian the administration has had to over time to respond to the historical situations that always represents an era with newer demands and requirements.

The second question is linked with the structure of administration. As is argued earlier, Indian administration confronts new policy priorities intermittently. India has clearly overgrown the past system of governance. Tasks before the government have expanded significantly, both in volume and complexity. Now the question is, is the structure of administration inflexible or flexible enough to address the new structural requirement? The answer is obvious as a precursory view of the Indian administration suggests. It is also obvious that new challenges need new structures. In two major ways, this has historically been done. On the one hand new departments have been created to take care of new requirements which were not so significant in the past. For instance, the concern for environment is a recent phenomenon and a new ministry was formed to deal with issues of environment. That it is also a global concern immediately links it with global agencies and also agencies/departments across the nation. So, environment, given its global implications, is both a domestic and transnational issue, which needs to be tackled differently and for which different structures are required to be put in place. This is also true of most of government departments which function in collaboration with others in view of the growing complexities of governance in the context of the consolidation of what is euphemistically called, the LPG (Liberalized–Privatized–Globalized) regime.

The third question raises a fundamental theoretical issue relating to the Weberian conceptualization of bureaucracy being a rational organization. Since the Indian administration keeps changing to adapt to the changing socio-economic milieu, how can it be rational in the Weberian sense? The answer to this question involves an empirical assessment of the Indian administration over a historical period of time. A perusal of the nature of Indian administration clearly suggests that similar to what Weber thought, the Indian administration endorses, as David Beetham (1995, 79) argues, 'a process of social levelling and the destruction of privilege particularly that based on birth'. Besides challenging birth-related privileges, Beetham (1995, 79) further suggests that the bureaucracy thrives because '[n]ot only did it grow up historically in association with demands for equality before law, but [also because] the principles of "rational" administration themselves, based on specialist knowledge and the employment of experts demanded a broadest possible social base of recruitment'. Rationality is maintained because of the social cohesion that the administration represent which stems not only from 'the common economic position and interests of its members, [but also] from the prestige of the life-style which distinguishes them' (Beetham 1995, 79). It is universally true that the bureaucracy is a secluded social entity and the aloofness from the wider social context is sustained by being 'rational'. Despite being differently textured historically, the Indian administration follows the Weberian dictum of rationality by following impersonal rules and regulations also the recruitment procedure, based on objective qualification and not birth. There is hardly a contradiction between being conceptually Weberian and historically conditioned because the former focuses on the structural characteristics of public administration that articulates its responses in accordance with the prevalent socio-economic and political circumstances. So being Weberian does not seem to be contradictory with being historically conditioned.

What is fundamental here is the idea that Indian administration is not static, but a vibrant socio-political institution that relocates its centre of gravity in accordance with the historical requirements of time. This explains why Indian administration continues to nurture some of the colonial traits even six decades after independence. There is undoubtedly structural continuity in so far as Indian administration is concerned though in terms of its nature it has undergone a sea change following the 1947 British withdrawal from India. This is also to suggest that Indian administration by being receptive to changing socio-economic impulses seems to have the characteristics of a living social organism that is adjustable to newer contextual inputs. While explaining structural continuity one should not also ignore the political significance of liberalism that continues to be respected, cutting across social strata even in the context a globalizing India. What is striking is the fact that despite being historically viable in independent India, liberalism was gradually introduced in India during the long duration of colonialism and does not appear to have influenced India's founding fathers when they were asked to make a choice. And, as a result, the structure of administration that colonialism bequeathed was retained and was imbued socio-politically with completely different priorities and preferences.

VII

Indian administration is a unique experiment which cannot be understood, let alone conceptualized with reference to the so-called universal models of conceptualizing public administration. In view of the complexities of its journey over different historical contexts, it is hardly possible to explain the peculiarities in Indian administration in a simplistic monocausal way of the one-size-fits-all formula. One needs to be sensitive to the journey to be able to capture the distinctive characteristics that it has acquired from different historical phases. Here there are two aspects of the journey that one has to keep in mind: on the one hand, it is obvious that administrative transformation in India is contingent on the prevalent socio-economic circumstances; and there is another equally important aspect, which is drawn on the changing nature of leadership. For instance, the Nehruvian style of consensus building through dialogue and discussion was completely disrupted with the consolidation of personality-based politics in India at the behest of Indira Gandhi when Indian administration lost its impersonal character to a significant extent. That it had inner vitality was evident when the Indian administration came back to the rail following the replacement of constitutional authoritarianism in the aftermath of the 1977 national election. This reinforces the argument that 'the administration is part of the support system of democracy [along with the electorate]: the one votes and the other sustains the mandate' (Prasad 2006, 163). With the execution of policies complementary to democracy, Indian administration is a powerful aid for a definite kind of constitutionalism that has flourished over contrasting periods of history. In this sense, it has far exceeded its instrumental function of being involved in the mere execution of impersonal rules and regulations. Its role is also one of strengthening democracy in its true spirit and manifestation by truly being accountable to the people at large. Besides internal accountability, ascertained through a hierarchy of control, Indian administration is also subject to external accountability following the adoption of the Right to Information Act 2005 and the acceptance of the Citizens' Charter, among others. These are aspects of the democratization of Indian administration that have successfully adapted to the rapidly changing socio-economic realities of India in which it is no longer paternalistic in its attitude, but rather a partner in the processes of socio-economic transformation along with other governmental and nongovernmental players.

Democracy is sustained by the Constitution of India 1950 which, by laying-out an elaborate structure of administration, has hardly left any space for confusion. Perhaps the most exhaustive constitution in the known civilization, Indian Constitution seems to have passed the test of time. The most revealing example happens to be the survival of the democratic Constitution in the aftermath of the 1975–77 Emergency when constitutional authoritarianism rose its ugly head temporarily. The reasons are to be located in the popular zeal for democracy. The then administration, which positively responded to the authoritarian rule, presumably to please the political masters, readily changed its preferences once the Emergency was withdrawn in 1977 and the democratic-constitutional values and practices were upheld.

Does it mean that the Constitution failed us or we failed the Constitution? Here a perceptive comment by Rajendra Prasad, the Chairman of the Constituent Assembly appears to be most instructive. In response to a question of whether the Constitution is strong enough to halt distortion, Prasad argued that 'Constitution, like a machine, is a lifeless thing [which] acquires life because of the men who control it and operate it, and India needs today nothing more than a set of honest men who will have the interest of the country before them'.[8] This is the crux of the argument that to make the Constitution functional in accordance with its true spirit, the role of the administration that articulates constitutional values in terms of actual decisions is as critical as that of the citizens. The Constitution is a powerful voice that the administration cannot afford to ignore provided the citizens are also alert and ready to fulfil their assigned democratic duties by being active participants in the ongoing political processes. As a bridge between the citizens and administration, the Constitution of India discharges an equally powerful role that is critical in sustaining the democratic structure of governance and in contributing values which are complementary to its meaningful functioning even in apparent chaotic circumstances. In other words, in the dialectical interconnection between the administration and citizens, the Constitution plays a critical role by not only laying out the fundamental principles of governance, but by also suggesting how to articulate them in a democratic manner.

There is one fundamental point that is reinforced in the above discussion: an analytical study of Indian administration enables us to understand the interface between democracy, the Constitution and citizens in a historical perspective. While administration is definitely an instrument, it is unable to act as it pleases given the interface conditioning both its style of functioning and the decisions that it formulates. In the process, the interface becomes a critical determinant in so far as the Indian administration is concerned. This has serious theoretical implications because a mere instrumental view of Indian administration is severely restrictive since its functioning is dependent on the interface which brings forth newer possibilities out of the dialectical interconnection involving democracy, the Constitution and citizens.

VIII

Comprising 15 interrelated chapters, *Indian Administration: Evolution and Practice* provides an exhaustive study of the phenomenon in a historical perspective. Based on the arguments that (a) public administration is context-driven and (b) conceptualizing public administration as a universal design is theoretically myopic, the book substantiates the claim that a mere structural explanation of Indian administration shall always be misleading given the fact that its roots are well-ingrained in the prevalent socio-economic and political circumstances. Structures are undoubtedly important aspects of an administration though their behavioural pattern, it is further argued, shall remain inexplicable unless they are placed in a historical context. This is a fundamental point that one cannot afford to ignore if one seeks to understand Indian administration in its complex manifestation.

There are three implicit divisions in which the book is conceptualized: since administration is characterized by both structures and processes, the chapters are articulated accordingly; besides these, each chapter also dwells on those major issues that various wings of Indian administration deal with. Written in the textbook mould, the book allows adequate space to those fundamental features of Indian administration that are holding its kernel. It is difficult to classify aspects of administration in watertight compartments because it is primarily about the processes in which they are enmeshed in a very complicated manner. More so in the case of Indian administration which has had varied pasts. One should thus read these chapters in that fashion although they are separated analytically. One fundamental point that runs through the book is that despite having been analytically demarcated, the chapters are dialectically interconnected to comprehend the structure, features and nature of Indian administration.

Although the contents have not been divided, three interrelated parts are imbedded in the way the chapters are demarcated. The first two chapters focusing on the evolution of Indian administration and the philosophical foundation of its latest incarnation respectively are introductory in character. With the laying out of the field with an introduction, the second implicit part comprising eight chapters, from Chapter 3 to Chapter 10, is an endeavour towards illuminating both the structure and functioning of various administrative efforts in India. Instead of dwelling on specific departments, this part concentrates on institutions of governance and the mechanisms that they usually resort to while responding to administrative concerns. Of these chapters, Chapter 10, besides dealing with the forms of the civil services in India, is also devoted to analyzing their nature in response to various Pay Commission Reports aiming at reforming the Indian bureaucracy. Apart from elaborating some of the contemporary issues of Indian administration (Chapter 15), with five chapters (from Chapter 10 to 14), the third part delves into actual policy making and its manifold impact on citizens. While Chapter 11 deals with public policy in India and seeks to capture the phenomenon in a historical perspective, Chapter 12 is an elaboration of efforts at reforming the administration since the appointment of the First Administrative Reforms Commission in 1964. Chapters 13 and 14 are about specific administrative steps towards fulfilling citizens' welfare needs. Based on the argument that administration is a citizen-centric endeavour, these chapters also highlight the dialectical interrelationship between citizens and the administration in which the former usually puts the latter in constant check by always being vigilant.

In 15 detailed chapters, one of which deals with some of the major issues of contemporary relevance, the book is an attempt to explore the complex dynamics of Indian administration which is structurally Weberian, but has clear imprints of post-Weberian characteristics by being receptive to external stimuli in the form of civil society activism, among others. By being adaptive, it has adjusted well with India's changing socio-economic and political realities. Contextual in nature, Indian administration thus fulfils a historical role which remains inexplicable if judged in the traditional hierarchical form of organization in the Weberian mould. That it is not static is a testimony to its vibrant nature. While seeking to fathom governance in India, one thus needs to be sensitive to the changes that it has undergone over various phases of history. In this sense, Indian administration is not only an interesting empirical reality, but also provides theoretical challenges for conceptualization for two reasons: first, in view of its clearly context-specific character, it cannot be understood, let alone conceptualized, in a typical Weberian format; second, given the increasing importance of impulses from within the domestic and global milieu in Indian administration, it is almost impossible to grasp its nature without taking them into account. Since public administration is inherently situation-driven, as this study confirms, the attempts towards building universal model shall be anything but conceptually useful because of the obvious limitations, as shown earlier.

NOTES

1. Supportive of liberal democracy of the Western variety, Amartya Sen thus argues that democracy is always preferable because there is a plurality of virtues: first, an intrinsic importance of political participation and freedom of human life; second, the instrumental importance of political incentives in keeping governments responsible and accountable and third, the constructive role of democracy in the formation of values and in the understanding of needs, rights and duties'.
2. This point is drawn on Bidyut Chakrabarty and Rajendra Pandey (2008, 3–6).
3. According to Alam (2004, 22), 'democracy in India is an assertion of the urge for more self-respect and the ability to better oneself'.
4. For details of the UP case, see A. G. Noorani (2000, 328–39).

5. While elaborating the office of profit controversy, I have drawn on an unpublished article by J. S. Verma (2006), the former chief justice of India. I am thankful to Justice Verma for having shared this unpublished article, a part of which was printed in *The Times of India*.
6. *S. R. Bommai vs Union of India, AIR*, The Supreme Court of India, December 1994.
7. The figure is taken from Sumanta Banerjee (2006).
8. Rajendra Prasad's statement in the Constituent Assembly (29).

REFERENCES

Adeney, Katharine, and Andrew Wyatt. 2004. 'Democracy in South Asia: Getting beyond the Structure-agency Dichotomy'. *Political Studies* 52 (1): 1.

Alam, Javeed. 2004. *Who Wants Democracy?* New Delhi: Orient Longman.

Austin, Granville. 1999. *Working a Democratic Constitution: A History of the Indian Experience*. New Delhi: Oxford University Press.

Banerjee, Sumanta. 2006, 9 September. 'Salvaging an Endangered Institution'. *Economic and Political Weekly*: 3838.

———. 2006. 'Assembly Polls, 2006 : Elections, *Jatra* Style, in West Bengal'. *Economic and Political Weekly* XLI (10): 864.

Beetham, David. 1995. *Max Weber and the Theory of Modern Politics*. Cambridge: Polity Press.

Chakrabarty, Bidyut, and Rajendra Pandey. 2008. *Indian Government and Politics*. New Delhi: SAGE.

Chakrabarty, Dipesh. 2007. 'In the Name of Politics: Democracy and the Power of the Multitude in India'. In *From the Colonial to the Post-colonial: India and Pakistan in Transition*, edited by Dipesh Chakrabarty, Rochona Majumdar and Andrew Sartori, 36. New Delhi: Oxford University Press.

Chandravarkar, Rajnarayan. 2007. 'Customs of Governance: Colonialism and Democracy in the Twentieth Century India'. *Modern Asian Studies* 41 (3): 448.

Guha, Ramchandra. 2007. *India after Gandhi: The History of the World's Largest Democracy*. London: Picador.

Jaffrelot, Christophe. 2005. *India's Silent Revolution: The Rise of the Low Castes in North Indian Politics*. New Delhi: Permanent Black.

Kaviraj, Sudipta. 2000. 'Modernity and Politics in India'. *Daedalus* (Winter): 156–57.

Kothari, Rajni. 2002. *Memoirs*. New Delhi: Rupa & Co.

Low, D. A. 1997. *Britain and Indian Nationalism: The Imprint of Ambiguity, 1929–1942*. Cambridge: Cambridge University Press.

Manor, James. 2005. 'The Presidency'. In *Public Institutions in India: Performance and Design*, edited by Devesh Kapur and Pratap Bhanu Mehta, 116. New Delhi: Oxford University Press.

Mitra, Subrata. 1991, August. 'Crisis and Resilience in Indian Democracy'. *International Social Science Journal*: 567–68.

———. 2004, November. 'Constitutional Design, Democratic Vote Counting and India's Fortuitous Multiculturalism'. Working paper, Heidelberg, Heidelberg University, Germany.

Morris-Jones, W. H. 1974. *The Government and Politics of India*. Reprint, New Delhi: B I Publications.

Naipaul, V. S. 1991. *A Million Mutinies*. London: Heinemann.

Nandy, Ashis. 1989. *The Intimate Enemy: Loss and Recovery of Self under Colonialism*. Reprint, New Delhi: Oxford University Press.

Nehru, Jawaharlal. (13 December 1946) 2003. 'Resolution: Aims and Objects'. *Constituent Assembly Debates*, vol. 1, book no. 1. Reprint, New Delhi: Lok Sabha Secretariat.

Noorani, A. G. 2000. *Constitutional Questions in India*. New Delhi: Oxford University Press.

Prasad, Kamala. 2006. *Indian Administration: Politics, Policies and Prospects*. New Delhi: Pearson.

Prasad, Rajendra. *Constituent Assembly Debates*, vol. 12.

Rudolph, L. I. and S. H. Rudolph, 2002. 'Redoing the Constitutional Design: From an Interventionist to a Regulatory State'. In *The Success of India's Democracy*, edited by Atul Kohli, 141. Cambridge: Cambridge University Press.

Sen, Amartya. 1999. *Development as Freedom*. New Delhi: Oxford University Press.

Verma, J. S. 2006. *The Times of India*, 4 September.

Evolution of Indian Administration

1

LEARNING OBJECTIVES

1. To grasp the evolution of Indian administration with reference to socio-economic circumstances.
2. To understand the peculiar features of Indian administration in the context of socialistic pattern of society and neoliberalism.
3. To conceptualize parameters that are critical to clearly comprehending the complexities of Indian administration.

Indian administration is a mixed bag. Empirically, it has clear imprints of British administration while conceptually, it carries legacies of administrations that preceded the British rule. In this sense, Indian administration can be seen as both, a continuity and a break with the past: continuity because it carries forward administrative traditions of a bygone era, and a departure since independent India's public administration is expected to discharge completely different kinds of responsibilities in the changed socio-economic and political milieu following the withdrawal of the British from India. The structure of administration that had evolved during the long colonial rule was useful for governance even after independence reinforcing the argument that mere structural continuity was not an impediment towards fulfilling socio-economic goals of democratic India. Imbued with entirely different ideological purposes, the Indian administration in its new avatar was found to be adequate by the founding fathers even after independence. This also confirms the argument that public administration is contextual in nature and cannot be formatted in universally accepted specific models.

The pre-British, particularly Mughal, administrative forms and functions were absorbed by the imperial rule. A cursory look at colonial revenue administration reveals how similar it was with what the Mughal emperor, Akbar, had devised in the second half of the sixteenth century. His Finance Minister Todar Mal overhauled the revenue system of Akbar's Mughal Empire. In order to consolidate the sources of revenue, especially from land, he introduced revenue districts and employed officers to manage the collection of revenue. Instead of arguing for a flat rate of revenue across the Empire, Todar Mal fixed the rate in accordance with the yields per year. By being subject-friendly, he seemed to have strengthened the human aspect of revenue administration which was usually very ruthless in the past. Not only did it create a goodwill for the ruler, but it also helped the administration to collect revenue rather effortlessly.

The East India Company replaced Mughal rule in the middle of the eighteenth century which continued for almost 100 years when in 1858 India was brought under the British crown. Although a new system of administration was consolidated, it had clear imprints of the administration of the bygone eras. In a similar way, once India became politically free, her administration was not entirely new, given the continuity of the structure of administration that the British had built to fulfil their partisan interests. What is striking is how the structure of colonial administration becomes relevant even after decolonization. A persuasive response can be given to address the concerns of those who felt ideologically uncomfortable when nationalist leadership accepted the prevalent administration which served colonial interests even after political freedom from the British rule. The response can be articulated at two levels: at one level, the idea that structures are mere instruments and hence they cannot influence the decision-makers' sense; at another substantive level, the conceptualization that structures behave in accordance with those who run them in order to fulfil definite socio-economic goals. Besides having faith in the prevalent administration, the founding fathers were governed by political instability and the communal blood bath during the transfer of power in 1947.

Two points remain critical here: first, it is evident that the administration of independent India cannot be understood, let alone conceptualized, without adequately comprehending past administrative practices and the rules and regulations, given the visible signs of continuity between the present and its past manifestation. The other point is that since public administration is organic in character, the dynamism of its Indian counterpart cannot be theoretically articulated unless one is drawn to the contextual compulsions shaping its nature. The aim of this chapter is therefore twofold: (a) to identify those major landmark decisions, including legal enactments that significantly influenced the evolution of public administration over different phases of India's political history and (b) to articulate those important strands of administrative thought that remain useful in conceptualizing the unique character of Indian administration. What is primary here is to understand Indian administration with reference to changing historical contexts that decisively influences its articulation. The chapter is thus illustrative of the argument that public administration is invariably contextual and Indian administration is not an exception.

The chapter focuses on the British administration given its critical role in shaping what emerged after India attained political independence in 1947. Colonial administration had also adopted some of the past practices and legal stipulations showing perhaps the continuity between the erstwhile administration and the one that came in the wake of the British rule. Furthermore, there were definite strands of administrative thought in ancient political discourses, especially in the writings of Kautilya. Before dwelling on the specificities of the British administration, the chapter is devoted to those major trends in administration which are useful in comprehending Indian administrative thought. Instead of providing a very general discussion, we have picked up three representatives from two different historical periods to highlight critical ideas which remain significant in conceptualizing India's administrative history. Besides Kautilya who, by evolving fundamental conceptual categories of administration, laid the foundation of Indian administrative thought, three thinkers from the mediaeval period, namely Barni, Abul Fazal and Todar Mal, articulated important ideas to theorize administration in historical contexts. Not only did they provide persuasive conceptualizations, but they also built context-sensitive theoretical models of administration which despite being specific to the era they represented, are also useful in developing a functional administration. From the conceptual point of view, these ideas provide important conceptual categories in administrative thought though they may not be exactly appropriate in theoretically decoding contemporary Indian administration.

KAUTILYA (C. 350–283 BC)

In ancient Indian political thought, Kautilya and his *Arthasastra*[1] are widely acknowledged as the thinker and text that best delineate the broad contours of the political and administrative systems in ancient India. A political realist who accepted monarchy as the most suitable form of government, Kautilya provides a broad analysis of the basic issues of statecraft. A key aspect of the Kautilyan theory of state was articulated in his conceptualization of *Saptang* (seven organs). Focusing on the seven vital organs—the *Swami* (the ruler), the *Amatya* (the minister), the *Janapada* (the territory with people settled on it), the *Durga* (the fortified capital), the *Kosha* (the treasury), the *Danda* (the army) and the *Mitra* (the ally or friend)—the *Saptang* theory seeks to define the state as an organic entity rooted in these seven elements. The kind of the state that emerges from an analysis of the *Saptang* theory seems to be one enmeshed in the characteristics of a strong monarchy with a stable and systematic administration.

While seeking to operationalize the theory of the state, Kautilya made extensive use of the twin concepts of *Dharma* and *Danda*. Explaining *Dharma* as social duty involving obedience to the customary and sacred laws, Kautilya provided supremacy to *Dharma* comprising well-defined norms governing human conduct which were uniformly applicable to citizens irrespective of rank or position. He also maintained that in order for *Dharma* to function properly in society, the unmistakable role of *Danda* was not to be ignored. Besides being coercive, standing out as the prime instrument of discipline in society, *Danda* was also to instantiate in the personality of the king the right to punish a citizen if there was a gross violation of the established norms of the state, which were fundamentally determined by its sacred and customary laws. Accordingly, disciplining an aberrant citizen appeared to be an important duty of the King since failure in doing so would result in unnecessary disturbances and miseries for the otherwise peaceful and happy life of citizens. *Danda* thus remained a critical instrument to maintain peace and order in the kingdom.

Arthasastra further provides a conceptually coherent theory of interstate relations and diplomacy. In ancient Indian literary works, the whole idea of interstate relations was believed to be conceptualized through the notion of *Mandala* (circles). Hence, Kautilya also attempted to explain the dynamics of interstate relations in ancient times through his *Mandala* theory. The essence of the theory lies in delineating the position of a kingdom as an ally or enemy vis-à-vis the intending conqueror with respect to its spatial placement in the *Mandala*. Taking the *Vijigishu* (the conqueror or the ambitious king) as the reference point, Kautilya explained the theory in terms of four basic circles. For instance, in the first circle, the *Vijigishu*, his friend and his friend's friend existed as the three primary kings forming a circle of states, each possessing the five elements of sovereignty such as the *Amatya*, the *Janapada*, the *Durga*, the *Kosha* and the *Danda*. Consequently, a circle of states comprised 18 elements. This characteristic applied similarly to the other three circles of states, with the *Ari* (enemy of the *Vijigishu*), the *Madhyama* (the indifferent king) and the *Udasina* (the neutral king) placing kings at the core of each of the three circles. In summary, drawing on the texture of the four circles yielded the *Mandala* theory its structure of four primary circles of states, 12 kings, 60 elements of sovereignty and 72 elements of states. In the realm of interstate relations, in addition to the *Mandala* theory, Kautilya also elaborated upon what he called the *Upayas* (peace politics) and the *Shadgunyas* (six-war tactics). These were supposed to give operational advice to the conqueror as to how to conduct interstate relations in times of peace and war. Finally, Kautilya also put forward a detailed system of diplomatic relations amongst states and preferred a well-designed espionage system to be maintained by the king in order to remain immune from any internal or external threats to his life and state.

ZIAUDDIN BARANI (1285–1357)

The medieval period represents a distinct phase in the history of Indian political thought owing to the introduction of new aspects in the socio-economic and politico-administrative life of the people with the arrival of Muslim rulers. The unique feature of the Islamic way of life that existed in medieval times was a belief in the universality of the law of the Koran, as drawn from the teachings of the Prophet Mohammad. Consequently, the *Shariat*, based on the precepts of the Quran, was taken as the final authority on the very existence of life, with the rationale of the state and government being to serve the purposes of *Shariat*. The typical mode of political thinking now took the form of chronicles and the work of historians. In this regard, and taken as the representative thinker of medieval times, Ziauddin Barani developed a capacious account that sought to articulate the complex political life of the middle ages by focusing on the functional aspects of the institution of the Sultan with reference to the Islamic faith on the one hand and the social dynamics of life among the common people on the other.

Enriched and authenticated by his first-hand experiences in the functioning of the monarchy during the Sultanate period, two distinguished works of Barani stand out: *Tarikh-i-Firozeshahi* and the *Fatwa-i-Jahandari* in which he laid down secular principles of governance by advocating *Zawabit* (state laws in which the role of the Koran and *Shariat* appeared less central than previously). The basic rationale for the acceptance of the *Zawabit* by Barani, rather, seems to have been his realization that with the changing character of society, notably the increasing complexity of administering diverse peoples and unwieldy empires, it might not be possible to rule strictly in accordance with the stipulations laid down in the *Shariat*. In favouring *Zawabit, Barani was supporting a mode of governance* whose foundations were non-religious and secular. Although he maintained that the *Zawabit* should not be overtly contradictory to the precepts of the *Shariat*, he asserted that the former should be given due weight within the state as its aim was on the one hand, to introduce functional flexibility into the working of governmental departments and on the other, to foster loyalties to the king and the state.

THE MUGHAL ADMINISTRATION

This section has two parts: the first part deals with the ideas of Abul Fazal and Todar Mal who laid down specific types of governance during the Mughal reign, while the second part focuses on the actual structure of the Mughal administration.

Conceptual Points

Abul Fazal (1551–1602) was another thinker who pursued Barni's political discourse in the context of the Mughal rule that finally came to an end in the mid-eighteenth century following the British conquest. His *Ain-i-Akbari* was not merely a legal treatise but also provided an administrative structure in which the role of individual was also duly recognized. Divided into five books, this fundamental text primarily focused on the principles that the ruler was expected to honour while executing his deeds. Opposed to tyranny, Fazal stressed the importance of separation of power to avoid concentration of power in a single authority. Nonetheless, he was not in favour of restricting the power to the emperor suggesting perhaps a continuity to the tradition that Barni had left behind. Despite the limitations which were clearly contextual, Fazal's socio-political thought was a break with the past given the importance that he had accorded to Hindu–Muslim amity for administrative efficiency in India where Hindus constituted a majority.

In 1580, Akbar instituted a system, called the *Dahsala* or the *Bandobast Arazi* or the *Zabti* system. Under this, the average produce of different crops as well as the average prices prevailing over the previous 10 years were calculated. One-third of the average produce was the state's share, which was to be paid in cash. The credit for developing this system, *Ain-i-Dahsala*, goes to Todar Mal. *Ain-i-Dahsala* does not mean a 10-year settlement, but was based on an average of the produce and prices over the previous 10 years (Saran and Das). For the measurement of land, the *bigha* was adopted as the standard unit of area. While fixing land revenue, both continuity and productivity of cultivation were taken into account. Land which was being continuously cultivated was known as *polaj;* land which remained fallow (*parauti*) for a year paid full rates when they were brought under cultivation. *Chachar* was land which had not been cultivated for more than 3 years. It paid a progressive rate, the full rate was charged in the third year. *Banjar* was cultivable waste land. To encourage cultivation, relief was given to the cultivators for five years; the revenue was charged then.

The revenue was to be paid in cash. This was done in a well-defined manner: after the assessment of land revenue in kind, it was converted into cash with the help of price schedules (*dastur-ul-amal*) prepared at the regional level or *dastur* level for various food crops. For this purpose, the empire was divided into a large number of regions, called *dastur* at *pargana* (cluster of villages) level having the same type of productivity. The government supplied *dastur-ul-amal* at the tehsil level which explained the mode of land revenue payment. Each cultivator received a *patta* or title deed and *qubuliyat* (deed of agreement for payment of state revenue). A number of other systems of assessment were also followed during Akbar's reign. The most common was called *batai* or *ghallabakshi* (crop-sharing). This was of three types: first was *bhaoli* where crops were reaped and stacked, and divided in the presence of those who had a stake on the crops; the second type was *khet batai* where the fields were divided after sowing; the third type *was lang batai* where the grain heaps were divided. In Kashmir, the produce was gauged on the basis of ass loads (*kharwar*) and then divided. Under *batai,* the peasants were given the choice of paying in cash or kind, but in the case of cash crops, the revenue was to be deposited only in cash. This was what was followed under normal circumstances. Peasants were given remission in land revenue if the crops failed on account of natural calamities, like drought or floods; they were entitled to *amil* (advance cash) as *taccavi* (loan) for seeds, implements and animals in times of need (Agarwal).

Administrative Structure in the Mughal Era[2]

The basic aspects of administrative functioning during the Mughal period were divided into departments under the headship of certain high officials of the empire. However, the appointment of various officials as the heads of different departments was not in conformity with some sound principles of personnel administration but on the basis of the sweet will of the King and the *mansab* held by an officer. *Mansab* was a typical notion of the Mughal administration, drawn from military vocabulary and denoting the official designation of rank and profit of an officer who in case of necessity was required to supply a specified number of troops in the service of the King. Thus, the elite corps of officers of the Mughal administration consisted of the *mansabdars* of different ranks and could be seen as precursors of the modern times gazette civil services. The appointment of these *mansabdars* was exclusively in the hands of the King and they held the post only during their life time without any hereditary claim on the *mansab*. Though merit was a consideration in granting the *mansabs* from time to time, it was in most cases a kind of patronage which the King used to bestow only upon those people who had proved their loyalty and efficiency in his eyes. Without any formal training in the task of administration, the *mansabdars* were mostly officials who learnt the art of administration by actual performance of the task over a period of time. The *mansabdari* system started fading away with the decline in the quality of the Mughal administration, though the British tried to emulate the same system during the colonial rule by according the various titles like Zamindars, Rai Bahadur and Khan Bahadur, etc. However, with the adoption of a democratic and egalitarian socio-political order in the country after independence, the whole concept of according a privileged position to a few individuals on the basis of their personalized services to the government was done away with.

Unlike the personnel administration of the Mughal Empire which owing to its obvious elitist and discriminatory character did not find much favour even with the British and was totally abolished in independent India, the characteristics of the provincial administration of the Mughal rulers continued to exist in one form or the other in many parts of the country. On the pattern of the Mughal provinces called *subah,* the country was divided into various presidencies during the British time which were thereafter converted into the modern day states and union territories. Each *subah* was an independent unit of governance during the Mughal period under the overall inchargeship of an official called the *Subedar* entrusted with the task of what may be called as the law and order functions of the province. Existing parallel to the *subedar* was an officer known as the provincial *diwan* who was assigned with the specific task of revenue collection, besides looking after the appointment of other officials of the province and maintenance of the provincial fort. Thus, we find a clear demarcation in the functional domain of the two officials with independent charge of the law and order and the revenue departments respectively, though placing both officers on the equal footing seemingly violated the principle of the unity of command and was fraught with the dangers of clash of personalities between the two high dignitaries. The two officers were also authorized to make a number of appointments at lower levels of the administration of the province in order to carry out their functions smoothly. Hence, while on the side of the *subedar*, his main assistant was an officer called *fauzdar*, the *diwan* was assisted by officers called *amins*, *kroris* and *tahsildars*.

Amongst the administrative units which bear a huge resemblance to the system prevailing during the Mughal Empire, the local or district administrations stand out prominently. Like the modern times when each state is divided into various districts as the main unit of administration, the Mughal period saw the division of a *subah* into various administrative units called *sarkar*s which were further divided down the line into different *pargana*s or subdivision levels and *mawdah* or a host of villages and *naglah* or a small hamlet. These administrative units still exist in a number of states of the country like Uttar Pradesh. Like modern day practice, the administration of the *sarkar* was divided into two broad heads: law and order and the revenue collection. While the *fauzdar* was in charge of law and order of the *sarkar*, revenue collection was the responsibility of an officer called the *amin* who was further assisted by an official called the *khazandar* for collecting money from the cultivators. At the *pargana* level, the *shigar* used to be the officer-in-charge, whose counterpart in modern times is known as the *parganadhikari*. His chief assistants in the field were the *qanungo* who dealt with the survey, assessment and collection of revenues. The *patwari*s were and remain the lowest ranking revenue officials entrusted with the task of conducting real ground level activities in the villages and listen to the grievances of villagers on issues relating to revenue collection. During the Mughal period when the King used to remain confined to his palace, it was these officials from the level of the *shigar* to that of the *patwari*s who remained the reflection of the King in the minds of the common people. In present time, with the arrival of democratic decentralization though, people's representatives have become the important link between the government and the people, and officials with almost the same nomenclature have remained the backbone of the revenue administration of the government.

The law and order administration of the Mughal Empire also became the precursor for the modern day police system, though substantial changes were made in the system by the British during the long span of their rule in India. Since the King himself was in charge of the safety and security of his kingdom from external aggression and internal disturbances, hence at the central level there was no official specifically assigned with the task of looking after law and order problems for the Empire. In certain cases, his prime minister, called *vakil,* used to assist the King mainly in advisory capacities on the issues concerning the domestic affairs of the kingdom. However, from the provincial level and below, the subject of law and order was vested with the most important official of the province, namely the *fauzdar.* Though he was tasked with a few more functions, yet his most significant responsibility pertained to the maintenance of law and order in the province whose breach was considered to be a serious lapse on his part. An important lacuna with regard to the law and order administration of the Mughal rulers was the omission of the vast rural areas in a *sarkar* from the point of view of appointing a specific official responsible with the matter. Rather, taking urbanized areas as the unit of administration, a *kotwal* was appointed to him for the maintenance of the law and order in the *sarkar.* Leaving the vast mass of the rural areas to fend for themselves on the issue of law and order, the onerous responsibility was vested with the *chaukidar* who was paid and maintained by the village community out of their own resources. Thus, the maintenance of law and order appears to be one of the most neglected aspects of the civil administration of the Mughal rulers.

In contrast to the pathetic condition of the administration of law and order, the revenue administration of the Mughal Empire was a highly developed and well knit one. In fact, right from the King till the lowest rank official of the kingdom, the concern for revenue administration was apparent in the nature of responsibilities allocated. Under the overall supervision of the king, the diwan or *wazir* used to be the chief revenue official of the state. Assisted by a number of subordinate officials, the *wazir* advised the King on basic policy perspectives of the kingdom and took care of the day-to-day affairs of the revenue or finance department. Down the line, the provincial *diwans* were appointed by the King but functioned under the subordination of the *wazir* with regard to his day-to-day activities. However, the real functionary charged with the responsibility of augmenting the revenues of the kingdom was an official known as the *krori* or the collector of the revenue of one crore dam. It was the office of the *krori* which after numerous combinations and permutations appears to have become the office of the collector in modern times. Two assistants of the *krori* in the discharge of his revenue functions included the amin officer-in-charge of the assessment of the revenue, and the *fotahdar,* that is, the officer who was to be paid revenues by the villagers in the real sense of the term. Further down the line, the *qanungo* was entrusted with the responsibility of conducting a survey of all the landed property, keeping records of the tax payers and being well versed with the revenue related rules and regulations whereas the *patwari* was in charge of taking the revenue department down till the common tax payers by being in touch with them and providing them with any information or messages regarding matters of revenue. The elaborate system of revenue collection, in contrast to the neglect of the law and order functions, brings forth that the Mughal administration was mainly a revenue collection administration and does not provide a holistic picture of civil administration during the medieval times.

In final analysis, it can be said that the Mughal administration basically helped the British in building up an Anglicized system of administration which was suitable for carrying out the functions of the colonial state. Contextualized in the perspective of the minimalist role of the state, the Mughal administration appeared to be interested in the performance of only those functions without which the existence of the state itself would be in jeopardy. Not surprisingly, therefore, is the finding that the most important preoccupation of the administration during the Mughal period was the collection of revenue, for the proper conduct of which there existed a very elaborate and fine-tuned administrative set-up. Besides that, the only other department getting the direct attention of the ruler seemed to be the administration of law and order, without which the shape of the state itself would not have remained intact. Still, the administration of law and order stood only in subordination to the administration of land revenue, though in normal course of times the two looked to be coterminous with each other. Though the Mughal administrative set-up was marred by a number of shortcomings in terms of its structure, staffing patterns and functional dynamics, credit needs to be given to the vision and endeavour of rulers of the time for at least conceptualizing and putting into place a system of administration which was able to hold the vastly expanded boundaries of the empire and provide a semblance of civilized life to the people by discounting any possibility of chaos and disorder in the society.

THE BRITISH LEGACY IN INDIAN ADMINISTRATION

The nature of the British administration also varied: under the East India Company, the Crown was not directly involved in administration; it was peripherally linked as the supreme authority controlling the Company that functioned under the overall administrative jurisdiction of the British queen. Empowered by the Crown, two institutions were entrusted with the operation of the Company in India: the Court of Proprietors and the Court of Directors. These two Courts were largely independent and decided the course of action for the Company in India. The Queen's charter authorized the Courts to fulfil its goal in India without almost any restrictions. The Company functioned in a ruthless manner, guided solely by its commercial interests. Although there were attempts by the Company's rulers to bring about reforms in administration, they remained largely academic in nature. Complaints against the 'misrule' of the Company poured in and as a result, the House of Commons appointed a Committee of Secrecy to look into the authenticity of the complaints. The findings of the Committee went seriously against the Company. The result was the adoption of the Regulating Act of 1773, the first formal articulation of the British supremacy over a part of India that abolished the Dual Government of the Company.

The Regulating Act, 1773

This Act was the first measure of the British Parliament that facilitated direct interventions in the affairs of the Company. Although the power of the Company's Directors remained unaltered, the regulation that the Company was required to keep the Treasury Bench informed, reduced its independence drastically. The Governor of Bengal, Warren Hastings was now designated as the Governor General who was to be assisted by a Council of four members, recommended by the Crown. According to the Act, the supreme authority rested not with the Governor General, but with the Council, guided by the principle of majority while taking a decision vis-à-vis India. While in India, the Council remained supreme, but it had to function under the supervision, direction and control of the Court of Directors in London.

The Act was a major milestone in India's public administration for four specific reasons: First, by restraining the Company, the Act simply endorsed the importance of values in administration. As the Company was involved in public administration in India, it could hardly avoid its obligations towards the ruled. The intervention by the Crown clearly suggested that the British government was not at ease with the way the Company was managing its affairs in India. So, the Act was largely an outcome of an ideological concern of the rulers in England for the governed in India. There is no denying the fact that colonial interests remained paramount, though the Act contributed to a social and political ambience that led to the adoption of ameliorating legal enactments in the course of time. Second, rejecting individual-based administration, as epitomized by the Governor, the Act also made the Council accountable to the Crown. This was a significant break from the past because public administration was not merely governance, but governance with a purpose. So, apart from laying down the structure of administration, the 1773 Act sought to change the ideological basis of the Company rule that was guided by the well-established principles of administration and had evolved in the long tradition of Westminster democracy under the Crown. Third, the Act marked the beginning of centralization. The Governor-General-in-Council became the supreme ruler in India and the Governors of the three presidencies of Bengal, Madras and Bombay were reduced to subordinate governments. Within the overall control of the Governor General, the Act however demarcated administrative domains of the Governors of the presidencies which was in turn critical to the evolution of public administration in India. By involving the Council in administration, the Act also inaugurated a new trend in the Company's rule that no longer, remained, at least theoretically, as arbitrary as before. The Governor General was required to consult the Council and was also made accountable to the British Parliament. Finally, the most outstanding feature of the Act was the establishment of a Supreme Court in Calcutta. This Court was founded under the Letters of Patent with Elijah Impey as the Chief Justice and three other judges. Primarily, a Court of record, it also had civil, criminal, ecclesiastical, admiralty, equity and supervisory jurisdiction over the whole Presidency and any other person in the employment of the Company even outside the Presidency.

As is evident, the Act was most critical to public administration in India because (a) it laid down the skeleton of the governmental system of modern India and (b) all subsequent enactments can be said to have either enlarged or amplified the basic text of the 1773 Act. Despite its limited appeal in today's context, the Act was radical in its approach and content. By holding the Company responsible to the Parliament, the Act sought to shape the Company's administration in accordance with principles of 'formal' democracy. Although the Act recommended unitary command by suggesting the supremacy of the Governor-General-in-Council, it was also a device for 'limited' decentralization because the Governors of the presidencies remained independent, at least administratively, within their respective domains.

The Regulating Act of 1773 was not sufficiently equipped to address the administrative distortions in India under Company rule. The parliamentary committee under Edmund Burke exposed the arbitrary functioning of the Governor General and Chief Justice and recommended for their recall. But it was not possible because the Board of Proprietors refused to respect the recommendation. This led to a constitutional crisis because it also demonstrated the lack, if not absence, of parliamentary control over Company rule in India. In response, the Pitt's India Act of 1784 was enacted. According to this Act, the Court of Directors were allowed 'free hands' to manage commercial affairs of the Company in India while in the political sphere, authority was vested in a new body, known as the Board of Control comprising six Commissioners. Appointed by the King, the Board had in it the Chancellor of the Exchequer, a Secretary of State and four Privy Councillors. The Board retained full powers of 'superintendence, direction and control' of all operations of the civil and military governments of the British territorial possessions in the East Indies. The Court of Proprietors lost its hegemony in Company's affairs except in the election of Directors who were given the authority to make appointments of all posts in India, though the Crown was authorized to recall any person in the employment of the Company.

In the evolution of public administration in India, the Pitt's Act was an important benchmark for two reasons: First, the Act established the supremacy of the British Crown in territories controlled by the Company. Administration was now an elaborate arrangement involving those appointed by the King and accountable to the Parliament. Through various structural mechanisms, the British government sought to create a system of governance in India which was qualitatively different from any of the preceding administrations. Second, this Act introduced a new policy in relation to the Indian princes by laying down that the Company needed to follow a policy of 'non-interference' in their affairs. In other words, the Company was restricted to those areas which were already under its control. The non-intervention policy was short-lived and by the end of the eighteenth century, especially with the arrival of Wellesley as the Governor General, the British Empire in India was transformed into the British empire of India. Wellesley accomplished his task both by military stringency and by strategic 'subsidiary alliances' with the Indian princes. What was remarkable about Wellesley, apart from his role as an empire builder, was his concern for an efficient administration because he believed that without skilled administrators, the Empire could not survive. With this intent, he founded a college at Fort William for the training of the Company's civil servants. From here, one can trace the genesis of the Indian Civil Service that was to be founded soon.

The Charter Act, 1833

Of all the Acts, enacted by the British Parliament to govern the East India Company in India, the Charter Act of 1833 was perhaps the most watershed legislative intervention in India's public administration. Why was such an Act necessary? The administration, both in India and Britain, confronted new circumstances following the rapid expansion of the British Empire in India. The administrative machinery was not adequate for holding the empire together. In Britain, parliamentary reforms led to a new form of governance largely due to the influence of the Enlightenment philosophy with its emphasis on enlightened liberalism. There was a clamour for free trade with India, unrestricted immigration of Europeans into India, reform of laws and improvement of education in India. Two ardent liberals who brought about changes in the British attitude during this period were Macaulay and James Mill. While the former, also a parliamentarian, was the Secretary to the Board of Control and the latter was the Examiner of India correspondence at India House.

As the Company lost its commercial monopoly in India following the acceptance of the Charter Act, all restrictions to European immigration into India were removed. Besides, the Act introduced new devices of administrative control in India which were as follows: First, the Governor General, now designated as Governor General of India was vested with supreme authority insofar as civil, military and revenue administration were concerned. In the centralized administration, the Governors of other provinces were subordinates to the Governor General who became the pivot of British administration in India. Second, all decisions of the Governor General and Governors, overriding the decisions of their respective Executive Councils were to be supported by recorded statement of the reasons. This was a rider in the stipulation to restrain those holding supreme authority. Third, all legislative powers were vested in the Governor-General-in-Council and the provincial governments lost their legislative powers. Laws approved by the Governor-General-in-Council came to be designated as acts and the endorsement of the Supreme Court for their validity was withdrawn. These acts were applicable to all Courts. Fourth, a Law Member who was to be an English Barrister was to be appointed to the Governor-General-in-Council in an advisory capacity. This appointment was certainly a significant step in the constitution of the Imperial Legislative Council. Macaulay, the first Law Member, was also entrusted with the task of codifying laws for India in his capacity as the President of the Indian Law Commission that came into being at the behest of the Governor General. Finally, the Charter Act was also a powerful statement against discrimination in employment under the Company in terms of religion, place of birth, descent, colour or any of these. Although this principle was theoretically endorsed, in practice it was otherwise, for reasons connected with colonialism.

Public administration in India gradually became complex with the expansion of the British Empire. While the 1773 Regulation Act ushered in an era of centralized administration of the Company, the 1833 Charter Act marked the culmination of that process by establishing the authority of the Crown over the administration in India. The Governor General became supreme along with the Council. As evident, the Indian administration was largely Weberian in spirit and content: it was hierarchical and centralized involving various layers of administration within the overall structure of the British rule. Its purpose was defined by colonialism that remained a determining influence, for obvious reasons, until India's independence in 1947.

The Act for the Good Government of India, 1858

Perhaps the most distinctive Act that radically altered the nature of public administration in India was the Act of 1858 which brought the East India Company's century-old rule to an end. In order to strengthen the colonial rule in the aftermath of the 1857 abortive revolt of the Indian army, which was characterized as the first war of independence, this Act stipulated devices to improve the administrative machinery by which the Indian government was to be superintended and controlled by the Crown in England. As the 1858 Queen's proclamation that led to the adoption of this Act underlines, [The Queen appoints Viscount Canning as] the First Viceroy and Governor General in and over our said territories, and to administer the government in our name, and generally to act in our name and on our behalf, subject to such orders and regulations as he shall, from time to time, receive through one of our Principal Secretaries of State.

Furthermore,

> [W]hen, by the blessing of Providence, internal tranquility shall be restored, it is our earnest desire to stimulate the peaceful industry of India, to promote works of public utility and improvement, and to administer the Government for the benefit of all ours subjects resident therein. In their prosperity will be our strength, in their contentment our security, and in their gratitude our best reward.

As is evident, the Proclamation provided significant inputs to the Act of 1858. By abolishing the Court of Directors and the Board of Control, the Act transferred the government, territories and revenues from the Company to the Crown. India was to be governed by the English Sovereign that, by implication, suggested the importance of the British Parliament for governance in India. As the pivot of colonial administration, the Secretary of State for India discharged all powers vested earlier in the Board of Control and Court of Directors. As a member of the cabinet, the Secretary of State drew his salary from the revenues, generated from India. He was authorized to place the annual statement of accounts of all government revenue and expenditure in India and to submit a report of all moral and material progress in India. To assist him in the discharge of his constitutional and administrative responsibilities, he was provided with a Parliamentary and a Permanent Undersecretary. A council, designated as the India Council, was constituted to help him perform his duties most efficiently. The Council was mainly an advisory aid and its role was thus limited though on various occasions it acted in a decisive manner to influence the decisions of the Governor General through other constitutional bodies. The Act of 1858 was not qualitatively different from the earlier Acts in the sense that it made no spectacular changes in colonial administration except that it vested the entire revenue of the country in the hands of the Governor-General-in-Council. Provincial governments became totally subsidiary to the Council. Another paramount Act which introduced non-official members in the administration was the 1861 Indian Councils Act. The function of the Council was limited to legislation and had no authority to control the executive though it empowered the provincial governments to legislate on provincial matters. The Executive Council was expanded to include the Advocate General of the provinces, in addition to four non-official members who were invariably Indians.

The Indian Councils Act is a remarkable piece of legislation for two important reasons: First, it was an important step towards the decentralization of power and in that sense it was a break with the past. For the first time, steps were taken to provide an alternative to centralized British administration. Second, it also introduced Indians in the administration and by recommending the inclusion of non-official members. It was a deliberate political design to accommodate elite Indians in public administration and had an enormous impact, especially in the aftermath of the 1857 uprising. Although those who were nominated were either Indian princes or big land owners, it was undoubtedly a significant beginning towards involving Indians in public administration.

In the early part of the Crown administration, two processes seem to have worked. On the one hand, attempts were made to strengthen the Governor-General-in Council and on the other hand, steps towards devolution, especially of, financial power. In this connection, the 1870 Mayo resolution is most remarkable which stated,

> Local interest, supervision and care are necessary to success in the management of funds devoted to education, sanitation, medical charity and local public works. The operation of the resolution in its full meaning and integrity will afford opportunities for the development of local self-government, for strengthening municipal institutions and for association of the natives and Europeans to a greater extent than before in the administration of affairs.

Several Acts were enacted to constitute municipalities in Bombay, Calcutta and Madras. The most eventful development in this regard was undoubtedly the 1882 Ripon Resolution that defended the introduction of local self-government by underlining that it was introduced 'not primarily with a view to improvement in administration. It is chiefly desirable as an element of political and popular education'. In pursuance of this goal, the 1885 Bengal Local Self Government Act was adopted which led to the formation of district local boards in Bengal.

The trajectory of the British rule in its initial phase suggests a phased decentralization of administration and growing involvement of Indians in administration. Two substantial events changed the course of colonialism: (a) the founding of the universities of Calcutta, Madras and Bombay that helped develop an articulate opinion of educated Indians on the British rule. It captured the growing discontent amongst Indians who always remained, for obvious reasons, peripheral in administration. (b) The inauguration of the Indian National Congress in 1885 which created a new platform to ventilate the grievances of the ruled. This also became a forum for the Indians to articulate demands for better rule. The outcome of all this was the 1892 Indian Councils Act. As the Act underlines,

> [Its aim was] to widen and expand the functions of the Government of India, and to give further opportunities to the non-official and native elements in Indian society to take part in the work of the Government, and in that way, to lend official recognition to that remarkable development both of political interest and political capacity that had been visible among the higher classes of Indian society since the Government of India was taken over by the Crown in 1858.

The Act provided for the enhanced membership of the Councils. It was mandatory for the government to consult representative bodies and institutions, approved by the government, before selecting nominees for the Councils. Besides legislative powers, the Councils were also empowered to pull up the Executive on financial matters though it had no power to either revise or reject decisions on this matter. However, the growing weight given to the Councils was indicative of a sea change in colonial rule. As Morley, the Secretary of State, articulated,

> [T]here are two rival schools of thought, one of which believes that better government of Indian depends on efficiency, and that efficiency is, in fact, the end of British rule in India. The other school, while not neglecting efficiency, looks also to what is called political concessions. (Pylee 1965, 68)

This declaration laid the foundational principles of British administration in India. As a first step, a Royal Commission was appointed in 1907 to look into an administration that seemed to have lost its viability in the context of growing discontent amongst the ruled. The aim of the Commission was to provide an administration which was able to adapt to the changed social, economic and political realities of India. While recommending the corrective measures, the Commission was guided by the following factors; (a) the difficulties of ruling the vast subcontinent from a single headquarter and the inevitable failure of the statesmanship and efficiency in administration; (b) the difficulties of applying uniform schemes of development for the provinces which were socio-culturally diverse; (c) to instil a sense of responsibility among those engaged in provincial and local administration and (d) to strengthen colonial rule by educating people on the values of strong administration. On the basis of the recommendation of the Commission, a bill was introduced in 1908 which became the 1909 Morley–Minto Reforms. As a political scheme seeking to strengthen colonial rule in India, the 1909 Act introduced a profound change with long term effects on the representation of communities in Councils. Once the Muslim League was founded in 1906 there were demands for a 'separate electorate' for Muslims. In his plea to the Governor General, the Muslim League chief, Aga Khan defended the need for a separate electorate for the Muslims on the basis of their 'numerical strength', 'political importance' and 'contribution' which they made 'to the defence of the Empire'. Endorsing the argument, Minto assured Aga Khan that Muslims 'may rest assured that their political rights will be safeguarded' (Pylee 1965, 68). So, the 1909 Act is a watershed in the history of representation in India. Muslims were recognized as a separate community with their electoral rights also guaranteed accordingly. The British policy of 'divide and rule' was thus formally articulated. The British policy of 'divide and rule' was thus formally articulated and public administration became partisan, for obvious reasons. Meanwhile, the Nationalist Movement gained momentum and the political atmosphere in India changed. The 1909 Morley–Minto Reforms failed to address the genuine grievances of the ruled. Various other Acts were also enacted to reinforce the repressive system of governance that was articulated by the 1909 Reform scheme. With the outbreak of the First World War, a change in the attitude of the British government was visible and this was largely 'strategic' in order to solicit the support of Indians in its war efforts. The result was the adoption of the 1919 Montagu–Chelmsford Reform scheme which was guided by the committed goal of the government 'to increase association of the Indians in every branch of the administration and the gradual development of self-governing institutions in India' (Pylee 1965, 89). On the surface, the Reform scheme, appeared to be novel and drew on the commitment to make public administration India-friendly, as the four major principles that formed the core of the scheme, suggested:

1. There should be, as far as possible, complete popular control in local bodies and the largest possible independence for them of outside control.
2. The provinces are the domain in which the earlier steps towards the progressive realization of responsible government should be taken. Some measures of responsibility should be given at once, and the aim of the British government is to provide complete

responsibility to the Indians in their governance to the extent possible under the present circumstances.

3. The Government of India must remain wholly responsible to the Parliament and having such responsibility, its authority in essential matters must remain indisputable pending experience of the effect of changes now to be introduced in the provinces. Meanwhile, the Indian legislative council should be enlarged and made more representative and its influence in the processes of policy making needs to be enhanced.

There is no denying that the 1919 Act was a politically appropriate strategy in a context when the Nationalist Movement was growing in importance, especially after the arrival of Mahatma Gandhi on the scene. Although the administration was guided by the colonial spirit, by involving loyalist Indians in governance, the British rulers provided a new design of public administration in India. In the new dispensation, structural changes in administration were made. The most remarkable step was the adoption of dyarchy. The dyarchy was an administrative device that demarcated functions between those which were to be given to popular control and those which needed to continue to remain with the British rulers: the former were called 'transferred subjects' and the latter 'reserved subjects'. The Governor-General-in-Council was in charge of the reserved subjects while Governors, acting with the ministers in the provinces, remained supreme in so far as the transferred subjects were concerned.

Despite being unique, dyarchy was doomed to fail simply because of its ideological roots lying in colonialism. Even the Alexander Muddieman-led committee which was constituted to examine the functioning of dyarchy concluded that it crumbled because of its inherent weaknesses and dissensions due to the following factors: (a) the demarcation of authority between reserved and transferred was meaningless since the de facto power always rested with the former; (b) as a result, there was hardly effective dialogue between the provincial ministers and the Governors or the Governor General; (c) Indian ministers were further handicapped since the Indian civil service officers hardly cooperated with them; and (d) excessive control by the finance department of the Government of India over transferred subjects.

As was evident, public administration was constantly being restructured to placate the Indians in governance. Although the actual power rested with the British authority, dyarchy was a critical step towards administrative devolution and it radically altered the complexion of British power in India which largely revolved around the Governor-General-in-Council. Dyarchy empowered the Governors who exercised independence in regard to transferred subjects in the provinces. Furthermore, the involvement of Indian ministers had introduced changes, though cosmetic in character, in public administration. Apart from gaining experience in administration, Indian ministers acquired first hand knowledge of how the administration functioned in a most partisan manner. This helped them articulate a nationalist agenda which was now readily acceptable to the people at large since it was experience-based. So, dyarchy was very critical to conceptualizing the changing nature of public administration in British India at least in the first two decades of the twentieth century.

The Government of India Act, 1935

While colonialism and centralization of power seemed to go hand in hand, public administration in British India underwent changes at least in its content. A change is visible if one follows the evolution of public administration since the adoption of the 1772 Regulating Act. Perhaps the most (and last) significant constitutional measure in India during the British rule was the 1935 Government of India Act that drew on the inputs from the Indian Statutory Commission, the All Parties Conference, the Round Table Conferences and the Joint parliamentary Committee of the British Parliament. Seeking to establish a federal form of government in which the constituent provinces had autonomous legislative and executive powers, the Act paved the way for a parliamentary form of government in which the executive was made accountable within certain bounds to the legislature. This radically altered public administration in India, including the civil services. Although the well-espoused federation never came into being, the Act was nonetheless a powerful comment against the integrated administrative system of the colonial variety. A perusal of the Act draws our attention to the following features:

1. Provincial autonomy was recognized by giving the provinces a separate legal identity and liberating them from central control except for certain specific purposes.
2. A federation of India was established demarcating domains between the provincial governments and the federal central government.
3. Dyarchy, discontinued in the provinces, was introduced at the centre. Subjects of foreign affairs and defence were 'reserved' to the control of the Governor General; the other central subjects were transferred to ministers in the provinces.
4. The federal principle was recognized in the formation of the lower house of the central legislature though the de facto ruler remained the Governor General.
5. Separate electorate was retained following the distribution of seats amongst the minority communities, as devised by the 1932 Communal or MacDonald Award.

The Act redefined the term 'public' in public administration. The introduction of provincial autonomy enabled Indian ministers to directly get involved in administration though they had to function under the overall restriction of colonialism. Hence, it was characterized as 'a gigantic constitutional facade without anything substantial within it' (Pylee 1965, 117). The Act was also a sign of the determination of the British government to warp the Indian question towards electoral politics. By involving Indians in administration, the Act had brought more players in the arena of public administration. There is no doubt that the Act introduced Indian politicians to the world of parliamentary politics and as a result of the new arrangement, stipulated by the Act, politics now percolated down to localities which had largely remained peripheral so far. The available evidence also suggests that the Act was the price the British paid for the continuity of the Empire. What thus appeared to be a calculated generous gesture was very much a politically expedient step. In fact, the surrender of power, though at the regional levels, caused consternation amongst the votaries of the British power in India, who saw an eclipse of British authority in this endeavour.

An uncritical look at these selective, but major, landmark constitutional initiatives during the colonial rule may lead one to conclude that these were initiated by the British for the Indians. Hence the spirit of nationalism was underrated. If one goes beyond the surface what becomes evident is that public administration underwent changes largely because of British efforts to defuse popular discontent. Hence the argument that every constitutional drive was initiated by the Raj is totally unfounded. History reveals that there were situations which forced the British authority to adopt measures to control agitation. For instance, the Congress campaign in the 1880s contributed a lot to the introduction of the 1893 reforms. Behind the 1909 Morley–Minto Reforms lay the *Swadeshi* Movement and militant nationalism. Similarly, the 1919 Mont–Ford Reforms were attempts at resolving crises that began with the Home Rule League and climaxed with the 1919 Rowlatt Satyagraha and the Non Cooperation Movement of 1910–21. To a large extent, the Gandhian Civil Disobedience Movement (1930–32) accounted for the introduction of constitutional measures seeking to involve Indian politicians in public administration.

Furthermore, the interpretation of those constitutional designs remains partial unless linked with the broader socio-economic and political processes in which they were conceptualized. An attempt to analyse the structure and dynamics of constitutional politics without reference to the broader social matrix and economic nexus is futile because the political-Constitutional structure reflects economic and social networks, religio-cultural beliefs and even the nationalist ideology which impinged on the organized world of administrative and Constitutional structure. So an urgent and unavoidable task for an analyst is not to completely ignore the broader socio-economic context but to ascertain its relative importance in shaping a particular constitutional initiative. For instance, the 1932 Communal Award was believed to have been initiated by the British to expand political activity amongst the Muslims in Bengal and Punjab. But, as studies have shown, it was also a concession the British were forced to grant in order make the maintenance of the Empire easier. The sharing of power with the native elites was thus prompted by considerations other than merely British initiatives.

ALL INDIA CIVIL SERVICES AND PUBLIC ADMINISTRATION

The civil services in India—in terms of their structure, role, behaviour and interrelationships—have evolved over a long period in history since the designing of the system around the middle of the nineteenth century.[3] The Macaulay Committee Report, 1854 is a watershed in the growth of bureaucracy in India. By recommending a civil service based on the merit system, the Committee sought to replace the age-old patronage system of the East India Company.[4] Defending the idea of a generalist administrator—'all rounder'—the Fulton Committee 'portrayed an ideal administrator as a gifted layman who, moved from job to job irrespective of its subject matter, on the basis of his knowledge and experience in the government' (The Macaulay Committee Report 1975, 125). The efficiency of the members of the ICS as administrators may have been exemplary, but there is no doubt that they were motivated primarily by imperial interests and hence 'the interests of the country were too often postponed to the interests of the [Crown]' (Trevelyan 1907, 6–7, quoted in Cohn 1990, 545).[5] Furthermore, there was a Weberian aspect to the ICS. Drawn from the well-off sections of the society, the civil servants, trained in some of the best universities, were chosen on the basis of a competitive examination. Those within the ICS were therefore secluded from the rest given their exclusive class, caste and educational backgrounds. In other words, they had a special status within society that Weber felt was essential to a true bureaucracy. Given their peculiar characteristics, British officials in India formed a most unusual kind of society with no organic links with the society they were to serve.[6] The Indian civil service held a pivotal position in the system of administration that flourished during the colonial rule. Recognizing its immense importance in sustaining the empire, Lloyd George thus declared in the House of Commons in 1922 that '[t]hey are the steel frame of the whole structure. I do not care what you build it—if you take the steel frame out, the fabric will collapse'.[7]

The Government of India Act, 1919 introduced administrative decentralization by transferring certain powers to Indian ministers in the provinces. The dyarchy gave further impetus to the demand for Indianization of the civil services. In 1921, only about 13 per cent of the officers were Indians. This challenged the spirit of the reform scheme. As against the demand for Indianization of superior services, the serving European officers sought to scuttle the move by submitting a memorandum to the British Prime Minister, Lloyd George. In his response, Lloyd George made his celebrated 'steel frame' speech. As he emphatically argued, he could foresee no period when 'they (those in service) can dispense with the guidance and assistance of a small nucleus of British civil Servants'. He further elaborated,

> I do not care what you build on it. If you take the steel frame out, the fabric will collapse. There is one institution we will not interfere with, there is one institution we will not deprive of its functions or of its privileges, and that is that institution which built up the British Raj—the British Civil Service in India.

The issue of retention of the All India Services was always controversial, as nationalist leaders considered the retention of these services as 'anachronistic' and 'incompatible' with provincial self-government. The nationalist members of the Reforms Inquiry Committee, 1924 and the members of the Indian Central Committee, 1928–29 that was constituted to liaise with the Indian Statutory Commission sharply argued for the abolition of central services and underlined the significance of 'provincialization' of the civil service. The Joint Committee on Indian Constitutional Reforms did not however endorse this point of view and the All India Services remained integral to the Raj. The question of retention of the All India Services had again figured prominently in the discussion in the Constituent Assembly in independent India.

Although there were some dissenting voices, the nationalist leaders, including Jawaharlal Nehru and Vallabhbhai Patel, were keen to continue with the steel frame. The stock argument ranged around the highest standard of efficiency, progressive and wide outlook, freshness and vigour in administration and efficiency at different levels (centre, province and district) that could be maintained if the All India Service was retained. As Patel (1949) has argued in defending the continuity of the services,

> [A]s a man of experience, I tell you, do not quarrel with the instruments with which you want to work. It is a bad workman who quarrels with his instruments. Take work from them. Everyman wants some sort of encouragement. Nobody wants to put in work when everyday he is criticized and ridiculed in public.

In independent India, the Indian Administrative Service (IAS) succeeded the ICS.[8] Despite its imperial roots, Indian political leaders chose to sustain the structure of the ICS presumably because of its efficient role in conducting Indian administration in accordance with prescribed rules and regulations supporting a particular regime.

However, during discussions in the Constituent Assembly, the house was not unanimous as regards the fate of the ICS. The argument opposing its continuity was based on its role as an ally of imperialism. 'The Civil Service as the Steel Frame ... enslaved us [and] they have been guilty of stabbing Nation during our freedom struggle. [W]e should not, therefore,' as the argument goes, 'perpetuate what we have criticized so far'.[9] Vallabhbhai Patel was probably most vocal in defending the ICS and its steel frame. Since they were 'patriotic, loyal, sincere [and] able, Patel was not in favour of tampering with the bureaucracy especially when the country was reeling under chaos towards the close of the British rule'. As early as 1946, he convened the provincial Premier's Conference to evolve a consensus on the future of which was then the All India Services (AIS). In view of their long association with public administration, officers belonging to the AIS 'are most well-equipped to deal with new and complex tasks'. Not only 'are they useful instruments, they will also serve as a liaison between the Provinces and the Government of India and introduce certain amount of brashness and vigour in the administration both of the Centre and the Provinces' (Maheshwari 1984, 211). Later while speaking in the Constituent Assembly, he categorically stated that, '[y]ou will not have a united India if you do not have a good All India Service' which had the independence to speak out its mind and enjoyed a sense of security. He also attributed the success of the Constitution to the existence of an All India Service by saying that, 'if you do not adopt this course, then do not follow this Constitution. ... This Constitution is meant to be worked by a ring of service which will keep the country intact'. 'If you remove them', Patel thus apprehended, 'I see nothing but a picture of chaos all over the country'[10] because he believed,

> [A]n efficient, disciplined and contented civil service assured of its prospect as a result of diligent and honest work is the hallmark of a sound administration under a democratic regime even more than under authoritarian rule. The civil service must be above party, and we should ensure that political considerations either in its recruitment or in its discipline and control are reduced to the minimum if not eliminated altogether.

Even Jawaharlal Nehru who was very critical of the ICS for its role in sustaining the imperial rule in India,[11] seemed persuaded and supported its continuity for 'the security and stability of India ... including coping with the slaughter and its aftermath in Punjab, crushing opposition in Hyderabad, and containing it in Kashmir'.[12] Patel's views were translated in Article 311 of the Constitution of India that stated that no civil servant shall be dismissed or removed or reduced in rank except after an enquiry in which he has been informed of the charges and given a reasonable opportunity of being heard in respect of those charges.[13]

So, an instrument that consolidated the imperial rule in India 'with so slight use of force'[14] survived in completely different political circumstances[15] primarily because of continuing support for it first from the British Government and then from the Congress Government. Furthermore, its continuity did not pose any threat to the dominant classes that reigned supreme following the 1947 transfer of power in India. The new civil service for all practical purposes was, as a former bureaucrat has commented, 'the continuation of the old one with the difference that it was to function in a parliamentary system of government, accepting the undoubted primacy of the political executive which in turn was responsible to the people through their elected representatives in the legislature' (Alexander 1998). Besides its structure, which was more or less, an expansion of the steel frame, the continuity was at a deeper level. While the colonial civil servants had a paternalistic attitude towards the people, and ruled largely by negative discretionary powers, '[t]heir successors, noting the vast unmet development needs of the people, substituted positive discretionary powers of patronage and subsidies, reinforcing the colonial syndrome of dependency on the *mai-baap* state' (Sudarshan 1999).

Apart from its functional utility, that the steel frame was retained more or less *intact* was due to fact that, as B. P. R. Vithal (1997) himself an IAS officer, argued, 'the Congress leaders who took office...shared the social background of the senior civil servants whom they inherited from the colonial state'. Thus, for example, Nehru felt at ease while working with senior civil servants. Similarly, Rajagopalachari felt more at home with ICS officers who were placed with him when he was the Prime Minister of Madras (1937–39) than with certain elements in the Congress party. The political processes subsequent to Independence gave rise to changes in the class composition of the political executive that were far-reaching and rapid than changes in the social composition of the civil services. While the political executives, trained in vernacular education, hailed largely from rural and semi-urban areas, those in the steel frame were generally urban-based and English-educated. The growing disparity in the class background of the political executive and the civil servants led to frequent frictions between the administrators and politicians in the Westminster parliamentary system of governance when the latter assumed a leading role in building a new nation.

Following independence, government functions also expanded in scope and content. With the introduction of the parliamentary form of government and the setting up of people's institutions right down to the village level, there has been an inevitable rise in the level of expectations which the state tries to meet by going beyond its traditional sphere of functioning. People's institutions were set up with the objective of creating self-governing institutions at the village level. The objective remains distant for ever. Similarly, independence and the Five Year Plans were perceived by people as synonymous with economic and social equity and well-being, and freedom from want and oppression. In the early days of the planning era, people did not crib much about shortages, which they confronted with fortitude because the future held hope and promise for them. With the passage of time, they felt disgruntled since their hope of creating an equitable India seemed to have been entirely belied. The ethos of self-governance, decentralization and community development were flagged in with considerable élan and fanfare. For example, the three-tier Panchayati Raj system and urban local bodies were conceived of as a properly meshed network of institutions to accelerate the development process.[16] The 73rd and 74th Amendments (1992) to the Constitution sought to advance the concept of 'self-governance' by providing for (a) regular elections, (b) minimal suppression of Panchayati Raj bodies through an administrative fiat and (c) regular finances through statutory distribution by state finance commissions. The aim, argues Kuldeep Mathur, 'is to reduce the margin of political and administrative discretion and to allow the decentralised institutions to gather strength on the basis of people's involvement'.[17] But, due to various reasons, the political process became what may be termed as 'reversed' and highly centralized and personalized systems of government developed both at the Central and State levels. There has been a massive erosion of institutions, whether they are the Parliament or parliamentary institutions, or the party system and democratic procedures in the running of parties, or the judiciary, or indeed the press. Describing the crisis and erosion of institutions as 'the natural and expected consequences of a political process that has undermined both the role and authority of basic institutions' (Kothari 1988, 287), Rajni Kothari has sought to grapple with a peculiar reality in which public administration appears to be largely de-linked with the basic institutions of the democratic system that have flourished in India following Independence.[18]

CONCLUDING OBSERVATIONS

Indian administration displays a creative blending of past traditions with modern experiments over several centuries. As is shown earlier, the Mughal administration had influenced British policy-makers when they set in motion a new administrative system following the establishment of Company rule which was refined with the 1858 decision to bring India under the Crown. On the surface, the ideas of Kautilya and Barni or, for that matter, Fazal may not have had direct impacts on Indian administration; they nonetheless remain critical milestones in Indian administrative thought. These thinkers sought a meaningful alternative that arose from their critiques and an organic engagement with the existing socio-economic and political milieu. In Kautilya's case, one notices the concern for a strong state in light of the chaotic circumstances of the Maurya rule. Barani's commentary on contemporary political governance was accompanied by attention to the complexities of medieval Indian political life. Here he attempted to conceptualize statecraft in a non-religious way that was not yet entirely secular in a modern sense but one that did have elements corresponding to the search for secular values. Fazal sought structural changes in administration by underlining the critical importance of the coming together of Hindus and Muslims for mutual benefit. Todar Mal's contributions in revenue administration remain a decisive milestone in administrative thought. There are, of course, additional sources of pre-modern Indian thinking about politics, but through their well-argued discourses on the basis of well-devised conceptual blocks, Kautilya, Barani, Fazal and Todar Mal appear to have provided significant methodological insights, especially with regard to state and governance in politically volatile circumstances. These are helpful for comprehending some of the major theoretical concerns in contemporary Indian administrative thought.

The period between 1909 and 1947, when major Constitutional experiments were undertaken under colonialism, sharply shows mutation in the formation of Hindus and Muslims as communities opposed to each other in the political arena. What was distinctive about this period was the growth of communities as political units always in a permanent adversarial relationship with the members of the 'other' community. This was further consolidated following the introduction of the communal electorate in the 1937 provincial elections. With the acceptance of the principle of majority, Muslims automatically became the most powerful community in Bengal and Punjab by their sheer demographic strength. In other words, religious identity as a demographic category became probably the single most crucial criterion in determining the distribution of governmental power in these Muslim-majority provinces. The 1935 Government of India Act reiterated the divide and rule strategy by formally recognizing that Muslims needed to be treated separately as a distinct, but neglected minority in India. This was a decisive Constitutional intervention because not only did it establish the principle of majority as sacrosanct in democracy, but it also made the Muslims self-conscious of their critical importance in governance in India. It is now possible to argue that the 1935 Act definitely shifted the centre of political activity in Bengal to the east of the province. Not by virtue of any inherent superiority of the Muslims but simply because in a democratically elected legislature, as a contemporary report underlines, 'the weight of numbers tells and the teeming millions of East Bengal—60 per cent of their being Muslims outweighed in point of numbers the more educated Hindus of the South, West and extreme north of the province'.[19] The migration of power to the countryside took place in the context of a major realignment in the social bases of political power.

The 1935 Government of India Act was certainly a powerful constitutional intervention that the colonial rulers seriously made to accommodate nationalist zeal, of course, within the colonial administrative format. This is also illustrative of efforts at legitimizing the growing democratic aspirations of the ruled in India through a constitutional device. Interestingly, the 1935 Act remained the strongest influence during the making of the 1950 Constitution for free India. Some 250 clauses of the present Constitution were, in fact, lifted from the Government of India Act. Although the political system of independent India draws its sustenance from universal adult franchise and political sovereignty, rules were undoubtedly derived from its colonial past. The most striking provisions that the Constitution of India derived from its 1935 counterpart are 'the Emergency provisions' that enable the President to suspend the democratically elected governments and fundamental rights of the citizens.

There is no doubt that the post-colonial state in India inherited its habits of governance from colonial practices. And, its *weltanschauung* (world view) is based on 'the mixed legacies of colonial rule' that upheld rule of law, bureaucracy, citizenship, parasitic landlords, modern political institutions and 'two-track tradition of protest and participation' (Mitra 2004, 29–34). What accounts for the relative stability of colonialism in India was certainly its ability to adapt to the changed socio-political circumstances as also the gradual but steady 'internalization' of domination by the subjects of colonial rule, which provoked an analyst to characterize colonialism as 'an intimate enemy' (Nandy 1989) because the dominated viewed the virtues of being dominated for their own betterment. Colonialism was thus not seen as an absolute evil but rather complementary to India's rise as an independent nation in the future. This statement may not be politically correct. Nonetheless, it can safely be argued that colonialism provided critical impetus to various processes that finally resulted in serious political mobilization against imperialism in India. Whether nationalism or democratization—both had their roots in the long history of colonialism and in this sense colonialism remained a significant force behind the rise of India as an independent nation in 1947.

REVIEW QUESTIONS

1. Trace the evolution of public administration since the days of Kautilya.
2. What is so distinctive about Ziauddin Barni's contribution to public administration? Elaborate.
3. Critically evaluate the nature of public administration during the Sultanate era.
4. 'Public administration was individual-centric in the pre-British era'. Elaborate.
5. Critically evaluate the institution-dependent public administration that emerged immediately after the British takeover of India.

6. In what respects did the 1773 Regulating Act and 1833 Charter Act remain critical in conceptualizing public administration in British India? Elaborate your response.
7. 'The 1858 Declaration lays the foundation of distinctive administrative traits in India'. Do you agree? Elaborate your response.
8. In what fashion is the 1935 Government of India Act a precursor of post-independent India's administration? Elaborate your response.
9. What is the steel frame in India? How was the continuity of the steel frame justified in the Constituent Assembly of India? Elaborate your response.
10. 'Indian public administration is neither indigenous in spirit nor exogenous in manifestation'. Comment.

NOTES

1. *Arthashastra* is an ancient Indian treatise on statecraft, economic policy and military strategy which identifies its author as Kautilya (c. 350–283 BC), a Takshashila-based scholar who also became the Prime Minister of the Maurya Empire (321 to 185 BC) in ancient India.
2. Drawn on the discussion that was pursued in Chapter 10 of Bidyut Chakrabarty and Rajendra Pandey (2008).
3. For a detailed account of the civil service in India during the British rule, see Mason (1997).
4. As the Report underlined, '[h]enceforth, an appointment to the civil service of the Company will not be matter of favour but matter of right. He who obtains such an appointment will owe it solely to his own abilities and industry' (The Macaulay Committee Report 1975, 125).
5. Given their stake in the British administration, it is but natural that whatever they did, they were simply acting in the imperial interests, and in the process, preserving or enhancing their superior positions. However, there is a school of thought defending that the imperial logic never appeared crucial in administration since 'the ICS [was] Jeremy Bentham's prototype of the benevolent social guardian committed to achieving the common good'. For details, see Stokes (1959, 159).
6. While explaining the nature of the British civil servants, Bernard S. Cohn (1990, 500–53) developed this argument further by drawing upon their post-recruitment training first at the Haileybury School and later in Oxbridge colleges that hardly took into account the rapid socio-structural shifts in India during the colonial rule.
7. Lloyd George was quoted in Mason (1997, xv). Duffrin was probably more categorical in appreciating the role of the Indian civil service. According to him, '[t]here is no service like it in the world. If the Indian civil service were not [as they are], how could the government of the country go on so smoothly? We have 250 million subjects in India and less than 1,000 British civilians for the conduct of the entire administration'. Duffrin's statement was quoted by Jagmohan (1998).
8. For a succinct account of the evolution of the Civil Service in India both during the British rule and its aftermath, see B. Shiva Rao (1968, Chapter 23, 708–23).
9. Shibban Lal Saksena's statement in *the Constituent Assembly Debate* (1999, 46). Prominent among those who criticized the decision to retain the ICS was M. Ananthasaynam Ayyanger who failed to understand the logic of providing 'guarantee to those persons who have played into the hands of others [and] cared only for money and the salaries they got'. Ayyangar's statement in the *Constituent Assembly Debate* (1999, 42).
10. Vallabhbhai Patel's speech in the Constituent Assembly. See *The Constituent Assembly Debates* (1999, 48–52). Seeking persuade his colleagues in the Constituent Assembly, he further argued, 'if these service people are giving you full value of their Services and more, then try to learn to appreciate them. Forget the past. We fought the Britishers for so many years. I was their bitterest enemy and they regarded me as such.... What did Gandhiji teach us? You are talking of Gandhian ideology and Gandhian philosophy and Gandhian way of administration. Very good. But you come out of jail and then say, "These men put me in jail. Let me take revenge". That is not Gandhian way. It is going far away from that' (*The Constituent Assembly Debates* 1999, 48–52).

11. As late as 1934, Nehru (1941, 445) characterized the Indian civil service as 'neither Indian nor civil nor service [and] it thus essential that the ICS and similar services disappear completely'.
12. Jawaharlal Nehru's speech in the Constituent Assembly. See *The Constituent Assembly Debates* (1947, 793–95).
13. For a detailed discussion in the Constituent Assembly during the preparation and finally acceptance of Article 311, see Rao (1968, 713–23).
14. While explaining the continuity of the steel frame for almost 200 years, Mason (1997, 345–46) stated, the administration in India 'had the immense advantage over those in the later African territories that it was possible to set up the framework of government before the invention of the electric telegraph and close control of England. Use was made of Akbar's machinery and whatever local institutions could be adapted. The whole was controlled by a cadre of district officers, rigorously picked, but trained almost wholly by doing what in fact they were learning to do. Because they were so few they had let their subordinates do their own work. Confidence that they would be backed up from above was hallmark of their profession and they acquired a confidence in themselves and a confidence that they would be obeyed, which meant that they were obeyed. Few administrations can have ruled so many with so slight use of force. Everything was done through Indians and by Indians to whom power was delegated'.
15. P. C. Alexander (1998), himself an IAS, thus argues, '[t]he new civil service for all practical purposes was the continuation of the old one with the difference that it was now to function in a parliamentary system of government accepting the undoubted primacy of the political executive'.
16. For an interesting, though slightly dated account of the panchayati system in West Bengal, Uttar Pradesh and Karnataka, see Atul Kohli (1987) and for studies of urban government of Delhi, see Ajoy K. Mehra (1991).
17. According to Mathur (1999, 22), '[t]he success of the Seventy-third and Seventy-fourth Amendments making decentralised structures part of the Constitution has yet to be seen—not only because they were only instituted in 1993, but also because the states have shown little evidence of implementing the requirement through their own statutes'.
18. The process, known as 'deinstitutionalization' invariably leads to a non-policy government that 'operates by means of spoils and preferments that take into account the particular situations of persons and communities'. Very common in the sub-Saharan Africa, 'such government tends to be "private government" both in the sense that government offices are treated as private property and in the sense that spoils, unlike policies, must be managed in a discreet and even clandestine fashion. They cannot be advertised, nor can they be publicly debated', see Hyden (1997).
19. India Office Records, London, Tyson Papers, Eur F. 341/41, John Tyson's note, 5 July 1947.

REFERENCES

Agarwal, Mamta. 'The Revenue System in the Sultanate and Mughal Period'. Retrieved from http://www.historydiscussion.net/history-of-india/the-revenue-system-in-the-sultanate-and-mughal-period-indian-history/676 (accessed on 24 April 2015).

Alexander, P. C. 1998. 'Civil Service: Continuity and Change'. In *Independent India: The First Fifty Years*, edited by Hiranmory Karlekar, 62. New Delhi: Oxford University Press.

Chakrabarty, Bidyut, and Pandey, Rajendra. 2008. *Indian Government and Politics*. New Delhi: SAGE.

Cohn, Bernard S. 1990. *An Anthropologist among the Historians and Other Essays*. New Delhi: Oxford University Press.

Hyden, Goran. 1997. 'Democratization and Administration'. In *Democracy's Victory and Crisis* (Nobel Symposium no. 93), edited by Axel Hadenius, 252. Cambridge: Cambridge University Press.

Jagmohan. 1998. 'Riveting the Steel Frame of the ICS'. *Hindustan Times*, 1 November.

Kohli, Atul. 1987. *The State and Poverty in India: The Politics of Reform*. Cambridge: Cambridge University Press.

Kothari, Rajni. 1988. *State against Democracy: In Search of Human Governance*. New Delhi: Ajanta.

Lok Sabha Secretariat. (1949, 10 October) 1999. *Constituent Assembly Debate*, vol. X. 3rd print, New Delhi: Lok Sabha Secretariat.

Maheshwari, S. R. 1984. *Indian Administration*. Reprint, New Delhi: Orient Longman.
Mason, Philip. 1997. *The Men who Ruled India*. Reprint, Kolkata: Rupa & Co.
Mathur, Kuldeep. 1999. 'Strengthening Bureaucracy: State and Development in India'. *Indian Social Science Review* 1 (1, January–June): 22.
Mehra, Ajoy K. 1991. *The Politics of Urban Development: A Study of Old Delhi*. New Delhi: SAGE.
Mitra, Subrata. 2004, November. 'Constitutional Design, Democratic Vote Counting and India's Fortuitous Multiculturalism'. Working Paper, South Asia Institute, Heidelberg University.
Nandy, Ashis. 1989. *The Intimate Enemy: Loss and Recovery of Self under Colonialism*. Reprint. New Delhi: Oxford University Press.
Nehru, Jawaharlal. 1941. *An Autobiography: With Musings in Recent Events in India*. Reprint. London: John Lane the Bodley Head.
Nehru, Jawaharlal. 1947. *The Constituent Assembly Debates*. vol. 1.
Pylee, M. V. 1965. *Constitutional Government in India*. London: Asia Publishing House.
Patel, V. 1949. Vallabhbhai Patel's Speech in the Constituent Assembly, The Constituent Assembly Debates, 10 October, Vol. X, p. 51.
Rao, B. Shiva (ed.). 1968. The Framing of India's Constitution (Select Documents). vol. V. New Delhi: IIPA.
Saran, Anand M., and Das, Bhairab L. 'Life of Raja Todarmal—His Bravery, His Taxation Policy, His Place of Birth and His Caste'. Retrieved from http://www.engr.mun.ca/~asharan/TODARMAL/TODARMALV6.pdf (accessed on 28 April 2015)
Stokes, Erik. 1959. *The English Utilitarians of India*. Oxford: Oxford University Press.
Sudarshan, R. 1999. 'Governance of Multicultural Polities: Limits of the Rule of Law'. In *Multiculturalism, Liberalism and Democracy*, edited by Rajeev Bhargava, Amiya Kumar Bagchi and R. Sudarshan, 111. New Delhi: Oxford University Press.
The Macaulay Committee Report (1854). 1975. *The Fulton Committee Report*, vol. 1. London: HMSO.
Trevelyan, George. 1907. *The Competition Wallah*. 2nd ed. London.
Vithal, B. P. R. 1997. 'Evolving Trends in the Bureaucracy'. In *State and Politics in India*, edited by Partha Chatterjee, 224. New Delhi: Oxford University Press.

2

Philosophical and Constitutional Framework of Indian Administration*

LEARNING OBJECTIVES

1. To understand the complex evolution of Indian administration with reference to the constitutional principles.
2. To elaborate the processes that are critical in grasping the evolution of Indian administration in a historical perspective.
3. To conceptualize the growth of Indian administration in clear theoretical terms.

A Constitution is the foundation on which administration is based. As a value-setting device, the Constitution guides administration in a specific direction. In this sense, administration articulates constitutional design in the form of decisions. Being ideology-driven, the Constitution is not just a pack of rules and regulations, but comprises those value preferences which are rooted in a particular socio-economic and political milieu. In other words, the Constitution is an ideologically charged document with a definite purpose to fulfil. This is the most fundamental in any study of the interface between the Constitution and administration. The interface needs to be studied dialectically because a deterministic understanding of the interrelationship, privileging one over the other, would be self-defeating. Even a cursory look at the interface reveals that the Constitution and administration are interconnected dialectically, although the nature differs according to socio-economic and political circumstances. This reinforces the fact that without grasping the dialectical interpenetration between the Constitution and administration, neither the Constitution nor the administration retains its vitality as powerful ideological instruments for setting in motion a specific path for political governance.

There is another point of massive theoretical significance: the interaction between the Constitution and administration is constant and not a one-time shot which further confirms that the two are organically linked. One can thus think of the interrelationship in the form of a diagram showing the interaction between the Constitution and administration within a specific milieu, fulfilling an ideological goal. One should also be aware of the fact that this interrelationship is not always friction free because any administration which transforms with changes in its personnel may not continually be tuned to fundamental constitutional values. Likewise, the Constitution cannot remain static in view of its organic linkages with the socio-economic and political reality from which it has evolved. This is likely to create uncertainty which is usually circumvented if there exists an ideology that cements the Constitution–administration bond for a common socio-political and economic goal.

* This chapter is drawn on Chakrabarty, B. and Pandey, R. 2008. *Indian Government and Politics*. New Delhi: SAGE.

While conceptualizing such an interrelationship, one cannot avoid referring to the role of history. India is a good example where neither the Constitution nor administration is absolutely new, but a continuity of the past. Structurally and also in terms of its nature, Indian administration in the aftermath of decolonization in 1947 was hardly a break with the past. Similarly, the 1950 Constitution of India replicated much of the British constitutional provisions and practices, though of course, within the changed ideological circumstances following the withdrawal of the British in 1947. Hence change was obvious, although in the early years of India's independence, cases of administration overruling the Constitution in what was identified as 'the exigency of situation' were not uncommon. The scenario however has changed, as has been the case with other stable political systems, once the values of democracy, socialism and republicanism have been accepted as sacrosanct for governance. With the consolidation of these fundamental values, the 1950 Constitution of India became not a mere instrument of authority, but a pathfinder for administrators who could not afford to ignore constitutional directions in view of the systemic requirements. The Constitution has also been instrumental in creating circumstances where political differences have been usually sorted amicably through the well-established mechanism of dialogue and negotiations except perhaps for some stray instances. Nonetheless, the fact remains that the Indian Constitution has created circumstances in which values supporting what the founding fathers had nurtured while leading the freedom struggle, have flourished. So, the administration–Constitution interface is nothing but a complementary network in which governance is structured and executed. This is conceptually most fundamental because (a) it enables us to capture the complex interrelationship between the Constitution and administration and (b) it also shows the importance of an ideology in sustaining an atmosphere in which the Constitution and administration remain complementary to each other.

The deep roots of ethos and functional vibrancy of democratic life in India may arguably be taken to be the fruition of the long cherished endeavour of the fathers of the Constitution who not only envisioned India to be a modern nation based on the norms of the rule of law, the secular character of the society, the democratic nature of the polity and ordinarily, primacy of the people's fundamental rights over other imperatives of the state; but also made comprehensive and mostly, precise provisions in the Constitution to facilitate the march of the nation in the desired direction. Given the immense importance of the Constitution in shaping administration, it is thus obvious that no discussion of administration will remain complete without a thorough understanding of the value-preferences that the Constitution seeks to pursue. This chapter attempts to delineate the salient features of the Indian Constitution encompassing the whole spectrum of vital issues ranging from the spirit of the Constitution as expressed in the provision on the Preamble, the Fundamental Rights and Duties and the Directive Principles of State Policy, to the broader functional arena of the political system like the federalism, the Parliamentary System and the amending procedures of the Constitution.

THE FOUNDING PRINCIPLES OF THE CONSTITUTION

For several reasons, the framing of an acceptable-to-all Constitution for free India was an extremely arduous task which the Constituent Assembly shouldered efficiently and produced the longest democratic Constitution in the world. First, the partition of the country and the subsequent mayhem in Punjab and Bengal led to a shocking state of nervousness amongst the leaders who immediately set on to devise ways and means to instil in the people confidence in the governability of the country. Moreover, the onerous task of ensuring the integration of the 500 plus princely states in the Indian Union appeared quite challenging in view of the ambivalent, if not totally defiant, positions taken by the rulers of the princely states like Junagadh, Hyderabad and Jammu and Kashmir.

Second, the carving out of Pakistan did not mean the conversion of India into a homogenous country as more than 10 per cent of the total Muslim population of the country stayed behind in India and whose religious and cultural identities needed to be protected. At the same time, India itself was home to numerous communities speaking different languages, professing different faiths, practicing different customs, following different traditions and emphasizing different cultures. In the face of such a diverse cultural base of the people, it was really a stupendous task to provide for sufficient constitutional provisions to protect distinct religious-cultural identities, without compromising with the unity and integrity of the country.

Thirdly, the tone and tenor of the national movement had aroused high levels of expectations amongst the common people in general and the hitherto marginalized sections of the society like the scheduled castes, scheduled tribes and the other backward people in particular, to experience a new dawn with the inauguration of the Constitution of the independent India.

Finally, the spirit of liberal democratic traditions was so strong amongst a majority of the national leaders, particularly Nehru, that independent India was bound to usher into a full blown democracy, irrespective of its preparedness to experience the mass scale of democracy based on universal adult franchise on the one hand, and the lurking dangers to the unity and integrity of the nascent nation from the dynamics of electoral politics on the other. Combined together, these riddles of Constitution making in independent India acted both as challenges as well as opportunities for the Constitution makers to show their fullest constitutional acumen and innovativeness.

Faced with the complex responsibilities of taking care of scores of seemingly mutually competing and sometimes contradictory claims on the Constitution of independent India, the Constitution makers had to adopt a policy of drafting a lengthy and all-encompassing document which contained not only the classical tenets of a Constitution like provisions defining the powers and functions of the various organs of government at both the union and the state levels, the fundamental rights guaranteed to the people etc., but also a number of unconventional provisions like the Directive Principles of State Policy to make the Constitution an instrument of socio-economic change in the country.

The Constitution makers, therefore, had to draw on all the available Constitutions and other legislative documents to provide for the building blocks to erect the edifice called the Constitution of India. To be precise, they banked heavily upon colonial construction, that is, the Government of India Act, 1935, to get the foundational base of the Constitution of India, an ironic epitome of the fact that they could not move much away from the system of governance devised by the British for India.

Thus, keeping the core drawn from the Act of 1935, the framers of the Constitution looked upon other Constitutions like the American and the Irish Constitutions for the operational dynamics of not only the democratic system of government in the country through the provisioning of fundamental rights, but also that of the visions of new India, marching on the path of rapid socio-economic transformation through the guiding force of the Directive Principles of State Policy. However, the physical structure of the Constitution of India, as drawn from the above mentioned sources, would have remained hollow and infertile, had the breathing spirit to it not been provided by the Objectives Resolution,[1] drafted by Nehru himself and approved by the Constituent Assembly on 22 January 1947. Finding its manifestation through the Preamble of the Constitution, which declared the pious goals of the Constitution to secure to all its citizens; justice, social, economic and political; liberty of thought, expression, belief, faith and worship; equality of status and of opportunity and to promote among them all fraternity, assuring the dignity of the individual; this resolution put into black and white the very raison d'être for which the Constitution of India was supposed to come into existence.

With the broad structure and essence of the future polity of the country being obvious, the Constituent Assembly arrived at seven basic decisions pertaining to the nature of the new state, namely, written Constitution, federal structure of the polity, republic from of state, parliamentary democracy, membership of the Commonwealth of Nations, secular nature of state and the welfare character of the state (Kapur and Mishra 2001, 62). These decisions were, in fact, the cherished dreams of the leadership of the national movement whose fulfilment was sought to be attained through the mechanism of the new Constitution. The various provisions of the Constitution of India therefore appear, in a way, nothing more than the bricks and mortars to facilitate the construction of the structure of a constitutional polity in the country.

Analyzing the inherent philosophical moorings of the Indian Constitution, Austin discerns a 'seamless web', consisting of three strands namely, protecting and enhancing national unity and integrity; establishing the institutions and spirit of democracy and fostering a social revolution to better the lot of the mass of Indians (Austin 1999, 6). Bestowing equal weightage and significance to all the three strands in time and space, Austin asserted the mutual dependence and inextricable intertwinedness of these strands and warned that undue strain on, and slackness in, any one strand would distort the web and risk its destruction and, with it, the destruction of the nation (Austin 1999, 6). However, despite the mutual dependence and inextricable intertwinedness of the three strands, as stressed by Austin, it may be argued that there was a certain degree of prioritization amongst the three strands and the framers seemed to be fairly clear on the first things first when framing the Indian Constitution. Framed with much painstaking perseverance and imbued with the long cherished dreams of the national leaders, the Constitution of India reflected the wisdom of the framers in not only meeting out the challenges at hand like preserving the unity and integrity of the nation, threatened by communal violence, but also a prophetic vision of heralding in an era of what Gandhi called 'Ramrajya'. To put it differently, the first and foremost priority of the framers at the time of independence, and probably afterwards, appeared to be guarding the unity and integrity of the county, for which they were willing to afford so much of unfettered powers to the Central government even at the risk of rendering the federal set-up of the polity meaningless. It appears paradoxical that though very few mentions were made in the Constitution in terms of the unity and integrity of the country, sweeping powers and unwritten discretion was provided, in addition to the retention of colonial constructions like the All India Services (like the IAS, formerly ICS and the IPS, formerly IP), to the Central government. It would therefore not be impertinent to argue that the preservation of the unity and integrity of country was the running consideration pervading from the first to the last word of the Constitution.

Having been reassured of the indestructibility of India as a nation, the framers set on to infuse the ethos and spirit of democratic governance in the country, within the broad spectrum of the parliamentary system, based on the sanctities of universal adult franchise. Banking heavily, if not exclusively, on periodic elections, to be conducted by an independent constitutional body, the framers' trump card, with regard to democracy, turned out to be the classical negative rights of western mould, ensuring for common people basic minimum constitutional guarantees through which they could feel as being the citizens of an independent country and enjoy the freedom of not only choosing their rulers, but also live a life of their volition, notwithstanding, the traditional character of Indian society and the socio-economic backwardness of the mass of the people. Thus, unlike the absolute value of unity and integrity, democracy did not become an absolute value for the framers who, nonetheless, wished it to underpin Indian polity and evolve in the course of time.

The value of social revolution, as referred to by Granville Austin (1999, 26–27), appears only at the last stage of contemplation by the framers, after ingraining fully the values of unity, integrity and democracy in the Constitution. Though fully aware of the indispensability and unavoidability of a subtle social revolution in the country in order to make democracy meaningful and sustainable, the framers seem to be convinced of the primacy and pivotal position of the other two values, which were bound to become the substructure over which the superstructure of social revolution could be erected. In sum, undoubtedly, the Indian Constitution appears to be a seamless web characterized by the three strands of unity and integrity of the country, institutions and spirit of democracy and social revolutionary fervour. Yet, the shape of this web does not appear to be circular where it is not possible to figure out the sequence and placing of the particular value. Indian Rather, it can be argued that the shape of the web could probably be pyramidal in which the three values are arranged in ascending order with the base position occupied by the value of unity and integrity of the nation, the next position accorded to the value of the democracy and finally the value of social revolution, in order of their dispensability from top to bottom.

As is evident, the 1950 Constitution of India was not only a product of the uncertain socio-political circumstances following the withdrawal of the British from India, but also the ideological commitment of the founding fathers for a democratic India. This was articulated in 22 parts in which the Constitution was divided. Over a three-year period (1946–49), the makers of the Constitution deliberated on each and every provision before it was incorporated. The charge that the 1950 Constitution was a borrowed doctrine is not entirely unfounded given the fact that most of the provisions were taken either from the 1935 Government of India Act or other Constitutions of different countries. Nonetheless, what emerged as the Constitution of India was a conclusive document illustrating how the founding fathers had confronted and sought to meaningfully address the challenges that they faced. So the Constitution was not merely a compilation of provisions, but an urge to fulfil the exalted goal of democracy, socialism and secularism, as is visible when one scans through the major features of the Constitution, including the Preamble to the Constitution of India.

THE PREAMBLE

The Preamble is often referred to as the soul of the Indian Constitution affording a key to its letter and spirit. Delineating the core concerns of the polity in independent India, the Preamble seeks to express a solemn resolve which becomes the guiding light for posterity in the country. Though the framers of the Constitution were sagacious enough to ingrain all the vital values underpinning the Indian polity in the Preamble, the government headed by Mrs Indira Gandhi, for obvious political considerations, effected an unnecessary amendment in the original Preamble to the Constitution by inserting the words 'socialist' and 'secular' along with the original words sovereign, democratic, republic as well as 'integrity' along with the original unity of the nation, through the 42nd Amendment on 18 December 1976.

Arguably, the insertion of these words appears unnecessary and unwarranted due to the futility of the purposes they were supposed to serve. Undoubtedly, a dominant faction of leadership during the national movement, led by Jawaharlal Nehru, was overwhelmingly intoxicated by the mesmerizing characteristics of socialism and would have in all probability gone for steering India on the socialist path of development. If there were any doubts on this count, the matter was finally settled at the Avadi Session of the Congress in 1954 by professing India to follow the 'socialistic pattern of society'. Above all, the policy of centralized planned economic development through successive Five Year Plans, initiated by the government of Nehru as well as the unbridled nationalization of financial institutions by Mrs Indira Gandhi, left not even an iota of doubt that India was totally on the socialistic path of economic development.

Similarly, the idea of secularism was probably as deep rooted in the mindset of Indian leadership as well as the masses like the idea of democracy. Significantly, as Indians fought their colonial rulers for independence, they also became well versed with certain values which although appeared western, but became synonymous with the value system of Indians—two such values being that of democracy and secularism. At the same time, vehemently opposed to the two-nation theory of the Muslim League and wary of the creation of a theocratic state of Pakistan in their neighbourhood, the framers of the Constitution were probably so sure of secularism being an indestructible characteristic of the Indian socio-political life that they found it absurd to ingrain any formalistic sense in the Preamble to the Constitution.

As regards the insertion of the word integrity in the Preamble, it seems obvious that the original phrase—'unity of the nation'—would have been taken as all inclusive, encompassing the term integrity in its ambit. Alternatively, after passing through the horrifying reality of the partition of the country, the framers appeared to be sufficiently assured that whatever remained of India would, for times to come, remain an integral part of the country, provided it remained united. Yet, in view of the centrifugal tendencies which emerged in the country after a few years of independence, it would not seem impertinent, if not undesirable, to insert the word integrity into the Preamble to the Constitution. Crucially, the only point of dispute appeared to be that the motive behind these insertions was more political, than idealistic or constitutional.

As amended in 1976, the Preamble, unambiguously, exemplifies the broad contours of Indian political life and serves a number of useful purposes, for, the expressions used in it connote certain fundamental aspects of the polity from which there is no escape for various stakeholders in the political life of the nation. First, though the use of the phrase, 'We, the people of India', may appear customary, its implications are far reaching for a nascent and fragile nation like India, marching on the unchartered path of democratic governance with competing hopes and aspirations from diverse quarters of society. Thus, by establishing the sovereignty of the people, the Preamble reduces all other units of governance in the country to a secondary position, robbing from them any possibility of usurping the powers of other units as well as organs of government. At the same time, it also implies that the powers which are given to the government in India, are sourced not from the states or any section of society or the former rulers of the Indian states but from the people at large, as a result of which no section of the people can challenge its authority and contend that it is not bound by the authority of the state because it has not accorded its consent to it. More importantly, since the states of the Union were not consulted in the formation of the Union, which was created by the people of India, they cannot claim a right of secession from the Union. Therefore, the Preamble not only affords a stable democratic polity for the nation, but also consolidates the unity and integrity of the nation.

Second, the Preamble puts in black and white the nature of the polity which must conform to the hard earned ideals of sovereign, socialist, secular, democratic and republic. Needless to say, the nature of Indian polity would not have been different from what it is today, had the words socialist and secular not been added to the original Preamble. While sovereignty affords a respectful place of pride to India in the comity of nations, the ideal of democratic republic manifests the basic outline of the nature of polity, guaranteeing people the fundamental right of choosing their representatives to foster democratic governance in the country. Unavoidably, the mention of India becoming a republic becomes a compulsive requirement in view of the previous incarnation of India as a British Dominion where the head of state was the British monarch. Hence, by making India a republic, the framers of the Constitution carried out a crucial, if not total, break with the British suzerainty, even if nominal in practical terms.

Third, the Preamble presents a wish list outlining the aspirations of the people which they expect the government of India to secure for them. Spelt out in terms of justice, equality and fraternity, these ideals act as a benchmark to guide policies and programmes of the government in the future to cast India into the mould of a welfare state. Leaving no room for ambiguity on the dimensions of justice, the Preamble demarcates that justice needs to be in terms of social, economic and political, to be construed in the broadest sense of the term so that the nature of the state in India does not become lopsided. The framers were quick enough to supplement the ideal of justice with that of the ideal of equality of status and opportunity to provide for a holistic framework of an egalitarian society in India. In the meanwhile, the Preamble does emphasize the promotion of fraternity amongst the citizens by assuring the dignity of individuals in society. Aware of the propensity of certain sections of society to advocate the subordination of individual dignity to the cause of farcical societal interests, the framers did not mince words to clarify that societal good could be ascertained only by ensuring individual good in society. Thus, the framers wished to create a social democracy in India, which as Ambedkar elaborates, 'means a way of life which recognizes liberty, equality and fraternity which are not to be treated as separate items in a trinity. They form a union of trinity in the sense that to divorce one from the other is to defeat the very purpose of democracy. Liberty cannot be divorced from equality; equality cannot be divorced from liberty. Nor can liberty and equality be divorced from fraternity'.[2]

Fourth, the Preamble makes it amply clear that the unity and integrity of the country is a precondition for other cherished ideals to become a reality in the scheme of things in independent India. Discounting any scope for tempering with the unity and integrity of the nation, the essence of the letter and spirit of the Preamble conclusively bars all stakeholders in the nation, be it individuals, groups of people, the state or any other entity, from casting aspersions on the unity and integrity of the country, in case of which the people of India and/or the government of India are enjoined to safeguard the unity and integrity of the nation.

Finally, the utility of the Preamble is discerned in its serving as a beacon light to the higher courts in the country that are called upon to discharge the grand duty of interpreting the Constitution. At the times of interpreting a controversial law or any constitutional provisions, where the meaning of the law in point is not clear or ambiguity or uncertainty prevails in the minds of the constitutional lawyers or judges, the only reference point left to the court is the language of the Preamble through which they persevere to mark out the real intention of the framers of the Constitution. It is argued that the Preamble is the repository of the spirit of the Constitution and hence, the only reference point for those engaged in interpreting the constitutional provisions should be the ideals embodied in it.

Looking at the vitality of the Preamble in the Constitution of India, it would be pertinent to analyze the position and sustenance of the Preamble. On the question of whether the Preamble forms the part of the Constitution or not, the incontrovertible position of the Supreme Court, since the Kesavananda Bharati Case, has been that the Preamble is very much a part and parcel of the Constitution.[3] Further as the former Chief Justice of India, M. Hidayatullah (1982, 51) points out,

> Preamble resembles the Declaration of Independence of the United States of America, but is more than a declaration. It is the soul of our Constitution which lays down the pattern of our political society which it states is sovereign, democratic republic. It contains a solemn resolve which nothing but a revolution can alter.

FUNDAMENTAL RIGHTS

The inclusion of a detailed scheme of fundamental rights in the Constitution marks the culmination of a long and sustained desire of Indians to be bestowed with the basic liberties of a free and happy life. Indeed, the formation of the Indian National Congress in 1885 was, among other things, aimed at ensuring the same rights and privileges for Indians that the British enjoyed in their own country (Austin 1966, 52–53), although the first systematic demand for fundamental rights came in the form of The Constitution of India Bill, 1895.[4] The Bill stipulated to secure to all citizens the freedom of speech and expression, the right to personal liberty, the inviolability of one's house, the right to property, equality before law, equality to admission to public offices and the right to petition for the redressal of grievances. However, the idea of Indians being called as the citizens of India was still absent, even in the minds of prominent Indian leaders, including the leaders of the Congress, who in the wake of the publication of the Montagu–Chelmsford Report (1919) impressed upon the British Government for the 'declaration of the rights of the people of India as British citizens.' The echo of the demands of Indians for certain fundamental rights was also heard in the draft of the Commonwealth of India Bill, formulated by the National Convention under the inspiration of Mrs Besant in 1925.

Thereafter, numerous resolutions were passed and committees were appointed to put forth perspectives of Indians on the nature and scope of fundamental rights, as aspired by the people of India.[5] Significantly, the Cabinet Mission Plan (1946), while accepting the demand for the Constituent Assembly and the necessity of a written guarantee of fundamental rights in the Constitution of independent India, suggested the appointment of an Advisory Committee on the Rights of Citizens, Minorities and Tribal and Excluded Areas, bestowed with the responsibility of preparing a list of fundamental rights and also to suggest their inclusion in the Union or the State List. Afterwards, the major boost for the provisions of fundamental rights came with the introduction of the Objectives Resolution by Jawaharlal Nehru. While adopting the Resolution on 22 January 1947, the Constituent Assembly solemnly dedicated itself to draft a Constitution for the governance of India wherein justice, social, economic and political, equality of status, of opportunity and before law; freedom of thought, expression, belief, faith, worship, vocation, association and action, subject to law and public morality was to be guaranteed and secured to all the people of India. In the light of the perspective provided by the Objective Resolution, the Constituent Assembly formed the Advisory Committee for reporting on Minorities, fundamental rights and on the tribal and excluded areas under the chairmanship of Vallabhbhai Patel and consisting of 53 other members. Streamlining its functions, the Advisory Committee, in turn, set up five sub-committees one of which was vested with the responsibility of suggesting the blueprint of fundamental rights for independent India. The draft report of the Sub-Committee, accompanied by explanatory notes on various clauses of the outline of fundamental rights, was circulated to its members who came up with insightful inputs on these clauses and after consolidation of the views suggested by the members, the final report of the Sub-Committee was submitted to the Chairman of the Advisory Committee on 16 April 1947.

The final shape to the provisions on fundamental rights was given by the Advisory Committee. Basing its formulations on the recommendations of the Sub-Committee, the Advisory Committee agreed on the desirability of dividing the rights into justiciable and non-justiciable, thereby paving the way for the compartmentalization of the erstwhile fundamental rights into two distinct categories of Fundamental Rights and the Directive Principles of State Policy. At the same time, even within the sphere of fundamental rights, it was decided to bestow certain rights upon all persons while few rights were to be guaranteed to citizens only, though the application of rights was extended to all the states of the country. The report of the Advisory Committee was accepted and adopted by the Constituent Assembly which by way of creating two chapters—III and IV made provisions for the Fundamental Rights and the Directive Principles of State Policy respectively.

Originally, the Constitution contained seven fundamental rights. But the right to property was repealed in 1978 by the 44th Constitutional Amendment during the rule of the Janata Government, reducing these rights to six only which are classified as: Right to Equality

(Articles 14–18), Right to Freedom (Articles 19–22), Right against Exploitation (Articles 23 and 24), Right to Freedom of Religion (Articles 25–28), Cultural and Educational Rights (Articles 29 and 30) and the Right to constitutional Remedies (Article 32). These rights have been protected against undue infringement by the state except for certain specific circumstances provided under the Constitution, though their amendability has been upheld by the Supreme Court under Article 368 of the Constitution in the Kesavananda Bharati Case (1973).

Described, along with the Directive Principles of State Policy, as the conscience of the Constitution, by Austin, the fundamental rights arguably constitute the soul of the Constitution. However, in material terms, as pointed out by N. A. Palkhiwala, they constitute the anchor of the Constitution and provide it with the dimension of permanence. The Constitution envisages the fundamental rights as the common platform on which divergent political ideologies and practices may meet. They provide the iron framework within which experiments in social and economic changes may be tried out.[6]

These rights, therefore, have been given a very important position in the constitutional law of the country, for, all laws in force in the territory of India immediately before 26 January 1950 and all legislations enacted thereafter, have had to conform to the provisions of Part III of the Constitution.

Moreover, the scope of fundamental rights are wide enough to encompass practically all those rights which human ingenuity finds essential for the development and growth of the personalities of citizens of the country. Significantly, the focus of attention of the framers in this regard was on the citizens mainly, if not exclusively, as many of these rights are not guaranteed to aliens. For instance, the rights contained in Article 15 (Prohibition of discrimination on the basis of religion, race, caste, sex, place of birth or any of them), Article 16 (Equality of opportunity in the matters of public employment), Article 19 (Right to Freedom) and Article 29 (cultural and educational rights) are available to citizens only. Nevertheless, the best part of the provisions on fundamental rights is the fine-tuned machinery which guarantees these rights in practice, as under Article 32, the Supreme Court has been given the original jurisdiction to entertain the petition of a person whose fundamental right has been infringed upon and is empowered with various Writs which can be issued to secure the enjoyment of these rights.

Despite being taken as the bedrock of democratic life in the country, the fundamental rights have not been made absolute since several reasonable restrictions have been placed on their enjoyment. Set to secure the public good on the one hand and the unity and integrity of the nation on the other, reasonable restrictions can be imposed specifically in the interests of the sovereignty and integrity of India, security of the state, friendly relations with foreign states, public order, decency, morality, health, etc. and for the protection of the interests of any Scheduled Tribes. Though these restrictions, no doubt, appear to be an attempt on the part of the framers to strike a balance between individual liberty and the social good, in the course of the functioning of the Constitution, it was rightly apprehended that the state might, under the garb of reasonable restrictions, put undue infringement on the enjoyment of these rights. Consequently, the endeavour of the Courts in the country has been to put a rigorous check on the reasonableness of the restriction, as and when they are imposed to curtail the rights of the people. The proclamation of a state of emergency provides another circumstance wherein the enjoyment of fundamental freedoms guaranteed under Article 19 may be suspended. Similarly, Article 33 empowers the Parliament not to grant some of the fundamental rights to the persons employed in the armed forces.

Reasonable restrictions notwithstanding, the fundamental rights appear to be big restrictions on the legislative, executive and to some extent judicial powers of the state. In making laws, the legislatures must see to it that such laws do not in any way infringe upon any of the fundamental rights guaranteed to people, for, if any of these laws as a whole or in part are found inconsistent with any of the fundamental rights, they would be declared null and void by the competent court. More precarious is the position of executive authorities who bear the brunt of the Court when they are found to be acting in any unconstitutional manner. The 2005 Soharabuddin fake encounter case of Gujarat has proved to be an act in which several senior IPS officers of the state were reported to have participated. The same canon of constitutional propriety applies to the judiciary also as no decision which is in contravention to the provisions of fundamental rights can be pronounced by any court in the country. If such a decision is delivered, it is bound to be set aside by the higher courts. More importantly, the restrictions of the fundamental rights do not apply only to state agencies but only to private individuals and organizations. For instance, Article 17 stands for the abolition of untouchability, Article 15(2) prohibits the inability of any citizen in the use of shops, restaurants, wells, roads and other public places on account of his religion, race, sex or of birth, and Article 23 bars the practice of beggary or forced labour in any form. Thus, the state, in addition to obeying the Constitution's negative injunctions of not interfering with certain liberties of citizens, must fulfil its positive obligation to protect citizens' rights from encroachment by society (Austin 1966, 51).

FUNDAMENTAL DUTIES

Impregnating the high sounding and zealously guarded domain of fundamental rights with a moderate dose of ethical citizenship responsibilities, the fundamental duties were inserted in the Constitution in 1976 through the 42nd Constitutional Amendment Act. Drawn from the Constitution of the former Soviet Union and placed in Part IVA of the Constitution under Article 51A. The set of 10 fundamental duties are supposed to be only moral exhortation to the citizens of the county to inculcate a sense of patriotic and sensible citizenship, without any legal justiciability.

Though not justiciable and therefore, with little consequence in practical terms, the provision of fundamental duties was opposed by many people who also brought out several inconsistencies in these duties. For instance, one of the fundamental duties asks every citizen of the country to develop the scientific temper and spirit of enquiry. But with a bulk of the people still illiterate, how is it possible to imbibe the habit of thinking with clarity and precision if they are unable to get the basic inputs of such a thinking. Nevertheless, the fundamental duties have become a part of the Constitution and despite their non-justiciability; they continue to exercise some sort of social and collective restriction on those who are fond of enjoying unfettered rights without discharging even an iota of duty to the society and the nation.

THE DIRECTIVE PRINCIPLES OF STATE POLICY

The provision of the Directive Principles of State Policy in the Constitution was the culmination of the humanitarian and socialist ideas nurtured by a majority of the leaders of the national movement who aspired for not only a political democracy for India, but also socio-economic democracy. Crystallizing in the 1931 Karachi resolution of the Indian National Congress, the leaders made a constitutional declaration of social and economic policy in the recognition of the vision of a welfare state in place of a regulatory state in the colonial mould. Ideally, the Karachi resolution must have led to the incorporation of the declaration of social and economic policy in the form of justiciable fundamental rights but the stark reality of the insufficiency of economic resources and the overbearing prevalence of conservatism in the society, at the time of framing the Constitution, seems to have dissuaded the framers to make the social and economic ideals the justiciable fundamental rights. The way out, therefore, seemed to be to place social and economic ideals in the form of directive principles, which though non-justiciable, would remain fundamental in guiding state policy. Borrowed from and patterned on the Irish Directive Principles of Social Policy, these directive principles also sounded attractive to the framers due to their long standing proximity with the Irish nationalist movement. Later on, when it came to the fine of tuning the various directive principles, other shades of cherished ideals like Hindu mythological beliefs and Gandhian ideas of social and economic reconstruction, along with secular socialist perspectives on Indian society also found adequate reflection in the final list of the directive principles.

Placed in Part IV of the Constitution (Articles 35–51), the directive principles signify the positive obligations of the state towards its citizens, for, as Article 37 envisages that though not enforceable by the Court, they are nevertheless fundamental in the governance of the country and it shall be the duty of the state to apply these principles in making the laws. Thus, the two fundamental issues in the context of the nature of the directive principles relate to their legal status in the Constitution as well their position vis-à-vis the fundamental rights. As regards the legal status of these principles, the vision of the framers was crystal clear that these principles would not be justiciable in the sense that the fundamental rights are, though, they would not be mere proclamations or the pious wish list only. As K. C. Markandan (1966, 147–48) argues,

> Far from being a proclamation or promulgation of principles, the directive principles constitute a pledge by the framers of the Constitution to the people of India and a failure to implement them would constitute not only a breach of faith with the people but would also render a vital of the Constitution practically a dead letter.

However, the real test of the vitality of the directive principles in the Constitution came through their recurring clashes with the fundamental rights, in which the Supreme Court tried to clear the air in various landmark judgements. The root cause of the conflict between the directive principles and the fundamental rights lies mainly, if not exclusively, in the provisions contained in Clause 2 of Article 13 which envisaged that the state shall not make any law which takes away or abridges the rights conferred by part III of the Constitution and any law made in contravention of this clause shall, to the extent of contravention, be void. Accordingly, the first case of clash between the two arose in the case of the *Champakam Dorairajan vs the State of Madras* in which the Supreme Court held that the directive principles could not override the fundamental rights, though it did accept that the fundamental rights could be amended under the provisions of Article 368, relying on the doctrine of harmonious construction of various provisions of the Constitution. Thereafter, the accepted position was that though ordinarily the directives principles could not override the fundamental rights, certain reasonable restrictions could be put on the fundamental rights in order to implement the directive principles by way of due amendment in the Constitution.

A climb down on the part of the Supreme Court appeared in 1967 in the case of *Golak Nath vs the State of Punjab*, when the Court denigrating the value of the doctrine of harmonious construction, held inter alia that the Parliament had no power to amend any of the provisions of Part III of the Constitution so as to take away or abridge the fundamental rights enumerated therein, making the fundamental rights unamendable in any situation. Finding itself in a piquant situation, the government got the 24th and 25th Amendments made in the Constitution, which came for the scrutiny of the Supreme Court in the case of *Kesavananda Bharati vs State of Kerala*. Falling back again on the doctrine of harmonious construction, the Court, propounding the doctrine of basic structure of the Constitution, held the primacy of the directive principles over the fundamental rights in respect of certain articles but rejected the rights of the legislature and the executive to make laws or issue orders amounting to amending the 'basic structure' of the Constitution. Later, in the case of *Minerva Mills Ltd. vs the Government of India*, the Supreme Court stuck to the position that the primacy of the directive principles over fundamental rights could not be claimed to be unqualified and any amendment to the Constitution, altering its basics structure was bound to be void.

Notwithstanding the long drawn controversy on the constitutional status of the directive principles, a perusal of various principles reveals interesting features regarding the scope and diversity of the same. As pointed out earlier, the provision of directive principles afforded various shades of perspectives an opportunity to provide their ideals a place in the Constitution, which are three in the main.

First, a substantive number of the directive principles were aimed at the establishment of a welfare state by bringing about a subtle socio-economic transformation in the country. For instance, Article 38 broadly defined the core content of the directive principles, envisaging that the state would strive to promote the welfare of the people by effectively ensuring a social order in which justice—social, economic and political—would pervade all the national institutions in the country. The other directive principles of this sort pertain to the equitable distribution of material resources in society, welfare of women and children, equal pay for equal work, improving conditions of work and free and compulsory education for children up to the age of 14, etc.

Second, a large number of the directive principles aspire to implement the Gandhian principles of social life, such as the establishment of village panchayats, cottage industries, uplifting of the conditions of Scheduled Castes and Scheduled Tribes, prohibition, improve the breeds of cattle and stopping the slaughter of cows and calves, etc.

Finally, certain directive principles dealt with the streamlining of governance in the country and the promotion of international peace. Thus, while the directive principle on the separation of the judiciary from the executive was aimed at streamlining the governance in the county, the directive principles relating to the securing of international peace and security, maintenance of good and honourable relations between nations, fostering respect to international law and treaty obligations and settlement of international disputes by arbitration and other peaceful means were meant for the global peace and tranquility.

The efforts at operationalizing the lofty ideals, enshrined in the Constitution in the form of directive principles portray a picture of belied promises. Though reduced to a secondary position by the framers themselves by not making them justiciable, albeit with stipulations of time and resources, the directive principles were supposed to be the fundamental guiding spirit behind the programmes and policies of the government. However, the government at various points of time was keener to look for alibis to neutralize the execution of the directive principles than to pool economic resources, secure social sanction and muster the political will to put them into practice. Hence, in the early years of independence, the argument of judicial impediments were advanced to explain negligible progress in the implementation of the directive principles. When the judicial impediments were ultimately warded off, the bogie of the insufficiency of resources was raised. But the true colour of governmental perspective on the directive principles started emerging during 1990s when successive governments, under the garb of liberalization of the economy, not only ignored these directive principles, but also started drifting away from them. The so called labour reforms was a case in point. Even those directive principles which had been implemented, like the one relating to the Panchayats and free and compulsory education to children up to the age of 14, appeared to have been implemented more to score a point over the Opposition than with the true spirit of bringing about a socio-economic transformation in the country. In such a scenario, the only plausible way out to get the directive principles implemented in letter and spirit is through the waging of a mass movement, pioneered by concerned people of society.

FEDERALISM

While deliberating to decide on the shape of independent India, the framers of the Constitution seemed to be in a somewhat dilemma, not owing to differences amongst themselves but due to the incongruity in their past experiences, the present set-up and the future prospective scenario of the country. Historically, owing to the vast diversity in the spatial character of the country, coupled with the localized structure of society and economy, as well as the dispersed structure of political authority, both the people and the local governments had enjoyed considerable degree of autonomy for a very long period of time till the establishment of the British rule in the country. Adept at running a unitary government at home, the British rulers, in an urge to tighten their grip over the whole country, ruptured the existing order to replace it with a highly centralized colonial administration. Caught in this paradoxical past and the present, the framers were called upon to devise a system for the country which would serve the future polity on a satisfying and durable basis.

Apart from the previous experiences, the state of things at the time of independence, particularly concerning the unity and integrity of the nation, also weighed heavily in the minds of the framers who were brainstorming on the shape of things for independent India. Though there was no doubt that the country would be accorded a decentralized system of governance, there existed certain discordant notes on the extent of such a decentralization. For instance, while agreeing that the Union Government should collect revenues and then distribute it among the states, the members vehemently urged for an increased share of revenue for the state governments. Thus, as Austin reveals, the singular aspect of the drafting of the federal provisions was the relative absence of conflict between the 'centralizers' and the 'provincialists', for, the framers had embraced the doctrine of 'cooperative federalism' as the guiding spirit of the Indian federal set-up (Austin 1966, 186–87).

Ultimately, the final shape of the provisions on federalism emerged to be typically Indian with no parallel in any other Constitution of the world. While structurally the Constitution created a federal polity in the country but provisions were also made to create a strong central government such that the labelling of such a system as a federation appeared improper. The Constitution, therefore, branded India as a 'Union of States', instead of a federation, the technicality of which was explained by Ambedkar as such,

> The Drafting Committee wanted to make it clear that though India was to be federation, the federation was not the result of an agreement by the states to join in a federation, and that the federation not being the result of an agreement, no state has the right to secede from it. The federation is a Union because it is indestructible.

Moreover, operationally, as he explained, it would be 'a federal Constitution in as much as it establishes what may be called a Dual Polity (which) ... will consist of the Union at the Centre and the States at the periphery, each endowed with sovereign powers to be exercised in the field assigned to them respectively by the Constitution'. Still, the Constitution avoided the 'tight mould of federalism' in which the American Constitution was cast so that it could become 'both unitary as well as federal according to the requirements of time and circumstances' (Ambedkar 2003, 33–34).

The most significant development in India's constitutional history is the consolidation of the parliamentary form of government that broadly corresponded with the Westminster model.[7] What is equally striking is the growth of federalism in India in spite of a parliamentary government that, in its classical form, flourished within a unitary system of government. While Britain is identified as a classical model of parliamentary government, the United States is always referred to as an ideal form of federal government. Both these political systems have evolved specific constitutional practices in consonance with their ideological preferences and socio-economic requirements. What largely explains the emergence of specific types of governance in both the United Kingdom and the United States is the peculiar historical circumstances in which they emerged as nation-states. In view of a gradual decline of monarchy in Britain, the parliament became sovereign reflecting popular aspirations, articulated through a well-devised system of elective democracy. While in the United States, the decision of the constituent units to merge for a strong political system led to the rise of a union that held power for sustaining a confederal arrangement. This is however not to suggest that there is a 'conflict' between parliamentary governments and federalism as theoretical categories. Federalism does not necessarily imply 'divided' sovereignty, incompatible with the notion of parliamentary supremacy just like the fact that parliamentary governments seek to establish 'unfettered' majority rules. Historically speaking, while framing the Dominion Constitutions (for Australia and Canada) in the early 1900s, 'parliaments' that came into being were not made 'supreme'. Instead, it was the Constitution that enjoyed supreme authority, exercised through a judicial review (by the Privy Council). It would therefore be most appropriate to argue that there are various politico-constitutional devices to avoid distortions in majority rule. Federalism is only one such device that privileges territorial entities, which may or may not be culturally or historically defined communities. While the parliamentary system is conceptually unitary, federalism is just otherwise. This is a puzzle that needs to be understood in a specific historical context. The British parliamentary model remained a major reference point for the Indian Constitution makers. Federalism seemed to have provided an institutional arrangement to accommodate India's pluralist socio-political character. What was apparently contradictory emerged as the most appropriate institutional set-up for governance in India.

Parliamentary federalism, as it evolved in India, is a unique hybrid system of governance in which apparently contradictory tendencies are sought to be managed. What has emerged in India during the course of more than half a century does not correspond with any of the classical models of government? The Indian political structure is neither strictly unitary nor purely federal; it is a form in which the elements of both can be traced and are evident. Distinct from the classical types for obvious reasons, the Indian political system offers a unique model drawing upon both the British tradition of parliamentary sovereignty and the American federal legacy in which regions seem to be prior to the Centre. This is essentially a hybrid system of governance that has emerged due to a peculiar unfolding of socio-political processes in the aftermath of India's rise as a nation-state. Parliamentary federalism is therefore not merely a structural device for the distribution of powers between different layers of government it is also the articulation of a basic philosophy accommodating diverse regional interests in the name of a nation.

A look at the functioning of federalism in India during the last almost five decades reveals unique twists in operationalizing the constitutional provisions in letter and in spirit, based on the political exigencies of the times. During the reign of Jawaharlal Nehru, in the formative years of the constitutional government in India, centre–state relations progressed fairly, if not absolutely, seemingly due to the existence of the Congress-led governments at both the centre and the states, though marked tendencies towards centralization were apparent in many areas of governmental functioning. Institutionalizing centralization, as Austin charges Nehru with, notwithstanding, the underlining characteristics of Nehru's regime were harmonious coexistence with the state governments on the one hand and the apparently centralizing moves justified by the circumstantial compulsions of the times, on the other.

Things started taking an unsavoury turn with the arrival of Indira Gandhi at the helm of affairs of the Central Government. Groping for a way out to escape her vulnerability to pressures from the heavyweight state Congress leaders, she appeared to have developed an intuitive tendency towards centralization and eventual monopolization of all powers in her hand, irrespective of its detrimental effects on the structure and functioning of democratic institutions in general and federal relations in particular. Formidable election victories of 1971 and 1972 emboldened Mrs Gandhi to change the constitutional character of federal relations through the apparently ill-conceived 24th and 25th Amendments, evoking sharp, if not subversive, reactions from the non-Congress state governments, the staunchest of which came in the form of the Tamil Nadu government appointed Rajamannar Committee Report.[8] Attaining an alarming proportion in the 1970s, Mrs Gandhi's monopolizing tendencies reached their peak in 1975 with the declaration of Emergency in the country. After remaining subdued for quite some time, the opposition Chief Ministers raised a banner of 'constitutional revolt' during the early 1980s in protest against subtle moves to turn the country into a unitary system, putting Mrs Gandhi into a tight position, to which she responded by appointing the Sarkaria Commission on Centre–State Relations in 1983. As Mrs Gandhi's tenures as Prime Minister posed more serious challenges to the structure and functioning of the federal system in the country, her safety valve creation of the Sarkaria Commission came out in 1987 with the most reasoned arguments, diagnosing the ills of the structure and functioning of the centre–state relations and suggesting plausible remedies for the same.

The contemporary phase of the working of the federal system in the country, which is said to have begun in the late 1980s, with the onset of an era of coalition and relatively weaker governments at the centre, has been marked by a reversal of roles of sorts for the major players of the game. To put it differently, if during the times of Jawaharlal Nehru and Indira Gandhi, the central government, by hook or by crook, tried to bully the state governments and overcentralize the already centralized constitutional framework of centre–state relations in the country, in the present phase of centre-state relations, the overbearing coalition partners, with their roots and political vision predominantly, if not totally, confined to particular states, so much guide and sometimes dictate the policies and actions of the central government making India appear as a classic case of a federation where the states are autonomous and the central government functioning in accordance with their sweet wishes. What is remarkable, however, in this context, is the fact that even the parties which were staunch supporters of the demand for state autonomy like the National Conference and Dravida Munnetra Kazhagam, (DMK), did not press for any serious efforts at recasting the basic parameters of centre–state relations in the Constitution, when they were, as in the case of the former or are, as in the case of the latter, in a position to dictate their terms to the central government. Rather, the move of the National Democratic Alliance (NDA) government, for obvious political reasons, to appoint a National Commission to Review the Working of the Constitution under the chairmanship of Justice M. N. Venkatachelliah, proved to be a whimper as the Commission in its report stood by the broader recommendations of the Sarkaria Commission and failed to caste any aspersion on the structural and functional viability of the Constitution of India. Crucially, thus, the constitutional provisions on centre–state relations have proved to be all weather, if not infallible, ones capable of meting out the requirements presented by, either dictatorial governments like that of Mrs Gandhi or helpless governments like that of Man Mohan Singh, without undergoing any permanent dent leading to the subversion of the Constitution.

PARLIAMENTARY SYSTEM

The system of parliamentary democracy, which informs all the institutions of governance in the country, did not become the crowning glory of the Constitution all of a sudden or without serious debate and discussion in the Constituent Assembly. Indeed, roots of the demand for a parliamentary system of governance in the country could arguably be traced back to the early twentieth century when Indians persistently demanded the establishment of parliamentary institutions in the pattern of the British polity which would afford them an opportunity to associate with governmental activities in the country. Though the colonial rulers consistently refused to accede to the wishes of the natives on the grounds of the unsuitability of Indians to run such kinds of institutions on the one hand, and the undesirability of parliamentary institutions as such, for India, on the other, the longings of enlightened Indians for some sort of parliamentary system to be established in the country became progressively hardened with every refusal of the British India Government for the same. Afterwards, in most, if not all the documents proposing the model of political set-up for independent India, like the Nehru Committee Report, the Sapru Report, the Draft Constitution of Free India published by the Socialist Party and the Hindu Mahasabha as well as by individuals like M. N. Roy, the argument for a parliamentary system of government figured prominently as the ideal model of governance for India after independence.

However, when the Constituent Assembly set on to decide the kind of political institution for the governance of the country, more than the lust, if not infatuation with the parliamentary system, the urge to devise a mechanism which would foster a rapid socio-economic revolution, weighed more dominantly in the minds of the framers. Having decided in favour of rapid evolution, as against violent revolution, as K. Santhanam (1948) put it, the obvious question before the framers, as Austin reveals, was: what form of political institutions would foster or at least permit a social revolution? As Austin informs further, two competing systems of political institutions were available to the framers to opt for: first, looking back into the nation's rich heritage and finding indigenous institutions capable of meeting the country's needs, the framers would base the Constitution on the village and its panchayats and erect upon them a superstructure of indirect, decentralized government in the Gandhian manner; second, opting for the Euro-American constitutional traditions, reflected in the form of parliamentary system, although it meant continuing in the direction the country had taken during the colonial period (Austin 1966, 27–28). Reminiscent of the old liking of Indians for parliamentary institutions, the Constituent Assembly's decision in favour of the latter option was arrived at with an overwhelming majority, with only one member raising a voice supporting the village panchayats, although the broad contours of his scheme of things also appeared to be in the mould of representative democratic governance.

Explaining the rationale behind the choice for the parliamentary system, Jawaharlal Nehru speaking in Lok Sabha on 28 March 1957, said,

> We chose this system of parliamentary democracy deliberately; we chose it not only because, to some extent, we had always thought on those lines previously, but because we thought it in keeping without own old traditions, not the old traditions as they were, but adjusted to the new conditions and new surroundings. We chose it—let us give credit where the credit is due—because we approved of it's functioning in other countries, more especially in the United Kingdom.

Further, providing a more deep seated account for the adoption of the parliamentary system by the Constituent Assembly, Austin (1966, 39–49) points out four compelling reasons.

First, the alternative of the panchayat based system of governance, rooted in the Gandhian frame of analysis, did not find favour with the framers as 'the Congress had never been Gandhian' on the one hand, and the near universal acceptance of the parliamentary system as the fait accompli for the country by all sections of Indian society.

Second, the commitment of many members of the Constituent Assembly to 'socialism' also emboldened the pursuits of going for a parliamentary system, for, socialism and democratic government were taken as supplementary to each other. Holding that democratic Constitution could not survive without a subtle move to secure social and economic equality, a majority of the Indians, with the probable exception of the communists held the view that 'there could be no socialism without democracy' which could be ordained by the parliamentary system of governance.

Third, the immediate challenges, posed on the well-being of the people on the one hand, and the unity and integrity of the country, on the other, also tilted the balance in favour of the parliamentary system. At the time of the inauguration of Interim Government in September 1946, livelihoods of the people were threatened due to famine-like conditions in many parts of the country, rising food prices, precarious grain reserves and a clash of interest between the surplus and scarcity provinces. Similarly, the threat to the unity of the nascent nation came from rising communal passions in the wake of the Direct Action Day call by Jinnah, the reluctance of a few princely states to join the Indian Union and the Communist rebellion in regions like Telangana. The cure to these ills was considered to lie in the parliamentary system as only that could afford a fair degree of centralization of powers in the hands of the central government without compromising the structure and functioning of democracy in the country.

Finally, the unflinching faith of the members of the Assembly in the need for universal adult franchise as the basic factor to herald social revolution in the country also weighed decisively in favour of parliamentary democracy because the parliament so elected was construed to represent the people as a whole, ensuring representation to all sections of society and fostering the socio-economic revolution to usher true democratic governance in the country. The somewhat, if not absolute, successful functioning of parliamentary democracy for the last six decades of post-independence period in India fulfilled the dreams of the framers to have a system of governance, capable of meeting all sorts of challenges to the welfare of both the people as well as the nation, without compromising the democratic ethos and spirit of institutions of governance. Embedded with the virtues of both responsibility and responsiveness, it ensured daily as well as periodic assessments of the functioning of the government. Significantly, the parliamentary system has facilitated the successful meeting of challenges to the social, economic and political life of the nation expeditiously due to the absence of any working at cross purposes between the executive and legislative branches of the government. Above all, the parliamentary system has afforded the people from all parts of the country, following various socio-cultural customs and traditions and distinct political ideologies to find a voice in the governance of the country through their representation in the parliament, going a long way to strengthen national spirit and belongingness in them.

Despite the institutional soundness and having sustained the unity and integrity of the country alongwith securing the mental and material well-being of the people, the functional dynamics of the parliamentary system in India has not been without its share of responsibilities in terms of the ills plaguing the country today. The inconsistent nature of polity over the years, beginning with the democratic governance of Nehru, through the authoritarian dispensation ordained by Mrs Gandhi, till the climax of weak and spineless government of Man Mohan Singh, it has been the classic case of unpredictability regarding the nature of government under a parliamentary system. More importantly, recourse to tactics of populist politics has again proved to be the nemesis of democratic governance in the country as shrewd and self-serving politicians and political parties have not hesitated in raising the bogey of either hollow or divisive issues to score a point over their political adversaries and gain parliamentary majority for themselves. Precisely a side effect of the parliamentary system, the policies like Mrs Gandhi's 'Garibi Hatao' sloganeering, V. P. Singh's 'Mandal' gamble and the Bhartiya Janata Party's 'Ram Mandir' ploy were all emotive issues to exploit the masses for vote politics rather than to bring about any remarkable changes in their lives. And the contemporary phase of coalitional politics, accompanied with the formation of unstable, if not defying the formation of any government at all, governments at both the centre and the states also appear to be the obvious consequence of an intense socio-economic and political churning taking place in the country, due to the dynamics of the parliamentary system. Yet, these undesirable, if not pernicious trends in the democratic politics of the country, may be taken as transitional hiccups in the evolutionary phase of a nation from being a traditional, backward, divided and politically inactive society to a progressive, developed, diversified and mass democratized nation, to facilitate which the framers banked upon the parliamentary system of governance for the country.

AMENDING PROCEDURES

The issue of amending procedures of the Constitution was one of the least debated and controversial ones dealt with by the Constituent Assembly probably due to the lesser importance attached to it by members on the one hand and the lack of adequate knowledge and 'immediate experience' amongst the average members of the Assembly on the other. Barring a few customary references in the reports like Nehru's (1928) and Sapru's (1946) as well as in the draft Constitutions of K. M. Munshi and K. T. Shah, K. M. Panikkar (1948), etc., a well thought out scheme of amending procedures was not available to the framers till mid 1947 when B. N. Rau presented his framework of amending procedure providing two fold procedures for amending the Constitution. These included first, the amendments needed to first be passed by a two-thirds majority in both the houses of Parliament and then ratified by a like majority of provincial legislatures. Second, the transitional provisions could be amended by a simple majority in the Parliament. However, the main dilemma before the framers was, presumably, to reconcile the competing allurements of amending the Constitution by a simple majority to keep the Constitution dynamic, living, serving the needs of the society with the changing times and circumstances on the one hand; and to make its procedures for making amendments in it rigid enough to thwart any frivolous attempt to alter the basic framework of the federal polity of the country. After due deliberations on the practices followed with reference to the American, the Australian and the Irish Constitutions, the Constituent Assembly agreed to provide a threefold method for amending the Constitution under the provisions of Article 368, drawing appreciation from experts like K. C. Wheare who complimented the framers for striking a balance by protecting the rights of the states while leaving the rest of the Constitution to be amended easily (Wheare 1988, 143).

Labelled as 'one of the most ably conceived aspects of the Constitution',[9] the provisions under Article 368 appear to have met the aspirations of the framers to make the Constitution a living document while making it extremely difficult to rob it off its basic characteristics. Of the three methods of amending the Constitution, two were specifically provided for in the Article whereas the third was provided for in about 22 other Articles. Thus, first, the Constitution can be amended by introducing an amending Bill in either house of the Parliament which needs to be passed by a majority in each house with two-thirds of the members present and voting, after which it is sent for Presidential assent and at the receipt of which it becomes an amendment.

The second method relates to the Articles enumerated under the proviso to Article 368 items (a) to (e), dealing with the method of election of the President of India; the distribution of legislative powers between the Union and the States; the extent of the executive power of the Union and the States; representation of the States in the Parliament; the provisions relating to the Supreme Court and the High Courts; and the amendment of the Constitution itself. To amend any of these Articles, the amending Bill needs to not only be passed by a majority of the total membership in each house and a majority of not less than two-thirds of the members present and voting in each house, but also ratified by at least one half of the state legislatures.

Third, the Constitution can be amended by a simple majority vote in the two houses of the Parliament, followed by the assent of the President. The basic percepts, with which this provision deals with include the formation of new states, alteration of state boundaries, changing the name of states, delimitation of constituencies, qualifications for citizenship, quorum in the Parliament, etc. to name a few, and these are to remain in force until the Parliament brings about changes in them. Though a formal amendment in all such cases is not effected, yet they have the effect of making changes in the constitutional law.

In view of the overt provisions made in Article 368 on the methods of amending the Constitution, a subtle debate emerged amongst scholars regarding the scope and nature of the Parliament's power to amend the Constitution. One school of thought, rooted in legal positivism, contended that, owing to the elaborate provisions made in the Constitution, the Parliament needed to confine itself to what was provided for in this regard, without any attempt to derive implied powers of amendment. Responding, in a way, to the provisions of Article 13(2) which bars the state from making any law which takes away or abridges the Fundamental Rights, the other school of thought held that the amendment of the Constitution needed to be viewed in the context of the socio-economic needs of the country, instead of the strict legal provisions provided for in this regard. These two contrasting, if not conflicting views on the amendability of the Constitution have found their reflection in the ongoing game of one-upmanship between the Parliament and the Supreme Court even till today.

Though questions on the limits of the amending powers of the Parliament were raised soon after the inauguration of the Constitution in 1951 in the case of *Sankari Prasad vs the Union of India*, the Supreme Court took the position till 1967, that the Parliament had unfettered powers to amend the Constitution. This position was dramatically reversed by the Supreme Court in the case of *Golak Nath vs the State of Punjab* in 1967, ruling that the Parliament had no power to amend the provisions on Fundamental Rights, leading to serious resentment in political circles that started attempting to find a way out of this all imposing judgement. Responding by way of the 24th and 25th Amendments, the government sought to turn the tables on the Supreme Court by not only nullifying what the Court had provided for in the Golak Nath case, but also extending the whip to the office of the President by providing that when a constitutional amendment was presented to him for his assent, he needed to give his assent and that he would not have any discretion in this regard. Creating again an opportunity for a stand-off between the government and the Supreme Court, the 24th and 25th Amendments were challenged in the Supreme Court in the case of *Kesavananda Bharati vs State of Kerala* in 1973.

The historical judgement in the Kesavananda Bharati case tried to restore the precarious balance between the government and the judiciary on the issue of the amendability of the Constitution by

> [O]verruling Golak Nath, upholding the 24th and 25th amendments and striking down the 'escape clause' in the 25th amendment's Article 31C. The essence of the statement of the nine judges was that Article 368 did not enable Parliament to alter the basic structure or framework of the Constitution.[21]

The Court, thus, through the doctrine of implied limitations and the doctrine of basic structure, tried to ensure the permanence of the basic constituent aspects of the Constitution, on the one hand, and give the maximum possible leverage to the Parliament to amend the socio-economic provisions to usher in an era of a welfare state in the country on the other. The core of the decision in the Kesavananda Bharati case was reiterated by the Supreme Court in the case of *Minerva Mills Ltd vs the Union of India*, thereby asserting the irreversibility of the doctrine of the basic structure in relation to the amendability of the Constitution. However, an aberration, in the form of the Ninth Schedule of the Constitution, existing since 1951, which made certain laws and amendments immune from judicial review after they are placed in the said schedule by the Parliament, created an anomalous situation in which the Parliament was accorded an indirect escape route to amend the basic structure of the Constitution and shield it from the scrutiny of the Court. Removing this anomaly, the Supreme Court, in the case of *IR Coelho vs the State of Tamil Nadu* held that the Ninth Schedule was created for a specific purpose and was not to be used as a shield to keep certain laws and amendments out of the purview of judicial review (*The Statesman* 2007), which may even have had the propensity of subverting the basic structure of the Constitution.

In contemporary times, issues regarding the amending procedure and ancillary questions appear to be settled in favour of a dominating position for the Supreme Court, which has progressively attained a position of commanding heights in the constitutional framework of governance in the country, partly due to the pernicious acts of commissions on part of the government on the one hand, and deplorable acts of omissions by the government, on the other. In both cases the people have had to move the Court to get the wrongful undone and the rightful done through judicial pronouncements. Such an unsavoury predicament of the constitutional framework needs to be cleared in favour of a reasoned balance in the jurisdictions of various organs of the government. Taking the doctrine of the basic structure of the Constitution as the reference point for amendments, both the Parliament as well as the Supreme Court should try to work the Constitution, in so far as amendments are concerned, rather than subverting it.

CONCLUDING OBSERVATIONS

Drafted to be the embodiment of numerous ideals cherished by prominent leaders of the national movement in terms of the shape of social, economic, political, cultural and religious systems and parameters of life of a modern and forward looking people, the Constitution of India represents the crux of what came out to be a fairly acceptable scheme of things amongst the competing perspectives on the contours of future Indian polity. As pointed out earlier, the major problems before the framers of the Constitution seemingly arose at two levels: macro and micro. At the first level, the core concern of the framers related to the adoption of the macro level institutions to manifest the foundational mechanism of the polity in terms of the parliamentary system of democracy, the federal nature of the polity etc. Though there existed a good deal of pointers on what needed to be the macro model of the polity in independent India, there, indeed, were certain alternative models which some members of the Constituent Assembly advocated for adoption by the Assembly. For instance, a few members of the Assembly argued for the superiority of the Swiss system of government in comparison to the British, ostensibly for the sake of better representation and protection of the interests of minorities and other sectional groups.

More deep rooted issues came to the fore once the puzzle at the macro level was sorted out. As India was a mammoth country with innumerable diversities, broken political customs and conventions, wide social cleavages and widespread religious and cultural variations, the issue of fine-tuning the political system of the country was not over just by adopting the parliamentary system, born and operationalized in a western country whose circumstances and socio-economic milieu were drastically different from those of India. Hence, while retaining the spirit of the parliamentary system of democracy, the fathers of the Constitution had to bring about suitable alterations in the classical parliamentary system, such as having an elected head of state in place of a monarchical system and providing for a powerful and independent judiciary in place of a subservient judiciary to the parliamentary supremacy in order to make it propitious to provide for a long lasting system of governance for the country. Similarly, looking at India's geographical size with well-entrenched diversities, in addition to the political aspirations of the people at the regional and local levels, the preference for a federal set-up for the country was obvious. The real issues, however, arose when the classical form of federalism was juxtaposed with the issue of zealously safeguarding the unity and integrity of the nation, as a result of which a number of modifications were introduced in the federal system of the country, prompting several scholars to call Indian federalism as a sub-federal order rather than a true federal one. Yet, the sole concern of the framers of the Constitution appeared to exclusively be concerned with devising the most suitable form of political system for the country, rather than placing India into one or the other straitjacket political systems prevailing in different countries of the world. This was also to be irrespective of academic evaluation and critiquing of the Indian system on the basis its departure from the norms of the classical form of the system.

The founding fathers succeeded in providing a constitutional mechanism by innovating a system of governance moulded in the parliamentary system of Britain and the federal set-up of America but also going miles ahead of these western countries by ensuring to the Indian people what these countries could not dream of, leave alone talk of in terms of its fruition. In other words, the claim to fame of these classical western democracies has been the guaranteeing of certain political and civil fundamental rights to their people in the name of ensuring an equal and free life for them. But as has been argued by the Socialist thinkers, political and civil rights turned out to be a farce in societies where the common person was not able to secure adequate social and economic well-being for himself/herself. On this count, the framers of the Indian Constitution appeared to have scored over both the western capitalist societies as well as the communist ones, by affording to their people not only political and civil fundamental rights, but also aspiring to ensure for them reasonable levels of equitable and satisficing social and economic lives through the provisions of the Directive Principles of State Policy coupled with the availability of resources in the country. Thus, the provisions on the Fundamental Rights and the Directive Principles of State Policy ensured the pith and substance to the skeleton of parliamentary democratic system ordained for the country. Combined together, the combo political and civil rights, ensured through the provisions of Part III and the social and economic rights, enshrined in Part IV of the Constitution, have placed the Indian Constitution at such a high pedestal that neither the capitalist Constitutions nor the socialist ones are able to graduate to that level, thereby making the Indian Constitution a model to be emulated by the newly democratizing countries of the world rather than looking for hitherto predominant western Constitutions.

In final analysis, the Constitution of India appears to be a unique construct bearing testimony to the pious vision and infallible wisdom of its framers. By way of the Preamble, the founding fathers were able to put in black and white the purposes for which the Constitution exists. Though the enormous complexities of Indian life compelled the framers to formulate the lengthiest Constitution in the world, its dynamism and resilience have been brought to the fore by the fact that it has been amended more than 124 times in a life span of just 64 years. Over the years, however, the soul of the Constitution has come to be defined in terms of the basic structure whose inviolability has been declared by the Supreme Court time and again. Thus, by now, the Constitution seems to have braved all sorts of challenges coming either in the form of the 42nd Amendment or the review of its working by the NDA government (1999–2004), with the doctrine of basic structure acting as the impregnable shield against any attempts at subverting its very essence while leaving other parts of it amendable by the Parliament in order to make it propitious for the changing circumstances in the country.

REVIEW QUESTIONS

1. What are the philosophical–constitutional values that are critical to Indian administration? Elaborate.
2. 'Bereft of constitutional and philosophical values, the Indian administration is just an inert structure.' Do you agree with this view? Elaborate your response.
3. How does the Constitution of India govern Indian administration? Elaborate your response.
4. Critically evaluate the role of the Preamble to the Constitution of India in shaping Indian administration.
5. Do you agree with the view that the Indian administration is bound by the constitutional provisions governing Fundamental Rights and Fundamental Duties in India? Elaborate your response.
6. 'Federalism is a critical influence in so far as Indian administration is concerned.' Do you agree with the view? Elaborate your response.
7. 'Parliamentary procedures and legislative outcomes are critical determinants of Indian administration.' Elaborate.
8. How do you conceptualize the importance of the parliamentary system in contemporary Indian administration? Elaborate your response.
9. 'Amendments are a constitutional design to contextualize Indian administration.' Do you agree with this? Elaborate your response.
10. In what respects, is the Indian administration a context-driven exercise? Elaborate your response.

NOTES

1. For details on Objectives Resolution, see *Constituent Assembly Debates* (2003, 59).
2. Quoted in R. C. Agrawal (1998, 15).
3. *Kesavananda Bharati vs the State of Kerala*, 4 S. C. C., 225, paras 94–98 (1973), 324.
4. For details, see B. Shiva Rao (1965).
5. For a historical perspective on the evolution of the demands for fundamental rights in India, see Austin (1966, 52–75).
6. Cited in V. D. Mahajan (1984, 70).
7. The Westeminster Model is a democratic parliamentary system of governance that had emerged in the UK; being a British colony, India was introduced to this form of democratic government in the wake of colonialism.
8. Though dated, the Rajamannar Committee Report contains the most sincere critique of the structure and functioning of the centre–state relations in the country. For details, see Report of the *Centre–State Relations Enquiry Committee* (1971).
9. Quoted in Austin (1999, 264).

REFERENCES

Agrawal, R. C. 1998. *Constitutional Development and National Movement of India*. New Delhi: S. Chand and Company.

Ambedkar, B. R. 2003. *Constituent Assembly Debates*, vol. VII. 4th Reprint. New Delhi: Lok Sabha Secretariat.

Austin, Granville. 1966. *The Indian Constitution: Cornerstone of a Nation*. New Delhi: Oxford University Press.

Austin, Granville. 1999. *Working a Democratic Constitution: The Indian Experience*. New Delhi: Oxford University Press.

Hidayatullah, M. 1982. *Democracy in India and the Judicial Process*. New Delhi: Metropolitan.

Kapur, A. C., and K. K. Mishra. 2001. *Select Constitutions*. New Delhi: S. Chand and Company.

Livingstone. 1956. *Federation and Constitutional Change*. Frazer, London.

Lok Sabha Secretariat. 2003. *Constituent Assembly Debates*, vol. 1. 4th Reprint, New Delhi: Lok Sabha Secretariat.

Mahajan, V. D. 1984. *Select Modern Constitutions*. New Delhi: S. Chand and Company.

Markandan, K. C. 1966. *Directive Principles in the Indian Constitution*. Jalandhar: ABS Publications.

Rao, B. Shiva. 1965. *The Framing of India's Constitution: Select Documents*, vol. I. New Delhi: Indian Institute of Public Administration.

———. 1971. *Report of the Centre–State Relations Enquiry Committee,* Chairman: Justice P. V. Rajamannar, Government of Tamil Nadu, Chennai.

The Hindu. 2007. 12 August.

The Statesman. 2007. New Delhi, 12 January.

Wheare, K. C. 1988. *Modern Constitutions*. New Delhi: S. Chand and Company.

Structure of Central Administration

3

LEARNING OBJECTIVES

1. To know the structure and organization of the Central Government.
2. To understand the functions and role of the Central Secretariat.
3. To discuss the role of the Cabinet Secretariat.
4. To examine the importance of the Prime Minister's Office (PMO).
5. To explore the nature and functions of attached and subordinate offices.

Under India's federal structure there are three levels of governance: central, state and local. At the central level, the Union Government looks after national affairs. At the state level, there are state governments to serve the people of the states. At the local level, which is closest to the people, there are local governments in rural and urban areas. For the smooth functioning of the Government at each level there exists an administrative set-up. Administration in India is thus carried on at different levels: centre, state, district and local levels.

The organizational set-up at central level is very vast, consisting of the Secretariat, ministries and departments, Cabinet Secretariat, the Prime Minister's Office and a number of attached offices and field offices. As on 16 March 2015 there were 25 apex offices, 51 ministries, 60 departments and more than 98 commissions of the Central government of India. This chapter shall primarily deal with these administrative and organizational set-ups at the central level in India.

THE CENTRAL SECRETARIAT

Under the Indian Constitution, all executive actions are taken in the name of the President. But the President is a mere constitutional head. A council of Ministers, with the Prime Minister at its head, aids and advises the President in the exercise of his functions. The real executive power vests in the Cabinet or the council of ministers with the Prime Minister, acting as the nucleus. As these ministers cannot perform numerous functions, they require assistance. For administrative convenience, the Government of India is divided into Ministries and Departments which together constitute the Central Secretariat. The Secretariat is the office which assists ministers heading various ministries in discharging their responsibilities.

The word 'Secretariat' literally means the office of the Secretary. The Secretary, being the principal advisor to the Minister, needs to be equipped with an office to assist him in the performance of his functions. The term finds its origin to the time when there was the secretaries' government in India. After independence, the power of governance came into the hands of popularly elected Ministers making the Ministry, and not the Secretary, the real centre of authority. Therefore, in the altered political situation, the term Secretariat has come to be a synonym for the Minister's office.

Evolution of the Central Secretariat

The Central Secretariat, like some other administrative institutions, is a legacy of the British rule in India. In the beginning, the Secretariat in India was the office of the Governor General. The original role of the Central Secretariat was to furnish requisite information for the formulation of policies and to carry out the orders of the Company's Government. The Regulatory Act of 1773 for the first time created the 'supreme government', with controlling power over the 'presidency government'. It consisted of a Governor General and four councillors in whom all the powers of controlling the military in India vested. This system continued throughout the British rule. With the expansion of the Company's rule, it took on a number of governmental functions and thereby the role of the secretariat expanded along with its size.

It was Lord Cornwallis who took some important steps to organize and strengthen the Secretariat. He created the office of the Secretary General, which later came to be known as the Chief Secretary with all powers and responsibilities. Lord Wellesley also took keen interest in reorganizing the Secretariat. He raised the status of the secretaries by raising their salaries and correspondent responsibilities. The functions of the secretaries were extended to research and planning in addition to their ordinary routine business of execution.

By the end of the eighteenth century, the supreme government consisted of a Governor General, three councillors and a secretariat consisting of four departments (each of these was under a Secretary and all of them worked under the overall control of the Chief Secretary). During the Montfort reforms in 1919, the Government of India consisted of a Governor General and seven members. There were nine secretarial departments and the total strength of the secretariat touched 46. This figure remained unchanged till the beginning of the Second World War in 1939.

The Second World War made a real contribution in evolving the Secretariat as a policy-making body. It was redesigned in the light of war scarcities and war support policies of the colony. The task of policy making got separated from execution and Lord Curzon introduced the transitory cadre of staff on deputation. Due to the urgency of personnel, the post of 'officer on special duty' (OSD) was created in the department of home affairs to look after the civil defense work. A lot of expansion in the Secretariat took place to look after many other areas. The strength of the Governor General's council increased from 7 to 14 and the number of secretariat departments reached 19.The total strength of officials also increased to 200, under the belief that such an expansion was a temporary war-time phenomenon and would be restored to its old position once normalcy was restored with the end of the war. But, the post-war reconstruction programmes and later the advent of independence did not permit any reduction in the size of the Secretariat. Rather, the advent of independence and the problems therein and the expanding social welfare functions of the new popular government further expanded the Secretariat. Thus, the number of departments in the Secretariat increased from 19 in 1945 to 74 in 1994, and likewise, the number of attached and subordinate offices also increased from 20 in 1947 to 100 in 1991.

The Role and Functions of the Central Secretariat

In the current administrative set-up, the Central Secretariat occupies a key position. It assists the Government in the fulfilment of its responsibilities. It assists the ministers in the formulation of governmental policies. As policies can be framed only on the basis of relevant data and information, the Secretariat makes them available to the Minister, thereby enabling him/her to formulate policies. In brief, the Secretariat:

- helps the minister in the policy making process.
- helps in framing rules and regulations.
- helps in financial management and budgeting.
- helps in coordinating with other branches of the government and maintaining contact with state administration.
- helps in evaluating the work done by executive agencies.
- assists the minister in discharging his responsibilities to the Parliament.

Thus, the Secretariat is the highest office of the Government.

> It has lent balance, consistency and continuity to the administration, and serves as a nucleus for the total machinery of a ministry. It has facilitated inter-ministry coordination and accountability to the Parliament at the ministerial level. As an institutionalized system, it is indispensable for the proper functioning of the government. (ARC 1967, 30)

The secretariat is called a think tank, because it provides vital information regarding governmental policies and activities. It acts as a channel of communication between the states and important institutions like the National Institution for Transforming India (NITI Aayog) and Finance Commission. It serves as a nucleus for the overall machinery of a ministry and facilitates inter-ministry coordination. The superior position of the Secretariat has been recognized by the Government through higher pay scales and special allowances for the officials of the secretariat. Thus, the Secretariat is an essential institution in the public administration of the country, being both inevitable and desirable.

Organizational Structure of the Secretariat

The Central Secretariat is a combination of various ministries and departments. The term 'ministry' came into practice only after independence in 1947. A ministry is under the charge of a minister, which may include one or more departments, each under the charge of a secretary. Large ministries like defense, home, external affairs and finance have more than one department. A department is an organizational unit headed by a Secretary. If a ministry has more than one department, it may have more secretaries, but only one senior officer will represent the ministry. A Senior Secretary is designated as the Principal Secretary. For the smooth functioning of a ministry; it is divided into the following segments headed by an officer-in-charge.

- Department — Secretary/Additional Secretary/Special Secretary
- Wing — Joint Secretary/Additional Secretary
- Division — Director/Deputy Secretary
- Branch — Under Secretary
- Section — Section Officer

A ministry consists of one or more departments which are headed by a **Secretary** or in some cases by an additional/special Secretary. He is the administrative head of the ministry/department and the principle advisor to the minister. He represents his ministry/department before the various Committees of the Parliament. He receives weekly reports of the cases disposed by his subordinate staff. In a ministry there may be as many secretaries as the number of departments. The senior most secretary coordinates the work of the other secretaries.

The secretary briefs the minister about the consequences of a policy. He represents his ministry in all national and international committees along with the minister. The secretary is free to give instructions for certain cases directly submitted to him. Thus, the secretary possesses the highest authority in the department.

Where the volume of work of a secretary is too large, he may be assisted by a **Joint or Additional Secretary** who takes charge of a wing. The function of a Joint Secretary is to relieve the Secretary of a bulk of work, and where necessary deal directly with the Minister. However, the Secretary is kept informed on all direct dealings with the minister. Regarding all business falling under his wing, the Joint Secretary occupies the maximum independence of functioning and responsibility.

Below the rank of Joint Secretary, a number of departments in the Government of India have the post of a **Director**, who is placed above the Deputy Secretary. The responsibilities of Director are more or less the same as that of a Deputy Secretary. This post is a creation of the 1960s to satisfy the ego of some officers.

A wing of a ministry is divided into divisions for the efficient and smooth disposal of business allotted to the ministry. Two branches generally constitute a division which is headed by a **Deputy Secretary.** A Deputy Secretary assists the Joint Secretary in the discharge of his functions. He has to use his discretion in taking orders from the Joint Secretaries, Additional Secretary or Secretary on important cases, either verbally or by submission of the relevant papers. Overall, the Deputy Secretary occupies an important position in the Central Secretariat.

A branch consists of two sections and is under the charge of an **Under Secretary.** He acts as a link between the Deputy Secretary and the Section Officer under his supervision. He is accountable to the Deputy Secretary for the smooth functioning of the branch. He exercises authority not only in regard to the speedy disposal of work, but also on the maintenance of discipline in sections under his control. Normally, it is the Under Secretary who needs to initiate action on all inward communications. He needs to submit more important cases to the Deputy Secretary which the latter is enabled to deal with quickly.

The above officers perform their functions keeping in mind the interests of the Government of India as a whole. For example the Secretary is the secretary to the Government of India, not to his minister alone. Unfortunately, S. R. Maheshwari observes that there is too much departmental thinking and the Secretary, today, ordinarily thinks in terms of his Ministry/ Department only, which is bound to hamper overall efficiency and coordination efforts. This thinking does not end at the Secretary's level; it has to an extent percolated downwards into the department. The Deputy Secretary often thinks only in terms of his division and the Under Secretary, of his branch. All this is certainly not conducive to the attainment of organizational goals and organizational harmony, an organization being defined in the broadest terms, as comprehending the Government of India as a whole (Maheshwari 2001, 74).

The lowest in the administrative structure is the **Section Officer** helped by a number of assistants, stenographers, upper division clerks, lower division clerks and peons. Together they constitute an office. The efficiency of higher level functionaries is, to a large extent, conditioned by the competence of the office. It is the foundation that sustains the entire super structure. It serves as the organizational 'memory', being a repository of specialized knowledge and precedents. This 'memory' function is important in the context of the tenure system which makes the officers birds of passage. Normally, an office has a Section Officer, four assistants and a number of upper and lower division clerks. The Section Officer presides over the office. At the lowest level, the lower division clerk is responsible to perform routine duties, such as collection of previous papers, maintenance of files and registers, dispatch of email, etc. The upper division clerk has a similar type of function to perform but, in addition, he notes on simple cases and assists in their disposal. The section officer ensures that the notes prepared by his subordinates are factually correct. He is the first line supervisor in the Secretariat's hierarchy and is expected to settle minor cases using his own discretion.

Staffing Pattern at the Secretariat

Most of the higher officials of the Secretariat ranging from the under secretary to the Secretary level are manned by officers of the Indian Administrative Service and the Central Services (Class I). They come on deputation from the states, after gaining experience in field administration. After rendering their services in the Secretariat for a period of three to five years, they return to their respective states with rich experience of policy formulation and evaluation. This kind of official arrangement is known as the tenure system and was introduced by Lord Curzon in 1905 who never forgot 'the men in the districts', and believed that 'India may be governed from Simla or Calcutta, but is administered from the plains.' In his opinion, the district was the central point of administration and all important administrative work was carried out at the district level. Therefore Lord Curzon felt that officers who had the experience of district should be brought to the Secretariat. He believed that it was a good idea to keep the Secretariat in touch with the field realities. After rendering their services in the Secretariat for some time the officers needed to go back to the district to renew their field experience, which tended to fade away during their service in the secretariat. Thus, officers at the district were believed to be people with real-life administrative experience.

The staffing pattern of the Secretariat by officers drawn from the states has been supported by a number of committees and commissions. In a reply to the recommendation of the Secretariat Procedure Committee (Llewellyn Smith) that the tenure of the Secretaries and the Deputy Secretariat should be extended from the existing three to four years, the Government of India categorically stated in 1919 that:

> The post of Secretary and deputy secretary must be temporary, since it is necessary that the secretariat should be in living contact with the administrative work in the provinces. For the same reason they hesitate to adopt the committee's recommendation, for each year spent by an officer in the secretariat materially weakens that contact. Moreover it is desirable to enlarge the category of officers who had experience of secretariat work. The field to draw upon is already inconveniently small and the Government of India fears that any lengthening of the tenure of office might result in the further contraction of this field. On these grounds, the Government of India have decided to maintain the existing arrangements whereby, except in the foreign and Political and Legislative departments, the tenure of office is limited to three years, though in the case of any officer, it may be extended beyond the period by order of the Governor General. (Government of India 1991, Para 72)

The Simon Commission (1930) also supported the practice of rotation of officers and remarked that

> it is an accepted principle that efficient Secretariat service, both in the provinces and at Delhi, depends upon a constant interchange of personnel between the districts and the secretariat, the provinces and the Centre ... experience gained with the central Government or at the provincial secretariat is, in the system of Indian administration, as much an asset to the provinces or districts as recent and intimate knowledge of the districts and provinces is inevitable in the provincial and the central secretariats. Circulation between them makes for vigour of the whole. (Report of ISC 1939, para 315)

While arguing in favour of the tenure system, the Wheeler Committee (1936) made the following comments:

- the experience will train civil servants to assume responsibilities and cultivate a sound judgement,
- the short period of three years neither alienates nor disrupts,

- the stint of service in the Central Secretariat, would benefit the provinces,
- it is preferable to rotate such benefit among all officers to prevent jealousies and discontent, and
- it is an easy way out to remove unsuitable officers and post them elsewhere.

The Maxwell Committee (1937) also supported the tenure system. The Committee said,

> [T]he officers of a permanent cadre at the secretariat would lose touch with the life of India, which will be a handicap in the performance of their task, and the presence in the provincial secretariat of officers who had experience in the central secretariat and vice-versa helped to provide a link between the central and provincial Governments.

The Committee recommended that the tenure of the officers at the Central Secretariat needed to be separated as far as possible by periods to be spent in the provinces and the districts where their touch with reality was revived. Similarly, officers with Secretariat experience needed to become available to the field as they would know how to get field problems solved from the secretariat.

The Administrative Reform Commission (1967) strongly endorsed the tenure system and suggested the removal of all barriers hindering the smooth flow of personnel between the Secretariat and the field. It recommended that the tenure system be rigidly endorsed and 'officers must go back to the parent departments or state government as the case may be for a substantial length of time—not less than the period spent outside the department/state before being considered for another assignment.'

Thus different committees and commissions endorsed in favour of the tenure system. It was seen as a positive instrument to balance centre–state relations and good for the healthy functioning of the federal system. It was also argued that it helped in framing national policies based on realities. The system also benefitted the states as they got back officers possessing a wide range experience and knowledge of the working of the central government as well as national policies. The tenure system gave an opportunity to officers to work in different environments thereby breaking the monotony of service. The Secretariat could easily get rid of the inefficient and incompetent persons who could be removed without any difficulty at the end of the tenure. Finally, the tenure system strengthened administrative unity and ensured independence of the civil services.

Despite the above mentioned advantages of the 'tenure' some arguments have been given against this system also. While the work of the ministries has become specialized in nature but the tenure system does not ensure the same. Second, at present, district experience is not necessary in many activities performed by the Central Government. Finally, the tenure system has strengthened the office at the cost of the officer. A new officer depends too much on his office, which gives rise to many evils associated to 'office-dominated administration'.

It is to be noted that the tenure system does not apply to all Government departments. For example, departments, like the Indian Audit and Accounts, Posts and Telegraphs, Customs, Income Tax and Foreign services mostly depend on their own specialized officers. The creation of the Central Secretariat Service has brought a new challenge to the practice of the tenure system because a number of posts of Under Secretaries, Deputy Secretaries and even Joint Secretaries are being filled from this service. The primary objective of having the tenure system was that the higher level civil servants engaged in policy-making and advising ministers must possess first-hand as well as fresh experience of working in the field to keep the actions and decisions of the central government as close to reality and as meaningful to the people as possible. Keeping this objective in mind the practice of the tenure system still remains a part of the staffing pattern of the Central Secretariat.

Sources of Placement

Under the tenure system, senior positions from the Deputy Secretary and above are filled on the basis of the **Central Staffing Scheme (1957).** As per this scheme, these posts are filled by officers of the following categories:

1. Officers of the Central Administrative pool,
2. Officers from the state cadres of All India Services on tenure deputation,
3. Officers from central services (Class I officers) on tenure deputation basis,
4. Officers of the selection grade of Central Secretariat service,
5. State civil service officers whose names are included in the select list for appointment to the IAS,
6. Other civil service officers, in consultation with the Union Public Service Commission.

Thus, the central government mostly depends on officers taken on deputation for fixed tenures to manage senior posts in the Secretariat. After completing their tenure at the Central Secretariat, most senior officers on deputation go back to their respective states with rich experience of policy formulation and monitoring.

The Central Secretariat Service (CSS)

There are three services in the Central Secretariat, which provide support and continuity to the governmental system in the Central Government Secretariat.

1. Central Secretariat Service (CSS),
2. Central Secretariat Stenographers Service (CSSS),
3. Central Secretariat Clerical Service (CSCS).

The Department of Personnel and Training of the Ministry of Personnel, Public Grievances and Pensions is the cadre controlling authority of all the three CSS. The sanctioned strength of the three services was 23,860 in 2013.The Institute of Secretariat Training and Management provides systematic pre-entry training to new entrants in grades III and IV of this service. The CSSS and the CSCS are designed to provide assistance to members of the CSS and other top level officers in the central secretariat.

The CSS is a major source of recruitment to Central Secretariat posts. It came into existence in 1948 by replacing the old Imperial Service. Presently it consists of five grades, namely Assistant, Section Officer, Under Secretary, Deputy Secretary and Director. Some of the Joint Secretary-level posts are also held (under the central staffing scheme) by the CSS officer. The CSS has been devised primarily to manage middle level posts in the Central Secretariat. It is a permanent bureaucratic set-up of the Central Government, ensuring continuity in administration and policies.

Prior to restructuring of the CSS in 2003, direct recruitment to the CSS took place at two levels. The section officers were recruited, to the extent of 20 per cent through the civil services examinations conducted by the UPSC. The second level of direct induction, to the extent of 50 per cent took place at the Assistant level through the All India Graduate Examination conducted by the Staff Selection Commission. After 2003, direct recruitment at the level of Section officers was discontinued. As such, direct recruitment into the CSS is now available only at the level of Assistants through the Graduate Level Examination of the SSC.

However, the direct recruitment quota has been increased from 50 to 75 per cent. In addition to the minimum qualification of graduation, computer proficiency has also been introduced at this level. The remaining 25 per cent of vacancies are filled by the promotion of Upper Division Clerks of the CSCS.

The CSS provide staff not only for the Central Secretariat, but also for most of the attached and subordinate offices and all posts from the level of Assistant up to Under Secretaries are included in this service. The CSS is a common service for all the ministries. This improves the opportunities and prospects of promotion for all the employees of the service.

Expansion of the Secretariat

In recent years the Secretariat work has increased manifold as the government has assumed increasing responsibilities in regulating trade and industry, controlling restrictive practices, promotion of economic development and the government's increasing accountability to the Parliament. As a result of these factors, there has been a remarkable growth in the number of posts at various levels in the Central Secretariat. For example there were 7 Secretaries in 1900 compared to 141 in 2001. Similarly at the Under Secretary level, the number has increased from 9 to 1,363 during the same period.

With the passage of time, the Secretariat has been subject to a number of **criticisms**. It is said that the Secretariat is an overgrown institution—a typically pampered child. It has too many officials to dispose of self-created work. The officials in the Secretariat either engage in unnecessary work which leads to the hiring of additional staff, or remain underworked chanting grievances. Its personnel also suffer from a sense of superiority, even arrogance, which is reflected in their behaviour towards the executive agencies. Though the Secretariat is primarily a policy-making body, but today it is performing a number of functions, which essentially belong to the executive agencies. This has on the one hand prevented the Secretariat from concentrating on policy-making and on the other such encroachment has weakened the authority of the executive agencies. The tenure system was devised for the exchange of personnel between the Secretariat and the field officers for policies based on field experiences but in practice this purpose in not being served because now officers continue in the Secretariat for a long period of time. In many cases, the Secretariat is the principle cause of delay because of the lack of adequate delegation of executive agencies, cumbersome procedures of doing work and a widespread desire to postpone decisions.

Despite a number of criticisms, the role and significance of the Secretariat is indispensable. It is the central body which provides a delivery system for policy formulation, continuity in policy administration, monitoring and review of the implementation of policies and schemes, coherent institutional memory etc., which are germane to good governance at the headquarter of the Central Government. As far as the tendency of empire-building of the Secretariat is concerned, substantial delegation of powers and functions is necessary from the former to the executive agencies. It will definitely ensure the purity of the Secretariat.

THE CABINET SECRETARIAT

To assist the council of ministers in the business of governing the country, a Cabinet Secretariat has been provided. It is the most important administrative agency of the Government of India with a dual function of the secretariat of the Union Council of Ministers, and as the co-coordinating institution of all other administrative agencies. Before independence, the

Executive Council of the Governor General was responsible for all governmental functions. As the amount and complexity of the business of the government increased, the work of the various departments was distributed amongst the members of the council with only the more important cases being dealt with by the Governor General or the council collectively. This procedure was legalized by the Councils Act of 1861 during the time of Lord Canning, leading to the introduction of the portfolio system and the inception of the Executive Council of the Governor General. The Secretariat of the Executive Council was headed by the Private Secretary to the Viceroy, but he did not attend the council meetings. Lord Willington first started the practice of having his private secretary by his side at these meetings. Later, this practice continued and in 1935, the Viceroy's private secretary was given the additional designation of Secretary to the Executive Council.

The Constitution of the Interim Government in September, 1946 brought a change in the name of the Executive Council's Secretariat and designated it as the Cabinet Secretariat. After independence, it developed into an organization for effective coordination between the ministries. As we know, the cabinet consists of senior ministers of the council of ministers headed by the Prime Minister. It occupies a central position in administration. The cabinet is responsible for higher level appointments, formulation of national policies on different issues, solution of interdepartmental problems and general coordination in the government.

It is against this background that one has to appreciate the role of the Cabinet Secretariat. It is under the direct charge of the Prime Minister. The administrative head of the Secretariat is the Cabinet Secretary who is also the ex-officio chairman of the Civil Services Board. In the Government of India (allocation of business) Rules, 1961 the 'Cabinet Secretariat' finds a place in the first schedule to the rules. The efficient functioning of the cabinet depends on the Cabinet Secretariat. It is the responsibility of the Cabinet Secretary to assist in:

1. coordinating major administrative activities and policies of the Government of India,
2. preparing the cabinet agenda and its minutes, keeping its records and tracking the progress made by ministries and departments in executing cabinet decisions,
3. acting as a custodian of papers of the cabinet meetings,
4. resolving difficulties or delays which may arise in the administrative field whether between departments of the Government of India or between the Government of India and the state governments,
5. watching the progress of important administrative measures of the Government of India, which affects more than one department,
6. submitting to the Cabinet and the Cabinet committees such matters as require their decision or direction, thus functioning as Secretary to the Council of Ministers,
7. assisting in decision-making in the Government by ensuring interministerial coordination, ironing out differences amongst Ministries/Departments and evolving consensus through the instrumentality of the standing/ad hoc committees of Secretaries,
8. laying down the rules of business and reallocating the business of the government among the various ministries and departments within the framework of the directives of the Prime minister, after these have been approved by the President, and
9. informing the President, Vice-President and Council of Ministers about the major activities of the government conducted in all ministries and departments.

It is clearly evident that the Cabinet Secretariat has a very important place in the central administration. It is a source of authority, the assistance of which enables the central government to undertake any matter of serious responsibility. Today, the Cabinet Secretariat is in a position to carry out its responsibilities with greater competence, efficiency and effectiveness.

Organization of the Cabinet Secretariat

The Cabinet Secretariat has three wings: civil, military and intelligence.

The **civil wing** provides secretarial assistance to the cabinet and its committees and the committee of the secretaries. Secretarial assistance includes submission of cases to the cabinet and committees, preparation and maintenance of records of the decisions taken by the cabinet and its committees and the initiation of follow-up action in the implementation of decisions reached by the cabinet and its committees. It is also responsible to lay down the rules of business and the allocation of the business of the government of India to the various ministries and the departments within the framework of the directives of the Prime minister after the approval of the President. It is also the responsibility of the Cabinet Secretariat to establish coordination along with securing timely action by all the ministries and departments on policy decisions which the cabinet as a whole or the Prime Minister have directed.

The main task of the **military wing** is to supervise carefully the work of the meetings of the Defense Committee, National Defense Council, Military Affairs Committee and many other committees associated with defence. It is also responsible for the security of the Prime Minister and his colleagues. Within this wing there is a Special Protection Group (SPG) which looks after the physical protection of the Prime Minister and his blood relatives.

The **intelligence wing** is primarily responsible to collect, evaluate and present intelligence pertaining to external threats to national security. It also takes account of internal factors having a bearing on national security. There is also a Research and Analysis Wing (RAW) headed by a director. The RAW takes care of the work relating to foreign intelligence activities and counter intelligence abroad.

In 1988 the **Directorate of Public Grievances** came into existence as an important organ of the Cabinet Secretariat. It is an independent appellate body which entertains public grievances against the actions and decisions of some of the central government institutions like railways, post office, public sector banks, etc.

Under the Cabinet Secretary, there are several secretaries heading various departments, for example, Secretary Coordination–Civil (heads the Department of Cabinet Affairs), Secretary Security/Military (under whom comes the Special Protection Group) and Secretary RAW (heads the Research and Analysis Wing), Secretary Performance Management Division (also holds the post of Chairman, National Authority, Chemical Weapons Convention) and Secretary, Public Grievances. As on 13 February 2015, there were 48 officers above the rank of Under Secretary in the Cabinet Secretariat.

The Cabinet Secretary

The Cabinet Secretary is the seniormost civil servant of the country who heads the Cabinet Secretariat. He is drawn from the senior most officers of the Indian Administrative Service. The efficiency of the Cabinet Secretariat owes a lot to the managerial capacity of the Cabinet Secretary. The main function of the Cabinet Secretary is to assist the Council of Ministers, dealing primarily with cabinet affairs. He/She is the chairman of the Committee of Chief Secretaries. Through this forum, he/she can get necessary information about any state administration. He/she keeps contact with other ministers, and the secretaries of other ministries and departments look towards him for guidance and advice.

As the head of the civil service, the Cabinet Secretary has to keep up the morale of the civil servants, and he often acts as a link between the civil servants and politicians at the central level. So far as the Cabinet is concerned, the minutes and decisions are taken down by the Cabinet Secretary who, in fact offers secretariat advice and assistance to the Cabinet. He attends all the meetings of the Cabinet and circulates the Cabinet decisions, on confirmation by the Prime minister, among the ministers and the secretaries. He has also to oversee the fact that the decisions of the Cabinet are implemented by the respective ministers and departments. The other important role is in relation to the Prime minister, as the Cabinet Secretary advises the Prime minister on whatever important matters his advice is sought. He provides the eyes and ears for the Prime Minister to keep abreast of the business of the government as a whole (Bhattacharya 2000, 57). Table 3.1 contains the list of Cabinet Secretaries appointed since 1950 in India.

Table 3.1 Cabinet Secretaries since 1950

Cabinet Secretary	From	To
Shri N. R. Pillai	6 February 1950	13 May 1953
Shri Y. N. Sukthankar	14 May 1953	31 July 1957
Shri M. K. Vellodi	1 August 1957	4 June 1958
Shri Vishnu Sahay	1 July 1958	10 November 1960
Shri B. N. Jha	10 November 1960	8 March 1961
Shri Vishnu Sahay	9 March 1961	15 April 1962
Shri S. S. Khera	15 April 1962	18 November 1964
Shri Dharam Vira	18 November 1964	27 June 1966
Shri D. S. Joshi	27 June 1966	31 December 1968
Shri B. Sivaraman	1 January 1969	30 November 1970
Shri T. Swaminathan	1 December 1970	2 November 1972
Shri B. D. Pande	2 November 1972	31 March 1977
Shri N. K. Mukarji	31 March 1977	31 March 1980
Shri S. S. Grewal	2 April 1980	30 April 1981
Shri C. R. Krishnaswamy Rao	30 April 1981	8 February 1985
Shri P. K. Kaul	8 February 1985	22 August 1986
Shri B. G. Deshmukh	23 August 1986	27 March 1989
Shri T. N. Seshan	27 March 1989	23 December 1989
Shri V. C. Pande	23 December 1989	11 December 1990
Shri Naresh Chandra	11 December 1990	31 July 1992
Shri S. Rajgopal	1 August 1992	31 July 1993
Shri Zafar Saifullah	31 July 1993	31 July 1994
Shri Surendra Singh	1 August 1994	31 July 1996
Shri T. S. R. Subramaniam	1 August 1996	31 March 1998
Shri Prabhat Kumar	1 April 1998	31 October 2000
Shri T. R. Prasad	1 November 2000	31 October 2002
Shri Kamal Pande	1 November 2002	14 June 2004
Shri B. K. Chaturvedi	14 June 2004	13 June 2007
Shri K. M. Chandrasekhar	14 June 2007	13 June 2011
Shri Ajit Kumar Seth	14 June 2011	13 June 2015
Shri Pradeep Kumar Sinha	14 June 2015	Till date

Source: http://cabsec.nic.in/about_cabinet.php

After independence a debate ensued about the position of the Cabinet Secretary and apprehensions were expressed about it becoming a kind of super-secretary. The Ayyangar Committee (1949) examined the position and recommended,

> He should be an administrative officer of the highest rank ... and he should be entrusted, as head of the cabinet secretariat, with the positive function of securing coordination as well as timely and effective action by all departments of the government of India in all matters in which the cabinet as a whole or the prime minister is interested.

The Ayyangar Committee's recommendation was accepted and since 1950 the Cabinet Secretary has been the seniormost civil servant of the land. The Administrative Reform Commission (1966–70), fixed his term for three years so that the functionary could provide effective leadership to the civil service. Accordingly, the principal functions of the Cabinet Secretary include:

- Principal Advisor to the Prime Minister,
- Principal Advisor to the Cabinet and the Cabinet Committees,
- Head of the civil service—its conscience keeper,
- monitoring and coordinating activities of various ministers and departments,
- acting as the link between the Prime Minister's Office and various administrative ministries,
- Head of the Cabinet Secretariat, and thus controls all the activities undertaken by the cabinet secretariat and finally, and
- above all, be the link between the political system and the civil service (Maheshwari 2001, 45).

Thus, the Cabinet Secretary occupies the top position in the Indian administrative system. The crucial and sensitive role played by the Cabinet Secretary can be understood from the following remarks of S. S. Khera, a former cabinet secretary himself:

> The Cabinet secretary provides the eyes and ears for the Prime minister to keep in touch with the process of official business in the central government. But he is in no sense the watchdog on behalf of the prime minister ... The cabinet secretary's is a very general staff function, not a line function in relation to the ministers. His business is to help, not to oversee. (1975, 181–82)

The leadership qualities of a civil servant are tested most during his tenure as the Cabinet Secretary, which is indeed a dream post for every bureaucrat. As the top-most bureaucrat, he is a motivator, leader and a visionary to all civil servants. His style of functioning significantly influences the entire bureaucratic set-up in India.

The Cabinet Committees

The Prime Minister selects the team of ministers in the Cabinet and allocates them portfolios. In most cases, the Prime Minister sets up different Cabinet Committees with select members of the Cabinet and assigns specific functions to such Cabinet Committees for the smooth and convenient functioning of the Government. This mechanism saves precious time of the Cabinet. A Cabinet Committee relieves the Cabinet of much preliminary work, leaving it free to concentrate on major issues and problems.

In India, the Cabinet Committee is of two types—standing and ad hoc. At any moment of time, it is usual to expect upwards of 10 Cabinet Committees of a standing nature. In addition, ad hoc Cabinet Committees are set up by the Prime minister as and when required. A Cabinet Committee can be either set up with a broad mandate or with a specific mandate. Many a times, when an activity/agenda of the government acquires prominence or requires some special thrust, a Cabinet Committee may be set up for focused attention. In all areas delegated to the Cabinet Committees, normally the decision of the Cabinet Committee in question is the decision of the government of the day. However, it is up to the Prime Minister to decide if any issue decided by a Cabinet Committee should be reopened or discussed in the full Cabinet. Every Standing Committee shall consist of such ministers as the Prime Minister may from time to time specify. Conventionally, while ministers with Cabinet rank are named as 'members' of the Standing Committees of the Cabinet, Ministers of State, irrespective of their status of having 'Independent Charge' of a Ministry/Department, and others 'with rank of' a Cabinet Minister or Minister of State are named as 'special invitees'.

The established practice is for a matter first to go to the appropriate Cabinet Committee where it is thoroughly thrashed out and conclusions are reached. The Cabinet Committee consists of ministers directly concerned about the issue or those who are knowledgeable about it. As the pros and cons of the matter have already been examined, the Cabinet, when it comes to this body, need not always go into all the details. This saves the cabinet's time. As on 3 December 2014 there were the following six Cabinet Committees:

1. Cabinet Committee on Political Affairs
2. Cabinet Committee on Economic Affairs
3. Appointments Committee of the Cabinet
4. Cabinet Committee on Parliamentary Affairs
5. Cabinet Committee on Accommodation
6. Cabinet Committee on Security

In the above list, the first four are the more important Cabinet Committees. The Political Affairs Committee deals with all policy matters pertaining to domestic and foreign affairs. The Economic Affairs Committee directs and coordinates governmental activities in the economic sphere. The Appointment Committee decides all higher level appointments in the Cabinet Secretariat, public enterprises, banks and financial institutions. The Parliamentary Affairs Committee looks after the progress of government business in the Parliament. The first three committees are chaired by the Prime Minister and the last one by the Minister of Home Affairs. Of all the Cabinet Committees, the most powerful is the Political Affairs Committee, often described as a 'Super Cabinet'.

THE PRIME MINISTER'S OFFICE

Besides the Cabinet Secretariat, there is the Prime Minister's Secretariat known as the Prime Minister's Office (PMO) to assist the Prime Minister in his own official capacity. Beginning as a modest and slim organization, it now is not only big but also important, which is also an indication of the concentration of power in the Prime Minister's hands. The PMO occupies the status of a department of the Government of India under the Allocation of Business Rules, 1961. It is primarily a link between the Prime Minister and his ministers on the one hand, and the President, Governors, Chief Ministers and foreign representatives, on the other.

The PMO is headed by the Principal Secretary to the Prime Minister who has often been a senior civil servant. He wields a great deal of influence as all decisions made by the Prime Minister are processed through that office. The Principal Secretary is assisted by an Additional

Secretary, and a number of Joint Secretaries, Directors and other junior officials. The Prime Minister's Office, as the name suggests, assists the Prime Minister in the performance of his political, parliamentary and public responsibilities. Which files are to be submitted to the Prime Minister and what would be the subject matter of those files, such things depend on whether the Prime Minister himself holds direct charge of the Ministry or whether there is a Cabinet Minister or State Minister in charge of the ministry. In the case of the former, all matters are submitted to the PMO. Only some very important policy issues are submitted to the PMO. In general, the jurisdiction of the PMO extends over all such subjects and activities which are not specially allotted to any individual ministry/departments. The main functions of the PMO are:

1. To deal with all matters that have come to the Prime Minister,
2. To assist the Prime Minister in discharging his overall responsibilities as the Chief Executive,
3. To help the Prime Minister in corresponding with the press and the public,
4. To assist the Prime Minister in examining cases submitted to him for order under prescribed rules,
5. To assist the Prime Minister in discharging his responsibilities as the Chairman of the NITI Aayog.
6. In general, standing by the Prime Minister as Chief Advisor on all important domestic and international affairs.

Since Indira Gandhi's time, the PMO has been an organ of awesome power and authority in the Government of India. Being closest to the Prime Minister, this office is more powerful than the Cabinet Secretariat. The Prime Minister's office in a way basks in the reflected glory of the political chief. In the real sense, today the PMO is the Government of the Government of India. The crucial role played by the PMO puts it naturally at the centre stage of national administration. As a catalyst and coordinator, the PMO's role is understandable. What creates problem is its super cabinet role which the ministers naturally resent. B. G. Deshmukh observes that over the years, the PMO has grown into a high profile body. Quite often, it has exceeded the powers of the Cabinet Secretariat and actively interfered with the working of various ministries and departments. People who constitute the PMO have acquired power and authority of their own in the name of the Prime Minister. Sometimes even the PMO comes to assume much more authority and power than the Prime Minister originally intended (Deshmukh 1997).

Therefore, it is desirable that, the PMO should not grow at the expense of the other organs of the government—the cabinet secretariat and the ministries. Also, it is the quality of advice that counts and not the quantity of staff engaged by the PMO. How the Prime Minister looks at his own organization and what kinds of advice he needs will be the chief determining factor of the PMO's existence and expansion.

THE ATTACHED AND SUBORDINATE OFFICES

The Secretariat is the topmost policy-making body of the Central Government. It is the brain of the government. The execution of policies is entrusted to a number of other organizations created for such specific purposes. Two main forms of such organizations are:

- attached offices and
- subordinate offices.

The **attached offices** are usually responsible for providing the executive direction required in the implementation of policies laid down by the ministry to which they are attached. They also serve as repositories of technical information and advise the ministry on the technical aspects of questions dealt by them. Policies can be framed only on the basis of adequate data, technical and other relevant information, and providing the same is the responsibility of the attached offices. For example, the Directorate of Intelligence Bureau and the Border Security Force are attached offices of the Ministry of Home Affairs. Usually such offices are headed by technical officers designated as the Director General, Registrar, Director, Chief Engineer, etc.

The attached offices play a dual role. They provide technical information for policy formulation as well as executive direction for policy implementation. Therefore, they are considered as field organizations because they not only issue executive directions to the subordinate offices, but also are responsible for the proper implementation of policies. They have to coordinate activities of subordinate offices and keep the Secretariat informed about the various challenges faced in the implementation of the policies.

The **subordinate offices** are responsible for the actual execution of policies and programmes. They usually operate under an attached office. For example, the Forest Survey of India and the Botanical Survey of India are subordinate offices under the Ministry of Environment and Forests. They are at the lowest levels of administration and come in direct touch with the clientele of the programme implemented by them on behalf of the government. They are required to submit a number of periodical reports to their attached office and also keep the concerned ministries informed of their activities. The subordinate office is thus the cutting edge of administration. Normally it functions under an attached office, but where there is no attached office under a ministry, it operates directly under the ministry. Being field agencies concerned with implementation work, the subordinate offices have a large number of technical field staff along with the usual ministerial staff for administrative work. These offices are generally headed by a technical officer. In comparison to attached offices, these offices only have limited administrative and financial powers. Although, it is the subordinate office which is responsible for the actual execution of policy and decisions made by the government, it appears to have been accorded a distinctly inferior status, as is indicated by the label 'subordinate'. Though the employees in these offices do the same type of work and possess the same qualifications as the Secretariat personnel but, the pay scales of personnel in the subordinate office are the lowest, their service conditions are not very attractive, and their future prospects are the dimmest. The attached offices have succeeded in acquiring parity with the Secretariat in all matters, but the subordinate offices are considered inferior as compared to the attached offices. Hence, the first Central Pay Commission (1947) recommended the abolition of such distinctions.

THE BOARDS AND COMMISSIONS

The Indian administrative system works with a network of ministries, departments, attached and subordinate offices which have already been discussed. Besides these agencies, there are some other executive agencies like Bureaus, Boards and Commissions, which implement policies at different levels.

If an organization reposes its responsibility in a single official it is known as a **bureau**, but if it is a group, the organization is called as board or a commission. Bureaus have homogenous structures and perform a single task. Their head are responsible to and work under the direction of the head of the organization. A bureau is more suited for administrative functions and is designed for those services which demand quick decisions and immediate action. The single head ensures better discipline and accountability. A good example of a bureau is the Central Bureau of Investigation (CBI) in India. As against single headship there is plural or **Board or Commission** type headship. In this system headship is not vested in one single individual but in a board or a commission. Each board or commission is however, headed by a Chairman. This type of headship is both useful and advantageous in organizations where policies and techniques have to be put on sound footings and where discussions and new techniques are to be developed. The system is very useful for organizations where collective interests are to be reconciled. Even this system is a good check on the use of discretionary powers. Collective decisions usually have maturity and give benefit of knowledge. In this type of headship, there is psychological satisfaction that all decisions will be taken impartially. It is believed that the partial attitude of one head will be countered by the other. These bodies can be classified on two different basis: first, classification according to the nature of their authority; and second, classification on the basis of their legal status. On the basis of their **nature of authority** the boards and commissions can be classified into three categories: advisory boards and commissions like small scale industrial boards, boards and commissions performing policy-making functions such as the NITI Aayog, and boards and commissions performing policy-making and executive functions, such as the Railway Board. The advisory boards/commissions are usually associated with the head of the organization for the purpose of advice only. They only tender advice which may or may not be accepted by the head of the department. They neither share departmental responsibility nor its policy. The boards and commissions which perform policy-making functions are high-powered bodies. Some boards and commissions perform both policy-making as well as its execution. The Railway Board is a good example of the same.

On the basis of their **legal status** these bodies can be classified into three categories: In the first category we can place **Constitutional Commissions** like the Election Commission, the Union Public Service Commission, the Finance Commission, the National Commission for Scheduled Castes and Scheduled Tribes and the Commissioner for Linguistic Minorities. These commissions are appointed by the president and do not come under the administrative control of any particular ministry in their day-to-day working. The members of these boards enjoy security of tenure and cannot be removed from their office without following a special provision as laid down in the Constitution.

The second category could be of those boards/commissions which are created by an Act of Parliament and known as **Statutory Bodies** like the University Grants Commission, the Central Board of Direct Taxes, the Central Board of Excise and Customs, the National Commission for Minorities, the National Commission for Backward Classes and the National Commission for Women. These statutory boards and commissions work under the administrative control of the ministry concerned. While some of them are ministries, the others are also free to a large extent from regular departmental procedures. They enjoy a great deal of autonomy in their day-to-day working, but their members do not enjoy the same degree of security, independence and prestige as compared to the constitutional ones.

The third category could include such boards/commissions which have been created by an **executive order or by a resolution of the Union Government** and could be termed as attached boards or commissions placed directly under the control of relevant ministries. In this category we may place the NITI Aayog, the National Commission for Safai Karamcharis, the Central Social Welfare Board, the Staff Selection Commission, the All India Handloom Board, etc. These boards are mostly advisory in nature. Their members do not have any definite tenure and have limited autonomy. However, some of them may be very important and high powered like the NITI Aayog.

Thus, there has been proliferation of new agencies after independence to perform the new and complex functions undertaken by the Government. Today a board or commission like plural executive has become an integral part of administrative institutions. The single head is the best where major policies and objectives of the government are well defined and where executive promptness is required to protect the interest of society. But, where the government has to undertake new planning and constant consultations are required for deciding policies for changing situations, the board or commissions are more suitable. They ensure administrative integrity, flexibility, impartiality, autonomy and accountability.

CONCLUDING OBSERVATIONS

To sum up, the administrative set-up of the Central Government is very vast, consisting of the Secretariat, Ministries and Departments, Cabinet Secretariat, the Prime Minister's Office and a number of attached and field offices. Each institution has its own importance and collectively they make the functioning of the government smooth, rational and efficient. Though the central administrative structure is a legacy of the British rule in India, but it has improved over time as per the requirements and wishes of the nation and its people. But, critics also point out that 'babu bureaucracy' still dominates the scene. In this regard, the recommendations of the Second Administrative Reforms Commission (2009) are very relevant to tackle such lacunae. It suggests reductions in decision-making levels, clear demarcation of responsibilities, rationalization of staff pattern, introduction of performance agreements and Memorandum of Understanding (MOU) to inculcate a dynamic administrative work culture in the Central Government. We hope that the implementation of these recommendations will definitely make the central administration more accountable, transparent, effective and efficient to address the challenges of the nation.

REVIEW QUESTIONS

1. Discuss the structure and basic features of the central administration in India.
2. Examine the structure and functions of the Central Secretariat.
3. Critically discuss the role of the Cabinet Secretariat.
4. Examine the role of the Cabinet Secretary in the Indian Administrative System.
5. 'The Prime Minister's Office (PMO) has become a centre of power in India'. Discuss.
6. Write a note on the structure and role of key Ministries and Departments.
7. Examine the structure and functions of some important Boards and Commissions in India.
8. Distinguish between attached and subordinate offices.
9. Discuss the importance of the Cabinet Committees in the Indian Administrative System.
10. What are the main problems in the structure and functioning of the central administration in India? What are your suggestions to tackle them?

REFERENCES

ARC (Administrative Reform Commission). 1967. *Report of the Study Team on the Machinery of the Government of India and Procedure of Work*. Government of India Managers of Publications, New Delhi.

Ayyangar, N. Gopalaswamy. 1949. *Report on the Reorganization of the Machinery of the Government*. Government of India Printing Press, New Delhi.

Bhattacharya, Mohit. 2000. *Indian Administration*. Kolkata: World Press.

Deshmukh, B. G. 1997. 'Prime Minister's Office—We Cannot and Need Not Do without it'. *The Indian Journal of Public Administration* (July–September).

Government of India. 1991. Report of the Government of India, Secretariat procedure Committee, Para 72.

Khera, S. S. 1975. *The Central Executive*. New Delhi: Orient Longman.

Maheshwari, S. R. 2001. *Indian Administration*. 6th ed. New Delhi: Orient Blackswan.

Report of ISC (The Indian Statutory Commission). 1939. vol. 1, survey, London, H.M.S.O.Cmd.3568.

State Administration

4

LEARNING OBJECTIVES

1. To know the structure and organization of state administration.
2. To understand the function and role of the State Secretariat.
3. To discuss the role of the Chief Secretary.
4. To examine the function and role of the State Finance Commissions.
5. To explore the relationship between state and local governments.

In the previous chapter, we have discussed the administrative set-up at the central level. State administration by and large follows the pattern and structure of the Central Government. Administration at the state level operates in the context of national uniformity as well as local diversity. Like the central administration, the state administration is also divided into a number of ministries and departments. The state ministries are headed by secretaries. Besides secretaries, who advise the ministers on all matters of policy, there are heads of departments, whose number corresponds to the number of important subjects administered by a state. It is the departmental head who carries out the policies and programmes of the government at the headquarters as well as in the districts through its field staff. State administration is an important link between the centre and the local bodies. On the one hand, it is an important mechanism to implement schemes and programmes of the central government; and on the other hand it transfers powers and functions to the local bodies as per the provisions of 73rd and 74th Constitutional Amendments.

The organizational set-up of state administration has a number of important institutions and actors, namely the Secretariat, Ministries, Departments and Directorates, Chief Secretary, State Finance Commissions, etc. This chapter primarily deals with these administrative and organizational set-ups at the state level in India.

THE SECRETARIAT

The State Secretariat is the highest office of the state government. It ensures consistency and objectivity in the administrative system. The state administration is divided into a number of ministries and departments. Like the ministries in the Union Government, the state ministries are headed by Secretaries as their administrative heads. The business of the government is allocated to ministers by assigning one or more departments to the charge of a minister. The expression Secretariat is used to refer to the complex of departments whose political heads are ministers while the administrative heads are the Secretaries. The secretary is the secretary to the Government as a whole, not to an individual minister. The entire administrative machinery of the state is divided into a number of departments. The Secretariat is a conglomeration of all these departments. The Secretary is the chief advisor to the minister and head of the department under his charge. He/she is responsible for carrying out the policies and decisions taken by his political chief and advises him/her by providing the necessary information required for facing the legislature and its committees.

The Secretariat is divided into a number of administrative departments. Each department has a hierarchical structure with a number of officers and the Secretary at the top of the hierarchy. The secretarial hierarchy consists of the Secretary, Deputy Secretary, Under Secretary and Assistant Secretary. These officers are subject to the tenure system and are appointed to the Secretariat for a fixed term. With a few exceptions, these senior officers are mostly generalist. The office component of the Secretariat includes personnel below the rank of Under Secretary. They are: Superintendent/Section officer, Assistants, Upper division clerks, Lower division clerks, Stenotypists and at the bottom class IV employees, who are engaged in manual works. All these personnel are Secretariat officials because they work in the Secretariat for very long.

The Secretariat is divided into a number of departments. The number of departments varies from state to state. For example, Sikkim has 15 departments, while most of the states have more than 35 departments. But, some of the common departments in most of the states are: Home, Finance, General administration, Revenue, Agriculture, Public works, Industries, Health, Education, Law, Rural development, Transport, etc. Each department keeps records of administrative data and information of their relevant fields. The main concern of the Secretariat is to see how policies are actually being executed. Thus, the Secretariat constitutes the brainpower and administrative memory of the government. It helps the Ministers in the following matters:

- formulation of policies and programmes of the government,
- supervising the execution of policies and programmes by the field agencies,
- budgeting and controlling expenditure,
- discharging their responsibilities to the legislature,
- acting as the spokesman of the government,
- matters related to senior appointments, transfers and cases of disciplinary proceedings against gazette officers,
- maintaining coordination with the Central Government as well as with the local bodies, and
- acting as a think tank of the state government.

It is clearly evident that the Secretariat is the apex policy-making body of the state governments. Though it plays a crucial role in state administration, but it has been observed that its attitude and behaviour is expansionist and it has even arrogated some powers and functions which do not belong to it. S. R. Maheshwari observes that a number of factors are responsible for this expansion. The most important factor he indicates is parliamentary democracy itself. Under this system, the minister is responsible to the legislature for the efficient functioning of his department and he has to answer parliamentary questions concerning his charge. Naturally, therefore, he wants to have a say in most matters. This, to an extent, explains the centralization of functions in the Secretariat and its expansion (Maheshwari 2001, 553). Thus, today the Secretariat occupies a significant position in the state administration.

The Chief Secretary

The Chief Secretary is the chief of the Secretariat in every state. He heads the civil services in the state. He works as an interdepartmental coordinator and gives general guidance to other officers. He acts as the chief communication link between his state government on the one hand and the Union Government and other state governments on the other. More than *primus inter pares*, he is admittedly, the chief of the Secretaries. The office of the Chief Secretary is considered very important and therefore has been excluded from the operation of the tenure system. In practice, he retires as the Chief Secretary, or moves to the Central Government to take up more important assignments.

The Chief Secretary occupies a key position in the state administration. In the office of the Chief Secretary, the state government has an institution and its parallel does not exist in the Central Government. Unlike the Central Secretariat, there is no separate Secretary to the Cabinet in the states. The Chief Secretary, thus, also acts as the Cabinet Secretary in states. In this capacity, he is a liaison officer between political and administrative executives. All files for the decision of the Cabinet must pass through him. The crowning position of the Chief Secretary makes him the keystone of the Secretariat. He is the real ruler in the state in the sense that his words are commands for all the employees of the state. Within him lays the real responsibility of coordination of government work and he stands as the bulwark of the administrative structure of the state Government. The Chief Secretary, generally, performs the following functions:

- he is the chief adviser to the Chief Minister,
- he supervises and controls over the entire Secretariat,
- being the head of the civil service he is authorized to make postings, transfers, etc. of state officials,
- as Secretary to the Cabinet, he prepares the agenda for cabinet meetings, maintains records of the proceedings, etc.,
- he is the primary channel of communications between his state government, on the one hand, and the central government and other state governments, on the other,
- he looks after all other matters not falling within the jurisdiction of other state Secretaries,
- being chief of all the Secretaries, he presides over a large number of committees and
- he acts as the Chief Coordinator of state administration.

The Chief Secretary is chosen by the Chief Minister of the state. The practice is that the Chief Minister consults the Union Government while appointing the Chief Secretary, but this consultation is not mandatory. Likewise, the Chief Minister may consult the Cabinet or a few of his ministerial colleagues on the matter, but the final decision is that of his/her own. However, some important factors are taken into account by the Chief Minister in this respect like, seniority, service record, performance and merit with the most important factor being the personal rapport of the officer with the Chief Minister. Besides these factors, different states have evolved different conventions regarding the appointment of the Chief Secretary. For example, in Andhra Pradesh, it had once been a tradition to appoint the seniormost officer as the Chief Secretary. It was done keeping in mind that such a member would possess a wide variety of experience in administration (Muttalib and Aleem 1988, 65). In Rajasthan, on the other hand, on many occasions, a number of senior officers were superseded while appointing the Chief Secretary. However, the superseded officers, to avoid embarrassment, were given grades equal to the Chief Secretary and were posted outside the Secretariat, as Chairmen of public enterprises or as the Chairman of the Board of Revenue (Arora and Goyal 2013, 336).

Till 1973, the Chief Secretary was not necessarily the seniormost official in all the states. On the recommendation of the Administrative Reforms Commission (1968), the post was equated to that of the Secretary to the Government of India in 1973, both in status and emoluments. As far as the tenure of the Chief Secretary is concerned there exists no fixed term. The Administrative Reforms Commission (ARC 1968, 26) recommended that the tenure of the

Chief Secretary should be three to four years but this suggestion has not been accepted mainly because in doing so, a Chief Minister may find himself burdened with a Chief Secretary appointed by his predecessor. Thus, practically, a Secretary's tenure depends to a large extent upon his/her administrative experience, rapport with the Chief Minister and on his/her ability to take an objective stand on sensitive issues.

The foregoing discussion makes it clear that the Chief Secretary plays a crucial role in state administration. He/she has enormous authority, power, dignity, status and influence. Therefore, he/she is rightly called as the 'kingpin of the state administration'.

THE DIRECTORATE AS AN EXECUTIVE AGENCY

As has already been mentioned, the Cabinet minister and the Secretary together constitute the Secretariat. On the other hand, the office of the Executive Head is known as the Directorate. A Secretariat is a staff agency while a Directorate is regarded as a line agency. In other words, a Secretariat is concerned with policy-making, while a Directorate is concerned with policy implementation. The Directorates translate into action policies framed by the Secretariat. They are the executive arms of the state government. In most of cases the Directorates are headed by Directors.

Executive Agencies are generally located outside the Secretariat and constitute distinct organizational entities. In a large number of cases, the heads of the executive agencies are known as Directors, like, the Director of Education, the Director of Social Welfare, the Director of Public Health, the Director of Transport and so on. However, there are other nomenclatures used to refer to the heads of the executive departments, like, the Department of Police is known as the Inspector General of Police, the head of the Jail Department as the Inspector General of Jails, the head of the Forest Department as the Chief Conservator of Forests, the head of the Cooperative Department as the Registrar of Cooperative Societies, the head of the Sales Tax Department as the Commissioner of Sales Tax, the head of the Irrigation Department as the Chief Engineer Irrigation, etc. Thus, different heads of the executive departments are addressed by different names. The state government controls the workings of the departmental heads through the Secretariat. The departmental heads enjoy specific administrative and financial powers delegated to them. The main functions of the Directorates are:

- to provide technical advice to the minister,
- to inspect execution of work by district departmental staff,
- to make appointments, confirmations, postings, transfers and promotions of departmental officers,
- to conduct departmental research and experiment programmes to improve departmental efficiency,
- to organize in-service training programmes for departmental staff,
- to exercise disciplinary powers over subordinate officers as per rules,
- to prepare departmental budgets, and
- allocation of grants and reappropriations of budget as per the rules.

The heads of the executive agencies are assisted by Additional Directors, Joint Directors, Deputy Directors and Assistant Directors. There is a permanent office of a department which is occupied by the lower level bureaucracy. Each department is headed by a specialist officer known as the Director, Registrar, or Chief Engineer, but in some cases a generalist IAS officer may also take the charge of a technical department. In such a situation, the generalist–specialist debate becomes prominent in the state administration. Apart from the state level, executive agencies also function at the sub-state level. The state level executive department establishes officers in the region where a region is simply a territorial unit below the state but above the district level. When this process proceeds further down the line, the district, block and village level field agencies of a Directorate emerge. Through the creation of field agencies, the administration is able to reach the doorsteps of the people it serves. Thus, all executive departments have their field agencies.

In the existing state administration there are disparities between the State Secretaries and Departmental Heads regarding their status, rank and remuneration. The State Secretary is considered to be higher than the heads of field agencies. The present service pattern has placed the generalist administrator at a higher position than the technical field officer.

PATTERN OF RELATIONSHIP BETWEEN THE SECRETARIAT AND THE DIRECTORATES

From the above discussion it has become clear that the Secretariat is the policy-making body, whereas the Directorate is the executive agency. Though both of them are separate entities, they are closely interrelated organizations. They work in close collaboration with each other. And in actual administration, often the line of demarcation between the two is not rigidly drawn. The Directorate is conceived as a technical, supervisory and advisory unit. At one end, it keeps in close touch with field-level operations of a department, while at another, it functions as a link organization between the Secretariat and the field organization. However, the Secretariat department often enters into the functional areas of the Directorate, in its enthusiasm to take control of field problems as well. And with the centralization of authority the Secretariat tends to become powerful and its relationship with the Directorate is naturally disturbed.

The institution of the Secretariat has attracted considerable criticism. The Secretariat as a concept is meant to encourage division of work between policy-making and policy executing agencies and the specialization of work which results from such compartmentalization of work. The idea of the Secretariat is also meant to promote delegation of authority from policy-making to policy-implementing agencies. However, in practice, these advantages of the Secretariat system have failed to fully materialize. The manner of functioning of the Secretariat and its overbearing attitude has tended to generate tensions in the Secretariat–Directorate relationship.

Critics point out that the Secretariat has an expansionist attitude. It does not confine itself to policy-making; instead it freely engages in matters of the executive nature. This encroachment has definitely weakened the authority of the executive agencies. It is also found that the Secretariat generally hesitates to delegate the required authority to the executive agencies. As a result of this, implementation of policies is delayed. Besides, the initiative of the executive agencies is hampered through repeated consultations with, and approvals from the Secretariat. The practice of evaluating the work of specialist of the field agencies by generalist administrators of the Secretariat is also criticized. It is untenable that the Secretariat should scrutinize the schemes and proposals prepared by the line agencies as the lay generalists have possibly nothing to contribute in such technical matters.

The Secretariat practically deals not only with the policy matters but also those of their execution, this has further enhanced its importance. The Secretariat has expanded its functional area through unauthorized encroachments in the executive domain. The fact that the Secretariat has come to be identified with the real power structure in the state government system and is even considered as 'the government' has unduly led to an expansion in the influence and authority of the Secretariat. It has aggravated the tension between the Secretariat and the Directorates.

Thus, the relationship between the Secretariat and the field agencies has been a big problem in state administration. A number of Committees and Commissions have been set up to resolve this problem and a number of suggestions have been put forward. It has been observed that the powers delegated to different departmental heads are not uniform, and uniformity in such powers has been suggested. The Secretariat also needs to delegate required authority to the departmental heads. The departmental heads also must allow their subordinates to fully exercise the delegated authority. Another suggestion is the conferment of ex officio Secretariat status on the heads of the executive departments. The result is that by virtue of holding office as a head, the incumbent of the position holds a suitable rank in the Secretariat. The clear advantage is that the two offices (those of the Director and the Secretary) are now combined in a single officer. The Director, by virtue of being an ex officio Secretary, can sign on behalf of the government. The need for scrutiny of schemes in the two offices is thus obviated. The same officer, in his capacity as Director, proposes the scheme and, in his capacity as Secretary, scrutinizes it.

The Administrative Reforms Commission's (ARC, 1966–70) team on 'the machinery of the Government of India and its procedure of work' has recommended that a distinction between the Secretariat as a policy-making body and the non-Secretariat organizations as executive agencies be completely abolished and the office of the executive agencies be merged with the corresponding departments in the Secretariat. The idea is to provide for adequate interactions between the policy-making and the policy implementing agencies of the government and remove the invidious distinction between the Secretariat and non-Secretariat parts of the administration. However, the ARC expressed itself against a general abolition of the distinction between the Secretariat and the executive agencies. It recommended the integration with the Secretariat of only those executive departments which were concerned with development programmes.

What could be a suitable pattern for the relationship between the Secretariat and the field agencies? There are different opinions from different quarters. But it can be observed that the question of the Secretariat–Directorate relationship is a vexed one. Readymade solutions to remodel this relationship are difficult to come by. But it can surely be said that both have to function in close collaboration with each other. Thus, the Directorate and the Secretariat have to work in tandem to ensure the Headquarters' coordinating role and the Directorate's duty to keep track of field situation.

THE STATE FINANCE COMMISSIONS

Democracy as a way of life is gradually percolating to the rural as well as urban populations through various levels of institutions, the Gram Panchayats and Urban Local Bodies being the essential foundations. Democratic decentralization becomes positively more meaningful, relevant and versatile when adequately endorsed with financial and administrative decentralization. State Finance Commissions are established so that they can help in improving the financial condition of local bodies such as the Panchayati Raj institutions (PRIs) and municipal bodies in the states. State Finance Commissions have been set up in various states of the country according to the guidelines that have been laid down in the Constitution of India, Article 243 (I). According to this article, the Governor of the state shall set up the Finance Commission within the period of one year that begins with the 73rd Amendment act of the Indian Constitution, 1992 and after that at the end of every five years. Article 243Y of the Constitution further provides that the Finance Commission constituted under Article 243 (I) shall make similar recommendation vis-à-vis the municipalities.

The Finance Commissions in the states usually comprise the Chairman, Member Secretary and other members. State Finance Commissions receive grants from the Finance Commission set-up by the Central Government. The functions of State Finance Commissions include:

- to review the economic condition of the various Panchayati Raj institutions and municipal bodies in the state,
- to take such steps that help in boosting the financial condition of the various municipal bodies and Panchayati Raj institutions in the state,
- to allot funds to the various Panchayati Raj institutions and municipal bodies in the state from the Consolidated Fund of the state,
- to act as an arbiter between the Central and the state governments with regard to issues that are of financial nature,
- to transfer funds that are granted by the Central government to the state government,
- to distribute between the various municipal bodies and Panchayati Raj institutions that are there within the state and the state government, the total proceeds of taxes, fees, tolls and duties that are charged by the state government, and
- to determine the taxes, tolls, duties and fees that may be levied by the various Panchayati Raj institutions and municipal bodies that are there within the state.

The states where State Finance Commissions have been set up include: Andhra Pradesh, Assam, Bihar, Kerala, Nagaland, Orissa, Tamil Nadu, West Bengal, Jammu & Kashmir, Goa, Gujarat, Manipur, Arunachal Pradesh and Himachal Pradesh. The state governments need to promote the State Finance Commissions as this would help in improving the economic condition of the states by bringing in more funds from the Centre for the states. Also it would help in improving the financial condition of the Panchayati Raj institutions and municipal bodies in the states. All this would also help in the all-round development of the state.

The Fourth Finance Commission—Rajasthan (2010–15)

Rajasthan has had the privileged position of becoming the forerunner in the sphere of the Panchayati Raj System. In pursuance of the constitutional and statutory provisions, the Governor of Rajasthan constituted the Fourth State Finance Commission on 13 April 2011, which submitted its report in September 2013. The Commission was constituted with a mandate to recommend principles and methodologies as regards the devolution of funds to the Panchayati Raj Institutions (PRIs) and Urban Local Bodies (ULBs).

The basic principles which the Commission has kept in view are as under:

- to ensure better accountability of any unit of local governance; its ability to raise revenues from its own sources, that are required to match as closely as possible with its expenditure needs,
- the strength of local government system depends upon the extent of finances available to assigned responsibilities, and
- government grants and incentives on the basis of population, geographical area and all round performance of the PRIs and ULBs.

The Commission in its report made practical suggestions for the PRIs and ULBs to enhance and mobilize their own tax and non-tax resources, so as to make Rajasthan a premier state in the overall scenario as aspired for the entire country. The state government transferred five subjects namely, Agriculture, Elementary Education, Medical Health, Social Justice and Empowerment and Women and Child Development to the PRIs along with the related funds, functions and functionaries. The Commission studied and assessed the financial requirement of the Local Bodies, with reference to their constitutional and other responsibilities, and recommended the principles and criteria needed to govern the transfer of net proceeds of the state's own tax revenue and the criteria for inter allocation of the share between the Local Bodies. Apart from that, the Commission also made extensive recommendations for strengthening the financial position of Local Bodies through higher internal resource mobilization and making them more effective in their role.

Recommendations

The Commission recommended that 5 per cent of net own tax revenue (excluding entry tax and land revenue) of the state government be devolved to the local bodies for the award period, i.e., 2010–15. In addition 100 per cent of land revenue, 25 per cent of entry tax, 3 per cent of royalty on minerals, 2 per cent cess on excise duty and 10 per cent surcharge on stamp duty were also recommended to be devolved. The total devolution of ₹10,183.96 crore for the award period is shown in Table 4.1.

It would be useful to examine here the quantum of vertical devolution of financial assistance from the state government to local bodies, by going through the recommendations made by the Finance Commissions of different states. Table 4.2 lists out those states where the Finance Commissions have recommended devolution in terms of the percentage of state revenues. In Karnataka, Andhra Pradesh, Gujarat and Haryana, the finance commissions have recommended the sharing of both tax and non-tax revenues, while the global sharing of these revenues has been recommended only for three of the four states. The percentage share varies from 10 (Gujarat) to 40 (Karnataka) with Andhra Pradesh (10.38) aligning itself closely with Gujarat. In Haryana, the Finance Commission has recommended shares in specific tax and non-tax revenues. Out of the remaining states, in the case of 10 states, the Finance Commissions have recommended sharing of the net proceeds of own tax revenues, the percentages varying between 1 (Sikkim) to 27 (Goa) with Assam (2), Rajasthan (2.25), Kerala (3.5), Madhya Pradesh (4) and Punjab (4) being close to the lower end and Orissa (10), Uttar Pradesh (12.5) and West Bengal (16) at the higher end. In Uttaranchal, the devolution in the first year of the award period came

Table 4.1 Devolution of Funds to Local Bodies in Rajasthan for the Period 2010–15

		(₹ In Crore)
(i)	5% of State's own net tax revenue (excluding entry tax & land revenue)	7,214.66
(ii)	100% of Land revenue	1,064.51
(iii)	25% of Entry tax	337.50
(iv)	3% of Royalty on minerals	390.86
(v)	2% Cess on excise duty on liquor	99.81
(vi)	10% Surcharge on stamp duty	1,076.62
	Total	**10,183.96**

Source: Report of Fourth State Finance Commission, Rajasthan (for 2010–15). 2013, September. Jaipur, Rajasthan.

Table 4.2 States Having Devolution as a Percentage of State Revenues, 2010

S. No.	State	Basis of Devolution
1.	Andhra Pradesh	10.38% of Tax and non-tax revenue including share of central taxes
2.	Assam	2% of State net tax revenue
3.	Goa	27% of State own tax revenue and share in central taxes to PRIs and 9% for municipalities
4.	Gujarat	10% of Annual revenue of state
5.	Haryana	Share in specific tax and non-tax revenue
6.	Karnataka	40% of Non-loan gross own receipts of state government during 2003–4 to 2007–8
7.	Kerala	3.5% of State own tax revenue
8.	Madhya Pradesh	4% of Net divisible pool of own tax revenue
9.	Orissa	10% of the Average of state gross own tax revenue
10.	Punjab	4% of Net receipts of all state taxes
11.	Rajasthan	2.25% of Own tax revenue.
12.	Sikkim	1% of All taxes
13.	Uttar Pradesh	12.5% Share in divisible pool of all state taxes except entertainment tax for ULBs and land revenue for PRIs
14.	West Bengal	16% of State tax revenue

Source: Government of Uttarakhand (2010).

to 9.1 per cent of the state's own revenues (excluding interest receipts, dividend, profits, royalties on minerals and sale proceeds from forest produce, etc.; SFC 2010).

Considering the fact that local bodies were deprived of their legitimate share in the increased revenue of the state (as the devolution was recommended on a per capita basis and not as a percentage of the state's revenues), the Uttarakhand State Finance Commission (2010) felt that there was enough justification for increasing the devolution percentage to at least 10 per cent of the state's own revenues (both tax and non-tax excluding interest receipts, dividend, profits, royalties from minerals and sale proceeds from forest produce etc.). In view of these considerations, the Commission recommend that 10 per cent of the state's own revenues (both tax and non-tax excluding interest receipts, dividend, profits, royalties from minerals and sale proceeds from forest produce, etc.) should devolve on local bodies in each of the five years of the award period (2006–7 to 2010–11). This would be in line with states like Gujarat, Andhra Pradesh, Uttar Pradesh and West Bengal (SFC 2010).

With the passage of the 73rd and 74th Constitutional Amendments, the Panchayati Raj Institutions and the Urban Local Bodies have acquired a legally mandated status and paving the way for direct democracy at the primary levels. We can call it the world's largest experiment in local democracy. Local democracy has become an effective prescription for all that is desirable—enhanced participation, greater public accountability, effective programmes of poverty alleviation and even reducing social and economic inequalities. Important constitutional provisions also include the setting up of a State Finance Commission for every state after every five years. The primary concern of the Commission has been to suggest ways and means to strengthen institutions of Local Governance. It is commonly accepted that the devolution of assigned functions, if they are to be both realistic and meaningful, must be matched by economic power and authority. This would give Local Bodies the power to control as well as perform their duties well and hence they could be legitimately asked to shoulder responsibility coupled with accountability.

STATE CONTROL OVER LOCAL GOVERNMENTS

The term 'local government' literally means the management of local affairs by the people of a locality. It is based on the principle that local problems and needs can be looked after by the people of the locality better than by central or state governments. The administration of local affairs is entrusted to representatives elected by the people of the locality in regular intervals. In India, the local government is the third stratum of government, the first two being the Central and state governments (Figure 4.1). India is known to be the world's largest democracy. In the constitutional sense, democracy is the system of government, in the administration of which, every adult citizen of the country enjoys some direct or indirect share. Keeping in view the real spirit and high ideas of democracy, local government forms an indispensable part of governance and administration in India.

The local government's jurisdiction is limited to a specific area and its functions relate to the provision of civic amenities to the population lying within its jurisdiction. But the activities of local governments are not less in number. Local governments have been undertaking new activities which either regulate the conduct of citizens or are in the nature of services such as the provisioning of mass transport, construction of houses for the poor, supply of electricity, health centres, parks, play grounds, etc. In fact, local governments today are much more important in the daily life of a citizen than the state or Central government.

Though rural and urban local governments have been empowered by the 73rd and 74th Amendment Acts, it does not mean that they have unlimited authority and freedom. Some measures of control over local bodies are not only desirable, but also necessary. Therefore, these bodies are kept under the control of state governments for proper direction, unification and coordination of civic services and for securing consistency and continuity in the

Figure 4.1 Administrative Structure in India

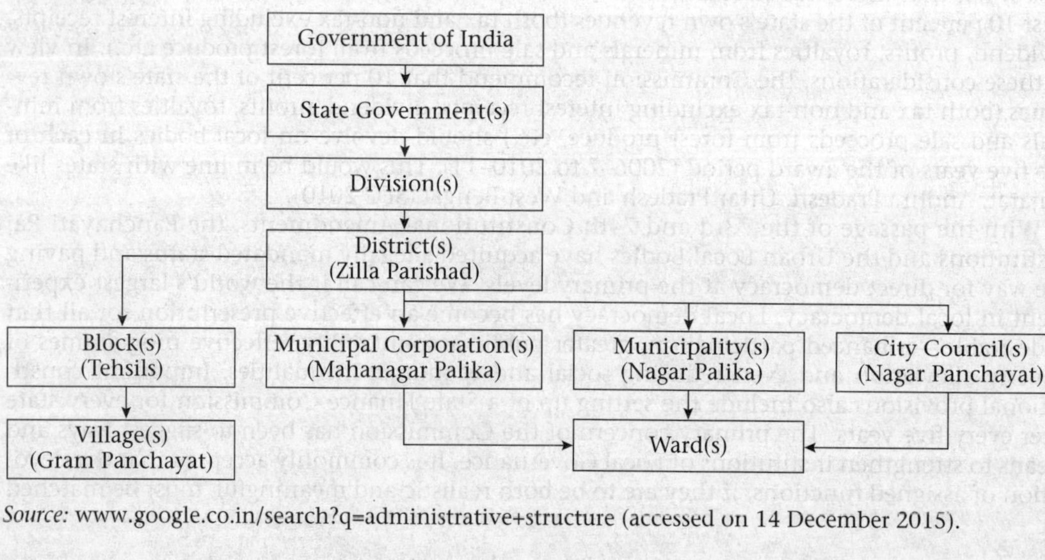

Source: www.google.co.in/search?q=administrative+structure (accessed on 14 December 2015).

formulation and implementation of national policies. The Central and state governments are free to prescribe the limits within which a local government has to operate and also reserve the right to issue directions from time to time. A local government functions within the provisions of the statute which has created it. It is subordinate to the state or provincial government which exercises control and supervision over it. The state governments exercise supervision and control over local governments to ensure minimum standards of service and their proper functioning through legislative, administrative and financial control. Local governments are also subject to judicial control for their acts or omission and commission. The following are the main mechanisms of state control over local bodies.

Institutional Control

This control is the cornerstone of the pattern of control over the PRIs relating to the basic structure of local bodies. Under institutional control, state governments have the power to regulate membership structure, composition, election, size of councils, functional jurisdiction, staff and inter-institutional disputes of the panchayats. Institutional control tends to ensure that when these statutory bodies function, they do not violate the spirit and letter of law that has created the Panchayati Raj bodies.

Administrative Control

Through administrative control, day-to-day administration of local bodies is regulated by state governments. Each state has an administrative department from the state level to the block level to exercise administrative control over Panchayati Raj Institutions (PRIs). The main mechanism of administrative control includes the supersession and dissolution of PRIs, power to cancel and suspend resolutions, removal of members of PRIs, inspections and tours, approval of bye-laws, instituting enquiries, enforcement of non-confidence motions, etc. The main purpose of administrative control is to prevent the implementation of policies and decisions which are not according to the basic goals and purposes of the institution concerned (Narain, Kumar and Mathur 1970, 51).

Financial Control

Financial control is the most effective method of control over local bodies. This control is exercised to keep the expenditure by local bodies within prescribed financial limits and to check the misuse of funds. It includes the regulation of finances, budgets accounts and audit of the PRIs. The audit of accounts of PRIs is done by auditors appointed by state governments. Sanctioning of budgets is also an important instrument of control. Heavy dependence of the PRIs on state assistance automatically makes them agree to accept state control over themselves (Singh and Singh 1986, 261).

Judicial Control

State governments also regulate local bodies through judicial control. But courts entertain cases only when any action by the local bodies is challenged by the state governments on legal grounds.

Supervisory Control

State governments demand periodical reports from local bodies about their functioning. These reports work as a tool in the hands of state governments to get themselves acquainted with the latest state of affairs of the PRIs. Monthly, quarterly, half yearly and annual reports on different programmes and schemes are required from and submitted by the PRIs.

PROBLEM OF EXCESSIVE CONTROL AND ISSUES OF CONFLICT BETWEEN STATE AND LOCAL GOVERNMENTS

It is clear from the above discussion that state governments enjoy enormous powers to exercise control over the self-governing institutions but there are several occasions when these powers are misused by the party in power to settle scores. For the effective functioning of the local bodies, such practices need to be stopped. State control over local bodies has been so rigid that it has reduced local self-governing bodies to the status of subordinate agencies of state governments thereby having their autonomy completely suppressed. Most of the time, state control and supervision are negative rather than constructive. The focus of such control is on fault finding rather than encouraging the local bodies. The power wielded by the state governments to dissolve local bodies' acts as a hammer on the authority of the latter. Sometimes this type of controlling power is used by the ruling party for political interests. In some cases, local bodies have to take prior approval of the state governments, which prevent them from working independently. Mostly local bodies do not have adequate funds. So they have to depend on state governments for financial aid. This financial assistance is uncertain, irregular and inadequate. The heavy dependence of local governments on state assistance leads to excessive financial control over these bodies.

Besides the above weaknesses, there are a number of other issues of conflict between state and local bodies. Local governments, both rural and urban, provide examples of the lack of clarity in the division of functional responsibilities. This occurs in several specific ways. First, the same general expenditure or service category is often the statutory responsibility of the state government as well as its subordinate local governments. Second, even where broad areas are explicitly divided, this is not necessarily done in a manner that promotes incentives for efficiency: the division of capital expenditures by the state and operations and maintenance by the local governments for the provision of a given service is the main example of this. Third, there has been a tendency for state governments to encroach on what might otherwise be well-defined municipal responsibilities, through the creation of special purpose agencies, or through the intervention of state government departments. Fourth, even when local functional responsibilities have been clear, they have been relatively narrowly defined, leading to inefficiencies such as the repeated repair of earthen (rural) roads rather than the construction of more durable alternatives. Fifth, the assignment of functional responsibilities has not always been efficient, in terms of allowing local governments control over activities with economies of scope or complementarities: law and order, or judicial services more generally, have been stressed as the most important case of this happening. Finally, the state bureaucracy is endowed with vast power in the administration of local bodies. Deputy Commissioners despite the creation of the Directorate of Local Bodies and the office of the Regional Deputy Directors still play a predominant role in the management of local affairs.

The above incidences make it clear that state control over local bodies requires some basic changes because the attitude of the government has not fully changed from being the superior to being a partner. Political commitment or will is required to imbibe democratic values. No doubt, state control is a must, but it should not make local bodies dancing dolls. There are several loopholes in state control over local bodies which need to be plugged in order to establish positive and effective control. Government officials should shed the tendency of dominance and act as real guides and friends to the non-officials. All possible efforts should be made to make means of control result oriented (Singh and Kumar 2005, 227). Local Governments should not be considered as subordinate agencies of the state government. There should not be too much internal and external control over the local bodies who should be given adequate autonomy to address their local issues effectively and efficiently.

CONCLUDING OBSERVATIONS

This chapter makes it clear that administration at the state level operates in the context of national uniformity as well as local diversities. Like the central administration, state administration also has a number of important administrative organizations and institutions like, the Secretariat, Ministries, Departments and Directorates, Chief Secretary, State Finance Commissions, etc. State administration is an important link between the Centre and the local bodies. On the one hand, it is an important mechanism to implement schemes and programmes of the Central government; and on the other hand it transfers powers and functions to local bodies as per the provisions of the 73rd and 74th Constitutional Amendments.

We have also seen that local governments form an indispensable part of governance and administration in India. The panchayats and municipalities have been empowered by the Indian Constitution, but that does not mean that they have unlimited authority and freedom. They are kept under the control of the state government in order to ensure proper coordination, direction and unification of local services and proper implementation of national programmes and policies. However, state control over local bodies is so rigid that it has reduced local self-governing bodies to the status of subordinate agencies to the state governments with their autonomy completely suppressed. No doubt, state control is a must, but it should not make the local bodies mere puppets.

The importance of local government lies in sustaining democracy. If democracy has to function properly, as many citizens as possible need to be encouraged and provided with opportunities to take a continuing interest in its activities and problems. The success of national democracy largely depends upon the success of democracy at the grass-roots level. All problems are not supposed to be solved by central and state governments. In fact, there are some problems which occur at the local level and need to be solved locally in accordance with local needs, environment and wishes of the people. To be acquainted with all these things, the government will need to step down to the local level in order to solve local problems in an effective manner. Local Governments contribute immensely to national prosperity. The Central and state governments should therefore act as their friends and benefactors and not as their powerful rivals or disinterested spectators.

REVIEW QUESTIONS

1. Discuss the structure and basic features of state administration in India.
2. Examine the organization and functions of the state Secretariat.
3. Write a note on the structure and role of key Ministries and Departments at the state level.
4. Critically discuss the role of the Chief Secretary.

5. Discuss the role of the state Directorate as an executive agency.
6. Examine the pattern of relationship between the Secretariat and the Directorate at the state level.
7. The State Finance Commission plays an important role in the empowerment of Panchayati Raj institutions. Discuss.
8. Write an essay on state control over local governments.
9. Excessive control of the state over local self-governing institutions leads to the demolition of autonomy of these local bodies. Discuss.
10. What are the main problems in the structure and functioning of the state administration in India? What are your suggestions to tackle them?

REFERENCES

ARC (Administrative Reforms Commission). 1968. *Report on State Government*. Government of India, New Delhi.

Arora, Ramesh K., and Rajni Goyal. 2013. *Indian Administration: Institutions and Issues*. 3rd ed. New Delhi: New Age International Publishers.

Government of Uttarakhand. 2010, 16 April. *Second Finance Commission Report*, State Finance Commission Report, Uttarakhand. Retrieved from http://gov.ua.nic.in/sfc/English_HTM/CHAPTER6.htm (accessed 12 April 2015).

Maheshwari, S. R. 2001. *Indian Administration*, 6th ed. New Delhi: Orient Blackswan.

Muttalib, M. A., and M. A. Aleem. 1988. 'Andhra Pradesh.' In *State Administration in India*, vol. I, edited by A. P. Padhi, p. 127. New Delhi: Uppal.

Narain, Iqbal, Sushil Kumar, and P. C. Mathur. 1970. *Panchayati Raj Administration*. New Delhi: Indian Institute of Public Administration.

Report of Fourth State Finance Commission, Rajasthan (for 2010–15). 2013, September. Jaipur, Rajasthan.

Singh, Mohinder, and Vijay Kumar, 2005, April–June. 'State Control over Panchayati Raj Institutions'. *The Indian Journal of Political Science* LXVI (2): 140, 142.

Singh, Sahib, and Swinder Singh. 1986. *Local Government in India: A Study in Rural and Urban Development Administration*. Jalandhar: New Academic Publishing Company.

District Administration

5

LEARNING OBJECTIVES

1. To know the organization of the district administration in India.
2. To understand the changing role of the District Collector.
3. To explore the relationship between the Collector and the Panchayati Raj institutions in India.
4. To discuss the relevance of the District Collector in India.

The district is the basic unit of administration below the state level in India. In fact, it has always existed as the unit of administration throughout the history of Indian administration. The main purpose behind the creation of the district administration is to facilitate the functioning of the state governments. The main functions of the district administration are to maintain law and order, collect revenue and attend to the welfare of the people. The district is placed under the charge of a district officer, called as District Collector—who virtually acts as the eyes, ears and arms of the state government. In the ever expanding role and scope of governance at the state level, the district administration plays an extremely crucial role in assisting the policy-makers in implementing their policies. As the head of this district administration, the District Collector plays a pivotal role in leading the official machinery. The district is truly a unit of administration with which almost every citizen comes into direct contact with. It is the real strength and power of the state government.

This chapter deals with the organizational set-up of the district administration, the changing role of the District Collector and the impact of democratic decentralization on district administration in India.

DISTRICT ADMINISTRATION: HISTORICAL CONTINUITY

The present-day district administration has historical roots. The territorial structure of administration in India can be traced to the Mauryan period where revenue villages were called *gramas*, a group of revenue villages was called *stana or taluk*, several *stanas* were called *aharas* or the district, a group of districts was called 'Pradesh' or the region (state) and several 'pradeshs' were called the 'Janapada' or a province. The head of the district administration had revenue as well as police functions. In the Mughal period, the head of the district was the *faujdar*, a military officer, who was under the control of the *subedar* (governor).The *amil* or *amulguzar* was the officer in charge of collecting revenue, who also had certain police and judicial powers. To balance him, there were the zamindars who also exerted similar powers. The authority that corresponded to the district collector during the Mauryan period was known as the *rajuka*, the *visayapati* during the Guptas and the *karori-faujdar* during the Mughal period. It proves that the institution of the Collector is not alien but a model native to the Indian administrative system.

British Intervention

When the British East India Company appeared on the scene, the 'native' model appeared to be convenient for the realization of the two-fold objectives it had set before itself, namely the collection of revenue and the consolidation of its authority in an alien land. The office of the Collector was first created under the East India Company on 14 May 1772 which also symbolized the transformation of the Company into a regular administrative organization. The 'district' was made the basis of Indian administration in 1786 when the office of the District Collector was made permanent. In 1787, the administration of revenue, civil justice and the magistracy were unified into the office of District Collector.

Since the Sepoy Mutiny of 1857, the district as an administrative unit was the mainstay of imperial rule in India, and the District Collector occupied a unique position in Indian local administration, incomparable to any other executive functionary at that level in the world. The years between 1857 and 1909 witnessed strong concentration of power in the hands of the Collector. In him was created a 'little Napoleon' who, being part and parcel of the steel frame made it possible, for the British to govern and control the vast subcontinent (Arora and Goyal 2013, 360). During this period, the Collectors used to play the role of a Magistrate as well as Collector of Revenue.

The Collector had to adjust his autocratic rule and at times benevolent administration to a climate of representative politics with the establishment of the Legislative Councils by 1919. The introduction of the constitutional reforms of 1919 known as the Montagu–Chelmsford reforms provided for the elections of the Legislative Councils and the transfer of quite a few departments to the elected ministers. The provincial autonomy under the Act of 1935 further diluted the Collector's authority in the sense that he had to now work in collaboration with the elected ministers. The Congress won the elections in 1937 and introduced several schemes for rural development and the Collector was put in charge of these schemes in the villages (Singh 1994, 167). Consequently, the collector had not only to adapt himself to work along with the elected politicians, but also under their supervision. Nevertheless, till the advent of independence, the Collector enjoyed a lot of power and prestige.

District Administration in Post-independent India

Independence and the adoption of the welfare state necessitated a complete reorientation of the district administration. The main focus now was on welfare and developmental activities. The single greatest assertion to the responsibility of the district administrator came through the expansion of rural development programmes. As the number of activities, institutions and departments involved in rural development increased, the coordinating and synthesizing role of the Collector in the development efforts of the government assumed greater importance.

However, the introduction of Panchayati Raj institutions proved to be a radical change in the functioning of the district administration as it called for empowering local bodies. The result was a reduction in the role of the District Collector, who was now primarily restricted to supervising and controlling authority. Despite such changes the fact was, as appropriately remarked by K. K. Das (1963) 'there is not, and never has been, an official quite like the collector anywhere else'.

Organization of the District Administration

The district administration headed by the District Collector is drawn from the Indian Administrative Service (IAS) and is responsible among others for the general control and direction of the police which is headed by the Superintendent of Police. The district is divided into a number of subdivisions called 'talukas' for the purpose of administrative convenience. For better supervision of many talukas, there is a grouping of the talukas, each group of talukas coming under a division which is headed by an officer called the 'tehsildar', who collects revenue and supervises land records. These tehsildars are state level officers and are called subdivisional or revenue divisional officers. At the bottom of district there are basic units which are the villages. The representative of the government in the village is the village accountant, known as the patwari, who is considered to be the 'eyes and ears of the Collector'. The patwari is mainly responsible for the maintenance of land records, as a result of which, he holds an important position in lower level bureaucracy, operating at the grass roots. In some states the blocks and talukas are synonymous in district administration. The District Collector through the Zilla Parishads, Blocks and Gram Panchayats administers development programmes and supervises them.

The other district level officers are the Superintendent of Police, the Chief Medical Officer, the District and Sessions Judge, the Executive Engineer, the District Education Officer, the District Food and Supply Officer, the District Social Welfare Officer and the District Development Officer. These officers head their respective departments. The District Collector coordinates and supervises the work of these officers who have technical control and supervision over their own departments. These officers keep him informed of their activities and report any serious issues likely to impact the law and order to him. The position of the Collector in the state hierarchy is as below.

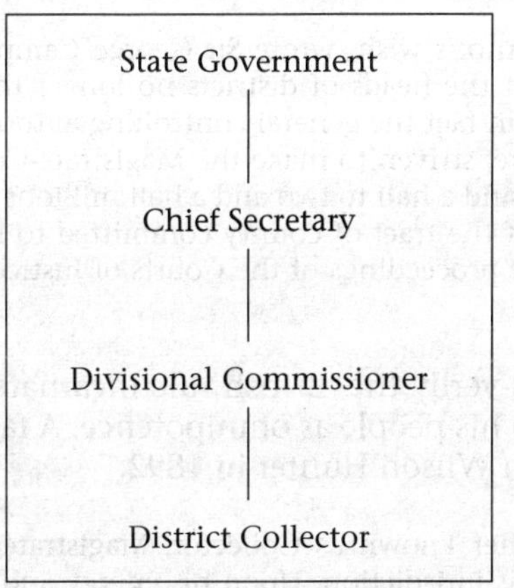

The District Collector belongs to the general administrative department of the state government, while the officials over whom he exercises control and supervision belong to a variety of departments in the district hierarchy of which he may or may not have a formal assignment. As head of the district administration, the Collector is involved in a network of interrelationships with other district level functionaries (Maheshwari 2013, 577). The district is, thus, a multiple one, having a galaxy of officers for administering the affairs of government.

DISTRICT COLLECTOR: THE KINGPIN OF DISTRICT ADMINISTRATION

A District collector, also called a District Magistrate or Deputy Commissioner, is the chief administrative and revenue officer of an Indian district. He is appointed by the state government from the IAS cadre. He usually works under the supervision of the Divisional Commissioner who is a senior IAS officer. He is responsible for implementing all government programmes at the district level. He is appointed by the state government, from among the pool of IAS officers in the state. The members of the IAS are either directly recruited by the Union Public Service Commission or promoted from the State Civil Services (PCS). Direct recruits are posted as Collectors in their thirties whereas promoted members from state civil services generally occupy this position in their forties. The Second Administrative Reforms Commission (2009) suggests that in complex and problem-prone districts, an IAS officer should be posted as a DM on completion of 10–12 years of service. A District Magistrate is transferred from his post by the state government.

Changing Role of the District Collector

Though the office of Collector has some roots in the past, the scope of his functions has varied from time to time. Under the British rule, a single officer positioned at the district headquarters, commonly called the Collector, was assigned the responsibility of maintaining law and order, peace and harmony, collecting revenue and administering justice in the district. For a majority of villagers in India, the Collector symbolized the 'government'. The conception of his office, as it became established in Bengal after many experiments, and as it was extended throughout British India, is expressed in the following quotation:

> It is the Lieutenant-Governor's wish, wrote Sir George Campbell, the Lieutenant-governor of Bengal, in 1872, to render the heads of districts no longer the drudges of many departments and masters of none, but in fact the general controlling authority over all departments in each district ... he has, therefore, striven to make the Magistrate-Collector of a great Bengal district, generally comprising one and a half to two and a half millions of inhabitants, the real executive chief and administrator of the tract of county committed to him, and supreme over everyone and everything except the proceedings of the Courts of Justice. (Report of the Indian Statutory Commission 1930)

The District Collector was verily the 'British rule incarnate'. The father and mother of the district, respected, trusted, to his people as omnipotence. A fairly vivid description of his position was given by Sir William Wilson Hunter in 1892:

> The district officer, whether known as Collector, Magistrate or as Deputy Commissioner, is the responsible head of his jurisdiction. Upon his energy and personal character depends ultimately the efficiency of our Indian Government. His own special duties are so numerous and so various as to bewilder the outsider; and the work of his subordinates, European and native, largely depends upon the stimulus of his personal example .... He is expected to make himself acquainted with every phase of his social life of the country. He should be a lawyer, an accountant, a surveyor, and a ready writer of State papers. He ought also to possess no mean knowledge of agriculture, political economics and engineering. (Maheshwari 2013, 575)

The Report of the Indian Statutory Commission (1930) made the following observations regarding the status of a Collector during the British rule:

> It is difficult to convey how great is the prestige of the Collector of a District among the inhabitants whom he serves. To most of them, as we have said, he is the embodiment to Government. The authority which he derives from his statutory powers is augmented by the constant exercise to advice and direction in matters where he is expected to give a lead. He wields large powers of patronage; he is responsible for making a vast number of minor appointments, for instance, of village headmen and accountants, of revenue officials and office clerks. His recommendations for honorary magistrateships and nominated membership of all local self-governing bodies are ordinarily accepted. He can grant seats at ceremonial functions such as 'durbars' (much prized as social distinctions), and the coveted Indian titles and honours, and other rewards, are usually conferred at his suggestions. The preservation of this influence is of the utmost concern to the Administration. Many everyday matters which might involve merely tedious disputes, or even civil action, quickly reach conclusive settlement were brought before the Collector. The same influence becomes of manifest public advantage when more serious conflict threatens. It is not by his success in putting down communal riots that a Collector is judged so much as by his success in preventing their occurrence.

Thus, during the British period, the Collector was the eyes and the ears of the government. The duty of assessing and collecting land revenue, which originally imparted to this office its title, was by no means his only duty. Other public functionaries posted in the district looked to him for help, advice, sometimes even orders and even the citizens almost instinctively flocked to him whenever they had grievances to be redressed or had any problem the solution for which they did not seem to know or agree with. It makes clear that during the British period, the Collector was the most powerful officer at the district level.

Role of the Collector in Independent India

Since independence, the office of the Collector has fundamentally changed in terms of its power and prestige. The main factors influencing the emergent role of the Collector include: democratic set-up in the country, vigorous attempts at decentralization, increasing developmental responsibilities and the rise of public consciousness. To elaborate the point in the words of Mohit Bhattacharya,

> After independence, government had to take up the work of speedy socio-economic development. From law and maintenance to people's welfare orientation, there was this basic change in the outlook of district administration. Agriculture and industrial production had to be increased, poverty, malnutrition, ill-health had to be tackled on war footing. Infrastructural development like roads construction, electricity generation, irrigation expansion, operating of new railway lines—all these had to be done as quickly as possible. These new activities meant opening of new offices at the district level and below. The district collector, being a generalist administrator, had to coordinate all these development activities. (2000, 69–70)

Another change was seen in the perception of the newly recruited civil servants. Whereas the British Collectors viewed themselves as uncrowned sovereigns of an empire and the people merely as subjects to be governed, the new breed of IAS officers were full of enthusiasm and idealism for the betterment of the people. The social composition also underwent a change. Whereas earlier the Collectors belonged to the upper strata of society, more currently, due to the spread of education and the reservation of seats, a more egalitarian set-up has emerged. Some of the Collectors belong to the low-income groups and hence, a greater degree of sympathy and understanding for the underprivileged sections can be expected of them. It is this composition of the IAS which has immense potential for affecting the ultimate power of bureaucracy and its controllability by social forces.

A. K. Dubey has pointed out that the initial reaction of the democratically constituted governments and legislatures to the civil servants was one of distrust and even hostility, because an important plank of the national struggle against the British was the denunciation of the civil service which was initially mostly British. He has summarized the developments thus:

> So the suspicion was there in minds of the new political masters as well as the civil servants. However, this phase was soon over as the civil servants displayed deep sense of loyalty to the constitution and patriotism. The District Officer symbolized, the traditional Indian concept of authority as an efficient and benevolent institution. Thus the all-embracing institution of the District Officer continued to be cherished across the years after the independence. Moreover, acceptability of district as a dependable administrative unit coupled with non-specialist nature of the district administration helped the institution survive through the change in political context. (Dubey 1995, 22–23)

Thus, the colonial bureaucratic set-up got legitimacy and continued to survive in the Indian administrative system.

DEVELOPMENT IMPERATIVES AND ROLE OF THE DISTRICT ADMINISTRATION

After Independence, the single greatest accretion to the responsibilities of the district administrator came through an expansion of rural development programmes. As the number of activities, institutions and departments involved in rural development increased, the coordinating and synthesizing role of the Collector in the development efforts of the government assumed greater importance. The year 1951 saw the beginning of the first Five Year Plan. From the maintenance of law and order and collection of revenue, the major emphasis shifted to the development of human and material resources and the elimination of poverty and wants.

With the inauguration of the National Extension and Community Development Programme in 1952, the Collector was given further responsibility of handling all the developmental functions in the district, in addition to the regulatory functions. For the successful implementation of these programmes it was considered essential to harness into service the traditional prestige and position of the Collector. He was asked to take upon himself/herself the functions of promoter and coordinator of all development activities. The district administration thus, continued as an organic whole, occupying a pivotal role in development administration.

A shift from the regular functioning of revenue and law and order of the Collector was also included in the First Five Year Plan. A steady support to the system of administration of development programmes was documented in the First Five Year Plan. The Second Five Year Plan stressed the relative importance of the administrative system of democratic governance. The reorganization of the district administration, integration of the activities of various development departments, linking up of local self-governing institutions with administrative agencies, regional coordination, supervision of district development programmes and strengthening and improving the machinery of general administration were made in the Second Plan. This exercise was followed in the Third Five Year Plan too. However, the Plan called for more intensive efforts and a greater sense of urgency towards strengthening equality of opportunity and the socialistic pattern of society.

In the course of Fourth and Fifth Five Year Plans, the organizational dimension of district administration for development emerged and it valued a new pattern of relationship between the district officer and the officer of technical department, between the administration and democratic bodies and between the district officer and the State department. During the Fourth Plan period, the Planning Commission recommended that all state governments should establish regional/district planning units equipped with qualified and competent technical staff. As a result, the office of the Collector was further strengthened as the head of the planning machinery at the district level besides it being an overall co-coordinator of different departments.

The district level administration acquired greater complexity during the Sixth Five Year Plan. It strengthened the district with the appointment of the District Development Officer who had complete authority and responsibility of development work and enjoyed the same status as the Collector. Apart from decentralization of the administrative machinery and the provisioning of adequate co-ordinating mechanisms at the local level, involvement of people at every stage of planning and implementation was also felt necessary. Therefore, an institutional mechanism for this purpose was adopted by bringing in representatives of the people. Some state governments established the system by entrusting development work to an officer of the rank of the District Collector as the Chief Executive Officer (CEO) of the Zilla Parishad.

DEMOCRATIC DECENTRALIZATION AND THE ROLE OF THE COLLECTOR

By the late 1960s, there was a realization that a bureaucracy-led development was not the answer to the problems of the third world nations and this brought a change in development approach. By sheer experience throughout the developing world, an important lesson was learnt that development needed to come through people's participation in policy making as well as policy implementation. This realization paved the way for democratic decentralization in India.

As a result of the recommendations of the **Balwant Rai Mehta Committee (1957)**, the position of the Collector in the field of development underwent a change. The Committee recommended a three-tier system for democratic decentralization, namely the Zilla Parishad at the district level, the Panchayat Samiti at the block level and the Village Panchayat at the village level. Though the Committee had recommended that the Collector should function as the Chairman of the Zilla Parishad, a different view gradually began to emerge which was opposed to the retention of the Collector in any dominant position in the Panchayati Raj set-up as it was felt that would not be in consonance with the spirit of decentralization.

The result was a broad variation in the Collector's powers and functions with regard to the Panchayati Raj institutions. Besides that there was no constitutional safeguard for these bodies. Being denied of any constitutional status and the lack of will on the part of the political masters, the Panchayati Raj system failed to deliver goods.

Another Committee, which deserves special mention in the evolution of democratic decentralization in India, is the **Ashok Mehta Committee (1977)** as it was appointed to inquire into the working of PRIs and suggest measures to strengthen them. The Committee felt that a combination of factors had conspired to undermine PRIs, such as an unsympathetic bureaucracy, absence of political will, lack of involvement in planning and implementation on a substantial scale and the domination of local institutions by the economic and social rural elite (Desouza, 371).

The Committee underscored the functional necessity of decentralization and recommended a two-tier system for the Panchayati Raj institution. It also recommended that the district be the basic unit since it was a viable administrative unit for which planning, coordination and resource allocation were feasible and for which technical expertise was available. It was the first to demand constitutional recognition for the panchayats. The Committee even drafted a model bill, which they appended with their report, seeking an amendment to the Constitution along these lines (Kumar 2006, 23).

The Janata Party did not stay in power long enough to implement the decisions of the Ashok Mehta Committee, and reportedly, in an initial meeting, the recommendations of the Committee were not received well by the state governments (Sethi 1989). However, the influence of the report of this Committee was significant. Infact, the states of Karnataka, Andhra Pradesh and West Bengal passed new legislations based on the same.

Another attempt to empower local bodies and give them constitutional status was made in the 1980s. On the basis of initiatives taken by the former Prime Minister, late Rajiv Gandhi, **workshops for Collectors and District Magistrates** were conducted by the Department of Personal and Training, Government of India, during December 1987 and June 1988 at Bhopal, Imphal, Hyderabad and Jaipur. The district heads interacted freely with the former Prime minister and as a result, a consensus emerged in favour of strengthening democratic institutions at the district and below levels. The officials opined that if genuine responsive governance could be operable it needed to be responsible, representative and responsive to the urges of the people. Needless to add that there was insufficient devolution of powers and functions at the district and below levels of our polity. Finally, these four workshops facilitated the crystallization of ideas highlighting the need for a constitutional buttress to ensure periodical and timely elections to self-government institutions like PRIs and urban local bodies.

Since the consensus was arrived by the district Collectors/Magistrates themselves, it became easier for the Government of India to move in the direction of arming local self-government institutions. These developments led to the abortive 64th Amendment which tried to create a stronger Panchayati Raj system in the first place. On the basis of consensus arrived at by all the political parties on the need for establishing a Panchayati Raj system throughout the country, the 73rd Constitutional Amendment Bill was passed in December 1992. Thus, the efforts made in the series of workshops on responsive administration led to the emergence of a new Panchayati Raj System in 1993.

THE 73rd AMENDMENT ACT, 1992, AND THE ROLE OF THE COLLECTOR

The 73rd Amendment Act, 1992 is a landmark in empowering local governance in India. The main features of the Act include the provision for a uniform three-tier Panchayati Raj system at the village, block and district levels, uniform five-year terms for panchayats, 33 per cent reservation for women and the establishment of a state-level Election and Finance Commission. It is for the first time that the panchayats were given constitutional status.

New Patterns of Relationship between the Collector and the Panchayati Raj Institutions

After the empowerment of the Panchayats, the role of the Collector changed immensely. Since the Act avoided covering the relationships and powers of the district Collector vis-à-vis these institutions, the state models vary from a situation of no control of the Collector as in

Bengal to nearly full control in Orissa, Karnataka and Haryana. So mainly two different patterns have emerged. First where there is greater power and delegation to people's representatives and a reduction in the power of the bureaucracy at the district level. For example, in Andhra Pradesh, the Chairman of the Zilla Parishad is permitted to exercise administrative control over the Chief Executive Officer who is equivalent to an IAS or DM, for the purpose of implementation of the resolution of the Zilla Parishad or any standing committee.

In Uttar Pradesh and Madhya Pradesh, the Zilla Panchayat has the power to control and supervise the administration of the District Rural Development Agency (DRDA) within its jurisdiction. The Karnataka model shows that the Collector who till now remains very powerful performs limited functions. The whole planning process came to be integrated at the district level and the DRDA was merged with the Zilla Parishad (Singh 1997, 557).The responsibility of conducting elections to PRIs which was earlier assigned to the Collector, has been given to the state level Election Commission (1993). The establishment of the state level Finance Commission also reduces some of the earlier jurisdiction of the collector in the financial matters of the Panchayati Raj institutions. These examples reveal that democratic decentralization has curtailed the powers of the Collector drastically in some states. Now his role is reduced to one of guidance and advice.

However, there is another pattern in which we find that the Collector has got a dominating role in relation to the panchayats. For example, in Andhra Pradesh the Sarpanch and Upsarpanch can be suspended if in the opinion of the Collector, they abuse the power vested in them. The Karnataka Panchayati Raj Act 1993 not only provides the power of supervision along with the control over execution of all works of the Zilla Panchayat by the Commissioner, but also the power to dissolve the Gram Panchayat. Likewise, the Bihar Panchayati Raj Act (1993) also gave control of the PRIs to the state government and the bureaucracy. In the Act, the state legislature has been empowered to use emergency power against the panchayats, which is exercised through the Collector at the district level.

It is generally believed that introduction of the 73rd Amendment Act has reduced the power of the Collector. But, it is not so, because the new Act has vested the bureaucracy with the power to control, monitor and even to recommend suspension and dissolution as the agent of the state Government. While local bodies have been given 29 programmes on which they only can plan, the final authority for implementation of these programmes is vested in the hands of bureaucracy. There is also a provision for the establishment of various committees like the Education Committee, the Public Health Committee, etc., to implement the plans but these committees are under the control and supervision of the bureaucracy. There are also some other factors like lack of administrative experience on the part of political leaders, lack of education among the rural masses and absence of leadership among women and backward sections of society which strengthen the overall role of the Collector in the district in spite of changes brought out by the Panchayati Raj system.

The recommendations of the Second ARC (2009) envisaged a new role for the Collector vis-à-vis the panchayat bodies. The Commission noted that the Collectors were so overburdened that many of them were not fully aware of how many Committees they were required to preside over. Such widespread functions without well-defined roles resulted in a lack of clarity and diffusion of the Collector's responsibilities. Also, after the establishment of PRIs/ULBs as the third tier of government, there was no need to assign any role/function to the Collector in respect of activities which were transferred by the state government to these bodies. As such, the Commission was of the view that there was need to redefine the role and responsibilities of the Collector in a clear manner. His job profile needed to consist of (a) a well-defined set of exclusive activities both statutory as well as non-statutory as a functionary of the state government, (b) the general work of coordination with various departments/agencies of the state and the Union governments at the district level, and (c) in the interim period till the time the local elected Institutions matured into district governments—as the Chief Executive Officer of the proposed District Council (ARC 2009, 71).

THE DISTRICT COLLECTOR: POWER AND FUNCTIONS

Irrespective of its genesis and of the practices prevailing during pre-independence era, the office of the District Collector has now become a uniform institution throughout the country. The contents of its functions may vary to an extent, but by and large, the functions of a Collector are similar in all the states except, in terms of development functions in which the pattern varies significantly. The District Collector is responsible for all governmental actions in the district as the agent of the state government. It is truism that the powers conferred on him/her are extensive and to some extent discretionary in nature. For instance, it is specified in the Bombay Revenue Department Manual that 'nothing can or should pass in the district of which Collector should not be kept informed' (Potter 1964, 68). By undertaking extensive tours, he should be both accessible as well as responsive to their felt needs. As per the **Second Administrative Reforms Commission (2009)**, the portfolio of the Collector's office generally performs the following functions and activities (though there may be variations across states):

- acting as the Head of Land and Revenue Administration, including the responsibility of district finance (expenditure and audit);
- acting as the District Head of the Executive Magistracy and overall supervision of law and order and security with some say in police matters;
- as the licensing and Regulatory Authority in respect of the various special laws such as Arms, Explosive and Cinematography Acts etc. in the district;
- conduct of elections—for Parliament, State Legislature and Local Bodies;
- as the Officer-in-charge of Disaster Management;
- as the guardian of public lands with the responsibility to prevent and remove encroachments which are often a source of tension between vested interests and the district administration;
- public service delivery, either by facilitating or directly delivering services assigned to the district administration from other departments. (In this respect, the Collector often acts as the Chairman of the Board for Parastatals or as Chairman or Member of various standing and interdepartmental committees);
- facilitation of interaction between the civil society and the state government;
- handling issues of local cadre management such as recruitment, in-service training and promotion; and
- act as the Chief Information and Grievance Redressal Officer of the district.

Some of the important functions of the Collector are elaborated below.

Revenue Administrator

As already discussed, the office of Collector was created to collect revenue. He still carries on this responsibility. He is the head of the Revenue Department of the district. The Collector handles all the matters connected with land reforms and revenue administration. In that capacity he exercises the power of general supervision and control of land records and their staff. His functions regarding land revenue are of several types such as collection of land revenue, canal dues, distribution of loans and recovery of dues, distribution of distress due to losses to crops caused by natural calamities and disasters, relief to fire sufferers, assessment of loss of crops due to floods and drought, relief to affected farmers, assessment and realization of agricultural tax, collecting and furnishing multifarious agrarian statistics concerning rain fall, crops, ensuring proper administration of land and proper sale and mortgages of land, etc.

For the proper performance of revenue administration, the Collector is assisted by other revenue officers. The district is divided into subdivisions, tehsils, kanungo circles and patwari circles which are headed by the tehsildar, kanungo and patwari to assist the Collector.

Ensuring Law and Order

As the District Magistrate, the Collector is responsible for the maintenance of law and order in the district. He plays this role with the help of the district police headed by the Superintendent of Police. As a district magistrate he promulgates orders in case of any danger of breach of peace and public order. He can inspect police stations and ask for any information and records dealing with crimes. He can order into an accident caused by explosions, issue warrants for the arrest of suspected offenders on apprehension of breach of peace.

Chief Coordinator

One of the most important roles of the Collector is to coordinate activities of different departments and agencies at the district level. The different departments usually carry on their activities independently. It is through the intervention of the Collector that a degree of coordination is achieved among the departments. The functions of the local self-governing bodies are integrated with those of the district level departments under the leadership of the Collector. He also works as a linkman between the state government and the local bodies. This role has been reemphasized by the Second ARC (2009, 80), which recommends that steps be taken to ensure that the Collector plays an effective coordination role in activities and programmes of other departments at the district level.

Development Administrator

In the post-independence period, the Collector has been primarily concerned with the implementation of various development schemes. There are numerous programmes related to agriculture, irrigation, animal husbandry, education, health, etc. Beginning with the Community Development Programme (1952) a number of welfare programmes have been introduced for the benefit of weaker sections of society. It is the overall responsibility of the Collector, to facilitate developmental programmes and welfare schemes in the district.

Crisis Administrator

During a major crisis, like floods, droughts, earthquakes etc., the Collector assumes full charge of relief operations. All other departments are directed to assist him in relief management. In case of a famine, he is the chief authority under the Famine Code to undertake relief measures. Similarly, during floods, he has to organize rescue operations, take steps to check epidemics, call the army for help and supply food and essential items. It is during a crisis that the effectiveness and credibility of the district administration is put to test.

Connecting Link between the State Government and PRIs

The Collector acts as an effective link between the PRIs and state government. He can bring to the notice of the state government the people's felt needs and aspirations and endeavour to ensure that these are given due attention by different departments as well as get are reflected in the actions taken by the state government. (Biju 1998, 137–39).In general, the Collector is expected to see that the priorities and targets set by the state government are met by the PRIs through the people's active participation. Thus, he needs to do a lot of advocacy with the state government on behalf of the PRIs. At the same time, he has to play a coordinating role between the District Level Officers and their respective heads of departments.

Since the achievement of independence, and more particularly, since the advent of planned development, the country has looked to the district administration to serve as the principal instrument for the country's development. Its efficiency determines whether development really reaches the people. It is also the perspectives and approaches of the district administrators which, in many ways, determine the content of development. Whether development concentrates merely on rapid economic growth or extends to social reform, distributive justice and human resource development, depends in good measure on the attitude of the district administration.

The Second Administrative Reform Commission (ARC) (2006) made remarkable comments on the changing role and the current relevance of the institution of the Collector. It narrates that the post of the District Collector has been the most important feature of field administration in India for the last 200 years. Before Independence, when the economy was primarily agrarian, the Collector as head of the land revenue administration also enjoying wide powers under criminal laws, was considered the ultimate guardian figure—responsible for the well-being of residents in his jurisdiction—the representative of the British Empire, capable of doing anything and everything. In the post-independence era, when the economy diversified, and the pace of industrialization and the growth of tertiary activities picked up, other functionaries too gained in importance. But, even now, in most parts of the country, excepting the metropolitan/mega cities, the Collector is the most recognized face of the administration. He is considered to be the principal representative of the government at the district level, who could be approached to solve virtually all problems ranging from land disputes, to scarcity of essential commodities, to inadequacy of relief in times of crisis, to community disputes and even to issues of family discords.

CONCLUDING OBSERVATIONS

Thus, even after attaining independence, the Collector continues to be the most important as well as most sought after government official of district administration. In fact, the District Collector is the kingpin of district administration. However, his role has gradually changed from that of an able coordinator to that of a facilitator in the implementation of various development programmes. The focal point of district administration is the Collector and District Magistrate. He represents the government at the district level and it is his job to solve the grievances of the people and also to take the policies of the government to the people and ensure that the same do not remain on paper alone. He has to lead, coordinate, push and harmonize various departments and diverse aspects of the government functioning at the district level. These responsibilities amply justify his preeminence in the Indian administration. Thus, Rajni Kothari (1970) rightly observes: 'the office of the Collector as the Chief Representative of the Government in the District is, in many ways, unique and its supposed stature and authority have engendered a sort of institutionalized charisma that is in some ways unparalleled in modern administrative development'.

REVIEW QUESTIONS

1. Discuss the basic features of District administration in India.
2. Examine the organization and functions of District administration in India.
3. Write a note on the evolution of the institution of Collector in India.
4. Critically discuss the role of Collector in the Indian Administrative System.
5. The District collector is the eyes and ears of the state government. Discuss.
6. Examine the pattern of relationship between the Collector and the Panchayati Raj Institutions.
7. What are the main recommendations of the Second ARC on the role of the Collector?
8. Write an essay on democratic decentralization and the District Collector.
9. Excessive control of bureaucracy over local self-governing institutions leads to the demolition of autonomy of these local bodies. Discuss.
10. What are the main problems in the structure and functioning of the district administration in India? What are your suggestions to tackle them?

REFERENCES

ARC (The Second Administrative Reforms Commission). 2009, April. *Fifteenth Report: State and District Administration*. Government of India, New Delhi.

Desouza, Peter Ronald. 2002. 'Decentralization and Local Government: The "Second Wave" of Democracy in India'. In *India's Living Constitution: Ideas, Practices, Controversies,* edited by Zoya Hasan, E. Sridharan and R. Sudarshan, p. 371. New Delhi: Permanent Black.

Dubey, A. K. 1995. *District Administration in India*. New Delhi: Uppal Publishing House.

Kumar, Girish. 2006. *Local Democracy in India: Interpreting Decentralization*. New Delhi: SAGE.

Maheshwari, S. R. 2013. *Indian Administration,* 6th ed. New Delhi: Orient BlackSwan.

Report of the Indian Statutory Commission. 1930. His Majesty's Slationery Officer, vol. I, Survey, London.

Singh, Hoshiar. 1994. Aspects of Indian Administration. Jaipur: RBSA Publisher.

Singh, Pratap. 1997. *Legislative Status of Panchayati Raj in India: Major Issues*. New Delhi: IIPA.

Local Governance in India: Rural and Urban

6

LEARNING OBJECTIVES

1. To discuss the concept of local governance.
2. To know how democratic decentralization has paved the way for local governance in India.
3. To examine the impact of the 73rd Constitutional Amendment Act on Panchayati Raj institutions.
4. To explore the role and functions of urban local bodies in India.

Participation of people in the governance of a nation is the essence of democracy. Such participation is possible only when the powers of the state are decentralized to the districts, blocks and villages where people can sit together, discuss their problems and formulate as well as monitor the implementation of their programmes. Decentralization is a prime mechanism through which democracy becomes truly representative and responsive. Thus it is called the crux of democratic governance. India embarked on ambitious decentralization initiatives in the 1990s via a couple of landmark amendments to the Constitution (73rd and the 74th Constitution Amendment Acts) to reinforce local democracy by empowering local self-governing institutions in both rural and urban areas. The decentralization experiment in India, popularly known as 'democratic decentralization', has enabled self-governing local institutions to play a pivotal role in the provisioning of public services, creation and maintenance of public goods and the formulation and implementation of developmental activities.

The present chapter dwells on the concept of local governance, contribution of democratic decentralization via the 73rd and 74th Constitutional Amendments in strengthening local governance in India and the role of rural and urban local bodies in empowering people.

FROM GOVERNMENT TO LOCAL GOVERNANCE

There has been a shift from government to governance at the local level. Local governance or new local governance, as a few prefer to call it, can be defined as a process of governing at the cutting-edge level involving a huge constellation of agencies and actors including the conventional government, nongovernmental and quasi-governmental sectors, civil society organizations, business elites and so on. Decision-making processes in new local governance, unlike local government, are considered to be collaborative efforts with multiple agencies involved in the process as joint stakeholders. In other words, it has sought to curve out a new discursive space for nongovernmental organizations, self-help groups and people's initiatives within political society. In contrast to the local government, which used to be conceived in formal and legal institutions, new local governance has moved away from such formal and legal patterns. It works through open networks and fosters cooperation amongst diverse governmental as well as nongovernmental actors. The Second United Nations Conference on Human Settlements (Habitat II) in 1996 defines it as:

> Urban governance is the sum of the many ways individuals and institutions, public and private, plan and manage the common affairs of the city. It is a continuing process through which conflicting or diverse interests may be accommodated and cooperative action can be taken. It includes formal institutions as well as informal arrangements and the social capital of citizens. (Ruet and Lama-Rewal 2009, 9)

Based on the post-bureaucratic notion of an organization, the new local governance encourages networking and negotiations over formalism. Moreover, in new local governance, 'the traditional conduits of local politics and policy implementation', as rightly put by Raco and Imrie, 'have to coexist, collaborate and compete with a plethora of new agencies, networks and organizations, all jostling for resources, power and influence' (Raco and Imrie 1999). In addition to this, the new local governance has also welcomed the entry of business elites into the local decision-making process, which, is no doubt a redeeming feature of it. Business has a love–hate relationship with politics in a democratic set-up. Neither business houses nor politicians have ever felt comfortable about the interrelationship. In most cases the relationship is kept under the carpet. Local governance, by allowing business elites in the decision-making processes, takes the curtain off the discrete relationship between business and politics, and makes the process more transparent.

The new paradigm also calls for a host of structural, procedural and attitudinal changes for streamlining the process. Structurally, the paradigm of local governance seeks to transform the state-controlled bureaucratically managed local administration to a more flexible, market-based one. Maximum emphasis in the new local governance has been placed on decentralizing authority to local bodies, flattening of hierarchies, slimming of bureaucracy, etc. Apart from the administrative overhauling of the typically centralized local government, the new paradigm also advocates in favour of giving local bodies an extra ounce of financial freedom by slackening the stranglehold of state over local finance. Similarly, at the **procedural** level, the new paradigm is sought to bring about several procedural changes, namely contracting out of services, introduction of performance measurement techniques, introduction of quality assurance yardsticks like Quality Service Initiatives, Quality Circle, Total Quality Management, Citizen's Charter and so on.

Another important element of change that the new local governance wants to imbibe is **attitudinal** or perceptual changes in local government vis-à-vis the citizens. Citizens, especially those in post-colonial countries have so long been treated as passive recipient of goods and services. In the new local governance, citizens are viewed as the centre of the development discourse. Naturally traditional perceptions about the citizen have been redefined as one of 'active customers' who are to be always kept in good humour. Hence, serving citizens has become the central focus of administration. Consequently, the gap between the public and private gets increasingly blurred, thereby paving the way for greater Public–Private–NGO interface. In fact, the success of local governance is largely contingent upon attitudinal changes.

However, the winds of change in local governance as sketched briefly above, do not originate overnight. Several factors are responsible for this paradigm shift in local governance. Denters and Rose (2005) have categorized these factors into two broad categories, that is, the macro environment and the micro environment. In the macro environment, local governments have had to encounter three major forces, namely urbanization, globalization and Europeanization; and in the micro environment local government has had to function within an environment of heightened customer enlightenment, leading to an increasing demand overload (Denters and Rose 2005). Almost on a similar vein, Carolina Andrew and Michael Goldsmith (1998) argue that

> much of this process is the result of external changes over which individual local governments have had little influence: increasing economic interdependence; the process of globalization; changing technologies; or the fall of communism in Eastern Europe, for example ... And some will be generated from within local governments themselves, be they processes on delaying, privatization and contracting out of services; attempts at improving customer care and citizen relationships.

The above factors compel local governments to reorient and reinvent themselves with an evolving environment.

DECENTRALIZATION: A VEHICLE FOR LOCAL SELF-GOVERNANCE

The Concept

Conceptually speaking, at the heart of any decentralization scheme there exists a conscious effort of de-centring power (be it administrative, political or fiscal) with a view to improving the status of the people. The etymological root of the English word decentralization can be traced back to a Latin word, which means 'away from the centre'. It is also couched as the most valued antidote to authoritarianism and bureaucratization. As a flexible and fluid discourse, it suits every ideological pursuit. If one starts tracking the evolution of the concept of decentralization, he or she will find that the concept has no fixed ideological fountainhead. More interestingly, it has been used by both the left and right for their respective interests. While for the Rightists, decentralization is the mechanism to de-centre nation-states and thereby pave the way for marketization; whereas for the Leftists it provides the opportunity of social mobilization.

Decentralization is a broader concept, which encapsulates in fact all the above kinds of transfer of power. For example, Cheema and Rondenilli (1983) have defined decentralization as 'transfer of planning, decision-making or administrative authority from the central government to its field organizations, local administration units, semi-autonomous and para-statal organizations, local governments or NGOs' (Cheema and Rondenilli 1983). Moreover, decentralization is not a static arrangement of sharing administrative or fiscal authority. It is in fact a continuum, from centralization to full autonomy (Meenakshisundaram 1999).

Decentralization is also seen as a process of transfer of responsibility, authority and functions from a 'superior' governmental unit to a 'lower' governmental unit (Friedman 1983 as cited by Baldev Singh 1996, 12). These functions may relate to planning, management, resource raising and allocation. The operational jurisdiction of the 'superior' unit is obviously large. However, the 'lower' unit may exercise some degree of autonomy from the 'superior' unit. The study team on community projects and the National Extension Service appointed by the Government of India in 1957 defined decentralization as a process whereby the government diverts itself completely of certain duties and responsibilities and devolves them on to some other authority (Committee on Plan Projects 1957, 7). A decentralized local authority, in this sense, would have a separate legal existence, its own budget and the authority to allocate substantial resources on a range of different functions, and decisions would be made by the representatives of the local people, who constitute the body.

Main Characteristics of Decentralization

The concept of decentralization has the following characteristics: **First**, it is both a philosophy and an institutional mechanism, which seeks to de-centre power from its traditional centres to far-flung areas with a view to empowering local communities. **Second,** autonomy forms the heart of decentralization. It is the yardstick through which the nature of decentralization can be measured. **Third,** decentralization has no fixed ideological sanctuary; it is in fact used by both the Left and the Right for justifying their respective positions. **Fourth,** the recent spate of enthusiasm for decentralization can be attributed to globalization. The votaries of globalization are actively advocating localization through decentralization for development as the beleaguered nation-states of Asia, Africa and Latin America have been virtually relegated to mere economic agents of the global market. **Fifth**, decentralization facilitates people's participation by creating new institutional spaces beyond the centre and thereby ensures a further deepening of democracy. **Sixth**, decentralization also instils confidence amongst the local community for governing their own affairs.

Decentralization, thus, creates a sense of responsibility in local decision-making agencies with more or less independent existence and powers. The basic idea of decentralization is sharing the decision-making authority with lower levels in the organizations, thereby improving their efficiency, effectiveness and responsiveness.

Significance of Decentralization

Participation and control of governance by the people of any country is the essence of democracy. Such participation is possible only when the powers of the state are decentralized to the district, block and village levels wherein all sections of the people can sit together and discuss their problems as well as monitor the implementation of programmes. Decentralization is a prime mechanism through which democracy becomes truly representative and responsive. Thus it is called the crux of democratic decentralization. G. Shabbir Cheema and Dennis A. Rondenelli have identified the following advantages of decentralization:

1. Decentralization can be a means of overcoming the severe limitations of centrally controlled national planning by delegating greater authority for development, planning and management of field officials. Through decentralization, tailor-made plans according to the needs of heterogeneous regions and groups are possible.
2. It can cut through enormous amounts of red tape and highly structured procedures. By decentralizing functions and reassigning central officials to local levels, their knowledge of and sensitivity to local problems can be increased. It also ensures closer interaction between government officials and the local population.
3. Decentralization can allow for better political and administrative 'penetration' of national government policies into remote areas. Decentralization calls for greater representation of various political, social, ethnic and tribal groups in decision-making. It can increase the administrative capability of local institutions, government and private agencies, to take over some of the pertinent central government functions. It also relieves top management of their routine tasks.
4. Decentralization helps in institutionalizing the participation of citizens in development planning by creating alternative means of decision-making. It leads to a more flexible, innovative and creative administration that reduces the cost of planning and increases

the number of public goods. It also ensures political stability by increasing the participation of local people in decision-making.

Rajni Kothari sees decentralization as an alternative system of governance based on a 'people centred' approach to sorting out local-level problems. He argues that 'the entire process would be for locating people at the centre of power so that they become the basic engine of the development process and not, as hitherto, merely its beneficiaries' (Kothari 1999, 48).

Democratic Decentralization

The addition of the value-loaded prefix 'democratic' lends a special characteristic to the concept of decentralization. For, decentralization does not necessarily mean democratic nor does it have any intrinsic value attached to it. It could be used by a purely regimented system for administrative convenience (Jha and Mathur 1999). Therefore, decentralization should not be treated as an end in itself. In fact, it is the democratic ambience that makes decentralization an effective tool of empowerment.

Democratic decentralization in the context of developing countries has been conceptualized from two different perspectives, namely institutional and instrumental. From the instrumental perspective, democratic decentralization can be seen as an instrument of ensuring participatory development by empowering local communities. From an institutional perspective, it can be viewed as an institution of self-government. Hence decentralization is the mechanism or avenue through which the nature of local governance can be ascertained.

INDIA'S JOURNEY TO LOCAL GOVERNANCE

India has one of the oldest traditions of local self-governance, as the Panchayats or village councils have existed since ancient times. They were primarily the "informal bodies of village elders," assigned with different kinds of functions like provision of goods and services, maintenance of law and order, common welfare of villagers, and so on. These bodies enjoy a substantial amount of autonomy in terms of organization, functions and finance; bestowed upon them by village communities. Village communities have exercised virtually unmatched freedom of action in all spheres of governance. The uniqueness of this form of governance has been that it has absolutely spontaneous development and no external authority has ever devolved power and authority to these bodies. Moreover, there was no uniform pattern for this form of governance as village communities had no uniform pattern of organization (Srivastava 2002). The vibrant tradition of local democracy in India has remained almost unaffected and self-sufficient despite the vicissitude of political empires at the central level.

The successive Muslim invasions in India and the consequent beginning of Muslim rule did have very little impact on the functioning of these village communities. Even the Mughals, who had brought almost the entire subcontinent under one rule for the first time, were not keen on unravelling the localized form of governance either. Instead, they were mainly preoccupied with police and revenue matters and decided to settle them with the village headmen. Hence, the arrangement continued unaltered till the middle of the seventeenth century, despite several political vicissitudes at the central level. Even at the advent of British rule in India during the nineteenth century, this indigenous form of local governance was very much prevalent. Sir Charles Metcalfe's famous portrayal of this form of local governance before the

Select Committee of the House of Commons bears clear testimony to the tradition of local governance prevalent in ancient India. In his words:

> The village communities are little republics, having nearly everything they can want within themselves, and almost independent of any foreign relations. They seem to last where nothing else lasts. Dynasty after dynasty tumbles down; revolution succeeds to revolution; but the village community remains the same. This union of the village communities, each one forming a separate little state, in itself, has I conceive, contributed more than any other cause to the preservation of the people of India, through all the revolutions and changes which they have suffered, and is in a high degree conducive to their enjoyment of a great portion of freedom and independence. (Metcalfe as quoted by Srivastava 2002)

But there was no serious attempt as such to unlock the huge potential of these little village republics, either by the colonial rulers or by the post-colonial state, except a few polemics and individual efforts by a few visionaries like Tagore and Gandhi. The colonial rulers in India did absolutely nothing to resurrect these 'little village republics'. Colonial intervention in local governance was primarily driven by the twin motives of empire building and mercantilism. The colonizers had adopted a selective approach for local governance. In fact, in order to strengthen their objective of empire building, they built 'urban centres' like Calcutta, Bombay and Madras and left the rest of the country as the 'periphery', serving the 'centre' without having any kind of development.

The introduction of local government in rural areas through the Bengal Village Chowkidari Act, 1870 was far from the spirit of self-governing institutions. The underlying objective was solely to serve the interests of the Empire. The Act was introduced at a time when the Empire was reeling under severe challenges of governance in the wake of the Sepoy Mutiny of 1857. The colonial rulers had realized the danger of leaving sensitive issues like governance at the hands of the East India Company and took over the charge of the subcontinent in 1858. The Bengal Village Chowkidari Act, 1870 should therefore be viewed as a desperate effort on the part of the Empire to fortify British rule in India. The rural local government was mainly an offshoot of the Act. The real intention was to strengthen the economic and the security aspects of the Empire as the law had authorized the village panchayats to mop up local taxes for maintaining village chowkidars and also to set up reliable intelligence mechanisms deep into the countryside to keep a tab on the activities of the people. Naturally, whatever little rural reconstruction and urban development was done during the period, was basically a part of their housekeeping functions.

The British colonial state as a part of its housekeeping functions had adopted several Constitutional measures to streamline local self-government. Notable among them were the Ripon Resolution (1882), the Bengal Local Self-government Act (1885), the Bengal Village Self-government Act (1919), etc. Out of the said measures, the Bengal Village Self Government Act of 1919 may be regarded as the beginning of local self-government in India, providing a two-tier structure with union boards at the bottom level and district boards at the higher level. However, these self-governing structures were neither self nor local as these bodies were marked by perennial resource crunches, over-bureaucratization and dominance of the local landed gentry. They remained as mere appendages of the provincial government.

LOCAL GOVERNANCE: POST-INDEPENDENCE INITIATIVES

Independence brought a shift in power structure, but not in the attitude regarding local governance. Mahatma Gandhi also put forward a model of democratic decentralization suited to Indian conditions. Despite the repeated advocacy of Mahatma Gandhi for *Gram Swaraj,* it remained a far cry even in independent India. Inheriting the colonial mindset on local governance, the framers of the Constitution belied the hope of strong and vibrant local governance by confining it to a non-enforceable section of the Constitution, that is, the Directive Principles of the State Policy. In this context, the comments of two major architects of the modern Indian Constitution, as quoted by Baviskar and Mathew (2009), merit some space here as they adequately mirror the said elitist mentality, which prevented local governance in India the status it deserved in the Constitution.

'The love of the intellectual Indian for the village community', argued B. R. Ambedkar,

> [I]s of course infinite if not pathetic. It is largely due to the fulsome praise bestowed upon it by Metcalfe who described that they want within themselves, and almost independent of any foreign relation....That they have survived through all vicissitudes may be a fact. But mere survival has no value. The question is on what plane they have survived. Surely on a low, on a selfish level. I told that these village republics have been the ruination of India. I am therefore surprised that those who condemn provincialism and communalism should come forward as champions of the village. What is the village but a sink of localism, a den of ignorance, narrow-mindedness and Communalism? (Ambedkar as quoted by Baviskar and Mathew 2009)

Almost in similar vein, Nehru wrote, 'I do not understand why a village should necessarily embody truth and non-violence. A village, normally speaking, is backward intellectually and culturally and no progress can be made from a backward environment. Narrow-minded people are much more likely to be untruthful and violent' (Nehru as quoted by Baviskar and Mathew 2009).

Thus, India's dream of inclusive local governance had to wait for almost four decades before it was finally materialized in 1993. In the meantime, there were a few pioneering efforts, but they were mostly selective in nature, confined to the provincial level. Notable among them were Balwantrai Mehta Committee, Ashok Mehta committee and the democratic decentralization experiments by a handful of state governments like West Bengal, Karnataka, Kerala and so on.

Balwantrai Mehta Committee (1957)

The first major headway in institutionalizing panchayats came from an apparently non-related study by the Team for the Study of Community Projects and National Extension Service in 1957, popularly christened after the name of its Chairman Balwantrai Mehta. Though the study was originally intended to assess community development initiatives and to recommend improvement measures thereon, the findings, however, suggested the necessity of strengthening the panchayats for institutionalizing community participation in the Community Development Programme (CDP). The committee recommended a three-tier system of rural local government, that is, village panchayats at the village level, the panchayats samiti at the intermediate level and zilla parishad at the district level; with panchayats samitis being the most effective body.

However, the Balwantrai Mehta Committee Report failed to rejuvenate panchayats as the institutions of local governance. A couple of factors can be identified for the same and include: First, the motive behind the study was more to legitimize central government-led development programmes than to establish panchayats as real bodies of community participation. Second, the embedded elitist apathy regarding panchayats amongst the government and the administration was also factored in the failure of Balwantrai Mehta Committee.

Ashok Mehta Committee (1978)

Another Committee, which deserves special mention in the evolution of rural local government in India is the Ashok Mehta Committee. The Committee was appointed to inquire into the working of PRIs and to suggest measures to strengthen them. The Ashok Mehta Committee felt that a combination of factors had conspired to undermine PRIs, such as an unsympathetic bureaucracy, absence of political will, lack of involvement in planning and implementation on a substantial scale, and the domination of local institutions by the economic and social rural elite (Desouza 2002, 371).

The Committee underscored the functional necessity of decentralization and recommended a two tier system for the Panchayati Raj institutions. The Committee also recommended that the district needed to be the basic unit of administration since it was a viable administrative unit for which planning, coordination and resource allocation was feasible and for which technical expertise was also available. The Ashok Mehta Committee was the first to demand constitutional recognition for panchayats. The Committee even drafted a model Bill, which they appended with the report, seeking an amendment to the Constitution along the same lines (Kumar 2006, 23).

The Janata Party did not stay in power long enough to implement the decisions of the Ashok Mehta Committee, and reportedly, in an initial meeting, the recommendations of the Committee were not received well by the state governments (Sethi 1989). However, the influence of the report of this Committee has been significant. In fact, the states of Karnataka, Andhra Pradesh and West Bengal passed new legislations based on the Ashok Mehta Committee Report.

RURAL LOCAL GOVERNANCE

Panchayati Raj Institutions (PRIs)

Panchayati Raj Institutions (PRIs), as stated earlier, are the institutionalized pan-Indian form of rural local governance, and came into existence with the passage of 73rd Constitution (Amendment) Act, 1992. The Act heralded a three-tier structure of rural local governance—Gram Panchayats at the bottom level, Panchayat Samitis at the intermediate level and Zilla Parishads at the highest level.

The Seventy-third (73rd) Constitutional Amendment Act, 1992

The 73rd Constitutional Amendment Act, 1992 is considered to be a watershed in the history of local government in India. It virtually salvaged the age-old tradition and institution of local governance from a dependent status to one of self-reliance by conferring the much coveted constitutional status on it. Until the passage of the 73rd Constitutional Amendment Act, states were the only sub-national units officially recognized by the Indian Constitution. The provision for local government remained under the state list and hence there was no uniform pattern of it across the country. The Act heralded a three-tier system of Panchayati Raj Institutions across the country. The functional domain of rural local bodies was limited largely to the provisioning of some core services such as water supply, sanitation, local roads, etc. The 'developmental' activities were limited to the role of implementing developmental schemes sponsored by either the central or state the governments. The passage of the Act empowered local bodies to formulate and implement development plans of their own.

The Context

The legislative origins of the 73rd Constitutional Amendment Act can be traced back to the Constitution (64th Amendment) Bill, which was introduced in the parliament in 1989 by the government of the then Prime Minister Rajiv Gandhi. The introduction of the Bill was perhaps the first attempt to confer constitutional status on rural local governments. Though the bill failed to clear the test of the Rajya Sabha, its broader objective of reviving the country's century-old institutions of rural local self-government was highly appreciated. The major reservation against the said Bill was that it provided very little space for state governments regarding local governance. However, after much deliberation, the issue of conferring constitutional status on rural local governments came into being with the passage of the 73rd Constitution (Amendment) Act, 1992.

Though the manifest reason behind the Act was to bring about an efficient delivery mechanism for development, there were serious political compulsions before the political leadership to bring forward the issue of local democracy. For, the decades of 1970s and 1980s had witnessed several anti-establishment movements on the basis of ethnic, religious, linguistic identities across the country. The militant secessionist movements of the North-eastern states, Punjab, Northern hilly tract of West Bengal; and the demand for separate statehood in Bihar and Uttar Pradesh had challenged the credibility of the Indian state to govern. Under the circumstance, sharing the power with communities at the grass root level was conceived as a desperate attempt to release the mounting pressure on the Indian state. Moreover, this policy of decentralization was hailed because it was felt that it would substantially downsize the powers of the opposition-ruled recalcitrant and demanding state governments, and establish a direct linkage with District Collectors and the Panchayati Raj bodies, bypassing state governments (Bandopadhayay, Ghosh and Ghosh 2003).

Main Features of the 73rd Amendment Act

Whatever be the motive behind the constitutionalization of the panchayats, the Act changed the very contour of local governance at the rural level. Some of the redeeming features of the Act are as follows:

- The Act has heralded a three-tier Panchayati Raj Institutions with Zilla Parishad at the top, the Panchayat Samitis at the intermediate level and village Panchayats at the bottom.
- The Act has clearly devolved power, authority and responsibilities to rural local bodies to enable them to function as the institutions of self-government (Article 243G).
- The Act has made it mandatory for all levels of PRIs to conduct periodic elections every five years. In case of early or premature dismissals of PRIs, elections are to be held within a period of six months, with the newly elected members serving out the remainder of The five-year term (Article 243E).
- the Act has also made provisions for the reservation of seats for the scheduled castes and tribes in all panchayats at all levels in proportion to their respective shares in the Panchayat concerned. In addition to that, the Act also made mandatory reservation of

one-third of all seats in all panchayats at all level for women, of which one-third are to be reserved for the women belonging to schedule castes and tribes. The constitutional provision for the reservation of seats for scheduled castes and tribes also extends to the position of panchayats chairpersons at all three tiers of the PRIs with one-third mandatory reservation earmarked for them.

- The Act has stipulated the constitution of a state level Election Commission for a period of five year to ensure free and fair elections in local bodies.
- The Act also empowered the state government to constitute another independent state-level commission, that is, the Finance Commission for five years to review the overall financial position of local bodies and recommend the principle that should govern the allocation of funds and taxation authority to local bodies. The Governor of the state has been entrusted with the power of constituting the Finance Commission, which will review the financial positions of the panchayats and make recommendations thereon to the Governor.
- The Act also made provisions for the constitution of Gram Sabhas—the body of the electorate of the gram panchayats and established a more direct channel for people's participation. The underlying rationale was that the Gram Sabha would function as a fulcrum of the development process, where the community would participate both in the formulation and in the implementation of development plans. Moreover, this body would function as organs of local accountability and oversight.
- The 11th Schedule (Article 243G) has been added which gives the list of 29 functions to be performed by the PRI.

According to Article 243(G) of the Act, 'Panchayats shall be given powers and authority to function as institutions of self-government'. This would be done by delegating powers and responsibilities to panchayats at the appropriate level such as: (a) preparation of plans for economic development and social justice and (b) implementation of schemes for economic development. Art 243(H) authorizes a Panchayat to levy, collect and appropriate taxes, tolls and fees. These two articles clearly lay out the powers, authority and responsibilities of panchayats vis-à-vis the state governments. They empower rural local bodies to play a pivotal role in the provisioning of public services, creation and maintenance of local public goods and planning and implementation of development activities and programmes to alleviate poverty and promote distributive equality.

Working of the Panchayati Raj System

It is evident from the above discussion that there are some radical provisions in the 73rd Amendment Act. They seek to address some of the problems encountered by PRIs in previous years, such as, (a) granting PRIs constitutional status, (b) empowering socially and economically disadvantaged groups, that is, Dalits, adivasis and women (c) ensuring free, fair and regular elections (d) keeping terms fixed (e) identifying a list of items which would fall under the jurisdiction of PRIs and (f) addressing the issue of PRI finances (Desouza 2002, 379). Thus the Act has provided for a significant degree of fiscal, administrative and political decentralization from the state to the local levels.

Now that such a democratic decentralization experiment is with us for more than two decades, it is necessary to evaluate the experiment, which is often euphemistically called as a 'silent revolution'. In this section we interrogate the democratic decentralization experiment by asking a few important questions: Are we really ready for decentralization? Is democratic decentralization an end in itself? Does democratic decentralization truly empower the local community? The above questions require a lot of introspection. In this section we critically appraise the role of democratic decentralization in delivering development and social justice.

Weaknesses of the Panchayati Raj System

Despite much accolade and fanfare, the PRIs seem to have failed to bring about the much needed transformation in India society and polity. In fact, several shortcomings have surfaced within a decade of their functioning. **First**, the panchayat as the institution of local self-government has been suffering from an identity crisis because the meaning of self-government has not been clearly articulated. **Second**, the PRIs inherited a culture of subservience, deliberately inculcated by the colonial era, going against the complete realization of decentralization in post independent India. **Third**, though the new PRIs have an avowed stand on gender empowerment, as the 73rd Constitutional Amendment Act envisages one-third reservation for women, in reality, however, panchayats are witnessing a typical phenomenon of proxy participation, where male members of the women candidates wield power on her behalf. The infamous *pradhan-pati* syndrome is a case in point. **Fourth**, another major weakness of this system is the overpoliticization of the panchayats. In a parliamentary democracy, thanks to being in power for many years, often panchayat administration and party administration have become identical and inseparable, leading thereby to an overlap of responsibilities. Consequently, panchayat administration has become the extended branch of party administration as the same set of persons simultaneously discharge both the duties, leading thereby to a lot of confusion. However, politicization is nothing unique, as the Indian Panchayati Raj system has allowed political mobilization. In a democratic system, competitive political mobilization could have enhanced the status of the community, if political parties were allowed to mobilize freely. For, in this system, political parties are always needed to outpace their contenders by improving the quality of services. Distortions occur only when any political party or combination of parties hold powers unilaterally for a long time. **Fifth**, over reliance on the PRIs as the institutions of local governance, often leads to 'system overloads' as too many development projects vie for attention in the panchayats. **Sixth**, a strong centralizing tendency with the centrality of the development state has been implicit in the decentralization initiatives in independent India. Starting from the Balwantrai Mehta Committee to the recent 73rd Constitution Amendment Act, there has been a distinct tradition of centralization of power.

The functioning of the new Panchayati Raj system reveals the fact that although legislative and electoral formalities have been completed in almost all the states, at the operational level, there are large variations among them. The 29 subjects mentioned in the 11th schedule do not give the power to legislate to the local bodies, but only to take decisions. The State Finance Commission's recommendations are not mandatory in nature. It is completely up to the state government whether it wants to devolve or not to devolve the functions, functionaries and resources to the local bodies as per the constitutional scheme. As of 2007, only 3 of India's 28 states had passed executive orders devolving all 29 functions to the local level, as required by the Constitutional Amendment (Government of India 2008b). The high handedness of bureaucracy, with a few exceptions, over local autonomy still prevails. The experience gained so far is that, at the district level, various departments and agencies still implement programmes and functions under the overall supervision and control of the District Collectors. The PRIs, therefore, have to be content with backseat driving (Vithal 1997, 12).

The experience of democratic decentralization makes it clear that it cannot be a solution to one and all ills of governance. Rigid patriarchal structures inhibit the participation of backward castes and women in village governance. The 73rd Amendment stipulates that one third of all panchayat seats be 'reserved' for women, with a similar provision for the scheduled castes and tribes. In North India, where caste and gender inequalities are particularly resilient, local elites have tended to adapt this requirement by putting up 'proxy' candidates from the required groups, and continue to wield power through them. The submissive female sarpanch; sitting quietly in a corner while her husband (often initially mistaken for the sarpanch) answers the questions, is a familiar figure in the critical literature on Panchayati Raj in North India (Dreze and Sen 2002, 362). Moreover, a majority of the elected representatives are first timers with little or no prior knowledge of the functioning of PRIs. It is not easy for rural weaker sections to actively participate in the development process. The literacy level amongst SC/ST and women is quite low. The distribution of rural assets and powers is heavily skewed in India with the bottom 39 per cent of rural households (belonging to lower castes) owning only 5 per cent of all assets, while the top 5 per cent own 46 per cent of all assets. This makes the opportunities and social choice shrink for the really deprived villages at the grassroots.

Inadequate financial resources are another crucial constraint in the effective functioning of decentralized governance. The panchayats have to depend on the devolutions and the grants-in-aid from the state governments and they have not developed any independent sources to raise revenues. Besides, most states have not transferred funds for the subjects transferred to these local bodies. A study of 12 states has shown that, in nine of these, the tax revenue of the local bodies (both panchayats and urban local bodies) was less than 5 per cent of the total tax revenue of the state government (National Commission to Review the Working of the Constitution 2001, 29). Limited fiscal autonomy of the panchayats renders them excessively dependent on the Central and state governments.

The constraints and problems that mark democratic decentralization initiatives are myriad but should not create a panic, as the country at the moment is passing through a transitory phase and any kind of transition takes time bring forth show positive results. It is a fact that a silent revolution is taking place in rural India where people are becoming conscious of their rights. One of the most heartening aspects of the Panchayati Raj experiment has been the inclusion and participation of variously disadvantaged groups such as the Dalits, Adivasis and women. It is unarguable that the provisioning of quotas has generated widespread awareness. Studies have shown that the development outcomes in panchayats headed by women are impressive, even if empowerment impacts have been rather slower in materializing. (Jayal 2007, 13).The renewed movement towards democratic decentralization has eroded bureaucratic monopoly over the development processes and has shifted the locus of power to those who matter at the grassroots level.

The new Panchayati Raj system represents an institutional watershed which has brought 'the people' back into the political processes at the grass roots level. People have been given a voice. This voice, even in a situation of pervasive asymmetric power, will result in a flattening of the asymmetry, a process that can have only emancipatory consequences. To paraphrase B. B. Baviskar 'the 73rd Amendment Act can rightly be termed as "a silent revolution", which in many respect salvaged the institution of self-government from a mere "agent" of provincial government to one of "self-reliant" one' (Baviskar and Matthew 2009).

URBAN LOCAL GOVERNANCE

Structure

Unlike the rural governance, urban governance is not hierarchical. Article 243Q of the 74th Amendment Act, 1992 (which came into force in 1993) stipulates that there shall be three types of urban local bodies in India, namely nagar panchayats for transitional areas; municipal councils or municipalities for smaller urban areas and municipal corporations for larger urban areas. State governments are allowed to design their own Municipal Acts in accordance with the broad parameters outlined in the 74th Amendment Act.

Functions

Article 243W of the Constitution deals with the 'power, authority and responsibilities of municipalities', which clearly lays out the functions of municipalities including the list of functions enumerated in the 12th Schedule. The details of those functions are stipulated in the 12th Schedule of the Constitution as below.

Urban planning, including town planning; regulation of land use and construction of buildings; planning for economic and social development; roads and bridges; water supply for domestic, industrial and commercial purpose; public health, sanitation, conservancy and solid waste management; fire services; urban forestry, protection of the environment and promotion of ecological aspects; safeguarding the interests of weaker sections of society, including the handicapped and mentally retarded; slum improvement and upgradation; urban poverty alleviation; provision of urban amenities and facilities such as parks, gardens and playgrounds; promotion of cultural, educational and aesthetic aspects; burials and burial grounds; cremations, cremation grounds and electric crematoriums; cattle pounds; prevention of cruelty to animals; vital statistics including registration of births and deaths; public amenities including street lighting, parking lots, bus stops and public conveniences; regulation of slaughter houses and tanneries.

The 74th Amendment Act, 1992: Main Provisions

The 74th Amendment Act, 1992 ushered in a new phase of urban governance in India. However, it has a striking similarity with the 73rd Constitutional Amendment Act, 1992. This Act is incorporated in article 243 Part—IX A of the Indian Constitution. Major provisions of the Act are as follows:

- Urban Local Bodies, to be known as Municipal Corporations, Municipal Councils and Nagar Panchayats, depending on the population, shall be constituted through universal adult franchise in each notified urban area of the country.
- These shall be constituted for a period of five years.
- Not less than one-third of the total number of seats in each urban local body shall be reserved for women.
- These bodies shall be endowed with the power and authority to formulate and implement schemes for economic development and social justice on 18 subjects.
- In order that urban local bodies can perform the functions assigned to them, the legislature of a state shall assign to them specific taxes, duties, tolls and levies and authorize them to impose, collect and appropriate the same.
- Each state shall also constitute a Finance Commission which shall review the financial position of urban local bodies and recommend the principles which should govern the devolution of resources including grants-in-aid from the consolidated funds of the state of these bodies.
- The superintendence, direction and control of the preparation of electoral rolls for, and the conduct of, all election to the urban local bodies shall vest in the State Election Commission.

- The Act has made provisions for the constitution of Ward Committees in all municipalities with a population of three lakhs and more.
- District Planning Committees and Metropolitan Planning Committees shall be constituted to prepare a development plan.

The 74th Amendment Act thus gives constitutional status to the municipalities. It seeks to redefine their role; power, function and finances. This has ushered in a new era of urban governance and urban management in India. The Act is significant because apart from the traditional functions, it allocates to the municipal bodies the function of economic development and social justice, which suggests their elevation from being mere instruments for 'agency functions' to responsible bodies for development planning. The provision of State-Level Finance Commission is a landmark step in the direction of providing financial autonomy to Urban Local Bodies. Reservation of seats especially for women ensures the participation of socially deprived sections of society.

The new Act has become an instrument of political education. In the context of urban politics, people are learning to organize, to question established patterns of authority, to demand their rights, to resist corruption and so on. This learning process enhances their preparedness not only for local democracy alone, but also for political participation in general.

Major Challenges for Urban Local Governance

The 74th Amendment Act has surely revived urban local bodies in India, but they still face a number of problems. The first and most serious problem facing the urban local bodies is the acute scarcity of finance. In the absence of proper funds, powers become meaningless because the same cannot be translated into real efforts and outcomes. The new Act provides for the constitution of a State Finance Commission to look into the financial sources of local bodies, but the recommendations of the Commission are not binding on the respective states. People's participation in urban bodies is still negligible. A major cause of this kind of attitude is that people look towards municipal bodies with inherent suspicion and take it for granted that their problems and grievances will not be taken care of. Moreover, like the 11th Schedule, there is no clear demarcation of functions between different local units of urban local government, leaving it to the respective state. This has given the states the liberty to impose their own choices in this regard, which has at times created more confusion than order, regarding what is to be delegated and what is not.

In the changing scenario, Urban Local Bodies need to exclusively devote themselves to the task of development, and therefore should enjoy a large measure of autonomy. But the ground reality depicts a contrary picture. Criticizing the 74th Amendment Act, Nirmal Mukherjee argues that 'it is almost a carbon copy of the 73rd Amendment Act' and 'a hasty afterthought'. Comparing it with the 73rd Amendment Act he further notes that 'it looks as if some independent thinking went into the panchayat law and then, one day, the municipality *wallah*s suddenly woke up and said "we too, please" and were simply served the panchayat dish with municipal sauce'. Second, it 'thoughtlessly constitutionalizes as artificial dichotomy between rural and urban when all previous thinking has stressed a continuum between the two' (Mukherjee 1999). Another myopia with the Act is the 'panchayats for rural areas' bias or panchayats are locked into a 'rural only' bind. Besides the above issues, urban governance is facing new challenges as a result of the processes of liberalization, privatization, globalization and urbanization.

IMPLICATIONS OF THE 73rd AND 74th AMENDMENT ACTS

The Acts as mentioned earlier are phenomenal in many respects. In this section we specifically highlight some of the implications:

Constitutional Status

The first and foremost implication of the 73rd and 74th Amendment Acts is the conferment of constitutional status on local governments. Initially, the Constitution of India did not confer any special status on local governments except an entry in the state list of the Seventh Schedule of the Constitution and a specific Article in the Directive Principles of State Policy, expecting state governments to take initiatives for organizing panchayats.

Until recently, there was no uniform pattern of local self-governments across the country. The formation and nurturing of local governments was completely a matter of good will on the part of state governments. With the passing of the Acts, it has become mandatory for state governments to construct rural and urban local governments. Hence, the constitutionalization of rural and urban local governments has engendered an exclusive legislative domain for local governments or what is known as the 'third stratum' of government (Mukherjee 1999), paving the way for a direct linkage between the governance process and the community per se.

Administrative Powers

The Acts have provided much needed administrative autonomy in terms of functional devolution to both the urban and rural local bodies. For long, local bodies were considered as mere 'agents' of the state governments. They did not have any authority of taking administrative decisions independent of state control. But the new Acts have enabled local governments to manage their own affairs. For instance, the authority of local bodies to superintend overall development of the area concerned may be mentioned, which includes among others, the preparation of plans for economic development and social justice, implementation of various developmental schemes or any other developmental initiatives as the local bodies deem necessary.

Financial Autonomy

Another important implication of the said Acts is financial autonomy which is the sine qua non of any organization. Local bodies in India were known for their perennial financial stringency. The Acts have virtually salvaged cash-strapped local bodies (including both the urban and rural institutions) with substantial financial authority. For example, the new Acts have allowed panchayats and municipalities to mobilize their own resources, apart from the normal sources of finance, that is, the grants-in-aids, which they usually receive from the government.

The Act also have provisions for the mandatory constitution of State Finance Commission by state governments once in every five years to review the comparative financial positions of local bodies and to make recommendations to the state government on the following issues: (a) the distribution between the state and the local bodies (panchayats and municipalities) of the net proceeds of the taxes, duties, tolls and fees leviable by the state, which may be divided between them under this part and the allocation between local bodies (panchayats and municipalities) at all levels, respective shares of such proceeds; (b) the determination of the taxes, duties, tolls and fees which may be assigned to, or appropriated by the local bodies (panchayats & municipalities) and (c) the grants-in-aids to local bodies (panchayats and municipalities) from the consolidated fund of the state.

Transparency in Governance

Nowadays, transparency has become the buzzword. It is now considered to be a necessary precondition for ensuring integrity in local government and an inseparable element of good governance. Thus, the fourth significant implication of the Act is that it has brought transparency in governance. The Acts under consideration have also given due importance to the transparency factor. Article 243 J of the 73rd Amendment Act and Article 243 Z of 74th Amendment Act mention the provisions for the mandatory audit of accounts of panchayats and municipalities respectively.

Accountability in Governance

As a result of these amendments, local bodies are now accountable to fulfil the aspirations of the people. They have been assigned powers and functions to solve the problems at the grass root level.

Deepening of Democracy

It is often said that the secret formula behind the success of Indian democracy lies in the embeddedness of the democratic spirit of Indian society. The new Acts by setting up all-inclusive popular bodies, that is, the Gram Sabha at the bottom level (and the Gram Sansad below the Gram Sabha in the case of West Bengal) in case of panchayats and the Ward Committee in the case of municipalities, have paved the way for greater penetration of democracy into the interstices of Indian society. Moreover, the new Acts have regularized the election process across the country. Prior to the Acts, elections in these local bodies were more or less voluntary. Barring a few instances, they were in most cases occasional and sporadic. The new Acts have clearly stated that elections to the local bodies are to be held every five years. If a panchayat or municipality is dissolved prematurely, elections need to be held within six months, with the newly elected members serving out the remainder of the five-year term.

Gender Empowerment

Another redeeming feature of the new Acts is the institutionalization of the participation of women via the reservation of seats in the local bodies. Women folk in India, especially in rural India have been subject to systematic and systemic exploitation by the patriarchy. They have been systematically 'excluded' from the corridors of power. The Acts have substantially elevated the status of Indian women from that of being subjugated to being self-reliant. The Acts have stipulated in categorical terms that 'not less than one third of the total number of seats to be filled by direct election in every panchayats shall be reserved for women'.

There is no denying that in an unequal patriarchal society like ours, reservation of seats for women has invariably uplifted the status of women. However, it should not be taken as *the* way of empowering women. It is only a step towards empowerment, not empowerment in itself, as is often mistakenly equated. The issue of reservation boils down to an irreducible duality between differences versus equality. Feminist epistemology seems to have been caught in this perennial dilemma. Putting it bluntly, the debate rather centres around whether women should struggle for equal rights or valorize their differences from men folk and thus ask for preferential treatment.

Empowerment of the Disadvantaged

It is quite fashionable these days to talk about 'inclusive development', which calls for an all-embracing formula and framework of development so that the disadvantaged sections are not left out at the margin. Modern political philosophers like Ronald Dworkin, John Rawls et al have justified, at least in essence, the necessity of inclusive development in their argument for equity and social justice. A considerable portion of our Constitution has been devoted to the upliftment of the scheduled castes, scheduled tribes and other backward classes. In addition to that, the new Acts have enabled the least advantaged sections (i.e., the scheduled castes and scheduled tribes) to have a greater chance of representation at the local bodies by reserving one third seats for them in both urban and rural local bodies.

Popular Participation

The said Acts have institutionalized popular participation in local governance. The introduction of the 'participatory development' as an alternative paradigm of development in the 73rd and the 74th Constitutional Amendment Act, 1992 is a case in point. The Acts have formalized popular participation through the mandatory construction of Gram Sabhas or Ward Committees at the bottom level.

Decentralized Planning

Another important hallmark of the new Acts is the introduction of decentralized planning process. For long, planning was couched as a highly technical job, to be carried out by a group of seasoned mandarins. But of late, the notion of planning has undergone a sea change as now the 'bottom-up' approach is being favoured to the conventional 'top-down' model. Government efforts at decentralization of planning are becoming evident in both rural and urban local bodies. In case of rural local bodies, state-initiated rural development through scheme-based activities with the participation of the people in implementing these activities has been reversed and replaced by people-initiated rural development programmes with the participation of the government (Palanithurai 2005). People are now couched as the stakeholders of development. Article 243G of the Constitutional Amendment Act, for example, has recognized the panchayats as 'institutions of self-government' and entrusted to them the responsibilities of preparing plans for promoting economic development and social justice.

The State Panchayat Act has at least formally given the necessary powers and functions to the panchayats to formulate plans. However, barring a few states like Kerala, Karnataka and Tamil Nadu, the track record of grass-root planning in the rest of the country is anything but inspiring. In fact, Kerala has taken a giant stride in this direction. For example, Kerala's much hyped 'people's campaign for the Ninth Plan could be mentioned here. Under the programme, the panchayats were entrusted to prepare and prioritize projects in an integrated and scientific manner. The programme also ensured maximum participation of local people at every stage of the planning process. The decentralized planning model is not confined to panchayats alone. The 74th Amendment Act has also made some provisions for decentralized planning via a few structural innovations like Metropolitan Planning Committee, District Planning Committee, etc.

CIVIL SOCIETY: FACILITATING PEOPLE'S PARTICIPATION IN LOCAL GOVERNANCE

As already discussed, civil society is an important actor of local governance as it ensures people's participation in local governance. The following section deals with the crucial role played by various civil society actors.

Role of Civil Society in Rural Development

Rural development has a typical statist bias. Until recently, it was considered as a state-led and state-induced development programme. But of late, courtesy the neoliberal 'recipe' of rolling back the state and the consequent unification of markets, it was found that state was no longer in a position to carry forward the huge task of community development single-handedly. Confusions reigned supreme as a virtual battery of scholars soon plunged into the scene. A host of possibilities were conjured up which ranged from 'rural development sans state paradigm' to an eventual eclipse of rural development. But history proved those 'prophecies' false as rural development as a policy showed no sign of receding, even though countries like India had already entered the third generation of economic reforms. Quite to the contrary, rural development in India has been experiencing an altogether new paradigm of a GO–NGO–People-centric model, ever since she has plunged into being a free market economy.

Under the new circumstances, the importance of NGOs or civil society organizations has increased exponentially. Under the new paradigm, the NGOs and people are taken as joint stakeholders of development along with the seasoned campaigner state. Traditionally, the interaction between the state and voluntary organizations was either absent or was more of a regulatory nature. They were not considered as 'equal partners' in the nation-building process. Their activities remained confined to relief and welfare alone. However, the new paradigm calls for a consortium of government and nongovernment institutions with their common pool of resources to cater to the rural people. Nongovernmental organizations are therefore supposed to supplement and complement the state in the process of rural development. Together, they can effectively attain the larger goal of people's empowerment and integrated rural development for which the country has been struggling for decades. The 73rd Constitutional Amendment Acts 1992 (came into force in 1993) further endorsed 'the complementarities' between voluntary organizations and the panchayats in rural development.

Role of Civil Society in Urban Development

The very contour of urban governance has also undergone a sea change over the last couple of decades, thanks to the sweeping economic, political and social transformation in the wake of globalization. With the progressive dissolution of trade and tariff barriers across the globe and the resultant networking of global markets, cities are now emerging as 'management hubs' or 'logistic centres' (Harris 2003) in a 'Borderless World' (Ohmae 1994). Hence, urban governance, which was for long considered as an exclusive preserve of the state, is now being seen as a collaborative effort of all the stakeholders in the urban space, with each having their respective roles to assert (Kundu and Kundu 2004). The underlying impetus, however, comes from the *New Right movement* and its prescription of 'rolling back the state'. Hence, there has been a partnership between the state, the markets and the NGOs sector in the name of Public–Private Partnership (PPP).

NEW DIMENSIONS OF LOCAL GOVERNANCE

In the wake of globalization, local democracy faces new issues and challenges. The following section deals with such issues and the response of local institutions and people to the new challenges.

The Global–Local Debate

The global–local debate refers to an ongoing debate regarding development at the local levels. The basic debate is about what should be the guiding principles of local development, local ideas and innovations or external technology and expertise. There are two views on the same. According to the first view, locally developed technologies and arrangements are more convenient to local development. They believe that local arrangement is based on the idea of immediateness and relevance. They argue that local requirements vary from place to place. There are different cultures, traditions and ways of life, and hence a uniform arrangement is not applicable to all.

Supporters of the idea of localism believe that locally developed solutions gain high acceptance and suit the local requirements. In such arrangements people feel a sense of belonging, so they are always ready to implement the idea. Their active cooperation, readiness and enthusiasm become the main vehicle for the implementation of programmes. In this system, local knowledge and resources are employed in a more meaningful way, which saves time and resources required for training for the implementation of programmes. Locally arranged models ensure greater participation and give a feeling of empowerment to the people. Thus under this scheme, problems can be identified quickly and responsive and sensitive solutions are possible.

The supporters of the global idea believe that today the world is like a global village and local problems can be solved more effectively and economically with the help of external expertise and technology. They argue that local efforts are not sufficient for rapid development which is the need of the hour. Thus, to fulfil the requirements of a growing population new and advanced technologies are needed, which is only possible through global support and collaboration. Neglecting the present realities is myopic as well as extremely risky from the view point of local development. If we keep ourselves within our boundaries and never think beyond that, we are depriving ourselves of new experiences, knowledge and innovations. Such a kind of thinking will keep us backward in our approach and action, and is not fruitful for local development.

The above debate makes it clear that local problems can be solved better with local solutions. Local arrangements are better accepted by people, ensuring greater participation and effective implementation of programmes. There is a sense of belonging and participation amongst the people. So, this approach is more participatory, effective and economical in addressing local issues. But at the same time the changing circumstances need to be kept in mind. Today we are in a globalized world and today's citizens are global citizens. There are a number of problems and challenges which can only be resolved by global efforts and cooperation. Terrorism, global warming, climate change, border conflicts, new diseases like cancer, AIDS, swine flu etc. are a few examples in this regard. These issues can only be resolved by international efforts. So today, we cannot keep ourselves aloof.

As far as the application and adoption of external technology and resources at the local level is concerned, some precautions need to be taken. That technology and knowledge which suits our local needs and circumstances could be adopted. It also needs to be in accordance to our culture, values and traditions. Before adopting such technology, the local people should be taken into confidence. It should be implemented only when the local people are convinced that it is going to help them. Thus, global ideas and experiences have to be participatory, sensitive and accommodative to local needs and requirements. In this way the local–global debate can be converted into a fruitful, productive and constructive approach for promoting development in the local area.

New Localism

The concept of 'New Localism' owes its popularity to the United Kingdom and to the policy changes announced by former Prime Minister Tony Blair in the early 2000s. It represented the devolution of power to local governmental agencies, but only within a framework of national priorities and goals. Of importance, and what has particularly characterized the movement as new, is the continued primacy of the Central government in setting the agenda that surrounds local autonomy and action (Crowson and Goldring 200, 2). Thus, it was introduced as a cautious devolution of power to the local level in an attempt to implement national goals in a more coordinated and uniform way.

'New Localism' primarily evolved to provide a uniform agenda and framework for local governance throughout the UK. The specific focus of localism in the UK included the freedom to meet central goals in health care and education and in improving the overall responsiveness of public services to children and family needs. Accompanying elements of the new localism are the notions that there should be reductions in central governmental approval functions, much more neighbourhood governance and direct engagement in implementing national goals, responsiveness to client needs and desires and an encouragement of local authorities to wrap multiple services around shared problems, like health, employment, education and the police.

Thus, New Localism is a cautious devolution of power to local bodies in order to implement national policies in a better way. It is new in two ways. First, it recognizes the role of the Central government in bringing changes at the local level, something that was strongly resisted by local people in the 1980s in the UK. Second, besides local institutions, it involves local communities and voluntary agencies in the provisioning of services to the people. Thus, it is more accommodative and participatory in nature.

Thus, the concept of New Localism is not a denial and refutation of national goals, policies and reform measures. It is, rather, a refocusing of attention upon the local districts, communities and neighbourhoods in the context of national and even global objectives. In this sense it is an arrangement where urban local governance is provided with a uniform framework under an order of the Central government. Thus, New Localism has emerged from a realization of the limitations of centrally driven policy implementation. It recognizes that local problems cannot be solved by standardized policies imposed from above, and that local institutions need space to adapt and innovate within the public policy process. Thus, it is a pragmatic response to the complexities and diversities at the grassroots level.

Urban Development Dynamics

There are a number of factors and forces which have changed the nature and character of cities in the last three decades, particularly in India. Liberalization, privatization, globalization and urbanization are the significant ones. Different studies indicate the new development dynamics and its ramifications on the cities and its people. Some of the work locates the intensification of urban exclusion as a result of the systematic deployment of neoliberalism as a structural adjustment policy (Davis 2004; Harvey 2008), others understand it within the rubric of socioeconomic changes ushered in by globalization (Appadurai 2002; Broudehoux 2009) and yet others see it as the rise of a new bourgeois governmentality in urban governance (Baviskar 2003). In 'The Urbanization of the Empire', Mike David (2004) argues that structural adjustment policies imposed forcibly on the Third World have destroyed import substitution industrialization, shrunk public sector jobs by ushering in waves of privatization, and decimated the rural sector as well. The result is an increase in urban unemployment, rural to urban migration and further pressures on urban informal jobs. The consequence has been the emergence of a new form of imperialism that colonizes the urban poor of the world through joblessness, poverty and informalization.

Within India, Mahadevia (2002) describes a desperate entrepreneurial urge on the part of civic governments to become 'world class' by emulating the cityscapes of the First World. She indicates a rapid transfer of municipal budgets from social infrastructure towards beautification and slum eviction, a trend that she refers to as 'Manhattanization'. The 'purified spaces' of the 'beautified city' normalize a 'bourgeois urbanism' (Chatterjee 2004) that informalizes labour, legitimizes the downward spiral of wages, sharpens socioeconomic inequalities and institutionalizes displacement and social exclusion of minority groups. Another study shows that in the name of making the Capital City clean and green, lakhs of industries were closed and relocated from Delhi. The process has made a majority of workers jobless, declined their bargaining capacity, forced them to work in a more exploitative market economy and brought with it isolation, frustration and social tension for the working classes and their families (Prakash 2012, 50). Thus workers have had to pay a high price for a 'clean' Delhi.

CONCLUDING OBSERVATIONS

In the foregoing analysis, an attempt has been made to situate the wave of decentralization that has been sweeping across since the 1990s. Decentralization has been identified as one of the important prerequisites of good governance. Traditionally it was conceptualized as an organizational innovation to ease off the pressure of an over-bureaucratized public organization. But with the onset of globalization, the concept of decentralization has become the surrogate of markets. The new local governance involves a multiple of actors for service delivery to the people. It has transformed governance into a more participatory, transparent and accountable system.

India embarked upon the decentralization experiment in 1992, through a couple of path-breaking legislations. The 73rd and 74th Amendment Acts have been appreciated for bringing about tectonic shifts at the subterranean level of Indian polity. They have transformed the very complexion of local governance from that of a subjugated status to one of self-reliance. These amendments have accorded constitutional recognition to rural and urban local bodies. They have addressed the persistent problems of irregular elections, suppression, inadequate representation, insufficient devolution of power, lack of administrative and financial autonomy and inadequate resources. The new process has democratized local self-governments in the rural and urban areas and brought substantive democracy at the grass roots level.

It was expected that with the constitutional empowerment of local bodies in 1992, the very complexion of local governance would be transformed. However, reality resurfaced soon after the initial hype died down in the form of overpoliticization, lack of accountability, lack of clarity in the delegation of power and authority, state intervention and the resultant lop-sided developments. Hence to make local governments true self-governing institutions, the following steps need to be taken: **First**, people need to be properly mobilized to shoulder the responsibility of governing themselves. In most cases, the necessity of self-rule is felt by the academics or planners, and then imposed upon the people from above. To make local governance truly participatory, the opinion of the people concerned needs to be honoured. **Second**, the so-called third stratum needs to be strengthened by ushering in multi-level partnerships at the sub-state level by harnessing several stakeholders of development including the government, nongovernmental sectors, civil society organizations and private business houses. **Third**, local governance needs to be seen from a holistic perspective, where rural and urban self-governing institutions are not treated in a compartmentalized way. Rural and urban development cannot be conceptually segregated, as the success of one is squarely contingent upon the success of the other. Hence, we should look beyond the 'rural or urban only bias' of the Constitution amendment acts.

REVIEW QUESTIONS

1. What is decentralization? Discuss the significance and approaches to decentralization.
2. Decentralization leads to greater democratization of administration. Discuss.
3. Distinguish between delegation and decentralization. Discuss the merits and demerits of decentralization.
4. What is democratic decentralization? Examine democratic decentralization in the context of 73rd Constitutional Amendment Act for panchayats.
5. Analyze the functional and fiscal decentralization of administration in the context of rural India.
6. Discuss the problems in the process of decentralization in rural administration.
7. What are the main features of the 74th Amendment Act?
8. Discuss the implications of the 73rd and 74th Amendment Acts.
9. Critically examine the functioning of Panchayati Raj institutions in India.
10. Briefly examine the major rural–urban development programmes and their management in India.

REFERENCES

Andrew, Caroline, and Michael Goldsmith. 1998. 'From Local Government to Local Governance: And beyond?' *International Political Science Review* 19 (2): 101–17.

Appadurai, A. 2002. 'Deep Democracy: Urban Governmentality and the Horizon of Politics', *Public Culture* 14 (1): 21–47.

Broudehoux, A. 2009. 'Seeds of Dissent: The Politics of Resistence to Beijing's Olympic Redevelopment', in *Dissent and Cultural Resistance in Asia's Cities*, edited by M. Butcher and S. Velayutham, pp. 14–32. London and New York: Routledge.

Baviskar, A. 2003. 'Between Violence and Desire: Space, Power and Identity in the Making of Metropolitan Delhi', *International Social Science Journal* 55: 89–98.

Baviskar, B. S., and George Mathew (eds). 2009. *Inclusion And Exclusion in Local Governance—Field Studies from Rural India*. New Delhi: SAGE.

Chand, P. 2012. "Implications of Industrial Relocation on Workers in Delhi". *Social Change*, 42 (1) March: 49–68.

Chatterjee, P. 2004. *The Politics of the Governed: Reflections on Popular Politics in Most of the World*. New York: Columbia University Press.

Cheema, G. S. and D. A. Rondinelli (eds). 1983. *Decentralization and Development: Implementation in Developing countries*. Beverly Hills, California: SAGE.

Crowson, Robert L. and Ellen B. Goldring. 2010. *The New Localism in American Education*. San Francisco: Wiley-Blackwell.

Davis, M. 2004."The Urbanization of the Empire: Mega Cities and the Laws of Chaos," *Social Text 81*, 22 (4) Winter: 9–15.

Denters, Bas, and Lawrence E. Rose. 2005. *Comparing Local Governance—Trends and Developments*. New York: Palgrave Macmillan.

Desouza, Peter Ronald. 2002. 'Decentralization and Local Government: The "Second Wave" of Democracy in India'. In *India's Living Constitution: Ideas, Practices, Controversies*, edited by Zoya Hasan, E. Sridharan and R. Sudarshan, p. 371. New Delhi: Permanent Black.

Dreze, Jean, and Amartya Sen. 2002. *India: Development and Participation*. New Delhi: Oxford.

Harris, Nigel. 2003, 21 June. 'Globalization and the Management of Indian Cities'. *Economic and Political Weekly* XXXVIII (25).

Harvey, D. F. 2008. "Right to the City", *New Left Review, 53* (September–October): 23–40.

Jayal, Niraja Gopal. 2007. *Local Governance in India: Decentralization and Beyond*. New Delhi: Oxford.

Jha, S. N., and P. C. Mathur, eds. 1999. *Decentralization and Local Politics*. New Delhi: SAGE.

Mahadevia, D. 2002. "Communal Space over Life Space", *Economic and Political Weekly*, November 30, 2002.

Kumar, Girish. 2006. *Local Democracy in India: Interpreting Decentralization*. New Delhi: SAGE.

Meenakshisundaram, S. S. 1999. 'Decentralization in Developing Countries'. In *Decentralization and Local* Politics, edited by S. N. Jha and P. C. Mathur, p. 68. New Delhi: SAGE.

Mukherjee, Nirmal. 1999. 'The Third Stratum'. In *Decentralization and Local Politics*, edited by S. N. Jha and P. C. Mathur. New Delhi: SAGE.

National Commission to Review the Working of the Constitution. 2001. 'Review of the Working of the Constitutional Provisions for Decentralization (Panchayats)'. Consultation Paper, New Delhi.

Ohmae, Kenichi. 1994. *The Borderless World: Power and Strategy in Global Marketplace*. London: HarperCollins.

Palanithurai, G. 2005. 'Development Roles Reversed: People's Initiative and Government's Participation'. In *Decentralization and Local Governance*, edited by L. C. Jain, p. 123. New Delhi: Orient Longman.

Raco, Mike, and Rob Imrie. 1999. 'How New is the New Local Governance? Lessons from the United Kingdom'. *Transactions of the Institute of British Geographers*, New Series 24 (1): 45–63. Retrieved 6 May 2008, from http://www.jstor.org/stable/623344

Ruet, Joel, and S. T. Lama-Rewal, eds. 2009. *Governing India's Metropolises*. London: Routledge.

Singh, Baldev. 1996. *Decentralization, Panchayati Raj and District Planning*. New Delhi: Atlantic Publisher and Distributers.

Srivastava, Ravi. 2002. *Evaluation of Anti-poverty Programmes In Uttar Pradesh: Study Report*. New Commission.

Vithal, B. P. R. 1997. 'Evolving Trends in the Bureaucracy'. In *State and Politics in India,* edited by Partha Chatterjee. New Delhi: Oxford University Press.

7

Civil Services in India

LEARNING OBJECTIVES

1. To know the evolution of the civil services in India.
2. To understand the changes in civil services in the post-independence era.
3. To examine civil service reforms in India.
4. To explore the contribution of the Indian Civil Services.

The administration of a country is run by officials who are called civil servants. In real terms, civil servants form the 'heart of public administration'. Hence, it is important to appoint the right kind of civil servants and to set up appropriate public organizations where civil servants are placed on recruitment and training. This chapter deals with the evolution, importance, constitutional base, recruitment, training, promotion and code of conduct of the civil services in India. It also discusses other important issues related to the civil services like their staff associations, political rights, employer–employee relations, grievance redressal mechanism, civil services neutrality, civil service activism and constitutional protection to civil servants. Finally, the chapter concludes with the recommendations of recent Committees and Commissions for making the civil services an efficient mechanism to serve the people.

CIVIL SERVICE, PUBLIC SERVICE AND BUREAUCRACY: DIFFERENT CONNOTATIONS

In common practice, the terms 'civil service', 'public service' and 'bureaucracy' are often used interchangeably with each other. It will be useful here to understand the connotation expressed by each of them. The original use of the term 'bureaucracy' referred to a cloth that covered the desks of eighteenth-century French officials. It was a way of describing a government ruled by officials. Over time, the term 'bureaucracy' acquired a negative connotation. It was used to describe procedures which were unreasonably time-consuming, and led to the harassment of people and the petty tyranny of officials (Das 2013, vii). Because of the negative connotation associated with bureaucracy, the term 'civil servant' came to be used instead.

There is very little difference between a bureaucrat and a civil servant, although the latter also means a full-time employee of the government. The term 'civil service', as it is used now, has two distinct meanings. First, it is a branch of the governmental service in which individuals are employed on the basis of merit as tested in an examination. Second, it refers to a body of employees in any government agency other than the military and the judiciary (Das 2013, viii). Thus, the term 'civil service' primarily refers to government officials appointed on the basis of merit tested by an examination.

While the civil service is a more restrictive term, 'public service' refers to a system of employment maintained by the government for supplying essential services or commodities (Maheshwary 2013, 280). In that sense, all government employees including the military and the judiciary are members of the public service. Civil servants are public servants also, but judges and military officers are not necessarily civil servants. Thus, the term 'public service' is much broader than civil service.

CIVIL SERVICES IN INDIA: AN EVOLUTIONARY PERSPECTIVE

Civil services in India evolved during the colonial period, first during the company rule, and then during the direct British government rule. All Company servants, to start with, came from England and had to execute a covenant before coming to India to the effect that they would serve the Company with good conduct and be loyal, and hence the usage, 'Covenanted Service'. There was no concept of an office, only a variety of tasks were given to the servants of the Company.

By 1765, the term 'civil servant' started appearing in the records of the East India Company to describe its officials. This was done to distinguish between those engaged in civil and military activities. Before that, the lowest functionary of the East India Company was called a 'factor', meaning a commercial agent. The trading station where the factors worked was called a 'factory'. In 1765, the Company ordered for only writers (clerks appointed by the company) to be recruited, and the point of entry to the civil service of the East India Company became that of the 'writer'. To be appointed as a writer, it was necessary to get a nomination from a director of the Company, which used to be made only on financial considerations (Das 2013, 13). This practice encouraged corruption, which became such a scandal that the British Parliament had to intervene and pass the Charter Act of 1793, which made it mandatory for the directors of the company to take an oath that they would not make any nomination in exchange of money or gifts.

The Indians had no place in the public services till 1833. The Select Committee 1831–32, under the chairmanship of Thomas B. Macaulay, dealt with the issue of Indianization. The committee wanted that Indians also be admitted to the higher civil services which would strengthen their attachment to British domination and lead to considerable savings in the expenses of the Government. The Charter Act of 1833 provided that no man shall be, by reason of his religion, place of birth, descent, colour or any of them, disqualified from holding any place, office or employment under the Company.

In 1837, an amendment bill allowed the company board to adopt limited competition as the basis for selection. The Board of Directors used their patronage till 1853. The Macaulay Committee was appointed in 1853, which strongly recommended the open competition system for recruitment to the civil services and listed the subjects to be offered in the competitive examination. It also recommended the age of 18–23 years for admission to the tests. The examinations were to be held in London. Consequently, the first examination under the new system for recruitment to the Indian civil service was held in 1855. The merit-based system put in place in 1855 by implementing the Macaulay Committee continues to the present day.

CIVIL SERVICES UNDER THE BRITISH CROWN

The East India Company's rule came to an end in 1858 and the British Crown assumed direct responsibility for the Government of India. With the transfer of power to the Crown, the Services were also brought under its control. The Act of 1858 gave the responsibility to determine the conditions of services to the Governor-General-in-Council. The 1861 Indian Civil Service (ICS) Act created a schedule of positions which were to be filled, under normal conditions, through a competitive examination. In 1878, the Secretary of State ordered that each member of the Covenanted Civil Service would be bound to serve anywhere in India. In this way, these services became All India Services.

The Atchison Commission of 1887 divided the public services into three categories: The Imperial Services for which appointments were made by the Secretary of State in England, the Provincial Services for which appointments were made by the provincial governments but with the approval of the Government of India, and the Subordinate Services comprising Lower level employees who also were appointed by the provincial governments.

The Mont–Ford Report (1918) suggested increasing the association of Indians with every department of administration. The Government of India Act, 1919 introduced the decentralization of administration by transferring certain subjects to the provinces placed under the control of Indian ministers. In 1921, it was found that Indians accounted only about 13 per cent of the Indian Civil Service. It gave further impetus to the demand for more Indianization of the services. At the time of the introduction of dyarchy, there were nine All India Services. The Government of India Act, 1919 provided for the establishment of the Public Service Commission of five members based on the British model to conduct examinations in India for recruitment to the All India Services. In 1921, in addition to the written examinations, a viva-voce examination was introduced.

On the basis of the recommendations of the Lee Commission (1923), the recruitment and control of the Central Services was delegated to the Government of India. The 1935 Act provided elaborate safeguards to secure in part that the existing civil servants did not suffer due to political changes more than what was inevitable, and in part that future servants would be recruited under conditions which as far as possible maintained sound traditions (Keith 414). The Act further provided for the establishment of a Federal Public Service Commission for two or more provinces.

The question of retention of the All India Services again comes up for discussion in 1946 when Indian independence was close at hand. As the interim government assumed power on 2 September 1946, the question came up whether a central or provincial civil service (PCS) should replace the ICS. Sardar Patel, the Home Minister, was aware of the need for increased provincial autonomy, but was afraid of 'provincial susceptibilities'. Thus, he successfully argued for a Central Service which would be efficient, impartial and free from local and communal bias, party allegiances or political influence (Mishra 1997, 301). A quota of 25 per cent was set for promotions from the PCS to the Indian Administrative Service, the successor to the ICS. Article 312 of the Constitution of independent India regularized the existence of two All India Services, namely the Indian Administrative Service (IAS) and the Indian Police Service (IPS) (Tummala 1996, 36). It also included provision for the creation of the new All India Services. Thus, a new chapter began in the history of the Indian Civil Services.

CIVIL SERVICES IN INDEPENDENT INDIA

When India became independent, many things changed, but the basic framework of the Civil Services continues. The ICS was succeeded by the Indian Administrative Service (IAS). In post-independence India, the IAS has emerged as an elite corps to man important decision-making positions in the administrative system. The pattern of IAS supremacy is also visible in the state government and local bodies. Today, the IAS is the core of the country's administrative structure, sharing its tasks with a number of All India, Central and State services, providing strong administrative links throughout the country. The following is the present classification of the Civil Services in India:

1. All India Services
2. Central Services
3. State Services

This section will deal with the structure and classification of the All India and Central Civil Services.

ALL INDIA SERVICES: THE STEEL FRAME OF INDIAN ADMINISTRATION

All India Services are those services which are common to both the central and state governments. Presently, India has three All India Services, namely the Indian Administrative Service (IAS), the Indian Police Service (IPS), and the Indian Forest Service (IFS). The Constitution under Article 312 contains the provision for setting up of the All India Services. The following arguments can be put forward in the favour of the All India Services:

1. Mechanism of promoting national integration
2. Providing a national vision of development
3. Ensuring uniform administrative systems
4. Coordinating the link between the Centre and the states
5. Providing independent and impartial civil services at the national level
6. Sharing the rich experience amongst different states

Recruitment and Placement

The All India Services and the Central Services in India are recruited on the basis of open national level competitive examinations conducted by the UPSC. There is a provision for the reservation of posts to the extent of 50 per cent in all categories of the civil services for those belonging to the Scheduled Castes, Scheduled Tribes and Other Backward Classes.

The officers of the All India Services serve the Central government, Union territories as well as state governments. The Ministry of Personnel, Public Grievances and Pension is the Cadre controlling authority for these services. The authorized strength of the Indian Administrative Service in 2011 was 6077, while the actual serving officers in the service were 4356 (Government of India 2010).

The Indian Administrative Service (IAS) is the most important among all the services in the country. This is partly because of the advantage that the IAS enjoys over other civil services in pay scales and faster promotions, and partly from the job content of the positions that their officers hold. The IAS officers, on their appointment, are allotted to a particular state. It is in this state that they specialize and learn the language of the state, customs, laws, and so on, and pass examinations in these subjects. All their postings in the field such as in the subdivision, district, etc., are in the same state. A part of their career is usually spent in the Central Government (Das 2013, 32). Important posts in the states are reserved for the IAS in order to promote quality, impartiality, integrity and an all India outlook in the administrative system.

The Central Civil Services

The Central Services belong to the Central government and serve different departments of the Central government. Their personnel are controlled by their respective ministries or departments. The members of the Central Services serve in the Central Government and the offices of the Central Government in the states and union territories. Unlike the All India Services, Central Service officials do not work under the state governments while working in the states.

The Central Services in India have four classifications: Group A, Group B, Group C and Group D. Group A comprises 59 important services which includes the Indian Foreign Service, the Indian Audit and Accounts Service, the Indian Postal Service, and the Central Secretariat Service. Group B consists of 33 corresponding services to Group A. Recruitment to Group A and B services are done by the UPSC. The Group C Central services consist of clerical personnel and their recruitment is done by the Staff Selections Commission. Group D consists of manual personnel like peons, gardeners etc. Thus, Group A and Group B comprise gazetted officers while Group C and Group D are the non-gazetted class.

A New Pattern of the Civil Services Examination

The scheme for the Civil Services Examination till 2011 was what was in vogue since 1979 (post Kothari Committee). Based on Professor S. K. Khanna's—former Vice Chairman, UGC Committee—recommendations, the scheme of the Civil Services (Prelims) Examination was changed from the year 2011. The Union Public Service Commission, subsequently formed another Committee headed by Professor Arun S. Nigavekar, as a continuum to the recommendations of the Professor Khanna Committee. The Commission's recommendations on the Nigavekar Committee (2011) for considering changes in the scheme of the Civil Services (Main) Examination was considered by the Government and accordingly a revised format of the Civil Services (Main) Examination, was implemented from the year 2013.

To become a part of the Indian Civil Service, the candidate has to be an Indian. The age limit for Indian Civil Services as on January 2015 was 21–30 years and the upper age limit was relaxed for SC/ST candidates by five years. Candidates possessing a degree of any of the universities recognized by the government are eligible for appearing in the examination. The examination is conducted annually. The competitive examination comprises three successive stages:

1. Preliminary examination (objective)
2. Main examination (written)
3. Interview

The Preliminary Examination

The preliminary examination is meant to serve as a screening test only. In 2011, the pattern of the preliminary examination was drastically modified, scaling up the marks for General Studies from 150 to 200 and replacing the paper on an optional subject with a CSAT of 200 marks. The current (2015) examination consists of the following two papers:

1. Paper I-General Studies ——— 200 marks
2. Paper II-Civil Service Aptitude Test (CSAT) ——— 200 marks

Both these papers are objective with multiple-choice questions set both in English and Hindi. Each paper is of two-hour duration and those who clear the exam appear in the main examination.

Main Examination

Only those candidates who qualify in the preliminary test appear in the main examination. The number of candidates to be admitted to the main exam is about 12 to 13 times the total number of vacancies to be filled in that year. The written examination consists of seven papers (see Table 7.1).

The UPSC has revised the pattern of the Civil Services Main examination from 2014. It is now designed to test the academic talent of the aspirant, along with his ability to present his knowledge in a clear and coherent manner. The main examination is intended to assess the overall intellectual traits and depth of understanding of the candidates rather than merely the range of their information and memory.

Now there are nine papers to be answered in the main examination. All of them are descriptive in nature. There are two qualifying papers: (a) any modern Indian language and (b) English, and these are of 300 marks each. These marks are not counted in the main examination. The candidate is allowed to use any one language from the Eighth Schedule of the Constitution or English as the medium of writing in the examination.

According to the new pattern, there are 'four' General Studies papers, 250 marks each totalling to 1000 marks. The scope of the syllabus of General Studies is of degree level. There is only 'one' optional subject to choose from the list of subjects. It comprises of two papers, 300 marks each. So, the total marks for the optional papers is 600. The scope of the syllabus of the optional papers is higher than the Bachelor's degree but lower than the Master's degree. The total marks for the written examination is 1750. The interview/personality test is of 275 marks.

Table 7.1 Papers to Be Counted for Merit

Paper	Subject Name	Marks
Paper-1	Essay	250
Paper-2	General Studies–I (Indian Heritage and Culture, History and Geography of the World and Society)	250
Paper-3	General Studies–II (Governance, Constitution, Polity, Social Justice and International relations)	250
Paper-4	General Studies–III (Technology, Economic Development, Bio-diversity, Environment, Security and Disaster Management)	250
Paper-5	General Studies–IV (Ethics, Integrity and Aptitude)	250
Paper-6	Optional Subject–Paper 1	250
Paper-7	Optional Subject–Paper 2	250
	Sub Total (Written test)	1750
	Personality Test	275
	Grand Total	2025

Source: http://civilservicesmentor.com/mag/new-ias-mains-scheme (accessed on 14 December 2015).

Interview

The interview/personality test is for 275 marks and the candidates can give their language preference for the same. The UPSC makes arrangements for the translators.

The candidate will be interviewed by a Board which has before them a record of the candidate's career. He will be asked questions on matters of general interest. The object of the interview is to assess the personal suitability of the candidate for a career in the public services by a Board of competent and unbiased observers. The test is intended to judge the mental calibre of a candidate. In broad terms, it is really an assessment of not only his intellectual qualities but also his social traits and interest in current affairs. Some of the qualities to be judged include mental alertness, critical powers of assimilation, clear and logical exposition, balance of judgement, variety and depth of interest, ability for social cohesion and leadership, intellectual and moral integrity.

THE UNION PUBLIC SERVICE COMMISSION (UPSC): RECRUITMENT BODY

Historical Background

The Indianization of the superior Civil Services became one of the major demands of the political movement compelling the British Indian Government to consider setting up of a Public Service Commission for recruitment to its services in the territory. The first Public Service Commission was set up on 1 October 1926. However, its limited advisory functions failed to satisfy the people's aspirations and continued stress on this aspect by the leaders of our freedom movement resulted in the setting up of the Federal Public Service Commission under the Government of India Act 1935. Under this Act, for the first time, provision was also made for the formation of Public Service Commissions at the provincial level.

The Constituent Assembly, after independence, saw the need for giving a secure and autonomous status to the Public Service Commissions both at the federal and provincial levels for ensuring unbiased recruitment to the Civil Services as also for the protection of interest of the service. With the promulgation of the new Constitution for independent India on 26 January 1950, the Federal Public Service Commission was accorded constitutional status as an autonomous entity and given the title—Union Public Service Commission.

Constitutional Provisions

The Union Public Service Commission has been established under Article 315 of the Constitution of India. The Commission consists of a chairman and 10 members. The terms and conditions of the service of the chairman and members of the Commission are governed by the Union Public Service Commission (Members) Regulations, 1969. The Commission is serviced by a Secretariat headed by a Secretary with two Additional Secretaries, a number of Joint Secretaries, Deputy Secretaries and other supporting staff.

The Union Public Service Commission has been entrusted with the following duties and roles under the Constitution:

1. recruitment to services and posts under the Union by conducting competitive examinations,

2. recruitment to services and posts under the Central Government by a selection process through interviews,
3. advising on the suitability of officers for appointment on promotion as well as transfers-on-deputation,
4. advising the government on all matters relating to methods of recruitment to various services and posts,
5. disciplinary cases relating to different civil services and
6. miscellaneous matters relating to the grant of extra ordinary pensions, reimbursement of legal expenses, etc.

The major role played by the Commission is to select persons to man the various Central Civil Services and posts and services common to the Union and States (the All India Services). The composition of the Commission includes 10 members along with its chairman.

Training of Civil Services

After independence, the IAS training school was set up in Metcalfe House in Delhi, where all the probationers were imparted one-year training. On the basis of the recommendations made by the Appleby Report (1953), the Indian Institute of Public Administration was set up in 1954. This was followed by the establishment of the National Academy of Administration at Mussoorie in 1959 with the merger of the Training School in Delhi and the IAS Staff College in Shimla. In 1985, a new Ministry of Personnel, Public Grievances and Pension, was created with the Department of Personnel and Training as one of its three departments.

Currently, all Group A services are required to undergo a two-year induction training. The content of the training programme varies from service to service. Induction training for the All India Services and Central Services Group A consists of a Foundation Course and a Professional Course. The Foundation Course is common to the IAS, IPS and other Central Services Group A. For the non-Group A services, the pattern varies. While some have mandatory induction training, others do not and report directly to their departments for their posting. The latter are expected to learn on the job.

In-service Training

The training given to civil servants is of two kinds namely, in-service training and mid-career training. Foundation and Professional Training are part of the in-service trainings. The Foundation Course provides the foundation for a career in the public service. It is a bridge between the academic world of college education and the actual field. Spread over a period of 15 weeks, this course is conducted at the Lal Bahadur Shastri National Academy of Administration, Mussoorie. A major portion of the training period (12 out of 15 weeks) is devoted to course work with three weeks to village study and extracurricular activities like trekking and river rafting, essentially aimed at developing leadership qualities and team spirit. The subjects taught include management, economics, public administration, law, politics, Constitution of India, Indian history and culture. All officers belonging to the All India Services and the Central Group A, recruited by the UPSC through the Civil Service Examination, have to undergo Foundation Training.

Professional training for other services focuses on more subject-specific inputs keeping in mind future requirements of the civil servants. For example, Income Tax officers are imparted 16 months training at the National Institute of Direct Taxes in Nagpur. After professional training, the officers go for an eight to ten weeks on-the-job training. Similarly, training for the Customs and Excise officers is imparted at the National Academy of Customs Excise and Narcotics, Faridabad.

Mid-career Training

Mid-career training is given in-between the service after gaining some experience. The purpose of such training is to refresh and update civil servants about their field and area of specialization. Both the National Academies at Mussoorie and Hyderabad impart such training to IAS and IPS officers respectively. For example the Mussoorie Academy runs a six-week refresher course for civil servants having a seniority of 10–15 years.

Managing Personnel Issues

Any country whose administration is run on the basis of the merit principle requires an efficient personnel management policy. Timely resolution of issues related to promotion, financial issues, and other grievances protects the rights of the civil services as well motivates them to serve the people in a better way. This section deals with such related issues of the civil services.

Promotions

Promotion criteria covering the higher Civil Services in India are set by the UPSC. There are time bound promotions for the IAS and officers of the Central Civil Services. An IAS officer begins his career in the state with two years in probation. This period is spent at training schools, the Secretariat, or field offices. He is given the position of Deputy Magistrate and has to look after law and order and general administration including developmental work in the area under his charge.

After the probation and two years of services as a Junior Scale Officer, an IAS officer is put in the senior scale. Then he may function as District Magistrate or Director of a Department. Senior Scale comprises Senior Time Scale (Joint Secretary), Junior Administrative Grade (Additional Secretary) and Selection Grade (Special Secretary). Selection Grade is given on promotion after 13 years of regular service. The next promotion within the state is that of a Commissioner-cum-Secretary after 16 years. This promotion also entitles them to Super Time Scale. Then after 25 years of regular service, an IAS officer may be promoted to above super time scale which is designated as Principal Secretaries or Financial Commissioners in some states. Each state has many Secretaries/Principal Secretaries and only one Chief Secretary. The Chief Secretary in the state is the top ranking civil servant and may be assisted by Additional Chief Secretaries. Thus, there are better promotion avenues for higher civil services in India.

Civil Service Code of Conduct

The goal of this code of conduct is to establish norms of conduct for the civil service and inform citizens about the conduct that the civil servants need to have for the purpose of improving the quality of the civil service; ensuring better administration in promoting public interest;

contributing to the prevention and elimination of bureaucracy and corruption in public administration, as well as creating an environment that enhances citizens' trust in public authority.

Based on the recommendations of the Committee on Prevention of Corruption (1964) headed by Shri K. Santhanam, the conduct rules for government servants were revised with a view to maintaining integrity in the public services. The Central Civil Services (Conduct) Rules, 1964 were notified laying down the code of conduct for Central government employees. The Commission recommended that every government servant shall at all times:

1. Maintain absolute integrity.
2. Maintain devotion to duty.
3. Do nothing which is unbecoming of a government servant.
4. Every Government servant holding a supervisory post shall take all possible steps to ensure the integrity and devotion to duty of all government servants for the time being under his control and authority.
5. No Government servant shall, in the performance of his official duties, or in the exercise of powers conferred on him, act otherwise than in his best judgement except when he is acting under the direction of his official superior.
6. The direction of the official superior shall ordinarily be in writing. Oral direction to subordinates shall be avoided, as far as possible. Where the issue of oral direction becomes unavoidable, the official superior shall confirm it in writing immediately thereafter.

Thus, the codes of conduct are guidelines for civil servants to make them accountable to the people and for performing their duties with devotion and integrity.

POLITICAL RIGHTS OF CIVIL SERVANTS

Civil servants in India have rights to vote and form associations, but they are prohibited from participating in political activities. They can neither become member of a political party nor subscribe to its funds. The objective behind this is to keep the civil services neutral and unbiased in delivering services to the people. Whatever political party comes into power, civil servants have to be loyal to the government and to the objectives of the Constitution. Thus, civil servants have the right to vote and the right to form organizations for fulfilling their professional objectives, but not the right to take part in active politics of the country.

Civil Service Neutrality

Neutrality is the hallmark of the civil services in India. It means that a civil servant must not identify himself with political parties and their groups and preserve their neutrality in matter of public policies. They are required to serve whosoever occupies the office of the minister. Civil servants not only implement policies and decisions by the political masters but they also advise them on policy-making. They can play this role better only when they observe complete neutrality in political matters.

Civil Service Activism

Civil service activism is about the extra ordinary role of a civil servant played for protecting the interest of the common masses. It includes regular meetings with the people, asking about their grievances and helping them as quickly as possible. Sometimes innovative reform programmes are initiated to address public issues. It is also about taking strict action even against the policies of their own minister that go against his constitutionally allocated duties. Steps taken by T. N. Seshan for electoral reforms and those for police reforms initiated by Kiran Bedi are good examples of civil service activism.

Civil Service Reforms

Reforms are an obvious response to the new challenges confronting state institutions managing public affairs. At the root of such an exercise lie efforts at enhancing administrative capabilities in the changed scenario. In recent times, the problem of administrative reforms has received continuing attention in India both at the Centre and in the states. In the 1996 Conference of Chief Secretaries, it was unanimously decided to address the administrative ills that appeared to have seriously handicapped Indian administration. It was further highlighted that one of the major factors for the failure of administration was the indifferent attitude that bureaucracy had displayed while dealing with delivery of basic services to the citizenry. Being bogged down by procedure-orientation, sluggishness, corruption and non-accountability for results, bureaucracy in India became alienated from the people to a significant extent. In the light of the discussion in the Conference, it was also agreed upon to institute instruments of accountability, such as grievance-redressal mechanism, the citizens' charter, an inter-ministerial working group on the Right to Information and Transparency, meaningful civil service reform, among others. As a follow-up of the measures that the Chief Secretaries Conference suggested, the Chief Ministers Conference, held on May 27, 1997 evolved an Action Plan to overhaul civil services to (a) make administration accountable and citizen-friendly, (b) implement the Right to Information to ascertain transparency in administration, and (c) improve the performance and integrity of public services.

As a checklist of items, the Action Plan is drawn on the primary concern to improve administration which was reportedly neither citizen-centric nor adapted to the changing socio-economic circumstances. Hence it was not possible for the administration to function as an effective aid for governance presumably because administration seemed to have become a captive of vested interests. The idea was to change not only the texture public administration but also its functioning by keeping in mind that bureaucracy was merely an instrument for public well-being. Three major steps were accordingly devised: first, in order to make bureaucracy transparent, each government department, especially those that had a large public interface, should have Citizens' Charter within three months. Besides laying out what the citizens expected from these departments, the Charter was also a bridge between the government and governed. Second, seeking to make bureaucracy sensitive to the citizens, the Action Plan also insisted on grievance redressal mechanism in government departments within three months. It was felt by the participants in the Conference that unless there was a redressal mechanism, the idea of accountability made no sense; the aim was to fix responsibility in case there was a deliberate lapse on the part of the bureaucrats, meant to streamline the delivery of services to the citizens. Third, the Action Plan also underlined the importance of democratic decentralization in governance to involve the stakeholders in improving administration and delivery of services at the grassroots. It was made possible with the promulgation of the 73rd and 74th Amendment Acts (1992) which constitutionalized participation in the decision making by the people at a level where the interface between the administrators and stakeholders was almost missing. Revolutionary in their aims, these amendment acts seemed to have radically altered the texture of grassroots administration by making the stakeholders integral to governance. By recognizing the role of voluntary agencies, these constitutional designs also expanded the horizons of local administration which no longer remained bureaucracy-specific.

The Conference came out heavily against secrecy and lack of openness in bureaucracy which were, felt the participants, the main sources of corruption. Two devices were thus suggested: on the one hand, it was agreed upon to create a working group on the Right to Information; it was also insisted, on the other hand, that steps needed to be taken immediately to introduce in the Parliament a legislation to replace the 1923 Official Secrets Act by the Right to Information. The suggestion was readily accepted and in 2005, with the adoption of the Right to Information Act, it became an empowering legislation which made bureaucracy more responsive. In the making of this Act, the Conference can thus be said to have articulated the views of civil society activists, especially the members of the Mazdoor Kisan Shakti Sangathan, which led a sustained campaign for the right to information. As is evident, the aim was to improve civil services by instituting mechanisms for combatting administrative debasement and inefficiency.

Fifth and Sixth Pay Commissions

In the annals of administrative reforms, the 1997 Fifth and 2006 Sixth Pay Commissions remained a critical turning point in two complementary ways: on the one hand, these pay commissions, while seeking to reconceptualize civil services in the context of globalization, were the efforts to articulate the neoliberal thrust in public administration; by defending privatization of public services, they seem to have, on the other hand, challenged the Weberian idea of bureaucracy being `hegemonic' in governance. One of the principal aims of these pay commissions was to create conditions in which agencies other than governmental bureaucracy were important in administration. For instance, in order to downsize governmental activities, they strongly argued for `contracting out' of the services and also offering contractual jobs—an idea that corresponds with the World Bank Governance model of administration.

The other significant recommendations of the Commission concerned 'openness' in administration. Defending the repeal of 'the Official Secrets Act of the old colonial days', the Commission insisted on openness which 'means giving everyone the right to access to information about the various decisions taken by the government and the reasoning behind them'. As an integral part of civil service reform, the Commission insisted on the formation of efficient grievance redressal machinery that has to be effective, speedy, objective, readily accessible and easy to operate' (Government of India 1997b, 93).

Drawing upon the examples of Canada, UK and Malaysia where effective grievance redressal cells have been functioning efficiently, the idea of a Citizen's Charter—defining the rights of customers of government schemes and services—was mooted by the Commission. The recognition and the procedures suggested in this connection were of crucial importance from the point of debureaucratizing the government and making it citizen-friendly. The issues, raised by the Pay Commission figured prominently in the Conference of Chief Ministers, 1997 where an action plan was adopted to (a) make the administration accountable and citizen-friendly, (b) ensure transparency and right to information and (c) adopt measures to cleanse and motivate the civil services.

The Government of India constituted the Sixth Central Pay Commission on 5 October 2006 which submitted its report on 24 March 2008. It was the first Central Pay Commission to be constituted in this century of rapid technological advances and after coming into force of the Right to Information (RTI) and Fiscal Responsibility and Budget Management (FRBM) Acts.

The Government machinery, therefore, had to gear up for better performance under stricter fiscal discipline and delivery mechanisms. These imperatives are reflected in the 'terms of reference' of the Sixth Central Pay Commission which made it incumbent on the Commission to recommend systematic changes for (a) transforming Central government organizations into modern, professional and citizen-friendly entities that are dedicated to the service of the people; and (b) harmonizing the functioning of the Central government Organizations with the demands of the emerging global economic scenario.

The Sixth Central Pay Commission, therefore, had to not only evolve a proper pay package for government employees but also make recommendations rationalizing governmental structure with a view to improving delivery mechanisms for providing better services to the common man. The main recommendations of the Commission which have a bearing on good governance are as follows:

Reduction of layers: the Commission recommended reducing the layers within the government structure so that decision-making and delivery is expedited. From 35 standard pay scales, the grades were reduced to 20, spread across four distinct running pay bands, one apex scale and another grade for the post of Cabinet Secretary/equivalent.

Restoring pride in the public services: government employees have to be motivated to take pride in the public services. Thus the Commission recommended various measures for job enhancement and job enrichment. The functions being discharged by Assistants and Private Secretaries would now on be carried out by Executive Assistants. Upgradation of all posts in Group D in the government to Group C along with their retraining and multitasking would provide enlargement and enrichment of functions and responsibilities to a large section of government employees.

Delegation with accountability: restoring delegation with accountability at each level in the decision-making process was one of the main thrust areas proposed by the Commission. Upgradation of critical cutting-edge jobs like teachers, staff nurses, constables, etc., was recommended. Strengthening decentralized levels with parity between field offices and the Secretariat was also recommended as the motivation and performance of the field and programme officers is critical to improve service delivery to the common man.

Ensuring availability of the best possible talent for government: The Commission recommended for lateral entry at higher levels in the government to ensure availability of the best possible talent from within and outside government with performance contracts. It suggested a shift from career-based to post-based selection in the higher echelons of government in order to get the best domain based expertise. A higher start and better incentives have been recommended at the initial entry level so as to attract younger talented profile. No increase in the retirement age was recommended as an active younger employee profile was considered as best suited for the tasks ahead. Additionally, it argued for a market driven compensation package for young scientists and posts requiring special expertise and professional skills.

Performance-related incentive schemes: the introduction of performance-related incentive scheme (PRIS) was designed to reward performance, innovation, creativity and responsive delegated administration of stakeholder interface for inclusive outcomes and service delivery. This was to be a budget neutral tool for results-based management with performance targets, standards and indicators and greater accountability.

The Sixth Pay Commission is a watershed in the evolution of the India's civil services for a variety of reasons. This was not a Pay Commission in the ordinary sense of the term since it also sought to reshape the bureaucracy in the light of emerging global trends. By suggesting significant changes in the administrative hierarchy, the Commission translated into reality the drive towards 'debureaucratization'.

Review Committees on the Civil Service Examinations

The Union Public Service Commission (UPSC) in 2001 appointed a committee of experts under the chairmanship of Professor Yogendra Kumar Alagh to review the existing scheme of the civil services examinations. The main complaint about the prelims pattern of exams was that it was more a test of memory than knowledge. The Committee after its study concluded that a mismatch existed between the suitability or aptitude and the service allocated to a candidate. The Alagh Committee recommended an aptitude test with emphasis on comprehension, logical reasoning, problem-solving and data analysis. Based on these recommendations the UPSC finally decided to change the pattern of the preliminary examination. This entrance test was to be rechristened 'civil service aptitude test' (CSAT) and would be in practice from the year 2011–12. In the new scheme there would be two objective papers in the prelims: (a) General studies (already in practice) and (b) Aptitude test, each carrying 200 marks and of two hours duration. However there would be no optional subject based paper and the new scheme would now test the candidates on their aptitude, decision-making skills and analytical abilities rather than their memorizing abilities.

The Hota Committee on Civil Services Reforms, 2004 was another initiative by the government to examine the whole gamut of a civil service reform. The Committee made the following important recommendations (Hota 2004, 15):

1. Age for entrants to the civil services should be 21–24 years for general candidates with a five years age concession to members of SC/STs and three years for OBCs.
2. Annual performance plans for officers.
3. After 15 years of rigorous review, if an officer is not found honest and performance oriented, he be weeded out of the service.
4. The duties, functions and responsibilities of all senior posts are to be laid down and publicized.
5. Article 311 of the Constitution to be amended to enable the President/Governor to dismiss/remove public servants in case of corrupt practices/having assets disproportionate to known sources of income.
6. Antiquated rules and procedures in the government must be discarded and new simplified ones put in place.
7. E-governance to be encouraged to augment efficiency and ensure transparency in government.
8. Civil servants should be encouraged to move laterally to non-governmental organizations.
9. To increase the representation of women in the civil services; it is proposed that within 15 years, at least 25 per cent members of the higher civil service should be women as against 13 per cent women at that time.

It is widely recognized that the civil services have played an important role in preserving unity, providing stability and maintaining order in a vast country like India, prone to various conflicts—ethnic, communal, regional, etc. Nonetheless there are concerns about the performance of the civil service in the context of realizing a result oriented government. It has been pointed out the civil service in India is more concerned with internal processes than with results. The systematic rigidities, needless complexities and over centralization in the policy and management structures within which the civil service functions are too complex and often too constraining. Rapid and fundamental changes are taking place in the country in terms of rapid economic growth, urbanization, environmental degradation, technological change and increased local awareness and identity. The response time to adapt to these changes is much shorter than it used to be. As instruments of public service, civil servants have to be ready to manage such changes.

The Moily Committee on Administrative Reforms

Based on the need to reform the civil services as highlighted in the foregoing paragraphs, the second Administrative Reform Commission was set up by the government on 31 August 2005 under the Chairmanship of Veerappa Moily to prepare a detailed blueprint for revamping the public administration system. The Commission was asked to suggest measures to achieve a 'proactive, responsive, accountable, sustainable and efficient administration for the country at all levels of the government'. The Commission has presented 15 reports to the government for consideration. Some of the important recommendations of the Commission include:

1. A National Institute of Public Administration to be established to offer Bachelor's Degree courses in public administration/governance/management.
2. The permissible age for appearing in the civil services examinations to be 21 to 25 years for general candidates; 21 to 28 years for candidates from OBC and 21 to 29 years for candidates from the SC/ST and physically challenged candidates.
3. The number of permissible attempts should be three, five and six and six respectively.
4. As a capacity building measure, every government servant should undergo mandatory training at the induction stage and also periodically during his/her career.
5. A central Civil Services Authority to be set up which, among other things, would formulate guidelines for appointments at the 'Senior Management Level' in the government of India.
6. Citizen centricity with the aim of ensuring citizen's welfare and citizens' satisfaction is critical for any government, which aims to provide good governance. The Commission suggested a number of strategies and tools which could be employed to make the administration citizen-centric, namely the adoption of appropriate modern technology, Right to Information, Citizens' Charter, grievance redressal mechanisms and active citizens' participation (Government of India 2009a, 2009b, 45).
7. In order to ensure ethics in governance, the Commission recommended the establishment of a national ombudsman to be called as 'Rashtriya Lokayukta'.
8. It suggests that the State Vigilance Commission/Lokayukta may be empowered to supervise the prosecution of corruption related cases.
9. Greater devolution of power and responsibilities in order to empower local institutions of governance. The Commission was of the opinion that a comprehensive exercise needed to be taken up regarding the broadening and deepening of the revenue base of local governments.
10. The Commission also recommended that all offices with a large public interface should have an online complaint tracking system.

11. The Commission in its first report titled 'Right to Information: Master Key to Good Governance' recommended that the Official Secrets Act, 1923 be replaced and substituted by a chapter in the National Security Act. The Manual of Office Procedure needed to be revised in the light of the provisions of the RTI Act, 2005 with regard to 'communications of official Information'. The ARC also suggested that Members of Parliament and Members of the State Legislative Assembly be declared as 'Public Authorities' under the Right to Information Act, except when they were discharging legislative functions (Government of India 2006, 11).

Thus, the Second ARC presented a comprehensive document dealing with the civil service reforms in India.

CONCLUDING OBSERVATIONS

The civil service is the most important instrument for implementing people's will and aspirations as expressed in the Constitution. To a large extent, it has been successful in bringing socio-economic change in the country. But it also has a negative image in the eyes of the people due to corruption, red-tapism and the nepotistic tendencies of the bureaucracy. Thus, the civil service has to undergo radical structural, procedural and attitudinal changes if it has to serve the people as an effective instrument of change and progress. It has to cultivate much wider social awareness and responsiveness as well as social sensitivity apart from the traditional virtues of integrity, efficiency and impartiality. We hope that the recent administrative reforms India has initiated would be able to reorient the civil services into a dynamic, efficient and accountable apparatus of public service delivery.

REVIEW QUESTIONS

1. Discuss the importance of the civil services.
2. Examine the evolution of the civil services in India.
3. Write a note on the All India Services.
4. Critically discuss the role of the civil services in the Indian administrative system.
5. Discuss the power and functions of the UPSC.
6. Write a note on the training of civil services in India.
7. What are the main recommendations of the Second ARC on the civil service reforms in India?
8. Write a note on the main features of the Fifth and Sixth Pay Commissions.
9. What are the main functions of the training centres of the civil services in India?
10. What are the main problems in the structure and functioning of the civil services in India? What are your suggestions to tackle them?

REFERENCES

Das, S. K. 2013. *The Civil Services in India*. New Delhi: Oxford University Press.

Government of India. 1997a. *Action Plan for Effective and Responsive Administration: Statement Adopted at the Conference of Chief Ministers*. Government of India, New Delhi.

Government of India. 1997b. *The Report of the Fifth Pay Commission*. Vol. 1, Government of India Press, New Delhi.

Government of India. 2009a, February. *Citizen Centric Administration: The Heart of Governance*. Second Administrative Reforms Commission, Government of India, New Delhi.

———. 2009b, February. *Right to Information: Master Key to Good Governance*. Second Administrative Reforms Commission, Government of India, New Delhi.

———. 2010. *Report on Ethics in Governance*. Second Administrative Reform Commission, Government of India, New Delhi.

Keith, Arthur B. 1937. *A Constitutional History of India 1600–1935*. London: Methuen and Co. Ltd.

Maheshwary, S. R. 2013. *Indian Administration*. 6th ed. New Delhi: Orient Blackswan.

Mishra, B. B. 1997. *The Bureaucracy in India: Analysis and Development Up to 1947*. Delhi: Oxford University Press.

P. C. Hota Committee on Civil Service Reforms. 2004, July. *Report of Union Public Service Commission, 2003–04*.

Tummala, Krishna K. 1996. *Public Administration in India*. New Delhi: Allied Publishers Limited.

Administrative Reforms in India

8

LEARNING OBJECTIVES

1. To understand administrative reform as a theoretical category.
2. To conceptualize administrative reforms in India with reference to the socio-economic and political circumstances.
3. To highlight the distinctive characteristics of administrative reforms in India.

Administrative reform is basically related to the idea of changes in administration that are brought about through deliberate efforts. It should however be borne in mind, as Machiavelli warns, that

> [T]here is nothing more difficult to arranged, more doubtful of success and more dangerous to carry than initiating changes in state's constitution. The innovator makes enemies of all those who prosper under the old order and only lukewarm support is forthcoming from those who would proper under the new. (1979, 59)

Administrative reform is therefore 'a risk, a gamble in which the odds are heavily against success ... [and] it can take generations for administrative behaviour and values to change appreciably' (Caiden 1999, 820). There are, thus, hardly any magical keys to administrative reform. It is a long-term process that requires talent, zeal and commitment, scarce resources and, above all, time, whereas governments tend to look for short-term and quick solutions. Reform is, argues Gerald Caiden (1999, 827), 'tossed around like a boat in a storm [since] from conception to finality is a long, arduous and difficult journey beset with numerous obstacles, unforeseen perils and unexpected surprises'. Underlining the criticality of the political ambience in which administrative reforms are sought to be undertaken, Caiden further argues that they are 'an artificial instrument of administrative transformation against resistance'. While elaborating administrative reform as a conceptual category, he thus identifies three important characteristics viz., first, it entails a thorough reconstruction of the machinery of the government which, in effect, means a complete or partial overhauling of the prevalent administrative structure that appears to have lost momentum in the changed circumstances; second, it aims at systematic transformation and not piecemeal change, permanent alternations and not cosmetic touches in structure, territorial organization, budget management, planning process and personnel practices to reduce corruption, incompetence and red tape; third, the different sectors and programmes are rationalized and reorganized for more effective performance, and finally, the machinery of the government is simplified and streamlined to eliminate unnecessary duplication, reduce inconveniences and minimize pluralism.[1]

ADMINISTRATIVE REFORMS IN INDIA

Turning to the 'reforms' scenario in India, one has to run through a long period of bureaucratic ups and downs since the advent of colonial rule. During the imperial rule, the core purpose of administration was to bolster colonialism where people's interests were absolutely peripheral if not entirely absent. Hence administrative reforms had, for obvious reasons, a single priority of perpetuating the British rule. With independence, the nature and spirit of administration were bound to be radically different since its moral foundation had undergone dramatic changes. Indian historical experience, both during the British period and in its immediate aftermath, led to the emergence of a public administration that was ill-suited to needs and aspirations of the people. The reasons are not difficult to seek as studies have shown that the bureaucrats who were brought up and trained in the colonial administrative culture are wedded to the Weberian characteristics of hierarchy, status and rigidity of rules and regulations and concerned mainly with the enforcement of and order and collection of revenues. While for the colonial regime, this structure was most appropriate, it was completely unfit to discharge functions in the changed environment of an administration, geared to the task of development. As the government became the main institution for development in the democratic set-up that India adopted following independence, the role of officials underwent changes. Their sole objective is to 'emphasize results, rather than procedures, teamwork rather than hierarchy and status, [and] flexibility and decentralization rather control and authority' (Bhatt 1979, 259). Seen as 'the development administrator', the bureaucrat needs to therefore be characterized by 'tact, pragmatism, dynamism, flexibility, adaptability to any situation and willingness to take rapid, ad-hoc decisions without worrying too much about procedures and protocol' (Bhatt 1979, 281).

Following independence, government functions also expanded in scope and content. With the introduction of the Parliamentary form of government and the setting up of people's institutions right down to the village level, there has been an inevitable rise in the level of expectations and performance have widened. People's institutions were set up with the objective of creating self-governing institutions at the village level. A true democracy as advocated by Gandhi ensures that local, state and national representatives are accountable to the people for local, state and national matters respectively through effective transparency. Such one-to-one accountability may promote responsible politics and competent professionals and social workers to politics. The objective remains distant. Our present system, based on diffused accountability, as mentioned in the consultation paper of the National Commission for Review of the Working of the Constitution (2000, 19), 'breeds corruption and attracts self-seekers to politics'. For this breed, the paper further underlines, 'interests of national development, welfare of the people and needs of good governance take lower priorities, if any'. Similarly, independence and the Five Year Plans were perceived by people as synonymous with economic and social equity and well-being, and freedom from want and oppression. In the early days of planning, people did not crib much about shortages, which they confronted with fortitude because the future held hope and promise for them. With the passage of time, they felt their hopes were 'belied' and they were 'nowhere near the promised land of honesty, plenty and happiness'. The ethos of self-governance, decentralization and community development were flagged in with considerable élan and fan-fare. For example, the three-tier Panchayati Raj system and the urban local bodies were conceived of as a properly meshed network of institutions to accelerate the development process. The 73rd and 74th Amendment Acts (1992) to the Constitution sought to advance the concept of 'self-governance' by providing for (a) regular elections, (b) minimal suppression of Panchayati Raj bodies through an administrative fiat and (c) regular finances through statutory distribution by the State Finance Commissions. But, due to various reasons, the political process became what may be termed as 'reversed' and highly centralized with personalized systems of government developing at both the central and state levels. There has been a massive erosion of institutions, whether they are the Parliament and parliamentary institutions, or the party system and democratic procedures in the running of parties, or the judiciary, or indeed the press.

Given the new challenges of economic development and social change, the prevalent administrative structure was both structurally inadequate and functionally unprepared in India's changed socio-political circumstances. So there was a need for administrative reforms whereby the structure would respond to systemic changes in the Indian polity following the British withdrawal. While redefining the nature of the civil service in independent India, Jawaharlal Nehru thus commented that since 'the state has become a dynamic state—not a static state—Services (administrators) have to adapt themselves to the changes...have to adopt methods to the changed conditions of work and the changed objectives of work'.[2] Several steps were undertaken in the aftermath of the 1947 transfer of power. The first step was undoubtedly the Secretariat Reorganization Committee (1947), appointed by the imperial government even before the actual transfer of power. In its report, submitted in August, 1947, the Committee commented extensively on 'the unresponsive' nature of the administration that was simply 'incapable' of handling 'the new challenges' in the aftermath of the British withdrawal (GOI 1949, 19–21). This line of thinking was pursued in 1951 in two subsequent reports—*Public Administration in India* and *Efficient Conduct of State Enterprises*, prepared by A. D. Gorwala for the Planning Commission. Recommending the introduction of 'organization and method' procedure in the government departments and public enterprises, Gorwala suggested steps to ensure 'efficiency' and 'discipline' in the civil service. What separates this report from the earlier ones is the adequate emphasis on 'the coordination between politicians and administrators' for 'smooth and efficient' functioning of public administration (Gorwala 1951). Gorwala's report was submitted on 30 April 1951. The report stated that though the administrative machinery had remained sound, the increasing work load had been adversely affecting the performance of personnel. Its major recommendations included (a) maintenance of high standards of integrity and efficiency in administration, (b) the machinery be reorganized for ensuring speed, effectiveness and accountability (c) some basic structural changes be therefore required to improve the quality of services and (d) arrangements made for imparting training to officials and recruitment through the Public Service Commissions to avoid nepotism and patronage. In his in-depth study of the Indian administration in 1953, Paul Appleby suggested radical reforms of the administrative structure that was 'archaic', 'feudalistic' and 'unimaginative' and hence was simply 'inadequate' to fulfil the primary goal of a nation with 'a long history of colonialism'. In his report, Appleby criticized 'the structure which subordinated the national Government to State, district and municipal control making implementation of programmes of national importance difficult'. He therefore suggested some structural changes like (a) the creation of middle-level functionaries and the recruitment of more executives at all levels, (b) a more flexible system of recruitment to meet particular needs and requirements, (c) the setting up of panels of qualified persons in place of the existing practice of selecting individuals, (d) arranging refresher courses for the serving personnel, (e) setting up of an Organization and Management Division in each department to monitor the work and (f) finding ways to improve administration through specialized studies and reviews undertaken by the Institute of Public Administration. Moreover, he was critical of the tendency of the Ministry of Finance to centralize powers and not to delegate them to operational ministries. Furthermore, while commenting on the nature of subordinates at the cutting edge level of bureaucracy, Appleby expressed concern at the growing level of corruption by saying that

> it is not surprising that it is at these cutting edges—post offices, district sub offices, in agricultural extension and in many places—where corruption is most common and where personal

> disgruntlement is the great handicap in the way of pushing on programmes ... actually undertaken and not merely verbalized. (2003, 33)

He referred to the diffusion of responsibility from the top to the lower levels and the lack of 'facilities for administrative delegation'. Because of this diffusion of responsibility, it was difficult to ascertain 'accountability'. There was, according to him, 'too much scrutiny and too many impediments before the fact and too little systematic review and scrutiny after the fact' (Appleby 1953, 38). He was critical of the tendency of the Ministry of Finance to centralize powers and not to delegate them to the operational ministries.

What drove Appleby in this exercise was his concern for change in an administration that was unlikely to go with change, given its colonial roots? In other words, the administration that served the imperial rulers did not appear to be appropriate for a free nation with its own socio-political and economic agenda. In fact, it is clear in Appleby's report that the prevalent bureaucratic set-up that sustained the foreign rule was a mismatch with India's national aspirations. What was most surprising to him was the acceptance of 'an administrative machine' simply because of its 'instrumental' significance. As a result, the later efforts at administrative reform appear to have focused more on structural changes believed to be crucial in radically altering the inherent ideological foundation of the Indian public administration. The report of the Second Pay Commission (1957–59) is illustrative here. Appointed in 1957, the primary task of the Commission was to examine 'the principles' that needed to govern 'the structure of emoluments and conditions of service' of Central Government employees. In order to ascertain efficiency, the Commission suggested the classification of government offices into 'attached' and 'subordinate' on a functional basis and bringing the relevant Secretariat and the attached offices under 'a single headquarter organization'. The other remarkable recommendation, drawn on the British pattern of Whitley Councils, was about the creation of a machinery for negotiation and settlement of disputes between the employers and employees. Although this recommendation was almost shelved, growing corruption in then administration led to the appointment of the Shanatam Committee, 1964, that looked into the problem of administrative corruption. Its recommendations were largely procedural in the sense that the roots of corruption lay in the violation of established systems and procedures. What was path breaking was its recommendation for the creation of the Central Vigilance Commission as a permanent administrative wing to keep a sustained vigil on civil servants.

The most comprehensive enquiry, ever undertaken in the aftermath of decolonization was the Administrative Reforms Commission that came into being in 1966 under the stewardship of Morarji Desai. Two important ideas seemed to have governed the constitution of this Commission: first, the changing nature of administration—from a mere law and order maintenance agency to an apparatus responsible for development—radically altered the traditional conception of administration; second, the ideological goal of a socialist pattern of society called for drastic overhauling of the machinery of the government that had so far discharged the responsibility in a very stereotypical manner. So, the Commission was given a very wide mandate and was entrusted with the task of

> [G]iving consideration to the need for ensuring the highest standard of efficiency and integrity in the public services and for making public administration a fit instrument for carrying out the social and economic goals of development as also one which is responsive to the public.[3] (GOI 1966–70)

As was evident, the Commission sought to redefine public administration by recognizing the importance of 'public' in administration. Furthermore, the adoption of a socialistic pattern of society brought about radical changes in the conceptualization of the role of the administration. Guided by the objective of establishing a socialistic pattern of society, the

Commission was entrusted with a 41-point charter, grouped into ten specific areas of enquiry which were as follows: (a) the machinery of the government of India and its procedures of work; (b) the machinery for planning at all levels; (c) centre–state relationships; (d) financial administration; (e) personnel administration; (f) economic administration; (g) administration at the state levels; (h) district administration; (i) agricultural administration and (j) problem of redressal of citizen's grievances. In the 20 reports that the Commission submitted, there were 581 recommendations that covered the entire gamut of Indian administration. Some of the most important recommendations relate to the structural transformation of the Central government including the composition of the Cabinet and other governmental departments responsible for developmental plans and programmes. Suggesting a maximum strength of forty five for the Central Cabinet, the Commission defined the role of the Prime Minister as a guide, coordinator and supervisor of a collectivity, known as the Cabinet. The Commission also provided a checklist of what the Prime Minister should do, which was largely in conformity with the Westminster form cabinet government where the premier is a pivot of the government. The other substantive recommendation involved the minister-secretary relationship that lies at the root of an efficient administration. In other words, critical of 'neutrality' in the civil service, the ARC supported a bureaucracy that clearly upheld the political will of the country, as articulated by the Prime Minister and his Cabinet. Since the government was committed to socialistic principles, the civil service that was responsible for the implementation of this goal was expected to reorient its role in the changed circumstances. Although the Commission maintained the obvious distinction between policy making and its execution in public administration, there was no rigidity in its characterization of the role of the political and permanent executives. As both of them constituted integral parts of an organic hole, it would be simply unrealistic, as the Commission held, to overlook mutual interaction between the two.

While the Commission devoted a great deal of energy to the structural reform of the Central government, personnel administration also received equal importance for it was human content that ultimately decided the character of public administration. Just like the 1953–55 Hoover Commission that believed that 'the government cannot be any better than the man and woman who make it function', the ARC also insisted that 'the road to the top must be open to every competent and qualified government servant [and] to higher management in the Secretariat, talent must be drawn from every cadre and class of government servants'. Drawn on this philosophy, the ARC articulated its suggestions in four different ways: first, a rational system needs to be devised for recruitment to policy making positions with personnel possessing the required qualifications and competence. This involves an optimum use of different services for Secretariat assignments and also the adoption of special measures to build necessary specialization in the Secretariat; second, senior management personnel must be selected from all relevant sources—generalists and specialists—and for this purpose, talent needs to be discovered and developed in all the services, especially among those who have not so far been inducted into higher management positions in the Secretariat to any significant degree; third, a rational pay structure requires to be installed so as to truly reflect actual responsibilities, associated with each job and finally, to boost morale in the civil service, talented lower rank personnel should be given greater scope than what exists to move up the hierarchy on the basis of competence and performance.

The ARC report is probably the most exhaustive checklist of steps to streamline the administration in the changed socio-political environment. Drawn on 'certain basic considerations', the most significant recommendation happens to be the appointment of a *Lokpal* (at the centre) and a *Lokayaukta* (in the states) apart from the introduction of the concept and technique of performance budgeting. Perhaps the two most important areas touched upon by the ARC in its reports are (a) the minister–civil servant relationship wherein the need for the depoliticization of the services is emphasized and (b) the creation of a climate and culture of administration wherein the growth of personal relationships between individual civil servants and the minister should be arrested. However, a closer look at the recommendations suggests that the Commission, instead of radically altering the structure, was favourably inclined towards mere 'cosmetic' changes within the administration. It is pertinent to mention here that administrative reform appears futile unless accompanied by political reform. In other words, since public administration is hardly neutral, its nature is contingent on that of the 'political' in which it is located. So the ARC report, despite being voluminous but not so illuminating, was hardly effective in substantially transforming the Indian administration which had, for obvious reasons, colonial roots. Notwithstanding the declared objective of making the administration responsive to the people, the ARC remained a well-researched document on Indian administration with no far-reaching impact.

During the period between the appointment of the ARC in 1966 and the inauguration of the Fifth Pay Commission in 1997, there were no major committees except for three isolated attempts: (a) to improve the pattern of the combined services competitive examination by introducing a preliminary tier of examination to eliminate a large number of candidates having less potential for success as a sequel to the Kothari Committee Report 1976; (b) to revitalize the Panchayati Raj system of governance at the grassroots by converting the three-tier structure into a two-tier structure (Mehta Committee, 1979) which has contributed significantly to the adoption of the 73rd Amendment Act in 1992 and (c) to change the system of economic administration (Jha Committee, 1986). Following these efforts, the most dramatic administrative reform scheme was articulated by the Fifth Pay Commission, 1997 that radically altered the prevalent conceptualization of reforms by tuning to the compulsion of liberalization and the emergence of a new economic order. Similarly, the reconstitution of grassroots governance in the light of the 73rd Amendment Act, 1992 introduced new dimensions in rural administration by seeking to bring in the hitherto peripheral sections of society into the decision-making processes.

It is obvious that even before the onset of liberalization, several measures were adopted to revitalize the administration and these owed their origin to completely different socio-economic concerns where reforms were largely internally generated while post-liberalization efforts are mostly externally driven. In these series of reform schemes, the recommendations of the National Police Commission (NPC), 1981 were different not only in thrust but also in probably raising some of the most crucial questions in a context when those possessing legitimate instruments of coercive power tended to distort the public nature of their authority at the slightest pretext.

NATIONAL POLICE COMMISSION REPORT

A critical look at police behaviour reveals an important dimension of its history, one that continues to influence its nature even after 50 years of independence. It will not be an exaggeration to argue that the Indian police remains the same at least in substance since it was formally inaugurated with the promulgation of the Police Act 1861 in the shadow of the 1857 armed struggle against the British with the main objective of ensuring imperial rule. Replacing the old *daroga* system that became redundant with the spread of British supremacy in India, the new system was introduced with a view to expanding its network as widely as possible. The police was an instrument of control, an instrument that was, for obvious reasons, unsparingly used to advance the cause of British imperialism. It therefore had no societal trust. Despite the fact that the colonial state animated the theory and practice of the rule of law in its constitutional deliberations, the police was steeped in partisanship, its role was vicious and its image was deliberately nurtured as adversarial to society. Notwithstanding severe indictment within four decades of its existence by the Police Commission 1902, no reform was allowed by the colonial government either in its organization or in its work culture. The police therefore emerged as a time-tested instrument that was allowed to function almost without shackles.

It is not difficult to understand why the colonial state preferred the Irish Constabulary model to the Metropolitan model that sought to provide a new image to the police which hardly drew upon force. For obvious reason, the British government never allowed its colonial states to adopt the Metropolitan Bobby model, drawn upon community policing that hardly resorted to coercion except under exceptional circumstances. Not only was the Irish Constabulary a time-tested force in Ireland, the model also seemed to be most appropriate in firmly establishing and maintaining British hegemony in circumstances when the colonial state was most vulnerable. Primarily a coercive instrument, the police hardly had interactions with the people because it was believed that a well-defined distance with the people was necessary to ruthlessly implement the official decree of the Raj.

For the colonial state, the choice of the Irish Constabulary was obvious. What is surprising was the continuity of the same model even after India became free. Despite being critical of the British police that sustained the most oppressive administrations, nationalist leaders, including Vallabhbhai Patel and Jawaharlal Nehru, allowed the system to continue simply because of its efficiency in law enforcement under colonialism. Even Gandhi was in its favour. Drawn on and inspired by ahimsa, he therefore perceived the police as conducive to radically different socio-economic and political order in which 'the spirit of violence will have all but vanished and internal disorder will come under control' (Gandhi 1940). Those who opposed the continuity of the Irish Constabulary due to its ideological underpinnings seemed to have been persuaded in view of the sudden outbreak of communal violence immediately after the transfer of power. What was readily acceptable due the exigency of the situation became a permanent feature of independent India since the political leadership, regardless of ideology, began to relish a partisan police that allowed the government to use a legitimate coercive force as and when required to pursue a political goal. The Gujarat carnage is perhaps the best available illustration to show how the police went berserk at a critical juncture to please the political bosses. However, it would be wrong to suggest that the police always acts in accordance with the ruling authority's dictation. Again, the Gujarat case demonstrates the extent to which the local police reflected the mood of the majority community. By getting involved in the mayhem, either through actions or non-actions, the Gujarat police had articulated its response to the riot merely as an integral part of the majority community. By sharing the emotions of the majority community, the police had hardly remained secular. Gujarat is probably the latest example of police being an active partner in the Hindutva campaign. Perhaps the most glaring example of a police force that tends to become communal at the slightest provocations is the Provincial Armed Constabulary (PAC) in Uttar Pradesh. Examples can easily be multiplied showing the complicity of the PAC with those for Hindutva. What stands out was its role during the 1992 Ayodhya catastrophe when the PAC was reported to have directly participated in the demolition of the controversial Islamic historical relic.

In view of the growing communalization of the police force, perhaps this is an appropriate time to have a fresh look at the 1981 report of the NPC. Before the NPC was inaugurated, several police commissions were appointed by various states, of which Kerala was the pioneer in instituting a Police Reorganization Commission in 1959. Appointed in the aftermath of the 1975–77 Emergency, the NPC made several recommendations on police reforms in its eight-volume report, submitted in 1981. What was ironical however was that those who argued strongly for police reform since they suffered most due to police brutality during the Emergency are in power at the centre since 1996, and yet, there has been a complete silence on what was hailed as 'a path-breaking document' that would radically alter our approach to police and policing in India.

The NPC has touched upon a wide range of issues concerning the police in India. Two areas that appeared to have bothered the Commission most were (a) the misuse of police and (b) accountability and police performance. For the Commission, the Emergency was a reference point when the bias of the ruling authority seemed to have determined police behaviour. The police was used not merely as an instrument of the state, or the government in power, but also of the politicians who had lost the legitimacy to rule. Jayprakash Narayan's appeal to the police to disobey the illegal order of their bosses in the wake of the *Chhatra Sangarsh* movement in Bihar was perhaps the first articulated signal towards the possible devastation due to police complicity with the government of the day.

According to the NPC, the police themselves at the behest of politicians distorted the role of the police during the Emergency. And, the Commission thus exhorts that 'the police subculture should take into account the fundamental rights of the people, the supremacy of laws and not of executive fiat, and our constitutional goal towards a developed and egalitarian society' (GOI 1981, ch. LXII, 14). There are innumerable examples to show that 'putting down political dissent became a tacitly accepted objective of the police system in most of the states'. In order to express their loyalty to the ruling party, the police always dealt with the law and order situations 'with a political eye'. The NPC was candid while seeking to conceptualise 'the police brutality and its cancerous corruption' by underlining that

> no thinking and planning are in evidence because the senior administrative ranks are perpetually insecure and are exhausted by the continual effort to survive, in an atmosphere where their assessment by the executive—administrative and political—is not always based on merit. Clearly the police organization as it stands today is unfit to discharge its duties. (GOI 1981, ch. LXII, 14)

To contain the misuse of the police, two major recommendations were made viz., (a) there should be a tenured office of the Chief of Police, selected by a panel drawn by a Committee comprising the Chairman of the UPSC, the Union Home Secretary, the senior most amongst the Heads of Central Police Organizations, the Chief Secretary of the state and the existing Police Chief of the state and (b) there should be a six member permanent State Security Commission with a fixed term of three years to annually review the performance of the police.

The other serious recommendation involves measures to ascertain police accountability while discharging duties. There are three types of interlinked accountabilities that the police should seek to ensure, namely accountability to the people, accountability to the law and organizational accountability.

There is a well-defined mechanism within the organization to ascertain 'internal accountability' for the police. But this by itself does not ensure accountability to the people for which mere recommendations will not suffice. So, accountability in this context presupposes two-dimensional responsibilities: on the one hand, the police is to discharge its responsibilities in accordance with both organizational rationality and systemic rationality, based on the law of the land; accountability also involves, on the other, duties to be discharged to the satisfaction of the party for whose benefit the duties are being performed. What it suggests is the importance of certain well-defined norms whereby a constant vigil is maintained by the people. Over the years, it has been observed that the police seem to be completely alienated from the people whose agents the police functionaries are and to whom they are ultimately accountable. It is not surprising that the use of third degree methods and custodial deaths have been on the rise. The police seem to be the easily available coercive instrument to the elected representatives as and when they require to forcibly suppress any mass agitation against the misuse of public office by them. The NPC noted down that on innumerable occasions the police has acted like a mercenary force ignoring completely its societal role in defending the people regardless of religion, clan and creed.

There is no doubt that these recommendations, if implemented, will radically alter not only the image of the police but also their functioning in a multi-religious society like India. What is most disturbing however is the reluctance of even those who have suffered from police atrocities to take care of the recommendations when in power. The reasons are not difficult to seek. The police appear to be a handy instrument at the disposal of the ruling authority to pursue sectarian interests with legitimacy. The roots of this blatant distortion therefore lie elsewhere. If society is vitiated by the communal virus and any anti-Muslim bias gets translated into violent action with the slightest provocation, it would be wrong to blame only the police for distortions in our secular fabric. The NPC's recommendations seem to have provided a good reference point to deal with those fundamental socio-political issues which, though directly linked with the functioning of the police, are equally significant in grasping what provokes mass hysteria at regular intervals in India.

RECENT TRENDS IN ADMINISTRATIVE REFORMS IN INDIA

Reform efforts in the government are a continuing process in every country. As shown earlier, in India, the Administrative Reform Commission (1966–70) produced a series of reports concerning almost all the departments of the government of India. Every Pay Commission Report in India carries with it many recommendations for changes in public administration per se. What is important to note is that these reform proposals have been discussed within the framework of traditional public administration. The accountability of the civil service to the elected elements within the overall accountability structure laid down in the Parliamentary system of government has not been in question. There has been general consensus that public administration can be reformed effectively by a combination of strategic management, structural organization and through the development of better personnel management systems.

In the 1980s, the global socio-economic and political scene started changing rapidly. The failure to control the economy in the developed West led to the rejection of old solutions of control, which led to the increasing importance of neoliberal right wing ideology.

As is evident, concern for administrative reforms in India is not of recent origin. What is new is the context in which this is being articulated. With the adoption of the New Economic Policy in the early 1990s, there have been attempts at dismantling the centrally directed framework of economic development. This is also the beginning of the period when international donor agencies exercised immense influence in the domestic economy by attaching conditionalities while giving aid. These conditionalities were, at the outset, mere prescriptions for the administration of aid but later they become modalities for reform in the overall framework of governance itself. Given the rising tide of 'neoliberalism', no country is free from this. Such a changed empirical context has contributed to a new conceptualization in the form 'reinventing government' that actually seeks to articulate the transformed role of public administration.

Reforms in administration in India in the 1990s were basically driven by economic liberalization measures. The Indian response was clearly articulated in the 1996 Conference of Chief Secretaries which suggested several corrective steps to arrest the ongoing drift in civil service before it was too late. The efforts to transform an aloof, impersonal and paternalistic bureaucracy into one which was citizen-friendly and sensitive to user needs remained the basic concern of those participating in the conference. What was suggested in the conference had its root in the arguments, put forward by Rajiv Gandhi, the former prime minister, in favour of a 'responsive administration'. In his series of speeches at the workshops of District Magistrates and Collectors that spanned across almost two years (between 1987 and 1988), Rajiv Gandhi (1988) argued that:

> [the] paternalistic model of [our] administration is not suitable for a society where the main thrust of administration is on development. It was agreed that the regulatory functions of administration should not seen as an end in themselves, as they tended to be in colonial times, but as a means of reinforcing and sustaining the processes of broad based development. [A] more representative and more responsive administration would be better placed to relate the purposes of administration to the larger goals of our national life—democracy, socialism, secularism and non-alignment.

The other point that was also made relates to 'the dependency syndrome' of the people. The bureaucracy continues to remain 'a doer' and not 'an enabler'. The people in general wait for the government to do 'the simplest things which they can do themselves'. The system has become 'so top-heavy and top-oriented' that at every level, people look to the level above for a solution. What is therefore needed is 'to push the administration down, not just in the administration but also sometimes out of the administration to the community'. By involving people in both planning and executing developmental programmes at the grassroots, the administration will become both 'responsive' and 'representative' in character.

Given the new emphasis in contemporary public administration, it is now clear that traditional public administration is hardly an appropriate tool to conceptualize contemporary governance. Critical of the pyramid like structure of administration, the new wave has been articulated in a model where 'centralization and top downs get edged out, compelling innovation and dictating empowerment of functionaries at the cutting-edge' (Sharma 2003). With the flow of power downwards, those who matter at the field level gain strategic importance and the administration is forced to shift its attention from a hierarchically informed and bureaucratically designed response to a citizen-friendly approach vis-à-vis public affairs. So, the mere instrumental importance of administration seems to be gradually phasing-out giving way to a proactive system of governance where the citizens are not merely recipients but clients having a significant influence on both the content and style of governance. So, in the changed perspective, the focus of these reforms is 'on reshaping the boundaries and responsibilities of the state, through privatization, the restructuring of public services and the introduction of private market discipline into public administration' (Minogue 1998). Contemporary public administration is not just about efficiency, it also upholds democratic participation, accountability and empowerment. There is therefore constant tension between (a) how to make government efficient and (b) how to keep it accountable. There is also a corresponding tension between 'the conception of people as consumers in the context of relations between state and market' and the conception of 'people as citizens in the context of relations between state and society' (Minogue 1998). What it clearly suggests is the increasing importance of citizen's participation in public affairs. Several steps have been taken to restructure administration in response to impetus from both domestic and external sources. Of these steps, the adoption of the 73rd and 74th Amendment Acts of 1992 and the implementation of the Fifth Pay Commission Report appear to be significant because of the felt-impact on the prevalent governance. Arising from the perspectives outlined earlier, these were momentous steps which could be potentially path-breaking and contained the seeds for radical transformation in both the content and style of governance. Interestingly, these two measures—the Amendment Acts and the Pay Commission recommendations—coincided not only with the liberalization impetus of the Central government, but also with the World Bank's marked emphasis on 'good governance' and decentralization. As the fundamental impulse of policy making moves away from centralized state institutions towards the market, these amendments, in principle, need to facilitate the creation of structures that devolve power to localized bodies. The underlying principle of Panchayati Raj is the use of local knowledge, popular experience and participation in the making of decisions that impact local people. There is no doubt that the reformed Panchayati Raj institutions are supposed to reconstitute the decision processes on the basis of local participation on a continuous basis and thus, in principle, represent an institutionalized shift in power towards lower, hitherto 'disempowered' sections of the rural population.

Notwithstanding the shortcomings of the prevalent system of local governance which are linked with the existing social and economic bases of power, these amendments, especially the 73rd Amendment Act, provide an alternative to the state-led and re-distributive developmental models. The renewed movement towards democratic decentralization and citizen-centric government has eroded bureaucratic monopoly over development processes and has shifted the locus of power to those who matter at the grassroots. This has been a reality due to a variety of factors. With constitutional recognition to rural and urban local bodies, state-level Election Commissions and Finance Commissions and the granting of mandatory status to the *gram sabahas*, bureaucrats are seen as mere facilitators and promoters of development and not regulators and directors. Within the theoretical format of democratic decentralization, the bureaucracy is a catalyst for change rather than an agent of change. Thus, it is a significant step in eroding the overwhelming paternalistic authority hitherto enjoyed by the bureaucracy.

If the 73rd and 74th Amendments denote 'the political route' to people's empowerment, the Effective and Responsive Administration package that arose out the Chief Ministers Conference, 1997 in New Delhi was an articulation of 'the managerial route' to redefine power equations between the government and the citizens. The imperative need was for governments at all levels to reinvent themselves and redefine their roles and responsibilities to bring about reforms in all areas which had an interface with the people. The public image of the bureaucracy, it was candidly confessed, was one of inaccessibility, indifference, procedure-orientation, poor quality and sluggishness, corruption-proneness and non-accountability for results. The need of the hour was therefore 'to assure the people of India of an efficient, open, responsible, accountable, clean and dynamically adjusting administration at all levels'. Immediate steps needed to be taken to restore people's confidence in the capacity and fairness of administration. Very significantly, the Conference recognized that 'governance has to extend beyond conventional bureaucracies to involve actively citizens and consumer groups at all levels, to empower and inform the public and disadvantaged groups and to ensure service and programme execution through autonomous elected local bodies' (1997, 1–2). There were, thus, three important aspects of the new agenda for civil service reform: (a) there was a crisis in administration which was not people-sensitive or citizen-friendly; (b) there was an urgent need to bring about reform in administration to make it people-sensitive, efficient and cost-effective and (c) there was also need for a change in mindset so that governing could be conceived *afresh* as 'governance'—a wider term than mere formal 'government'—opening, in the process, possibilities for the inclusion of other actors, such as citizens, consumer groups, elected local bodies or those who were linked with the administration in some way or the other. The managerial reform package seeking to transform the public administration suggested the following three measures: (a) accountability-fostering measures; (b) measures for promoting transparency and openness and (c) measures directed at civil service performance and integrity. So, reform was nothing but an enlargement of opportunities for all, not just for select few.

In view of the earlier well-directed designs for civil service reform, the recommendations of the Fifth Pay Commission were another milestone in this direction. True to the spirit, expressed in the 1996 Chief Secretaries conference, the Fifth Pay Commission recommended: (a) downsizing the government through corporatization of activities which involves 'manufacturing of goods or the provision of commercial services'; (b) transparency, openness and economy in government operations through 'privatization of activities where government does not need to play a direct role' and also 'contracting out of services which can be conveniently outsourced to the private sector' (GOI 1997, 122–23) and (c) contractual appointments in selected areas of operations 'for the purpose of maintaining a certain flexibility in staffing both for lateral entry of experts, moderating the numbers deployed depending on the exigencies of work and ensuring availability of most competent and committed personnel for certain sensitive/specialized jobs' (GOI 1997, 175).

The Central government was advised to go for a 30 per cent reduction in the strength of the civil services, as the Pay Commission felt that it would be unwise to let the government sector continue as 'an island of inefficiency' and 'inertia'. The normal procedure of voluntary retirement after completing 20 years was to be continued. Alongside this, the Commission recommended a special scheme of voluntary retirement in the departments where surplus manpower was identified. In such cases, there was to be a provision for the selective retirement of persons, the initiative always resting with the Government and for 'a golden handshake'.

The other significant recommendation of the Commission was concerned with 'openness' in administration. Except for what was detrimental to the interests of the nation, the security of the state or its commercial, economic and other strategic interests, were not be made public, 'nothing should be held back just to subserve the interests of individual bureaucrats and politicians' (GOI 1997, 151). Every important government decisions involving 'a shift in policy' needed to be invariably be accompanied by a White Paper 'in the nature of an explanatory memorandum'. As an integral part of Civil Service Reform, the Commission insisted on the formation of 'an efficient grievance redressal machinery [that] has to be effective, speedy, objective, readily accessible and easy to operate' (GOI 1997, 157). Drawing upon the examples of Canada, UK and Malaysia where effective grievance redressal cells have been functioning efficiently, the idea of a Citizen's Charter—defining the rights of the customers of government schemes and services—was mooted by the Commission. The recognition by the Commission of citizen's right to information and the procedures suggested in this connection were of seminal importance from the point of debureaucratizing government and making it citizen-friendly. The issues, raised by the Pay Commission figured prominently in the 1997 Conference of Chief Ministers where an action plan was adopted to (a) make the administration accountable and citizen-friendly, (b) ensure transparency and right to information and (c) adopt measures to cleanse and motivate the civil services.

The latest in government–citizen relationship is the concept of the Citizen's Charter. Democracy demands that the citizen's voices be heard and taken note of in the delivery of services to him/her, particularly if those services are rendered by government agencies. In fact, the parameters of services need to be defined according to the requirement of the citizens. It is at this interface between the citizen and the service provider that trust is demanded and is also the point at which, very frequently, trust breaks down. There arise problems relating to transparency, accountability and responsiveness of the public administration. The Citizen's Charter was perceived as an instrument that could be used to chisel out the possibilities of a healthier relationship between the service provider and its user. In India, it was also seen as a vehicle for building greater awareness of mutual responsibilities amongst both, the government and the citizens.

Under the Charter, citizens have been brought at the centre of all government activities changing the prevalent concept of treating citizens as passive recipients of government service. The idea behind the Charter is tapping citizens' responses to the actual working of government organizations. Normally, the Charter would cover all public services and aim at demanding from the government and service organizations (post office, railways, etc., for instance) accountability, transparency, quality and choice of services, provided by them to the people. The Charter is not, at all, a list of new principles of governance; instead, it merely reiterates those norms which ideally should constitute the foundation of public administration. It is, therefore, an attempt to bring back the basic values of public administration that have been eroded due to various socio-political reasons, connected also with the evolution of the British political system.

CONCLUDING OBSERVATIONS

Administrative reform is a continuous challenge for those seeking to understand the processes of governmental renewal, which derives its impetus from the ideology that the existing political and governmental systems do not meet contemporary demands. In other words, administrative reform does not take place in a vacuum and is always inspired by the failure of the prevalent system of governance to respond effectively to the social and political needs of the governed. In the context of 'breathtaking change', bureaucratic institutions that developed during the industrial era seemed to be inadequate and the importance of globalization as the conceptualization of new issues involving the government and the governed could not be glossed over in such a scenario. So, a new perspective—underlining the role of market or market-type mechanisms in redefining the nature of governance—emerged in which administrative reform was articulated. What was new was a distinctive formulation synthesizing traditions of public administration with contingent changes in public service provision and influences from the private and voluntary sectors. The process, known as the pluralization of the state redefined the contour of reforms where the state was just a mere agency along with others involved in public affairs. Administrative reform is thus a practical scheme of governance highlighting a clear theoretical advancement in the discipline of public administration.

Administrative change is inevitable because (a) public administration regularly negotiates with the changing priorities of a society of which it is a part and (b) it seeks to incorporate not only new administrative techniques but also the ideas that grow out of socio-economic and political churning. Constant governmental renewal thus appears to be the outcome of the search for an appropriate administration that keeps pace with the changing reality. So, it would not be wrong to argue that governmental renewal is primarily inspired by 'ideologies, philosophies and policy approaches on which interventions in society are based' (Nelissen et al. 1999, 18). Governance is a legitimizing device of governmental action that is justified by the rationale from which a government draws its sustenance. In a democracy, for instance, administrative reform is usually articulated in measures reflective of the predominant politico-ideological values. Not only do they provide rationales for governmental action, but also they are yardsticks for assessing policy alternatives. As is shown, the reform efforts in India reveal the extent to which the changing priorities of the political system act decisively in governmental renewal. Whether in the pre-liberalization phase or in its aftermath, administration reinvented itself to accommodate the dominant values on which its legitimacy was drawn. Before the onset of globalization, the distinctive feature of public administration was that despite having nurtured the colonial structure it had successfully injected new dynamism in governmental activities reflective of a conscious search for an alternative both in spirit and content. Globalization, with its ideological package of 'structural adjustment', means an altogether different and intricate external environment seeking to radically alter both the administrative setup and the values on which it is based. Several steps have already been undertaken to undermine the bureaucratic grip over public administration in India. The recommendations of the Fifth Pay Commission seem to have upheld this spirit while suggesting several steps aimed at administrative reorganization in India. Changes in administration are, however, mostly cosmetic in nature. Thus, although the reform efforts have direction they lack the appropriate ideological backing which in turn appears to have weakened the entire project.

REVIEW QUESTIONS

1. How do you conceptualize administrative reform as a theoretical category? Elaborate your response with reference to its features.
2. 'Administrative reform is a hurdle'. Elaborate.
3. Write a critical essay on the nature of administrative reforms in India.
4. 'Administrative reforms in India are not a purely contextual exercise nor can they be imposed from above'. Do you agree with the view? Elaborate your response.
5. Do you agree with the view that the first Administrative Reforms Commission remains a milestone in administrative reforms in post-independent India? Elaborate your response.
6. Evaluate the nature of the first Administrative Reforms Commission with reference its major recommendations for overhauling Indian administration.
7. 'The Second Administrative Reforms Commission, 2005, is a break with the past'. Do you think so? Elaborate your response.
8. Can ethics be injected in governance? Elaborate your response with reference to the steps that the Second Administrative Reforms Commission, 2005, has suggested.
9. Critically assess the importance of the Moily Commission, 2005 in reforming Indian administration.
10. In what respect has the Second Administrative Reforms Commission been an endeavour to accommodate the market-forces in contemporary India? Elaborate your response.

NOTES

1. Gerald E. Caiden's foreword in Mohammad Mohabbat Khan (1980).
2. Jawaharlal Nehru's (1975, 42–43) speech 'a word to the services' (delivered on 9 December 1955).
3. A parallel is drawn with the 1953 Hoover Commission that made a series of recommendation to improve the US administration in the aftermath of the Second World War.

REFERENCES

Appleby, Paul. 1953. *Public administration in India: Report of a Survey*. Delhi: Managers of publications.

Bhatt, Anil. 1979. "'Colonial Bureaucratic Culture and Development Administration: Portrait of an Old-fashioned Indian Bureaucrat," *Journal of Commonwealth and Comparative Politics,17* (3): 259.

Caiden, Gerald E. 1999. "Administrative Reforms-proceed with Caution. "*International Journal of Public Administration, 22* (6): 815–832.

Gandhi, M. K. 1940. 'The Nature of the Police Force', *Harijan*, 1 September.

GOI. 1949. *Report of the Secretariat Reorganization Committee*. Government of India, New Delhi.

———. 1966–70. *Administrative Reforms Commission's Report*, Ministry of Home Affairs, Government of India. New Delhi.

———. 1981, May. *Eighth and Concluding Report of the National Police Commission*. Government of India, New Delhi.

———. 1997. *The Report of the Fifth Pay Commission*. Vol. 1. Government of India Press, New Delhi.

Gorwala, A. D. 1951. *Report of Public Administration* and also *Efficient Conduct of State Enterprises*. Government of India, New Delhi.

Khan, Mohammad Mohabbat. 1980. *Bureaucratic Self-preservation: Failure of Major Administrative Reform Effects in the Civil Service of Pakistan*. Dhaka: University Press Limited.

Machiavelli, Niccolo. 1979. *The Prince*. Suffolk, UK: Penguin Classics.

Minogue, Martin. 1998. 'Changing the State: Concepts and Practice in the Reform of the Public Sector'. In *Beyond the NPM: Changing Ideas and Practice in Governance,* edited by Martin Minogue, Charles Polidano and David Hume, 17. Cheltenham: Edward Elgar.

National Commission to Review the Working of the Constitution. 2000. *Review of Election Law, Processes and Reform Options*. Consultation Paper, New Delhi.

Nehru, Jawaharlal. 1975. *Jawaharlal Nehru and Public Administration*. New Delhi: Indian Institute of Public Administration.

Nelissen, Nico, Marie-Louise Bemelmand-Videc, Arnold Godfroij, and Peter De Goede, eds. 1999. *Reinventing Government: Innovative and Inspiring Visions*. The Netherlands: International Books.

Sharma, Arvind. 2003. 'Administrative Reforms in India: A Synoptic View'. In *Governance and Development: Issues and Strategies,* edited by Pradeep Sahni and Uma Medury, p. 111. New Delhi: Prentince-Hall.

9

Public Policy in India

LEARNING OBJECTIVES

1. To explain the meaning and the complex unfolding of public policy as a conceptual category.
2. To understand the evolution of public policy as an area of public administration in India.
3. To comprehend how public policy is executed in a neoliberal India.

Public policy is a frequently used term in our daily life. We often read in the newspaper about public health policy, education policy, environmental policy, agricultural policy, industrial policy and so on. Public policies are primarily framed by the government to satisfy public needs and demands. They are the means by which the ends of a collective community are served. Without policy, the government and administration are rudderless. Successful policies make successful governments and administrations and hence there is a saying that when policy fails, the government fails. This chapter is divided into two sections: the first section deals with the theoretical dimensions of public policy, i.e. the concept, relevance, types, models and approaches; the second section deals with the functional dimensions of public policy namely: the formulation, implementation and evaluation processes.

GROWING IMPORTANCE OF PUBLIC POLICY AS A FIELD OF STUDY

Public policy is a relatively new subfield in political science. Its development as an area of study emerged out of a recognition of the fact that traditional analyses of government decisions were incomplete descriptions of political activities. As the relationships between society and its various public institutions became more complex and more interdependent, there emerged the need for more comprehensive assessments of what governments did, along with how and why they pursued some policy alternatives over others (Gerston 1974, 3). Focus on public policy processes developed with the emergence of modern society and industrialization. During the nineteenth century, representative governments began to evolve in some parts of the world. With increased political participation by larger portions of the public, government decisions assumed greater importance and legitimacy. Clashing values with respect to social, economic and political questions had profound implication for politics and government. With these changes, governments began to focus on the problems of their citizens (Gerston 1974, 4). Contemporary public policy and policy analysis particularly has an American and twentieth-century flavour. It was in America where initiatives towards a more unified approach to the study of public problems and policy really began as reflected in the work of Harold Lasswell (*Psychopathology and Politics*, 1930 and *The Analysis of Political Behaviour*, 1948), which culminated in the publication of Lasswell's essay on 'The Policy Orientation', in the book titled *The Policy Sciences*, co-edited by Daniel Lerner. Harold Lasswell stands behind initiating the movement on public policy. In the late 1960s, as Edward S. Quade notes, a number of converging factors, such as war, poverty, crime, race relations and pollution could be credited for producing great interest in policy sciences. In recent times, the study of public policy has evolved into what is virtually a new branch of the social sciences viz., the so-called 'Policy Sciences'.

WHAT IS PUBLIC POLICY?

Before coming to the term 'public policy' it would be fruitful to understand its two components—'public' and 'policy'. We know that public administration emerged as an instrument of the state to serve 'public' interest rather than 'private' interest. In this sense 'public' consists of all the people in general having something in common rather than a few individuals having their personal interests. In political life, the government is the main vehicle to serve the needs and demands of the 'public'. The term 'policy' refers to overall programmes of action towards a given goal. Robert Presthus (1975, 14) defines policy as 'a choice made by an individual or group of individuals that explains, justifies, guides or outlines a certain course of action'. Thus policy can be broadly defined as a proposed course of action of an individual, a group; an institution or government, to realize a specific objective or purpose; within a given environment.

As an approach to understanding political change, public policy has almost as many definitions as there are policy issues. Let us consider a few definitions to get a better understanding of the concept. Thomas R. Dye states that 'public policy is whatever governments choose to do or not to do' (Peters 2012, 5). This definition includes all actions and inactions of the government as public policy. Seeking to extend the linkage, B. Guy Peters (2012, 5) adds that public policy is the 'sum of government activities, whether acting directly or through agents, as it has an influence on the lives of citizens'. James E. Anderson defines public policy as 'a purposive course of action followed by an actor or set of actors in dealing with a problem or matter of concern' (1975, 3). This concept of policy focuses attention on what is actually done as against what is proposed or intended by the government and public officials thereby differentiating a policy from a decision, which is a choice among competing alternatives.

Larry N. Gerston seeks a definition that responds to the actions and exchanges of both people and governments in dynamic public policy as 'the combination of basic decisions, commitments and actions made by those who hold or affect government positions of authority' (Anderson 1975, 7). Yehezkel Dror defines public policy-making as a 'dynamic process which decides major guidelines for action directed at the future, mainly by governmental organs. These guidelines (policies) formally aim at achieving what is in the public interest by the best possible means' (Dror 1974, 12). Public policies are those policies developed by governmental bodies and officials, through non-governmental actors and factors which may influence policy development. The special characteristics of public policies stem from the fact that they are formulated by what David Easton has called the 'authorities' in a political system, 'elders, chiefs, executives, legislators, judges, administrators, counselors, monarchs and the like'. These are he says, the persons who 'engage in the daily affairs of a political system' are 'recognized by most members of the system as having responsibility for these matters', and take actions that are 'accepted as binding by most of the members so long as they act within the limits of their roles' (Easton 1965, 212).

On the basis of the above definitions of different scholars we can spell out some of the implications of the concept of public policy. First, public policy is concerned with purposive or goal-oriented action rather than random behaviour. Second, public policy is a course of action adopted and pursued by governments to serve public interest. Third, public policy is what governments actually do and what subsequently happens, rather than what they intend to do. Fourth, public policy may be either positive or negative in form. In its positive form, it may involve some form of government action to affect a particular problem, while in its negative form, it could involve a decision by government officials not to take action, to do nothing, on some matter for which governmental involvement is sought. Lastly, public policy has a legal and authoritative base. Members of a society find it legitimate to pay taxes, obey traffic rules and pollution control norms because of their legal binding and coercive power.

THE SIGNIFICANCE OF PUBLIC POLICY

Public Policy is a significant component of any political system. It is primarily concerned with the public and their problems. The role of public policy is to shape society for its betterment. W. Parsons while narrates the role of public policy says 'the wider purposes of public policy as involving enlightenment, the fuller development of individuals in society and the development of consensus, social awareness and legitimacy, rather than simply the delivery of goods and services'. Public policies thus involve improving the democratic and political capacities of the people, and not simply the efficiency and effectiveness of the delivery of services. This implies that public policy has a participatory and democratic character.

Public policy has a developmental role. Well-planned policies help in the socio-economic development of a nation. After independence, India formulated a number of policies aimed at socio-economic transformation. Planning Commission was set up. The Five Year Plans were formulated. Policies regarding agricultural development, industrial growth, poverty eradication, rural development, etc., were framed. Today we can see the positive results of these policies. Public policies also helped India in its nation-building task. India could defend itself not only from external aggression but also succeed in keeping divergent groups, caste, linguistic and religious sects united. Thus, since independence, public policies in India have helped in achieving socio-economic development and maintaining national unity and integrity.

As far as the significance of public policy to political science is concerned, Thomas R. Dye (1998, 3) gives three reasons for the same: scientific, professional and political purposes. First of all, public policy can be studied in order to gain greater knowledge about its origin, the processes by which it is developed, and its consequences for society. This, in turn, will increase our understanding of the political system and society in general. Public policy has professional utility also. An understanding of the causes and consequences of public policy permits us to apply social science knowledge to the solution of practical problems. Factual knowledge is a prerequisite to prescribing for the ills of society. If certain end values are desired, then the question of what politics would best implement these ends is a factual question requiring scientific study. In other words, policy studies can produce professional advice.

Finally, public policy has political utility. It ensures that a nation adopts the right policies to achieve the right goals. It is frequently argued that political science cannot be silent or impotent in the face of great social and political crises, and that the political scientist has a moral obligation to advance specific public policies. This task is accomplished by politicians having knowledge of public policies.

Public policy has assumed considerable importance in response to the increasing complexity of society. Public policy helps in explaining the causes and consequences of government activities. Public policies help us not only to understand social ills but also provide devices and mechanisms for moving a social and economic system from the past to the future.

Types of Public Policy

In a political system, the government performs a number of activities. It regulates conflicts within society, it organizes society to carry on conflicts with other societies, it distributes a great variety of symbolic rewards and material services to the members of society and extracts money from society in the form of taxes. Theodore Lowi (1964) suggests that policies may be regulatory, distributive and redistributive in nature and each type of policy is associated with a particular political process.

Regulatory policies are concerned with the regulation and control of individual conduct through coercive techniques. These policies deal with the regulation of trade, quality of education, safety measures, etc. This type of regulation is conducted by autonomous institutions that work on behalf of the government. In India, the Securities and Exchange Board of India (SEBI), the Telecom Regulatory Authority of India, the Bureau of Indian standards and the Reserve Bank of India (RBI) are examples of regulatory agencies. Distributive policies grant goods and services to specific groups of the population. All public welfare programmes are distributive. Agricultural subsidies to farmers, subsidized food for the poor and government health services are examples of such policies. Redistributive policies aim at redistributing resources from one group to another. The main objective of such policies is to set up an equitable society through the redistribution of social and economic rewards. Income tax policies are often cited as examples of redistributive policies.

Fred M. Frohock (1979) adds two more policies in Lowi's three-fold dimension of public policy. These are capitalization and ethical policies. Subsidies and tax concessions received by the business class come under capitalization policies. Such distribution, in theory if not in practice, is aimed at increasing the productive capacity of any society's institutions. Although normally included in distributive policies, capitalization policies are not like the primary consumptive distribution of welfare programmes. Ethical policies are aimed at establishing correct practices for some moral issues. For example, the US Supreme Court's decision in 1973 (*Roe vs. Wade*) made abortion a legally acceptable alternative in the first three months of term. The Court did not settle the moral issue of abortion, and many people still view abortion as morally wrong, even though it is legally permitted. But the public policies, following the Court's decision, set out what ought and ought not to be done in an area marked off by deep moral convictions. In effect, the Supreme Court's decision established legally permissible practices on a moral matter (Frohock 1979, 13).

The Policy Environment

Policy-making cannot be adequately understood separate from the environment in which it takes place. Demands for policy actions are generated in the environment and transmitted to the political system, at the same time; the environment places limits and constraints upon what can be done by policy-makers. James E. Anderson identifies two environmental factors, namely, political culture and socio-economic variables and their influence on policy-makers. Political culture means widely held values, beliefs and attitudes concerning governmental policies and actions.

Differences in public policy and policy-making in various countries can be explained, at least partly, in terms of political–cultural variations. Sociologist Robin W. Williams has identified a number of 'major-value orientations' in American society. These include individual freedom, equality, progress, efficiency and practicality. Values such as these and others, such as democracy and individualism clearly have significance for policy-making. The political culture helps in political behaviour. Differences in political culture help in ensuring that public policy is more likely to favour economic competition in the United States because individual opportunity is a widely held value here, while it is more likely to tolerate industrial cartels in China because economic competition has not been highly valued here.

Socio-economic conditions also influence political activities to a great extent. Public policies can be viewed as arising out of conflicts between different groups of people, private and official, processing differing interests and desires. One of the prime sources of conflict, especially in modern societies, is economic activity. Conflicts may develop between the interests of different groups. Groups that are underprivileged or dissatisfied with their current relationships with other groups in the economy may seek governmental assistance to improve their situation. Thus, there have been labour groups, dissatisfied with their wages resulting from private bargaining with employers that have sought minimum wage legislation. A society's level of economic development will impose limits on what the government can do in providing public goals and services to the community. The scarcities of economic resources will, of course, be more limiting in many underdeveloped countries of the world than in an affluent society such as the United States. Social conflicts and change also provoke demands for government action. In the 1990s, there was a growing demand for reservation in India from the backward classes. They put pressure on the government to evolve a policy of reservation for their upliftment. Those with conflicting interests and values opposed such demands, with the consequence that public officials found themselves hard-pressed to desire acceptable policy solutions.

It can be fairly drawn from this discussion that social, economic and political factors need to be considered to understand how policy decisions are made and why some decisions are made rather than others.

The Official Policy-makers

Official policy-makers are those who possess the legal authority to engage in the formation of public policy. These include legislators, executives, administrators and judges. Each performs policy-making tasks at least somewhat different from the others. Legislatures are concerned with the central political tasks of policy formation and law making in a political system. In the course of approving legislatures, the legislature performs other important functions like deliberating, scrutinizing, criticizing and publicizing government policies and their consequences for the public on the floor of the house. Usually it lays down the broad objects which the administration has to pursue and in more important cases also the machinery and the procedures through which these are to be pursued.

Modern governments everywhere depend vitally upon executive leadership both in policy formulation and in its execution. In the Parliamentary form of government, all policies need to have the approval of the Cabinet and the ministers of the government introduce the countries; the executive probably has even more influence in policy-making than in developed countries. It is due to the lack of a strong bureaucratic base and little influence of the pressure groups that facilitates greater concentration of power in the hands of the government.

In the post-Second World War period, the classical doctrine of the politics–administration dichotomy has proved to be futile. Now there is a consensus that administrators are also involved in the policy formulation processes in more than one way. In complex industrial societies, the technicality and complexity of many policy matters, the need for continuing control and the lack of time and information among other reasons, have led to the delegation of much discretionary authority to administrative agencies formally, recognized as 'the rule making power'. Public officials today are associated with policy formulation in three important ways. First they supply facts, data and analysis (regarding the workability of a policy) to the ministers or to the legislature and impart content to a policy. Second, they are constantly in touch with the public, so they have a better understanding of their problems and the solutions required in the form of policies. Third, on account of lack of time and knowledge, the legislature passes 'skeletal' Acts and leaves the 'body' to be filled by the administration. It is here that the administrators have maximum scope for 'policy-making'. The judiciary also plays an important role in public policies. In countries where the courts have the power of judicial review, they have played an important role in policy formation. They have the power to determine the constitutionality of the actions of the legislature and the executive branches and to declare them null and void, if such actions are found to be in conflict with constitutional provisions. They play an important role in giving direction to the social, economic and political policies of national importance.

Unofficial Participants

Besides the official policy-makers, many other unofficial players may participate in the policy-making process like interest groups, political parties and individual citizens and they may considerably influence policy formation without possessing the legal authority to take binding policy decisions.

Political Parties

In modern societies, political parties generally perform the function of 'interest aggregation', that is, they seek to convert the particular demands of interest groups into general policy alternatives. Every political party has its own programmes or policies. These programmes, policies or values are presented to the people in the form of manifestos (before the elections) in order to gain their support. The professional purpose of the manifesto is that it lends a promise, that in case that party comes to power, it will implement the policies promised therein. Since the government is formed by the leaders of the political party that wins the majority of seats in the legislature, party cadres get involved in the formulation of policies to which they are committed.

Pressure Groups

Pressure groups are organizations with formal structures whose members share common interests. They strive to influence policies of the government without attempting to occupy political offices. The main function of these groups is to express demands and present alternatives for policy action. They constantly try to protect the interest of their members either by pressurizing the government of the bureaucracy to take decisions, which are likely to be in consonance with the interests of their members. They employ various methods such as publicity campaigns, lobbying, personal meetings with the officials or legislatures, writing letters or memoranda, etc., for this purpose.

Individual Citizens

In the present age, it is not possible for any government to impose policies on citizens perennially, if such policies don't reflect their will. Public policies have to be consistent with the interests of the citizens. A democratic government cannot adopt policies to which a large body of citizens is opposed. Thus, the citizens exercise an indirect influence on policy-making. The exercise of the right to vote enables citizens to make a choice of public policies. Elections are opportunities for citizens to select between the alternative policies thrown up by political parties.

WHO IMPLEMENTS POLICY?

Public administration is mainly a policy implementation organization. Many other actors like the legislature, the courts, pressure groups and community organizations help in the process. In modern political systems, public policy is implemented primarily by a complex system of administrative agencies. These agencies perform most of the day to day work of the government and thus affect citizens directly compared to other governmental units. Administrative agencies often operate under broad and ambiguous statutory mandates giving them a lot of discretion to decide what should or should not be done. Lack of time, interest, information and expertise on the part of politicians may also contribute to the delegation of authority to these agencies. Policy implementation is not an easy task. Without cooperation from the top administrators, little can be achieved. In policy implementation, administrators, especially senior executives, should have the functions discussed below. First of all, administrators must clearly understand the nature and significance of policies that the political masters have set. They are responsible for giving advice for the formulation of policies designed to achieve goals, and also mobilizing, organizing and managing the resources necessary to carry through these policies. Second, they should assist policy-makers to avoid ambiguities. They need to advise them on the importance of adopting policies which can be implemented. Third, they should be able to translate general policies and their objectives into operational targets. This function should also include analyses of probable costs and benefits for achieving the operational targets. As far as possible, they should adopt a rational approach and use management techniques to implement policies. Finally, they should be able to pay special attention to the coordination of policies and policy instruments. They should analyze the policy in question in relation to other policies to see if any inconsistencies exist, and examine whether it complements or supplements other policies to produce better results (Dror 1974, 12–13).

Bureaucratic organizations have been subjected to a number of criticisms. They are said to be afflicted with excesses of red-tapism, unresponsiveness, hierarchies and rigid rule frameworks. Despite these maladies, they hold importance. Kenneth Meier and Bohte (2007) write, 'when faced with a cute crisis, chronic problems, or even apathy, the positive state [Government] responds, and the response usually includes a bureaucracy'. To a large extent, bureaucratic agencies are responses to the directions of public policies.

While the administrative machinery is the primary implementer of public policy, legislative bodies are also involved in policy implementation. Although the role of legislative bodies is not very crucial; they may affect administrative organizations in several ways. It subjects administrative discretion and delegation to institutional control. Parliamentary approval is required for many top level administrative appointments, and this may be used to influence the implementation process. The judiciary also plays an important role in policy formulation. Some laws are enforced primarily through judicial action. The courts affect administration through their interpretation of statues and administrative rules and regulations and their review of administrative decisions in the cases brought before them. Courts can facilitate, hinder or largely nullify the implementation of particular policies through their decisions. Political parties also affect the policy implementation process. They try to influence both the executives and the bureaucracy, to implement policies which serve their purpose. Sometime they prevent the implementation of a policy that may be contrary to their ideology. The civil society groups, non-governmental organizations and community organizations also help bringing about implementation. The Panchayats after the 73rd Amendment Act (1992) have acted as an integrating device for grassroots agencies. In short, a variety of participants affect the implementation of a given policy.

POLITICO-IDEOLOGICAL AND INSTITUTIONAL SETTINGS

Public policy is a constructed design in a specific context. This is why it is difficult to have a universal mode of analysis of public policy. Contrary to the one-size-fits-in formula, a careful analysis of the making of public policy suggests that its articulation is always situation-specific. There is however a general point that needs to be kept in mind: public policy is a wave and with certain broad politico-ideological characteristics presumably because of the uniform context in which it is structured. With the transformation of the context, the nature of public policy is bound to change, as will be shown below by a detailed discussion of the processes leading to the making of the Constitution for independent India after the attainment of political freedom. There are two interrelated aspects in the making of public policy which are critical here: on the one hand, the interface between the context and actual public policy reflects the ideological predilection of contemporary political dispensation while, on the other, it also mirrors a desire to go beyond the present which is what makes public policy transcendental. The example of *Zawabit* (state laws) that Barni insisted in his *Fatwa-i-Jahandari* proves the point. By consistently arguing for state laws in preference to the *Shariat* Laws, he prepared a strong ground for secular laws. In his perception, to rule a religiously diverse India, the administrator was expected to remain neutral while administering rules and regulations and with a clearly religious rule, tilted in favour of a community, remained a hurdle for an efficient administration. Although Barni made this argument in the context of medieval India, it continues to hold water even today since it established a principle insisting on the priority of state laws over those which were meant to protect narrow communal interests.

This is evident in contemporary India. With the removal of the British rule, the nationalist leaders while preparing independent India to face the challenges of a new nation undertook various steps to articulate an ideological preference for a socio-religiously diverse country. The concern was to bring disparate communities together for a common cause. They thus engaged themselves in evolving broad principles appropriate to build a well-knit society. The task was not an easy one, especially in the context of the traumatic experience of the 1947 partition. What was the way out? For the founding fathers, three major ideological influences seemed to have been critical in the making of public policy in India: colonialism, nationalism and democratization. The colonial, nationalist and democratic responses to the processes for the making of public policy remained crucial in comprehending Indian politics after decolonization. Two points need to be kept in mind: first, although colonialism and nationalism ere surely antagonistic to each other, there is no doubt that the former provoked circumstances in which nationalism emerged as a powerful ideology to articulate the voice of the colonized. Second, colonialism also led to a slow process of democratization by gradually involving people who were favourably disposed towards the alien administration. The colonial state had permitted some measures of representation to carefully selected Indian interests. But it had also ensured that the state remained a distant object from the ruled. The British political elites, influenced by the Enlightenment principles, seemed inclined to some values which ran counter to their colonial interests; they thus evolved a unique mixture of policies involving measures to protect their self-interests along with their belief in the fundamental principles of the Enlightenment philosophy. The British imperial attitude in India thus seemed to be highly ambiguous reflected in the endeavour 'to negotiate their liberal regard for self-rule as the best form of government and their vested interests in being imperial masters'.[1] There is no doubt that the post-colonial state in India inherited its habits of governance from colonial practices. And its *weltanschauung* (world view) is based on 'the mixed legacies of colonial rule' that also upheld the rule of law, bureaucracy, citizenship, parasitic landlords, modern political institutions and the 'two-track tradition of protest and participation' (Mitra 2004, 29–34). Nonetheless, a careful look at the evolution of institutions in India clearly shows that they evolved creatively to adjust to changing circumstances. The Westminster model of Parliamentary democracy that India adopted was not a clone, but rather was responsive to the situation-specific ethos and existent socio-cultural milieu. Furthermore, the changing socio-economic profile of the legislative assemblies and national Parliament has also been indicative of a trend towards a genuinely inclusive democracy. Given the growing politicization of the peripheral sections of society, the elite-centric governance is seen to be fading away with the consolidation of people-centric governance. The change of political authority at regular intervals through elections is an eloquent testimony to the depth of the democratic processes, which are not merely articulated in periodic elections. The introduction of adult suffrage transformed the texture of India's public policy beyond recognition. Democracy is therefore no longer confined to the electoral participation of voters; rather, it is also articulated in the everyday struggles of people while exercising their rights as citizens. In consequence, the terms of political discourse in contemporary India no longer resonate the values of the erstwhile Congress era, but are the outcome of the processes of a deepening of democracy. Raising the voice of the regions, those representing the regions, seem to have created a platform for effective dialogue between the centre and the periphery. The history of independent India is thus a testimony to the creative articulation of a democracy that is neither ethnocentric nor exactly imitative of western experiences, but *sui generis*.

A careful analysis of the making of India's Constitution over a period of three years between 1946 and 1949 reveals how the founding fathers crafted a new course of action to translate the democratic aspirations of a politically free India following decolonization. Furthermore, although the Constitution was a continuity at least in structural and procedural terms, it was also a clear break with the past since the 1950 Constitution drew on an ideology that sought to establish a liberal democratic polity in India in the aftermath of the withdrawal of the British. There can be no greater evidence of the commitment to constitutionalism and rule of law on the part of the founding fathers than the Constitution that they framed despite the serious difficulties due to the partition. The commitment to liberal democratic values, as the Constituent Assembly proceedings suggest, remained paramount in the making of the Constitution. For instance, though the Constitution makers valorized the idea of popular sovereignty, they redefined it and adopted the liberal representative principles to create a Nehruvian statist political order. Popular sovereignty was thus defined in the Habermasian proceduralized sense in which 'popular opinion and will formation in informal and voluntary public spheres could seek to influence the channels of legitimate law making' (Sen 2007, 112).

SOCIALISTIC PATTERN OF SOCIETY

The Constitution was to foster the achievement of many goals. Social revolution was one of them. It aimed to fulfil the basic needs of the common man and it was hoped that this revolution would bring about fundamental changes in the structure of Indian society. The members of the Constituent Assembly did not work in a vacuum; they were members of the nation's Parliament between 1947 and 1950 and were also at the head of both the provincial, and the union governments and were therefore aware of problems including food shortage, communal riots, etc. 'The state', Jawaharlal Nehru thus argued, 'has become a dynamic state—and not a static state—in which administrators have to adapt themselves to the changes ... have to adopt methods to the changed conditions of work and the changed objectives of work' (*The Hindustan Times* 1950).

There were three possible ways: (a) the Left alternative—where the state was the owner of the means of production, (b) the Rightist alternative where the state would not interfere and (c) the mixed economy in which the state would involve itself in ventures for 'public utilities' to ensure all-round development in the country. Jawaharlal Nehru, India's first democratically elected premier, entrusted the state with the task of steering capitalist development in India thereby seeking to ensure equitable distribution of wealth. It was 'an approach that sought to combine goals of growth and reduction of disparities, while avoiding the violence and regimentation of revolutionary change' (Frankel 2005, 3). It was, as Nehru characterized, 'a third way which takes the best from all existing systems—the Russian, the American and others—and seeks to create something suited to one's own history and philosophy' (Karanjia as quoted in Frankel 2005, 3). Seeking to articulate the 'third way', the economic model that India adopted in the aftermath of independence was the model of state-led import substituting industrialization.

The Preamble to the Constitution of India enshrined principles to lay the foundation of a socialistic pattern of society. The Directive Principles of State Policy (part IV of the Constitution) emphasize that the goal of the Indian polity is not unbridled laissez faire but that of a welfare state where the state has a positive duty to ensure to its citizens' social and economic justice with dignity, consistent with the unity and integrity of the nation. By making them fundamental in the governance and making the laws of the country and duty of the state to apply these principles, the founding fathers made it the responsibility of future governments to find a middle way between individual liberty and the public good, between preserving the property and privilege of the few and bestowing benefits on the many in order to liberate the powers of men equally for contributions to the common good.[2]

In this model of state-directed development, the most significant instrument was the Planning Commission that came into being in January, 1950 despite serious opposition from the Gandhians within the Congress Working Committee. However, the Cabinet Resolution that finally led to the creation of the Commission underlined three major principles as special terms of reference in the preparation of the plans which largely defused the opposition. These principles included: (a) that the citizens, men and women equally, have the right to an adequate means of livelihood; (b) that the ownership and control of the material resources of the country are so distributed as best to serve the common good and (c) that the operation of the economic system does not result in the concentration of wealth and means of production to the common detriment (Frankel 2005, 85).

The 1977 Industrial Policy Resolution upheld the importance to the cottage industries and also declared that PSU should be profitable and efficient. The 1980 Industrial Policy Resolution reiterates the 1956 Industrial Policy Resolution presumably because of Indira Gandhi's insistence on the socialistic pattern of society which swayed Jawaharlal Nehru and his colleagues in the past. The state should play a progressive active role in the development of industries. The industries were classified according to the Resolution as: (a) industries manufacturing arms and ammunition, production and control of atomic energy and the ownership and management of railway transport and (b) basic industries viz. iron, coal and steel, aircraft manufacture, ship building, mineral oils. I & II are state's domain and the rest can be given to the private enterprises.

The Congress commitment to the principles of socialism was reiterated in the 1955 Avadi annual session of the Congress. In view of the declared objective of being a socialist pattern of society, the state shall play a vital role in planning and development. The 1956 IPR underlined the significance of cottage industries for (a) large scale employment and (b) moral boost and consequently confidence. The 1980 IPR reiteration of the 1956 IPR due to Mrs Gandhi's faith in socialism.

NEOLIBERAL ECONOMIC REFORMS IN INDIA

With the onset of macroeconomic reforms in the 1990s, state-led developmental plans seemed to have lost significance in a situation where the non-state actors grew in importance in redefining the state's agenda.[3] India adopted reforms in perhaps a very guarded manner. One probably cannot simply wish away the theoretical justification for state intervention in a transitional economy. Socialist principles may not have been forgotten, but the importance of the state for the social sectors cannot be minimized unless a meaningful alternative is mooted. This is reflected in the obvious distortions in India's economy. On the basis of an empirical study of Andhra Pradesh and other supporting data, it has been argued that 'two economies—one affluent and the other predominantly agricultural economy—are emerging ... and this division can be seen across the social and regional landscape of India' (Frankel 2005, 625). The technology-based, export-oriented and city-centric economy flourishes in the new economic environment while the agricultural economy remains backward and those associated with this 'have little expectation of a better future [and] remain preoccupied with the daily struggle to secure a livelihood' (Frankel 2005, 625).

It is true that economic liberalization is a significant influence and yet, the importance of the prevalent 'politico-institutional context' cannot be undermined while conceptualizing the impact of economic reforms in India. In a significant way, the institutional legacy of 'a well-entrenched state' has affected the post-reform possibilities in India. As a commentator has argued, 'India's bureaucratized regime—the license–quota–permit raj—has had major, unintended consequences on post-transition patterns: all [state] governments and central regimes continue to rely on state-led strategies of reform; there is no "Washington Consensus" or "neoliberal" route to reforms in India' (Sinha 2004, 51). There is no doubt that economic reforms brought about radical changes in India's political economy. Yet, the old regulatory regime of the bygone era remained critical in the path and processes of liberalization in a very decisive way. What thus proliferates across India is 'state-guided routes to liberalization rather than market fundamentalism' (Sinha 2004, 55). This has resulted in obvious tensions in the economy which are neither appreciative of market hegemony nor fully supportive of the erstwhile state-led development paradigm. In fact, herein lie the roots of severe social discontentment, fuelling ideological political movements, including the militant Maoist movement, challenging the state for its failure to protect the marginalized. The situation has thus become far more complicated because there is evidence to confirm that the state has miserably failed to address genuine socio-economic grievances of the majority of the people especially in rural India which leads to the consolidation of people-centric political movements. Given their distinctive contextual nature, they cannot be understood in the derivative theoretical discourses.

CHANGING ECONOMIC HORIZONS

The introduction of macroeconomic reforms in 1991 posed a serious challenge to state-led development plans and programmes. Given the clear failure of the Nehruvian socialistic pattern of society that was espoused so zealously by the political leadership immediately after India's decolonization in 1947, the 1991 New Economic Policy did not appear to have raised many eyebrows. Nonetheless, the principles governing a socialistic pattern of society cannot be said to have completely disappeared; instead, the Indian state seems to have adopted a context-specific strategy in which state intervention is appreciated so long as a meaningful alternative is unavailable. Furthermore, one cannot simply gloss over the larger political-philosophical issue involved here. The argument that the march of the market economy has been resisted by the Indian elites' infatuation for socialistic principles does not appear persuasive in the light of the visible mass opposition to economic liberalization. As Pranab Bardhan (2008, 136) has argued, 'our collective passion for group equity, for group rather than individual rights and the deep suspicion of competition in which the larger economic interests are given an opportunity to gobble up the small, work against the forces of market and allocational efficiency'. This passion was particularly strengthened by Gandhi who being opposed to market-driven capitalism, was drawn to 'small is beautiful' perspective while conceptualizing his distinctive model of economic development. Economic reforms have created conditions in which those persuaded by the Gandhian moral critique of market expansion and competition are drawn to the left radical forces for building active grassroots movements all over the country for the protection of the environment, women's rights and the traditional livelihood of the indigenous people. In such circumstances, development or market seems to be synonymous with 'dispossession of the little people and with despoliation of the environment'. Major strands in the political culture thus, as Bardhan rightly concludes, 'provide a non-too-hospitable climate for market reforms' (Bardhan 2008, 137).

Economic liberalization in India ushered in reforms 'by stealth' (Jenkins 1999, 172–207)[4] as it was more or less accepted as a *fait accompli* to avoid the massive balance of payment crisis in 1991. Apart from domestic compulsions, internationally two major events undermined 'the basic premises of the earlier social consensus regarding the development strategy' (Tendulkar and Bhavani 2007, 85). The first was the collapse of the former Soviet Union and its East European satellite states that moved towards 'a market-oriented economic system' eschewing altogether the model of planned economic development. Second, the spectacular success of 'the socialist market economy' of China with the opening of its economy since 1978 and its concomitant favourable economic fall-outs that cast serious doubts on India's development strategy, based on economic nationalism.

This is reflected in the obvious distortions in India's economy. On the basis of an empirical study of Andhra Pradesh and other supporting data, the author thus argues that 'two economies—one affluent and the other predominantly agricultural economy—are emerging ... and this division can be seen across the social and regional landscape of India' (Frankel 2005, 625). The technology-based export-oriented city-centred economy is flourishing in the new economic environment while the agricultural economy remains backward and those associated with this 'have little expectation of a better future [and] remain preoccupied with the daily struggle to secure a livelihood' (Frankel 2005, 625). The contribution of agriculture to national income has, in recent years, fallen dramatically but more than 600 million Indians still depend on farming. This is a matter of concern, for obvious reasons. In fact, the growing divergence between the share of agriculture in GDP and in the work force alerts 'to the urgent imperative of raising farm productivity in India [which] languishes far below potential' (Shah 2008).

While agriculture remains 'a bargain sector', industrialization is hailed as 'the panacea' for India's economic ills since the economy is growing fast even when agriculture stagnates. Seeking to articulate the typical Indian response to liberalization, the Industrial Policy Resolution 1991 thus suggested several steps to 'unshackle the Indian industrial economy from the cobwebs of unnecessary bureaucratic control' though within the overall control of the state. Four specific steps were recommended: first, the government decided to abolish 'industrial licensing policy' except for a short list of industries related to security and strategic concerns, social reasons, hazardous chemicals and overriding environmental reasons. Second, the government also endorsed 'direct foreign investment up to 51 per cent foreign equity in high priority industries'. To avoid bottlenecks, an amendment to the Foreign Exchange Regulation Act 1973 was suggested. Third, it was also decided to withdraw protection of 'the sick public sector units' and there would be 'a greater thrust on performance improvement' to ensure accountability of those involved in these state-sponsored enterprises. Finally, the Policy sought to remove 'the threshold limits of assets in respect of those companies functioning under the MRTP (Monopolies Restrictive Trade Practices) Act'. By seeking to amend this Act, the Policy suggested the elimination of 'the requirement of prior approval of the Union Government for establishment of new undertakings, expansion of undertakings, merger, amalgamation and take over and appointments of Directors under certain circumstances'. The Indian response to economic liberalization is most creative, if judged contextually. The Nehruvian socialist pattern of society cannot be so easily dispensed with for historical reasons while globalization may not be an appropriate strategy for economic development in a poor country like India because in its present form, argues Joseph Stiglitz, it seems like 'a pact with the devil'. A few people may have become wealthier, but for most of the people, closer integration into the global economy, 'has brought greater volatility and insecurity, and more inequality' (Stiglitz 2006, 292).[5] Economic liberalization is thus a double-edged device which while improving the lives of some Indians also left millions more untouched. Hence it has been rightly pointed out that the essence of economic liberalization in India can be captured by a Buddhist proverb suggesting that 'the key to the gate of heaven is also the key that could open the gate to hell'. Indeed, the danger and opportunity are so intricately intermingled in economic reforms that 'the journey to the promised land of [economic prosperity] could easily turn into a hellish nightmare of poverty and widening inequality for the majority' (Bhaduri and Nayyar 1996, 159).

The above analysis is helpful in conceptualizing the making of public policy in India since public policy is not made in a vacuum. The prevalent socio-economic context holds the key to understanding the processes that are critical for comprehending the nature of public policy. As is evident now, the erstwhile emphasis on a socialistic pattern of society does not seem to be tenable in the changed socio-economic context. It is true that India is not a liberalized economy in the sense that her south-east Asian neighbours are though she has welcomed economic liberalization in certain prime economic sectors for inclusive growth. The policy-makers had new priorities in the new environment and as a result the focus gradually shifted from state-led planned economic development to the importance of the market forces. The protection that the public enterprises received in the earlier dispensation was gradually withdrawn and the policy of disinvestment is being pursued with zeal. Even the Maharatnas are now subject to market competition and weak public sector units are being phased out since they are no longer viable in the face of stiff competition.

Re-conceptualizing public policy in the context of the consolidation of the liberalized–privatized–globalized (LPG) regime in India, policy-makers have provided a new direction to the making of public policies which were inconceivable in the erstwhile state-led planned economic development. The change is visible in three ways: first, policy-making no longer remains a prerogative of either the bureaucrats or politicians and has the gradual involvement of stakeholders from different walks of life. Now, in the changed milieu, NGOs and civil society actors cannot be bypassed and their role is most critical in conceptualizing and making of public policy. Second, the growing importance of global or transcendental actors who may not be directly involved in the preparation of policies, but remain critical given their importance as donors. Without the funds that these powerful players provide, developmental activities are likely to be halted and thereby their voices gain significance. By being integrally connected with the processes of development, not only do they consolidate their voice, they also emerge as key players in policy-making. Third, the rising importance of citizens in policy-making, which is no longer an exclusive domain of politicians or bureaucrats. An alert citizenry provides critical inputs to the making of policies which the state cannot afford to ignore because of the obvious adverse consequences. There are innumerable examples to show that in recent years, some of the major policies were accepted by the government because of citizens' mobilization on a particular issue. Being armed with, for instance, the Right to Information Act 2005, citizens are no longer mere recipients but instigators of change. With their growing consolidation for gender sensitivity, for example, they continue to influence government policies in a very significant manner.

CONTINGENT CIRCUMSTANCES AND POLICY-MAKING

In the context of the LPG regime that has emerged following the adoption of the New Economic Policy 1991, public policy-making cannot be insulated from external sources which have become very critical given the obvious importance of external players in India's development. With their critical role in policy-making, the global actors, whether the World Bank, IMF or other foreign donors, global actors have become part and parcel of policy activities which, in the past, remained an arena where the domestic players had the final say. The situation underwent a sea change following India's decision to integrate with the global economy. Nonetheless, in the making of public policies, the domestic context continues to remain critical. By drawing on some of the major examples, it will be shown how domestic circumstances shape public policy.

First, the Mandal Commission Report 1978 brought about radical changes in India's policy-making in two fundamental ways: not only did it introduce reservation for the Other Backward Classes who constitute more than half of India's demography, on the one hand, it also brought back the importance of one's caste identity, on the other, making it a prime consideration in so far as the formulation of public policy was concerned. With the acceptance of this report by the state in 1990, the Mandal Commission became a new reference point in contemporary Indian politics. Although the policy of reservation does have a past when those belonging to the scheduled castes and scheduled tribes were given reservation, the Mandal formula stood out because it guaranteed protection to a majority of the population who were denied their due in public jobs. This ushered in a new era in the policy domain which radically altered the texture of policy-making by recognizing caste as an important criterion in formally distributing public jobs.

Second, the Right to Information (RTI) Act 2005 is an empowering device that has also brought about significant changes in the policy domain. Replacing the Official Secret Act 1923, this legislation enables citizens to seek information within a stipulated time frame; the denial of required information amounting to the denial of a right which immediately attracts punishment. The RTI is a revolutionary step because it has not only transformed the attitude of government officials who are now bound to respond to any request for information but also that of the citizens who are now empowered to raise issues affecting them and demand their resolution by applying the well-established democratic-legal means. In public policy-making, this Act remains a significant input because it provides policy-makers with the inputs which may not be otherwise available. The RTI thus reconfirms the significance of citizens in public policy which is regularly renewed with their pro-active role in decision making.

Third, similar to the RTI, the Right to Education Act (RTE) 2009 is another significant piece of legislation that reinforced the importance of citizens in public policy-making. The Act makes education a fundamental right of every child between the ages of six and fourteen and specifies minimum norms in elementary schools. Based on the dictum that no child should be left behind, this Act creates circumstances in which those who are denied this right can go for judicial endorsement. So the RTE is an enabling law which also allows citizens to assert themselves if they are deprived of what is a constitutionally guaranteed right. Despite the fanfare over the RTE, there are criticisms because the quality of education provided by government schools is very poor due to lack of quality teachers and lack of adequate infrastructure. The campaign that the RTE has unleashed by making the right to education a fundamental right has not resolved the problems of primary education India, as various researches have shown.[6] Nonetheless, as a major public policy intervention, the RTE has provoked new initiatives on the part of citizens who by being alert and assertive are integrally connected with the processes of policy-making. With them as partners, citizens have become as critical as the bureaucrats or politicians in the policy domain.

Finally, several flagship programmes launched by the government of India have also made citizens an integral part of public policy-making. These programmes were the outcome of the government of India's initiative to reach out to those sections of India's population who have so far remained peripheral to the policy domain. The citizens cannot be bypassed if they demand benefits out of these programmes. Of all these programmes, the Mahatma Gandhi National Rural Employment Guarantee Act (MGNREGA) 2005 was most revolutionary because it established the right to employment as an inalienable right in India. In order to translate the assurance that the founding fathers gave in the Part IV (Directive Principles of State Policy) of the Constitution which guarantees the right to work (Article 41) and to provide dignity to the rural populace through an assurance of livelihood security (Article 21), this Act pledges to offer livelihood security in rural areas by providing at least 100 days of guaranteed employment in a financial year, to every adult member in each household willing to engage in unskilled manual work. Employment is guaranteed with minimum wages, and if employment is not available, the applicant is entitled to an unemployment allowance which also means that the MGNREGA is a legal entitlement. An outcome of the bottom-up and demand-driven processes, the Act is a major public policy intervention in recent years which, despite being a political device to win votes, has resulted in significant changes at the grassroots. Not only has the Act made people rights conscious, it has also effectively challenged the roots of exploitation by vested interests in rural areas. By insisting on their rights for employment, the rural adult population not only makes policy-makers sensitive of their responsibilities, but also creates circumstances in which they play key roles in policy-making.

These selective examples highlight three important points: first, public policy is a complex domain in which the role of the bureaucrats and politicians is as important as that of the citizens. Public policy is made on the basis of a dialogue involving the state and the citizens in which the two are dialectically connected. Second, by being interactional, public policy is also directional whereby the views of the stakeholders are articulated. Challenging the conventional notion that public policy is the exclusive domain of bureaucrats and politicians, an argument supporting citizens' active role in policy-making can thus be made. Third, the above policy devices also show the changing nature of the policy context which is critical to understand the gradual involvement of citizens in the policy processes. As a careful study of the contingent circumstances reveals, public policy is also an arena where various actors operate to attain their respective goals which directs our attention to politics or a specific kind of power relationship that shapes and guides policy responses in a particular socio-economic and political milieu. This is perhaps most fundamental in conceptualizing public policies and the processes that are integral to their formulation.

PUBLIC POLICY PROCESS IN INDIA

Policy-making is the government's vital function in a democratic country like India. The process of policy-making begins with the ideas and opinions people have about the actions that they want the government to undertake. There are also demands by civil society organizations or interest groups on the political system for action on some perceived problems. People with demands, supported or opposed by interest groups, seek commitments from the government to put their ideas into action (Sapru 2010, 152). In the Indian Parliamentary system, the activities of the government are carried out by a Council of Ministers, headed by the Prime Minister. In the Council of Ministers, the Cabinet occupies an important place, as it is the agency that takes important decisions pertaining to government policies. The Cabinet formulates all the policies and sends them to the Parliament for approval. The Parliament consisting of the Lok Sabha and the Rajya Sabha discusses them before the endorsement by its members. Policies are approved once they are accepted by a majority. Once it is approved in the Parliament, they are sent to the President of India for assent. The President is free to either approve or withhold; on occasions, the Bills can be sent back to the Parliament with the comments and recommendations of the President. The Parliament is authorized to make changes, if its members so desire, in light of the suggestions, made by the President. If the Bill is sent back to the President, there is no way he/she can disapprove it again; it is mandatory for him/her to approve the Bills once they are returned by the Parliament after following the due processes of discussion or otherwise. After having completed these processes, the Bill is converted into an official policy which is then binding on everybody.

Another stage in the public policy process is policy implementation. The real fruits of a policy can be enjoyed when the policy is implemented effectively. In India, various institutions like the legislature, executive, judiciary, civil services, civil society organizations, among others, participate directly or indirectly in the process of policy implementation. The legislature plays an important role in the policy implementation process by expressing its opinion during the question hour session and also when the Bill is discussed on floor of the House. There are several committees like the Public Accounts Committee, Estimates Committee and various select committees that scrutinize the government's decisions. Every year during the discussion on the annual budget, members usually take part in the discussion. The judiciary also plays a critical role in the policy implementation processes. Any policy formulated by the government which is repugnant with the Constitution is declared ultra vires to the prevalent rule of law. The introduction of Public Interest Litigation (PIL) also strengthens the Supreme Court of India to take cognizance of illegal governmental activities, if any. This is a powerful instrument for the judiciary to hold the government in check in case of any deviation from the rule of law. The role of the executive is no less insignificant. With aid from the civil services, the executive is primarily responsible for the implementation of policies. An efficient civil service is always a great help to policy-makers. Civil servants, with their expertise, provide support to the ministers who may not have the required skills to execute the decisions that they make. Only on the basis of healthy cooperation between the permanent and political executives, an efficient policy regime can be built. Despite occasional friction, the relationship between them remains cordial, and hence the policies that the government makes with assistance from the permanent executive are usually implemented without hiccups.

After being successfully implemented, policies are evaluated in order to assess whether they are congruent with the intentions of the policy-makers; or whether the results have been in conformity with what was expected. In India, the official policy evaluation agencies are the legislature and its various committees, the Comptroller and Auditor General, commissions of enquiry and the departmental evaluation reports. Evaluation activity is also carried out by agencies which are not connected with the government. University research scholars, private research institutes, pressure groups and organizations with public interests are also engaged in the evaluation of public policies. They also provide people with information on specific policies. This is an effective channel whereby policy-makers are made accountable to the people who always remain vigilant and alert. These instruments thus fulfil a significant role in realizing one of the fundamental aims of democracy in India which does not merely mean elections at regular intervals, but a constant interaction between the rulers and the ruled within the framework of governance.

CONCLUDING OBSERVATIONS

Public policy-making is a very complex, dynamic process with its various components making different contributions to it. It decides major guidelines for action directed at the future, mainly by governmental organs. These guidelines formally aim at achieving set goals which are considered to be most appropriate for the governed. The policy-making process is one way of understanding the means through which conflicting demands are heard; reconciled and resolved in an orderly, if not always satisfactory, fashion. Fundamentally, it provides some explanation of the cacophony known as 'politics' in an ever changing society. This means that public policy seeks to articulate values which are critical in governance. In a democracy like India, the importance of the people remains most decisive in so far as public policy-making is concerned. While mirroring public choice, policy-makers are expected to take into account the stakeholders as integral to the policy processes. The role of bureaucrats and politicians is significant, but not exclusive especially with the legal empowerment of the populace in recent years. The citizens cannot be bypassed and neglected if the policy-makers decide to make policies which are durable and effective.

With the consolidation of democratic institutions in India, policy-makers are constantly subject to various kinds of checks and balances. Besides regular elections when the electorates exercise their rights, there are many politico-social movements which also ascertain the importance of the *vox populi*. People voluntarily participate in these movements to challenge the existing dispensation of political power. The Mazdoor Kishan Sangharsh Samiti movement in Rajasthan that spearheaded the campaign for the right to information led to the promulgation of the RTI in 2005. As an empowering legislation, the RTI Act has changed the texture of Indian policy-making in which it hardly remains an exclusive domain of the politicians and bureaucrats. In principle, this Act allows access to information but in reality however, is an enabling device as far as the stakeholders are concerned because any denial of information means deprivation of a basic democratic right to information. There seems to be an organic connection between the politico-ideological movements and the policies since the latter are usually devised to address the concerns that these campaigns highlight.

The above discussion also endorses the fact that diverse policy-making contexts shape different reform dynamics. The differences in the context which are shaped by socio-economic texture, public opinion, political parties, governing conditions, among others, remain most critical in the making of public policies. Following this argument, one can easily categorize India's policy concerns over a historical period of time since she became politically free in 1947. Immediately after independence, the ideological commitment to the socialistic pattern of society remained paramount during the Nehruvian era. An ideational change was visible from 1975 till 1990 which rendered deregulation and globalization appealing to policy-makers; by 1991, with the acceptance of the New Economic Policy, India reached a different stage of history when the erstwhile socialistic pattern appeared to have considerably lost its salience. There have thus been three interrelated phases of policy-making in India which are reflected in the nature of public policy: deregulation was an anathema in the era of state-led planned economic development; it was hailed as rejuvenating for the Indian economy once the LPG regime evolved its organic roots in India. What is thus fundamental is the notion that there is hardly a universal model of public policy given its contextual nature. This also reinforces the argument that the one-size-fits-all formula is theoretically myopic since the context differs from one historical age to another. For instance, while the Nehruvian consensus lost its viability, to a significant extent, in the post-1991 era for obvious reasons, it was considered most appropriate for nation building in India in the aftermath of decolonization. In a similar way, public policies which are drawn on political preferences are shaped accordingly. De-regulation, disinvestment and policies towards liberalized trade initiatives which are now championed as most relevant for India's growth were despised as politically futile in the past since they were derived from India's uncritical support for globalization.

There is a significant dimension that is linked with the growing importance of globalization in contemporary India. Public policies have become internationalized given the increasing salience of global actors even in the making of public policies which are relevant to domestic affairs. By agreeing to decontrol the prices of petroleum products, Indian policy-makers seem to have been influenced by market forces which are operative at the global level. This is a clear case to substantiate the point that this decision is reflective of how policy-makers responded to the contingent circumstances in which global considerations remained paramount. Another example presents a different trajectory: a 2014 example shows that India's decision to not concede to the conditionalities of the World Trade Organization (WTO) regarding the food subsidy was governed by her commitment to the Right to Food. With its determination to fight it out, the government of India forced the WTO to withdraw conditionalities on its support to Indian agriculture. Despite being different in texture, these two examples demonstrate two different stories: on the one hand, the policy-makers agreed to follow an international trend because it helped the Indian consumers, and being adamant against the WTO's dictates, the Indian state also exhibited its independence vis-à-vis pressure, exerted by an international agency. These examples also confirm how India's domestic strength, both political and economic, enables her to play a role in accordance with the nation's priority.

In the contemporary context, the study of public policy has become far more complex given that it is not only linked with domestic circumstances but also with its global counterparts. While seeking to understand the complex nature of public policy, one is thus drawn to the equally complex socio-economic churning that gets reflected in any specific public policy. The fundamental point that this chapter highlights relates to the context-driven nature of public policies which remains elusive if one seeks to conceptualize them in a derivative theoretical format. So, policy-making is a context-driven exercise which cannot be grasped in disregard to the socio-economic circumstances in which it is articulated.

REVIEW QUESTIONS

1. What is public policy? Elaborate your response with reference to its major features.
2. 'Public policy is a mirror, reflecting the ideological contours of a country'. Comment.
3. 'Public policy is a context-driven and goal-awaited exercise'. Comment.

4. What are the major factors that impinge on the making of public policy in India? Elaborate your response.
5. Write a critical essay on the processes of public policy-making in India since independence.
6. What are the major governmental institutions that play a critical role in making public policy in India? Elaborate your response with examples.
7. How do external agencies influence public policy-making in India? Elaborate your response with examples.
8. Can public policy and its making in India be conceptualized independent of the forces supportive of a liberalized, privatized and globalized (LPG) regime? Elaborate your response.
9. Can socio-cultural peculiarities be a factor in the making of public policy in India? Elaborate with examples.
10. How do you explain the changing nature of public policy in contemporary India? Elaborate with instances.

NOTES

1. D. A. Low (1997) has brought out this ambiguity in his *Britain and Indian Nationalism: The Imprint of Ambiguity, 1929–1942.*
2. Articles 38 and 39 spell out the sentiments. Article 46 underlines the concern for the weaker sections, including scheduled castes and scheduled tribes.
3. For details, see Varshney (2007).
4. Since economic reforms were not 'strategy-based' but 'crisis-driven' Indian had hardly had a choice and was thus more or less forced to accept 'the conditionalities', imposed by the donor agencies.
5. This argument was forcefully made by Bussmann (2007).
6. For details, see Mukherjee (2014, 138–40).

REFERENCES

Anderson, James E. 1975. *Public Policy Making*. New York: Thomas Nelson & Sons.

Bardhan, Pranab. 2008. *The Political Economy of Development in India*. New Delhi: Oxford University Press.

Bhaduri, Amit, and Deepak Nayyar. 1996. *The Intelligent Person's Guide to Liberalization*. New Delhi: Penguin.

Bussmann, Margit. 2007, March. 'When Globalization Discontent Turns Violent: Foreign Economic Liberalization and Internal War'. *International Studies Quarterly* 51 (1): 79–97.

Dror, Yehezkel. 1974. *Public Policy Making Reexamined*. New York: Leonard Hill Books.

Dye, Thomas R. 1998. *Understanding Public Policy*. New Jersey: Prentice Hall.

Easton, David. 1965. *A System Analysis of Political Life*. New York: Wiley.

Frankel, Francine R. 2005. *India's Political Economy, 1947–2004*. New Delhi: Oxford University Press.

Frohock, Fred M. 1979. Public Policy: Scope and Logic. New Jersey: Prentice Hall.

Gerston, Larry N. 1974. *Public Policy Making: Processes and Principle*. 2nd ed. New York: M. E. Sharpe.

The Hindustan Times, New Delhi, 11 March, 1950

Jenkins, Rob. 1999. *Democratic Politics and Economic Reform in India*. Cambridge: Cambridge University Press.

Karanjia, R. K. 'The Mind of Mr. Nehru: An Interview', quoted in Frankel, Francine R. 2005. *India's Political Economy, 1947–2004*. New Delhi: Oxford University Press.

Low, D. A. 1997. *Britain and Indian Nationalism: The Imprint of Ambiguity, 1929–1942*. Cambridge: Cambridge University Press.

Lowi,Theodore J. 1964. "American Business, Public Policy, Case Studies and Political Theory," *World Politics,16* (4): 677–715.

Meier, Kenneth and John Bohte. 2007. *Politics and the Bureaucracy: Policymaking in the Fourth Branch of Government*. New York: Thomson and Wadsworth.
Mitra, Subrata. 2004, November. 'Constitutional Design, Democratic Vote Counting and India's Fortuitous Multiculturalism'. Working Paper, South Asia Institute, Heidelberg University.
Mukherjee, Rahul. 2014. *Political Economy of Reforms in India*. New Delhi: Oxford University Press.
Peters, B. Guy. 2012. *America's Public Policy: Promise and Performance*. 9th ed. Washington: C & Q Press.
Presthus, Robert. 1975. *Public Administration*. 6th ed. New York: The Ronald Press Company.
Sapru, R.K. 2010. *Public Policy: Art and Craft of Policy Analysis*. New Delhi: PHI Learning Private Limited.
Sen, Sarbani. 2007. *Popular Sovereignty and Democratic Transformations: The Constitution of India*. New Delhi: Oxford University Press.
Shah, Mihir. 2008. 'Governance Reform Key to NREGA (National Rural Employment Guarantee Act) Success'. *The Hindu*, 14 March.
Sinha, Aseema. 2004, January. 'The Changing Political Economy of Federalism in India: A Historical Institutional Approach'. *India Review* 3 (1): 51 and 55.
Stiglitz, Joseph. 2006. *Making Globalization Work: The Next Steps to Global Justice*. London: Allen Lane.
Tendulkar, Suresh D., and T. A. Bhavani. *Understanding Reform: Post-1991 India*. New Delhi: Oxford University Press.
Varshney, Ashutosh. 2007. 'India's Democratic Challenge'. *Foreign Affairs* 86 (2, March/April): 93–106.

Planning and Economic Development in India

10

LEARNING OBJECTIVES

1. To understand planning and economic development as conceptual categories.
2. To comprehend the peculiar evolution of state-directed planned economic development in India.
3. To explain the processes leading to the dismantling of centralized planning in the context of neoliberal India.
4. To understand the formation of the National Institution for Transforming India (NITI) Aayog as an alternative to the state-directed development paradigm.

The aim of this chapter is to comprehend the role of institutionalized processes in development from the time India became politically free in 1947. As history has shown, India's approach to development has always remained contextual. This was evident when the nationalist leaders opted for the Soviet-type centralized planning as perhaps an effective means for development. The idea was widely acclaimed, regardless of the ideological differences among those who presided over India's destiny following decolonization. The Planning Commission which was constituted in 1950 was hailed as an instrument for bringing about quick development in India. India's trajectory of development however proved otherwise: instead of being instrumental in contributing to uniform development in the country, the Planning Commission failed to accomplish the goal. It was felt that centralized planning did not appear to be effective in attaining the goal that the nationalist leadership sought to attain. In other words, the panoptical state-led development approach did not appear to be relevant in the context of the declining importance of the state in the processes of development; the idea of the state being just an actor along with other actors gained ground in the globalizing world. Following the acceptance of the New Economic Policy in 1991, it was stated in so many ways that the Planning Commission had become redundant given the growing significance of decentralized planning as the only way to achieve all-round economic development in India. Centralized planning appeared to be futile since it was not possible to address specific issues which were context-driven and which therefore never received adequate attention in the much-hyped one-size-fits-all formula. That the planned development of the erstwhile era was inadequate for development in a diverse country like India was appreciated though no specific steps were taken to address this till 2015 when the National Democratic Alliance government constituted the National Institution for Transforming India (NITI) Aayog in place of the former Planning Commission to serve the needs and aspirations of the people of India better. Replacing the six-decades old Planning Commission, the NITI Aayog, conceived more in the nature of a think-tank, was conceptualized as a politico-ideological instrument seeking to substitute centralized planning with a bottom-up approach where the Aayog would support the formulation of plans at the village level and aggregate them at higher levels of government.

Given India's growth trajectory since independence, the Aayog is envisaged to endorse the norm of cooperative federalism enabling the constituent states to formulate schemes according to their distinctive needs rather than be dictated by the centre. The needs of a state such as Maharashtra which is highly developed may not be the same as that of a backward state like Jharkhand and therefore centralized planning may not be apt by any figment of imagination in these circumstances. Hence the mandate for the NITI Aayog conceptualizes the distinctive needs of each state differently in accordance with its specific requirements. Like the erstwhile Planning Commission, the Aayog will continue to advise and monitor the progress of developmental schemes that the states adopts; it will no longer have the executive functions of framing plans and allocating for the plan-driven schemes. The impact of the Planning Commission on India's development cannot be so easily ignored since it has been in place for more than six decades following the withdrawal of colonialism in India in 1947 while the NITI Aayog is too new to have any sway on the trajectory of growth in the country. This chapter is therefore structured to provide adequate attention to the role of planned development along with the way the new Aayog is expected to discharge its responsibilities in the context of the growing consolidation of a neoliberal politico-ideological regime in India. What is striking is the fact that while the Planning Commission was considered an ideological baggage borrowed from the former Soviet Union, the NITI Aayog represents an effort towards articulating India's neoliberal endeavour for sustainable economic growth. Ideologically drawn, both the planned development of the erstwhile era and its opposite, as conceptualized by the NITI Aayog remain important pillars of India's growth trajectory since independence. Centralized planning may have become futile though it undoubtedly had a role in the state-directed-development era. Differently textured, the NITI Aayog is a bold initiative to conceptualize India's approach to development in the changed environment of steady globalization.

PLANNING AND ECONOMIC DEVELOPMENT

With the formation of the Planning Commission in 1950, India ushered in the state-led development era in which the state became a critical economic actor. Despite its historical antecedents, the idea of state-directed planned economic development gained significant salience in independent India, especially with Jawaharlal Nehru, India's first Prime Minister at the helm of affairs. Given his staunch opposition to the Gandhian model of democratic decentralization, Nehru always preferred the state-driven economy as perhaps the only driving force for India's rapid socio-economic regeneration in the aftermath of the colonial rule. The strategy worked well, though not to the extent it was expected to by those supporting planned economic development. The reasons for its failure can easily be identified; one of them was definitely the tussle between those in favour of the planned economy and those who were opposed to it. It was strongly felt since the beginning of India's journey as an independent nation in 1947 that democratic decentralization of the Gandhian variety would have been far more appropriate in view India's socio-economic and political diversity, and the balance was struck in 1992 with the promulgation of the 73rd and 74th Constitutional Amendment Acts which formally recognized the importance of democratic decentralization as a governance format. Nonetheless, the role of the state for planned economic development continued to remain as critical as in the past. The importance of the Planning Commission was diluted, though not finished in the light of the growing significance of parallel constitutional agencies embracing decentralized planning. Another attack on the Planning Commission came in the form of the New Economic Policy 1991 which, by endorsing a guarded policy of economic liberalization, posed a serious intellectual challenge to its continuity especially with the growing importance of market forces which marginalized the state, to a great extent, as an arbiter in economic strategies for development. So, the idea of state-directed development already had powerful critics when the Bharatiya Janata Party-led government of the National Democratic Alliance came to power in 2014. Those endorsing the relevance of the Planning Commission lost out since it failed to attain the objective of uniform economic development in India; and, hence the arguments for its abolition gained ground. Despite its effectiveness as a strategy at the outset, the policy of state-led planned economic development became gradually redundant due to (a) the consolidation of forces marginalizing the state as a determinant of economic growth and (b) its clear failure to achieve what was expected when it was mooted immediately after the dawn of independence in India. There are two fundamental questions that need to be addressed: first, has the idea of state-driven economic development lost its relevance just because of its failure to accomplish the stated-goals or due to its vacuous claims in contrast to the rising importance of a market-driven counter ideology providing an alternative to the erstwhile strategy of state-directed economic development? There is a connected second question: whether the market-driven strategy will be useful for peripheral societies, including India, where the proportion of people living below poverty line is staggeringly alarming.

It is difficult to find conclusive answers to these questions although the discontinuity of the Planning Commission will certainly raise pertinent questions on the development strategies that India adopted since she became politically free in 1947. This chapter therefore, besides analyzing the rationale of planning and the Planning Commission, dwells also on the issue of planning in the era of liberalization and brings out the political dimensions of economic reforms since their initiation in the early 1990s. While seeking to understand the processes leading to the obliteration of the Planning Commission, the chapter further focuses on the debate highlighting whether giving hegemony to market-driven strategies is an appropriate device in India where the state, with its insistence on inclusive development, cannot afford to ignore its role in effecting what is usually defined as balanced and all-round economic growth.

THE CONCEPT OF PLANNED DEVELOPMENT

Stated in simple terms, conceptually, planning means deciding what should be done in a given situation, after careful consideration of the alternatives and thereafter working out the details of how it could be done as quickly and economically as possible (Sarup and Brahme 1990, 9). In other words, owing to resource constraints and an urgency to achieve certain minimum level of economic development, developing countries all over the world have found it expedient to adopt the method of planned economic development to have quick and balanced socio-economic development with the strategy of making the best possible use of available resources without any wastage and over run of time. Thus, through planning, the underdeveloped and developing countries have been able to guide the priorities, direction and pace of their socio-economic development instead of leaving them on the vagaries of market forces whose universal objective remains the maximization of profit for private entrepreneurs, without any concern for the fulfilment of the basic needs of the people. The present chapter strives to unravel the basic issues involved in planned economic development of the country, beginning with the First Five Year Plan in 1951. Besides looking at the genesis of planning in India and the factors for its adoption as the dominant strategy of development, it also seeks to put into perspective the structure and functioning of the planning machinery, with special focus on the Planning Commission as the central arch of the whole edifice of planning. The contemporary relevance of planning in the era of liberalization and an analysis of the political dimensions of economic reforms in recent years form the other core contents of the chapter.

The Genesis and Development of Planning in India

Despite remaining in one form or the other, an inevitable part and parcel of human activity, planning as a formidable and fascinating strategy for rapid and sustained economic development started taking roots and drawing attention from all parts of the world after its astoundingly successful experimentation in the ex-Soviet Union in the late 1920s. As a number of Indian leaders, including Nehru, were quite influenced, if not infatuated, with the ideological soundness of communism and became admirers of the economic, though not political, system of planned economic development as practised in the Soviet Union, arguments eulogizing the infallibility of planning as the best strategy for economic development started doing the rounds in the country in the late 1920s (Austin 1966, 235). This is partly true because the idea of planning also had clear indigenous roots going back to the nineteenth century, especially in the writings of Dadabhai Naoroji, R. C. Dutt and M. G. Ranade with their emphasis on the importance of state-led industrialization for the eradication of national poverty. They consistently argued that private initiatives, because of their profit motives would never take interest in efforts which were crucial for the country's development, but were unlikely to give them profit. Hence, the state was obliged to take part in developmental projects in a planned way. Following the 1917 Russian revolution, socialist ideas were accepted as a ready-made solution to India's poverty. That Jawaharlal Nehru and a majority of his colleagues endorsed the idea was evident when the former readily agreed to head the planning committee once the newly-elected Congress President, Subhash Chandra Bose invited him. It was appointed by the Congress to look into the modalities of operationalizing planned economic development in the country. It emerged as one of the dear demands of the Congress in its parleys with the Cabinet Mission, though without result, ultimately sneaking into the proceedings of the Constituent Assembly, where it was decided to place 'Economic and Social Planning' as one of the subjects in the Concurrent List of the Constitution.

Interestingly, the prevalent perception of planning in the minds of the capitalists in Western countries as an inherently Marxist formulation aimed at monopolizing the ownership of economic resources in the hands of the government, did not deter the renowned capitalists in India from pitching for the adoption of a strategy of planned economic development of the country. In their booklet, A Plan of Economic Development for India, they, among other things, provided for a blue print, called the Bombay Plan, seeking the creation of very comprehensive plans by a National Planning Committee and its execution by a Supreme Economic Council working alongside the National Planning Committee under the authority of the Central government (Austin 1966, 236). Echoing somewhat similar aspirations on the desirability of planning for the economic development of the country, a Gandhian plan, prepared by Shriman Narayan a die-hard follower of Mahatma Gandhi, also presented a strategy for formulating socio-economic developmental policies for the nation through the mechanism of a planning body, rooted, albeit, in the Gandhian perspectives on the social and economic reconstruction in India. The final endorsement for planning in India came in the form of the 'People's Plan' drafted by one of the most intellectual innovators of the country, M. N. Roy, on behalf of the Indian Federation of Labour, in the hope of presenting the viewpoints of the working class in the ongoing debate on planning in the country. The cumulative impact of all these efforts in making planning the fait accompli of the strategy of economic development, thus, strengthened the hands of people who were bent upon planned economic development, brushing aside reservations of people like Vallabhbhai Patel and other right-minded leaders of the Congress Party.

Although rooted in the early socialist orientations of Jawaharlal Nehru,[1] the idea of national planning, in the later years, got transformed from an alternative to the market system to a method of coordinating and guiding the various components and imperatives of economic development in independent India. The support, in one form or the other, which started pouring in for some sort of national planning for faster economic development, was based on the understanding of the notion of planning in which all the players in the national economy would find a space for themselves to remain in the game, in spite of a predominant role assigned for the state. Significantly, in order to drive home this point, Nehru, apparently, as an illustration, in his presentation of the Resolution on Industrial Policy before the Constituent Assembly in April 1948, indirectly, declared the adoption of the policy of a mixed economy under which, among other things, a sizeable role was visualized for the private sector in the economic development of the country. The basic operational milieu in the course of a mixed economy was supposed to be provided by inputs like political democracy, governmental planning, regulation and control of the economy, vibrant public sector, and a system of tax reliefs and state financial aids to the private sector (Panthem 1982).

Conclusively, thus, as Amiya Bagchi writes, planning emerged as a more or less unanimous choice between three prominent streams of forces at work on the prospective strategy of development for India: (a) the nationalist conservative trend which wanted the state to supplement the efforts of private enterprises in areas where they lacked resources or initiative, (b) the official technocratic stream which regarded planning as an effective administrative tool for poverty alleviation, and (c) those for whom planning was part of a socialist ideology, whose central objective was the establishment of a just society (Bagchi 1995). Being the outcome of a whole host of ideological and pragmatic imperatives, planning, in the final analysis, turned out to be 'an amalgam of objectives and strategies often lacking internal coherence and consistency. What Nehru and the planners finally settled for was a satisfactory rather than a maximum rate of growth with the acceptance of a certain level of inequality' (Bagchi 1995, 86).

ROLE OF THE PLANNING COMMISSION

The endorsement of the concept national planning from different quarters and the probable institutional mechanisms suggested in the various plans could not provide any final idea on the nature and functions of the institutional machinery to be created for planning in the country. Partly, due to the apprehensions of the rightist faction in the party, the Congress failed to arrive at a smooth decision to set up a Planning Commission as the key organization in charge of the affairs of formulation and implementation of the Five Year Plans. In the subsequent tug of war leading to some angry and bitter debates in the meeting of the Congress Working Committee on 25 January 1950, an agreement was reached on a Cabinet Resolution to provide for the creation of the Planning Commission.

Structured in the mould of a staff agency, the prime role of the Planning Commission was designed so as to assess and augment the material, capital and human resources of the country; to formulate a plan for their balanced use; to define the stages of implementing the plan; to indicate the requisites of plan execution; and to determine the machinery for the effective execution of the plan. Accordingly, the structure of the Commission was visualized to be a judicious mix of both political leadership at the top level and general staffing of the Commission by experts at other levels. The leadership of the Prime Minister, no doubt, was eminently needed for a body without any constitutional or statutory basis to add to its prestige and efficient functioning in the initial years but in subsequent years it was found to be undesirable, if not counter-productive, for a balanced and consistent role of the Commission. The First Administrative Reforms Commission (ARC) had noted that taking advantage of the Chairmanship of the Prime Minister, the Planning Commission has 'steadily added to its functions and personnel and has stepped into the area of the executive authority of the centre and the state governments' (GOI 1968, 121). But in later years, the Planning Commission fell to the neglect of Prime Ministers like Rajiv Gandhi who instead of making use of the experience and expertise of the Commission in the effective execution of the planning processes arrogated the power to the Prime Minister's Office for carrying out vital functions of the Commission like the formulation of plans. Thus, as an insider, pointing out the impact of vagaries of the attitude of the Prime Minister towards the Commission, has noted 'if the Prime Minister wants to use the Planning Commission as the pivot of economic planning and development, it will acquire a lot of importance. If he does not want to use it, the Commission becomes useless' (Sethi 1992). The ARC, therefore, recommended to discontinue the practice of the Prime Minister's formal and mandatory association with the Planning Commission, though acceding to the view that he should be invariably kept informed of the important decisions taken by the Commission and when he deems fit, he may also attend the meetings of the Commission and chair it.

Quite often than not, the overcrowding of the Planning Commission with ministers from the Central Cabinet also militated against the expert nature and functional autonomy of the Commission. Indeed, the objective of the creation of the Planning Commission was to have a body, outside the normal hierarchy of the government, consisting of professionals, to objectively assess and augment the resources of the country in order to formulate feasible plans within the broad policy guidelines of the government. Over the years, the Commission appears to have turned out to be no less than a government department with the usual bureaucratic structure and functions, engrossed in routine matters, instead of acting as a staff agency to suggest innovative and feasible policy alternatives to the government. The need, therefore, is to restore the professional autonomy of the Commission by fine tuning its structure through a reduction in its overbearing political component in order to keep its relevance intact in the era of liberalization and privatization.

The functioning of the Planning Commission, in normal course, need not have evoked any adverse comments and reactions from the people both inside and outside of the organization. The near unanimous acceptance of planning as the fait accompli of economic development afforded for the Planning Commission a very propitious pedestal for guiding and regulating the ways and means of securing a fast and sustainable development in the conditions of the people. However, the functional dynamics of the Planning Commission have produced more critics than supporters, fetching not only a bad name for the idea of planning as a plausible course of action for the economic development of the country, but also providing seemingly sound logic to drastically curtail, if not totally wind up, the scope of functioning of the Planning Commission.

The most strident criticism of the functioning of the Planning Commission during its more than 64 years of existence has been that its vision has become blurred owing to a disproportionate increase in its position and functional domain, as a result of which it has distracted from its core function of formulating plans after due assessment and augmenting of the available resources. Rather it has become an executive department of the government engrossed in the performance of certain secondary functions of an executive nature. In utter disregard to the aspirations of its founding fathers and the other proponents of planned economic development, the Planning Commission, instead of confining itself to the formulation of the perspective, five-year and annual plans, has bothered itself more with execution and evaluation of the plans, which need to have been the responsibility of the development administration of the country. As Jawaharlal Nehru pointed out so succinctly, 'the Commission which was a small body of serious thinkers, had turned into a government department complete with a crowd of secretaries, directors and, of course, a big building' (cited in Basu 1992, 308). In nutshell, the concentration of power of allocating plan grants in the hands of the Planning Commission mandarins without any corresponding responsibility to the Parliament or other elected bodies has perverted their vision so much that they have emerged as one of the most formidable irritants in cordial centre–state relations in the country. Though, conceptually, experts have opined against the consideration of central grants to be a subversion of the federal system,[2] what has gone against the spirit of smooth centre-state relations is the tendency on part of the Planning Commission to examine in detail not only the total size of state plans but even the sectoral plans, including individual schemes. Moreover, the concept of tied grants, disbursed at the instance of the Planning Commission's earmarking of resources, compromises with the autonomy of the states and flexibility in using these resources as per the priorities of individual states.[3] Though there may be some degree of exaggeration in the complaints of the states in terms of the functioning of the Planning Commission, the fact cannot be ignored that the Commission has, more or less, allowed itself to be an instrument of political vindictiveness in the hands of the certain narrow-minded governments at the centre to settle scores with the non-conformist governments of various states. Moreover, in its enthusiasm to plan for the whole country, the Commission betrayed an utter ignorance of the immense diversities prevailing in the country and has gone ahead to work on the basis of practical uniformity across the nation. Hence, planning for economic development has practically superseded the federal Constitution with the result that it has been functioning almost like a unitary system in many respects (Santhanam 1960, 56).

The nature and scope of the functioning of the Planning Commission has also adversely impacted the scale and context of the functioning of certain constitutional bodies like the Finance Commission which have been designed to act the fulcrum of efficient and cordial centre-state financial relations in the country. Itself bereft of any constitutional status, bulldozing of the constitutional bodies by an extra-constitutional body like the Planning Commission would probably never augur well for the establishment of responsible government institutions as per the visions of the Constitution makers of the country. Indeed, it appears to be a fraud on the Constitution to allow executive-decreed bodies like the Planning Commission to take charge of vital subjects such as governance in the country, more so, by subordinating constitutional bodies which have been created for the same purpose. Also, such a state of affairs does not appear to have the direct or indirect sanction of the fathers of the Constitution, for, had they wanted this, they would have made explicit provisions in the Constitution in this regard, keeping in view their propensity to provide even for minor issues of the polity, unmindful of its ramifications for the length of the Constitution.

Though the apprehensions on the potentiality of the Planning Commission to 'become some sort of super body over the cabinet' (quoted in Austin 2003, 618) did not prove to be exactly true, its overbearing impact on national economic policy-making could not escape the attention of scholars who found the cabinet to be 'relegated to the fringe' (quoted in Austin 2003, 618) by the Commission in this regard. Going a step ahead in exposing the leviathan called the Planning Commission, Ashok Chanda has pointed out that the Commission's undefined position and wide terms of reference had catapulted it into the position of 'the Economic Cabinet, not merely for the Union but also for the States' (cited in Jha 1984). Consequently, most of the studies on the working of the Planning Commission, including the ones sponsored by the central government have not minced any words in suggesting a restriction in the scope of the functioning of the Commission in terms of formulating plans and other ancillary activities, and the transfer of decision making for plan programmes on the state subjects from the centre to the states, and the strict absence of the Commission in getting involved with the implementation of the plans.[4]

In view of these critical observations on the structure and functioning of the Planning Commission, it appears to have been robbed off much of its sheen, if not credibility and prestige, like most of the institutions cumulatively called the public sector. Still, the old glory of the Commission remained untouched due ostensibly to the absence of any better alternatives to replace the existing ones. It is in this context that the wave of liberalization, setting on in early 1990s, swept the whole planning process, including the institutions involved in it, off their feet and thus also arose the need for a new raison de tare to keep these seemingly anachronistic institutions and processes in sync with the rapid transformations being experienced in the economic sphere of most of the developing countries in the world.

PLANNING IN THE ERA OF ECONOMIC LIBERALIZATION

The inauguration of the decade of the 1990s, in a way, proved unfortunate for governments and policies rooted in the ideology of socialism. In the wake of their opening up and subsequent exposure to the forces rooted in the market-model of life and development, there was an explosion of the accumulated resentment against communist governments leading to the demise of hitherto impregnable leftist bloc of countries. In developing countries, particularly India, the occurrence of a severe and unprecedented crisis in the economy, contemporaneously presented as an external payment crisis getting reflected in the loss of international investor-financier confidence thereby putting the country on a credit watch by several rating agencies, leading to the serious questioning, if not total crumbling of the prevailing macro level management of the economy. It was officially recognized that this crisis was not, however, simply due to deterioration in the trade account, but rather it was accompanied by other adverse developments on the capital account reflecting a loss of confidence in the government's ability to manage the situation (GOI 1991, 6).

Arguments were also advanced to attribute the causes for poverty and economic stagnation to the state's tendency to undermine the operation of market forces in the name of planned economic development of the country. As a way out of the situation, the need for structural adjustment and stabilization policies in tandem with a reduction in the role of the state in economic development was portrayed as indispensable. As a result, a concerted package of reforms, branded as the Structural Adjustment Programmes (SAPs) and initiated under the tutelage of the World Bank and the International Monetary Fund (IMF), was thrust upon the country in the name of the panacea for the economic crisis. Stressing the inevitability of sound macro-economic and financial policies, trade and financial liberalization, privatization and the deregulation of domestic markets, the strategy of SAPs promoted a minimal state that would desist from economic interventions and focus on sound monetary policies by unleashing market forces aimed at privatization, budget rationalization and the integration of the domestic market in the international economic system.

In such a scenario, free markets became the rage, but did that mean that central planning would be gasping for breath, being smothered out of existence by the devil called laissez faire? Setting the stage for a reorientation, if not a total recast of the planning system, the process of liberalization necessitated that the mandarins of Yojana Bhawan don new clothes lest their days of political and bureaucratic pre-eminence be soon over. In view of the changed socio-economic environment following the adoption of the New Economic Policy (1991), the Planning Commission seemed to have lost its viability. This also confirms that the neoliberal strategies appear to have become critical in India's economic growth.

The other argument that is made to justify the discontinuation of the Planning Commission relates to the gradual decline of the public sector. The Planning Commission is no longer relevant, the argument goes, because 'the country has moved away from the Nehru-Mahalanobis strategy which visualized substantial public investment, and hence the need for a plan to effect such investment' (Patnaik 2014). With the decision to dismantle the public sector, any particular engagement in development projects could now be planned and executed by the concerned departments. Hence, the Planning Commission had run out of steam in view of the declining importance of public investment. The argument has substance, and it is evident that the Planning Commission, as an overarching executive agency, has certainly run-out of its utility in the changed context of a liberalized India. Nevertheless, the 64 years of its history shall remain useful to understand whether the Indian state fulfilled its role in accordance with what the nation aspired to attain following the constitution of the Planning Commission in 1950 as an extra constitutional agency. In that respect, the long duration of this governmental organization provides us with a corpus of knowledge on India's economic growth in the aftermath of decolonization.

In light of the arguments questioning the relevance of state-led planned development, the inevitability of planning to co-exist with market forces, in the form of a guide and facilitator will probably remain a distinct feature of India's economic system in view of the state of economic development and the pressing need for the government to not dilute its responsibilities in the social sector. The model, available for emulation to the country, appears to be the French concept of 'Indicative Planning' whose crux lies in just indicating the broad directions of economic development instead of dictating it persuasively or coercively. In fact, conceptually, under indicative planning, the role of the state gets narrowed down to only acting as an advisor and persuader, using the moderate technique of moral persuasion from the high pedestal of being the people's representative, without recourse to any coercive or controlling methods.[5] In such a system, since a substantial part of the economy is owned and managed by the private sector, government planning is afforded to act only as a facilitator, promoter and partner, instead of a regulator, allocator and director. By way of planning, the major responsibility of the planning machinery is to provide for a long term perspective of economic development in the country. Contextualizing, thus, the role of the planning system in India in the framework of the one existing in developed countries like France, it needs to be emphasized that the public sector would remain a major player in the economic activities of the country, owing to its strategic significance, both for the safety and security of the nation and the socio-economic regeneration of the common masses. To that extent, planning may be allocative and regulative but in so far as planning for the whole economy (having a major bearing on the functioning of the private sector) is concerned, it is focused only on a few sectors, leaving minor operational dynamics to be decided by the private players themselves. Indeed, sometimes things may be other way round, when private entrepreneurs may put forward their own perspective on economic development of the country and request the government to come forward to extend a sympathetic consideration to their points of view and become a partner in their pursuits of planning and execution of plans for balanced economic development in various sectors of the economy.

Hence, acting as 'mutually complementary forces' in facilitating rapid economic development for the country, the private sector and state planning need to coexist together, albeit with planning continuing to be a significant variable in stipulating strategies for public investment and affording guidelines for routing private sector investment in the desired sectors. Significantly, by providing the minimum threshold level of investments in the non-core sectors like telecommunications, transport, aviation, etc., the planning machinery has facilitated for the private sector avenues to make new forays into these sectors and establish a large number of ancillary industries hovering around major public sector undertakings. As the Planning Commission itself noted, 'central planning and investment has provided the base over which the superstructure of further development can occur smoothly with planning playing an integrative role' (Planning Commission, 8).

It is, however, important to assess the transformed role of the planning process in the country in a detached form without the previous sentimental attachment with bodies like the

Planning Commission which had become the sacred cows of the government of India. In fact, the electoral rhetoric and bankruptcy of thinking at the Commission seem to have considerably undermined the ideological mission that it was expected to fulfil. Hence it hardly received any support from the people who felt that the Planning Commission lost its viability in the changed socio-economic milieu. But, with market financing now open to the public sector, the role of the Commission as an allocator has diminished, though, with its vast infrastructure and information gathering experience, it can and has to be allowed to work as a watchdog. Moreover, to be politically effective, the Commission has to show its superior economic expertise in suggesting guidelines for private investments.

One of the grudges against the process of planning has been that it has largely taken 'expenditure' as an index for the efficient use of funds by public sector agencies. However, as a World Bank (1995, 49) study has suggested, such an approach needs to be replaced by one which has improved profitability, productivity and savings-investments deficit. This kind of forward thinking would help save Public Sector Undertakings (PSUs) while offering incentives for the private sector to invest in areas where traditionally the public sector did not achieve astounding success. Politically, having handled the role of mediating between the state and the centre for the purpose of allocation of finances, and as a part of the National Development Council, the Planning Commission remains certainly an ideal forum to at least debate issues like the policy of Special Economic Zones (SEZs) and taxation reforms. Business may be wary but it is felt that as far as infrastructure is concerned, there should be a balance of ideologies between what the Commission prescribes and what industry wants to get. Although the economics of the market place certainly play a role in the provisioning and use of infrastructure, the government does need to provide the blueprint. In other words, once the government is clear about the policy on toll, industry would take over with a transparent auction process.

However, radical ideas which should be the domain of the perspective planning division have yet to find any takers in the Planning Commission. Ideally, the Commission should make available various alternatives to tide over a particular situation, otherwise, there is a danger of politicians getting carried away by their own compulsions and rhetoric. There, thus, exists an enormous potential for interaction between national planners and corporate planners, and the process can be strengthened through informal consultative mechanisms as in Japan or the Malaysian system of *Retreat*, where the Prime Minister brainstorms along with key ministers and the industry leaders. In crux, the Commission cannot be a regulator, but can be a guide in suggesting ways and means for India's socio-economic regeneration.

A SHIFT OF FOCUS: FROM THE PLANNING COMMISSION TO THE NITI AAYOG

The abolition of the Yojana Aayog (Planning Commission) and its replacement by the National Institution for Transforming India (NITI) Aayog in 2015 was an ideological response in the changed socio-economic milieu following the consolidation of the neoliberal political forces in India. Opposed to the post-colonial dirigisme state, the NITI Aayog was the outcome of India's preference for the free market strategy in which the role of private capital was considered critical in growth and development. Appreciative of sectoral planning that is tuned to India's socio-economic diversity, it is also part of an endeavour to get integrated with the global markets that have become critical players in domestic policies in the changed environment.

Conceptually, the NITI Aayog is rooted in Indian tradition. As the Cabinet resolution of 1 January 2015 suggests, the ideological roots of the Aayog can be found in Mahatma Gandhi's urge for 'constant development' which desires to 'maintain one's dogma in order to appear consistent' isanathema. Hence, it was argued:

> [In] the changed dynamics of the new India, the institutions of governance and policy have to adapt to new challenges and must be built on the founding principles of the Constitution of India, the wealth of knowledge from civilizational history and the present day socio-cultural context. (*The Gazette of India* 2015, 6)

The NITI Aayog is not a mere institutional innovation, it is reflective of the heartfelt desire of the people 'to seek elimination rather than alleviation of poverty'. For this what one needs is an overhauling of the system by introducing significant institutional reforms in governance and 'dynamic policy shifts that can seed and nurture large-scale change', the Cabinet Resolution insists. In the proposed institutional changes, the role of the stakeholders is also appreciated. Besides the critical importance of people in development, the Resolution further reinforces that the constituent states should have a decisive say in 'determining the architecture of economic growth and development' challenging the one-size-fits-all approach which was inherent in the era of centralized planning.

India is being radically transformed and the forces that have contributed to such transformation are, as per the Cabinet Resolution,[6] as follows:

1. The industry and service sectors have developed and are operating on a global scale now. To build on this foundation, new India needs an administration paradigm in which the government is an 'enabler' rather than 'a provider of first and last resort'. The role of the government as 'a player' in the industrial and service sectors has to be reduced. Instead, the government has to focus on enabling legislation, policy-making and regulations.
2. India's traditional strength in agriculture has increased manifold on account of the efforts of our farmers and improvements in technology. We need to continue to improve, and move from pure food security to focus on a mix of agricultural production as well as improvements in the actual returns that farmers get from their produce.
3. Today, we reside in a 'global village', connected by modern transport, communications and media, and networked international markets and institutions. As India contributes to global endeavours, it is also influenced by happenings far removed from her borders. Global economics and geo-politics are getting increasingly integrated, and the private sector is growing in importance as a constituent within that. India needs to be an active player in the debates and deliberations on the global commons, especially in relatively uncharted areas.
4. India's middle class is unique in terms of its size and purchasing power. This formidable group is increasing with the entry of the neo-middle class. It has been an important driver of growth and has enormous potential on account of its high education levels, mobility and willingness to push for change in the country. Our continuing challenge is to ensure that this economically vibrant group remains engaged and its potential is fully realized.
5. India's pool of entrepreneurial, scientific and intellectual human capital is a source of strength waiting to be unleashed to help it attain unprecedented heights of success. In fact, the social capital that is present in our people has been a major contributor to the development of the country thus far and therefore, needs to be leveraged through appropriate policy initiatives.
6. The non-resident Indian community, which is spread across more than 200 countries, is larger than the population of many countries of the world. This is a significant geo-economic and geo-political strength. Future national policies must incorporate this

strength in order to broaden their participation in the new India beyond just financial support. Technology and management expertise are self-evident areas where this community can contribute significantly.

7. Urbanization is an irreversible trend. Rather than viewing it as an evil, we have to make it an integral part of our development policy. Urbanization has to be viewed as an opportunity to use modern technology to create a wholesome and secure habitat while reaping the economic benefits that it offers.
8. Transparency is now a sine-qua-non for good governance. We are in a digital age where the tools and modes of communication like social media are powerful instruments for sharing and explaining the thoughts and actions of the government. This trend will increase with time. Government and governance have to be conducted in an environment of total transparency—using technology to reduce opacity and thereby, the potential for misadventures in governing.

As is evident, governance has become far more complex in today's context. A simplistic approach, which is inherent in centralized planning, does not seem to work in such circumstances, as the Cabinet Resolution underlines. In order to be effective, development strategies need to take into account the complexities of socio-economic realities while devising effective policies for inclusive growth and development. In other words, contrary to the one-size-fits-all approach, the new strategy needs to be multi-dimensional and sensitive to the specific requirements of various segments of society in a global perspective. This is a unique approach to socio-economic regeneration of a country as diverse as India where centralized planning does not seem to be effective in the changed environment. It has been argued in the Cabinet Resolution:

> we need to find out our own strategy for growth [and] the new institution has to zero-in on what will work in and for India [since] … no single model can be transplanted into the Indian scene [though the proposed institution must] incorporate influences from the world.[7]

It will be, the Resolution further insists, 'a Bharatiya approach to development'. What is distinctive in this approach is the insistence on finding context-driven solutions rather than having a pre-designed formula to tackle contingent issues. The erstwhile Planning Commission was guided by macro-formulae that hardly paid attention to the specific requirements of the constituent states while the proposed NITI Aayog, being sensitive to the unique demands of each state, shall evolve policy alternatives in accordance with what seems to be appropriate for them.

Chaired by the Prime Minister, the NITI Aayog shall have a Governing Council comprising the Chief Ministers of all the states and the Lieutenant Governors of the Union Territories besides experts with specialized knowledge who will be invited by the chair to contribute to the Aayog's functioning. Unlike the Planning Commission which drew on the macro-design of economic development, the Aayog will be assisted by Regional Councils which will be formed to address specific issues and contingencies affecting more than one state or a region. This is a unique design for providing a voice to the states and regions, which was not possible in the state-led development era since the states hardly had any say in the allocation of funds for specific projects. The idea will definitely work better as now the states as stakeholders will participate in the decision making processes thereby highlighting areas that need attention. For instance, Kerala with its highly developed social indicators may not require assistance from the Union Government for women empowerment while this may not be the case for the other states. The formation of Regional Councils to take care of the specific demands of regions is a unique design in India's development trajectory simply because they will be tuned to the ground reality while devising strategies for economic growth.

The objectives for which the NITI Aayog was created have been clearly spelt-out in the Cabinet Resolution. By taking care of national priorities, the NITI Aayog is equally sensitive to the distinctive needs of the constituent states in federal India, and these are the objectives which the Cabinet Resolution has highlighted in an unambiguous manner too. There are three types of interrelated objectives: first, as an institution with focus on national priorities, the NITI Aayog is to evolve 'a shared vision of national development priorities, sectors and strategies with the active involvement of the states in the light of the national objectives'. With its strong belief in the fact that strong states make a strong nation, the Aayog seeks to foster 'cooperative federalism through structured support initiatives and mechanism with the states on a continuous basis'. The second objective is to make the Aayog functional by being sensitive to the specific requirements of those at the grassroots. As the Resolution suggests, the NITI Aayog is to develop mechanisms to formulate 'credible plans at the village level and aggregate these progressively at the higher levels of government'; in order to achieve inclusive growth, the Aayog is also expected to pay 'special attention to those sections that may be at risk of not benefitting adequately from economic progress'; and finally, for sustained development, the NITI Aayog is also responsible for designing 'strategic and long term policy and programme frameworks and initiatives and monitor their progress and their efficacy'. The third objective relates to the contribution of the Aayog in generating knowledge which will be of use in improving its efficiency. As it is believed, the lessons learnt through the monitoring of projects and feedback from the stakeholders shall always remain critical inputs in so far as the designing for economic development goes. In the context of the growing importance of network among the stakeholders, the NITI Aayog cannot avoid partnerships with the key stakeholders and national and international likeminded think tanks in order to fulfil its objective of creating 'a knowledge, innovation and entrepreneurial support system through a collaborative community of national and international experts, practitioners and other partners'. Given the well-articulated design in which the Aayog functions, it is likely to be 'a state-of-the-art resource centre for good governance and best practices in sustainable and equitable development' in India.[8]

As the above objectives reveal, the NITI Aayog is not to merely devise plans for the country, it is also responsible for facilitating the implementation of the development agenda. This involves making implementation central to the planning process through an emphasis on tangible outcomes, realistic targets, strict time lines and robust monitoring and evaluation—a clear transition from 'the isolated conceptualization of merely planning to planning for implementation' (GOI 2015, 13). Seeking to articulate a model which is 'all-round, all-pervasive, all-inclusive and holistic' (GOI 2015, 16), the NITI Aayog is a clear break with the past given the objectives that it seeks to fulfil in contrast with its bete noire, the Planning Commission which was neither organic to the processes of economic change nor was sensitive to the rapidly changing socio-economic milieu when state-driven planning seems to have considerably lost its salience.

The formation of the NITI Aayog is a bold initiative, fully tuned to the neoliberal ethics of governance in which the government is merely an enabler rather than a doer. As the past has shown, the Planning Commission seems to have exhausted its potential in contributing to uniform development for the country as was expected when it was conceptualized. In the transformed context, when the dirigisme state was dismantled in view of changes in the domestic and international milieu, the Planning Commission ceased to be become as critical in economic planning as it was at the outset. In other words, the decline of the Planning Commission was contingent on the declining significance of the state-directed development paradigm in which the role of the state as a hegemonic force was always appreciated at the cost of other parallel actors in economic planning and development. Challenging this assumption of upholding the hegemonic role of the state, the creation of the NITI Aayog is a powerful step seeking to involve the myriad stakeholders in planning and its implementation. In this sense, the formation of the Aayog is an outcome of the disillusionment with the planned economy and the role of the Planning Commission which was reduced to a mere forum for the disbursement of the annual allocation of funds to the constituents states in accordance with its priorities. This strategy backfired in the light of the growing consolidation of the neoliberal ethics of governance in which the state ceased to be a critical force in governance. A context-driven design, the NITI Aayog is thus an endeavour for an appropriate mechanism for inclusive growth and *antyodaya* which means that development is futile unless it does not reach the poorest of the poor.

Conceptually, the Aayog is reflective of the disenchantment with state-driven economic planning and appreciative of neoliberalism as perhaps the most effective vehicle for sustainable growth. It is too early to comment on its future though, as its objectives suggest, it is likely to usher in a new era of thinking in so far India's development trajectory is concerned. In the current neoliberal dispensation, when the state is relegated to the background, the Aayog may be hailed as an appropriate institution given the growing importance of the stakeholders in its functioning. Furthermore, by discarding the top-down approach for bottom-up planning, the NITI Aayog also gives voice to those at the periphery who so far remain neglected in economic planning. The Aayog is also a clear step towards upholding the states' rights by forming both Governing Councils and Regional Councils. By replacing the National Development Council which was a state forum with these institutionalized councils, the new political dispensation in India has created institutions for dialogues and debates among the stakeholders implying that decisions cannot be imposed but shall be the outcome of deliberations among them. In this sense, the NITI Aayog is more than an institution for planning and its implementation, but rather a forum for strengthening processes for further democratizing governance in India in the neoliberal context.

CONCLUDING OBSERVATIONS

Planning is a vision, an integral part of the nationalist movement; it is rooted in the nationalist dream of linking knowledge and power to serve society. Although critics fumed at the commanding position taken over by the Planning Commission in deciding the strategy of socio-economic development in the country, the utility of the idea of planning and the machinery of the Planning Commission was widely acknowledged due to the scarcity of resources at the disposal of the government and the mammoth problems facing the Indian state due to severe resource constraints. In the aftermath of colonialism, the state became the principal arbiter in so far as India's socio-economic regeneration was concerned. Priorities were different and the state opted for a solution which was context-specific. Although India's growth chart may be very impressive, there is no doubt that her economic strategies worked well to address those issues which acted as impediments to growth. The Nehruvian state-led development planning did not appear to be perfect though it contributed to the consolidation of a self-dependent India. This was a great achievement suggesting perhaps the justification of the goal-driven, instrumental planning for a young nation which had great potential given the mass support for whatever the nationalist leadership had undertaken to change India's economic map. Conceptually persuasive and politically meaningful, arguments for state-led economic growth were easily accepted since they were aspirational and perhaps self-fulfilling.

However, the inauguration of the policies of liberalization, privatization and globalization since the early 1990s drastically transformed the scenario and the outlook in which the whole planning process and the mechanism of the Planning Commission were placed to work in earlier times. Not only did the scale of government spending by way of starting new economic ventures get reduced substantially, the earlier pattern of compulsory planning was also almost discarded in favour of indicative planning whereby the task of the Planning Commission only remained to indicate or point out the broad directions of economic development in the country. However, one thing remains very clear in the minds of the planners that notwithstanding the onset of the trend for indicative planning, the utility of traditional sectoral planning would remain intact as long as the social sector remained a priority area for the government.

With the change of the national government led by the United Progressive Alliance in 2014, newer issues, especially relevant to the planned economic strategy, have been raised. At the same time, the political configuration in India has become more plural with the ascendancy of regional parties in a majority of the states. The prevalent top-down model involving the transfer of central resources to the states on the basis of vague and outmoded principles failed completely to bring about inclusive growth in India with the targeted beneficiaries always remaining distant. The top-down and deterministic paradigm at the behest of the Planning Commission, with concomitant tendencies towards 'one-size-fits-all' solutions, became less effective given the growing importance of decentralized planning. As a result, the grassroots planning, or bottom-up model of planning, gained easy acceptance especially in the light of its success in various states which disbursed resources in accordance with inputs from the grassroots. So the strategy of economic liberalization not only introduced new players, it has also opened-up avenues for the involvement of those neglected but who actually are the real actors of socio-economic changes. It is difficult to make a conclusive point as to whether this will yield positive results. Nevertheless, one has reasons to feel excited given the fact that the withdrawal of an overarching organization like the Planning Commission and the encouragement of grassroots planning shall now contribute to alternative conceptualizations which have so far remained entirely an anathema to the present dispensation of public authority. In other words, the dismantling of the Planning Commission offers an opportunity to create a platform for new ideas, for finding out solutions to seemingly intricate issues and for designing systems to enable effective implementation. One may be persuaded to endorse the endeavour at creating a think tank, following the Chinese National Development and Reform Commission, which remains sensitive to the unique socio-economic needs of federal India by challenging the desire to impose 'the one-size-fits-in formula' while addressing the issues of economic growth. The NITI Aayog can thus be said to be an outcome of the search for an alternative conceptualization of development in the changed socio-economic and political milieu. Critical of centralized planning that has lost its viability in the neoliberal global world, the Aayog is also a context-driven response.

By involving the stakeholders in economic planning, the Aayog is an endeavour towards making planning inclusive. The Aayog is thus not merely an institutional replacement of the erstwhile Planning Commission, but the reinvention of planning in a new context in which the state no longer remains a hegemonic force given the rising importance of non-state actors in development. In view of its short duration, it is too early to comment on the Aayog's future in India though it has articulated a powerful voice against the state-directed-development paradigm that has remained uncontested till the adoption of the 1991 New Economic Policy in India. In brief, the formation of the Aayog can be attributed to arguments against centralized planning that have clearly failed to accomplish what the founding fathers strongly hoped when the Planning Commission was formed in 1950. In the transformed socio-economic milieu, the Commission not only lost its credibility, but also became a subject of severe controversy due to its failure to devise appropriate strategies for India's uniform economic development. Appreciative of India's diversity where the one-size-fits-all formula would not work, the NITI Aayog seems to be an adequately-equipped instrument for economic development since it takes into account the critical role of the stakeholders in evolving strategies for economic change and development.

There is one fundamental point that needs to be reiterated before concluding the discussion on the feasibility of the state-guided development paradigm that remained unchallenged till the assumption of power by the BJP-led National Democratic Alliance in 2014. Since planning does not seem to be a mere economic project given its articulation in a specific kind of politics, one cannot afford the role of politics in conceptualizing the nature and functioning of the Planning Commission. India's diversity as a political entity is the key here. There is thus a very simple argument that planned economic development was welcomed when it was politically supportive of a paradigm in favour of a controlled economy in which the hegemonic role of the state remained sacrosanct. In the changed environment of economic liberalization, when the state, instead of being 'a doer', has become 'an enabler', these ideas have obviously lost their salience. Politics of the day thus prevails with the sounding of the death knell for the state-directed development paradigm that Jawaharlal Nehru and his nationalist colleagues had espoused so dearly in India's formative years as an independent nation following the withdrawal of the British from India in 1947.

REVIEW QUESTIONS

1. How do you conceptualize planning as a mode of economic development? Elaborate your response.
2. Can planning be effective with the decline of the state as a domineering force? Elaborate your response.
3. Critically evaluate the role of the Planning Commission of India since its inception in 1950 following an executive order.
4. 'The decline of the Planning Commission and the dwarfing of the state remain integrally connected'. Do you agree with the view? Elaborate your response.
5. Do you agree with the view that the Planning Commission in India became redundant (or otherwise) with the consolidation of neoliberalism in India? Elaborate your response.
6. 'The dwindling of the Planning Commission is a symptom of a greater malice in India's political economy'. Do you agree with the view? Elaborate your response.
7. Critically evaluate the processes towards the growth and consolidation of the National Institution for Transforming India (NITI) Aayog in India.
8. 'The National Institution for Transforming India (NITI) Aayog is an alter ego of the erstwhile Planning Commission of India'. Do you agree with the view? Elaborate your response.
9. In what ways, it will be correct to suggest that the root of the National Institution for Transforming India (NITI) Aayog can be traced back to the failure of the state-led development paradigm in India?
10. Do you agree with the view that the National Institution for Transforming India (NITI) Aayog is an appropriate mechanism to uphold India's federal spirit? Elaborate your response.

NOTES

1. See, for details, Chakrabarty (1992).
2. See, for instance the views of D. D. Basu (1992, 308).
3. For a detailed exposition on the planning as an irritant in the centre–state relations, see Hegde (1998).

4. Two illustrative studies, representing the governmental as well as independent perspectives, may be, GOI (1968, 96–97) and Frankel (1978, 310–11).
5. For instance, bearing out the rooting of indicating planning in the country, the recent advice of the Prime Minister to have some sort of ceiling on the absurdly exorbitant salaries and perks of the Chief Executive Officers of certain big Indian multinational companies (MNCs) was in the nature of a moral advice without any sanction of the force of law. Not finding propitious to the health of their companies, the industry syndicates ignored such advice, without any further action on the part of the government. See, *The Hindu* (2007).
6. Cabinet Resolution of 1 January 2015—reproduced in *The Gazette of India* (2015).
7. Cabinet Resolution of 1 January 2015—reproduced in *The Gazette of India* (2015).
8. Quotes are from Cabinet Resolution of 1 January 2015—reproduced in *The Gazette of India* (2015).

REFERENCES

Austin, Granville. 1966. *The Indian Constitution: Cornerstone of a Nation*. New Delhi: Oxford University Press.

———. 2003. *Working a Democratic Constitution: A History of the Indian Experience*. New Delhi: Oxford University Press.

Bagchi, Amiya. 1995. 'Dialectics of Indian Planning: From Compromise to Democratic Decentralization'. In *Industry and Agriculture in India since Independence,* edited by T. V. Sathyamurthi, 47. New Delhi: Oxford University Press.

Basu, D. D. 1992. *Introduction to the Constitution of India*. New Delhi: Prentice-Hall of India.

Chakrabarty, Bidyut. 1992. 'Jawaharlal Nehru and Planning, 1938–41: India at the Crossroads'. *Modern Asian Studies* 26 (2).

Frankel, Francine R. 1978. *India's Political Economy, 1947–1977: The Gradual Revolution*. Princeton, NJ: Princeton University Press.

GOI. 1968. *Report of the Study Team: Centre–State Relationships*. Administrative Reforms Commission, Manager of Publications, Government of Indi, New Delhi.

———. 1991. *Economic Survey, 1991–92*. Ministry of Finance, Government of India, New Delhi.

———. 2015, 8 February. *NITI Aayog: From Planning to NITI: Transforming India's Development Agenda*. Government of India, New Delhi.

Government of India. 2015. *The Gazette of India*. Cabinet Secretariat Resolution,1 January, New Delhi, p. 6.

Jha, A. N. 1984. 'Planning, the Federal Principle and the Parliamentary Democracy'. In *Union–State Relations: Selected Article,* edited by Abhijit Dutta, 7. New Delhi: Indian Institute of Public Administration.

Hegde, Ram Krishna. 1988. *Planning and the State Rights*. Bangalore: Government of Karnataka.

Panthem, Thomas. 1982. 'Elites, Classes and the Distortion of Economic Transition in India'. In *Contemporary India,* edited by N. R. Inamdar, R. M. Bapat, P. N. Limaye, S. N. Tawale and Rajendra Vora, p. 221. Pune: Continental.

Patnaik, Prabhat. 2014. "End of the Planning Commission?" *Economic and Political Weekly, 29,* July 19.

Planning Commission. *Annual Report, 1993–1994*. Government of India, New Delhi.

Santhanam, K. 1960. *Union–State Relations in India*. New Delhi and Mumbai: Indian Institute of Public Administration and Asia Publishing House.

Sarup, Anand, and Sulabha Brahme. 1990. *Planning for the Millions*. New Delhi: Wiley Eastern Limited.

Sethi, J. D. 1992, 14 March. 'Autonomy of the Planning Commission'. *Mainstream*: 23.

The Hindu. 2007. 7 June.

The Gazette of India. (2015), 7 January. *The Gazette of India* 1 (6): 6–9.

The World Bank. 1995. *Bureaucrats in Business: The Economics and Politics of Government Ownership*. London: Oxford University Press.

11 Financial Management in India

LEARNING OBJECTIVES

1. To understand the nature of budgets and finance as conceptual parameters.
2. To focus on the peculiar unfolding of budgets and finance in India over a historical period.
3. To draw attention to the distinctive characteristics of budgets and finance in India.

The budget is critical to financial administration in any country for at least two fundamental reasons: on the one hand, it is a definite indicator of the financial health of a polity which is reflected in the statement of expenditure and income. It also charts out, on the other hand, the future of a country on the basis of certain well-defined projected variables relating to income and expenditure. One cannot thus ignore the budget if one would like to understand the true nature of financial administration of any country. Besides being critical to financial administration, the budget is also indicative, if not illustrative, of the 'politics' that go into its making. The budget is not merely a statement of expenses and income, it also confirms and sets in motion ideological priorities of the nation in question. India provides a good example. Before the adoption of the New Economic Policy 1991 which was also an endorsement of the policy of economic liberalization, India was governed by the Nehruvian socialistic pattern of society that favoured the widely practised economic policy of a mixed economy. It was obvious that the budgets that the then governments formulated remained a tool to accomplish this goal. In the changed circumstances following the decision to open-up the Indian economy, this was not the case and the nature of the government budgets thus underwent significant changes. Unlike in the past, the post-1991 budgets seek to articulate the new ideological thrust of the government by gradually shaking-off the earlier socialistic stance. The budget is thus perhaps one of those first governmental instruments which clearly shows new directions and also policies that the ruling authority is likely to embrace under the transformed socio-economic milieu. In view of the criticality and also multidimensional character of budgets, this chapter is devoted to a threadbare discussion of the budget in the context of India's financial administration. Besides dwelling on what is basic to the budget as a conceptual category, the chapter shall also endeavour to understand its nature in the context of India's rapidly changing socio-economic scenario. The main purpose here is to provide a thorough understanding of the budget and financial administration in India both as a process and also as an event: while, as a process, the budget is constantly unfolding, seeking to attain a goal, as an event, it is a specific instrument of the projected socio-economic growth for a specific time-frame.

BUDGET POLICY ORIENTATIONS OVER THE YEARS

The present budgetary system of India owes its origin to the colonial period when the Finance Department was established in 1843 to look after the financial affairs of the government. But the budget per se was presented for the first time in 1860 to herald the system of laying down the annual estimates of revenues and expenditures and their consideration and approval by the legislature. With minor modifications and sometimes additions in the existing system, the budgetary system of India, by and large, remained the same throughout the colonial rule. However, the two debilitating features of the colonial budgetary system in India were: absence of popular control over the budget and lack of socio-economic developmental perspective in the budgetary allocations. The colonial budgetary system was, therefore, given a go-by after independence and replaced by a responsive and development oriented budgetary system under the provisions of the Constitution of India.

The budget policy orientations during the early times of Jawaharlal Nehru remained confined within the prescriptions of the Indian Constitution as stipulated under the provisions of Article 112. Without effecting any drastic break with the colonial line-item budgeting system, the budgetary policy of Nehru got enriched with the initiation of planning as a vital component of the economic development in India. Gradually, as the plan allocations started outweighing the non-plan components the governmental economic stipulations, the budget appeared to have increasingly got reduced as an instrument of taxation rather than a policy document. Moreover, in the budget, the expenditure side of the estimates was accorded high status without matching accountability and result orientation. In Nehru's times, therefore, budgetary policy could not emerge as a formidable tool of socio-economic development for the country along with acting as an effective instrument of ensuring efficiency, economy and effectiveness in enormous government expenditures.

To eradicate the obvious flaws in the existing system of the budget, a number of appreciable policy measures were introduced during the times of Mrs. Indira Gandhi in the budgetary system of the country. Owing to its superior technical value, the demand for the introduction of performance budgeting was raised from a number of quarters including the Estimates Committee and Administrative Reforms Commission. But a precondition for the introduction of performance budgeting was sincere reforms in the accounting system so as to make it a tool of administrative efficiency. Hence, the government took the landmark step of separating the audit from the accounts in 1976, undoing a long-standing colonial feature of the budgetary system in the country. Subsequently, the system of performance budgeting was introduced in select developmental departments of the Central Government in 1977–78. Above all, instead of allowing planning to dominate the budgetary processes, the idea of a Planning, Programming and Budgeting system (PPBS) was accepted as a way to integrate planning with budgeting in India

With the dawn of economic liberalization in the country since the early 1990s, the policy orientations behind the budget in India appear to have undergone subtle transformations manifested in three ways. First, despite remaining an inalienable part of the overall budgetary process, the component of planning lost its commanding position in determining the focus and locus of the budget. Now, planning got reinvented to act only as a guiding instrument to indicate the broader contours of the socio-economic development plans of the government to be reflected in the budgetary provisions. Second, in order to bring about efficiency and economy in the financial functioning of the government, a number of managerial innovations and improvizations also found ready acceptance in the budgetary procedures. For instance, a quite effective measure of cost-cutting in government departments has been the technique of the Zero-based Budgeting, which has been borrowed from the private sector of the United

States. Finally, amidst the continuing populist and bureaucratic underpinnings in the budget, a subtle move has taken place to bring about some degree of fiscal discipline through budgetary techniques. Through such a move, not only would the unproductive fiscal profligacy of governmental agencies be minimized, the money so saved could be reinvested in the newly prioritized social sector development.

Quite evidently, thus, the trajectory of the budget policy orientations in India has been guided by the administrative expediency and ideological moorings of the governments. Taking the budget mainly in its instrumentalist value, the governments over the years have sought to utilize budgetary formulations to secure money for certain programmes and projects rather than using it as a policy instrument. The primary reason for this seems to be the advent of planning as the predominant determinant of the policy perspectives of the government for the socio-economic development of the country. Nevertheless, the urge for economic prudence and fiscal discipline have led the governments at various times to go for subtle improvizations in the budgetary and accounting procedures. As a result, the budget probably inadvertently got salience in the realm of government policy-making as the free-play of the market forces in the country led to large reductions in the overarching role of planning. In contemporary times, the budget seems to have regained its status as the major instrument of policy pronouncements for the socio-economic development of the country.

MAJOR ACTORS IN THE BUDGETARY PROCESS

The budgetary process in India is quite a complex one involving a number of actors and agencies at various stages. Given the democratic nature of the Indian polity, such a cumbersome process and a multitude of agencies is obvious since they perform distinct functions crucial to the successful and responsive functioning of the budgetary system. What is unique in such a system, just as in the case of other democratic systems, is that apart from stipulating money, what is equally, if not more, important is the system of accountability for spending such money. Significantly, the intimate relationship between the legislature and the executive in the context of India's parliamentary democracy makes the legislature share a number of substantive financial functions along with the executive. At the same time, the autonomous institution of audit also joins the other agencies in providing logical inputs in the overall functioning of the financial administration of the country. What follows is a brief elucidation of the major actors or agencies in the budgetary process in India.

The Parliament of India may be taken as the lead actor in the budgetary process of the country. In consonance with the norms of Parliamentary democracy, the Parliament is entrusted with the primary responsibility of acting as the custodian of public money in the country. Consequently, by way of discharging its onerous responsibilities as a fund-raising and fund-granting agency, it exercises almost absolute control over the budget of India through its powers of levying, abolishing or decreasing any tax or other budgetary allocations. Indeed, such a commanding position to the Parliament has been accorded by the Indian Constitution itself. Hence, under Article 112 of the Constitution, the President has been vested with the responsibility of laying before the Houses of Parliament the 'annual financial statement', the constitutional terminology used for the budget. However, of the two houses of Parliament, it is the lower house or the Lok Sabha that holds absolute control over the budgetary process with just a nominal role assigned for the upper house or the Rajya Sabha.

An equally important actor in the budgetary process in India is the Executive. In fact, the theoretical monopoly of the Parliament over the budget boils down to the monopoly of the Executive itself under the dynamics of Parliamentary democracy. In other words, as the Executive commands an absolute majority in the Lok Sabha, it is but natural that the wishes of the former are unhesitatingly fulfilled by the latter as the two are staffed by people belonging to the same party or ideological persuasions. Another reason for the dominance of the budgetary process by the Executive is its role as the administering agency for the budgetary proposals. In this capacity, the Executive, even in theory, has been assigned the role of evolving proposals for demand of money from the Parliament keeping in view the policies and programmes for socio-economic development, in addition to the other routine expenses such as defence and administration of the country. The budgetary process in India, therefore, seems to be a fine example of the harmonious and cooperative functioning of the two pivotal institutions of constitutional governance in the country.

As the core unit of the Executive, entrusted with the task of managing the operational dynamics of the budget, the Ministry of Finance may arguably be taken as the nodal agency of the budgetary process in India. Indeed, to a layman, the Ministry of Finance epitomizes the financial administration of the country in its entirety. Though technically untenable, yet such a notion is attributed to the Ministry of Finance keeping in view its role in the managing of finances of the country. For instance, right from estimating the final figures of the revenues and expenditures of the government for presentation before the Parliament, the Ministry is vested with the task of ultimately ensuring that the finances of the country are managed properly. The major contours of the functioning of the Ministry are discerned from its structural divisions in the three departments, that is, the Department of Economic Affairs, the Department of Revenue and the Department of Expenditure. Such an overarching role in the management of the finances of the country has made the Ministry of Finance one of the key ministries of the Government of India.

An indirect yet democratically unavoidable actor in the budgetary process of democratic societies is the institution of an independent audit. In India, such a function is discharged by the constitutional authority called the Comptroller and Auditor General (CAG) of India. Envisaged under the provisions of Article 148 of the Constitution, 'the office of CAG is meant to introduce the rigour and uniformity of government accounts on the one hand and to carry out the responsibility of conducting independent audit on the other' (Chakrabarty and Pandey 2008, 157). The CAG conducts such an audit on behalf of the Parliament to investigate and report on the fidelity, legality and efficiency of all the financial transactions carried out by government departments. The criticality of the role of CAG in the budgetary processes in India has been a byproduct of the Parliamentary democratic system of governance provided for under the Constitution. Over the years, it has emerged as one of the most stringent checks on the financial impropriety and profligacy of the government, though critiques have argued against such a role of audit in India.

Finally, the Parliamentary Committees constitute the last set of actors playing a significant role in the budgetary processes of the country. The role of these Committees exposes the inadequacy of control exercised by the Parliament over the finances of the government due to the paucity of time and lack of expertise. Previously, there used to be only two Committees—the Estimates Committee and the Public Accounts Committee of the Parliament to discharge the necessary functions of legislative control. But in recent times, with the creation of the departmental-related Standing Committees of Parliament, the role of the Parliament in the functioning of various departments of the government has become more comprehensive and focused. Nonetheless, the role of these Committees is distinct in relation to the budgetary process. The Estimates Committee, for instance, suggests economies in estimates of expenditures of various government departments in order to make them more realistic and economical. On the contrary, the Public Accounts Committee carries out a post-mortem of the Appropriation accounts in the light of the audit report of the CAG. In the process, it attracts the attention of the legislature to financial irregularities, if any, and suggests remedial measures for the same. Distinct to the others, the departmental-related Standing Committees carry out not just financial control over the concerned departments but also scrutinize their overall functioning from time to time.

In a nutshell, the major actors or agencies in the budgetary process of India are numerous and varied owing to the variety of functions each of them is supposed to perform. Such functions may be classified in three groups, each having their critical value in the smooth functioning of the budgetary system. Hence, while the broad functions of the Parliament as the fund-raising and fund granting agency is well-established, the role of the Executive and its sub-agencies such the Ministry of Finance as the proposer of financial estimates is equally universally accepted. What is, however, unique to India is apparently its elaborate system of legislative control over the budget through the mechanism of its own committees as well as the institution of an independent audit. Indeed, the successful functioning of financial administration in India can be credited to the reasonably satisfactory role played by these actors in the budgetary processes of the country.

THE BUDGET SYSTEM IN INDIA

In this section, the budget system of India is explained with reference to its classification, formation and composition.

The budgetary classification is generally considered a useful tool for providing meaningful information on the activities of the government and it sets out the form and structure for closer analysis and utilization by policy-makers. In other words, the budgetary classification serves the purpose of presenting a maze of data in a simple and systematic way such that non-technical Parliamentarians are able to understand the niceties of the budget and meaningfully take part in the deliberations on it. Keeping that in mind, the budget classifications in various countries of the world are carried out in two distinct ways. First, is the traditional method of budget classification, also known as the line-item method and it provides for the arrangement of data on the basis of departments that are supposed to incur the expenditures. On the contrary, the second method, also called the performance budgeting method or the functional classification method, seeks to classify receipts and expenditures on the basis of functions, projects, programmes and activities of the various departments.

The budget classification in India, for a long time even after independence, continued to be carried out in the format of the line-item method maintaining the opaqueness of budgetary provisions and rendering their proper evaluation almost inscrutable. Hence, following the recommendations of a number of committees and commissions as well as persuasions from development economists, the government decided to switch over to the functional classification of the budget in 1974. Consequently, now instead of just naming the department for the budgetary classification, government activities are categorized into three broad groups namely General or Regulatory Services, Social and Community Services and Economic Services. Even within these groups, the budgetary allocations are further classified under five heads viz., sectoral head, major head, minor head, sub-head and detailed heads of account.

For purposes of budget classification, General Services includes those regulatory or routine services of the government that do not involve any productive or developmental activities. These services are further clubbed together under six broad groups: (a) Organs of State such as the Parliament, the Head of State, Judiciary, Audit, Council of Ministers and Elections, (b) Fiscal services including the agencies for collection of taxes, (c) Interest payments and debt services, (d) Administrative services such as the Public Service Commissions, general administration, police, etc., (e) Pension and miscellaneous general services and (f) Defence services.

As against the General Services, the Social and Community Services consist of programmes and activities that aim at providing basic social services to the people. Forming the core of the social development programmes of the government, these services include education, health, housing, drinking water, social security including old-age pension, welfare of the scheduled castes and scheduled tribes, women, minorities and other marginalized sections of society. Besides, in recent times, under this head the government has initiated a number of flagship schemes such as the *Sarva Shiksha Abhiyan* (Education for All), the Mid Day Meal Scheme, the National Rural Health Mission, the Total Sanitation Campaign, the National Rural Employment Guarantee Scheme, the Integrated Child Development Services, the Jawaharlal Nehru National Urban Renewal Mission and the Pulse Polio Programme aimed at bringing about a turnaround in the fortunes of the masses of the country (*The Times of India* 2009, 11).

Lastly, the Economic Services cover those sectors of the government that are involved in productive and manufacturing activities including trade and commerce. These services are further classified into seven sub-groups including (a) General Economic Services including foreign trade and export promotion, (b) Agriculture and allied services such as cooperation, minor irrigation, animal husbandry, fisheries, forests, soil conservation, dairy development etc., (c) Industry and Minerals including heavy and medium industries, village and small scale industries, mines and minerals, (d) Water resources and Power Development, (e) Transport and Communications including Civil Aviation, Road Transport, Ports, Lighthouses and Shipping, (f) Railways and (g) Posts and Telegraphs. However, with the separate presentation of the Railways budget, the clubbing of railways under the head of economic services does not carry much weight in current times.

After the streamlining of budget classification through the adoption of techniques of the Performance Budgeting system, the formation of the budget has become quite meaningful and accountable in India. The formation of the budget follows the cycle of the financial year from April to March each year. However, owing to cumbersome procedures involved in the final formation of the budget, the process for the same begins around the month of September–October. Initiating the process, the Ministry of Finance issues a circular to the various ministries and departments inviting their estimates for the coming year. This is in accordance with the general principle of budgeting that he who spends the money should also prepare estimates in advance for presenting before the legislature. These estimates are subsequently transmitted to the Controlling Officers of the respective departments who are assigned the responsibility of giving final shape to the budget estimates of the department. The Controlling Officers, therefore, are empowered to scrutinize the estimates and either give their approval for the same or revise the estimates, if necessary, giving reasons for the same. Approved and consolidated, thus, the estimates of various ministries and departments then go to the Ministry of Finance in November–December. By the end of January or early February, the Ministry of Finance is able to prepare a consolidated statement of revenues and expenditures which is further fine-tuned by the third week of February to culminate the process of formation of the budget.

The completion of the process of budget formation results into the final product, technically called the 'annual financial statement.' The composition of this statement or the budget is, in the main, marked by the items of income and expenditure that are presented in the following format:

1. actual figures of the previous 3 years;
2. the sanctioned budget estimates for the current year;
3. revised estimates of the current year;
4. proposed estimates for the next financial year, with explanatory notes for any increase or decrease in estimates; and
5. actuals of the current year available at the time of preparation of the estimates and actuals for the corresponding period of the previous year (Thavaraj 1987, 496).

In order to provide for a ready-recknor of the budgetary provisions, the budget document contains a broad description of the receipts and expenditures of the government. The total receipts of the government are the sum total of the revenue receipts and the capital receipts. Similarly, the total expenditures of the government are calculated by summing up both the plan as well as non-plan expenditures. A remarkable feature of the budget document, indicating the health of the government finances, has been the two deficit indicators. While the revenue deficit indicates the excesses of revenue expenditures over revenue receipts, the fiscal deficit denotes the totality of revenue receipts and certain non-debt capital receipts as well as the total expenditures including loans, net of repayments etc. The difference between the two gives the figures for the fiscal deficit which also indicates the total borrowing needs of the government from all sources to meet the above mentioned difference.

The niceties of the budget system of India, therefore, get reflected in the classification, formation and composition of the budget. Though most, if not all, of the aspects of the budget system in India draw their lineage from conventions and rules rooted in the colonial framework, a number of modifications brought about over the years have added new vibrancy and coherence in them. The budgetary system in India, thus, appears to be a good example of continuity and change keeping in view the requirements of the changing times.

The Budget Process

While the budget process in any country is a complex and time-consuming one, the dynamics of a number of unconventional factors such as planning and Parliamentary democratic polity in India do not make the matter any easier. Indeed, the budgetary process in the country appears to have become an all the year round affair as one or the other aspects of the process is always in motion keeping budget officials on their toes. For instance, the initiation of the budgetary process by the third quarter of the year does not get completed with the enactment of the budget proposals by the Parliament in the month of March. Parliamentary approval is followed by the onerous task of budget implementation which within its ambit also combines the responsibility of budget accounting as well. The final act in the budgetary process is enacted by the audit of the Appropriation accounts maintained by the spending departments which in itself is an activity having its own follow up actions. Hence, what follows is a brief narration of the various significant activities involved in the budgetary process in India right from the stage of budget planning and moving through the stages of scrutiny, implementation, accounting to reach the final stage of audit.

Budget Planning

The budget planning stage involves numerous intricate activities that go into making the budget before its presentation to the Lok Sabha. To set the stage for budget planning and to accommodate the plan objectives for development in the budget provisions, a detailed discussion takes place between officials of the Planning Commission and the Ministry of Finance. In this discussion the two crucial issues that get finalized include the gross budget support for plans and ministry/department-wise plan allocations (Sudarsanan 2001, 65). Such an exercise appears to be a crucial step in budget planning in India given the predominant position accorded to planning in chartering out long term policies and programmes for the socio-economic development of the country. However, this is also argued as a weakness of the Indian budgetary system which is alleged to have been reduced to not more than an instrument of over-aching planning for the country. Nonetheless, irrespective of the merit of such a critique, it may be argued that since planning has become well-entrenched in the economic system of the country, it would not be possible to overlook the same. The only way out left, therefore, is to go for a coordinated approach by incorporating plan considerations in budgetary provisions. Hence, once the issues of plan concerns are addressed, the onus falls on the Ministry of Finance to set the ball rolling for the formation of the budget to be presented before the Parliament.

Budget Scrutiny

The scrutiny of the budgetary proposals in India takes place at two levels: administrative and legislative. Administrative scrutiny refers to the scrutiny carried out by the higher echelons of a particular department as well as the Ministry of Finance. For instance, the budgetary proposals emanating from the base estimating authorities are, as a norm, scrutinized by the Financial Advisor and head of the department. Only when the administrative approval of these officials is obtained, such proposals become part of the departmental budget. Further, if the proposal involves construction works, it needs to be submitted for scrutiny to the Public Works Department which may then give technical approval to the proposal. As the final step in administrative scrutiny, all the departmental budgets, particularly the 'new items' thereof, are minutely scrutinized by the Ministry of Finance and its decision becomes the final word on the subject.

After the budget is presented in the Parliament, the stage of legislative scrutiny begins. Previously, the legislative scrutiny of budgetary proposals in India was more generalized and formalistic given the technical nature of the subject and paucity of time at the disposal of the Parliament to go into the details of the budget. But with the inauguration of the system of departmental-related Standing Committees in 1993, legislative scrutiny of the budget has become more focused and sharp. However, bringing another aspect of this system, a commentator argues, '[T]his is a valuable contribution to legislative scrutiny of the budget proposals but the public focus of debate on the floor is now lost' (Prasad 2006, 147). In the end, the debates and discussions on various aspects of the budget culminate in its approval by the Parliament.

Budget Implementation

The nodal agency for budget implementation in India is the Ministry of Finance. Following the passage of the Appropriation Act (2015), the Ministry of Finance issues advisories to the spending ministries intimating the quantum of allocated funds to them. Thereafter, the responsibility comes to the controlling officers, who ordinarily are the heads of the departments, to allocate money to the numerous disbursing officers of the departments. However, the disbursing officers are given the right to spend money only to the extent permitted going beyond which necessarily requires sanctioning from the requisite authorities. At the same time, it is also mandatory for each spending department to maintain records of payments and receipts in the prescribed method of accounting. Thus, the system of budget implementation in India essentially involves, at the ground, functionaries such as controlling officers, competent officers to accord financial sanctions, drawing and disbursing officers and an efficient structure of accounts to keep record of payments and receipts. In the process of budget implementation, the concerned officers are expected to exercise the highest degree of continuous vigilance and financial prudence in order to have economical, efficient and effective utilization of the public money.

Budget Accounting

Constitutionally, budgetary accounting in India is the responsibility of an independent and constitutional authority called the CAG of India. In fact, the method and form of keeping accounts of the central as well as state governments are prescribed by the CAG with the approval of the President of India. Hence, the office of the CAG happens to be the custodian of the accounting and audit system in the country. The audit and accounts were separated in 1976 to provide for better administrative expediency and accountability. 'Under the Comptroller and Auditor General there is an Accountant General in each state, in whose office the accounts of the transactions (Central as well as State), which take place within the territorial limits of the state, are kept' (Bhattacharya 2008, 379). The uniqueness of Indian accounting, thus, lies in its executive functions despite retaining it under the overall monitoring and guidance of the legislative constitutional office of the CAG.

Budget Audit

The budget audit is the exclusive function of the CAG of India. Given the value and sanctity of the function, the office of the CAG has by implication been made analogous to that of a judge of the Supreme Court of India in terms of its independence and functional autonomy. An audit is, in fact, visualized as an extension of legislative control and accountability over the financial administration of the country. The audit in India is more sharp and focused with regard to expenditures which are called the Appropriation Audit. The objective of the Appropriation Audit is:

> to ensure that the funds voted by the legislature are utilized by the executive for the purposes for which they were intended with due regard to economy and efficiency. It comprises:
>
> 1. audit from the point of view of accountancy and classification;
> 2. audit from the point of view of authority;
> 3. audit of appropriation and finance accounts; and
> 4. audit from the point of view of propriety. (Thavaraj 1987, 644)

In brief, the budgetary process in India appears as an integrated entity reflecting the nature and structure of the socio-economic and politico-administrative set-up of the country. For instance, budget planning is arguably a standard statement on the budgetary dynamics of the socio-economic development goals and methods by which they have been acheived. However, in order to provide for wisdom, faithfulness, economy and accountability, an elaborate system of administrative and legislative scrutiny has been put in place. On the contrary, budget implementation illustrates the maturity and autonomy of administrative the apparatus in India with a view to facilitate the highest degree of initiative, enterprise and innovation in administering the development of the country. Lastly, budget accounting and audit become the hallmarks of financial accountability in true spirit of the Parliamentary democratic system of governance in India.

FINANCE MANAGEMENT IN INDIA

The management of finances in India involves a complex set of activities right from the generation of resources to their proper management for the socio-economic development of the country. In fact, finance constitutes probably the most significant aspect of the budget.

Government policies and programmes designed to bring about socio-economic development of the people get functional dynamism only through the support of finances. Indeed, budget and finance may be taken as two sides of the same coin.[1] In this regard, the Ministry of Finance functions as the nodal agency to manage finances in conjunction with certain other bodies like the Planning Commission. Two core issued involved in financial management in India are the generation of revenues and the proper expenditure of the same in such a manner that the socio-economic development of the country is maximized to the greatest possible extent. However, a common tendency evident in finance management in most developing countries appears to be the notion of deficit financing. Though in many cases deficit financing is ordinarily used as a means of augmenting resources of the government which are to be used for productive purposes, this usually is not the case in India. While taking recourse to deficit financing, the government is often seen spending the resources for unproductive purposes. This appears to be a significant aspect in the management of finances in India.

Finance Revenues and Expenditures

The revenue component of public finance in India consists of receipts on both the revenue or current as well as capital accounts. In turn, revenue receipts are further divided into tax revenue and non-tax revenue. Accounting for the major chunk of finance revenue of the government, tax revenue is drawn mainly from three types of taxes: taxes on income and expenditures, taxes on property or capital assets and taxes on goods and services. While the first two sets of taxes are known as direct taxes, the last category is called indirect taxes. Of the direct taxes, income tax constitutes the backbone of finance revenue in India. The other components of the taxes on income and expenditure include corporation tax and interest tax. Two key components of the taxes on property comprise the wealth tax and the gift tax. Within the category of indirect taxes, customs duties, central excise duty and the recently introduced service tax constitute the nucleus of the account. In contrast to tax revenues, the contribution of the non-tax revenues to the body of finance revenue is not that remarkable. It is drawn mainly from routine governmental enterprises such as currency, coinage, mint, interest receipts, dividends and miscellaneous non-tax revenues.

Capital account receipts of the government are drawn from four sources: (a) net recoveries of loans and advances made previously to state governments, Union Territories and public sector undertakings; (b) net market borrowings (i.e., gross borrowings from the market less repayment of public debt); (c) net small savings collections (gross collections less share of the states) and (d) other capital receipts such as provident funds, special deposits, etc. (Datt and Sundharam 2008, 894–95).

On the expenditure side, a new classification was adopted under the heads of non-plan expenditure and plan expenditure from the financial year 1987–88. Accordingly, non-plan expenditures are again sub-divided into revenue expenditures and capital expenditures. Revenue expenditure consists of revenue payments, defence revenue expenditure, subsidies in the fields in the areas of fertilizers, food, export promotion etc. debt relief to farmers, postal deficit, police, pension, other general services such as organs of state, tax collection, external affairs and likewise. There are also allocations to finance the social services such as health, education, social security, employment guarantee schemes, mid day meal scheme etc., in addition to massive outlays for the core sectors of the economy such as agriculture, industry, power, transport, communications, science and technology, mining and other infrastructural development projects. Finally, grants to the states and the Union Territories as well as grants to foreign countries are also disbursed from the revenue expenditures corpus of the government.

As referred to earlier, capital non-plan expenditure is mainly meant for financing activities such as defence capital expenditure, loans to public sector enterprises, loans to the states and the Union Territories, apart from the loans and grants to foreign governments.

As against non-plan expenditure, plan expenditure is expected to provide financing for long-term infrastructure development projects in the sectors such as agriculture, rural development, irrigation and flood control, energy, industry, mining, minerals, transport, communications, science and technology, environmental protection, social services and social security. Significantly, the key to understand plan expenditure is the prior stipulations for such expenditures in the Five Year Plan documents with appropriate divisions of the sum total of expenditures in a particular sector over the span of five years. Besides the financing of central projects, another critical aspect of plan expenditure happens to be central assistance for the plans of the states and the Union Territories. The finance expenditure component of public finance in India, therefore, consists of both non-plan as well plan expenditures with the budgetary provisions just giving a detailed description of these heads for a particular financial year.

Funds and Government Bonds

As part of the management of public finances, the government of India maintains its corpus of funds under three specific purpose accounts called funds and account. First, the Consolidated Fund of India, set-up under the provisions of Article 266 (1) of the Indian Constitution, acts as a fund to finance, among other things, expenditures called 'charged expenditures' in the conduct of operations of the vital organs of the state such as the judiciary and other constitutional offices. It consists of all the revenue receipts of the government by way of taxes such as income tax, central excise, customs and other non-tax revenues. Further, all loans raised by the government both from within and outside the country are also credited into this Fund. This Fund also feeds all the expenditures of the Government after proper authorization from the Parliament. Second, under the provisions of Article 267 of the Constitution of India, the Contingency Fund of India has been set up with a corpus of ₹50 crores to meet expenses arising in an emergency and due to unforeseen circumstances. Interestingly, once the Parliament sanctions money for the said emergency circumstance, the advance made from the Contingency Fund is reimbursed to it. Thus, this Fund is supposed to act as some sort of cushion to provide the government finance resilience in times of crisis. Finally, the Public Account, constituted under Article 266 (2) of the Constitution, is meant to service transactions relating to debt other than those included in the Consolidated Fund of India. As such transactions do not constitute normal receipts of the Government, no Parliamentary authorization is required for payments to be made from this Account. Thus, in brief, the Consolidated Fund of India, the Contingency Fund of India and the Public Account form the core of what may be called as the Government Funds in India.

Government bonds also constitute a significant component of the public finance system in India. Technically, a government bond is a bond issued by the Government of India denominated either in the country's own currency or in foreign currencies in which case they are called sovereign bonds. Such bonds are issued to raise money in order to finance the spending of the government given the insufficiency of funds raised from sources like taxation. The Government of India, for instance, proposes to borrow ₹450,000 crore in 2009–10 (*The Hindustan Times* 2009, 21) from the market to funds its massive socio-economic developmental programmes. In fact, a high fiscal deficit means higher government borrowing, primarily, if not exclusively, through the means of the government bonds in the Indian context.

In sum, the management of public finance in India is a complex and technical exercise requiring high degree of managerial skills and financial prudence. Being the operational part of the economic system of the country whereby the real challenges of generating, maintaining and spending financial resources are to be met, finance management has always remained a prime concern of the Government. Moreover, acknowledging the vitality of the activity, several definite provisions have also been made in the Constitution to provide for certain basic formulations on the issue. The inherent logic behind such constitutional provisions seems to be the concern of the framers of the Constitution to confine the management of finances within the parameters of democratic governance in the country. Clearly, therefore, barring few financial crises that have erupted occasionally, the overall management of finances in India has remained on a sound footing, bearing testimony to the prudence and farsightedness of the fathers of the Indian Constitution.

BUDGET SYSTEM REFORMS IN INDIA

The inheritance of a budgetary process designed to suit the requirements of a colonial economy was definitely not appropriate for the needs of a newly independent and development-oriented economy like India. Over the years, therefore, numerous subtle reform measures have been initiated in the budgetary processes of the country in order to bring it in sync with the requirements of a nation embarking on the path of rapid socio-economic development within the norms of a democratic polity. So, the basic contours of reforms in the budgetary processes have revolved around the themes of: relocating its orientations from a colonial economy to that of a development oriented one; making the budget a tool of socio-economic development for the country; reorienting its focus from outlays to outcomes; designing the budget as an instrument of ensuring effective politico-administrative accountability of administration to the legislative and executive bodies; and bringing about suitable technical reforms, say, in the system of accounting and audit.

To ensure that the budget system reforms did not cause any disruptions in the smooth functioning of the financial administration of the country, such reforms have been introduced in a piece-meal and evolutionary manner. Three distinct phases of the process of budgetary reforms may be discerned in India. First, with the inauguration of India as an independent nation, the budgetary system was subject to deep-seated reforms more so in terms of reorienting it to the development and accountability imperatives of a developing and fledging democracy than to bring about a radical change in the technical format of the budget. Second, in the wake of the recommendations of the First Administrative Reforms Commission (1968), a number of far-reaching changes were introduced in the technical format of the budget on the lines of the Performance Budgeting, accounting reforms, etc. Finally, in contemporary times, with the strengthening of the forces of liberalization and privatization, Parliamentary control over the budgetary process is also sought to be streamlined and deepened with the creation of a number of Parliamentary Standing Committees to closely scrutinize the budgetary allocations of various ministries and departments.

As explained earlier, the contents of budgetary reforms in India have encompassed almost the entire gamut of the budgetary process. The beginning in this regard seems to have been made by ideological reorientations in budgetary outlook from being colonial to becoming development-oriented. Further, in order to make such reorientation bear fruit, the line-item format of budget preparation was replaced by the performance budgeting system in 1977–78 for most of the developmental ministries of the Government of India. Moreover, as a preparatory move to introduce performance budgeting, and to streamline the audit and accounting system, the audit and accounts which were hitherto managed as an integrated system, were separated in 1976. At certain times, suggestions were also made to introduce the format of Zero-Based-Budgeting (ZBB). But such suggestions could not cut much ice given the complexity of the development imperatives of the country. The last substantive reform in the budgetary process of the country came in the form of the Standing Committees of the Parliament to insightfully and closely monitor the functioning of the concerned ministries and departments (Kashyap 1990, 3247). As a result of such reforms in the budgetary processes, the performance of the budgetary system in India has undergone remarkable improvements. For instance, the budget has not only emerged as a strong tool of socio-economic transformation, it has also made public authorities responsible for the execution of budgetary allocations more accountable and sharp-focused in attaining stipulated objectives. Yet, there still exist a number of grey areas where budgetary reforms have not been able to make much difference such as the rising fiscal deficit. As a result, the budget in India still remains burdened by the over-bearing fiscal deficit casting doubts on its ability to discipline government expenditure. Moreover, in order to take the process of budgetary reforms in India to any logical conclusion, the focus areas now need to be raising governmental revenue, increasing work efficiency, limiting subsidies to the poor, sorting out the complexities in the power sector, right sizing government, prioritizing governmental expenditures and linking agricultural and health policies (Vyasulu 2009, 21–23).

FINANCE SYSTEM REFORMS IN INDIA

Technically, the financial system in India consists of a myriad of institutions, activities and products having a strong bearing on the country's economy. The key functions of the financial system include the channelization of domestic savings and foreign capital into productive investments for the economy on the one hand, and the efficient delivery of financial services such as payments, savings, insurance, pensions etc. to the mammoth populace of the country on the other. Hence, in the post-independence times, the Indian financial system was built to serve the twin purposes of propelling the growth trajectory as well as providing social and economic stability to the people. The context and nature of financial system reforms in India, therefore, hover around the idea of bringing the system in sync with the fast changing dynamics of the global economy without causing a sudden and untoward upheaval in the life of the common people.

Given the complexity of the task in hand as well as the problem of stemming the tide of public outcry over the nature and product of financial system reforms, the Government thought it convenient to move in phases in so far as the finance system reforms in India were concerned. So, the first phase of these reforms began in the context of the unprecedented economic crisis the country faced in the early 1990s in the wake of a massive balance of payment crisis. With a government favourably disposed towards financial reforms placed at the helm of affairs at the centre, global financial institutions such as the International Monetary Fund and the International Bank for Reconstruction and Development found it convenient to press for fundamental reforms in the Indian financial system. As a result, a policy called the Structural Adjustment Programme, was initiated under the close monitoring of global financial institutions with a view to dismantle the structures and processes created to construct a socialistic pattern of society in India during the early years of independence of the country. Besides, the focus during this phase of reforms was also on liberalization of the interest rate and directed credit. However, as most of the reforms in the first phase were macro in nature, they were criticized for focusing on the bigger picture that could bog down progress in the country. Hence, an International Monetary Fund Report listed a number of specific (micro) steps that could get the reforms going and build up some momentum once people began to see the benefits. For instance, it was suggested that converting trade receivable claims to electronic format and creating a structure to allow them to be sold as commercial paper could greatly boost the credit available to small and medium sized enterprises (Prasad and Rajan 2008). Hence, with the dawn of the new millennium, the stage was set for the second phase of financial system reforms in India.

With the basic groundwork getting done in the first phase, the stage was now set for the initiation of the most comprehensive and penetrating reforms in the financial system of India. Given the complexity and the proportion of the areas and issues to be covered in this phase, an indicative list of such spheres may include:

1. Reducing the fiscal deficit, to reduce the risk of macroeconomic instability and increasing the availability of finance to the private sector
2. Improving the legal, regulatory and supervisory frameworks, in order to improve bank credit and risk management
3. Improving systems for dealing with weak banks
4. Developing capital markets further
5. Developing pensions and insurance to increase finance for long-term investments, Including infrastructure
6. Improving financial services to improve the welfare of customers and meeting the Challenge of globalization of financial services
7. Managing links to external capital markets (Hansen and Kathuria 1999).

In sum, the second generation of financial reforms in India are focused on the monetary and financial sectors despite the political sensitiveness of these areas. Indeed, without drastically reforming the monetary and financial sectors of the economy, the real fruits of a liberalized economy cannot be reaped by the people in the long term (Reddy 2004). Such reforms are likely to be more in the structural dispensation of the financial sector than in operational policy orientations. Indeed, the government is faced with the formidable challenge of containing the worrisome fiscal deficit while continuing to provide the necessary fiscal stimulus to revive the economy. It has also to institute a fiscal restructuring programme towards achieving fiscal consolidation in the medium term. The programme needs to draw lessons from the past and redesign the fiscal restructuring plan for the centre as well as the states. Experience shows that the mere passing of any legislation does not necessarily bring about fiscal discipline. It needs to be matched with the political will to ruthlessly implement such legislation irrespective of the storms created by unscrupulous people with vested interests in continuing with the existing system (Rao 2009).

Evaluative Remarks

Public budgeting seems to be the most difficult act in governance because it involves making and carrying out decisions regarding the acquisition, allocation and utilization of resources, particularly money, by the government. The reasons are not difficult to find. Besides technical expertise in addressing critical areas of public concern, the governmental authority preparing the budget needs to take into account the ideological priorities of the regime. Budgetary decisions are therefore a meaningful socio-economic index of knowing the nature of the polity both from the point of view of its economic health and political direction. This is also a clear device to identify the gaps between what the budget suggests and what it accomplishes.

There is no doubt that the budget is a time-tested mechanism in financial management which is governed by certain well-defined principles drawn on the economic priorities and the ideological predilections of the government in power. Two important and significant points emerge from this statement. As mentioned, the budget seeks to capture the concern of the stakeholders underlining the socio-political agenda of the government. What is most critical in this process is the overwhelming importance of 'democracy' as an aspired ideal. And, hence, despite socio-cultural differences, the most significant aspect of the entire process of budget preparation and implementation happens to be 'the unambiguous role of the public'. It is true that due to peculiar circumstances, the public may not be as visible as is expected; but, in the long run, the neglect will cost the decision makers dearly unless this is meaningfully addressed. What is basic to this argument is the importance of ideology in shaping the budget, drawing on the political priorities, as defined by the government in power. Whether it is India or elsewhere, the stakeholders seem to propel the government to action in accordance with what they consider as 'ideological priorities'. This is what separates India from other types of political systems where 'people' appear to be 'mere cogs' in the entire process of making and implementing the budget without a meaningful voice. This is also what makes the study of the budgetary processes in India so interesting and revealing because not only does this set in motion studies on the complexities of the entire exercise, but it also provides inputs for an enriching analysis of financial administration in India.

THE COMPTROLLER AND AUDITOR GENERAL OF INDIA (CAG)[2]

The CAG of India is the most important institution in the Indian Constitution along with other institutions. As Ambedkar had rightly said in the constituent assembly,

> Comptroller and Auditor General of India shall be the most important officer under the Constitution of India. For, he is to be the guardian of the public purse and it is his duty to see that not a farthing is spent out of the Consolidated Fund of India or of a state without the authority of the appropriate Legislature. In short, he shall be the impartial head of the audit and accounts system of India. (Basu 2012, 203)

Theoretically, the Indian Constitution establishes an independent CAG which ensures a guarantee to its people that the government is accountable and responsive to the Parliament. This is the founding principle of the Parliamentary system of Government that the Executive will be responsible to the Legislature and the essence of such control lies in the system of financial control by the Legislature. To discharge this function it is important that the Legislature have some kind of agency which would be fully independent from the Executive, and would scrutinize the financial transactions of the Government. Therefore it is important to asses this very important institution in contemporary times. The CAG is not only an institution but also a tool to maintain governance and to empower the people.

A Brief History

The CAG of India as a head of the Supreme Audit Institution of India (SAI) has a long history. It has evolved through the practice and tradition in British India. Just prior to the Mutiny of 1857 Lord Canning had initiated a major administrative reorganization. As part of this reorganization, for the first time, a separate department with an Accountant General was established. He was responsible for accounting and auditing of financial transactions under the East India Company. After the mutiny the British Crown took over the administration of India and passed the Government of India Act 1858. This Act introduced a system of annual budgets of Imperial income and expenditure in 1860. The budgeting system laid the foundation stone of the Imperial Audit. Sir Edward Drummoned took charge in November 1860 as the first Auditor General. Therefore, originally it was designated the Accountant General to the Government of India, and later designated as the Auditor General of India in 1860. The term Comptroller and Auditor General of India was first used in 1884. Under the Montague–Chelmsford Reforms of 1919, the Auditor General became independent of the government. The government of India Act 1935 strengthened the position of the Auditor General by providing for a provincial Auditor General in a federal set-up. He was given the status of a judge of the federal court in regard to the security of his service. The legacy of the 1935 Act continued in the period following independence. Till 1947, when the last British Auditor General Sir Bertie Monro Staig handed over the reins, the department remained an integral part of the British administration.

After independence, in a federal setup, a unitary Audit System was established, that is, the CAG of India would audit the centre as well as state governments. Before adopting this system in the Indian Constitution, a huge debate was taken up in the Constituent Assembly. The draft Constitution prepared by the Constitutional Advisor in October 1947 contained separate provisions for the appointment of the Auditor–General of the Federation and Auditor Generals for the Provinces. The Auditor General for the Federation was to be appointed by the President, and would have the same security of tenure as a judge of the Supreme Court. It was open to a Provincial Legislature to provide for by law, the appointment of an Auditor General for the Province. Appointment to the office of the Provincial Auditor General was to be made by the Governor in his discretion and he could be removed from office only in the same manner as a High Court judge (Kashyap 2004, 414). The Expert Committee on the financial provisions of the Union Constitution observed that the provisions of this draft were adequate for the purpose of securing the independence of the Auditor General. The Committee however favoured the continuance of a single Auditor General for the Government of India as well as for the provincial governments (Kashyap 2004, 414). Later on this advice was accepted by the Drafting Committee.

Position in the Indian Constitution

Our Constitution makers, realizing the importance of an independent agency for audit under the Parliamentary form of government, made the CAG fully independent so that it could function efficiently. In Part V of the Constitution of India, Articles 148, 149, 150 and 151 form the basic structure of the institution of CAG of India. According to Article 148 (1):

> [T]here shall be a Comptroller and Auditor General of India, who shall be appointed by the President by warrant under his hand and seal and shall be only be removed from office in like manner and on the like grounds as a Judge of the Supreme Court.

With this his salary and other conditions of service could be determined by the Parliament but once appointed, neither his salary nor his rights in respect of leave of absence, pension or age of retirement could be varied to his disadvantage. After retirement or resignation he would be not eligible for any office under the government of India or any state government. His salary and other expenses of his administration or office were charged upon the Consolidated Fund of India, it meant that they were not subject to vote.

Independent CAG in Independent India

Dr Ambedkar said in the Constituent Assembly (1949),

> Personally speaking for myself, I am of the opinion that this dignity and office is probably the most important officer in the constitution of India. He is the one man who is going to see that the expenses voted by Parliament are not exceeded or varied from what has been laid down by parliament in what is called the Appropriation Act. If this functionary is to carry out the duties and, I submit his duties are far more important than the judiciary, he should have been certainly as independent as the judiciary.

To keep this in mind our Constitution framers made this institution autonomous from the government so that it could discharge its functions free from the pressures of the government. The Constitution enabled the independent nature of audit by the CAG by providing:

1. Appointment by the President of India.
2. Special procedure for removal like a Supreme Court Judge
3. Salary and other administrative expenses charged on a consolidated fund, meaning that they are not subject to vote.
4. He/she cannot hold any other government office after his/her terms expires.

Powers and Duties of the CAG

Articles 149 and 150 of Indian Constitution deal with the power and duties of the CAG. According to the Article 149,

> The Comptroller and Auditor General shall perform such duties and exercise such powers in relation to the accounts of the Union and of the States and of any other authority or body as may be prescribed by or under any law made by Parliament and, until provision in that behalf is so made, shall perform such duties and exercise such powers in relation to the accounts of Union as of the States as were conferred on or exercisable by the Auditor General of India.

Beside the Constitution, the CAG of India (Duties, Powers and Conditions) Act, 1971 also talks about the duties and powers of the CAG in detail. This Act identifies the various subjects and items which come under the scrutiny of the CAG. According to this Act, it shall be the duty of CAG (Government of India)

1. to audit all expenditure from the consolidated fund of India.
2. to audit all transactions of the Union and the states relating to contingency funds and public accounts.
3. to audit all trading manufacturing, profit and loss accounts and balance sheets and other subsidiary accounts kept in any department of the Union or of a state.
4. audit of receipts and expenditures of bodies or authorities substantially financed from the Union or state revenues.

In 2007, the CAG issued, under Section 23 of the DPC Act, 'Regulations on Audit and Accounts' which defined in detail the scope, manner and extent of his auditing and accounting mandate.

Types of Audit

There are mainly three types of audit carried out by the CAG:

1. Compliance Audit
2. Financial Audit
3. Performance Audit

Apart from these traditional audits, the CAG has carried out many audits of information technology systems and environment related issues.

What Happens to the Audit Reports?

The reports prepared by the CAG are submitted to the President in the case of the Union and to the Governor in the case of the states. Article 151 of the Constitution says (a) the reports of the CAG of India relating to the accounts of the Union shall be submitted to the President, who shall cause them to be laid before each House of Parliament and (b) the Reports of the CAG of India relating to the accounts of the state shall be submitted to the Governor of the state, who shall cause them to be laid before the Legislature of the state. Once submitted in the respective houses, the reports are referred to the Central and state related Public Accounts Committee and Committees on Pubic Understandings (COPU). These specialized Committees scrutinize these reports and select those paragraphs/findings that are most critical to public interest. In this process the CAG provides them with technical assistance. Based on their study these Committees prepare reports with recommendations and submit them to their respective houses for further discussion.

Changing Role of India's Comptroller and Auditor General Over a period of time, the CAG has changed itself. We have already discussed the mandatory provisions of the CAG and Its importance to maintain democracy. Through the Indian Constitution, the CAG has been made an autonomous institution so that it can have surveillance on the government through its audit reports. Though we cannot say that it has not done anything, rather, its work had not been satisfactory. It has worked just as a wing of the government and its audit reports have not done much for bringing forth the transparency of the government. It was like the Election Commission which was inefficient till the 1990s. Till the early 1990s, the Election Commission, even though a 'constitutional' authority, functioned more or less as a wing of the executive branch—a mild friendly agency sympathetic to the party in power, unwilling to express itself strongly to fulfil its defined role as the guardian of purity in the electoral process (Subramanian 2012, 19). But in the 1990s this situation was changed. The Election Commission redefined itself in terms of what was expected in the Constitution rather than the party in power. In this process, the Election Commission itself played a very important role. With T. N. Seshan becoming the Chief Election Commissioner of India, the Election Commission became an active, independent, strong-willed umpire to oversee fair play in the electoral process. Seshan gave teeth to the organization with the EC gaining wide perception that it had a strong bark and a vicious bite when the occasion demanded it (Subramanian 2012, 19). Here came in the 'personality' factor in the reviving of the Election Commission. Much the same scenario applies to the CAG—its place as a constitutional agency was transformed with the arrival of Vinod Rai on the scene. The institution in the pre-Rai era did bark now and then, though it had no serious intension to bite—it was a friendly poodle in the service of the government, a toothless tiger, rather than a fierce watchdog of peoples' interest in ensuring propriety in governmental income and expenditure. Vinod Rai 'did a Seshan' to the institution of CAG (Subramanian 2012, 19).

Why it was Vinod Rai who made a successful history for the CAG? Was it that only the impact of his personality or something else? There is no doubt Vinod Rai did a wonderful job in reviving this very important institution called the CAG. It was Vinod Rai who came up many reports in which many scams were brought forth. Though nation has seen many scams in the past, the intensity of scams that we are facing today is very different from past. One by one so many scams are coming to light. The CAG's scrutiny of expenditures in the Commonwealth Games (CWG) of 2010, and soon thereafter the analysis of the 2G spectrum allocation have changed the way we look at the government. It was the outcome of the CAG report (2012–13) which shook the UPA II government and charged it as a corrupt government. He seemed to have redefined the functioning of India's Comptroller and Auditor General. Vinod Rai thus reinterpreted the position of the CAG. According to him the CAG is not merely an accountant. It was not made merely to conduct audits, prepare reports and place them in the Parliament. During a lecture at the Harvard Kennedy School in the United States, he said:

> The question that continues to repeatedly arise in our minds is whether the Parliament, and in fact, the public at large, expect us to be mere accountants and do arithmetic over government expenditure? If it was so, then why constitutions worldwide should – appoint such high dignitaries as Auditors General and give them independence, freedom from the executive and accord them a constitutional position. Evidently what was envisioned in the constitution was more than expecting them to be mere accountants.[3]

This is not the story of one day which suddenly changed this institution. There were so many factors that contributed to this change. Although Vinod Rai brought about important changes, the process of change had started much before his joining as the CAG. There was a difference between the working of the CAG pre 1991 and post 1991. The year 1991 was the time when the nation saw a major change in it. There were so many economic and political changes that occurred. In this period, there were many multi-faceted developments in the CAG's organization.

The 1990s witnessed an Indian Audits and Accounts Department (IA&AD) with vastly reduced portfolios of entitlement functions, since a considerable portion of these had already been transferred to the respective state Governments (Kumar 2008, 1).

Major Changes in CAG's Organization During the 1990s[4]

If we analyze the time from 1990 to 2010, it marks an era of multi-faceted developments in the CAG's organization. Some of these include:

1. 1990 witnessed an IA&AD with vastly reduced portfolio of entitlement functions, since a considerable portion of these had already been transferred to the respective state governments.
2. The period was characterized by very significant growth in computerization and Information Technology (IT) applications, tremendous improvements in infrastructure and other facilities, modernization of office systems and procedures.
3. The Department has taken several entirely new kinds of audit functions; for instance, the expenses, incurred by the Panchayati Raj institutions are now subject to accounting by the department which also scrutinizes the expenditure of the newly-created states since they do not have the required facilities at the outset.

4. New systems and procedures were introduced like the system of peer review, strategic plans and perspective plans. Mission Statements as well as Vision Statements for the Department were issued and a trend towards aligning the prevailing audit practices in line with the best practices globally became the hallmark of the present CAG's period.
5. A development of great significant was the decision of the CAG V.N. Kaul to issue the Regulations on Audit and Accounts in pursuance of powers vested in him under Section 23 of the CAG's (DPC) Act, 1971.
6. The period will be known for India's Sports Authority of India's (SAI) entry into the international auditing scene for the first time with its election as a member of the United Board of Auditors in 1992. The 1990s also marked in international forum like INTOSAI and ASOSAI. The period also saw the CAG getting actively involved in two global forums for SAI's namely INTOSAI and ASOSAI.
7. In the field of Government Auditing, the era is marked by several very momentous developments. Most significant of these were the new audits that came up as a result of the major liberalization reform that was ushered in 1991. In the audit department, a wave of globalization started. The IA&AD started its attempts to integrate with the best global auditing standards and practices. New areas of audit sprang up as a result of government policies on privatization. Performance audit became more accentuated by completely rebuilding its structure and methodology and defining the tools more clearly and objectively.
8. In the field of audit practices and procedures, several new systems were tested including the concept of outsourcing of certain field workers for carrying out beneficiary surveys. Also the department started hiring experts and consultants to help in complex technical areas.
9. This was also the era of building up several new institutions. An autonomous institution under the aegis of the CAG was setup in 1996 called the 'Institute of Public Auditors of India' as a 'think tank' in audit, accounting and accountability matters. The CAG set up an Audit Advisory Board in March 1999. It had 14 outside eminent members from fields such as academicians, engineers, retired civil servants, doctors, professionals, defense experts and other persons of repute apart from the CAG top management team.

All of this contributed to the progress made by this department and brought this institution to where it stands now. Because of its reports, people have come across big scams which government officials were engaging in for a long time. It is not only the contribution of Vinod Rai but also the time in which all the reports were brought out. Anna Hazare and his team started a movement against corruption which was supported by large numbers of people. Civil Society has a role to bring people who want to make the government accountable for its decisions at the centre stage. Young people joined this movement for a transparent and accountable government. Social media played an important role in spreading information quickly. The RTI is playing an important role in making the government more transparent and the media is supporting the same for a strong democratic government. Speaking at the third anniversary of the Moneylife Foundation in Mumbai, Vinod Rai said, '2012 will go down in the history of Indian democracy as defining year. A year in which citizen came center stage and debunked the old age myth of the silent majority' (2013). In a lecture delivered at the Harvard Kennedy School, he explained how the civil society and the citizens of India had supported this institution. He said:

> Today's youth is discerning, demanding and believers in respecting Institution created by the Constitution. He is not willing to see politicians subvert these institutions....The citizens coming center stage and wanting to be heard, is indeed phenomenon which debunks the myth of a silent majority.[5]

Today, the CAG has not has limited itself merely to make reports and place it before the Parliament but is also sensitizing people's opinion on it's on did observation.[6]

Vinod Rai made certain important changes in the working of this institution that helped this institution to work effectively and some of these include:

1. Now CAG has engaged itself in the business of upgrading governance as any other agency in the administration. It has changed its culture. Now they engage in positive reporting. They recognize good practices alongwith reporting the faults.
2. The CAG has started to convert the salient observations of their reports into small booklets which are well written and facilitate easy understanding. They have started distributing some pamphlets, which they refer to as 'Noddy' books, to the media, colleges, citizen's groups, non-governmental organizations etc. This is being undertaken in the firm belief that an awakened citizen, once sensitized about the inadequacy of government departments would exert pressure on these departments and maintain vigilance thereby ensuring better delivery of government services.
3. Now the institution of the CAG has started to support the concept of social audits for more widespread coverage of social sector issues. They hold the view that they do not have knowledge where government schemes are being implemented on the ground. So they have started engaging with credible citizen's groups which are helping them to be acquainted with the government welfare schemes. With these initiatives Vinod Rai has changed this institution for the better.

Evaluative Remarks

As a constitutional agency, the CAG in India has changed its role since it was instituted. Although it has been constitutionally empowered to discharge its independent role, there have been occasions when it was vitiated by heavy political interference. As a result, its independence was questioned and it was criticized as nothing but an appendage to the ruling party. There are however instances when the CAG rose to the occasion and performed its role as an independent agency acting as a conscience keeper of the government by adopting adequate steps to avoid financial impropriety. The audit of government expenses by the CAG have thus become a powerful constitutional instrument also bringing tax payers as stakeholders in the reckoning.

While evaluating the role of the CAG as an assessor of how the government spends the tax payers' money, one should also be sensitive to the context in which it functions. If it was a hegemonic role of a single political party, it might not have been possible for the CAG to remain true, for obvious reasons, to its constitutional obligation. Furthermore, the individual integrity of the CAG cannot be ignored. Despite the fact that the selection process is quite rigorous, there have been many instances of individual follies that have not tampered the CAG's reputation as a public institution. Nonetheless, the CAG is probably one of those few constitutional bodies that is still respected presumably because of its constant vigil on government spending.

Besides its role as an auditor, the CAG also puts the government on alert by raising issues in the public domain. By creating public opinion in case the government violates constitutional norms, it becomes an important institution of democracy in India. With its defined constitutional role, the CAG has not only put the government in check, it has also created an environment in which citizens are given an equally important role in governance. With the exposure of several scams in which even ministers have been involved, the CAG has gained the reputation as a tough instrument of governance that cannot be easily ignored given its constitutional power and its ability to consolidate mass opinion against the wrongdoings of the government. This is a remarkable achievement for a constitutional agency that, despite being identified as a government-appendage in the past, has gradually become a powerful public voice even in the midst of the consolidation of forces challenging democracy.

CONCLUDING OBSERVATIONS

The key to understand the financial health of a nation is surely the budget. In that sense, the budget is not just a statement of expenditure and income, it also reflects the politico-ideological priority of any nation. This means that the budget is a mirror of contemporary politics which go into its making. In the context of a planned economy like India, the distinctive nature of the budget is drawn on the broad economic policies in which it is formulated and implemented. As the above discussion demonstrates, two ideas are most critical in the conceptualization of the budget as integral to India's financial administration: while, on the one hand, it is an indispensable instrument for charting out the course of action in securing a specific path of development, it is also a process showing, on the other, both the elasticity and also the rigidity of the system in so far as financial administration is concerned. It is elastic because it is not averse to change and it is rigid because it cannot be changed at the drop of a hat since it is guided by well-defined priorities.

No discussion on financial administration in India shall remain complete unless one takes into account the role of the CAG in any post-mortem of government expenses and spending. With its constitutional responsibility, the CAG has become perhaps the most reliable instrument to establish integrity in administration. Given its vibrant nature in India, it has also fulfilled its political role in raising public opinion when the government or the spending authorities have deviated from what is considered 'proper' in the lexicon of financial administration. As the discussion has shown, the CAG, by always being alert to its constitutional obligations, appears to have surpassed, in recent times, its institutional role of a mere auditor; becoming one of the constitutional agencies that is critical to India's democracy. In other words, the CAG, while fulfilling its constitutional role, has set into motion processes protecting its sanctity in conjunction with India's democratic ethos.

There is a final point. A country's financial health is most secure when its citizenry remains alert and vigil. So ultimately what matters are the citizens who need to be sensitive to their constitutional responsibilities. This means that an alert and sensitive citizenry is the most effective shield against distortion and decay in government functioning. There are innumerable instances to illustrate the point that the role of citizens remains most critical in governance, especially in a democratic country like India. The Anna Hazare-led 'India against corruption' movement 2010 has shown once again how a powerful mass movement radically alters the ideological priorities of the ruling authority and how the processes towards preparing an effective Lokpal (Ombudsman) had begun with all earnestness by involving civil society actors who never remained integral to government decisions in the past. What is most striking is the fact that constitutional agencies, however powerful they are in constitutional terms, never become very effective unless they are embraced by the citizens. This means that constitutional agencies, in order to be effective, need to be linked with the wider frame of politics in which citizens remain most critical. By drawing attention to this dimension, the above discussion is the beginning of an endeavour highlighting the dialectical interconnection between government agencies and political processes in a context in which the role of citizens can never be undermined.

REVIEW QUESTIONS

1. How do you conceptualize the budget? Elaborate your response with reference its features.
2. Trace the evolution of the budget in India since the British era.
3. 'Budget is not merely a statement of income and expenditure, but an account of the financial health of the country'. Elaborate your views with examples from India.
4. What are the landmark budgetary reforms in India since independence? Elaborate your response.
5. Distinguish between traditional and performance budgeting with reference to examples.
6. What are the major processes in the making of the budget in India? Elaborate your response.
7. 'The role of the Comptroller and Auditor General and India's financial well-being are critically interconnected'. Do you agree with the view? Elaborate your response.
8. How do you explain the growing effectiveness of the Comptroller and Auditor General in India in recent years? Elaborate your response.
9. Critically evaluate the politics of budgeting in India.
10. In the context of the dismantling of the hegemonic state in India, the centralized system of budgeting seems to have lost its salience. Do you agree with the view? Elaborate your response.

NOTES

1. For a lucid account of the concepts and functioning of the budget and finance and their mutual relationship, see Asian Development Bank (2009).
2. This segment of the discussion is drawn on Sadhna Gupta, Comptroller and Auditor General in India, MPhil dissertation (Hindi), University of Delhi, 2014, unless otherwise indicated. We are thankful to Ms Gupta who prepared the text for the book.
3. The speech of Vinod Rai at the Kennedy School of Government. Retrieved from http://www.ndtv.com/article/india/govt-auditor-cag-vinod-rai-s-speech-at-harvard-kennedy-school-327674
4. This section presents a summary of the major developments in the CAG's organization during 1990s—the material is based on Vijay Kumar's (2008) book.
5. http://www.ndtv.com/india-news/govt-auditor-cag-vinod-rais-speech-at-harvard-kennedy-school-512634, Vinod Rai's lecture at Harvard University, 7 February 2013, accessed on 12 December 2015.
6. The speech of Vinod Rai at the Kennedy School of Government, Harvard University. Retrieved from http://www.ndtv.com/article/india/govt-auditor-cag-vinod-rai-s-speech-at-harvard-kennedy-school-327674 accessed on 28 April 2015.

REFERENCES

Asian Development Bank. 2009. *Macroeconomic Management and Government Finances*. New Delhi: Oxford University Press.

Basu, Durga Das. 2012. *Introduction to the Constitution of India*. Reprint. Nagpur: LexisNexis, Butterworths Wadhwa.

Bhattacharya, Mohit. 2008. *New Horizons of Public Administration*. New Delhi: Jawahar Publishers and Distributors.

Chakrabarty, Bidyut, and Rajendra Kumar Pandey. 2008. *Indian Government and Politics*. New Delhi: SAGE.

Constituent Assembly Debates. 1949. 'B.R. Ambedkar's intervention in the Constituent Assembly', The Constituent Assembly Debates, 25 November, Vol. X, p. 979.

Datt, Ruddar, and K. P. M. Sundharam. 2008. *Indian Economy*. 58th ed. New Delhi: S. Chand and Company.

Government of India. *Comptroller and Auditor-General's (Duties, Powers and Conditions of Service) Act, 1971*. Retrieved from http://saiindia.gov.in/hindi/home/about_us/mandate/DPC_act/DPC_act.html accessed on 17 April 2015.

Hansen, James A., and Sanjay Kathuria. 1999. 'India's Financial System: Getting Ready for the Twenty-first Century: An Introduction'. In *India: A Financial System for the Twenty-first Century,* edited by James A. Hansen and Sanjay Kathuria, 9. New Delhi: Oxford University Press.

Hindustan Times. 2009. New Delhi, 8 July.

Kashyap, Subhash C. 1990, 6 October. 'A New Parliamentary Initiative: Subject based Standing Committees of Parliament'. *Economic and Political Weekly*: 3247.

———, ed. 2014. *The Framing of India's Constitution: A Study*. Rev. ed. New Delhi: Universal Law Publishing Co. Pvt. Ltd.

Kumar, Vijay. 2008. *The Comptroller and Auditor General of India: A Thematic History, 1990–2007*. Vol. 1. New Delhi: Ashish Publishing House.

Mint. (2013), 2 April. 'Vinod Rai is the Face of a New, More Assertive Even Aggressive, Comptroller and Auditor General'. *Mint*.

Prasad, Eswar S., and Raghuram G. Rajan. 2008, 9 September. 'Next Generation Financial Reforms in India'. *Finance and Development* 45 (9): 37.

Prasad, Kamala. 2006. *Indian Administration: Politics, Policies and Prospects*. New Delhi: Pearson Longman.

Rao, M. Govind. 2009, 20 June. 'The Fiscal Situation and a Reform Agenda for the New Government'. *Economic and Political Weekly*: 85.

Reddy, Y. V. 2004. 'Monetary and Financial Sector Reforms in India: A Practitioner's Perspective'. In *India's Emerging Economy: Performance and Prospects in the 1990s and Beyond,* edited by Kaushik Basu, 62. New Delhi: Oxford University Press.

Sudarsanan, C. N. 2001. *Government budgeting: Principles and Practices*. Chennai: Sree Sudarsan Publications.

Subramanian, T. S. R. 2012, 27 October. 'CAG: A Necessary Evil or a Bulwark?' *Economic and Political Weekly*: 19

Thavaraj, M. J. K. 1987. *Financial Administration of India*. 2nd ed. New Delhi: Sultan Chand and Sons.

The Hindustan Times. 2009. New Delhi, 8 July.

The Times of India. 2009. New Delhi, 3 June.

Vyasulu, Vinod. 2009, 1 August. 'The Budget 2009–2010: Beyond Fiscal Rectitude'. *Economic and Political Weekly*: 21–23.

Citizens and Administration in India

12

LEARNING OBJECTIVES

1. To understand the citizen—administration interface.
2. To discuss the pre-conditions for a citizen-centric administration.
3. To figure out people's participation in administration.
4. To examine administrative accountability in India.
5. To illustrate the public grievance redressal machinery in India.

A citizen is a member of a political community who enjoys rights and assumes the duties of membership. In that sense, being a citizen is more than a status; it is about the entitlement of rights and privileges of a person that ensures a quality life. So, citizenship is more than a set of rights and obligations, it is an innate orientation on the well-being of the state and society. The ancient Greeks realized that, and the polity of Athens institutionalized citizenship through its diverse associations, councils and authorities within an urban framework. In such an environment, citizenship, in principle, meant participation in the co-production of policies. At the basis of this participation stood a belief in the 'happy versality' of man. Historian Geoffrey Hosking (2005, 1 and 2, lecture 3) suggests that citizenship in ancient Greece arose from an appreciation for the importance of freedom. Hosking (2005, 1 and 2, lecture 3) explained:

> It can be argued that this growth of slavery was what made Greeks particularly conscious of the value of freedom. After all, any Greek farmer might fall into debt and therefore might become a slave, at almost any time ... When the Greeks fought together; they fought in order to avoid being enslaved by warfare, to avoid being defeated by those who might take them into slavery. And they also arranged their political institutions so as to remain free men.

However in modern times, the status aspects of citizenship have been stressed heavily and the qualitative aspects of citizenship appear to be grossly underestimated. In their wake, public administration as a discipline, has been, until recently, more focused on the improvement of the state apparatuses than on the development of citizenship and the involvement of citizens in the making of governmental policies (Rouband 1999, 47). This dominant trend is responsible for the alienation of citizens and thus there has been an increase in citizens' grievances against the administration.

In this background the present chapter deals with some significant dimensions of the interactions between citizens and the administration, namely citizens' perceptions about administration, pre-conditions for a citizens-centric administration, people's participation in administration, forms of public accountability and the role of the public grievance redressal machinery in India.

THE CITIZEN–ADMINISTRATION INTERFACE

In a democracy, citizen–administration relations are significant because the support and consent of the governed is a prerequisite for the success of a representative government. The state and in actual terms, the administration have important responsibilities for providing major amenities such as life-education, health, employment opportunities; improved means of transport and infrastructure, etc., to its citizens. All this ensures a good life for the citizens. In public administration two noticeable trends have emerged in recent times. First, there has been an expansion in the size of the public bureaucracy as well as an increase in its powers and activities. Second, in the wake of the spread of general education, as well as political and social awakening, there has been a rise in the expectations of the people from the administration.

The relationship between law and public opinion in a democracy was discussed by A.V. Dicey at the end of the twentieth century (Dicey 1948). The importance of the subject grew sharply after the Second World War, thanks to the growth of welfare as well socialist ideologies in the new states. People in affluent societies were less concerned about the old concept of liberty than a love of material comfort and pleasure. The focus of the relationship between the state and society has shifted from political liberty to economic prosperity and social justice. The state has expanded its political base through a universal adult franchise. Administration has, therefore, of necessity penetrated into every aspect of civic life. The bulk of the citizens who are voters and beneficiaries of state services are more keen on getting services supplied than the subtle aspects of how they get them (Agarwal 2004, 270). The position of the citizens from being mere recipients of administrative help and services has now shifted to their being the prime movers in the affairs of governance.

There are different ways in which citizens interact with the administrative agencies in their day-to-day life. Mohit Bhattacharya (2008) illustrates five categories of such interactions. These could be in the form of:

1. **Clients:** In this form, citizens seek to obtain benefits or services from governmental agencies. For example, a patient visits a government hospital for a medical checkup or treatment.
2. **Regulatee:** As regulatee, the public interacts with many government agencies like the police, income tax authorities, licensing authorities etc.
3. **Litigants:** As litigants, the public moves the court against the 'unjust' actions of public agencies. For example, people seek redressal from the court when the motor vehicles authority may be delaying the issuance of a car license.
4. **Participants:** In this form people become direct participants in decision-making in public agencies at different levels. For example; parents become members of a school's guardians' committee, an irrigation project associates the farmers with the different decision-making processes of the project.
5. **Cutting-edge encounters:** In this form people approach the agencies which are responsible for day today primary services and facilities to the public. For example, people approach municipal employees for water, electricity, and sanitation facilities.[5]
6. **Protesters:** besides the above five, there could be another form of interaction that is, people as protesters. People often interact with government agencies on public policy as protesters, opposing the injustice in government policies and actions. For example, people oppose the construction of a dam in their locality.

Thus, citizens in day to day life constantly interact with the administration. The purposes of contact may be varied, for example, it may be for getting basic services like water, electricity and health services or it may be for getting a driving license or an income tax return from the income tax department. Sometimes people get the opportunity to directly participate in policy-making and the implementation of a governmental agency or project. When people do not get services in time or are harassed by public authorities, they seek redressal of their grievances from the court and when they do not see justice coming from any side, they resort to protests or criticize the unjust policies and actions of the government. Through these happy or unhappy interactions, citizens form opinion about public administration.

Citizen's Perceptions about the Administration

Though ideally speaking, the interaction between citizens and the administration is supposed to be trustworthy and purposeful, in reality, it is observed to be always plagued by conflicts, stresses and strains. Discontent amongst the citizens because of the wide disparity between the performance of administration and popular expectations has become a normal feature. The general feeling which persists amongst the people is that the policies are cumbersome, or the processes of administration are unjust. Yet another important problem is a deterioration in the standards of honesty and integrity in both, politics and administration because of corruption. Rigid observance of rules and regulations, non-acknowledgement of complaints, inordinate delays in the disposal of various matters account for the lack of faith of public in administration.

A number of research studies have been undertaken to examine the relationship between the citizens and administration in India. Some such important ones include studies on 'Police Administration' by Davis H. Bayley (1969), 'Rural Development' by Rakesh Hooja (1978) and 'Urban Government' by V. Jagannadhan (1978). The findings of these studies reveal interesting information on citizens' perceptions about public administration in India. The general perceptions of the people on administration that emerge out of these studies include:

1. Inordinate delays and waiting periods.
2. Favouritism in administration.
3. Need for middlemen (brokers) to get things done.
4. Unhelpful attitude of the officials especially lower level functionaries.
5. Citizens' ignorance about procedures involved in getting things done.
6. Rich-poor discrimination in administration: the rich having access to administration and the general tendency of officials to avoid the poor and underplay their needs and interests (Bhattacharya 2008, 257).

A recent study (ARC 2009) by the Centre for Media Studies (CMS) shows that a majority of citizens are not satisfied with the delivery of public services. In seven out of the eleven departments covered in the study, less than one-third of citizens were satisfied with the services delivered. In fact, in most need-based services such as the police, judiciary and municipalities, (which enjoy a greater discretion and power), not even 20 per cent of the households were satisfied with the services. Even in essential services such as the Public Distribution System (PDS), hospitals, electricity and water supplies, a mere 30–40 per cent of the households were happy with the services (Second Administrative Reforms Commission 2009). The Sixth Central Pay Commission's (2008) comments in this connection are worth noting:

> For the common man, bureaucracy denotes routine and repetitive procedures, paper work and delays. This, despite the fact that the Government and bureaucracy exist to facilitate the

> citizens in the rightful pursuit of their legal activities. Rigidities of the system over centralization of powers, highly hierarchical and top down method of functioning with a large number of intermediary levels delaying finalization of any decision, divorce of authority from accountability and the tendency towards micromanagement, have led to a structure in which form is more important than substance and procedures are valued over end results and outcomes. Non-performance of the administrative structures, poor service quality and lack of responsiveness, and the subjective and negative abuse of authority have eroded trust in governance systems which needs to be restored urgently. (GOI 2008, 365)

Thus, administration in India is generally perceived to be unresponsive, insensitive and corrupt.

Barriers in Citizen-centric Administration in India

It is evident from the above discussion that the general perception of the people about administration in India is very negative. The Second Administrative Reforms Commission (2009) during its visits to the states had several occasions to meet and hear from the public. Most observations by citizens were about the poor quality of services provided by the government, the indifferent attitude of government servants, corruption and abuse of authority and lack of accountability. A common complaint pertained to excessive red-tapism and the long time taken to get even routine work done. The Commission in its 12th Report on citizen centric administration (Second ARC 2009, 14–16) identifies the following five barriers in citizen-centric administration in India:

1. Wooden, inflexible, self-perpetuating and inward looking attitude of civil servants
2. Lack of accountability of civil servants
3. Red-tapism
4. Ineffective implementation of laws and rules
5. Low levels of awareness of the rights and duties of citizens

Thus, the reason for the administration not being citizen-centric can be attributed to the attitude and work of some government servants, the deficiencies in the existing institutional structures and the lack of awareness about rights and duties on part of the citizens. Thus, Robson (1967) observes:

> In mind of average citizen, bureaucracy still suffers from traditional defects associated with it. These are an excessive sense of self-importance on the part of officials or an undue idea of the importance of their office, an indifference towards the feelings of the convenience of the individual citizens, mania for regulations, formal procedures, a failure to recognize relations between the governors and the governed as an essential part of democratic process.

Ensuring Citizen-friendly Administration

The poor image of the government in the minds of large sections of the population points towards an inefficient and ineffective administration. This highlights the need for substantially reforming our governance systems. The main focus of such reform should be on making citizens central to all government activities and reorganizing the government to effectively address the concerns of common people. An analysis of the barriers to citizen-centric administration reveals that there are several pre-conditions which must be fulfilled in order to make administration citizen-centric. Some of these preconditions are discussed below:

Accountability: Accountability is defined as the state of being accountable, liable or answerable. To be accountable means to be obliged to report, explain or justify something. It ensures that something is carried out as expected. Accountability is a key requirement of good administration. It means public servants must be accountable to the public. They are not only accountable to the questions asked by the people but also have to respond to demands and provide services to the people.

Accessibility: a good administration has to be accessible by the people. If people have any problems, administrative officials should be ready to listen to them and accordingly respond to them too. There has to be no fear in the minds of the people about the status and rigidity of the bureaucracy. It also requires that there be no discrimination and the poor have easy access to the administration.

Transparency: transparency is an essential pre-condition for good administration. It is the antonym of secrecy, which is the traditional hallmark of public administration. It implies that governmental policies and functioning be known to the larger society. Transparency means that information is freely available and directly accessible to those who will be affected by decisions and their enforcement. It also means that information is easily understandable. Transparency enables citizens to keep themselves informed about policies of the government, the rights that they have and the services they can expect from the government. The Right to Information and the Citizens' Charter are means of ensuring transparency in administration.

Participatory: promoting citizen-centric administration also implies giving a voice to citizens in the governance process. It means the involvement of people in administrative activities, particularly the participation of beneficiaries in developmental activities, both at the formulation and implementation stage, for the success of programmes. People's participation is also an important safeguard against the abuse of administrative authority. It is a method of tapping human and material resources for development. Meaningful participation by citizens in governance can be promoted through the Panchayati Raj institutions, Bhagidari programmes and by involving citizens groups in certain aspects of governance.

Responsiveness: A responsive administration is an apparently moral concept in public administration in as much as it calls for the public functionaries' accountability directly to the people. It is a micro-level concept deriving its credibility and validity from the delivery system of a country's public administration. By being responsive, governmental institutions gain 'legitimacy' in the public realm, which automatically ensures their wider acceptance and thus, effectiveness in governance. A responsive administration entails a mechanism of redressal of grievances also.

Effectiveness and efficiency: The success of an administrative system also depends on the effective and efficient delivery of services to the people. Effectiveness is the extent to which an objective or goal is achieved. If an organization has successfully achieved its objectives, it is considered effective. Effectiveness is thus a matter of comparing results with the prior intentions. Efficiency on the other hand refers to the process by which the organization maximizes its objectives with the minimum use of resources.

In addition to the above mentioned necessary pre-conditions for a citizen-centric administration, decentralization and delegation of policies, adoption of modern technology, process simplification and integrity of the civil services are other features and norms for any successful administration.

In this connection, the remarks of Dr S. Radhakrishnan, former vice president of India, on the occasion of the First Annual day of the Indian Institute of Public Administration on 20 November 1959 are worth noting. He wanted the administration 'to be fair in all manners to the people and that the administrators must feel that they are not there merely to rule over the people but 'they are essentially servants of the people'. He also stated that 'administrators are not to regard themselves as a privileged class. They are not to grow into bureaucracy'. The higher civil servants, Dr Radhakrishnan said, 'must understand the needs and aspirations of the common man and woman and try to protect them from the petty officials who are inclined to harass them and show their authority'. Above all he said, 'it is my great anxiety that in this country we "should have administrative integrity first, efficiency next, economy third"—with these conditions we will be able to build a happier Indian Society' (Agarwal 2004, iii–iv). He thus placed 'integrity' in administration above all other requirements for citizen-friendly governance.

PEOPLE'S PARTICIPATION IN ADMINISTRATION

People's participation in the administrative processes is basic to its success. It means the direct involvement of citizens in the process of administrative decision-making, policy formulation and implementation. Peoples' participation also means collective and continuous efforts by the people themselves in setting goals, pooling resources together and taking actions which aim at improving their living conditions. To William Morrow, the term citizen participation means the direct participation of ordinary men and women, in contrast to public and private elites, in policy-making. Furthermore, it is employed to focus on the direct participation of the underprivileged and enfranchised in decisions that affect their lives (Morrow 1980, 190). Thus, People's participation is a mechanism of involvement and participation of the people in the decision-making processes of a nation.

Citizens' participation in governance embodies a shift in the development paradigm from citizens as the recipients of development to one that views them as active participants in the development process. Equally, it involves a shift from a 'top-down' to a 'bottom-up' approach to development involving increasing decentralization of power away from the Union Government and closer to the grassroots levels.

Ensuring Good Governance

The concept of citizens' participation in governance is essentially based on the premise that citizens have a legitimate role in influencing the decision-making process that affects their lives, their businesses and their communities. In other words, citizens' participation refers to the mechanism and modalities by which citizens can influence and take control over resources and decision-making that directly impacts their lives. At the ideological level, direct citizens' participation in governance is seen as contributing to a healthy democracy because it enhances and improves upon the traditional form of representative democracy to transform it into a more responsive and participative grassroots democracy. It is now widely accepted that active citizens' participation can contribute to good governance in the following ways:

1. It enables citizens to make government accountable, more responsive, efficient and effective.
2. It helps to make government programmes and services more effective and sustainable.
3. It enables the poor and marginalized to influence public policy and service delivery to improve their lives.

4. It helps individuals to develop a sense of civic maturity, they become more educated, tolerant and compassionate, which finally helps in improving the quality of policy.
5. It helps in recognizing that citizens have vital contribution to make for the betterment of public policy.
6. It helps to promote healthy grassroots democracy.
7. It develops better understanding between the government and the people.

Thus, people's participation in administration ensures a transparent, accountable, participatory, responsive, effective and efficient government. However, people's participation is not free from barriers. One of these is the existence of widespread inertia in the larger society resulting in apathy and passivity. In addition, under the name of people's participation, what may happen is a situation, which William Morrow (1980) calls 'abdication', 'pacification', 'co-operation' and 'client-building'. Citizens' participation does not necessarily lead to leaders representing their constituencies. Rather, they strike a tie-up with the local bureaucracy, which may silence them. The representatives, when interfacing with the bureaucrats represent their individual interests, and not their constituencies' cause. In such cases, participation becomes a kind of formality like paper work, and not the empowerment of the common people in its true sense.

The fact that participatory efforts occasionally are perverted does not mean that the perversions make the participatory movement meaningless to its original purposes. Citizens' participation demands certain preconditions which are needed for making citizens' participation more effective. Some of the important ones include: an enlightened political leader; acknowledgeable and competent citizens; conscientious civil servants; informed and co-operative public; ensuring that information required for taking decisions are clear and precise; well organized communication network; both authority and citizens must demonstrate willingness to take responsibility; to make a practical survey of the environment for which it is intended; and participation at all levels-both rural and urban (Avasthi and Maheswari 2010, 643). These conditions and actions are necessary, both on the part of officials as well as the common people for a true representative and participatory democracy.

ADMINISTRATIVE ACCOUNTABILITY

Accountability is an essential feature of all forms of democratic governments. The concept of accountability refers to the liability of government servants to give a satisfactory account of the use of official power or discretionary authority to the people. This is considered as an effective safeguard against the misuse of power and the abuse of public authority. The substance of accountability, according to Mohit Bhattacharya (2008), places at least four requirements on public administrators:

1. Make laws work as intended with minimum waste and delay.
2. Exercise lawful and sensible administrative discretion.
3. Recommend new policies and propose changes in the existing policies and programs as needed.
4. Enhance citizen confidence in administrative institutions.

The notion of accountability carries two basic connotations: answerability, which stands for the obligation of public officials to inform about and explain what they are doing, and enforcement, that is, the capacity of accounting agencies to impose sanctions on the power holders who have violated their public duties.

Administrative Accountability in India

In India, administrative accountability is enforced by means of various controls. The purpose of control is to ensure that public servants exercise their powers and discretion in accordance with the laws and regulations. Broadly speaking, there are two types of administrative control, namely internal and external. The internal control operates from within the administrative machinery. The techniques of internal control are: budgetary system, hierarchical order, enquiries and investigations, pressure groups, press, and annual confidential reports. External accountability over the administration in India is maintained through legislative, executive and judicial control.

The administration is made responsible towards the elected representatives because in a democracy the people are supreme. Thus the legislature has been given certain powers through the Constitution and through conventions that keep an effective check on malpractices, and abuse of authority by the administration. The legislature applies a number of methods for controlling the administration namely asking questions during the question hour, Parliamentary discussions, Parliamentary audit, non-confidence motion and complaints to the Ombudsman.

Executive control over the administration is another potent instrument in any responsible government. The executive exercises control over the administration through a number of means and techniques like, power of appointment and removal, rule-making power, ordinances etc., civil service code, delegated legislation, budgetary system and making appeal to public opinion. Another important instrument through which administrative accountability is ensured is judicial control and it may take the shape of judicial reviews, statutory appeals to the suits and writs against the government. The primary objective of judicial control over administration is the protection of the rights and liberties of citizens by ensuring the legality of the Administrative Act (Singh 2002, 216–17). Thus, budgetary measures, departmental inquiries, annual confidential reports etc. make the administrative system accountable internally. The external accountability over administration is ensured through legislative, executive and judicial controls.

Redressal of Public Grievances

The Chambers dictionary defines 'grievance' as 'a ground of complaint, a condition felt to be oppressive or wrongful'. A grievance may arise out of the non-fulfilment of certain demands and expectations. Mere demands may be related to policies of the government or to the performance of the administration in the implementation of policies framed by the government. A grievance is thus any sort of dissatisfaction, which needs to be redressed. Some of the common grievances faced by the people against the administration may be delineated in the following categories:

1. **Red-tapism:** delay in administrative functioning
2. **Corruption:** demand and acceptance of money for doing things
3. **Favouritism:** obliging the powerful and influential people
4. **Nepotism:** helping the people of one's own kith or kin
5. **Discourtesy:** use of abusive language or misbehaviour in public dealings
6. **Neglect of Duty:** not doing things as per the law
7. **Delay:** not doing things on time
8. **Discrimination:** ignoring the poor and weak sections and favouring the rich
9. **Mal-administration:** inefficiencies in achieving goals
10. **Inadequate Redressal Machinery:** absence of a machinery to attend to public complaints against officials.

The basic principle of a grievance redressal system is that if the promised level of service delivery is not achieved, then it is the right of a citizen to take recourse to a grievance redressal mechanism. This mechanism should be well publicized, easy to use, and prompt and, above all, citizens must have faith that they will get justice from it.

The Grievance Redressal Mechanism in India

The Government of India, the state governments as well as the various organizations under them have set up grievance redressal mechanisms to look into the complaints of citizens. At the national level, there are primarily two designated nodal agencies in the Union Government handling these grievances:

(a) The Department of Administrative Reforms and Public Grievances, Ministry of Personnel, Public Grievances and Pension
(b) The Directorate of Public Grievances, cabinet Secretariat

Besides these nodal agencies, there are other institutional mechanisms like the Central Vigilance Commission, the Lokpal and Lokayuktas which have the mandate to look into complaints of corruption and abuse of office by public servants. Many organizations, for example, the Reserve Bank of India, have set up ombudsman to look into grievances. Institutions such as the National and State Human Rights Commissions, the National and State Women Commission; the National Commission for Scheduled Castes and the National Commission for Schedules Tribes also look into complaints from the public in their prescribed areas. Today, with increased awareness levels, the aspirations of citizens have gone up along with their demand for the prompt and effective resolution of their grievances. The role of some of the important institutions and other initiatives for the redressal of public grievance in India are discussed further.

THE CENTRAL VIGILANCE COMMISSION

On the basis of the recommendations made by the Committee on Prevention of Corruption, popularly known as the Santhanam Committee, the Central Vigilance Commission (CVC) was set up by the Government of India in 1964. The CVC advises the Union Government on all matters pertaining to the maintenance of integrity in administration. It exercises superintendence over the working of the Central Bureau of Investigation—the principal investigating agency of the Union Government in anti-corruption matters—and also over the vigilance administration of various ministries and other organizations of the Union Government.

Organizational Set-up

As per The Central Vigilance Commission Act, 2003, the Commission consists of:

- A Central Vigilance Commissioner—Chairperson
- Not more than two Vigilance Commissioners—Members

The Central Vigilance Commission (CVC) has its own Secretariat, Chief Technical Examiners' Wing (CTE) and a wing of Commissioners for Departmental Inquiries (CDI). The Secretariat consists of a Secretary of the rank of Additional Secretary to the GOI, four officers of the rank of Joint Secretary, thirty officers of the rank of Director/Deputy Secretary (including two OSDs), four Under Secretaries and office staff. The Chief Technical Examiner's Organisation constitutes the technical wing of the Central Vigilance Commission (India) and is manned by two engineers of the rank of Chief Engineers (designated as Chief Technical Examiners) with supporting engineering staff. There are fourteen posts of Commissioners for Departmental Inquiries (CDI) in the Commission, 11 in the rank of Director and 03 in the rank of Deputy Secretary. The CDIs function as Inquiry Officers to conduct oral inquiries in departmental proceeding initiated against public servants.

Functions and Powers of the CVC

As per the CVC Act, 2003, The Central Vigilance Commission performs the following tasks:

1. Exercise superintendence over the functioning of the Delhi Special Police Establishment (CBI) in so far as it relates to the investigation of offences under the Prevention of Corruption Act, 1988.
2. Give directions to the Delhi Special Police Establishment (CBI) for superintendence insofar as it relates to the investigation of offences under the Prevention of Corruption Act, 1988.
3. To inquire or cause an inquiry or investigation to be made on a reference by the Central government.
4. To inquire or cause an inquiry or investigation to be made into any complaint received against any official under its jurisdiction.
5. Review the progress of the applications pending with the competent authorities for the sanction of prosecution under the Prevention of Corruption Act, 1988—Section 8(1) (f).
6. Tender advice to the Central government and its organizations on such matters as may be referred to it by them.
7. Exercise superintendence over the vigilance administrations of the various Central government ministries, departments and organizations of the Central Government—Section 8(1) (h).
8. Have all the powers of a Civil court while conducting any inquiry.

The CVC has been conceived to be the apex vigilance institution, free of control from any executive authority, monitoring all vigilance activities under the Central government and advising various authorities in the Central government in planning, executing, reviewing and reforming their vigilance work. Consequent to the promulgation of an Ordinance by the President, the Central Vigilance Commission has been made a multi-member Commission with 'statutory status' with effect from 25 August 1998. Vide a Government of India Resolution on 'Public Interest Disclosure and Protection of Informer' dated April 2004, the Government of India authorized the Central Vigilance Commission as the 'Designated Agency' to receive written complaints for the disclosure on any allegation of corruption or misuse of office from 'whistleblowers' and thereby recommend appropriate action.

THE LOKPAL AND LOKAYUKTA: COMBATING CORRUPTION

The Lokpal is an independent body that enquires into cases of corruption against public functionaries. The term *Lokpal* was coined in 1963 by Laxmi Mall Singhvi, a member of Parliament, during a Parliamentary debate about grievance mechanisms. The word was derived from the Sanskrit words *Lok* (people) and *Pala* (protector), meaning 'Protector of People'. The first

Administrative Reforms Commission (ARC), 1968, headed by Morarji Desai submitted an interim report on 'Problems of Redressal of Citizen's Grievances' in 1966. In this report, the ARC recommended the creation of two special authorities designated as the 'Lokpal' and the 'Lokayukta' for the redressal of citizens' grievances.

The Lokayukta in the States

After the recommendations of the first ARC (1968), many states constituted 'Lokayuktas' to investigate allegations or grievances arising out of the conduct of public servants including political executives, legislators, officers of the state government, local bodies, public enterprises and other instruments of the government. Maharashtra was the first State to introduce the Lokayukta through The Maharashtra Lokayukta and Upa-Lokayuktas Act in 1971. Under this Act, a member of the public can file specific allegations with the Lokayukta against any public servant for enquiry. The Lokayukta can also initiate a suo-moto inquiry into the conduct of public servants. Presently, there are more than 17 states in India who have set up Lokayuktas.

The Lokpal: The National Ombudsman

As a result of the ARC (1968), the Lokpal Bill was first introduced in the Lok Sabha in 1968. Since then the Bill has been introduced nine times in the Parliament, but due to various reasons it could not be passed into a law. The Lokpal and Lokayukta Act, 2011 was introduced in the Parliament following huge public protests led by anti-corruption crusader Anna Hazare who got massive support from the common masses. The Bill is one of the most widely discussed and debated Bills in India, both by the media and the people of India at large, in recent times. The Bill was tabled in the Lok Sabha on 22 December 2011 and was passed by the house on 27 December 2011 as The Lokpal and Lokayuktas Bill, 2011. The bill was passed in the Rajya Sabha on 17 December 2013 after making certain amendments to the earlier Bill and in the Lok Sabha on 18 December 2013. The Bill received assent from the President on 1 January 2014 and came into force from 16 January 2014 and is officially called as The Lokpal and Lokayuktas Act, 2013.

Salient Features of the Lokpal and Lokayuktas Act, 2013

The Lokpal and Lokayuktas Act, 2013, is an anti-corruption Act which 'seeks to provide for the establishment of the institution of Lokpal to inquire into allegations of corruption against certain Public functionaries and for matters connecting them'. The following are the main features of the Act:

Nomenclature: There will be a Lokpal at the Centre and Lokayukta at the level of the states,

Composition: The Lokpal will consist of a Chairperson and a maximum of 8 members, of which 50 per cent will be judicial members while50 per cent members of Lokpal shall be from SC/ST/OBSs, minority and women.

Selection: Selection of the Chairperson and members of Lokpal will be done through a selection committee consisting of the PM, the Speaker of the Lok Sabha, the leader of

Opposition in the Lok Sabha, the Chief Justice of India or a sitting Supreme Court Judge nominated by the Chief Justice of India.

Jurisdiction: The Prime Minister, ministers, current and former legislators, government employees, employees of firms funded or collected by the Centre, societies and trusts that collect public money, receive funds from foreign sources come under the purview of the anti-corruption law. However, bodies creating endowments for or performing religious or charitable functions have been excluded.

Investigation: All anti-corruption inquiries should be completed within 60 days and the investigations completed within 6 months. The Lokpal shall order a probe only after hearing the public servant. An enquiry against the PM has to be held in-camera and will have to be approved by two-thirds of the full bench of the Lokpal.

Prosecution: The Lokpal can initiate prosecutions through its Prosecution Wing before the Special Court and the trial has to be completed within two years. The Bill also incorporates provisions for attachment and confiscation of property acquired by corrupt means, even while the prosecution is pending.

Central Bureau of Investigation: For independence of the CBI, in the new Bill, a Directorate of Prosecution will be formed. Appointment of the Director of Prosecution will be on the recommendation of the Central Vigilance Commissioner.

Protection of Whistleblowers: Provides adequate protection for honest and upright public servants

Penalty: In case of false and frivolous complaints there is a provision of imprisonment up to one year and a fine of up to ₹1 lakh. In case of public servants, the imprisonment is up to seven years. In case of Criminal misconduct and habitually abetting corruption the jail term up to 10 years.

Lokayukta: Each state should set up a Lokayukta by law within 365 days. But the states will have the freedom to determine the nature and type of Lokayukta.

The Lok Pal Act, 2013 is a new mechanism to address the menace of corruption in India. The Act is significant in the sense that it includes even the Prime Minister under its purview. It is more inclusive, effective and time-bound. Adequate provisions are there to protect whistleblowers and honest and committed officers. The provision of penalties and punishments is a deterrent for corrupt and dishonest public servants. With the introduction of the new Act let us hope a new chapter of accountable, transparent and responsive governance begins in India.

E-GOVERNANCE

E-Governance is another mechanism to redress public grievances and thereby bring people closer to the administration. E-governance is the short form of 'electronic governance'. If service delivery is done through the use of information and communications technology (ICT), it is said to be E-governance. In general, E-governance denotes the use of ICT in any organization, that is, governing through the electronic mode. Increasingly, E-governance is being used to refer to the performance of governmental functions through the application of ICT, the most well-known part of which is the 'Internet'.

Thus, E-governance is about a process of reform in the way governments work, share information, and deliver services to internal and external clients. Specifically, an E-government harnesses information and communication technologies, such as the Internet, the web, and mobile phones, to deliver information and services to citizens and businesses. As a first step, information about services is published on a website and citizens can interact with the site to download application forms for a variety of services. The next stage involves the use of ICT in the actual delivery of services, such as filing a tax return, or renewing a license. More sophisticated applications can process online payments (Bhatnagar 2008, 247).

Bringing People Closer to the Administration

E-governance thus provides citizens the ability to obtain government services through electronic means, enabling access to government information and completion of government transactions on an anywhere, anytime basis. In this way it is a tool for bringing people closer to the government and administration. The idea is simply to create capabilities for providing citizens' access to government departments through electronic networks. The ultimate goal is to bring about better governance which has been termed as simple, moral, accountable, responsive and transparent (SMART; GOI 2002, 187), and the aim of which is to create a space for the regular involvement of citizens who, as customers of public services, now have direct access to governmental activities through the ICT. Thus, through E-governance, the aim of SMART governance is achieved, that is:

Simple: There are no elaborate procedures, no paper work and no need for frequenting government offices,
Moral: The system is cleaned up of corruption and other unethical practices,
Accountable: Since all the information is in the public domain, the government's accountability enhances,
Responsiveness: Through the use of ICT, the government can be in regular touch with the masses and get their feedback;
Transparency: The information which was shrouded in secrecy within dark file chambers will now become available to all on the click of a mouse.

A revolution in ICT has the potential of elevating the governance process to new levels. The ICT facilitates the efficient storing and retrieval of data, instantaneous transmission of information, processing information and data faster than the earlier manual systems, speeding up governmental processes, taking decisions expeditiously and judiciously, increasing transparency and enforcing accountability. It also helps in increasing the reach of the government—both geographically and demographically. Recognizing the increasing importance of electronics, the Government of India established the Department of Electronics in 1970. The subsequent establishment of the National Informatics Centre (NIC) in 1977 was the first step towards e-Governance in India as it brought 'information' and its communication into focus. Several important initiatives were undertaken by the Union and the state governments in the 1990s. All these culminated in the launch of the National e-Governance Programme in 2006.

In the developed countries, governance is a well-established mode in which governmental services are made available to citizens through Internet portals. In India, digital governance has been legalized by the Information Technology Act of 2000. The act provides:

> [L]egal recognition for transaction carried out by means of electronic data interchange and other means of electronic communication, commonly referred to as 'electronic commerce' which involve use of alternatives to paper-based methods of communication and storage of information, to facilitate electronic filling of documents with the government agencies.

This Act is a watershed in conceptualizing administrative reforms in India. More importantly, governance is certainly an attack on bureaucratic red-tapism, which causes unnecessary delays and corruption. It is a tool for achieving 'good governance especially with regard to improving efficiency, transparency and making interface with government user friendly' (Chakrabarty and Bhattacharya 2008, 52). The citizens can not only view government Acts online, they can also provide significant inputs through emails and electronic devices (Chakrabarty and Bhattacharya 2008, 52). Information-Communication Technology is, thus, an important tool for connecting citizens and the government.

The ICT-based E-governance has ushered in a new era in government innovations with capacities to (a) reduce the cost of government, (b) increase citizens' inputs into the government, (c) improve public decision-making and (d) increase the transparency of government transactions. The object of E-governance is 'to arm the citizens to act as watch dogs to government' (Chakrabarty and Bhattacharya 2008, 52). In view of these well-defined functional characteristics, e-governance is also a very meaningful step towards combating corruption. By reducing discretionary powers it curbs opportunities for arbitrary action, and also empowers the citizens by making their interventions in the transactions of governmental business regular through the ICT. The project E-sewa (service) that began in the West Godavari district in Andhra Pradesh (India), is a good example of the same. The project is a tool 'to bridge the digital divide in the rural areas' through the extensive use of information technology 'for providing access to various citizen to citizen (C2C) and citizen to government (C2G) services to the people in rural areas' (Chakrabarty and Bhattacharya 2008, 52). Managed by a women's self-help group, the project is a class by itself as it enables 'the local women-participants' to emerge as 'information leaders', who remain critical in realizing the goal of E-Sewa (Chakrabarty and Bhattacharya 2008, 52).

Thus, E-governance articulates public administration in a refreshing new way. It seeks to forge a link between the citizens and the government in terms of electronic public service. By doing so, it creates conditions for strong citizen's participation in government decision-making processes. The successful induction of E-governance requires a change of mindset. This, in turn, requires great political will and determination and a clear-headed and decisive leadership.

THE CITIZENS' CHARTER

The Citizens' Charter is an instrument which seeks to make an organization transparent, accountable and citizen friendly. The Citizens' Charter scheme in its present form was first launched in 1991 in the UK. The aim was to ensure that public services were made responsive to the citizens they served. A Citizens' Charter is basically a set of commitments made by an organization regarding the standards of service which it delivers. A Citizens' Charter is a public statement that defines the entitlements of citizens to a specific service, the standards of the service, the conditions to be met by users, and the remedies available to the latter in case of non-compliance of standards.

The Charter concept empowers the citizens in demanding committed standards of service. Thus, the basic thrust of the Citizens' Charter is to make public services citizen-centric by ensuring that these services are demand driven rather than supply driven. A Citizens' Charter is characterized by the following six principles (ARC 2009, 34).

1. **Quality:** improving the quality of services
2. **Choice:** for the users wherever possible
3. **Standards:** specifying what to expect within a time frame
4. **Value:** for the taxpayers' money
5. **Accountability:** of the service provider (individual as well as organization)
6. **Transparency:** in rules, procedures, schemes and grievance redressal

The Citizens' Charter, when introduced in the early 1990s, represented a landmark shift in the delivery of public services. The emphasis of the Citizens' Charter is on citizens as the customers of public services. So far, 111 Central Ministries/Departments/Organizations have formulated Citizens' Charters in India. It is a new revolution in making the administration more accountable, transparent and ensuring timely service delivery to the public.

RIGHT TO INFORMATION (RTI)

Right to Information (RTI) is the most effective and accessible mechanism to redress public grievances. It means the freedom of the people to have access to government information. It implies that the citizens should have free access to all files and documents pertaining to the government's working processes. The RTI has been seen as the key to strengthening participatory democracy and ushering in people centred governance since access to information can empower the citizens to demand and get information about public policies and actions, thereby leading to their welfare. Transparency in government organizations makes them function more objectively as well as predictably and also enables citizens to participate in the governance processes effectively. In a fundamental sense, the RTI is a basic necessity of good governance.

In recognition of the need for transparency in public affairs, the Indian Parliament enacted the Right to Information Act on 11 May 2005. The Act provides for the proactive disclosure of information, establishment of the Information Commission, appointment of public information officers, procedures for getting information, etc. It is a path-breaking legislation empowering people and promoting transparency. It provides for the setting up of a practical regime to enable and empower citizens to secure access to information under the control of public authorities. The Act gives citizens the right to request and access information held by the government at different levels, and places a corresponding duty on the government to provide information proactively and on request.

The Act defines 'information' broadly to include not only information kept in all forms of print and electronic media, but also physical samples of works. In terms of scope, the Act covers the whole of India (except the state of Jammu and Kashmir), and specifically, it gives to citizens the right to information held by public authorities established, owned, or substantially financed by the Central government, the state governments, and the administration of the union territories. This includes the panchayats, municipalities and other local bodies (Sharma and Devasher 2007, 356).

The RTI Act lays down the time limit as thirty days for normal applications and forty days where a third party submission is to be called for. In a novel approach, these time limits are reduced to a mere 48 hours when the information sought 'concerns the life and liberty of a person'. The application fee is ten rupees per request and no fee is charged from people living below the poverty line. The Act provides for the appointment of Public Information Officers (PIOs) in all administrative units/offices as may be necessary to provide information to persons requesting it. Assistant IPOs are also to be appointed at each sub-divisional or sub-district level. These provisions are designed to bring access closer to the people by ensuring that applicants can submit requests in their local areas. Every PIO can be penalized ₹250 per day up to a maximum of ₹25,000 for not accepting an application, delaying information without reasonable cause, and providing incomplete, incorrect and misleading information. Information must be in writing, including by e-mails, and the request must be submitted to the PIO. Where no response is received, this will be deemed as a refusal. But applications must be rejected in writing with appropriate reasons.

The Act also defines 10 categories of information that are exempted from disclosure because of their sensitive nature. These are information relating to national security, information given in confidence by a foreign government, cabinet papers, trade and commercial secrets. The Central Intelligence Agencies and security agencies like IB, RAW, Directorate of Revenue Intelligence, Central Economic Intelligence Bureau, special frontier force, BSF, CRPF, ITBP, CISF, etc. are also excluded from this Act. But information relating to corruption and human rights must be given with the approval of the Central or State Information Commission, as the case may be.

The Act provides for the establishment of an Information Commission at the Centre and in all the states comprising a Chief Information Commissioner and ten Information Commissioners. The Commission can make any order required to bring about compliance with the law, including releases of documents, appointment of PIOs and the publication of specified information. The Act says that the Central Chief Information Commissioner will be appointed by a committee consisting of the Prime Minister, a leader of the opposition and a Union Minister nominated by the Prime Minister.

The RTI Act, 2005 is one of the most empowering legislations available to the citizens of India. It can facilitate specific actions to solve existing and emerging problems. The Act should not be taken as a negative measure but rather as a positive approach to improve the machinery of governance at every level. The Act is expected to keep the civil services active via the feedback of the people through the information sought by them. Information asked by the people can also help the civil servants in ascertaining the satisfaction of the people. However, it is also to be kept in mind that the mere conferment of the RTI without changing the prevalent style of governance would make the entire exercise futile. In the context of our present scenario, characterized by lack of political will and the reluctant attitude of the bureaucracy to recognize people's right to information, the role of civil society organizations would be crucial and significant in ushering in a new era of open, transparent and accountable governance. The more these organizations come forward to enlighten and mobilize people at the grassroots, the more would be the realization of the immense potential of the RTI.

VOLUNTARY AGENCIES: NEW PLAYERS OF GRIEVANCE REDRESSAL

NGOs also play a very important role in supplementing government efforts in redressing grievances. In the Seventh Five-Year Plan, great emphasis was laid on the involvement of voluntary agencies and other interest groups in making the bureaucracy more responsive to legitimate demands of the citizens. They create an awareness of the rights of the public, interact with administrative departments/ministries for the formulation of policies and action programmes. They also provide counselling and spokesman services. Standing Committees of Voluntary Agencies (SCOVA) have already been set up in various departments, such as Youth Affairs, Sports, Pension and Pensioners, Welfare and Health and Family Welfare. In India, Seva Mandir (Udaipur), Saheli (Jaipur), Aastha (Udaipur) and Sulabh International are some of the NGOs working in the field.

In view of the gradual withdrawal of the state from the social sectors, voluntary organizations have grown in importance not only as alternatives to what is being pursued as development but also as a relatively new experiment in which the role of conventional agencies is largely being eclipsed. They play the role of activists, executing programmes and delivering services and also as 'the mobilizers of opinions, awareness and support of the people concerned with and affected by social, economic and political problems'.

The role of voluntary agencies is increasingly being recognized because they have the special advantage of knowledge of local conditions, not only to design programmes better but to also monitor them effectively. Their contributions in making people aware of various developmental schemes, adopted by the state is now highly appreciated. This suggests a clear shift in government attitude towards voluntary agencies and vice versa.

CIVIL SOCIETY: ARTICULATING CITIZENS' INTERESTS IN A MARKET ECONOMY

The governance paradigm has challenged the state-centric public administration. The inadequate state-directed development paradigm has given rise to an approach involving local people and local resources in a decentralized, people-centric self-development mode. What is critical in this conceptualization of development is that civil society that has emerged as the third sector along with the state and the market. As a significant departure from the conventional conceptualization of public administration, civil society-centred governance creates spaces for voluntary action in areas where the state has already retreated. Civil society gains salience in developing countries presumably because the state-directed development paradigm has failed to a large extent to eradicate poverty and in containing the emergence of an 'insensitive' and mechanical bureaucracy. Civil society contributes to the consolidation of decentralized bottom-up people-centric grassroots governance.

Public Administration, in its new avatar of governance, articulates a trilogy of state, market and civil society. Governance is not merely governmental, but a design which is both market-driven and civil society-induced. The market redefines citizens as clients or consumers while civil society expands the public sphere by including a whole range of civic actions that have hardly figured in the bureaucratic model of public administration. Civil society can thus be most effective in governance by mediating between the citizen and the state, by articulating citizens' interests to the government, by inculcating participatory norms and by restricting the government through citizens' involvement in its day-to-day functioning. Drawing from the shared accountability of stakeholders, the new governance paradigm secures accountability by reducing discretion or delegation in public bureaucracy through collaborative governance. This also makes participation meaningful and effective in the sense that the involvement of the stakeholders in decision-making brings about changes in organizational structure from a hierarchical and centralized to a more decentralized and flexible form for enhancing self-management. Civil society thus makes participation in governance people-centric and also development-oriented.

THE GOVERNANCE DISCOURSE AND THE CHANGING ROLE OF CITIZENS

The concept of citizenship is a key component in public administration. It fosters concerns for public interest and plays an important role in the creation of a harmonious society. However; the governance discourse which is a neo-liberal response to public administration is radically changing the role of the citizens. It is providing diverse channels for articulating and aggregating their interests in a democracy. Also, it is enabling them to act in different capacities as citizens, voters, consumers, clients or members of interest groups. It speaks for the empowerment of customers, not citizens, increased choices for citizens and an empowered government providing public choices in meeting the needs of the customer.

In the governance paradigm, the significance accorded to the consumer represents an economic view of human behaviour. There is a stark distinction between a citizen and a client or a customer. A citizen is an individual in a constitutional state, a repository of rights and duties endowed upon him by law, rules and regulations. Whereas a customer or client functions in a market atmosphere, holding certain rights and responsibilities, and is willing to pay for the services received (Medury 2010, 159). The governance approach thus, gives primacy to consumers instead of citizens, to their rights and participation in public services.

Most contemporary movements in public administration advocate increased citizen participation or involvement in administrative governance, yet have significantly different definitions of citizen's participation. The New Public Management advocates participation from a managerial perspective, building citizen's participation into managerial techniques often drawn from 'total quality management' and similar management movements in private sector (Osborne and Hutchinsons 2004, 15). In these models, the citizens are the consumers or customers of government services and their inputs are important in order to deliver high-performance products and services. Citizen's participation is encouraged in the form of citizen satisfaction panels or surveys, and in performance measurement.

The term 'public' in public administration seems to have lost its significance and the market has acquired salience in governance. Citizens have thus become clients, guided largely by neo-liberal individualism. Bureaucrats are 'rent-seekers' and not society's 'benevolent guardians', as Bentham believed (Chakrabarty 2014). Explaining the distortions in public bureaucracy within the 'public choice' perspective, governance provides a conceptual framework to define collective behaviour in terms of 'methodological individualism' in which the selfish interests of individuals seem to be the driving force in whatever they undertake in society.

Public administration is now 'governance' which is nothing but checklists of certain activities designed both to stabilize and also to consolidate neo-liberalism. In the changed circumstances, the citizen is a client or a customer having to pay the price for the services used. According to Uma Medury, the relationship between the state and the citizen, which has always been dialectical, now appears to be morphing into a relationship between a producer of services and customers. The goal of the administration tends to be the satisfaction of the needs of these consumers through their participation, consultation, etc. This sort of situation poses questions as to whether it is possible to transform a fundamentally political and dialectical relationship, and whether client satisfaction can diminish the dissatisfaction of citizens and restore confidence in the government (Medury 2010, 160). It seems that the 'public' aspect of administration is losing its significance and making space for private service providers.

CONCLUDING OBSERVATIONS

In the changing scenario, the position of citizens from being mere recipients of administrative support and services has now shifted to their being prime movers in the affairs of governance. It is a change from the local beneficiary status to active 'participant status'. In a democracy, the main purpose of public administration is to serve the people. An accountable, accessible, transparent, participative and responsive administration is inevitable to address the problems of the people. There are different ways in which citizens interact with administrative agencies in their day-to-day lives. Through these interactions people have observed that the administration in India is generally unresponsive, insensitive and corrupt. Thus citizens' grievances against the administration are on an increase and at the same time concerted efforts are being made by the government to reduce the growing discontent amongst the citizens by providing various channels for the redressal of their grievances. The Right to Information, the Citizens' Charter and E-Governance have emerged as more effective and accessible tools to redress citizens' grievances.

REVIEW QUESTIONS

1. Discuss the relationship between the citizens and the administration.
2. What is the citizen's perception about administration in India? Discuss
3. Examine the necessary pre-conditions for a citizen-friendly administration.
4. Write an essay on people's participation in administration.
5. What is accountability? Discuss administrative accountability in India.
6. What are the main factors responsible for the growing discontent of citizens with the administration?
7. What are the important grievance redressal mechanisms in India? Examine their effectiveness.
8. Discuss the impact of E-Governance on administration.
9. What is a Citizen's Charter? Examine its role in ensuring administrative accountability.
10. Write an essay on the 'Right to Information' in India.
11. Discuss the main provisions of the Lokpal and Lokayakta Act, 2013.

REFERENCES

Agarwal, U. C., ed. 2004. *Public Administration: Vision and Reality*. New Delhi: Indian Institute of Public Administration.

Avasthi, A., and S. Maheswari. 2010. *Public Administration*. Agra: Lakshmi Narain Agarwal.

Bhatnagar, Subhash C. 2008. 'E-Government: Building a SMART Administration for India's States'. In *The Governance Discourse: A Reader,* edited by Bidyut Chakrabarty and Mohit Bhattacharya, 247. New Delhi: Oxford University Press.

Bhattacharya, Mohit. 2008. *New Horizons of Public Administration*. New Delhi: Jawahar Publishers and Distributors.

Chakrabarty, Bidyut. 2014. 'The Study of Public Administration in India: A Chequered Journey(?)', *Indian Journal of Public Administration* 60 (1), January–March 2014.

Chakrabarty, Bidyut, and Mohit Bhattacharya (eds). 2008. *The Governance Discourse: A Reader*. New Delhi: Oxford University Press.

Dicey, A. V. 1948. *Lectures on Relation between Law and Public Opinion in England During the Nineteenth Century*. 2nd ed. London: Macmillan.

GOI. 2002. 'The Tenth Five Year Plan'. Approach Paper, Chapter 6, New Delhi.

———. 2008. *Report of the Sixth Central Pay Commission*. Government of India, New Delhi.

Hosking, Geoffrey. 2005. *Epochs of European Civilization: Antiquity to Renaissance*. United Kingdom: The Modern Scholar.

Medury, Uma. 2010. *Public Administration in the Globalization Era: The New Public Management Perspective*. New Delhi: Orient Black Swan.

Morrow, William L. 1980. *Public Administration: Politics and the Political System*. New York: Random House.

Osborne, D., and Hutchinsons. 2004. *The Price of Government: Getting the Results We Need in an Age of Permanent Fiscal Crisis*. New York: Basic Books.

Public Sector Group, Poverty Reduction and Economic Management Network. 2007. `Reforming Public Institutions and Strengthening Governance: Main Strategy, a World Bank Strategy'. In *Reinventing Public Administration: The Indian Experience*, edited by Bidyut Chakrabarty. New Delhi: Orient Longman.

Robson, W.A. 1967. *Politics and Government at Home and Abroad*. George Allen and Unwin.

Rouband, Luc (ed.). 1999. *Citizens and the New Governance*. Amsterdam: IOS Press.

Second Administrative Reforms Commission (ARC). 2009. *Citizen Centric Administration: The Heart of Governance*. Government of India, New Delhi.

Sharma, Pradeep K., and Mandakini Devasher. 2007. 'Right to Information in India: Legislation and Beyond'. In *Decentralisation: Institutions and Politics in Rural India,* edited by Satyajit Singh and Pradeep K. Sharma, p. 356. New Delhi: Oxford University Press.

Singh, Amita. 2002. *Public Administration: Roots and Wings*. New Delhi: Galgotia Publishing.

Social Welfare Administration in India

13

LEARNING OBJECTIVES

1. To learn the concept of social welfare and social welfare administration.
2. To examine the structure and functions of social welfare administration.
3. To discuss the contribution of social welfare administration in protecting the weaker sections of society in India.
4. To examine the social welfare policies and legislations in India since independence.

Social welfare is a dynamic concept. It believes that it is the responsibility of the community and the state to promote the well-being of the underprivileged and disadvantaged people of society. The concept was primarily developed in connection with the social problems of industrial society. Poverty, sickness, suffering, and social disorganization have existed throughout the history of mankind, but the industrial society of the nineteenth and twentieth centuries had to face so many social problems that older human institutions—family, neighbourhood, church and the local community—could no longer adequately address them. Thus, the need for a broader system of social services was required. Since that time, governments have been taking greater responsibility for the well-being of citizens. This chapter will primarily discuss the concept of social welfare, social welfare administration and its role in protecting the weaker sections of society in India.

THE CONCEPT OF SOCIAL WELFARE

In a broader sense, 'social welfare' is the organized provisioning of services and efforts by society to deal with social problems. This notion of social welfare has also been corroborated by some distinguished writers on the subject. According to Walter A. Friedlander:

> Social Welfare is the organized services and institutions, designed to aid individuals and groups to attain satisfying standards of life and health, and personal and social relationships which permit them to develop their full capacities and to promote their well-being in harmony with the needs of their families and the community. (1967, 4)

Richard Titmuss defines social welfare as 'all collective interventions to meet certain needs of the individual; and/or to serve the wider interests of society'. Harold Wilensky and Charles Lebeaux define social welfare as those formally organized and socially sponsored institutions, agencies and programmes which function to maintain or improve the economic conditions, health or interpersonal competence of some parts or all of a population (Wilensky and

Lebeaux 1958, 17). According to the Encyclopedia Britannica, social welfare is a system of laws and institutions with which a government attempts to protect and promote the economic and social welfare of its citizens, usually based on various forms of social insurance against unemployment, accident, illness and old age.

Amartya Sen argues that enhancing an individual's capabilities results in a greater likelihood for individual success as well as society's success. Enhancing freedoms is one means of development (Sen 2000). Sen argues 'unfreedoms', which can include famines, lack of healthcare and gender discrimination. In this regard, welfare provides individuals with the basic needs necessary to live a healthy life with the capability to enjoy freedoms that are inherently available to all. Therefore, it is essential to note the importance of welfare especially for the underprivileged in terms of government assistance. Andrew Heywood gives the following arguments in favour of social welfare:

1. It promotes social cohesion and national unity, in that it gives all citizens a 'stake' in society and guarantees at least some basic social support.
2. It enlarges freedom in the sense that it safeguards people from poverty and provides conditions in which they can develop and realize their potential.
3. It ensures prosperity by countering the effects of social deprivation and helping those who cannot help themselves.
4. It serves as a redistributive mechanism that promotes greater equality and strengthens a sense of social responsibility (Heywood 2005, 152).

Thus, social welfare in the broad sense encompasses the well-being of large number of people, including their physical, mental, emotional, spiritual and economic needs. In other words, social welfare includes the basic institutions and processes related to facing and solving social problems which affect a large number of people and which require some kind of concerted group efforts to resolve. The purpose of welfare is to assist individuals in need. The ultimate goal is to lift welfare recipients out of adverse situation and make self-sufficient.

Social Welfare: An Evolutionary Perspective

Generally, interest in social welfare activities emerged as a response to the spectre of urban poverty and social division created by industrialization in the western nations. It was primarily in the late nineteenth and early twentieth centuries that an organized system of state welfare provisioning was introduced in many countries. Germany is generally held to be the first social welfare state. Bismarck (1815–98) introduced for the first time a nationwide system of social insurance. Dramatic changes took place in the aftermath of the First World War. The Russian Revolution of 1917 led to the abolition of private property and institutionalized the ascendancy of the state through central planning and thus giving the state control over all economic activity. The United States did not have an organized welfare system until the Great Depression (1929), when emergency relief measures were introduced under President Franklin D. Roosevelt. The government was concerned with the growing public uprising against capitalism, so it established the welfare system to assist families with little or no income. During the Great Depression, the welfare state was seen as an alternative 'middle way' between communism and capitalism.

In the UK, the beginning of the modern welfare state was in 1911 when David Lloyd George introduced the National Insurance System which was later expanded by Clement Attlee (1945). The Beveridge Report (1942) was another landmark in the history of social welfare in the UK. This was a report, proposing social welfare provisions for the entire population of the country from 'cradle to the grave'. In pursuance of the report, Britain developed a comprehensive social security system to fight what Beveridge called the five giant evils of want, namely disease, ignorance, squalor and idleness. It gave priority to family allowances, tax-supported comprehensive health services, and a universal scheme of national income support insurance which was to provide subsistence income in unemployment, sickness and retirement and also to cover maternity, widowhood and funeral costs.

Another event was unleashed by the Second World War leading to the collapse of colonial rule in the world and the emergence of newly developing nations of Asia and Africa. These newly decolonized nations were clamouring for social insurance. This heralded the advent of the activist state for governance. Although a welfare consensus developed in the early post-1945 period as paternalistic conservatives, modern liberals and social democrats unified in support for the principle of welfare. The 1980s and 1990s witnessed a general retreat from welfare, even among the socialists, brought about in part by the pressures of economic globalization. Nevertheless, even today, welfare remains one of the central fault lines in ideological debates.

SOCIAL WELFARE ADMINISTRATION

The administration of social welfare activities is of crucial importance since all policies and programmes formulated for the welfare of the people and the financial allocations made for their upliftment would be of little avail unless there is an effective and efficient administrative mechanism manned by properly trained and motivated staff. 'Social welfare administration' can be defined as the process of transforming social policy into social services. It is the process of implementation, of translating policies into action programmes. According to Arthur Kruse (1960), the administrative process seeks to mobilize all the resources of the agency to the end that its purpose is translated into efficient and effective services. Forder (1974, 1) holds the view that social welfare administration is concerned with the study of welfare systems and particularly government sponsored social services.

Richard Titmuss (1985) defines social administration as the study of social services whose objective is improvements in the condition of life of individuals in the setting of family and group relations. It is concerned with the development of these services, both statutory and voluntary, moral values implicit in social action, the roles and functions of the services, their economic aspects and the part they play in meeting certain needs in the social process. All these are important and need to be explored in social welfare administration (Titmuss 1985, 14–15). John Kidneigh defines social welfare administration as 'the process of transforming a social policy into social services—a two way process: transforming policy into concrete social services and the use of experience in recommending modification of policy' (Kidneigh 1959, 58). This definition encompasses the idea that administration is the process of implementation and translating policies into action programmes. Rosemary Sarri (1971) lists out the following activities of social welfare administration:

1. Translation of social mandates into operational policies and goals to guide organizational behaviour,
2. Design of organizational structures and processes through which the goals can be achieved,
3. Securing resources in the form of materials, staff, clients and social legitimation necessary for goal attainment and organizational survival,
4. Selection and engineering of the necessary technology,

5. Optimizing organizational behaviour directed towards increased effectiveness and efficiency, and
6. Evaluation of organizational performance to facilitate systematic and continuous problem solving.

In brief, social welfare administration refers to the process of applying professional standards, competence and resources to secure the successful implementation of targeted programmes of social welfare through various social agencies, officials and voluntary, for the fulfilment of ideals, goals and aspirations. In order to make an agency more effective to render social welfare services to the community, it has to adopt certain administrative, financial and procedural modifications which every official and worker in the agency needs to understand.

Education and Training in Social Welfare Administration

Social welfare administration constitutes a branch, sub-division or a sub-set of public administration. Its scope extends from the diagnosis of social problems, initiating measures to eradicate them through social legislation and the creation of public awareness, to the provisioning of social welfare services for the deprived, disadvantaged and underprivileged sections of society with a view to alleviate their sufferings and to ameliorate their lot. Both as a discipline and a profession, it is yet in its nascent stage.

It is apparent that the Charity Organization Movement helped in bringing into existence schools of social work that taught knowledge and skills related to administration. The beginning of formal education started in 1898, when the New York Charity Organization Society established a summer school for volunteers and others who wanted to 'deepen their understanding of the poor people they were dedicated to helping'. In 1904 this offering was extended to a one year programme and to a two-year programme in 1910. At about the same time, educational innovations were appearing in other parts of the country. At the University of Chicago, in 1901, a series of courses in social welfare were offered under the Extension Department. This programme was formalized in 1908 with the incorporation of 'the Chicago School of Civics and Philanthropy', the forerunner of the school of Social Service Administration. The courses in these pioneering schools of social work provided students with some knowledge and skills related to social welfare as part of a common curriculum. At first, administration was not considered to be separate from direct services and practice. By 1914, however, a course in administration was offered by at least one school of social work.

First World War and the Great Depression gave added stimulus to the need for more formal education for those who would provide leadership in administering social service programs. In 1936, a paper on administration was presented for the first time at the National Conference on Social Work. Enough interest in administration had developed so that by 1944, when the new curriculum for the schools of social work was agreed upon, administration was included as one of the 'basic eight' adopted by the American Association of School which is substantiated by the fact that the American National Conference on Social Work (1946) sponsored a section on administration for the first time.

In order to meet the requirement of education and training in social welfare administration in India, Sir Dorabji Tata Graduate of Social Work, Mumbai (which now is known as the Tata Institute of Social Science), was the first to be founded in 1936, to be followed by the Delhi School of Social work in 1947–48, the school of social work at the University of Baroda and thereafter a large number of departments of social work in various universities and post-graduate colleges which have included social welfare administration as a major component in their curriculum while some universities and institutes like the Institutes of Social Sciences, Mumbai have also started independent courses in social welfare administration.

Principles of Social Welfare Administration

The following are the main principles which are recognized and practiced by social welfare agencies:

1. The objectives and functions of a social welfare agency should be clearly defined.
2. Its programme should be based upon actual needs, should be limited in scope and territory to a field in which it can operate effectively.
3. The agency should be soundly organized, should have a clear cut distinction between policy making and execution, units of command and effective coordination of all organization units and staff members.
4. The agency should operate on the basis of sound personnel policies and good working conditions. Personnel should be employed on the basis of their professional qualifications, should be paid adequate salaries and be adequate in quantity and quality to meet the needs of the agency.
5. The work of the agency should be characterized by a basic desire to serve human beings, an understanding of the individuals whom it seeks to serve, and of their needs.
6. The agency should operate on the basis of annual budgets, it should have adequate accounting systems and its accounts should be audited annually by a competent professional authority.
7. The agency should put itself to the test by self-appraisals at appropriate intervals to take stock of its successes and failures in the past year, its present status and programmes and the next steps it ought to take to achieve better performance in the service of its clientele.

Thus, social welfare administration functions on the principles of clarity of objectives, need based programmes, organizational soundness, qualified and trained personnel, adequate accounting system and a sense of service to the human beings.

SOCIAL WELFARE ADMINISTRATION AND PROTECTION OF THE WEAKER SECTIONS IN INDIA

It was after the attainment of independence that social welfare was given its due place in the objectives to be pursued by the government for the welfare of the people of India. The fathers of the Constitution had come to appreciate the role that the state was expected to play in the promotion of people's welfare and had, therefore, included certain provisions in the Constitution for the attainment of the ideal of a welfare state. The basic aims of a welfare state are clearly fore-shadowed in the Preamble of the Constitution and in virtually all of Part IV, containing the Directive Principles. The significance given to the concept of the welfare state by the Constitution makers can also be visualized in part-III concerning the Fundamental Rights and special provisions made for the Scheduled Castes (SCs), Scheduled Tribes (STs) and backward classes in the Constitution.

Table 13.1 Constitution of India Guarantees

Social Protection

- Equality before the law (Article 14)
- Special provision for the advancement of any socially and educationally backward classes including SCs and STs (Article 15 [4])
- Abolition of 'untouchability' and its practice in any form is forbidden (Article 17)
- Appointment of a Commission to investigate the conditions of socially and educationally backward classes (Article 340)
- The right for all minorities to establish and administer educational institutions of their own choice (Article 30)
- To specify the castes and tribal communities deemed to be SCs and STs (Articles 341 and 342)

Economic Promotion

- To promote with special care the educational and economic interests of the weaker sections and in particular of SCs and STs and protect them from any social injustice and all forms of exploitation (Article 46)
- Special Financial Assistance is charged from the Consolidated Fund of India each year as grant-in-aid for promoting the welfare of the STs and development of Scheduled Areas. (Article 275[1])
- The Claims of SCs and STs to appointments in services (Article 335)

Political Rights

- Administration and control of the Scheduled Areas and Scheduled Tribes in any State (Articles 244 and 339)
- Reservation of seats for SCs and STs in the House of the People and in the Legislative Assemblies of the States (Articles 330 and 332)

Source: Author's compilation from different sources.

SOCIAL WELFARE: THE INDIAN PERSPECTIVE

In India, the term 'social welfare' has come to be used in a restricted sense, namely the provisioning of social welfare services to the underprivileged groups including the SCs, STs, widows, orphans, women and children, socially maladjusted, beggars, prostitutes, delinquent and physically and mentally disabled, and therefore, social welfare programmes are directed to ameliorate their conditions (United Nations 1970, 65).

Constitutional Provisions

The Indian Constitution has made a number of provisions related to social welfare. Article 15 of the Constitution prohibits discrimination on grounds of religion, race, caste, sex or place of birth, Article 16 provides for the equality of opportunity in matters of public employment, Article 17 prohibits untouchability, under Article 38 the state is directed to secure a social order for the promotion of welfare of the people, Article 42 directs the state to make provisions for securing just and humane conditions of work and maternity relief. Article 46 promotes the educational and economic interests of the SCs, STs and the other weaker sections of society. The IX Schedule lays down the illustrative list of 257 enactments to protect the interests of SCs and STs. Article 164 provides for a minister in-charge for the welfare of SCs, STs and backward classes. Articles 330, 334 and 335 describe the provision for reservation of seats for the SCs and STs in the Parliament, legislative assemblies of states and in services and institutions. Article 338–339 has provisions for the setting up of a National Commission for the SCs and STs by the President of India. Article 340 relates to the appointment of a Commission to investigate the conditions of backward classes.

Legislative Measures

The government has enacted various legislative measures to combat social evils and to protect the weaker sections of society against social injustice as these are indispensable for supplementing programmes being implemented for their welfare. Some of these laws are: The scheduled castes and scheduled tribes (prevention of atrocities) Act, 1989, The Equal Remuneration Act, 1976, The Child Marriage Restraints Amendment Act, 1978, the Dowry Prohibition Act, 1961 (amended in 1984) Suppression of Immoral Traffic in women and Girls Act, 1956 (amended in 1978), the Commission of Sati (prevention) Act, 1987, Juvenile Justice Act, 1986, The Child Labour (Prohibition and Regulation) Act, 1986, the Maternity Benefit Act, 1961 (Amended in 1976), the Employees' State Insurance Act, 1948, The Employees Provident Fund and Miscellaneous provisions Act, 1952, The Payment of Gratuity Act, 1972, etc.

SOCIAL WELFARE MINISTRY IN INDIA

Realizing the importance of social welfare administration, the Government of India set up a Ministry of Welfare in 1985. The name of the Ministry was changed to the Ministry of Social Justice and Empowerment in 1998. The responsibility for implementation of social welfare schemes is shared between the central and state governments. The Central government is responsible for formulating policies and programmes besides coordinating and promoting the implementation of allied services by the states. Earlier the Ministry was also responsible for the welfare of women, children and SCs, but in 2007 the child development division was merged with the Ministry of Women and Child Development. In 1999, the Tribal Development Division was moved out to form a separate Ministry of Tribal Affairs. The Ministry was entrusted mainly with the task of empowering the following disadvantaged and marginalized target groups:

1. Scheduled Castes (SCs)
2. Other backward Classes (OBCs)
3. Persons with Disabilities (PWDs)
4. Senior Citizens
5. Victims of substance abuse

The Ministry performs its above tasks through legislations, schemes and activities of:

1. Educational and economic development and social empowerment of SCs and OBCs.
2. Rehabilitation, educational and economic development and social empowerment of persons with disabilities.
3. Support to senior citizens by way of their maintenance, welfare, security, health care and productive and independent living.
4. Rehabilitation, through 'whole person recovery' of victims of substance abuse (Government of India 2010, 1).

The Ministry is the nodal organization for the formulation of social welfare policies and programmes and also for ensuring their implementation. The Ministry is assisted in its functioning by a number of subordinate organizations, National Commissions and National Institutes over which it exercises administrative control. These are the National Commission for Scheduled Caste and National Commission for Backward Classes, National Commission for Safai Karamcharis, Commission for Economically Backward Classes, Rehabilitation Council of India, Dr B. R. Ambedkar Foundation, National Institute for the Orthopedically Handicapped, National Institute of Rehabilitation, Training and Research, and the National Institute of Social Defense. The Ministry of Welfare, since designated as the Ministry of Social Justice and Empowerment in 1999, is headed by a Cabinet Minister who is assisted by two ministers of state. The Ministry has a Secretary assisted by an Additional Secretary, four Joint Secretaries and one Deputy Director General in the rank of Joint Secretary who heads the Bureaus of Scheduled Castes Development, backward classes, social defence, disabilities and planning, research, evaluation and monitoring. There is also one post of Economic Advisor in the rank of Joint Secretary.

Welfare Provisions for the SCs

The Ministry of Social Justice and Empowerment is the nodal ministry for overseeing the interests of the SCs. According to the 2011 Census, the SCs constitute 16.6 per cent of population in the country comprising the category of weaker and marginalized sections of society. The Indian Constitution prescribes protection and safeguards for these castes by way of insisting on their general rights as citizens and with the object of promoting their educational and economic interests and removing social disabilities. The main safeguards are:

1. The abolition of untouchability and the forbidding of its practice in any form (Article 17).
2. The promotion of their educational and economic interests and their protection from social injustice and all forms of exploitation (Article 46).
3. The removal of any disability, liability, restriction or condition with regard to the access to shops, public restaurants, hotels and places of public entertainment or the use of wells, tanks, bathing ghats, roads and places of public resort maintained wholly or partially out of state funds or dedicated to the use of the general public (Article 15[2]).
4. Special representation in the Lok Sabah and State Vidhan Sabhas to SCs and STs till 25 January 2010 (Articles 330, 332 and 334).
5. Permitting the state to make reservations for the backward classes in public services in case of their inadequate representation and requiring the state to consider the claims of the SCs and STs in the making of appointments to public services (Articles 16 and 335).
6. Special provision for the administration and control of scheduled and tribal areas (Article 244 and 5th and 6th Schedule) (Sachdeva 2010, 418).

Under Articles 330 and 332 of the Constitution, seats are reserved for SCs and STs in the Lok Sabha and the State Legislature Assemblies in proportion to their population. At present (16th Lok Sabha, 2014), 131 (SC 84 and ST 47 seats) out of 543 Lok Sabha seats and 1,161 out of 4120 assembly seats of different states belong to the reserved categories. Following the implementation of the 73rd and 74th Amendment Acts, 1992, safeguards have been provided for the proper representation of members of SCs and tribes by reserving seats for them in both rural and urban local self-governing institutions in proportion to their population in the respective areas.

As per the provisions of Article 335 and 16(4) of the Constitution, 15 per cent vacancies are reserved for SCs in the All India Services for which recruitment is through open competition. Reservation in direct recruitment to Group C and D posts, which normally attract candidates, is fixed in proportion to the population of SCs and tribes in the respective states and Union territories. Reservation is also made at 15 per cent of the vacancies for the SCs in promotion of the result of the competitive examinations limited to departmental candidates in group B, C and D. Reservation is also provided for these castes in promotions on the basis of seniority, subject to fitness in Group A, B, C and D posts (Sachdeva 2010, 419).

National Commission for Scheduled Castes

In pursuance of the Constitution's 65th Amendment Act, 1990, a National Commission for Scheduled Castes was constituted in 1992 with wide functions and powers. The Commission consists of a Chairperson, Vice-Chairperson and five other members. Their tenure is of three years from the date of joining. The main functions of the Commission include:

1. To investigate and monitor all matters relating to the safeguards provided for SCs in the Constitution.
2. To enquire into specific complaints with respect to the deprivation of rights and safeguards of the SCs and STs.
3. To participate and advise on planning processes and the socio-economic development of SCs and STs.
4. To present to the President annually and at such times as the Commission may deem fit, reports on the working of those safeguards.
5. To make recommendations in terms of the measures that need to be taken by the Union or any state for the effective implementation of those safeguards and other measures for the protection, welfare and socio-economic development of SCs.
6. To discharge such other functions, in relation to the protection, welfare development and advancement of SCs as may be thought proper by the Central government. The Commission has been conferred powers of a Civil Court.

National Commission for *Safai Karamchari*

To promote and safeguard the interests and rights of *safai karamcharis* (sweepers), the National Commission for Safai Karamchari was constituted in 1994. Its main function was to recommend to the Central government specific programmes for the elimination of inequalities in status, facilities and opportunities for safai karamcharis under a time-bound programme. It was empowered to investigate specific grievances and matters relating to the implementation of programmes and schemes for the welfare of scavengers. The Commission is consulted on major policy matters affecting safai karamcharis, who suffer social humiliation and inhuman atrocities.

The National Safai Karamcharis Finance and Development Corporation was established in order to empower the safai karamcharis and their dependents to break them away from their traditional occupation as well as to provide leverage to them to work their own way up the social and economic ladder with dignity and pride. The Corporation provides financial assistance at concessional rates of interest for income generating activities to the scavengers.

Welfare Schemes for the SCs

The Ministry of Social Justice and Empowerment has implemented a number of schemes for the development of SCs. Some of them are discussed in the following sections.

Educational Development

To provide financial assistance to SCs students in post-matriculation, a 'Post Matric Scholarship' for SC students was launched in 2003. Financial assistance under the scheme includes a maintenance allowance, reimbursement of non-refundable compulsory fee charges by educational institutions, book bank facility and other allowances. Other schemes include pre-matric scholarships for children of those engaged in unclean occupations, hostels for SC boys and girls, the book-bank scheme, and free coaching for SC students.

For encouraging SC students to pursue higher education, of the Rajiv Gandhi National Fellowship was instituted. The scheme provides financial assistance to SC students for pursuing research studies leading to MPhil, PhD and equivalent research degrees in universities, research institutions and scientific institutions. Another important educational fellowship is the National Overseas Scholarship. It is meant to provide assistance to selected SCs students for Master courses and PhD programmes abroad in specified fields of engineering, technology and science only. The scheme provides for the fees charged by the institutions as per the actual monthly maintenance allowance, passage visa fee and insurance premium, annual contingency allowance, incidental journey allowance, etc.

In 2001, the Ministry of Social Justice and Empowerment launched the scheme of Coaching and Allied Assistance for the weaker sections including the SCs. The objective of the scheme includes providing quality coaching for group A and B examinations conducted by the UPSC, SSC, Railway Recruitment Boards and the State Public Service Commission, officers' Grade examination conducted by Banks, and Public Sector undertakings and training for finishing courses/job oriented courses for employment in the private sector like IT, bio-technology, and so on, who are in need of soft-skill as well. The scheme is implemented through reputed coaching institutions/centres run by the state government universities and private sector organizations.

Economic Empowerment

In order to promote economic development of the SCs, special control assistance was started in 1980. The main thrust of the scheme was on the economic development of the SC population in order to bring them above the poverty line through self-employment or training. The amount of subsidy admissible under the scheme was 50 per cent of the project cost, subject to a maximum of ₹10,000 per beneficiary. In 1989 the Government of India set up the National Scheduled Castes Finance and Development Corporation. The broad objective of the Corporation is to provide financial assistance in the form of concessional loans to all SCs families living below double the poverty line (presently ₹40,000 per annum for rural areas and ₹55,000 per annum for urban areas) for their economic development and upliftment and economic empowerment through various schemes. During 1 April 2004 to 31 December 2009, the Corporation had disbursed an amount of ₹845 crores covering 2.86 lakh beneficiaries (Government of India 2011, 985–86).

Welfare of the Scheduled Tribes (STs)

The tribal people of India, who come under the category of the 'scheduled tribes', constitute 8.6 per cent of the population of the country (Census 2011). The Union Government constituted a separate Ministry for Tribal Welfare in 1999 as a nodal agency for overall policy planning and coordination of programmes and projects for the welfare of SCs. The Constitution provides various safeguards for the promotion and protection of the interests of the STs. The provisions contained in Articles 19, 46, 146, 244, 330, 332, 334, 338, 339, 342 and the 5th and 6th schedules of the Constitution are relevant in this regard.

Tribal development has been, from the beginning, based on a two-pronged policy namely (a) protection and promotion of their interests, through legal-administrative support and (b) implementation of development schemes to raise their levels of living. The Tribal Sub-Plan (TSP) concept evolved and implemented during the Fifth Five-Year Plan period continues to be the main instrument for the development of the tribal people and tribal areas. The TSP is in operation in 17 states and two union territories. The TSP is funded through resources drawn from (a) state plans, (b) special central assistance (c) centrally sponsored programmes and (d) institutional finance. Under the centrally sponsored schemes, the programmes of girl's hostels for STs is in operation since the Third Five-Year Plan and has considerably helped in promoting the education of girls from the tribal communities. Tribal research institutes have been set up in Hyderabad, Guwahati, Ranchi, Ahmadabad, Bhopal, Kozhikode, Pune, Udaipur, Lucknow, Imphal and Kolkata. These institutions have been contributing to development efforts through research, evaluation, collection of data, training and providing professional inputs in the preparation of tribal sub-plan documents.

In order to promote education amongst the STs the government has introduced a number of programmes. The Post-matric Scholarships were started to provide financial assistance to ST students pursuing post-matriculation courses. The ashram schools have been established as residential schools for the ST children with the objective of providing an environment conducive to learning and to increase the literacy rates among the tribal students. In order to raise the literacy of tribal students, in 2009 a programme for strengthening education among ST girls in low literacy districts was introduced.

To encourage higher education among the STs, the Rajiv Gandhi National fellowship (2005–6)_was started. The objective of the scheme is to provide fellowships for those belonging to the STs to pursue higher studies. The fellowship follows the pattern of UGC fellowships awarded to research students pursuing regular and full-time MPhil and PhD courses. A sum of ₹45 crores was allocated under the scheme during 2009–10. The Ministry of Tribal Affairs introduced a new scheme for top class education for ST students in 2007–8 with the objective of encouraging 57 meritorious students for pursuing studies at the degree and post-degree level. These ST students would be awarded scholarships covering the full tuition fee and other non-refundable dues in respect of government/government funded institutions (Government of India 2011, 997).

Welfare of Other Backward Classes (OBCs)

Ever since the Mandal Commission Report (1990) highlighted the problems of backward classes, a new category called Other Backward Classes (OBCs) emerged in welfare administration of the country. The Mandal Commission had estimated the OBC population at 52 per cent of the total population. In pursuance of the Supreme Court judgement popularly known as the Mandal Judgment (1992), the National Commission for Backward Classes was set up in 1993 as a permanent body for entertaining, examination and advising the government on request for inclusion and complaints of over-inclusion and under-inclusion in the lists of OBCs of citizens. As per the provision of the Act, the advice tendered by the Commission was to ordinarily be binding upon the government.

After the Mandal Judgement in 1992, the government started providing 27 per cent reservation in vacancies of civil posts and services in the Central government in favour of OBCs. On 25 January 1995 the government issued instructions relaxing the upper age limit for OBC candidates in direct recruitment by three years and the number of attempts was increased to seven for the civil service examinations. Any attempt in improving the social and economic status of backwards communities lies in improving their access to education and assisting them in upgradation of merit through special coaching programmes. To ensure educational development among the OBCs, a number of schemes have been launched by the government, namely pre-matric examination coaching and hostels for OBC boys and girls. The National Backward Classes Finance and Development Corporation has been established with the objective of providing concessional finance to members of the backward classes living below the poverty line.

Welfare of Persons with Disabilities

The government has put into place a number of programmes for the welfare of persons with disabilities. A comprehensive law, The Persons with Disabilities (Equal Opportunities, Protection of Rights and Full Participation) Act, 1995 was created and enforced in 1996. The law deals with both preventive and promotional aspects of rehabilitation including education, employment and vocational training, provision of rehabilitation services for persons with disabilities and a grievance redressal machinery both at the Central and state levels.

The office of the Chief Commissioner for persons with disabilities is an important statutory functionary responsible for co-ordinating the work of the state commissioners for persons with disabilities, monitoring the utilization of funds disbursed by the Central government, taking steps to safeguard rights and facilities made available to persons with disabilities and also to look into complaints about the deprivation of rights of persons with disabilities.

Under the National Scholarship for Persons with Disabilities, every year scholarships are awarded to 500 students for pursuing post-matric, professional and technical courses. The scheme of assistance to disabled persons for the purchase/fitting of aids/appliances (ADIP scheme) assists the needy physically handicapped persons with durable, modern and standard aids and appliances, which can promote their physical, social and psychological rehabilitation. The government has set up the National Handicapped Finance and Development Corporation (NHFDC), an apex-level financial institution for extending credit facilities to persons with disabilities for their economic development. In order to effectively deal with the multi-dimensional problems of the disabled population the government has set up national institutes in each major area of disability, important among them being the National Institute for Visually Handicapped, Dehradun, and the National Institute for Orthopedically Handicapped, Kolkata. These institutes are mainly responsible for conducting innovative research, organizing training programmes for manpower development and delivering services for disabled people in the country.

GENDER EQUALITY AND FEMALE EMPOWERMENT IN INDIA

The promotion of gender equality and female empowerment is one of the goals of the UN Millennium Development Goals Report, 2011 released by the United Nations in June, 2011. The Report indicates that girls are gaining ground in education, although unequal access persists in many regions. In the developing nations, like India, 96 girls were enrolled in primary and in secondary school for every 100 boys in 2009.This is a significant improvement since 1999, when the ratios were 91 and 88, respectively. However, only three regions, the Caucasus and Caribbean, and South-Eastern Asia have achieved gender parity in primary education (defined as a gender parity index between 97 and 103). Exceptionally, in Eastern Asia, girls slightly outnumber boys in primary school. Progress for girls has lagged in most other parts of the developing world, and equal access to education in the early years remaining a distant target in Northern Africa, Oceania, Southern Asia, Sub-Saharan Africa and Western Asia.

The Report also says that following significant job losses in 2008–9, the growth in employment that occurred during the recovery in 2010, especially in the developing regions, was lower for women than for men. Women employed in manufacturing industries were especially hard hit. So far as political representation was concerned, the Report says that despite the growing numbers of women Parliamentarians, the target of equal participation of women and men in politics is still far off. By end-January 2011, women held 19.3 per cent of seats in the single or lower houses of Parliament worldwide. This is an all-time high. Still it confirms a pattern of slow progress over the past 15 years from a world average of 11.6 per cent in 1995 (United Nations 2011, 20–23). In such a background, the Report suggests the elimination of gender disparities in education, access to economic opportunities and equal participation of women in politics as paramount in enhancing women empowerment was to be achieved by 2015.

Female Empowerment in India

Women constitute 48 per cent of the total population of India (Government of India 2011). The development of women is of paramount importance and sets the pace for overall development. Since 1985, there is a separate Department of Women and Child Development functioning as part of the Ministry of Human Resources Development to look into matters related to women and children. Keeping in view its importance, a separate Ministry of Women and Child Development came into existence on 30 January 2006. The vision of the Ministry was to empower women to live with dignity, contributing as equal partners towards the development of the country in an environment free from violence, and providing opportunities for their growth and development in an environment free from exploitation.

From time to time several Acts of Parliament have provided direction for the welfare of women, like the Suppression of Immoral Traffic in Women and Girls Act 1956, the Hindu Succession Act 1956, the Dowry Prohibition Act 1961, the Maternity Benefit Act 1961, the Equal Remuneration Act 1976, the Sati (Prevention) Act 1987, the Pre-Natal Diagnostic Techniques (Regulation and Prevention of misuse) Act,1994, and the Protection of Women from Domestic Violence Act, 2005 and the Protection Against Sexual Harassment of Women at Work Place Bill, 2005.The most revolutionary of all was the Supreme Court Judgement in the case of Geeta Hariharan versus Reserve Bank of India 1999 which made it mandatory for all the departments of the Government of India to consider the name of the mother along with that of the father for all practical purposes such as school admissions, bank accounts, passports etc.

The National Commission for women (NCW) was set up in 1992 to deal with all facets of women's empowerment. The main task of the Commission is to study and monitor all matters relating to the constitutional and legal safeguards provided for women and to review the existing legislations and suggest amendments, wherever necessary. The Commission also ensures the speedy redressal of grievances of women. The Ministry of Women and Child Development is charged with the nodal responsibility of implementing and co-ordinating programme of women's welfare and development. The Ministry is implementing the following schemes for the welfare of women:

Support to Training and Employment Programme for Women

This programme launched in 1987, seeks to provide updated skills and new knowledge to poor and assetless women in the traditional sectors such as agriculture, animal husbandry, dairying, fisheries, handlooms, handicrafts, khadi and village industries, social forestry and sericulture for enhancing their productivity and incomes. It has made a significant impact on women in the traditional sectors by upgrading their skills and by mobilizing them into viable groups, arranging for marketing linkages, support services and access to credit. During 2009–10, 21,963 poor women benefited from this scheme.

Swadhar

The Swadhar scheme was launched in 2001–2 as a central sector scheme for providing holistic and integrated services to women in difficult circumstances, such as the destitute, widows deserted by their families, women prisoners released from jail and without any family support, trafficked women/girls, victims of sexual crimes, who are disowned by family etc. The project is implemented through the Social Welfare/Women and Child Development Department, reputed public/private trusts or voluntary organizations etc. provided they have the requisite experience and expertise in the rehabilitation of such women. During 2009–10, 16,860 women benefited by this scheme.

Working Women's Hostel

The scheme of assistance for the construction or expansion of hostel buildings for working women with day care centres for children is being implemented since 1972–73. Under this scheme, financial assistance is provided to non-governmental organizations, women's development corporations, local bodies, universities etc. for the construction of buildings for working women's hostels. By 2009, 887 hostels had been sanctioned throughout the country benefiting 64,922 women.

Short-stay Homes

The scheme of short stay homes was launched in the year 1969, and was meant to provide temporary accommodation, maintenance and rehabilitative services through voluntary organizations to women and girls rendered homeless due to family discords or crime. Under the programme temporary shelter to the needy women and girls is given for six months to three years. Children accompanying the mother or born in the home may be permitted to stay in the home up to the age of seven years, after which they may be transferred to children institutes or provided foster care services.

Family Counselling Centres

The scheme was introduced by the Central Social Welfare Board in 1983. The centres provide counselling, referral and rehabilitative services to women and children who are victims of atrocities, are family maladjusted and face social ostracism. They are also provided crisis interventions and trauma counselling in the case of natural disasters. The centres also create awareness and mobilize public opinion on social issues affecting the status of women.

Rashtriya Mahila Kosh (RMK)

The National Credit Fund for women known as the Rashtriya Mahila Kosh (RMK) was set up in 1993 as a national level organization under the Ministry of Women and Child Development to meet the credit needs of poor and assetless women in the informal sector. The RMK extends micro-finance services through a client friendly and hassle free loan mechanism for livelihood activities, housing, micro-enterprise, family needs, etc., to bring about the socio-economic upliftment of poor women.

Gender Budgeting

Gender budgeting is a powerful tool for achieving gender mainstreaming to ensure that the benefits of development reach women as much as men. It seeks to ensure the equality of outcomes and not equality of opportunities. The Ministry of Women and Child Development as the nodal agency for gender budgeting has taken great strides towards promoting gender budgeting across sectors, at different levels of governance. A powerful impetus to the process was provided by the Ministry of Finance in 2004, which mandated the setting up of Gender Budget Cells in all ministries and departments. So far, 56 ministries and departments of Government of India have set up gender cells.

National Mission for Empowerment of Women

The government launched the National Mission of Empowerment of Women (2010–15) on 8 March 2010, with a view to empowering women socially, economically and educationally. The mission shall monitor and review gender budgeting by Ministries/Departments as well as the effective implementation of various laws concerning women.

Political Empowerment of Women

The 73rd and 74th Amendments (1993) to the Indian Constitution have served as a breakthrough towards ensuring equal access and increased participation in the political power structure for women. Now there is a provision for 33 per cent reservation for women in local self-governing bodies. This has been hailed as a watershed achievement in the empowerment of women, as over one million rural women have joined village panchayat posts as *sarpanches* or *adhyakshas* or members of community administration.

The money and muscle power associated with the electoral process inhibits a large number of women from joining politics. Restrictions on mobility, lack of control over resources and low literacy are well known obstacles but the recent panchayat elections have evidenced a phenomenally large number of female elected leaders much beyond the reserved 33 per cent seats. Realizing the significance of women's participation in the political process, states like Uttarakhand and Jharkhand have reserved 50 per cent of their panchayat seats for women. It has in a sense given women a position of strength, recognition and a legal endorsement of their position to participate in governance.

The Government of India declared 2001 as the Year of Empowerment. In order to bring about the advancement, development and empowerment of women, a National Policy for the Empowerment of women was passed in 2001. The main objectives of the policy (Government of India 2001) include:

1. Creating an environment through positive economic and social policies for the full development of women to enable them to realize their full potential.
2. The *de-jure* and *de-facto* enjoyment of all human rights and fundamental freedom by women on an equal basis with men in all spheres—political, economic, social, cultural and civil.

3. Equal access to participation and decision making by women in the social, political and economic life of the nation.
4. Equal access to women to healthcare, quality education at all levels, career and vocational guidance, employment, equal remuneration, occupational health and safety, social security and public office, etc.
5. Strengthening legal systems aimed at the elimination of all forms of discrimination against women.
6. Changing societal attitudes and community practices by active participation and involvement of both men and women.
7. Mainstreaming a gender perspective in the development process.
8. Elimination of discrimination and all forms of violence against women and the girl child.
9. Building and strengthening partnerships with civil society, particularly women's organizations.

The Ninth Five Year Plan (1997–2002) made two significant changes in the conceptual strategy of planning for women. First, the 'empowerment of women' became one of the nine primary objectives of the Plan. To this effect, the approach of the Plan was to create an enabling environment where women could freely exercise their rights both within and outside the home, as equal partners, along with men. Second, the plan attempted the 'convergence of existing service' available in both women-specific and women-related sectors. To this effect, it directed both the Centre and the states to adopt a special strategy of the Women's Component Plan (WCP) through which not less than 30 per cent of funds/benefits was to flow to women from all the general development sectors. It also suggested that a special vigil be kept on the flow of earmarked funds through an effective mechanism to ensure that the proposed strategy brings forth a holistic approach towards empowering women (Goel 2010, 111–12).

In the Eleventh Five Year Plan (2007–12), for the first time, women have been recognized as not just equal citizens but as agents of economic and social growth. The approach to gender equality is based on the recognition that interventions in favour of women must be multipronged and should provide women with basic entitlements. It also emphasizes on strengthening the existing institutional mechanisms and creating new ones for gender mainstreaming and effective policy implementation.

The Twelfth Five-Year Plan (2012–17) steering committee on Women's Agency and Child Rights views the term 'women's agency' as a socio-political ideal, encompassing an abiding commitment to dignity and equality, envisioned in relation to the wider framework of women's rights. It is a process of gaining control over oneself, over resources and over existing societal perceptions and attitudes and can be achieved only when an improvement in the 'condition' of women is accompanied by an advancement in their 'position' through the enhancement of their economic, social and political freedoms, along with the opportunities and choices available to them.

The Constitution of India grants equality to women in various fields of life, yet a large number of women are either ill-equipped or are not in a position to propel themselves out of their traditionally unsatisfactory socio-economic conditions. They are poor, uneducated and insufficiently trained and are often absorbed in the struggle to sustain the family physically and emotionally and as a rule are discouraged from taking interest in affairs outside their homes. Oppression, discrimination and atrocities on women are still rampant. Patriarchy continues to be embedded in the social system in many parts of India, denying a majority of women the choice to decide on how they live. The overriding importance of the community in a patriarchal sense ensures that women rarely have an independent say in community issues. Female infanticide continues to be common. Statistics show that there is still very high preference for the male child in India. There is an imbalance in the male–female ratio in some states. Domestic violence is also found to be widespread despite the enactment of the Domestic Violence Act 2005 and dowry related crimes are still rampant in society. Except for a meagre number of urban and sub-urban women, Indian woman are still crying for social justice.

The Protection and Welfare of Children

Children (0–14 years) constitute 29.5 per cent of the Indian population as per the Census 2011. The Indian Constitution contains several provisions for the protection, development and welfare of children. Article 24 prohibits the employment of children in any factory or mine or in any other hazardous occupation. To substantiate it, Articles 39 (e) and (f) lay down that the state shall direct its policy in a manner that the tender age of children is not abused.

Keeping in mind this spirit of the Indian Constitution, the National Policy on Children was adopted in 1974 and the Integrated Child Development Services (ICDS) became operational in 1975. For the holistic development of the child, this to be the world's largest and most unique programme providing a package of services comprising supplementary nutrition, immunization, health check-ups, along with health and nutrition education. Ministry of Women and Child Development launched a new centrally sponsored scheme namely the Integrated Child Protection Scheme (ICPS) from the year 2009–10. The objectives of the scheme were to contribute to the improvement in the well-being of children in difficult circumstances, as well as to bring about reductions in vulnerabilities to situations and actions that lead to abuse, neglect, exploitation and the separation of children from their parents.

To respond to the emergency needs of the children in difficulty the government started child line services. Child line has a dedicated number (1,098), which is a 24-hour toll free telephone service available to all children in distress. In order to provide non-formal education and vocational training to working children, the scheme for the welfare of working children was commenced in January 2005. The Ministry of Women and Child Development launched a new pilot scheme called the Dhanlakshmi—a conditional cash transfer for girl child with Insurance cover in 2008. The objective of the scheme was to provide financial incentive for families to encourage them to retain the girl child in school and educate her. A National Commission for Protection of Child Rights was set up on 5 March 2007 for the proper enforcement of children's rights and the effective implementation of laws and programmes relating to children.

SOCIAL WELFARE POLICIES IN INDIA

The Government of India, from time to time has formulated a number of social welfare policies. In the following section we discuss three important social welfare policies concerning employment, education and health.

Mahatma Gandhi National Rural Employment Guarantee Act (MGNREGA)

The National Rural Employment Guarantee Act (NREGA), 2005 is considered to be a milestone in the history of rural development in India. It was brought into force by the Central government in 2006. The law was initially called the National Rural Employment Guarantee

Act but was renamed as the Mahatma Gandhi National Rural Employment Guarantee Act (MGNREGA) on 2 October 2009.

The Act was introduced with the aim of improving the purchasing power of rural people, by providing primarily semi or unskilled work to them, irrespective of whether or not they were below the poverty line. Unlike previous employment generation schemes, the MGNREGA for the first time legally guaranteed employment to India's poor population. The Act guarantees 100 days unskilled job per rural household. It further states that if the government fails to ensure employment to the rural poor, it has to dole out unemployment allowances to them. The underlying objective of the Act is to eradicate poverty from various pockets of the rural hinterland and to make villages self-sustaining through the creation of productive assets such as water tanks, soil conservation works, etc.

The MGNREGA was launched on 2 February 2006 from Anantapur in Andhra Pradesh and initially covered the 200 'poorest' districts of the country. According to the union rural development ministry's figures, initially more than 1.36 crore people—above one per cent of India's total population—were given jobs under the Act. In 2008–9, it provided employment opportunities to more than 4.47 crore households. Schedule I of the Act enumerates eight categories of work that are supposed to be the 'focus of the scheme':

1. Water conservation and water harvesting, drought proofing (including afforestation and tree plantation), irrigation canals (including micro and minor irrigation work).
2. Provision of irrigation facilities to land owned by households belonging to the SCs and STs or to the beneficiaries of land reforms or to the beneficiaries of the Indira Awas Yojana of the Government of India.
3. Renovation of traditional water bodies (including desalting of tanks).
4. Land development.
5. Flood control and protection works (including drainage in water-logged areas).
6. Rural connectivity to provide all weather access.
7. In addition, there is a residual category, that is, any other work, which, may be notified by the Central government in consultation with the state governments.

Under the Act, each state is supposed to formulate a Rural Employment Guarantee scheme within six months of its enactment. Broadly speaking, the village and intermediary Panchayats are entrusted with the task of implementation activities, while coordination activities are left for the district level. Planning, supervision and monitoring take place at all levels. The government decided to extend the Act throughout the country from April 2008. The Act was implemented in a phased manner—130 districts were added in 2007–8. With its spread over 625 districts across the country, this flagship program of the UPA Government has the potential to increase the purchasing power of the rural poor, reduce distress migration and create useful assets in rural India. Also, it can foster social and gender equality as 23 per cent workers under the scheme belong to the SCs, 17 per cent to the STs and 50 per cent are women (Government of India 2013). The National Sample Survey shows an eightfold increase in employment in public works after the implementation MGNREGA. There is also an increase in the share spent on rural employment schemes out of the total Central Plan expenditures. It has increased from an average of 11.8 per cent in the three years before the MGNREGA (2002–3 to 2004–5) to 13.3 per cent in the last three (2009–10 to 2011–12) (Government of India 2013, 42).

Despite its achievements, the MGNREGA has been criticized on a number of grounds. There are many reports which speak of the corruption and misuse of the funds provided for the scheme. Another important criticism is that the public works schemes' completed products (e.g., water conservation, land development, afforestation, provision of irrigation systems, construction of roads, or flood control) are vulnerable of being taken over by the wealthier sections of society. A monitoring study of the MGNREGA in Madhya Pradesh has showed that the types of activities undertaken were more or less standardized across villages, suggesting little local consultation. Further concerns include the fact that corruption in local governments leads to the exclusion of specific sections of society. Local governments have also been found to claim that more people have received job cards than people who have actually worked in order to generate more funds than needed, to be then embezzled by local officials. Bribes as high ₹50 are paid in order to receive job cards. There is criticism from construction companies that the MGNREGA has affected the availability of labour as now labourers prefer to work under the MGNREGA rather than working under construction projects. It is also widely criticized that the MGNREGA has contributed to shortages in farm labour. Even in July 2011, the government had to advise the states to suspend the MGNREGA during peak farming periods.

However, in a country with rampant rural poverty and unemployment, the scheme has been able to achieve two objectives—rural development and employment. Focused on the rural areas, it has been able to involve the local people in activities that help them directly namely, water conservation and harvesting, afforestation, rural connectivity, flood control, construction and repair of embankments, etc. Considering these facts the scheme has helped in empowering rural people.

Sarva Shiksha Abhiyan (Education for All)

Sarva Shiksha Abhiyan (SSA) is the Government of India's flagship programme for achieving the Universalization of Elementary Education (UEE) in a time bound manner, as mandated by the 86th Amendment to the Constitution of India making free and compulsory education to children (of 6–14 years of age a fundamental right. The SSA is being implemented in partnership with state governments to cover the entire country to address the education needs of 192 million children in 1.1 million habitations. The programme seeks to open new schools in those habitations which do not have schooling facilities and to also strengthen the existing school infrastructure through the provisioning of additional class rooms, toilets, drinking water, maintenance grants and school improvement grants. Existing schools with inadequate teacher strength are to be provided with additional teachers, while the capacity of the existing teachers is being strengthened by extensive training, grants for developing teaching–learning materials and strengthening of the academic support structure at the cluster, block and district levels. The SSA seeks to provide quality elementary education including life skills. It has a special focus on girls' education and on children with special needs.[1] The programme also seeks to provide computer education to bridge the digital divide.

There are a number of challenges in the effective implementation of the SSA. Will we ever achieve the goals of the SSA if we do not focus on the reform and decentralization agenda, along with the school autonomy and institutional development thrust? The answer according to Amarjeet Sinha is an emphatic no. The challenge for the SSA is to change the mindset of bureaucrats and teachers, to make them responsible towards meeting the learning needs of all children after providing the resources at their command to do so. The challenge is to create basic minimum learning conditions for all children in all schools and learning centres. The apathy of the state is reflected in the slow pace of effective decentralization and community control for local level accountability of the schooling system.

[1] Refer to the *Sarva Siksha Abhiyan* website for more details. Available at www/http://ssa.nic.in/, accessed on February 27, 2015.

With the proliferation of private unaided schools and parental preference for such schools, government funded schools today cater largely to the poor. Any significant improvement in their performance, therefore, will have positive consequences for poverty reduction. The withdrawal of children of the elite from government schools has also led to their decline as those charged with maintaining government schools do not suffer if the school functions irregularly or ineffectively. Sinha warns that the children who are not in school are from poor families in rural and urban India, are mostly girls and children from the Dalit, minority and tribal households, those making a living agricultural labourers, migrant labourers, construction workers, destitute women, or as lowly paid seasonal labourers. They also deserve quality schooling for their children. He hopes that the democracy will not fail them (Sinha). Thus, the success of the programme will also improve the lives of the poor and weaker sections of society.

National Rural Health Mission

The National Rural Health Mission (NRHM) was launched by the Central government in April, 2005. Its detailed framework for implementation which gave it the mandate for large scale health sector reforms was approved in July, 2006. The design of the NRHM was a very inclusive process. A large number of task forces were set up with the best of public health experts, civil society representatives and government servants to look at some of the key areas where interventions were required. These task forces examined issues like health financing, primary health structures, partnership with non-governmental organizations, medical and nursing education, rural health practitioners etc. It was through this consultative process that the framework for the NRHM was finalized.

The following are the main features of the Mission:

1. Provides support to states for strengthening the system of health care in rural areas through the provision of physical infrastructure, human resources, equipment, emergency transport, drugs, diagnostics and other support.
2. Covers all programmes in the health sector except HIV/AIDS, mental health and cancer.
3. Ensures untied funds to all health facilities starting from village health and sanitation committees to district hospitals.
4. Provides management support to strengthen capacity for the decentralized management of health.
5. Makes provisions for the constitution of community institutions at the health facility level.
6. Provides a community worker called ASHA in every village.
7. Allows states to innovate and promote flexible financing to allow local decision-making.

The NRHM has tried to push reforms with resources in partnership with the state and UTs in bringing about reforms and improvements in the health indicators. The NRHM framework for implementation has pushed the communalization of facilities, adequate and flexible financing with community accountability, monitoring progress against the Indian Public Health standards, innovations in human resources, engagement and building of capacity at all levels for the effective and efficient decentralized management of the health system. Independent studies have shown that the NRHM has led to an increase in outpatient cases, inpatient cases, institutional deliveries, availability of ambulances, presence of community health worker in every village, better availability of drugs and diagnostics and most importantly a sincere effort to craft a credible public health system.

CONCLUDING OBSERVATIONS

Social welfare administration is an effective mechanism for addressing social problems through measures such as: framing social legislation, creation of public awareness, and making provisions of social welfare services for the deprived, disadvantages and underprivileged sections of society with a view to alleviate their sufferings. The development of social welfare in post-independence India has been phenomenal in terms of the provisioning of the administrative machinery, financial outlays and the expansion of social welfare programmes for numerous sections of the disadvantaged and underprivileged. The setting up of the Ministry of Social Justice and Empowerment, the Ministry of Women and Child Development and the Ministry of Tribal Affairs as full-fledged ministries and organizations subordinate to them like the National Commission for SCs/STs, the Minorities Commission, the National Institute for the Handicapped and the National Institute of Public Cooperation and Child Development, are great landmarks in the evolution of social welfare administration in India. The programmes and initiatives undertaken by these institutions in uplifting the weaker sections of society are commendable.

However, despite a number of achievements, we need to do a lot in terms of addressing the spectre of poverty, inequities, and injustice in India. One-third of the world's hungry still reside in India. We have failed dismally in providing two square meals a day to more than 30 per cent of our population. Child labour still constitutes one-fourth of the country's total workforce in which 44 million children live in subhuman conditions, and about 3 lakh girls are engaged in flesh trade. The goal of universal primary education appears successful only on papers. The girl child continues to be discriminated. Women are being denied their legitimate rights of equality and are still subjected to atrocities including infliction of death due to non-fulfilment of dowry demands. Though women have been given 33 per cent seats in panchayats, still they are directed by their male partner. The incidences of atrocities on the dalits are mounting. Tribal people are being displaced in the name of developmental projects. The weaker sections of society suffer indignities and humiliations. The gap between the very rich and the very poor is devastatingly widening (Sachdeva 2010, 122). The administrative machinery has proved inefficient and unresponsive in addressing the problems of the weaker and downtrodden sections of society. Thus, the situation is grim.

Keeping in mind the above challenges, there is a need to make social welfare administration more effective and accountable. A number of measures can be initiated in this regard, like the proper monitoring of social welfare programmes, strict action against corrupt officials, preventing delays in the implementation of schemes, checking leakages of funds by middlemen and ensuring that services actually reach the target groups. Social security measures need to be extended to unorganized labour, atrocities on children, women and the SCs need to be checked with strong preventive measures like setting up Special Courts and Special Police Forces. There is need to ensure that the tribals are not alienated by encroachments on their indigenous way of living, culture and traditions on the pretext of development. By implementing these measures we can surely improve the condition of the disadvantaged sections of society and make them a part of national development.

REVIEW QUESTIONS

1. Write an essay on the evolution of the concept of 'Social welfare'.
2. What is social welfare administration? Discuss its main principles.
3. Evaluate the role of social welfare administration in India, with particular reference to the weaker sections of society.

4. How far has Social Welfare Administration benefited the OBCs in India? Discuss.
5. What measures have been taken by the Government of India for the upliftment of the SCs and STs? Discuss.
6. Discuss the organizational structure and functions of Social Welfare Administration in India.
7. Discuss the main policies and programmes undertaken by the government for the welfare of women in India.
8. 'Social welfare administration has to go a long way to get the recognition as an independent discipline'. Comment.
9. What are the main challenges before social welfare administration in India? Discuss.
10. Give your suggestions to make social welfare administration more effective and accountable.

REFERENCES

Beveridge, William. 1942. *Social Insurance and Allied Services*. New York: Macmillan.

Forder, Anthony. 1974. *Concepts in Social Administration*. London: Routledge and Kegan Paul.

Friedlander, Walter A. 1967. *Introduction to Social Welfare*. New Delhi: Prentice-Hall of India.

Goel, S. L. 2010. *Social Welfare Administration*. Vol. 2 (Social Justice and Empowerment). New Delhi: Deep and Deep Publications.

Government of India. 2001. *National Policy for the Empowerment of Women 2001*. Ministry of Human Resource Development, Government of India, New Delhi.

———. 2010. *Annual Report 2009–10*. Ministry of Social Justice and Empowerment, Government of India, New Delhi.

———. 2011. *India 2011*. Publication Division, Government of India, New Delhi.

———. 2013. *Twelfth Five year Plan (2012–17): Faster, More Inclusive and Sustainable Growth*. Vol. 1. Planning Commission. New Delhi: SAGE.

Heywood, Andrew. 2005. *Key Concepts in Politics*. New York: Palgrave Macmillan.

Kidneigh, John C. 1959. 'Social Work Administration: An Area of Social Work Practice'. *Social Work Journal* 31 (April): 58.

Kruse, Arthur. 1960. *Administration of Social Welfare Agencies* (Social Work Year Book). New York: National Association of Social Work.

National Rural Health Scheme. National Health Mission, Ministry of Health and Family Welfare. Retrieved from http://mohfw.nic.in\nrhm\documents\5 years-nrhm-final.fdf (accessed on 13 December 2015).

Rosemary, S. 1971. "Administration in Social Welfare," *Encyclopedia of Social Work*. New York: National Association of Social Workers.

Sachdeva, D. R. 2010. *Social Welfare Administration in India*. New Delhi: Kitab Mahal.

Sarva Shiksha Abhiyan. Ministry of Human Resource Development. Retrieved from www\http:\\ssa.nic.in\ (accessed on 13 December 2015).

Sen, Amartya. 2000. *Development as Freedom*. New Delhi: Oxford University Press.

Sinha, Amarjeet. 'Is It Really Possible?' Retrieved from www.india-seminar.com\2004\536\amarjeet-sinha.htm (accessed on 12 December 2015).

Titmuss, Richard M. 1985. *Essays on the Welfare State*. London: George Allen and Unwin.

United Nations. 1970. *Social Welfare Planning in the Context of National Development Plans*. New York: United Nations.

———. 2011. *UN Millennium Development Goals Report, 2011*. New York: United Nations.

Wilensky, Harold L., and Charles N. Lebeaux. 1958. *Industrial Society and Social Welfare*. New York: Russell Sage Foundation.

Environmental Administration in India

14

LEARNING OBJECTIVES

1. To understand the important environmental issues in India.
2. To know the legal and constitutional provisions of environmental protection in India.
3. To explore the response of the judiciary on environmental issues.
4. To examine the role of civil society in environmental governance in India.

Man, since his origin, has lived in harmony with nature. However, with the development of science and technology, man has endeavored to master the natural world. Due to his greed for accumulating wealth, natural resources have been exploited blindly. The result is what we see today. The cities and towns are highly polluted in terms of air and water quality and too noisy and unhygienic for healthy human living. Forests are denuded leading to disturbances in weather and the water table. Rivers and oceans are not only polluted but are getting shorn of their natural wealth through human voraciousness. Due to over exploitation, the earth is losing its fertility. The atmosphere is beset with the looming danger of global warming and ozone layer depletion. Man, today, is facing the crisis of his own survival. This chapter deals with environmental issues in India, the legal and constitutional provisions for environmental protection and the response of the judiciary and civil society to environmental challenges in India.

ENVIRONMENTAL ISSUES IN INDIA

Man's desire for ultimate joy and comfort has led him to exploit nature's free goods and services to the extent of reducing its natural capacity for self-stabilization. As a consequence of this disregard on the impact of these activities on the environment, numerous environmental problems have arisen. The major environmental issues in India are air pollution resulting from industrial development, water pollution from domestic and industrial effluents, deforestation, loss of biodiversity, solid waste, noise pollution and vehicular pollution in a growing number of cities. However, the protection of the environment presents the most fundamental challenge to the nation's desire to industrialize faster, to be self-sufficient in food and to be capable of fulfilling certain basic needs of the growing population. The challenge is to strike a balance between the environment and development. Some of the major environmental problems in India can be identified under the following sections.

Environmental Pollution

When the physical, chemical and biological projects of different components of environment, namely the air, water, soil, noise, etc., change to the detriment of living species it may be said that the environment has been polluted. Pollution thus occurs when environmental changes create or are likely to create dangers to public health and safety or when they are harmful to domestic, industrial, recreational or other legitimate uses of environmental components. The effects of environmental pollution are harmful especially with their immense impact on human survival and the quality of life. The major types of pollution can be studied under the following sections.

Air Pollution

The major component of the atmosphere is air without which no life can survive. Yet clean air is a rare commodity today, especially in big cities and towns. Today air pollution is a major environmental problem in cities. According to the Air (Prevention and Control of Pollution) Act, 1981 air pollution means the presence of solid, liquid or gaseous substances in the atmosphere in such concentration as may or tend to be injurious to human beings or living creatures or plants or property or the environment (CSE 1982, 132).

Air pollution is one of the biggest environmental problems in India. In most of the 23 Indian cities having a million plus population, air pollution levels exceed the World Health Organization (WHO) stipulated health standards. And in most of the cities, the levels are getting worse because of the growing number of vehicles, energy consumption and unbridled industrialization and burning of waste. Six of India's 10 largest cities, namely Mumbai, Calcutta, Delhi, Ahmedabad, Kanpur and Nagpur, face severe air pollution problems, with the annual average levels of total suspended particles (TSP) at least three times as high as the WHO standard (Jain 2005, 7). Due to coal being burnt in power plants, sulphur dioxide (SO_2) and fly ash emissions are constantly increasing. As CO, Ozone, lead and hydrocarbon are related to vehicular emissions, it is clear that their levels will increase rapidly with a concurrent increase in vehicular transport in India in the future.

Worsening air quality is a scary story unfolding in urban India. Clinching evidence of this has emerged from a recent study 'Global Burden of Disease' (2012), carried out by 450 experts of five international organizations including the WHO, which ranks outdoor air pollution as the fifth largest killer in India. The report says that the decade-long air quality management efforts have failed to contain the problem. The cocktail of toxic air is increasing health risks and compromising the 'livability' of Indian cities (CSE 2013, 35). The public health implications of heavily polluted air in Indian cities were made more stark when in June 2013, the International Agency for Research on Cancer classified outdoor air pollution and particulate matter as Class 1 carcinogens and the leading environmental causes of lung cancer deaths (CSE 2014, 148).

The World Bank Report (2013) provides more evidence to indicate the astounding health costs of dirty air in India. The World Bank's evaluation of health costs from a wide gamut of environmental damage including both outdoor and indoor air pollution, inadequate water supply, poor sanitation and hygiene, shows that outdoor air pollution tops the list. It is the highest among all damages, with a cost amounting to over ₹110,000 crores. Every year, outdoor air pollution claims 109,000 lives of adults and 7,513 lives of children below five years in India. The cost of outdoor and indoor air pollution together is the highest annual burden on India's economy accounting for nearly half of all damages. The Report states that the highest costs for outdoor and indoor air pollution are driven by high exposure of the young and productive urban population to particulate matter pollution. That leads to substantial cardio-pulmonary and chronic obstructive pulmonary disease mortality among adults. New cases of chronic bronchitis reported are about 48,000 per year. Annual hospitalizations due to air pollution are estimated at close to 3.7 lakh and emergency visits/outpatient hospitalization stand at 73 lakh per year. The cost of particle pollution-related health damage amounts to 1 per cent of India's GDP (CSE 2014, 149).

Water Pollution

Water pollution is another major environmental issue in India. Water pollution may be defined as the introduction into a water body of substances of such character and in such quantity that its natural quality is so altered as to impair its usefulness; affect the health of living organisms or render it offensive to the senses of sight, taste or smell.

Municipal sewage and industrial waste are the major sources of water pollution in India. More than 80 per cent of the total pollution load comes from municipal sewage. Waste management systems have not been able to keep pace with the huge volumes of organic and non-biodegradable wastes generated daily. As a consequence, garbage in most parts of India is unscientifically disposed and ultimately leads to an increase in the pollutant load of surface and groundwater courses. It is estimated that about 38,000 million litres per day (mld) of wastewater are generated in urban centres having population more than 50,000 in India (housing more than 70 per cent of urban population). The municipal wastewater treatment capacity developed so far in India is about 11,000 MLD accounting for 29 per cent of wastewater generation in these two classes of urban centres (CPCB 2013, 5). Thus less than one third wastewaters in cities is treated and the rest is discharged in rivers, resulting in the contamination of water and thus exposing 70–90 per cent people to unsafe drinking water.

Industries are another major source of water pollution in India. Poor environmental management systems, especially in industries such as thermal power stations, chemicals, metals and minerals, leather processing and sugar mills, have led to the discharge of highly toxic and organic wastewater. This has resulted in the pollution of surface and groundwater sources from which water is also drawn for irrigation and domestic use. Tanneries in Chennai, Kanpur, Agra and Calcutta and dyeing units in Gujarat, Madhya Pradesh and Chennai create heavy pollution loads without having effective treatment facilities. The industrial sector, contributing to about 20 per cent of the national income, accounts for about 8 per cent of the current water use. With rapid industrialization and urbanization, the water requirement for energy and industrial use is estimated to rise to about 18 per cent (191 bcm) of the total requirements in 2025.

Water quality is further affected due to the overuse of chemical fertilizers and pesticides. India uses about 5 million tonnes of chemical fertilizers and 77,000 tonnes of pesticides and insecticides, which usually find their way into the rivers or ground water. About 25 per cent reach the sea and pollute coastal waters affecting marine life. Water pollution is not restricted to surface water alone. There have been cases where the ground water is found to have become contaminated. Solid waste dumping is one cause for ground water pollution. The various kinds of harmful materials present in solid waste may dissolve in water and percolate down into the soil and contaminate the ground.

Water pollution is turning India's major rivers and other bodies to sewers. For example in Kolkata 860 million litres of untreated sewage is discharged through sewer outlets daily into the Hooghly River. Similarly in the river Yamuna 1900 mld solid waste comes daily from Delhi. The length and basin of river Yamuna in Delhi is only 2 per cent, when compared with Haryana and UP, but the pollution loads contributed by Delhi are 80 per cent of the total water (Chand 2013, 135). The entire 48 km stretch of the Yamuna river in Delhi is highly polluted due to the release of untreated sewerage as well as industrial effluents.

World Health Organization statistics indicate that half of India's morbidity is water related. Water pollution is responsible for a number of diseases like typhoid fever, dysentery, hookworm, jaundice, poliomyelitis pneumonia, influenza and whooping cough. In 1999, Prahladpur in North-West Delhi shot into the limelight with around 300 of its residents falling prey to jaundice. In the year 2000, there were around 66,000 reported cases of gastroenteritis infections. In the same year 955 people were reported to suffer from cholera. Also 1,106 people suffered from malaria (*TOI* 2001, 4). A major reason for water borne diseases was the mixing of sewer lines with the drinking water lines.

Noise Pollution

According to the WHO any unwanted or undesired sound is noise and the increase of noise beyond a certain limit is said to be noise pollution. The major sources of noise pollution are found to be road traffic, blaring of radios and TVs, audio and video records, railways, air crafts, building construction, etc. Further, increases in industrialization and urbanization are responsible for increased noise pollution in cities.

In January 2000, the Ministry of Environment and Forest, Government of India, notified the norms of permissible noise levels in urban and rural areas in India (Table 14.1). However, most Indian cities have far exceeded the maximum permissible limits prescribed by the government. Data available from the Central Pollution Control Board (CPCB) database (2011) shows that Delhi and Mumbai are the noisiest cities with 132 decibels (dB), while Bangalore registered 130.66 dB and Chennai had a noise level of 129.22 dB, all dangerously above permissible limits.

Noise in the major cities and towns in India is a growing menace. The World Health Organization's guideline (1999) says noise above 80 dB can cause hearing impairment, especially among children, above 30 dB can cause sleeping disorders and also impact spoken communication, cardiovascular activity and trigger negative social behaviour. In the first ever real-time data of noise pollution in 35 locations around seven cities released by the CPCB on 23 March 2011, a decade after India notified noise standards, indicates that the average day time noise levels in metros was much higher than the national standard of 65 dB ampere. A comparison with noise levels in some international cities indicates that those in Indian cities are living in the noisiest parts of the global urban landscape. Noise levels in busy parts of London, New York and Beijing were less than around the Income Tax Office in New Delhi and Bandra in Mumbai. Among the Indian cities, locations monitored in Mumbai were the

Table 14.1 Ambient Air Quality Standards in Respect of Noise

Area Code	Category of Area/Zone	Limits in dB (A) Leq.	
		Day Time	**Night Time**
(A)	Industrial area	75	70
(B)	Commercial area	65	55
(C)	Residential area	55	45
(D)	Silence zone	50	40

Source: The Noise Pollution (Regulation and Control) Rules (2000).

nosiest followed by Delhi, Chennai and Bangalore. Achworth Hospital in Bandra in Mumbai constantly has the highest noise pollution levels followed by the Income Tax Office in Delhi (*TOI* 2011).

A news article in *The Times of India* on 27 April 2011 (page 1 of 4) said that living in Chennai was equivalent to living in a factory—at least in terms of the noise all the residents are subjected to. Data from the Central Pollution Control Board (CPCB) shows that the noise levels everywhere in Chennai are over 100 dB—more than a typical factory. The average noise level in Chennai is actually higher at more than 129 dB. It must be noted that pain in the ear begins at 125 dB. The permissible limit is 85 dB fixed by the World Health Organization (WHO). It is not just Chennai. CPCB data shows that noise levels in all the major Indian metros are far above permissible limits and may have reached dangerous levels. The levels could cause hypertension, psychological diseases and depression.

Land Degradation

As per the estimates of the Indian Council of Agricultural Research in 2010, out of the total geographical area of 328.73 million hectare (mha), about 120.40 mha was affected by land degradation due to various reasons like, water and wind erosion, soil acidity, soil alkalinity, mining and industrial waste, soil salinity, waterlogging, etc. This results in an annual soil loss of about 5.3 billion tonne through erosion (CSE 2014, 88). Along with the soil, major plant nutrients are lost and are being replaced by artificial fertilizers. Deforestation, overgrazing, faulty agricultural practices and a constant search for firewood have resulted in landslides, flash floods, desertification and waterlogging. In an attempt to offset this loss, new land is constantly being brought into production. With the new agricultural practices, much of India's good farmland has become deficient in nutrients and organic materials. In the past, Indian farmers used organic manure to overcome nutrient deficiencies, but since the agricultural explosion they have been using increasing amounts of chemical fertilizers, adding further stress on the environment.

Another growing threat is the bulk diversion of fertile land to meet the increasing demand for industrialization, urbanization, housing and infrastructure development. As per the State of Indian Agriculture 2012–13 published by the Central Agriculture Ministry, the percentage of land used for non-agricultural purposes has increased from 3.3 to 8.6 per cent during the period 1950–51 to 2009–10. The diversion has not been restricted to private land. Common lands like grazing areas and forests are also being diverted, thus threatening the food security of the marginalized sections of the population, like tribal and forest dwellers. Currently, close to 22,000 sq. km of land is devoted to projects in the agri-business, infrastructure, mining and non-conventional energy sectors (CSE 2014, 88). Most of the land taken over by industries is common land and forests, traditionally used by local communities states like West Bengal, Jharkhand, Odisha, Andhra Pradesh and Haryana that reported higher rates of diversion than the national average are also the states that reported large-scale public protests over land acquisition.

Solid and Hazardous Waste

It is evident from the visible garbage in our cities and towns that the improper disposal of solid and hazardous wastes has become a major threat to the environment and public health. Solid wastes are becoming a scourge. The legal dumps are over flowing and the number of illegal garbage dumps in by lanes, parks and roadsides are on the increase. On an estimate, at least 8 per cent of India's landmass has become wasteland due to open garbage dumps and has lost its utility and fertility. Also these dumps are breeding grounds for infectious diseases like plague, cholera, TB, jaundice and numerous skin ailments. Hospital waste is among the most dangerous types of garbage because of its being contaminated with disease-carrying pathogens. The list of diseases caused due to improper disposal and treatment of hospital waste is endless, but a majority of these are deadly such as AIDS, hepatitis, TB, bronchitis, gastroenteritis and other skin and eye related disorders. Thus, the improper disposal of bio-medical wastes in the major cities and towns of India has become a matter of serious concern.

Delhi, the capital city, is facing an acute problem due to solid and hazardous waste. The present municipal waste generation in NCT of Delhi is 7,000 tonnes per day and the expected range of the waste quantity generated by 2021 is expected to be 17,000–25,000 tonnes per day (TERI 2001, 13). Disposal is mainly in landfills. Fourteen landfill sites have already been filled up. Four landfill sites at Gazipur (East Delhi), Bhalswa (North), Hastsal (South-West) and Okhla (South-East) are operational at present, though these will soon get filled. Due to growing pressures on land in Delhi and the projected increase in the quantum of solid wastes, the scope for disposal through landfill sites is limited. Too much land is being consumed accompanied by the increasing danger of ground and surface water contamination. Solid waste samples from the surface and various depths of the landfills have been found to contain high levels of faecal coliforms and faecal streptococci. The most critical hazardous waste generated in Delhi is from small-scale enterprises such as pickling units, electroplating units, anodizing units and sludge from Central Effluent Treatment Plant (CETP).

The current estimates of the quantity of infectious biomedical waste in Delhi is 20–25 tonnes per year, most of which finds its way (with or without treatment) into municipal waste dumps in the absence of any dedicated disposal facility. In addition, informal practices of rag picking and recycling of various hospital wastes contents poses a potential health hazard to rag pickers as well as to the general population who use such recycled waste items. Besides, most healthcare facilities use various hazardous chemicals in processes such as disinfections, radiotherapy and X-ray film processing. The wastes generated from such activities are invariably discharged into sewer drains. A survey conducted in Delhi in 2000 by an NGO Shrishti (GNCT Delhi 2001, 1) for ascertaining the status of biomedical waste management reveals that many of the facilities have installed treatment provisions such as incinerators, but most of these incinerators hardly run at desired temperature ranges and moreover burn chlorinated plastics. Thus, the possibility of emissions of toxic products of incomplete combustion (which may be more toxic than the parent compound) and emissions of compounds such as dioxins and furans cannot be ruled out.

The waste plastics markets all over India are so packed and crowded with waste spilling out, that frequent fires create environmental problems both for the workers as also for the residential areas around. Delhi is Asia's largest waste plastic market, handling and trading over 1,000 tonnes of waste daily, followed by Jolly Mohalla in Bangalore and Dharavi in Mumbai (TERI 2001, 95). The problem pertaining to the management of plastic wastes is its non-biodegradability. Through various stages of their use, they get disposed via municipal garbage dumps and finally collected as virgin plastics and are accepted as user friendly. The problem arises when plastics are recycled for repeated use. Because these are produced from wastes, there is apparent consumer resistance. What is worse is that a major volume of more than once recycled bags remains on ground and is not collected by the rag pickers as their resale value gets reduced. These—together with other food, vegetable oil and detergents packaging when not collected/recycled—become an eyesore.

Threats to Biodiversity

India has very rich biodiversity. It is recognized as one of the 12 mega centres of biodiversity. As per the records of the Ministry of Environment and Forests, the country has more than 45,000 plant species and 81,000 animal species representing 7 per cent of the world's flora and 6.5 per cent of its fauna. However, under the pressure of an exploding population and the growing demands of industries, our natural living resources are fast dwindling and several species of wildlife are being rapidly lost. At least 10 per cent of India's recorded wild flora and possibly a large fraction of its wild fauna are on the threatened list.

India has 172 species of animals considered globally threatened or 2.9 per cent of the world's total number of threatened species. These include 53 species of mammals, 69 birds, 23 reptiles and three amphibians. It has some of the rare animals in Asia and the world, such as the Asiatic Cheetah, Indian Rhinoceros, Bengal Fox, Marbled Cat, Asiatic Lion, Asiatic Wild Ass, Gaur and Wild Asiatic Water Buffalo. Similarly, there are more than 1,500 varieties of plants are at threat in India.

Deforestation

The forest cover in India is disappearing at a staggering rate of 1.3 mha each year. India has a forest cover of 21.05 per cent of the country's land surface as against the target of 33 per cent prescribed by the National Forest Policy (1952). The major causes of deforestation include the encroachment of forest lands for cultivation, shifting cultivation, diversion of forest land to non-forest uses, grazing, unauthorized and commercial felling and industrial use.

A report by the Centre for Science and Environment (2014) shows that between 1981 and 2012, 1,183,966 hectare of forest land was diverted, 14 per cent of this diversion was for power projects and over 13 per cent was for mining (Figure 14.1; CSE 2014, 84). Regularization of encroachments took up the largest chunk of diversions. The Report says that most of this happened in 1990 and 2001 (Table 14.2).

Figure 14.1 Forest Cover in India (Total Forest Cover 21.09%)

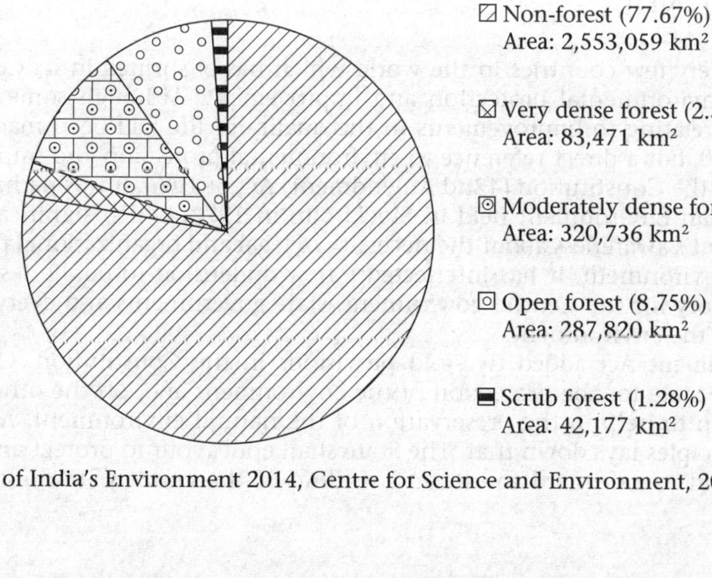

Source: State of India's Environment 2014, Centre for Science and Environment, 2014.

Table 14.2 Forestland Diversions in India (1990–2001)

Purpose/Sector	Forestland Diverted	
	Area (ha)	**Percentage**
Defence	46,087.93	3.89
Transport (railways and roads)	60,363.10	5.10
Social services	65,165.24	5.50
Irrigation	141,641.76	11.96
Mining	159,660.34	13.49
Power projects (hydel, thermal, wind and transmission lines	167,118.00	14.12
Others (including industries)	175,498.24	14.82
Regularization of encroachment	368,432.07	31.12
Total forestland diverted	1,183,966.68	

Source: State of India's Environment 2014, Centre for Science and Environment, 2014.

Deforestation is mainly responsible for a rise in temperature, low rainfall, air pollution and soil erosion. Deforestation accelerates water runoff and soil erosion. As wood supplies dwindle, Indian families are forced to use whatever substitutes are available, such as animal dung or crop residues, which would otherwise be returned to the soil as fertilizers. This compels farmers to use chemicals, which in the long run have an adverse effect on the productivity of the land. The National Environmental Engineering Institute reports that in several states, ground water is being drawn faster than its rate of recharge. Some parts of Haryana and Punjab have seen the levels sink by over 4 metres. Levels in Tamil Nadu have fallen between 25 and 30 metres due to over pumping.

CONSTITUTIONAL AND LEGAL PROVISIONS FOR ENVIRONMENTAL PROTECTION IN INDIA

India is one of the very few countries in the world which has enshrined in its Constitution a commitment to environmental protection and improvement. Although some provisions in the Constitution relating to improvements in the quality of life had been made since its proclamation in 1950, but a direct reference to environmental protection and improvements was introduced with the Constitution (42nd Amendment) Act of 1976. It was perhaps the UN Conference on Human Environment held in Stockholm in 1972, which significantly influenced the government's awareness about the necessity of legal and organizational frameworks for protecting the environment. It has interjected a new dimension to public responsibility by making it obligatory for the Central government, state governments and every citizen to protect and improve the environment.

The 42nd Amendment Act added two-fold provisions in the Constitution. On the one hand, it directed the state for the protection of the environment and, on the other; it cast a duty on every citizen to help in the preservation of the natural environment. Article 48 A of the Directive Principles lays down that 'The State shall endeavour to protect and improve the environment and to safeguard forest, and wildlife of the country' (Basu 1998, 446).

Article 51 A (g) specifically refers to the fundamental duty regarding the environment. The Article says, 'It shall be the duty of every citizen of India to protect and improve the natural environment including forests, lakes, rivers and wild life and to have compassion for living creatures' (Basu 1998, 447). Further the directive principles of State Policy in Article 47 clearly underline the environmental duty of the state to improve public health.

There is no direct provision for the protection of the environment in the fundamental rights. But the High Courts and the Supreme Court of India have read the right to wholesome environment as part of the right to life guaranteed in Article 21 of the Constitution of India. Article 21 enunciates that no person shall be deprived of his life or personal liberty except according to the procedure established by law. The slow poisoning by the polluted atmosphere caused by environmental pollution amounts to a violation of Article 21 of the Constitution. In fact, the right to life guaranteed in Article 21 of the Constitution embraces the protection and preservation of nature's gifts without which life cannot be enjoyed. Moreover, environmental degradation has a disastrous impact on the right to livelihood which is part of the right to life.

The legal sanction to protect different segments of the environment in India, has been provided by successive enactments and laws. It is a well-known fact that Pandit Nehru had tremendous interest in wildlife, but the honour goes to Indira Gandhi for enacting the Wildlife (Protection) Act, 1972. It is clearly evident from the title of the Act that its main objective is to protect wild animals and birds, particularly rare species, such as the lion and the great horned rhinoceros, which are fast disappearing.

The Wildlife Protection Act was followed by the Water (Prevention and Control of Pollution) Act, 1974. This is another major and significant Act in environmental protection in India. The Act came into force in 12 states. The objective of the Act is to prevent and control water pollution and also to maintain and restore the wholesomeness of water. For achieving the objectives of the Act, provisions were also made for setting up of Central and State Boards for the prevention and control of water pollution.

Of all the environmental problems facing the country, the problem of deforestation has received maximum public attention. In order to accommodate diverse interests associated with forest resources, under the changed socio-economic and political environment after independence, the Forest (Conservation) Act, 1980 was passed by the government. Under the Act, the Central government can constitute an Advisory Committee to advise the government regarding grants of approval under Section 2 and any other matter connected with the conservation of forests which may be referred to it by the Central government. The Central government makes rules for carrying out the provisions of the Act.

The Air (Prevention and Control of Pollution) Act, 1981, is another important Act which has been passed by the Government of India. The Act makes provision for the prevention, control and abatement of air pollution, for the establishment of Boards for conferring powers and functions relating thereto for matters connected therewith. These Boards have been empowered to establish air laboratories, to enable them to perform their functions efficiently.

The Bhopal Gas Tragedy of 1984 led to speedy progress towards environmental protection in the 1980s. The Environment (Protection) Act, 1986 was framed to prevent another such mishappening. The Act was passed for the following objectives: protections, regulation of discharge of environmental pollutants, handling of hazardous substances, speedy response in the event of accidents threatening the environment and giving deterrent punishment to those who endanger human environment safety and health. This is a more effective and bold measure to fight the problem of pollution as compared to all the previous laws in this regard.

The National Environment Tribunal Act, 1995, was enacted in 1995 in view of the fact that civil courts litigations take a long time (as happened in the Bhopal case).The Act was to provide strict liabilities for damages arising out of any accident occurring while handling any hazardous substance and for the establishment of a National Environment Tribunal for the effective and expeditious disposal of cases arising from any such accidents. The main objective of the Act is to give relief and compensation for damage to person, property and the environment.

The year 2011 is distinctive for the establishment of the National Green Tribunal (NGT) by the Ministry of Environment and Forest under the National Green Tribunal Act 2010 for the effective and expeditious disposal of cases relating to environmental protection and conservation of forests and other natural resources including the enforcement of any legal rights relating to the environment and giving relief and compensation for damages to persons and property and for matters connected therewith or incidental thereto. It is a specialized body equipped with the necessary expertise to handle environmental disputes involving multi-disciplinary issues. The Tribunal shall not be bound by the procedures laid down under the Code of Civil Procedure, 1908, but shall be guided by principles of natural justice. The Tribunal's dedicated jurisdiction in environmental matters shall provide speedy environmental justice and help reduce the burden of litigation in the higher courts.

The coming into force of the NGT Act implied an automatic repeal of two existing laws: the National Environment Tribunal Act 1995 and the National Environment Appellate Authority Act, 1997, and therefore, the closure of the National Environment Appellate Authority (NEAA)—a quasi-judicial body empowered to hear appeals against environmental approvals granted (or not) to projects. All the cases pending before the NEAA were to be heard by the NGT.

In pursuance to the International Convention on Biological Diversity (CBD), to which India was a signatory, the Biological Diversity Act, 2002 was notified in 2004. It addresses the access to biological resources and associated traditional knowledge to ensure equitable sharing of benefits arising out of their use to the country and its people. It included provisions like the prohibition on transfers of Indian genetic material outside the country without specific approvals of the Indian government; prohibition on anyone claiming an Intellectual Property Right (IPR), such as a patent, over biodiversity or related knowledge, without the permission of the Indian government; regulation of collection and use of biodiversity by Indian nationals, while exempting local communities from such restrictions; measures for sharing benefits from the use of biodiversity. It is a major legislative intervention to empower local communities by involving them in the protection of the biodiversity around them.

The Recycled Plastic Manufacturing and Usage Rules, 1999 prohibits vendors of foodstuffs from packing their wares in bags or containers made from recycled plastics. If foodstuffs are to be sold in plastic bags, the carry bags must be made of virgin plastic. The rules also specify that all carry bags must have a minimum thickness of 20 microns. The thin bags clog drains and gutters, preventing the flow of sewage and storm water. This causes floods in the city streets. In 2000, the Noise Pollution (Regulation and Control) Rules came into effect. These rules prescribe ambient air quality standards in respect of noise for industrial, commercial and residential areas as well as identified 'silence zones'.

India is party to the Montreal Protocol on substances that deplete the ozone layer. These are substances such as chlorofluorocarbons (CFCs) used in refrigerators. The production and consumption of such substances are to be phased out as per the Protocol. In this regard, the Government of India formulated the Ozone Depleting Substances (Regulations) Rules, 2000, the main features of which are:

1. Restriction on the production levels of ozone depleting substances (ODS) and annual reductions specified.
2. Ban on creating new capacity or expansion of capacity to manufacture ODS.
3. Exports restricted to countries who are signatories to the Montreal Protocol.

4. Ban on capacity expansion or setting up a new facility for the production of ODS based equipment.
5. No import or export of ODS or ODS based equipment without a licence (Rajagopalan 2008, 91).

Keeping in mind the emerging environmental scenario and to strengthen and make the existing laws more comprehensive, the Ministry of Environment and Forest prepared a draft in 2004 for the New Environment Policy of India which finally became effective in 2006 as the National Environment Policy (NEP), 2006. Its preamble says that it seeks to extend the coverage, and fill in gaps that still exist, in light of present knowledge and accumulated experience. It does not displace, but builds on the earlier policies. Sustainable development concerns in terms of enhancements of human well-being, broadly conceived, are a recurring theme in India's development philosophy. The present day consensus reflects three foundational aspirations. First, human beings should be able to enjoy a decent quality of life. Second, humanity should become capable of respecting the finiteness of the biosphere. Third, that neither the aspiration for a good life, nor the recognition of biophysical limits should preclude the search for greater justice in the world. The NEP is also a response to India's commitment to a clean environment, mandated in the Constitution in Articles 48 A and 51 A (g), strengthened by the judicial interpretation of Article 21. It is recognized that maintaining a healthy environment is not the state's responsibility alone, but also that of every citizen. A spirit of partnership should thus be realized throughout the spectrum of environmental management in the country. While the state must galvanize its efforts, there should also be recognition by each individual—natural or institutional—of its responsibility towards maintaining and enhancing the quality of the environment. The preamble of the NEP, 2006 sets the following objectives:

1. To protect and conserve critical environmental resources.
2. To ensure equitable access to environmental resources for all sections of society and in particular of poor communities, who are most dependent on environmental resources.
3. To ensure judicious use of environmental resources.
4. To integrate environmental concerns into policies, plans, programmes and projects for economic and social development.
5. To apply the principles of good governance to the management and regulation of the use of environmental resources.
6. To enhance resources for environmental conservation (GOI 2006, 8).

The objectives stated above are to be realized through various strategic interventions by different public authorities at the Central, state and local government levels. The following principles may, accordingly, guide the activities of different actors in relation to this policy:

1. Human beings are at the centre of sustainable development.
2. Environmental protection is an integral part of the development process.
3. Services of environmental resources are to be given economic value.
4. Polluters have to pay for the loss to the environment.
5. Public participation in environmental decision-making (GOI 2006, 10).

The Scheduled Tribes and Other Traditional Forest Dwellers (Recognition of Forest Rights) Act, 2006 is a key piece of forest legislation passed in India on 18 December 2006. It has also been called the Forest Rights Act or the Tribal Rights Act. The law concerns the rights of forest-dwelling communities to land and other resources, denied to them over decades as a result of the continuance of colonial forest laws in India. Supporters of the Act claim that it will redress the 'historical injustice' committed against forest dwellers, while including provisions for making conservation more effective and transparent. The demand for the law has seen massive national demonstrations involving hundreds of thousands of people.

The Act as passed in 2006 has the following basic provisions:

1. Right to hold and live in the forest land for habitation or for self-cultivation for livelihood by forest dwelling scheduled tribe or other traditional forest dwellers.
2. Right of ownership, access to collect, use and dispose of minor forest produce.
3. Other community rights for uses of entitlements such as fish and other products of water bodies, grazing and traditional seasonal resource access of nomadic or pastoralist communities.
4. Rights including community tenures of habitat and habitation for primitive tribal groups and pre-agriculture communities.
5. Right to protect, regenerate or conserve or manage any community forest resource which they have been traditionally protecting and conserving for sustainable use.
6. Right of access to biodiversity and community rights to intellectual property and traditional knowledge related to the biodiversity and cultural diversity.

Thus, the Forest Rights Act, 2006 makes provisions for the ownership over land that is being farmed by tribal or forest dwellers, rights of local people to minor forest produce, to grazing areas, to pastoralist routes, etc., the provision of rehabilitation in case of illegal eviction or forced displacement and gives forest management rights to the local people to protect forests and wildlife.

JUDICIAL RESPONSE TO ENVIRONMENTAL ISSUES IN INDIA

The proceeding section clearly shows that the Government of India has taken a number of steps in the constitutional, legal and administrative fields, in order to protect the environment from further degradation and pollution. In spite of such efforts made on part of both the Central and state governments, the problem of environmental degradation and pollution has not been controlled to the extent to which it possibly can be. A number of reasons are responsible for this. First, most provisions of the administrative and legislative laws remain only on paper, or are twisted out of shape during their implementation. Second, lack of proper coordination and cooperation among the administrative institutions is an important loophole in the whole institutional setup. A further weakness of the present official programme for environmental protection is its lack of recognition of the crucial role that NGOs can play in complementing the government's own efforts. From the legislation point of view, loopholes in the Environment Protection Acts hinder the progress of implementation.

As the executive has repeatedly failed to secure environmental safety and protection, people seek redressal from the judiciary. So, the judiciary has strenuously endeavoured over the past two decades to bring in laws for the service of the poor and disadvantaged sections of society. In the early 1980s, the role of the higher judiciary in India underwent a transformation. A new and radically different kind of case altered the litigation landscape. Instead of being asked to resolve private disputes, the Supreme Court and High Court judges were asked to deal with public grievances over flagrant human right violations by the state or to vindicate the public policies embodied in statutes or constitutional provisions. This new type of judicial business is collectively called as 'Public Interest Litigation' (PIL). Most environmental actions in India fall within this class.

PUBLIC INTEREST LITIGATION IN ENVIRONMENTAL CASES

Our Judiciary has exhibited an enlightened judicial creativity and foresight whenever it has had an opportunity to decide issues relating to the environment. A survey of the numerous judgements of the High Courts and the Supreme Court shows that most of the technical hindrances have been brushed aside by devising new tools of legal interpretation and construction.

The landmark judgement of the Supreme Court in the *Ratlam Municipality vs Vardhichand*[1] is representative of the new outlook of the judiciary towards environmental conservation. In this case, the Supreme Court laid down two founding principles. One, that no municipality in India can put forth lack of money as a ground for not discharging its primary duty of looking after the health and safety of its residents. Two, the absence of public conveniences and the prevention of industrial pollutants to the detriment of citizens health are violations of the human rights of decency and dignity which are non-negotiable first charges on a municipality.

In the Dehradun Quarrying case,[2] for the first time, the Supreme Court held that the fundamental right to a wholesome environment is a part of the fundamental right to life in Article 21 of the Constitution. The question of water pollution, especially that of the river Ganga came up before the Supreme Court in the case of *M. C. Mehta vs Union of India*.[3] This river passes through the industrial belt of three states and most of the industries are tanneries and leather industries. The Supreme Court ordered the closure of thirty tanneries in Kanpur which were releasing untreated effluents into the river Ganges. The court recognized that the closure of the tanneries might cause unemployment, but held 'life, health and ecology have greater importance to the people'.

The judiciary has come up to its judicial activism by giving new dimensions to the right of life and personal liberty, guaranteed by Article 21 of the Constitution. The right to healthy environment has been made and construed as a fundamental right by the apex court of the country while deciding various public interest cases filed by the enviro-legal expert Mr M. C. Mehta. Article 21 which gives the right to 'life' includes all attributes which are necessary for the enjoyment of life. In the *Munn vs People of Illinois*,[4] it was pointed out that by term 'life' something more is meant than mere animal existence. Pollution causes permanent disabilities leading to the malfunctioning or non-functioning of the vital organs of the body, which reduces a person to a mere animal existence and thereby denies him the right to life.

M. C. Mehta vs Union of India (Supra18.464) is yet another milestone of judicial concern to environmental protection. The Supreme Court, inter alia pointed out:

1. The Government should evolve a national policy for the location of chemicals and other hazardous industries in areas where the population is scarce and there is little risk to the community and care should be taken to minimize the pollution.
2. The Government of India should set up an Ecological Science Group consisting of independent, professionally competent experts in different branches of science and technology who would act as an information bank for the court and generate new information according to the particular requirements.
3. Environmental Courts should be set up with one professional judge and two experts drawn from the Ecological Science Research Group.
4. A principle of absolute liability should be there to compensate the harm caused to persons due to environmental pollution.
5. The measure of compensation must be correlated with the magnitude and capacity of the enterprise because such compensation must have a deterrent effect. This will also be in consonance with the legislative intention when provided with increased maximum punishment in the Environment Protection Act, 1986 for its violation.

In the Bhopal Gas Tragedy case, the Supreme Court also played a vital role. It showed its deepest concern for the life and liberty of the people which was affected by the leakage of the poisonous gas resulting into the pollution of the environment, affecting adversely the health of millions, the death of many and incapacitating lives forever. In *Union Carbide Corporation vs Union of India,*[5] the court directed the Government to immediately provide interim relief for the victims of the gas tragedy which was directed to be released in May 1993 under the directions of the Government of India to the Reserve Bank of India. The Court directed the Union Carbide Corporation to pay a sum of US$470 million to the Union of India in full settlement of all claims and liabilities related to and arising out of the Bhopal gas leakage disaster. The Supreme Court considered it a compelling duty, both judicial and humane, to secure immediate relief to the victims. The court held that the right to live in a healthy environment cannot be violated by anyone under the plea that if any harm is caused then the injured party shall be suitably compensated. The right to live in a healthy environment is supreme.

Environmental pollution is also caused by stone crushing activities and thus affects the right of citizens to fresh air and to live in a pollution free environment. Thus, in the *M. C. Mehta vs Union of India,*[6] the Supreme Court issued directions for stopping mechanical stone crushing activities in and around the Delhi, Faridabad and Ballabhgarh complexes. Keeping in view the sustainable development, directions were also issued for the allotment of sites in the new 'Crushing Zone' set up at village Pali in the state of Haryana to the stone crushers who were directed to stop their activities in the Delhi, Faridabad and Ballabhgarh complexes.

A historic judgement was delivered by the Supreme Court in the Delhi Gas Leak Case (*M. C. Mehta vs Union of India*) (Mathew 2000, 14). The petitioner had alleged the infringement of the right to life of several thousand people due to the severe polluting and hazardous activities of the Shri Ram Food and Fertilizers, manufacturing oleum and chlorine, situated in the heart of the city of Delhi. The Supreme Court ordered the management to pay compensation to the victims of the oleum gas leak. It allowed the partial operation of the plant after laying down several conditions to ensure maximum safety of the workers and the community living in the surroundings. Thus the Court not only widened the scope of Article 21 by including in it the protection of the environment but also included a liability in tort for those harmed by the pollution.

The Supreme Court has shown its deep concern regarding vehicular pollution in Delhi. In the *M. C. Mehta vs Union of India,*[7] the Supreme Court pointed out that keeping in view the mandate of Articles 47 and 48 A of the Constitution of India, it had issued directions from time to time with a view to tackle the problems arising out of chaotic traffic conditions and vehicular pollution in Delhi. However, the Court was distressed to find that the directions given by the Supreme Court from time to time did not evoke the response they were expected to. While giving the directions, the Court had treated it as a legal issue and proceeded to examine the impact of the right following from Article 21 of the Constitution vis-à-vis a decline in environmental quality. The Supreme Court pointed out that the directions issued by it were meant to be compiled with and emphasized that it was the obligation of the state to comply with the same. The Court also directed the 'Environment Pollution (Prevention and Control) Authority for the National Capital Region', constituted on 7 January 1998 under the chairmanship of Shri Bhurelal, to control vehicular pollution and connected matters and to submit a report about the action taken by it. The Authority proposed certain measures for the immediate improvement of the air quality and gave a time frame for long term improvements.

The Supreme Court in order to control vehicular pollution in Delhi said that the following steps should be taken immediately as delivered by its Order dated 28 July 1998:

1. Implementation of directions to restrict the plying of commercial vehicles including taxis, which are 15 years old, by 2 October 1998,

2. Restrictions on the plying of goods vehicles during day time to be strictly enforced by 15 August 1998,
3. Expansion of pre-mixed oil dispensers (Petrol and 2T oil) to be undertaken by 31 December 1998 and,
4. Ban on supply of loose 2T oils at petrol stations and service garages to be enforced by 31 December 1998.[8] These directions have already been complied with. The Supreme Court approved the directions given and the time frame fixed by the Shri Bhurelal Committee. The Court further directed that the above mentioned time frame would be strictly adhered to by all the authorities who would also take effective and adequate steps to bring to the notice of the public, both through the print and electronic media, the various directions issued by the Court from time to time. The Supreme Court cautioned all concerned that any failure to abide by any of the aforesaid directions would invite action under the Contempt of Courts Act, 1971, against the defaulters.

Thus, during the course of litigation, the Supreme Court shifted its focus from one scheme to another. In 1990, the emphasis was on the prosecution of defaulters. In 1991, the Court was anxious to have buses of the Delhi Transport Corporation converted from diesel to gas operation. In early 1992, the Court's attention shifted to bringing down emissions from public buses. Throughout 1994, the Court exerted pressure on the government to ensure that new vehicles are fitted with catalytic converters and that lead free petrol was introduced in the four metros by April, 1995. Thereafter the Court monitored the extension of the unleaded petrol distribution network and obtained assurances from the Centre in respect of reductions in the lead content of petrol and the notification of the year 2000 emission norms. In late 1996 and 1997, the Court pressed the Central government to convert its vehicles to operate on cleaner fuel, that is, Compressed Natural Gas (CNG) and also sought technical solutions to reduce harmful emissions from two and three wheelers and diesel trucks and buses. In 1999, the Court required all private vehicles registered after 1 June, 1999 to conform to the Euro I norms and those registered after 1 April, 2000 to meet the Euro II norms. Diesel takers were prohibited in the National Capital Region (NCR) unless they conformed to the Euro II norms.

In 1985, Mehta moved the Supreme Court, seeking direction to relocate 1,200 polluting industries away from Delhi. Mehta was appalled to see that contrary to the provisions of the Master Plan of Delhi, formulated in 1962, industrial units were operating in residential and non-conforming areas and causing pollution to the environment. Estimates placed the number of units at over 127,000. At least 10 per cent of these units were hazardous industries. The Master Plan of Delhi became the basis for the judgement delivered by a division bench on 8 July 1996 (and later on 6 and 9 October 1996) stating that:

1. 168 hazardous industries be moved from Delhi to suitable locations in the NCR, or closedown by 3 November 1996.
2. 513 and 334 units operating in residential and non-conforming areas be relocated between 30 January and 30 June 1997.
3. The Delhi administration ensure that 39,000 units, operating in non-conforming areas, be either relocated or closed down.

As a result of the Supreme Court order, 168 hazardous/large industries were closed/relocated by November 1996 and further, more than one lakh units operating in the non-conforming areas were also closed/relocated from Delhi.

The above mentioned judgements make it clear that the judiciary has exhibited its dynamism in evolving new dispensations to tackle the problem of pollution control. The doctrine of public interest litigation, replacement of the punitive sentencing policy with a new sentencing policy based on affirmative action, judicial search for less harmful alternatives of economic development plans, its attempts to encourage social activists to enforce social rights through cost awarding techniques are part of the new judicial activism.

The landmark judgements and orders of the Supreme Court have triggered a wave of environmental consciousness in the country. The striking features in all these cases have been the Court's attempts at encouraging petitions to utilize the instrument of Public Interest Litigation (PIL) for energizing the judiciary to play a more interventionist role in areas where the country's executive had failed to act. Judicial revolution in the field of environmental litigation has taken away in its sweep, out-mode doctrines and fashioned new remedies and strategies to fight environmental onslaughts. The law of public nuisance has been sharpened as a powerful weapon to promote public health and safety. The right to clean environment has been recognized as a part of the right to life guaranteed under the constitution.

CIVIL SOCIETY AND ENVIRONMENTAL GOVERNANCE IN INDIA

Another significant feature of Indian environmental governance is the role of the civil society in making people aware and involved in environmental protection. We can see the role of civil society in the Chipko Movement, Narmada Bachao Andolan, Anti-Tehri Dam protest, Chilka Bachao Andolan, Appiko and Silent Valley Andolan in South India. The main demand of these movements has been to protect the rights of the local masses over their *jal*, *jamin* and *jangal*. Civil society has attacked the anti-people policies of the government and awakened the masses about the destruction of the environment. The following section discusses some of the important environmental movements led by civil society in India.

Chipko Movement

The origin of modern environmental movements in India can be ascribed to the Chipko Movement in the central Himalayan region in the early 1970s. This movement was basically a people's movement to resist the cutting of trees. There were frequent floods in the Alaknanda river catchment area due to the cutting trees for developmental work like the construction of roads, river dam projects, etc. The people of village Gopeshwar formed an association called the Dasholi Gram Swarajya Mandal in 1970 mainly to provide relief to flood affected people in that area.

The origin of chipko (to hug) took place in early 1973 when the Forest Department refused to allot ash trees to the Dasholi Gram Swarajya Sangha (DGSS), a local cooperative organization based in Chamoli district, for making agricultural implements. On the other hand, the forest department allotted ash trees to a private company, that is, Symonds Co. This incident provoked the DGSS to fight against this injustice through lying down in front of timber trucks and burning resin and timber depots as were done during the Quit India movement. When these methods were found unsatisfactory, Chandi Prasad Bhat, one of the leaders, suggested the embracing of trees and thus 'chipko' was born. The local people considered chipko as a fight for the basic subsistence, denied to them by institutions and policies of the state (Guha 1989). This form of protest was instrumental in driving away the private company felling the ash trees. With its success, the movement spread to other neighbouring areas and then onwards the movement has been popularly known as the Chipko Movement internationally.

The Chipko Movement with its wide following and success can be termed as a watershed in environmental movements in India. It kindled the environmental aspects of development and gave rise to numerous conflicts and protests over natural resources and ecological issues. It helped to understand the close links between the livelihoods of the local people and the environment. It also signified the role of the local people, especially women, in protecting and conserving their environment.

Silent Valley Movement

An NGO in Kerala called the Kerala Sasthra Sahitya Parishad (KSSP) raised their voice to stop the Silent Valley Hydral Project in 1978. Silent valley is rich in tropical forests with enormous bio-reserves. The state government of Kerala wanted a hydroelectric project for the power hungry state inside a deep tropical forest in Silent Valley. This tropical forest was the only remaining one in the country. Environmentalists objected to the project and field a case in the High court, which they lost. However the movement raised an important issue and got the support of the public and the media and finally with the intervention of Mrs Indira Gandhi, the project was cancelled by the state government. It proved a milestone in protecting the ecological balance of the valley.

Narmada Bachao Andolan

This is one of the most popular movements in the environmental history of India. It was started to protest against the construction of dams (around 30 in number) on the river Narmada to produce hydroelectricity and provide irrigation facilities to the drought prone areas of Gujarat and Rajasthan. It was estimated that the construction of two big dams on the river Narmada would cost ₹30,923 cores and ₹8,190 cores by way of environmental loss. Besides this the project would submerge about 130,482 hectares of which 55,681 hectares were prime agricultural land and 56,066 hectares were forests. The two dams namely the Sardar Sarovar Project and the Narmada Sagar Project would have enormous utilities to the people in terms of the supply of electricity and irrigation but the estimated environmental costs were too much to ignore according to the report by environment scientist. It was estimated that more than 1 lakh people of 248 villages would be displaced by the project. Nearly 57 per cent of these people are tribal constituting 8 per cent of India's population.

Protests against the Sardar Sarovar Project started in the late 1970s, along with the clearance of the project, but received momentum only during the late 1980s. The pro-tribal Narmada Bachao Andolan (NBA) founded by Medha Patekar in 1989, has effectively exposed the ecological implications of the dam and the lacunae in the resettlement and rehabilitation policies of the government. During its earlier phase, the main demand of the NBA was complete stopping of the dam, but later on it focussed on reducing the height of the dam and a proper resettlement and rehabilitation policy for the displaced people. The movement gained wider public attention with the mobilization and organization of oustees, mostly tribal and the joining of eminent social workers like Baba Amte and Sunderlal Bahuguna. The movement succeed in getting international support which forced the World Bank to withdraw funding of the project. This may be termed as only a partial success of the movement as the ultimate success lies in convincing or pressuring the government to stop the project with people's support which is most unlikely in the present socio-economic conditions in India.

Appiko Movement

It was started in 1983 by the people of Balegadde village, Uttar Kannada district in Karnataka state. This district is a part rich forest of the Western Ghats. The people of this village protested the cutting of teak trees using the Chipko way of embracing the trees. The activists spread the movement throughout the region through *padayatras*, meetings, folk dances, etc. The movement mainly focused on the need to conserve and grow trees. This movement has played a crucial role in preserving the environment and ecosystem of Western Ghats.

Besides the above, there have been a number of other environmental initiatives and movements led by civil society in India. These include the Chilka Bachao Andolan for people's traditional rights over natural resources in Odisha, the Beej Bachao Andolan (Save Seed Movement) for protecting biodiversity, the Anti-Tehri Dam Movement for protecting the ecology and preventing people's displacement in the Garhwal region of Uttarakhand, the Rain Harvesting Movement by Tarun Bharat Sangh in Rajasthan, the Ganga Mukti Andolan for making the river Ganga pollution-free in Bhagalpur district of Bihar and the Pani Panchayat in Maharashtra for conserving soil and water. All these are the success stories of local people protecting their environment.

Thus, since the 1970s, a number of grassroots environmental initiatives and movements have been organized in India by civil society. They force us to think about alternative ways of harnessing natural resources to ensure ecological sustainability and social equity in society. These environmental movements have emerged as new forms of social movements that have successfully linked the degradation of nature with the survival of the masses. These movements challenge the present model of development which has been responsible not only for environmental destruction but also displacing the common masses.

CONCLUDING OBSERVATIONS

Governance of the natural environment in the world of today has emerged as, arguably, one of the most complex challenges ever faced by humanity. The variety of environmental changes generated by human activities, from the local to the global levels, are not new. However, the magnitude of the diverse changes and the resulting impacts on the functioning of the natural ecosystem's processes have grown very rapidly over the past two centuries, and more so in the second half of the last century. The Stockholm Conference on Human Environment in 1972 turned out to be a watershed event in the recognition of the challenges in environmental governance by the global community. Since then, the environment has got increasingly internalized in the governance agenda at all spatial levels of governance.

India was one of the participants of the Stockholm Conference (1972), the first international meeting on environmental protection, which shows its consciousness to environmental issues. There can be little doubt that the Indian state has since independence passed a number of laws, rules and regulations to protect the environment. India is one of the very few nations in the world which has enshrined in its Constitution a commitment to environmental protection and improvement. Despite these initiatives of the government and the constitutional provisions, the problems of air, water and noise pollution are on the increase. The main reason for this is the non-implementation of provisions to protect the environment.

Over the past four decades, the Indian Supreme Court has not only played a significant role in environmental protection, it has also secured a firm foothold in the environmental governance arena. The environmental judgements of the Court, in many cases, have had significant impacts on the overall environmental governance processes in India. Judicial activism, particularly in recent times, has given new direction to the protection and improvement of the environment.

REVIEW QUESTIONS

1. What are the significant environmental issues in India?
2. Air pollution is a big environmental challenge in India. Discuss.
3. What are the main provisions of the Indian Constitution regarding environmental protection? Discuss.
4. Discuss the important laws framed by the Indian government for environmental protection.
5. Do you justify the role of the Indian judiciary in environmental protection? Examine.
6. Public Interest Litigation has become an important tool of the judiciary to protect the environment in India. Discuss.
7. Write a short note on the 'Chipko' Movement.
8. Critically examine the role of civil society in environmental protection in India.
9. Write a note on the debate of Development vs Environment in India.
10. Write an essay on environmental governance in India.

NOTES

1. AIR (All India Reporter). 1980. SC 1622. *Ratlam Municipality vs Vardhichand.*
2. AIR. 1985. SC652. *Rural Litigation and Entitlement Kendra Dehradun vs State of UP.*
3. AIR. 1987. SC463. *M. C. Mehta vs Union of India.*
4. AIR. 1988. SC236. *Munn vs People of India.*
5. AIR. 1990. SC273. *Union Carbide Corporation vs Union of India.*
6. Supreme Court Cases. 1992. SCC256. *Mehta vs Union of India.*
7. AIR. 1998. SC62. *M. C. Mehta vs Union of India.*
8. Mehta. 1985. *M. C. Mehta vs Government of India*, Writ Petition (civil) Ho.13029 of 1985.

REFERENCES

Basu, D. D. 1998. *Introduction to the Constitution of India*. New Delhi: Prentice-Hall of India.

Chand, Prakash. 2013. Urban Growth and its Impact on Environment and Public Health: A Study of Delhi. New Delhi: Urban India: A Journal of the National Institute of Urban Affairs.

CPCB (Central Pollution Control Board). 2013. *Status of Water Quality in India 2011*. Ministry of Environment and Forests, Government of India, New Delhi.

CSE (Centre for Science and Environment). 1982. *The State of the Environment, 1984–85*. New Delhi.

———. 2013. *Good News and Bad News: Clearing the Air in Indian Cities*. New Delhi.

———. 2014. *A Down to Earth Annual State of India's Environment 2014*. New Delhi.

GNCT Delhi (Government of National Capital Territory of Delhi). 2001. *Eco-club Teachers' Manual*. Department of Environment, Forest and Wild Life, Government of India, New Delhi.

GOI (Government of India). 2006. *National Environment Policy 2006*. Ministry of Environment and Forest, Government of India, New Delhi.

Guha, Ramchandra. 1989. *The Unquiet Woods: Ecological Change and Peasant Resistance in the Himalaya.* New Delhi: Oxford University Press.

Jain, Ashok K. 2005. *Law and Environment.* Delhi: Ascent Publications.

Mathew, P. D. 2000. *For Ensuring a Safe Environment Law against Pollution.* New Delhi: Indian Social Institute.

Rajagopalan, R. 2008. *Environmental Education.* New Delhi: Oxford University Press.

TERI (Tata Energy Research Institute). 2001. *State of Environment Report for Delhi.* TERI, New Delhi.

The Noise Pollution (Regulation and Control) Rules. 2000. Ministry of Environment and Forest, Government of India, New Delhi.

TOI (The Times of India). 2001. 'The Birds have Flown the Banks of the River'. New Delhi, 7 June.

Major Issues in Indian Administration

15

PART I
CONCEPTUAL ISSUES

Generalist versus Specialist Debate

LEARNING OBJECTIVES

1. To explain the generalist versus specialist debate in public administration.
2. To understand the debate in the Indian context.

Public administration is the government in action. And governance requires both generalists and specialists; otherwise, its main goal shall always remain distant. In the light of such an argument, any distinction or separation between the generalists and the specialists seems to be futile. Given the growing complexities of contemporary public administration, the distinction is hardly meaningful so far as actual governance is concerned. So, the fundamental question that needs to be asked is whether the attempted separation is mere cosmetic or whether serves any purpose in re-conceptualizing public administration in the prevalent socio-economic context. A reality check reveals that an administrator who is professionally tuned needs to combine both the generalist as well as the specialized functions to fulfil what he/she is expected to do. For instance, in case of formulating a policy, an administrator is required to draw on specific inputs which are distinctly specialized; while implementing the same he/she needs to be a coordinator which is an important generalist function. As a coordinator of a department, his/her role remains critical in pursuing any course of action which is to be endorsed not only by the staff at various levels of governance, but also by the targeted beneficiaries. Here, in other words, the generalist experience as a manager is immensely significant in guiding a specific course for the administrative feat. While formulating a decision, an administrator will invariably need to be acquainted with the complex dimensions of the decisions which he/she is likely to take in a specific context; and for that not only he/she needs specialized knowledge, but is also required to draw on what appears to be critical to arriving at informed decisions. The moot point here relates to actual administrative functioning which cannot be understood, let alone grasped, without reference to the dialectical interconnection between the generalist and specialized aspects of public administration. There are two issues that need to be addressed to understand the distinction in specific socio-economic contexts: while, on the one hand, the discussion shall focus on the feasibility of such a distinction in an actual administrative setup; it will also, on the other hand, dwell on the specific Indian situation, which, despite having endeavoured to shake off the colonial hangover, has so far, failed to completely abdicate past influences in administration. This is not to suggest that the Indian administration is colonial in nature even after attaining political freedom in 1947, but to argue that given the pronounced structural continuity and its inbuilt tendency to remain 'aloof' from the wider socio-economic milieu, the Indian public administration does not seem to have been entirely transformed even after more than six decades of decolonization.

CONCEPTUAL AND EMPIRICAL ROOTS

The distinction needs to be grappled within socio-economic terms meaning that arguments in favour of either the generalists or the specialists be made keeping in view their relative importance in governance. In other words, in conceptualizing the distinction, the context remains most critical. It is therefore not odd to find that the generalists gained salience in colonized India where the British state required the generalists to discharge the twin functions of maintaining law and order and collecting and generating revenue, thereby abdicating other responsibilities almost completely, for obvious reasons. The situation had hardly changed as the generalists enabled the colonial powers to fulfil their primary objectives, disregarding completely the colonized with its iron-fist rule.

So, British colonialism strengthened arguments for the generalists for the obvious benefits that they had reaped while in governance. A product of the contemporary socio-economic milieu which endangered colonialism and its cohorts, the generalists remained an important cog in the administrative machinery that not only supported colonialism, but also created an environment in which they gained credibility primarily for their utility in governance. Furthermore, they gradually became indispensable for the administration as they continued to provide a framework of governance which was most effective despite being challenged by the nationalists during the freedom struggle.

In contrast with the British system, the American public administration endorsed specialists in governance. America needed specialists who were endowed with specialized skills to manage a vast country which did not have any format of governance that was complementary to its growth as a nation. By recruiting a corps of specialists, the administration prepared a specific design that remained integral to the democratic ethos of the government. The preference for specialists was thus guided by the felt need of the state that pursued an agenda of development and growth with their support. How then is the coordination between the political executive and the specialists affected? Here, the role of the Constitution and other statutory provisions come to play critical roles in putting things on rail. As a commentator has argued, 'in essence, coordination by rules and files was subordinated as a goal to the more preferred objectives of experiment, competition among specialist and innovation in policy and procedure' (Roy 1964, 1059).

It is now evident that the distinction between the generalists and the specialists needs to be understood with reference to the socio-economic circumstances in which they are located; in view of their clear socio-economic roots, their nature cannot be comprehended in isolation. By providing two different conceptualizations of administrators, both the British and American systems of governance remain useful inputs in so far as the general nature of public administration is concerned. One cannot thus make a conclusive argument because the issue of generalists and specialists is clearly context-driven, as is also evident in the context of the French public administration where bureaucrats at the top echelon of administration are always selected on the basis of their specialized knowledge of areas in which they are well-grounded; they are posted in departments, in other words, according to their specialization.

Empirically, the defence for generalists in India was made by reference to the Northcote–Trevelyan Report 1853 on the 'organization of permanent civil service in Britain'. The Report emphasized that the superior position in bureaucracy should be occupied by 'the most promising young men of the day [selected] by a competing examination on a level with the highest description of education in this country' (Northcote–Trevelyan Report, as quoted in Maheswari 1995, 146–47). This was justified further by suggesting in the Report that 'men capable of distinguishing themselves in any of the subjects we have named ... would probably make themselves useful wherever they might be placed' (Northcote–Trevelyan Report, as quoted in Maheswari 1995, 147). The impact of this report was evident in the Macaulay Report 1854 on the Indian Civil Service which emphasized that young men with excellent education, enthralled by the desire for creativity were likely to be superior to those who undertook specialized training in narrow fields. Reflecting the tenor of British liberal education, this was an idea which had run through the Indian civil service since technological differentiation and functional specialization were then relatively underdeveloped.

The impact of the long-drawn colonial rule was evident when the generalist civil service was readily accepted by those who presided over India's destiny after independence despite the opposition of Jawaharlal Nehru in the Constituent Assembly. It was also believed that the elitist bureaucracy comprising principally the generalists remained most competent, given their commitment to Weberian neutrality, in terms of advising the political executive who had just taken charge following the British withdrawal. What ensured their smooth sailing even after the launching of the First Five Year Plan and Community Development Programme in 1952 was their ability to adjust to the changed socio-economic environment. Underlining the need of specialists in administration, the Second Pay Commission (1957–59) sought to strike a balance between the generalists and the specialists as it was of the view that the importance of the generalists and the specialists could never be wished away as public administration was becoming far more complicated as time passed by. Persuaded by this argument, the Estimates Committee, in its 1966 report, suggested that the government should also take adequate steps to appoint specialists in those ministries and departments which required technical expertise; furthermore, the generalists should also take the technical experts into confidence in any decisions affecting administration per se. The generalists, the Committee suggested further, should never indulge in practices which were reflective of their arrogance and meanness.[1]

The intervention of the first Administrative Reforms Commission is perhaps most creative. In its 1969 report on personnel administration, the Commission made a distinction between 'general purpose service' and 'functional service' to denote the generalists and the specialists respectively. Those belonging to the general purpose services remained responsible for coordinating among the departments/ministries and by virtue of their mobility from one department to another during their career, gained expertise which may not have been possible for those, stuck in one particular job. For the specialists, two conditions needed to be met: on the one hand, they needed to have vocational education and also training for the job they were entrusted with, and on the other, they remained stationary since they did not have the required skills for mobility across the board.

CONCLUDING OBSERVATIONS

The debates can never be conclusive. There are persuasive arguments on both sides. For comparativist Fred W. Riggs, structural and functional differentiations are inevitable in development.[2] Such an argument defends the creation and sustenance of specialists in administration especially in those polities which are socio-economically 'underdeveloped' largely due to the lack of proper institutions for growth and development. When social life was simple, the generalists managed to perform tasks efficiently; but with the growing complexities of human existence, it did not seem to be so easy. Hence arguments for the specialists become far stronger than in the past. This was reiterated by the Fulton Committee 1968 which, while suggesting means for improving the British administration, regretted that technical experts, like scientists, engineers and those with specialized training were not given due importance in the administration in view presumably of the obsession for generalists who, with their training, seemed to have been well-equipped to handle any situation irrespective of its gravity (The Report of the Fulton Committee 1968, para 15, as quoted in Arora and Goyal 1995, 559).

The debate gradually lost importance in the 1970s and the distinction was characterized as 'spurious' (Lal 1964, 1357) presumably because of the growing acceptance of specialists in public administration. It was possible largely due to the changes in people's perceptions of administration which has been responsible for inclusive growth in India. A new era ushered in with the consolidation of the idea of a 'committed bureaucracy' which was geared to the socialistic pattern of society in India. In other words, contemporary politics had created an environment in which the issue did not revolve around the relative priority of generalists over specialists, but was focused on development and growth following a politically articulated model of state-led planned economic development. Therefore, conventional thinking on such issues seems to have become redundant in the changed socio-economic environment of economic liberalization when each nation, including India, has been confronted with different kinds of challenges involving not only the nation-states, but also non-state transnational actors. The demand is not for exclusive generalist or specialist cadres of administrators, but a corps that, by combining the qualities of both the generalists and the specialists, puts forward the best that is expected of them. Yehezkel Dror has perhaps made the most perceptive comment which is critical in conceptualizing how the debate has become futile. As he says:

> [T]he required qualities of public administration cannot be achieved by any mixture of 'experts and generalists' in the traditional sense. Only by overcoming this dichotomy not only in discourse, but in action, can we achieve the public administration qualities needed for handling new and difficult problems and for absorbing new very promising and very frightening knowledge under conditions of accelerated social change. We must develop a new breed of top administrators who are experts in a broad approach and experts in the uses of diverse knowledge, and we must achieve a mix between various types of new professionals and administrators who are equipped for symbiotic work. (Dror 1968, 6)

For any administration to function efficiently, what is thus required is a creative blending of the generalist and specialist qualities in a context when the society, economy and polity are intricately enmeshed in perhaps an equally complex socio-economic and political milieu. Instead of hovering on the relative importance of the generalists over the specialists or vice versa, a meaningful debate can be initiated by linking public administration with the prevalent power-relationship in which it is shaped. In other words, since the administration is more than a mere functional instrument of governance, it cannot be meaningfully conceptualized without ascertaining the linkages that it has with the wider environment of politics. Thus, one needs to couch the terms of the debate not in the language of conventional public administration where politics is more or less outlawed, but in the contemporary voice in which governance is understood less in structural terms but more as a process involving stakeholders who are dialectically engaged with the prevalent socio-economic and political order.

Political and Permanent Executive

LEARNING OBJECTIVES

1. To understand conceptually the distinction between political and permanent executives.
2. To comprehend the role of political and permanent executives in India.

In pure conceptual terms, the expression, political executive, refers to politicians who discharge executive roles while permanent executives are civil servants who are recruited through a due process. Also known as temporary executives, political executives bring in values in public administration which their counterparts translate into reality. So, the relationship between political and permanent executives is most intimate and governance remains vacuous if their role is assessed in isolation from each other. In other words, in the articulation of public administration as government in action, both these forms of executives, which are analytically divided, remain integral. Such a distinction may have made sense in the context of simple societies where public administration is conceptualized in institutional terms, ignoring the complex role that the socio-economic milieu plays in its articulation. The idea that public administration cannot be understood, let alone conceptualized, without reference to the socio-economic circumstances in which it is located is thus most fundamental. The roles of the executives, whether political or permanent, have also become far more complicated. This section thus makes two arguments: [a] despite being operational in two domains, in the actual socio-economic context, the distinction between political and permanent executives is clearly analytical and not, at all, realistic, and [b] the more the distinction is stretched, the less is the possibility of a clear understanding of their respective roles in governance.

ROOTS OF THE DEBATE

Despite its analytical validity, to grasp the nature of the two types of executives, one cannot just gloss over the debates over its feasibility as is also supported by the famous article by Woodrow Wilson 1887, entitled 'the study of administration'. Famously known as the dichotomy thesis, Wilson was in favour of compartmentalizing the two domains since they were clearly demarcated vocationally. According to Wilson, permanent executives are responsible for administrative action while political executives engage in implementing constitutional principles through administrative feats. While dividing the sphere of constitutional principles from the administrative domain, he thus argues that 'public administration is detailed and systematic execution of public law. Every particular application of general law is an act of administration ... The broad plans of governmental action are not administrative; the detailed execution of such plan is administrative' (Wilson 1887, 197–222 reproduced in Chakrabarty and Bhattacharya 2005, 94). While the distinction is clearly spelt out, in reality it gets blurred because governance is the outcome of interpenetration between those involved in making policies on the basis of constitutional principles and those who are in charge of their execution as policies. Wilson was aware of this two-way traffic between political and permanent executives, as he observes:

> [T]he study of administration, philosophically viewed, is closely connected with the study of the proper distribution of constitutional authority. To be efficient it must discover the simplest arrangements by which responsibility can unmistakeably fixed upon officials: the best

> way of dividing authority without hampering it, and responsibility without obscuring it. And this question of the distribution of authority, when taken into the sphere of the higher, the originating functions of the government, is obviously a central constitutional question. (Wilson 1887, 197–222, reproduced in Chakrabarty and Bhattacharya 2005, 94)

So, the dichotomy thesis, as Wilson himself clarifies, is clearly misplaced despite the fact that any analytical distinction of the domains of the political and permanent executives does not necessarily mean that they are differently located since they are entrusted with constitution-driven administrative responsibilities. Behind his conceptual separation between the two domains lies the belief that since they required different kinds of expertise, they needed to be treated differently, although in reality, the distinction was just cosmetic and analytical. So, Wilson's argument has two levels: at one level, as a Weberian, he strongly believed in bureaucratic neutrality; but, at another level, he, as a pragmatic administrator, was persuaded to endorse the dialectical interpenetration between the two complementary wings of administration, represented by the political and permanent executives respectively.

DECODING THE DEBATE

Persuaded by the Weberian logic of neutrality, those who presided over India's destiny in the aftermath of decolonization strongly felt that the interference by political executives in administration impeded the fulfilment of socio-economic and political goals that the polity sought to achieve. In tune with the Wilsonnian insistence on administration being demarcated from the political domain, the founding fathers expressed resentment when public affairs were extremely vitiated by excessive snooping by the political masters. As Vallabhbhai Patel (1949) noted most alarmingly that 'certain tendencies and developments in our administration and public affairs fill me with some disquiet and sadness of heart [because] our public life is degenerating'. Despite being partners in governance, the relationship between the permanent and political executive is usually tilted in favour of the latter given that the former generally remains at the mercy of the political authority for plum posts or choice-driven transfers and other benefits. It thus becomes a nexus in which both of them draw mutual benefits by bending rules, regulations or moral codes according to their convenience. Reflecting on this, the first Administrative Reforms Commission (1968) very poignantly wrote:

> [T]here is a disinclination among a quite number of Ministers to welcome frank and impartial advice from the Secretary or his aids and an inclination to judge by his willingness to do what they wish him to do ... This has also bred a tendency on the part of the increasing number of civil servants to attempt to anticipate the Minister's wishes and proffer their advice accordingly. A further development of this unhealthy trend is the emergency of personal affiliations leading to an element of 'politicization' among civil servants. All thus cut at the root of the healthy relationship between the two. (GOI 1968, para 56)

Instead of being coordinators of governance, the civil servants became instruments, as the above report suggests, of personal aggrandizement. Notwithstanding the constitutional guarantee against humiliation, as Article 311 stipulates, the permanent executives preferred to submit when their political masters said so to avoid unnecessary stress and trouble. This was most graphically illustrated by the Shah Commission Report 1977 which inquired into the bureaucratic excesses during the Emergency 1975–77 in India. While critiquing the feudal culture that appeared to have engulfed public life, the Commission attributed the lack of sensitivity, efficiency and accountability in public service to a mindset which justified it appropriate of the public office for private gain. This is perhaps the most appalling development that has destroyed the very foundation of Indian democracy which was hailed at the dawn of independence irrespective of class, clan and ethnicity.

Opposed to the concentration of power in the hands of a few individuals, given that the greed for power destroyed democratic principles, the founding fathers sought to create a framework in which both the political and permanent executives functioned, respecting their respective domains of functioning although this could not be separated into watertight compartments given their organic linkage with governance, they being primarily coordinators and not separate players. This had very definite theoretical implications in the conceptual domain. The traditional concept of bureaucracy being neutral of politics does not seem to be tenable simply because of the complexities of governance which requires interpenetration and not isolation of their respective roles. Political executives or ministers remain most critical in so far as policy making is concerned; but the role of civil servants has also been changing from being mere agents of the political executives to that of collaborators in the articulation and making of policy responses. Furthermore, the classical theory of bureaucratic neutrality presupposes a consensus on values which is almost impossible in a transitional society like India where dissent and conflict happen to be so common and integral in one's day-to-day existence. Hence the argument that neutrality of bureaucracy in the context of India's vibrant democracy does not seem to be plausible and academically penetrating.

HISTORY OF THE FRICTION BETWEEN POLITICAL AND PERMANENT EXECUTIVES

Instance of differences between political and permanent executives are plenty. There are however some striking examples when the differences led to the resignation of the political executive or removal of the civil servant who was involved in a fracas with the former. Some of them are frequently referred to while describing the nature of the relationship between these two partners of governance. One of the first incidents happened to involve the Finance Minister, T. T. Krishnamachari and his principal Finance Secretary, H. M. Patel over the purchase of the share of private companies by the nationalized Life Insurance Corporation, in 1957. The Minister was reported to have kept the Secretary in the dark about the entire deal which the former denied. It had snowballed into a major crisis for the government which was avoided with the resignation of the Minister, followed by the voluntary retirement of the Secretary. In 1966, Gulzari Lal Nanda resigned as the Home Minister by charging the Home Secretary, L. P. Singh of non-cooperation and insisted on his replacement which the Prime Minister never conceded. The Minister felt humiliated and resigned while the Secretary was allowed to continue. History repeated itself in 1971 when the then Railway Minister had a serious disagreement with the Railway Board Chairman, B. C. Ganguly when the former took decisions to change the job profile of the Railway Board Chairman. Since the Minister did not consult the Chairman, it was not acceptable to Ganguly which led to a bitter acrimony between the two. In this case, the Minister's discretion was carried forward and Ganguly was dismissed as the Chairman. Similarly, A. P. Venkateswaran was threatened of dismissal when the Prime Minister Rajiv Gandhi was peeved by his enthusiastic response to a journalist's question over the probable tour schedule of the latter during 1987. To save his face, Venketeswaran rushed a letter of resignation to the ministry and requested immediate relief from his responsibilities.

These examples are dated though they make one point clear that at the dawn of independence, especially during the Nehruvian era of governance, the permanent executives were given adequate protection if a whimsical decision of the minister affected them. This was not the case afterwards, especially in the era of a committed bureaucracy. The ministers or political executives had an upper hand to discipline bureaucrats when they purportedly became less committed to what the political executives decided. As a result, the permanent executives reportedly became mute observers of what their political masters did. The result was noticeable and the permanent executives tended not to raise their voice if they felt strongly against any ministerial decision which was likely to have negative consequences. With their hegemonic control over political authority, the temporary executives exercised their power by resorting to all kinds of punitive measures, including transfer, besides harassment that they were subject to if the ministers' orders went unheeded.

The situation however underwent changes in the coalition era especially since the Fourth General Election 1967 because of the uncertain political environment in which ministers had to interact with their secretaries and other subordinate staff. Political executives were handicapped and so were the permanent executives since the circumstances were so uncertain. It is true that instances of major discord during this era were not witnessed though it had gradually consolidated ministerial grip over the permanent executives except on rare occasions when the civil servants rose to the occasion to challenge the ministers despite the probable adverse consequences on their career and job prospects. Since the General Election 2014, which established a single party rule in India, the scene appears to have changed in which the permanent executives seem to be gauging the depths of the water in the changed environment. Political changes notwithstanding, the tradition seems to be continuing because the government in power is reportedly comfortable with pliable permanent executives, as seen by the recent instances of putting those officers in office who are unquestionably loyal to those holding ministerial assignments. Besides political loyalty, civil servants are also chosen by their political masters on the basis of their ethnic or religious identities disregarding, on various occasions, their professional competence. What is at stake under these circumstances is neither the personal reputation of the political or permanent executives nor the integrity of the system, but the sanctity of the system of governance which becomes a victim for insistence on private gains.

CONCLUDING OBSERVATIONS

As the discussion shows, the domain of politics and administration cannot be demarcated. Hence political and permanent executives cannot be separated in two watertight compartments; they are complementary to each other.

Governance involves cooperation and coordination between them since 'public administration has become a patchwork quilt of complex relationships and numerous decision points besides politics that has a clear bearing' (Self 1981, 4). One needs to be sensitive to this complex interrelationship if one desires to understand contemporary public administration. So, instead of highlighting the domain-conscious public servants, both political and permanent executives, the focus has shifted to interactive executives who have identical concerns in so far as governance is concerned. This also reinforces the fact that a mere technical understanding of public administration in any socio-economic context shall not be rewarding but rather would be self-defeating because it fails to capture the complexities in which governance in its contemporary manifestation is articulated.

In today's India, as elsewhere, public administration has undergone significant metamorphosis in the one-size-fits-all format. Besides those who are directly involved in governance, there are several other agencies which are critical in public decision making. For instance, a vigilant civil society, an ever watchful media and the Right to Information (RTI) Act require that political and permanent executives be held accountable and their actions constantly monitored. An alert judiciary is also there to ascertain that the rule of law is honoured and respected regardless of the circumstances. In the transformed environment, the distinction between permanent and political executives does not seem to be relevant because they are integral to the government machinery. So, the question that has become pertinent is how to get the best out of them in circumstances when the stakeholders cannot be so easily bypassed given the prevalence of instruments like the media, right to information, among others, through which they exercise their control. What we need is not keeping at bay either the politicians or the civil servants, but rather making them aware of their respective roles in rendering public service. This requires significant attitudinal changes which are slow to achieve in a transitional society like India where vested interests are as well-entrenched as the forces challenging them. Nonetheless, here lies the key for noticeable changes in public administration.

Ethics in Governance

LEARNING OBJECTIVES

1. To understand ethics in governance as a conceptual category.
2. To comprehend ethics in governance in India with reference the prevalent socio-economic and political milieu.

The India against Corruption campaign 2011–12 catapulted the issue of ethics in governance to the centre-stage of Indian politics. Demanding the introduction of a Jan Lokpal Bill, the participants came together to campaign for a less corrupt society and united under an octogenarian Anna Hazare. They saw a silver lining since it provoked a mass campaign all over the country. It is true that the movement did not fulfil its goal though it created awareness amongst the people which helped sustain the zeal to fight against malpractices in administration. Besides seeking to achieve its immediate objective, the Anna Hazare campaign once again raised the importance of ethics in governance which has acquired a significant place in contemporary theoretical discussions. This is more so because of the growing decadence in governmental practices largely owing to a decline in ethical values in public administration which perhaps has been singularly responsible for the rise of 'corruption' in a virulent form. The possible reason is located in the overgrowth of the state in which bureaucracy has allegedly become a 'rent-seeker', ignoring its role of being 'a benevolent guardian' or its foundational Weberian role of a 'neutral' dispenser of administration. However one describes the phenomenon, there is no doubt that this is a challenge that involves a thorough analysis of the circumstances and also the outcomes in a historical context because a dwindling of ethics in governance is not an overnight phenomenon, but an offshoot of a long-term process.

STATING THE ISSUE

It is difficult to conclusively define the term 'ethics' which is usually a context-driven conceptualization. Nonetheless, on the basis of the literature on administrative ethics, one can derive a meaningful definition of what ethics is all about. One of the prominent thinkers, FM Marx in his 1949 article in the American Political Science Review sought to conceptualize the idea by linking it with the prevalent political ideology that the machinery of government is expected to translate into social reality. Public administration can thus be viewed as an instrument for attaining the purpose of political order. 'The core of administrative ethics [thus] lies', argued Marx (1949, 1127–28), 'in the ideas that nourish the political system' implying thereby that the administrators are not free to follow their own personal values in the course of their professional activities, but are obligated to be 'conscious agents of a democratic community' and to direct their action 'toward promoting the healthy growth of a free society dedicated to the common good'. Ethics is therefore a set of standards that society places on itself to articulate its responses to societal needs. The mere adoption of rules—the compliance model—cannot inject ethics in human behaviour; what is thus required is also a set of mechanisms to execute rules and regulations by putting in place competent disciplinary agencies to investigate violations and deviations, and also to impose sanctions quickly in firmly promoting a culture of integrity in administration.

HOW WAS THE ISSUE ADDRESSED?

India since independence has set more than 45 committees and commissions to strengthen administrative capabilities by making the administrative machinery efficient and accountable. What began with the Tottenham Committee Report 1946 which also focused on the decline of discipline in the civil service has continued unabated till today. The most comprehensive endeavour ever made in independent India was the appointment of the Administrative Reforms Commission (ARC) in 1966 under the chairmanship of Morarji Desai. Two important ideas seemed to have governed the constitution of this Commission: first, the changing nature of administration—from a mere law and order maintenance agency to an apparatus responsible for development, and second the ideological goal of a socialistic pattern of society calling for a drastic overhauling of the machinery of the government that had so far discharged the responsibility in a very stereotypical manner. So the Commission was given a very wide mandate and was entrusted with the task of giving consideration to 'the need for ensuring the highest standard of efficiency and integrity in public services and for making public administration a fit instrument for carrying out social and economic goals of development as also one which is responsive to the public' (GOI 1966–70).[3] Keeping in view the objective of providing an efficient and corruption free administration, the ARC suggested the following steps:

1. In order to eliminate corruption in the public services, the government should adopt preventive, surveillance and deterrent punishment, and deal ruthlessly with the nexus of officials, criminal elements and venal political functionaries.
2. Rules and legal provisions should be amended to enable immediate and exemplary prosecution and removal of corrupt officials without resource to any political protection.
3. There should be no scope in the rules for any interference in the prompt prosecution and punishment of corrupt public servants, and permissions for such prosecutions should be given within a prescribed period to investigating agencies like the Central Bureau of Investigation where prior approval has already been given.
4. The investigating agencies and vigilance machinery should be strengthened by provisioning of adequate staff, powers, resources and independence accompanied by proper accountability for results. The preventive aspect of corruption in the government or the public sector depends on an independent and well-staffed vigilance setup.
5. Amendments should be formulated to the relevant rules on the lines of those proposed in the rules relating to the All India Services and denial of fair treatment and justice to

people other than those having access to money and influence. That is why there is a strong demand by the people for effective punitive and corrective measures to tackle administrative ills (Vittal 2002).

THE SECOND ADMINISTRATIVE REFORMS COMMISSION, 2005

The first ARC report was probably the most exhaustive check-list of steps to streamline the administration in the changed socio-economic environment. Drawing on certain basic considerations, the most significant recommendation was the appointment of Lokpal (at the union level) and Lokyakuta (at the state level), apart from the introduction of the concept and technique of performance budgeting. Based on the need to reform the civil services, the second Administrative Reform Commission was set up by the Government of India in 2005 under the chairmanship of Veerappa Moily to look into the issues crippling public administration in India. The Commission attributed the visible decline of ethics to a whole range of factors, including the socio-psychological decline of individuals responsible for redrawing India's path for development. In the light of a general degradation of public administration, the Commission thus observed that 'in our case, at times public office is perceived to be an extension of one's property. That is why sometimes, public offices are a source of huge corruption and a means of extending patronage' (GOI 2007, 6). The Commission was thus asked to suggest measures to evolve an efficient administration for the country 'to reverse the slide [in governance] by prescribing stringent standards of probity in public life instead of providing shelter to public figures of suspect integrity' (GOI 2007, Preface). The Commission presented 15 reports to the government for consideration. Among them, the report on *Ethics in Governance* would be of particular interest to all those who clamour for an ethical framework for politics in the country. The Commission, while taking cognizance of the salutary measures introduced in recent years at the prompting of the Supreme Court and a pro-active Election Commission, made a host of recommendations to usher in stability and accountability in the field of politics.

The Report begins with the ethical values in politics.[4] It says that politics and those engaged in it, play a vital role in the legislative and executive wings of the State whose acts of commission and omission in working the Constitution and the rule of law become the point of intervention for the judiciary. While it is unrealistic and simplistic to expect perfection in politics in an ethically imperfect environment, there is no denying the fact that the standards set in politics profoundly influence those in other aspects of governance. Those in politics have a clear and onerous responsibility. India was fortunate that high standards of ethical conduct were an integral part of the freedom struggle. Unfortunately, the ethical capital started getting eroded after the transfer of power. Excesses in elections (in campaign-funding, use of illegitimate money, quantum of expenditure, imperfect electoral rolls, impersonation, booth-capturing, violence, inducements and intimidation), floor-crossing after elections to get into power and abuse of power in public office became major afflictions of the political process over the years. Political parties, governments and more importantly the Election Commission and the Supreme Court took several steps since the late 1980s in an attempt to eliminate the gross abuses that had virtually become the norm. Yet, there is widespread view that much more needs to be done to cleanse our political system. The Commission made the following suggestions to introduce reforms in the political system:

1. A system for partial state funding should be introduced in order to reduce the scope of illegitimate and unnecessary funding of expenditure for elections.

2. The issue of disqualification of members on grounds of defection should be decided by the President/Governor on the advice of the Election Commission.
3. Section 8 of the Representation of the People Act, 1951 needs to be amended to disqualify all persons facing charges related to grave and heinous offences and corruption, with the modification suggested by the Election Commission.

The Constitution should be amended to ensure that if one or more parties in a coalition with a common programme mandated by the electorate either explicitly before the elections or implicitly while forming the government, realign midstream with one or more parties outside the coalition, then Members of that party or parties shall have to seek a fresh mandate from the electorate.

The Commission expressed concern over the decline of social accountability. Hence it was suggested by the Commission that social accountability initiatives be institutionalized; otherwise, they tend to become part of vocabulary with no or less substance. It has thus been argued that 'the impact is greatest and most sustainable when social accountability mechanisms are institutionalized—in other words, embedded with and systematically implemented by a civil society, state or hybrid institution' (Malena, Forster and Singh 2004, 14). As shown, conceptually, social accountability is an effective means to consolidate an environment supportive of drives towards instilling the values of ethics in governance. By creating new effective vertical mechanisms of accountability and strengthening the prevalent devices for horizontal accountability, social accountability can be said to be useful for better governance in which the role of stakeholders is as critical as those officially responsible for translating ideological priorities of the political bosses into legislative decisions. With focus on accountability and the machinery for its inculcation in public life, the Second Administrative Reforms Commission 2005 thus stands out not merely for its penetrating recommendations, but also for creating a momentum for change by raising a debate in the public domain on the dialectical linkages between the decline of ethics in governance and moral decadence of India's social fabric.

CONCLUDING OBSERVATIONS

The discussion of ethics in governance in India demonstrates that the issue has 'a much wider import than what happens in the different arms of government [and] ... an across-the-board effort is [thus] needed to fight deviations from ethical norms' (GOI 2007, 5). Reiterating that mere internal interventions cannot be conclusive in eradicating the source of administrative ills, the second ARC, like its first counterpart, attributed the decline of ethical values in administration to the overall decadence of India's politics since independence. Besides the pernicious impact of colonialism in independent India's administration, there is no denying that public governance has become a casualty largely due to its appropriation by narrow, partisan and sectional interests. Nonetheless, there have been serious endeavours in recent times not only to identify the sources of decadence, but also to device mechanisms for arresting such a decline. One can possibly refer to political institutions like the Election Commission or the Supreme Court of India, amongst others, which have taken several steps since the late 1980s in an attempt to eliminate the sources of the abuse of power by the powerful. Similarly, civil society clamour for cleansing the political system is another seriously pursued endeavour to challenge corruption in public life. These attempts shall yield results in a conducive environment because 'in the long run', as the Shanthanam Committee concludes, 'the fight against corruption will succeed only to the extent to which a favourable social climate is created' (Shantanam 1964, 101). Ethics in governance is thus a goal that will remain elusive unless it is conceptualized and articulated in the overall political environment that critically influences Indian administration and its voice.

Corruption and Administration

LEARNING OBJECTIVES

1. To understand corruption as a conceptual category.
2. To comprehend the nature of corruption in India with reference to wider socio-economic and political processes.

Corruption is endemic in administration since the bureaucracy is usually dubbed as 'a rent-seeking organization'. This is not a modern phenomenon. In his *Arthasastra,* a text that is traced back to the fourth century BC, Kautilya provided a graphic illustration of corruption by saying that 'just as it is impossible not to taste the honey (or the poison) that finds itself at the tip of the tongue, so it is impossible for a government servant not to eat up, at least, a bit of king's revenue' (Kangle 1972, 91). For Kautilya, corruption and administration were integrally linked. In common parlance, corruption means embezzlement of any kind which is not justified by norm, practices or rules. This also includes the use of public office for private gains where an official responsible for public office is engagement in activities for private enrichment. While seeking to define corruption, Carl J. Fredrich (1989) thus elaborates by saying:

> [Corruption is] a kind of behaviour which deviates from the norm actually prevalent or believed to prevail in a given context … It is deviant behaviour associated with a particular motivation, namely that of private gain at public expense … Such private gains may be monetary one, and in the minds of the general public, it usually is, but it may take other forms.

What Fredrich underlines is the fact that corruption is 'deviant behaviour' justifying private gain at public expense. Corruption is thus a transactional evil where a favour is extended in exchange for private benefits.

With such a definition, this segment is devoted to analyzing the corrosive effects of corruption in administration in two interrelated parts: On the one hand, the discussion concentrates on the possible roots of corruption in India, and on the other hand, it deals with those instruments and mechanism that India has evolved to combat corruption. This is however not to suggest that the entire administration is corrupt and vitiated; instead, the argument is couched in the form of queries relating to the insidious impact of the desire for private gains at the cost of taxpayers' money. It is difficult to carry out an exhaustive study of the phenomenon given the space constraint. Hence our aim is to flag-out the basic issues that we consider critical in conceptualizing corruption in the context of a developing country, like India, which is a simultaneously a booming economy as well.

STATEMENT OF THE PROBLEM

Corruption is ubiquitous in India. In 2012, India ranked 94th out of 176 countries in Transparency International's Corruption Preparation Index, along with Columbia, Greece, Mongolia, Senegal and others. In a study, conducted by Transparency International, it was found out that more than 62 per cent of the Indians had paid a bribe or influenced an officer to extract work in public offices successfully (2005, 103). Most of the largest sources of corruption include entitlement programmes and social spending schemes, attached to the Central government, including the Mahatma Gandhi National Rural Employment Guarantee Scheme and the National Rural Health Mission. The other important source of corruption involves the transport industry, especially vehicles that are used to ferry goods across the states, which are forced to pay cash in bribes annually to numerous regulatory and police stops on interstate high ways. This is an open secret and nobody seems to feel bad about it; owners of these vehicles willingly pay to ease-out their movement from one state to another.

While explaining the growing incidence of corruption in India, the Second Administrative Reforms Commission refers to three factors which are also rooted in India's historical past in colonialism: first, colonialism created a mindset that had a propensity to exercise power arbitrarily; second, the prevalence of a huge unorganized sector whose workers are not conscious enough to demand their rights while working; such a workforce can easily be manipulated by those holding positions of authority in public offices; third, factors responsible for corruption-prone mindsets include over-regulation, complicated taxation and licensing systems, numerous government departments with uncontrolled discretionary powers, monopoly by government controlled institutions in certain goods and service delivery and lack of transparent laws and processes.

HOW TO COMBAT CORRUPTION?

This is too difficult a question to respond to in categorical terms because so long as the mindset remains unchallenged, no institutional/legal mechanism is adequate to uproot corruption and its myriad sources from the polity. However, attempts have constantly been made to weed out the roots of corruption. One of the first serious efforts in this direction was made by the Shanthanam Committee 1964 which was set up by the first Administrative Reforms Commission. In order to tackle corruption in administration, the Government of India, introduced, in response to the recommendation of the Shanthanam Committee, several legal/institutional frameworks, including the Central Bureau of Investigation, the office of the Comptroller and Auditor General and the Central Vigilance Commission. These are well-equipped institutionalized agencies set up to contain corruption by being both preventive and punitive, that are authorized to punish deviant behaviour if it is provided through due processes.

There is also no dearth of legalized mechanisms to address corruption and corrupt practices in administration. Of all the preventive steps, the RTI Act 2005 legally makes it binding on government officials to provide information requested by citizens or face punitive action. This Act has considerably empowered the citizens allowing them access to information which had so far remained an exclusive domain of government officials under the archaic colonial Official Secrets Act of 1923. The other empowering Act happens to be the Right Public Service Legislation that has already been enacted in 19 constituent states of India. By providing time-bound delivery of services for various public services, rendered by the government to citizens and devising mechanism for punishing the errant public servant, this Act has been effective in containing corruption and enhancing transparency in public dealings and accountability for those involved in public service delivery. Similarly, the Prevention of Money Laundering Act of 2002 is also an attack on corrupt public servants by authorising the government to confiscate properties which are disproportionate to his/her income.

One of the major interventions in this regard has been the adoption of the Whistle Blowers Protection Act 2011 which provides a mechanism to investigate alleged corruption and abuse of power by public servants and also to extend protection to those exposing deviant behaviour of government officials for private gains out of public responsibilities. Of all these mechanisms, the institution of the Lokpal for the country as a whole and Lokayuktas for the states is perhaps a significant endeavour towards creating a corruption-free India. The Lokpal and Lokayuktas Act of 2013 which came into force in 2014 provides the establishment of an ombudsman-type of institution in India to enquire into the allegations of corruption against public functionaries. The Lokayuktas at the state level have come into being in several states though the appointment of a Lokpal for the country as whole remains a distant goal presumably because of the disagreement amongst political parties which are not favourably inclined towards creating a mega agency to combat corruption regardless of the political consequences.

CONCLUDING OBSERVATIONS

Corruption in administration is an issue that can never be addressed conclusively for three reasons: first, it is a pathological syndrome, the roots of which can be traced back to the colonial days when exercise of power by those at the helm of affairs was far more arbitrary than what is visible now. With its long reign, not only did the colonial state authoritatively consolidate such a design, it succeeded simply because the forces of opposition did not appear to be strong enough; second, the trend has continued in independent India with a dysfunctional vigilance machinery, the breakdown of organizational integrity, declining importance of accountability in public authorities, logjam of procedural chaos and vitiated environment of work (Prasad 2006, 324–26) and third, corruption is rooted and also flourishes because of a mindset that challenges neither institutional nor individual delinquency; well-entrenched and effective as a mechanism, corruption seems to have become integral to our governance and hence it is better to accept rather than crib since the situation shall not change so soon.

Is corruption inevitable? If that be so, the discussion on integrity in administration seems to be irrelevant. In view of the growing consolidation of public opinion against corruption in India, it will be difficult, if not impossible to sweep the issue under the carpet. A vibrant democracy along with an alert citizenry is perhaps the best shield against corruption. There is thus a need to develop a counter mindset to scuttle the other mindset championing the immutable character of the Indian administration which cannot function unless couched in corrupt practices. The argument that administration is static defies the fundamental laws of social change; this is further reinforced by the recent happenings in India when mass energy was released to integrate citizens with governance. The transformation is visible with the involvement of the stakeholders, including the press that has played a very critical role in creating an environment in which corrupt practices receive immediate public attention. The role of the oversight bodies, acting as watchdogs cannot also be undermined in the gigantic task of making India free from corruption, as the example from other countries show.

Challenges of Good Governance in India

LEARNING OBJECTIVES

1. To understand governance as a conceptual category.
2. To comprehend the distinctive features of governance in India.

Good governance is an ideological construct that has gained salience with the consolidation of neoliberalism across the globe. India is not any exception. The journey began with the adoption of the New Economic Policy 1991 that officially endorsed economic liberalization as a policy. A new era thus set in in which governance was no longer a domestic issue, but was contingent on external pulls and pressures that gradually became difficult to ignore. Nations no longer remained as independent as in the past, but became inter-dependent, and governance epitomised such inter-dependence in an unambiguous manner. The situation became far more complex when governance, despite being a domestic concern, was subject to external conditionalities which could not be avoided given the inevitable need for financial assistance from the developed north and global financial institutions. For the countries, caught in a loan-trap, it was difficult to be innovative and to remain obedient to the conditionalities that they were subject to in view of their loan obligations. It was a vicious circle from which there was no escape.

Governance is 'a conceptual riddle' (Chakrabarty and Bhattacharya 2008). Semantically, it refers to government-run administration. Hence, it should be studied within the format of public administration. However, given its roots in the concerns of the World Bank for recovering loans given to the Sub-Saharan African states, it became integrally linked with the neoliberal thrust in contemporary global politics. While conceptualizing good governance in the context of debt-ridden Sub-Saharan Africa, the World Bank was encouraged to foster 'grassroots and non-governmental organizations such as farmers' associations, cooperative and women groups' as integral to public administration (The World Bank 1989, 18). In the light of this principal objective, the World Bank (1992, 27) now defines good governance by stating:

> [It is] epitomized by predictable, open and enlightened policy making, a bureaucracy imbued with a professional ethos acting in furtherance of public good, the rule of law, transparent processes and a strong civil society participating in public affairs.

As is evident, there are four key elements in good governance: (a) public sector management, (b) accountability, (c) legal framework for development and (d) information and transparency. A dissection of the World Development Report 1992 further reveals that good governance involves (a) respect for the rule of law—it is the duty of civil society to ensure that the rule of law is maintained and protected, (b) special care for the disadvantaged and weak, (c) tolerance and broadmindedness to embrace unity and diversity—which means appreciation for multiculturalism, and (d) respect for institutions upholding the spirit of democracy, primarily procedural democracy of the western variety. So good governance comprises 'mechanisms, processes and institutions through which citizens and groups articulate their local obligations and mediate their differences' (UNDP 1997, 9). It is difficult to have a universal formula because the socio-economic context in which good governance is articulated differs from one country to another. Aware of this, the World Bank while addressing this aspect thus admitted:

> [H]istory, custom, law, society and political economy affect the way in which the ruled in a country hold rulers to account for their performance, the relative openness of a socio-political system or an economy, and the degree of predictability in government decision making and interaction with the public. (Brautigam 1991, 6)

Good governance gained currency at a moment in the evolution of public administration when the complexity of societal problem solving demanded a multi-pronged search for the refashioning of the mode of governance. As it eventually emerged, it came to represent transparency, accountability, integrity and legitimacy of the institutions, rules, practices and values on which a society discharged its social obligations. These characteristics are relative to the society in question because they cannot be articulated in absolute terms.

ADDRESSING THE CHALLENGES OF GOOD GOVERNANCE IN INDIA

Good governance has always been at the forefront of the development agenda in India. Beginning with the Eighth Five-Year Plan (1992–97) good governance has remained a pivotal concern for policy-makers. The Eleventh Five-Year Plan (2007–12) was most explicit in its demand for good governance as perhaps a panacea for a majority of administrative ills. It was thus most frankly admitted that many of the initiatives that the Government of India took to achieve the objectives of growth and poverty alleviation and inclusiveness at substantial public expenses 'have floundered because of poor design, insufficient accountability and also corruption at various levels' (GOI 2008a, 4–5). So, India's exalted aims of inclusive growth, reducing poverty and bridging the various divides that continued to fragment the social fabric could only be achieved, as the vision document of the Eleventh Plan suggests, 'if there is a significant improvement in the quality of governance' (GOI 2008a, 223). How to accomplish the goal? The plan document identifies six specific areas which are critical to establish practices of good governance: first, as a democratic country, the central feature of good governance is democratic elections that should be conducted in a fair manner ensuring effective representation of all sections of the population; second, the government should be transparent and accountable to completely eliminating sources of corruption at every level of governance; third, the government must be effective and efficient in delivering social, economic and public services without bias and prejudices; fourth, empowering the Panchayati Raj institutions to effectively devolve power and funds to grassroots functionaries to carry out the functions constitutionally assigned to them; fifth, the rule of law must be firmly established and there should be stringent punishments if they are violated and sixth, the system should function in a manner which is seen to be fair and inclusive, especially for the disadvantaged sections who need to be empowered to participate in governance as integral partners.[5]

Despite being an agenda initiated by World Bank, governance has ushered in a new era by critiquing the Weberian hierarchical form of public administration that needs to be truly participatory and democratic. The effort is towards strengthening the institutions of civil society and what the people need is not doles or financial packages, but empowerment in the financial, legal and institutional sense of the term. They need 'institutions which give them power to decide and legal rights to manage them ... by the mass involvement in those activities which bring them benefits' (Mathur 1996, 315). In the post-liberalization era, a number of steps were taken by the Government of India that aimed at improving the quality of governance. Given the constraint of space, mention shall be made only of those major initiatives that radically altered the texture of governance in India. Seeking to restore 'publicness' in public administration, one of the first major initiatives was the adoption of the RTI Act in 2005, which not only empowered citizens, but also effectively challenged the hegemonic bureaucratic control over access to information. This was therefore an empowering device in more than one sense: By replacing the Official Secret Act of 1923, the RTI Act 2005 was a major step in refashioning public administration to a significant extent. Another momentous step was the adoption of the Citizen's Charter. Primarily an adaptation of the UK model, the Indian Citizen's Charter has an additional component of 'expectations from the clients' or, in other words, 'obligations from the users' (Centre for Good Governance 2008, 3). What it ensures is the involvement of the stakeholders in the formulation of the Charter which, to be effective and meaningful, needs to meet the needs of the users. By devising an instrument to make the government accountable, the adoption of the Charter is a watershed in the history of India's public administration. By making administration responsive, the Charter has thus become an integral part of government functioning in contemporary India besides being an important key to citizen's empowerment as well.

The other most revolutionary step in this regard happens to be the adoption of the 73rd and 74th Amendment Acts in 1992 which brought about significant changes not only in the texture of governance at the grassroots, but also in the popular perception about governance. As against 543 elected members of the Lok Sabha and about 4,500 directly elected members of the state assemblies, there are about 3.2 million elected representatives in the panchayats of which as many as 1.2 million are women. There are more elected women in India alone than in the rest of the world put together. The move towards inclusive growth does not seem to be a mere slogan because this large contingent of elected members are involved in planning, implementing and supervising the delivery of essential public services.

As stakeholders, citizens have become integral to administration which is also an instrument for their well-being, and hence cannot be left out. This is a unique realization for those at the grassroots drawing upon what they gain in the government's outreach mission. Simultaneously with their involvement in grassroots governance, the major flagship programmes like the Mahatma Gandhi National Rural Employment Guarantee Act, the National Rural Health Mission and other comparable endeavours also provide the stakeholders with avenues for participation in activities which are critical for their survival. Panchayats no longer remain mere instruments of authority, but put forward a new framework for participation which is an anathema if public bureaucracy is conceptualized strictly in Weberian terms. By creating circumstances for meaningful participation, they appear to have creatively interpreted public administration in a post-colonial context. Governance has thus reconceptualized administration by making the stakeholders at various levels integral to administration. In the new dispensation, citizens are no longer recipients but rather are instigators of change.

CONCLUDING OBSERVATIONS

Good governance is not just a conceptual parameter, but a prescription to combat and also refashion a predatory state that has appropriated the government for partisan gain. This is also a shield for market-driven socio-economic regeneration since an orderly governance creates political stability and also institutions which are critical to smooth functioning of the market. So the notion of good governance in the neoliberal realm does actually support and also expedites processes for the status-quo for reasons connected with the market and its partisan functioning. By enhancing the state's capabilities within the neoliberal predisposition, good governance accords a powerful conceptual justification to endeavours drawing on self-motivation which is undoubtedly good provided there are well-established mechanisms to such efforts. And in case these are absent, they need to be created with state support at least in the initial stages; therefore over emphasis on good governance may result in a situation where the state withdraws hoping to be replaced by what is euphemistically characterized as 'popular initiatives'. Nonetheless, both as a conceptual category and a practical design, governance is a positive intervention in three fundamental ways: first, by shifting the focus from inputs to outcomes, it radically alters our perception about public administration that cannot be conceptualized as an event, but as an integral process in which the government is just a significant, player. Challenging hierarchical bureaucratic governance, it further reemphasizes the importance of the horizontal coordination of agencies involved in the delivery of public services. As against hierarchy, the principal concern here is to evolve teamwork involving the stakeholders. The second implication is far more serious especially in a developing country like India where the colonial bureaucratic structure of the bygone era has been more or less retained. Governance, despite being a market-friendly design, has unleashed forces supportive of institutional pluralism which are most radical given the well-entrenched bureaucratic hegemony notwithstanding the commitment of the founding fathers for creating a new India free from bias and prejudices of any kind. This is an opportunity in which the Indian public administration can be substantially refashioned in the neoliberal context where governance is not merely an act, but a coordinated act seeking to redesign public administration in a creative manner. In this sense, governance cannot be just a checklist of items, as per the World Bank, but a fresh wave of thinking based on a thorough critique of the age-old Weberian conceptualization of hierarchical and control-stricken public bureaucracy. Thirdly, governance is also an institutional mechanism required to address the well-entrenched inadequacies in India's public administration. It is now common knowledge that endemic corruption not only undermines the moral fibre of the polity, but has serious and irreversible practical consequences for politics, economic development and governance. With the growing involvement of the stakeholders in governance, those, indulging in corrupt practices attract immediate attention. This means that an alert citizenry is perhaps the most effective shield against corruption. Governance, by catapulting people on the centre stage, thus becomes an important vehicle for change in circumstances where stakeholders are linked amongst themselves for common goals.

Non-governmental Organizations, Civil Society Organizations and Development

LEARNING OBJECTIVES

1. To understand non-governmental and civil society organizations as conceptual categories.
2. To grasp the role of non-governmental and civil society organizations in contemporary Indian public administration.

In contrast with the state-directed development discourse, there also exists an alternative in which the non-governmental organizations (NGOs) and civil society organizations (CSOs) are preeminent. Failure of the state to bring about development led to the emergence of NGOs and CSOs as vehicles for development in areas where the state always remained peripheral, especially in developing countries. Although the expressions—NGOs and CSOs—are used interchangeably, their role is not exactly identical since the former are also involved in political processes while the latter are primarily engaged in social endeavours. Nonetheless, they, as development alternatives, offer innovative and people-centric approaches to service delivery. Conceptually, the perceived failure of the state-led top-down model of development exposed the limitations of the state and other profit-driven organizations; they were also products of circumstances when, with the ideological ascendancy of neoliberalism, the state gradually withdrew from the social sectors as a consequence of the structural adjustment programme of the early 1970s and later which eclipsed, to a significant extent, the role of the state in developmental activities. The World Bank Report 1994 on the structural adjustment in Sub-Saharan Africa was a clear articulation of future development plans for the 'third world' countries in which the role of the state was minimal. Underlining the importance of 'the rolling back of the state', the Report also sought to minimize restrictions of the free play of market forces. The neoliberal approach and its accompanying structural adjustment programmes lost their momentum by the mid-1990s and the state seemed to have regained its prominence in the context of the consolidation of the governance era. The state, in other words, became a critical player with the growing importance of governance in public discourses that embraced democracy and people's participation in governance. The process towards 're-governmentalization' may have reduced the significance of NGOs and CSOs in the era of governance though, by strengthening civil society, which is a space for bargaining, negotiating and also coercing, it also consolidated them 'as proxies for broader processes of citizen engagement that would enable them to act as a countervailing power against local and national governments' (Banks, Hume and Edwards 2015, 707). Despite changes in circumstances, the role of NGOs and CSOs does not appear to have dwindled presumably because of their critical role in development could not be bypassed since capital-intensive and technology-based industrial ventures would never be adequate to bring about inclusive development. As alternatives, the NGOs and CSOs constitute vehicles for people

> to participate in development and social change that would not be possible through government programmes; [they also constitute a space in which] it is possible to think about development and social change that would not be likely through government programmes; [they thus constitute] instruments for turning these alternative ideas, and forms of participation into alternative practices and hard outcomes. (Mitlin, Hickey Bebbington 2007, 1701)

So, definitionally, NGOs and CSOs are empowering devices in contrast to the state and market which being ideologically conditioned, obviously remain dogmatic and thus usually non-sensitive to popular initiatives and demands.

The state failure, as is argued, fuelled interests in NGOs and CSOs as development alternatives articulating a new paradigm. Their growing importance in development is a paradigm shift for a variety of reasons: Not only does it unleash processes whereby people get involved, but it also helps in conceptualizing the paradigm in which the state remains peripheral. Besides their role in service delivery, they also create an alert citizenry challenging 'unequal relationships and [pursuing] transformative agendas through their people-centred approaches' (Banks, Hume and Edwards 2015, 710). They thus act, it is further shown, 'as schools of democracy by providing resources and opportunities for association, collective action, mitigating societal conflicts, expanding political participation and providing channels of interest representation' (Banks, Hume and Edwards 2015, 711). As incubators of alternative development, NGOs and CSOs provide critical inputs to model an alternative discourse in a context when the state is withdrawing from key social sectors. The need is keenly felt more in developing countries where the state, by being inadequately equipped to meaningfully handle the developments, becomes a mute observer when it comes to even addressing the basic needs of the people. This is not to suggest that NGOs and CSOs are relevant only in developing countries because their role is equally decisive even in the developed countries in popularizing people-centric plans and programmes which may not attract the state's attention.

THE INDIAN REALITY

The aim here is to understand the role of NGOs and CSOs in India's socio-economic development in the changed environment in which the state has acquired a new character in the context of the growing importance of the governance agenda. The state continues to remain critical to development in a scenario in which the role of the NGOs and CSOs has also become significant given their importance in articulating an alternative to the conventional state-led planned development in India.

What is striking is the fact that even in the context of a socialistic pattern of society, the planners gave adequate importance to people's voluntary initiatives towards addressing issues of development. The First Five Year Plan (1951–56) thus stated that 'any plan for social and economic regeneration should take into account the services rendered by [voluntary] agencies and the State should give them maximum cooperation in strengthening their effort' (Planning

Commission 1951, as quoted in Lalitha and Kohli 1983, 16). The objective of the Plan was to support NGOs and CSOs in those areas where they had already made an impact with almost no support from the state. This was reiterated in the Third Five Year Plan (1961–66) which mentioned that 'popularly organized voluntary efforts may go a long way towards augmenting the facilities available to the community or helping the weakest and the [neediest] to a somewhat better life' (Planning Commission 1961, 292). What was most striking was a shift in policy direction. Not only was the importance of voluntary organizations highlighted but the fact that they were most crucial in helping those in the periphery was also recognized. The Third Plan was also a watershed because for the first time, the importance of NGOs and CSOs was strongly felt for policy purposes. In fact, from the Third Plan onwards, it was strongly felt that state-driven development was not adequate for India's socio-economic growth and that the NGOs and CSOs did have a supplementary role to play. The idea was further reinforced in a report of the Rural–Urban Relationship Committee 1966 that emphasized the role of voluntary agencies in mobilizing community support for local development activities by stating that 'local voluntary organizations can be very helpful in mobilizing popular support and assistance of the people in the activities of a local body' (GOI 1966, 113). So, during the Third Plan period, it was strongly asserted that the role of voluntary agencies, both NGOs and CSOs, could not be dispensed with given their critical importance in fulfilling the development agenda. The trend continued and the Seventh Five Year Plan (1985–90) which characterized voluntary agencies as 'the eyes and ears of the beneficiaries' reiterated that NGOs and CSOs constituted one of the most important sources of inputs for development planning in India. This was a clear break from the past because for the first time in India's development through planning era, it was admitted that voluntary agencies made people not only aware of the possible alternatives besides the top-down model of development, but also pushed for what they deemed appropriate for people's well-being. What figured in the Seventh Five-Year Plan was the outcome of a long-drawn process in which these agencies had significant roles for supplementing government efforts: the state had finally come to terms with voluntary agencies because their contribution in conceptualizing and also enunciating alternative development discourses was too significant to wish away.

In the context of the structural adjustment programme that India had partially adopted, NGOs and CSOs were readily accepted as partners of the development agenda. What was initiated in the Seventh Five-Year plan was reaffirmed further in the Ninth Five-Year Plan (1997–2002) which, by recognizing their role as integral to India's development, made them critical partners in India's development strategies. Even in the governance era, by admitting the NGOs and CSOs as critical players in development, the Tenth (2002–07), Eleventh (2007–12) and Twelfth (2012–17) Five Year Plans underlined further that meaningful development consisted in mobilizing the skills, strength and creative capabilities of the masses of people and securing their active participation in carving out a distinct space in India's development trajectories. What is vital here is their role in building a network involving the stakeholders at different layers of Indian society. The fast growing numbers of NGOs and CSOs also reveal that efforts are being made to address the needs of the myriad socio-economic segments which, so far, have remained peripheral and almost disconnected with the planned agenda. The implications are significant: Not only do they act as the eyes and ears of the people at the grassroots, but they have also become critical partners in the preparation of plans and programmes involving the stakeholders. With the gradual withdrawal of the state from important social sectors, the NGOs and CSOs seem to have filled the gap that has been left vacant; so they are complementary to the state's endeavours. A perusal of their role, in other words, suggests that given the growing complexities of development, especially in developing countries like India, it is difficult, if not impossible, for the state to conclusively address demands for inclusive development, and this is where the NGOs and CSOs become significant and critical in the entire development processes.

CONCLUDING OBSERVATIONS

An analysis of the role of NGOs and CSOs in development in India highlights three points which are of immense theoretical significance in grasping development processes particularly in developing countries (Chakrabarty 2006). First, their growing strength contributes significantly to the importance of civil society—an arena separate from the state and the market—that has largely been appropriated by the state. Comprising 'a criss-crossing network of various non-state institutions' (Dahrendorf 1996, 231), like families, associations of different types including trade unions and clubs—NGOs and CSOs are thus serious endeavours at creating 'a non-state autonomous sphere' (Rudolph 2000, 1762) in which ideological hegemony is contested across a range of organizations and ideologies challenging and also upholding the existing order. The second theoretical implication is linked with the rising importance of NGOs and CSOs in conceptualizing alternative forms of development highlighting the critical role of a set of organizational actors that are not part of the household, the state or the market. These include associations, people's movements, citizens' groups, consumer associations, small producer associations, cooperation, women organizations, and of course, development NGOs.[6] Suggesting a more action-based agenda, these forums rewrite the history of development by refashioning the prevalent tools of analysis which are not adequate to comprehend the contemporary development agenda. The third implications relates to the nature of development and its conceptualization. Development is absolutely political, highlighting the particular kinds of power-relationships in which it operates; not, at all, managerial or administrative, development is basically contingent on the nature of the state that invariably pursues a line of thinking according to its ideological priorities (Leftwich 1996, 6). By exposing the inherent limitations of the state-led development paradigm, NGOs and CSOs have firmly established that development cannot be measured by gross domestic product or gross national product but by 'the enlargement of human capabilities and the enhancement of quality of life for all' (Jayal 1997, 412). Instead of being mere technological transformations, development is, in other words, a return to politics in which the prevalent power-relationships remain most significant in conceptualizing its character. As both facilitators and participants, NGOs and CSOs thus remain critical players in the entire process in which neither the state nor the market seems decisive, but the involvement of the people and their initiatives are significant in the reordering of wealth and privileges by challenging the prevalent power-relationships.

The Public Sector in India in the Pre- and Post-liberalization Era

LEARNING OBJECTIVES

1. To understand the conceptualization of liberalization as a theoretical category.
2. To understand the impact of liberalization on public enterprises in India.

The euphoria over the public sector seems to have considerably waned with the ascendancy of neoliberalism in which the logic of the market reigns supreme. This was not the case once India became politically free in 1947 when the nationalist leadership preferred development strategies in which the public sector appeared to be the most appropriate instrument for

India's inclusive growth. Appreciative of its role in economic development, Jawaharlal Nehru, India's first Prime Minister who was also enamoured by the Leninist New Economic Policy of total state control of the economy, felt strongly for the state-led planned development model. Evolved out of the faith of the nationalists in the efficiency of the public sector as a vehicle for growth, it gradually became a dependable instrument for the economic regeneration of a former colony like India. There were two basic sources from which the leadership seemed to have drawn it inspiration: on the one hand, the meteoric rise of the former Soviet Union following the 1917 Revolution in which the role of the state remained most critical, convinced those who presided over India's destiny immediately after independence of the viability of the public sector-driven economic development strategy; and the obvious reluctance of the private entrepreneurs to initiate ventures for the nation's development without seeking profit led them, on the other hand, to go for state-driven planned economic development. The Congress party officially endorsed this strategy in its Avadi Session 1955 when the socialistic pattern of society was accepted and the public sector was given massive importance in India's economic regeneration.

THE INDIAN SCENE

The public sector thus received adequate attention since it conformed to the ideological mission that the Congress stalwarts had set for the young nation, as was evident in the Industrial Resolution (1948, para 1), which stated:

> [T]he nation has now set itself to establish a social order where justice and equality of opportunity shall be secured to all people. For this purpose, careful planning and integrated efforts over the whole field of national activity are necessary; and the Government of India propose to establish a National Planning Commission to formulate programmes of development and to secure its execution.

This seems to have set the tempo by guaranteeing a prominent role to the state in so far as economic growth was concerned. The state had exclusive responsibility for the establishment of those undertakings which contributed to public utilities and India's strategic concerns. What was initiated in 1948 was reinforced in the 1956 Industrial Policy resolution which earmarked a specific space for the public sector. Complemented by what is usually known as the *Mahalanobis* model which put industrial growth as the top priority, the 1956 policy stated in formal terms 'the critical importance of basic and heavy machine producing industries for accelerating the tempo of growth under the autarkic industrialization strategy' (Tendulkar and Bhavani 2007, 24). As a result, the public sector was given the responsibility of building heavy and basic industries and it was appreciated because it conformed to the nationalist aspirations. The state progressively assumed a predominant and direct responsibility in which the public sector remained a complementary endeavour.

CHANGES SINCE THE INDUSTRIAL POLICY RESOLUTION 1977

The scene had however undergone changes following the adoption of the Industrial Policy Resolution 1977 after the formation of the Janata Party government in 1977. Given the failure of the past resolution to bring about inclusive development, the new government felt the need to reframe industrial policies and especially the role of the public sector which had not fulfilled the expectations that it had generated when formed. The Industrial Policy 1977 thus insisted that the public sector would not only be the producer of very important and strategic goods of basic nature, but would also work at maximizing essential supplies for consumers besides contributing to the development of the small scale sector and ancillary units. It also raised doubts about foreign collaborations in areas where Indian entrepreneurs had the required technological knowhow. With the collapse of the Janata Party government in 1980, the Congress returned to power and it also brought about significant transformation in the Industrial Policy 1980. Two issues stand out here: for the first time, public sector units were subject to severe criticism for their inefficiencies especially in managing their affairs; they were given specific instructions to set their house in order. The other remarkable decision was to liquidate sick public sector units and merger of those which were potentially capable of revival with the healthy ones. The second issue relates to the liberalized licensing pattern for big industrial houses. This was also a first significant step that provided confidence to big industries which were given adequate appreciation for their role in India's growth perhaps due to the prevalent ideological predisposition of the ruling authority.

The support that the public sector had received from the political authorities was gradually withdrawn also because of the massive attack on the autarkic development model following the disintegration of the former Soviet Union. The tremors were also felt in India especially with the rise of a new leadership which did not appreciate the state-led economic model to the extent its earlier counterpart had. Although the Congress government led by Rajiv Gandhi (1984–89) did not abdicate the socialistic pattern of society in which the public sector remained preeminent, changes in policy directions were clearly visible. In his Lok Sabha speech, the Prime Minister despite having underlined the importance of the public sector in economic growth, opened the doors for the private sector in many reserved areas which had so far remained the exclusive domain of the public sector, in order to reduce the burden on the state and also urged private entrepreneurs to be creative in their approach to address global challenges. The change was reflected in the Seventh Five-Year Plan (1985–90) which argued for the gradual withdrawal of protection for public sector units and also made them face competition to establish their viability.

The beginning of the 1990s saw a paradigmatic shift when the Congress leadership openly advocated economic liberalization in a very guarded manner. The change was not only due to the feeling that the public sector was not adequately equipped to bring about inclusive growth, but also due to global changes following the breakdown of the former Soviet Union and the Warsaw Pact of the East European countries. The impact was so severe that the government of India had to think beyond the age-old emphasis on the public sector as a reliable engine for growth. With the adoption of the New Economic Policy 1991, the P. V. Narsimha Rao-led Congress government endeavoured to rejuvenate an India facing a heavy fiscal deficit, over-centralization and excessive bureaucratization of economic processes. Following his commitment to take India out of the fiscal crisis, Rao created an ambiance of hope and also possibilities of change. The year 1991 can thus be treated as a turning point in India's economic growth, with the release of wide ranging measures to deregulate the economy by discontinuing the licence-quota-permit-raj. The principal objectives of the Industrial Policy Resolution were to 'build on' the gains already made, correct the distortions or weaknesses that might have held back the progress, 'maintain a sustained growth in productivity and gainful employment and attain international competitiveness' (GOI 2001, 10). The new policy was to deregulate the industrial economy in a phased manner.

One of the major sources of lack of adequate economic growth was the lackadaisical performance of public sector units. Hence the 1991 Resolution focused on them to suggest various measures to halt further economic decay by encouraging (a) disinvestment of shares of a select set of public enterprises for raising resources and to encourage wider participation of the general public and workers in their ownership, (b) sick industries were to be phased out soon to avoid further pressure on the state exchequer and (c) greater autonomy to the management, but to be held accountable for specified results. These were significant steps to make the public sector relevant in an era of stiff competition. With the withdrawal of protective shields, a new era dawned in the history of public enterprises with the consolidation of a period of de-licencing, deregulating and dismantling of the inspector raj.

Unlike the Industrial Policy Resolution 1956 which reserved as many as 17 industries exclusively for public sector, the 1991 Resolution reduced the number to eight which were: (a) arms and ammunition, (b) atomic energy, (c) coal and lignite, (d) mineral oils, (e) mining of iron ore, manganese ore, gypsum, sulphur, gold and diamond, (f) mining of copper, lead, zinc, molybdenum and wolfram, (g) minerals, specified in the schedule to the atomic energy of 1953 and (h) rail transport. By 2010, five items were taken out in which the private sector was allowed to operate and only three are currently earmarked for exclusive public sector domain including (a) atomic energy, (b) minerals specified in the 1953 schedule and (c) rail transport.

Besides demarcating specific areas in which the public sector was allowed to operate, the 1991 Resolution also approved a Memorandum of Understanding with other companies that made their presence felt in the international market. In order to recognize the contribution of the successful public sector units, the Resolution further identified them as *Navratnas* and those less successful as *Miniratnas*. The Navratna status was granted to successful enterprises which were given enhanced financial powers for committing capital expenditures, starting joint ventures and also providing incentives to their employees. The Miniratnas were those enterprises which were profit-making, but did not have a good record of handling their employees who remained dissatisfied. Although there were initially 11 Navratnas, with the privatization of the Indian Petrol Chemicals Limited and the Videsh Sanchar Nigam, the number reduced to nine.[7] In light of the significant growth shown by these Navratnas since 1996, the government of India came up with another label of the Maharatna for these companies meaning that they would be allowed to make, without any government endorsement, an additional capital expenditure of ₹5,000 crore or 50 per cent of their net growth, whichever is less. By 2011, five former Navratnas were recognized as Maharatnas[8] for their contribution to India's economic well-being. These Maharatnas stand out not only as profit-making enterprises, but also for their efficiency in running business ventures in accordance with global standards. By designating successful public enterprises as Maharatnas, the Indian government found a unique way of recognizing their contribution for development in a scenario where the conceptual validity of the state-led planned economy seemed to have considerably disappeared.

An analysis of the Five-Year Plans since the Seventh Five-Year Plan (1985–90) reveals that public enterprises did not have a smooth journey given changes in the political priorities of the state. At first, the blanket support that the public sector used to get was withdrawn in the Seventh Five-Year Plan and the idea that they needed to face competition in order to justify government assistance was mooted. Signalling a sea change in India's economic future with the adoption of the New Economic Policy 1991, the Eighth Five-Year Plan (1992–97)—by agreeing to the steps that the Seventh Five-Year Plan—had suggested a reduce in the investment in the public sector to a significant extent. The trend continued into the Ninth Five-Year Plan (1997–2002). In order to retain the significant annual growth rate of 6.8 per cent, the Ninth Five-Year Plan further reduced public sector outlays and envisaged a bigger role of the private sector and market forces. Not only did the public sector receive only 33.4 per cent of the total investment much less than what was earmarked for the private sector, the Indian state agreed for foreign direct investments and also disinvestment of public sector units which were performing well. The disinvestment policy was followed rigorously during the Tenth Five-Year Plan (2002–07) when the proceeds from the disinvestment were diverted to fill the gaps, created by budget deficits of losses from departmental undertakings and other unproductive government's expenditure. The Eleventh Plan (2007–12) was no exception. The share of public sector investment dwindled further to 23 per cent as compared to 33 per cent in the Ninth Five-Year Plan. It was justified by saying that private investment (from both the global and its domestic counterpart) created a more favourable investment climate which contributed to a consistent growth rate in India despite uncertainties elsewhere. For the policy-makers, it was a great boost and despite strong criticisms of government withdrawal from the public sector, the policy was also preferred in the Twelfth Five-Year Plan (2012–17) as its approach paper clearly stipulates.

CONCLUDING OBSERVATIONS

The importance of the public sector has considerably declined in the post-liberalization era in view of the failure of state-led planned development to bring about inclusive growth in India. With their interventions in the economy, private entrepreneurs have undoubtedly contributed to growth though it has created economic disparities since the principles of social development have been replaced by the syndrome of economic growth. As is obvious, the private investors prefer to invest in profit-making areas ignoring social development while the public enterprises remain committed to inclusive development that cannot be attained if the desire for growth prevails over other considerations. This is however not to argue for blanket support to the public enterprises regardless of their performance. One cannot ignore the adverse consequences of blind support to them and in that respect, the decision to open up the economy was an eye-opener. It is now evident that the heavy losses that the public sector units incurred were largely due to over-bureaucratization of their functioning along with indiscriminate political interference and unconditional subsidies. Once these issues were conclusively addressed, the scenario would have changed; but no serious attempt was made. Following the acceptance of neoliberal economic reforms, the protection was gradually withdrawn. With the consolidation of forces for liberalization, the public sector units had to justify their existence by following the basic commercial yardsticks of profits before and after tax and also the ratio of sales to capital invested, among others. It created circumstances in which the public enterprises were forced to redesign their policies and mode of functioning. The emergence of the Navratnas, Miniratnas and now Maharatnas has shown that, with policy changes, the public sector can compete with private investors along with the fulfilment of its socio-economic obligations. What is needed is the political will to grab the bull by its horns rather that following the easy option of selling equities in the most profitable public enterprises to sustain growth.

Human Rights Administration in India[9]

LEARNING OBJECTIVES

1. To understand human rights as a conceptual category.
2. To comprehend the complex interrelationship between human rights and Indian administration in a historical perspective.

A concern for human rights is universal though steps towards formally protecting them were adopted in 1948 with the approval of the Universal Deceleration of Human Rights. Since then, serious endeavours have been made to institutionalize rules and regulations for protecting human rights across continents. As complementary to this effort, in 1991, a UN sponsored meeting of representatives of national institutions was held in Paris which adopted a set of principles guiding national institutions responsible for guarding human rights. Known as the Paris Principles, they gradually became an immediate reference point to address human rights violations in any part of the globe. Subsequently endorsed by the UN Commission on Human Rights and the UN General Assembly, these principles also provoked a campaign for the consolidation of the Human Rights Commissions as perhaps a shield against distortion and also the violation of inalienable human rights. Ironically, the genesis of the idea of having some sort of institutional mechanism for the protection and promotion of human rights in India can be attributed to the policies of western countries, notably the US, to link economic and financial assistance to developing nations with the condition of human rights protection (Mathew 1994, 7). Although the idea of conditional loans was always opposed by India, it was readily accepted in this case for it not only helped secure concessional loans and grants, but also enabled the state to constitute an agency for the protection and promotion of human rights in India. Moreover, the growing awareness amongst people regarding their democratic and civil rights, coupled with mounting pressures from human rights organizations in the country to have a law and institutional mechanism for the protection of human rights compelled the government to go for the enactment of a law laying down the broad provisions of a Human Rights Commission in the country. Owing to the lack of self-visualization on the issue of a Human Rights Commission in government circles, the first effort in such a direction in terms of providing for such a Commission met with discomfiture. The Human Rights Commission Bill introduced in Parliament in May 1993 was withdrawn in view of the scathing criticism it received from all quarters and persons involved in the propagation and promotion of human rights in the country. Subsequently, pouring its mind into the objections raised on the Human Rights Commission Bill for three months, the government came out with a Presidential Ordinance called the Protection of Human Rights (1993), providing for the constitution of a Human Rights Commission. Ultimately, the Protection of Human Rights Act, 1993 was enacted by the Parliament under the provisions of which the National Human Rights Commission (NHRC) was constituted.

The formation of an autonomous NHRC in 1993 was the outcome of both indigenous forces and external pressures. The first of its kind among the South Asian countries and also few among those established elsewhere, the NHRC gradually grew in importance by becoming proactive in protecting and promoting human rights in India. As a legal entity from the time it came into being following the enactment of the Protection of Human Rights Act 1993, it has also become integral to governance in the context of institutional decay. Nonetheless, by being true to its constitutional obligation, the NHRC has set into motion a process that has not only made citizens aware of their uninfringeable rights, but has also provided an institutional mechanism if these rights are violated. Seeking to reinforce the constitutional guarantee of basic rights, the 1993 Act, while underlining the Commission's distinct role, recognized human rights as rights relating to life, equality and dignity of an individual enforced by the Constitution or embodied in international covenants which are justiciable. Endowed with substantive powers, the Commission is undoubtedly an important institution sustaining India's democratic ethos and fervour in a meaningful way.

ACHIEVEMENTS OF THE COMMISSION

At the time of the inception of the NHRC, the sceptics were quite vociferous about their concerns on the structural and functional weaknesses of the Commission. However, during the long years of its existence, the NHRC has come out with flying colours in so far as the inculcation of a culture of respect for human rights is concerned in most circles of government as well as in the minds of the common people. In fact, the Commission has turned out to be the true custodian in terms of the protection and promotion of human rights in India with its sincere and spontaneous efforts to not only redress the grievances of the victims on a petition but quite often, it has also taken *suo moto* cognizance of any incident of violation of human rights with prompt remedial steps in order to provide relief to the aggrieved persons. Consequently, the Commission has not only been able to command a high degree of respectability and moral ground amongst the people but also amongst government functionaries a positive outcome of which has been the recommendations of the Commission getting due respect by the concerned departments.

A major invention of the Commission, which is also in tune with the times, appears to be its tendency of involving CSOs, in addition to educational and public oriented organizations, in its endeavours for the protection and promotion of human rights of those people who either suffer from some sort of social stigma or are faced with vested interests bent upon sabotaging the efforts of the Commission for the same. Hence, the problems pertaining to child prostitution, prison reforms, rehabilitation of the persons displaced by the ongoing mega projects, child labour, bonded labour, iron deficiency among pregnant women and problems of the mentally disabled etc. have been able to attract the attention of the Commission whose efforts would supposedly have gone in vain had it not received insightful inputs and active support from NGOs.

An astounding success story of the Commission happens to be its fruitful efforts in spreading human rights literacy and awareness amongst the different sections of society in accordance with one of its statutory obligations (Roy 2003, 382–400). Indeed, the issues pertaining to the human rights of various sections of the people seem to have become prominent in the public domain which is also indicative of citizens' faith in the Commission. If citizens are aggrieved by any act of omission and commission by both the governmental and non-governmental agencies, they have the right to approach the Commission. Illustrative here is the growing number of complaints to Commission for grievance redressal. Moreover, by succeeding to make lessons of human rights a part of the school curriculum for educating young minds about the value of protecting and promoting human rights, the Commission seems to be sowing the seeds of a vibrant society marked by an unflinching devotion to the cause of human rights rooted in the ancient Indian dictum of live and let live.

Finally, since its inception, the Commission has been able to formulate guidelines and issue directions to concerned agencies on a number of issues including the misuse of police powers, especially arbitrary arrests, setting up of human rights cells in state and city police headquarters, prison reforms, elimination of child labour, compulsory education, caste and communal violence, rights of persons with disability, human rights of mentally ill, abolition of manual scavenging, quality assurance in hospitals, review of certain laws and statutes affecting the human rights of citizens, implementation of international treaties and instruments of human rights, protection of human rights and dignity of AIDS affected patients and sex workers, institutional changes in the legal system etc. It is indeed true that the NHRC plays a critical role in making people aware of the issue of Human Rights in an unpresented way. By also being proactive on occasions when violation of rights is rampant, the NHRC has also become an integral part of India's civic awareness.

LIMITATIONS OF THE COMMISSION

As is the case with various other statutory commissions and institutions, the NHRC is also handicapped by a number of structural and functional shortcomings which come in the way of the efficient and effective performance of its functions. Structurally, despite the best efforts of the NHRC, the creation of a State Human Rights Commission has not been able to become a reality in all the states and Union Territories of the country. The obvious consequence of this has been that the complaints of the violation of human rights emanating from within the territories of a particular state also get directed towards the NHRC since there is no state level mechanism to take care of such cases. In such a situation, the time and energy of the Commission gets absorbed in redressing such grievances and the Commission is not able to spare its time or pay attention to streamlining the system of governance from a human rights perspective nor is it able to evolve innovative measures to make respect for human rights a way of life in the country.

The apathy of the state governments towards the cause of human rights is further deepened with the reluctance of a majority of the state to set up the Human Rights Courts at the district level under the provisions of the Protection of Human Rights Act, 1993. The institution of special court to deal with issues of particular nature or significance, such as, crime against women, drug/narcotics trafficking, among other, heralded a new chapter in Indian administration. Similarly, the setting up of Human Rights Courts at the district level in India's each district is a very serious endeavour towards dispensing justice in the cases of violation of human rights. But in the absence of such courts, cases pertaining to the violation of human rights go to the ordinary courts of law whose procedures and speed of delivering justice is well known, thereby resulting in the procrastination of such cases leading to a loss of faith of the common people in the deliverance of justice by the courts.

CONCLUDING OBSERVATIONS

The increasing importance of the NHRC in governance is contingent on the context as well. Mere institutional guarantees may not always be adequate for the protection and promotion of human rights. What is most critical is the role of the people who always remain victims of the excesses, committed by an over-zealous state. An alert citizenry is thus the key to the success of the Commission in fulfilling its role as per the statute. As its history since inception demonstrates, the NHRC did not appear to have attracted much attention presumably because it was dismissed as just another institutional device to placate the rising demand for another instrument which was likely to lose its significance as had happened with the others. It was fated, in other words, to gradually disappear. The scene however underwent a significant transformation once the Commission became assertive in its response to glaring cases of human rights violations. The cases that catapulted the NHRC on to the centre stage were the 1995 Punjab mass cremation and the 2002 Gujarat communal riots in which it took suo moto cognizance of the incidents for investigation. Once it was established that the state had a role to play in these two instances, the Commission gained significant prominence as an institution which fulfilled its mission even in adverse circumstances.

A perusal of the Commission's role since the very beginning also confirms that it has succeeded in carving out an independent, and also powerful institution which is linked with forces consolidating India's democratic fervour. Besides discharging its primary functions, the NHRC is thus involved in processes which are critical to India's democracy. Politically vibrant, socially relevant and intellectually innovative, the Commission has also created hope among those who do not have mentors and have thus remained at the mercy of the perpetrators of injustice having their human rights violated. The Commission has thus generated confidence across the various classes and communities in India which is certainly a source of optimism and is perhaps the principal reason for its growing importance in contemporary India.

REVIEW QUESTIONS

1. How do you define corruption? Elaborate your response with examples from contemporary India.
2. What are the major recommendations of the Second Administrative Reforms Commission 2005 for containing corruption in India? Elaborate your response.

3. 'Ethics in governance is a misnomer'. Do you agree with the view? Elaborate your response.
4. Distinguish between the generalists and the specialists in administration with examples from contemporary India.
5. Elaborate on the distinction between permanent and temporary executives with examples from contemporary India.
6. What are the major institutions responsible for protecting human rights in India? Elaborate your response.
7. 'Public sector has lost its salience with the consolidation of globalization in India'. Comment.
8. In what respects do voluntary organizations remain critical to development in contemporary India? Elaborate your response.
9. 'Governance in contemporary India is not merely structural but also ideological'. Comment.
10. 'Indian administration is politically contrived and ideologically construed'. Do you agree with the view? Elaborate your response.

PART II
EMPIRICAL ISSUES

Disaster Management in India

LEARNING OBJECTIVES

1. To know about the mechanisms of disaster management in India.
2. To understand institutional arrangements and constitutional provisions for disaster mitigation in India.

Disaster is an unwanted guest. The term 'disaster' originated from the French word 'Desastre' which is made up of two words—'des' meaning bad or evil and 'astre' meaning star. Thus, literally, disaster means a bad star. Further, the term 'disaster' may be defined as an unexpected happening, causing a huge loss of life and property. The UN defines disaster as the occurrence of sudden or major discomfort which disrupts the basic fabric and normal functioning of a society or community (GOI 2011, 14). Thus, disaster is a sudden, calamitous event that seriously disrupts the functioning of a community or society and causes human, material, economic or environmental losses that exceed the community's or society's ability to cope using its own resources. As a disaster is an event which falls beyond the coping capacities of the affected community thus, it calls for efforts from the society at large.

TYPES OF DISASTER

Disasters may be of two kinds:

1. Natural
2. Manmade

Natural disasters include: earthquakes, landslides, volcanic eruptions, floods and cyclones. Natural disasters affect human life and also the infrastructure of environment. So far as natural disasters are concerned, they take place areas which are vulnerable. Places located near a river are vulnerable to floods which far off places are not. Similarly, there are some places which are vulnerable to earthquakes. Geographers have marked some areas as vulnerable to earthquakes due to natural and geographical factors. For example, Japan is an earth quake prone country due to natural reasons.

On the other hand, manmade disasters are those for which human beings are responsible. Disasters such as aviation disasters, stampedes, building collapses and train accident are events that are caused by human errors and occur in proximity to human settlements. Thus, man is also responsible for disasters in society but it can be managed and controlled.

DISASTERS IN INDIA

India has been vulnerable, in varying degrees, to a large number of natural, as well as, man-made disasters on account of its unique geo-climatic and socio-economic conditions. It is highly vulnerable to floods, droughts, cyclones, earthquakes, landslides, avalanches and forest fires. Out of the 35 states and union territories in the country, 27 are disaster prone. Almost 58.6 per cent of the landmass is prone to earthquakes of moderate to very high intensity; over 40 million hectares (12 per cent of land) is prone to floods and river erosion; of the 7,516 km long coastline, close to 5,700 km is prone to cyclones and tsunamis; 68 per cent of the cultivable area is vulnerable to droughts and the hilly areas are at risk from landslides and avalanches (GOI 2011, 3). The loss in terms of private, community and public assets due to disasters is astronomical. The natural hazard that occurred in Kedarnath valley (Uttarakhand) due to torrential rainfall in June, 2013 is the latest evidence to show the amount of loss caused by disasters.

Disasters take a huge toll on human lives and property and severely hamper development. It may not be possible to prevent natural disasters totally, but with careful pre-disaster planning and preparedness, the adverse effects of the hazards and the economic loss therein can be reduced. Here comes the significance of disaster management.

DISASTER MANAGEMENT

Disaster management is the discipline of dealing with and avoiding both natural and man-made disasters. It involves preparedness, response and recovery in order to lessen the impact of disasters. The Disaster Management Act, 2005 defines disaster management as more like a continuous and integrated process of planning, organizing, coordinating and implementing measures which are necessary for:

1. Prevention of danger or threat of any disaster
2. Mitigation or reduction of risk of any disaster
3. Capacity building including research and knowledge management
4. Preparedness to deal with any disaster
5. Prompt response to any threatening disaster situation
6. Assessing the severity of the effects of any disaster
7. Evacuation, rescue and relief
8. Rehabilitation and reconstruction

Disaster management therefore is an integrated process that aims not only at post-disaster relief but also focuses on the pre-disaster mitigation of the risks. If factors creating risks can be identified, then efforts can be made for preventing damage and loss of life.

MITIGATING MEASURES TO DISASTER MANAGEMENT

In the case of natural disasters, management of the disaster may be a critical problem but the proper designing of plans and programmes can definitely reduce the loss of human life and property to a significant extent. It can be done by removing people and property from a threatened location and by facilitating timely and effective rescue of the vulnerable people from the possible epicentre to a far-off safe place. In such cases, preparedness is the main way of reducing the impact of disasters.

Provision of relief is one of the most important aspects of disaster management. After any natural disaster, the supply of relief is one of the main concerns of disaster management. Relief activities include, rescue, relocation, providing food and water, preventing disease and disability, repairing vital services such as telecommunications, electricity and transport, providing temporary shelter and emergency health care (Chakrabarty and Chakraborty 2014). Thus, proper planning and provisioning of relief measures are effective tools of disaster management. Public awareness and education along with the involvement of the local community and civil society are also part of an effective management of disasters.

DISASTER MANAGEMENT IN INDIA

India is considered as the world's most disaster prone nation. Millions of people are affected every year and the economic losses caused by natural disasters amount to a major share of the Gross National Product (2 per cent of GDP). Every year, a huge amount of resources is mobilized for rescue, relief and rehabilitation works following natural disaster occurrences. An analysis of what transforms a natural event into a human and economic disaster reveals that the fundamental problems of development that the country faces are the very same problems that contribute to its vulnerability to the catastrophic effects of natural hazards. The principal causes of vulnerability include rapid and unmanageable urbanization, huge urban and rural poverty and degradation of the environment resulting from the exploitation of natural resources.

The late 1990s and the early part of the twentieth century marked a watershed in Disaster Management in India. The Orissa Super Cyclone (1999) and the Gujarat Earthquake (2001) taught the nation a hard lesson.

EMERGENCE OF AN INSTITUTIONAL ARRANGEMENT IN INDIA

In India, a permanent and institutionalized setup began in the decade of 1990s with the setting up of a disaster management cell under the Ministry of Agriculture, following the declaration of the decade of the 1990s as the International Decade for Natural Disaster Reduction (IDNDR) by the UN General Assembly. Following a series of disasters such as the Latur earthquake (1993), the Malpa landslide (1994), the Orissa super cyclone (1999) and the Bhuj earthquake (2001), a high powered Committee under the Chairmanship of Mr J. C. Pant, Secretary, Ministry of Agriculture, was constituted for drawing up a systematic, comprehensive and holistic approach towards disasters. There was a shift in policy from an approach of relief through financial aid to a holistic one for addressing disaster management. Consequently, the disaster management division was shifted under the Ministry of Home Affairs in 2002 and a hierarchical structure for disaster management evolved in India (GOI 2011, 24).

ORGANIZATION AND STRUCTURE OF DISASTER MANAGEMENT

The Disaster Management Division is headed by a Joint Secretary (DM) in the Ministry of Human Affairs (MHA), who is assisted by three Directors, Under Secretaries, Section Officers, Technical Officer, Senior Economic Investigator, consultants and other supporting staff. The upper echelon of the structure consists of a Secretary (Border Management), Home Secretary, Minister of State in charge and the Home Minister.

The National Disaster Management Authority has been established at the Centre, the SDMA at the state and district authorities at the district level are gradually being formalized. In addition to this, the National Crisis Management Committee, also functions at the Centre. The nodal ministries, as identified for different disaster types, function under the overall guidance of the Ministry of Home Affairs (the nodal ministry for disaster management).

THE DISASTER MANAGEMENT ACT, 2005

This Act provides for the effective management of disasters and for matters connected therewith or incidental thereto. It provides institutional mechanisms for drawing up and monitoring the implementation of disaster management. The Act also ensures measures by the various wings of the Government for the prevention and mitigation of disasters and prompt responses to any disaster situation.

The Act provides for the setting up of a National Disaster Management Authority (NDMA) under the Chairmanship of the Prime Minister, State Disaster Management Authorities (SDMAs) under the Chairmanship of the Chief Ministers, District Disaster Management Authorities (DDMAs) under the Chairmanship of the Collectors/District Magistrates/Deputy Commissioners. The Act further provides for the constitution of different Executive Committees at the national and state levels. Under its aegis, the National Institute of Disaster Management (NIDM) for capacity building and the National Disaster Response Force (NDRF) for response purposes have been set up. It also mandates the concerned ministries and departments to draw up their own plans in accordance with the Government of India's national policy and plans.

The Act further contains provisions for financial mechanisms such as the creation of funds for response, the National Disaster Mitigation Fund and similar funds at the state and district levels for the purpose of disaster management. The Act also provides specific roles to local bodies in disaster management. Further with the enactment of the 73rd and 74th Amendments to the Constitution and the emergence of local self-government, the role of local authorities becomes very important. The DM Act, 2005 also envisages specific roles for local bodies in disaster management.

There has also been a concerted effort on part of the state to mainstream disaster mitigation initiatives in Rural Development schemes. One example is the coordination between the Ministry of Rural Development and the Ministry of Home Affairs (which is now the nodal ministry for the coordination of relief and response and overall natural disaster management), for changing the guidelines of schemes such as the Indira Awas Yojana (IAY) and the Sampoorn Grameen Rojgar Yojana (SGRY) so that the houses constructed under the IAY or the school buildings/community buildings constructed under the SGRY are earthquake/cyclone/flood resistant.

THE ROLE OF CIVIL SOCIETY

Since the local community is the first to respond in any disaster situation, there is a great need for community level initiatives in managing disasters. The initiatives taken by various agencies, including the state, need to be people-centric and the level of community participation needs to be gauged through the role played by the community in the process of planning and decision-making. Efforts need to also be made to strengthen local economies, thereby making people independent of external assistance. The voluntary sector has been in the forefront for mobilizing communities, thereby enabling them to cope with disasters in the past decades. Their initiatives and experiences have been consolidated and demonstrated on a larger scale with the help of the state. Development organizations working in communities share a good rapport with the community, which helps the state in implementing its plans more effectively. Village-level plans prepared after the super cyclone in Orissa could be seen as an example of the same.

FUTURE CHALLENGES

There is an urgent need to look at disasters from a development perspective. Disasters can have devastating effects on communities and can significantly set back development efforts to a great extent. The Yokohama Strategy (1994),[10] which is the outcome of the World Conference on Natural Disaster Reduction in May 1994, emphasizes that disaster prevention, mitigation and preparedness are better than disaster response in achieving the goals and objectives of vulnerability reduction.

The Government of India has adopted mitigation and prevention as essential components of its development strategy. The Tenth Five-Year Plan emphasizes the fact that development cannot be sustainable without mitigation being built into the development process.

In the long run, the onus is upon local communities to handle disasters with the help of the state and other such organizations. It is a well-known fact that community dynamics are quite complex in a country like India. There is a need to address the specific local needs of vulnerable communities through local traditions and cultures. The restoration of common property resources with the participation of local level bodies is a real challenge. The historical focus of disaster management has been on relief and rehabilitation after the event has occurred but now the focus is on planning for disaster preparedness and mitigation. Given the high frequency with which one or other part of the country suffers due to disasters, mitigating the impact of disasters needs to be an integral component of development planning. Thus, development projects need to be sensitive towards disaster mitigation. Disasters are part of human life. We have to face them, since we have to live in the environment of nature. Thus, we have to be careful about disasters, either natural or man-made. We can tackle and prevent disasters with sound management and precautionary measures.

Land Acquisition for Development

LEARNING OBJECTIVES

1. To understand the main issues in the Land Acquisition Act.
2. To know the nuances of the constitutional and legal premises of the Act.

The issue of 'land acquisition for development' can be attributed to the model of development adopted in post-independent India. Land acquisition refers to the process of acquisition of land by the central or state government of India from landholders for various infrastructure and economic development projects. However, a contentious issue that has been raised by the land owners is that they have not been adequately compensated.

In the 1950s, industrial and infrastructure projects were considered to be the path towards development and projects such as large dams generating water and power were supposed to help India 'catch up with the West' and promote modernity. It was unquestioned then that such mega projects would require the displacement of a large number of population. Forced uprooting of people was considered to be the 'cost' of development due to overarching national interest.

According to one estimate, every year, over 500,000 people are displaced by infrastructure construction, including hydroelectric irrigation projects, mines, industrial complexes and super thermal and nuclear power plants (Kothari 1997, 85–116). As the Kalinganagar (Orissa) and Nandigram (West Bengal) incidents of 2006 and 2007 respectively highlight, the displacements involved in large infrastructure projects remain an unresolved issue within 'development'. With big dams and irrigation projects like the Narmada and Tehri, Special Economic Zones spanning across the country, gas pipelines, and clean, beautiful metropolitan cities with vision Shanghai, India is certainly bound on the fast road to development. However, the question being raised again and again is: Development for whom and at whose cost?

The situation has deteriorated with liberalization and globalization. With the profit motive as its main motor, the corporate sector in general and the private sector in particular, require more land. The Central government expressed its intention to accede to this demand in the Rehabilitation Policy 1994 draft that began, It is expected that there will be large scale investments, both on account of internal generation of capital and increased inflow of foreign investments, thereby creating an enhanced demand for land to be provided within a shorter timespan in an increasingly competitive market ruled economic structure.

However, the problem is 'majority of our mineral resources...are located in the remote and backward areas mostly inhabited by tribals' (MRD 1994, 1–2). The Centre provided it legal backing through the Highways Act, 1995, the Special Economic Zones (SEZ) Act, 2005 and the attempt to change the Fifth Schedule in 2001 to make acquisition of tribal land easier. Most states too introduced legal changes to suit this purpose. For example, Karnataka amended its Land Reforms Act in 1995 to make the leasing of land possible for aquaculture and raised the land ceiling to 108 acres and is planning to remove the restrictions on tenancy. Goa has amended its industrial policy to encourage investments without giving priority to employment generation. Gujarat too is contemplating changes (Fernandes 2008, 95). This is likely to grow exponentially in the future because of the insatiable demand for land as a consequence of liberalization and globalization. Globalization involves a greater attack on land which is the source of sustenance of most rural communities.

Till 2013, land acquisition in India was governed by the Land acquisition Act, 1894. The Land Acquisition Act allowed the government to acquire private lands. The displaced people were only liable for monetary compensation linked with the market value of the land in question, which was still quite minimal. There have been a number of political and social protests against the acquisition of land by industrialists. The amount reimbursed has been fairly low with regard to the current index of prices prevailing in the economy. Furthermore, because of their low levels of human capital, the displaced people often fail to find adequate employment.

THE LAND ACQUISITION REHABILITATION AND RESETTLEMENT ACT, 2014

The Modi Government introduced a new Land acquisition Act in December, 2014 with the objective of protecting the rights of the land owners as well as removing the hindrances in acquiring land for developmental purposes. The 2014 Act focuses on providing not only compensation to land owners, but also extend rehabilitation and resettlement benefits to those losing their livelihoods from the land, which is to be in addition to the minimum compensation. The minimum compensation to be paid to land owners is based on a multiple of market value and other factors laid down in the Act. The Act forbids or regulates land acquisition when such acquisition includes multi-crop irrigated area. The Act has changed the norms for the acquisition of land for use by private companies or by public–private partnerships, including a compulsory approval of 80 per cent by the landowners. The Act also introduced changes in the land acquisition process, including a compulsory social impact study, which needs to be conducted before an acquisition is made.

The government recommended the promulgation of an ordinance (on 31 December 2014) making significant changes in the Land Acquisition Act including the removal of the consent clause for acquiring land for five areas of industrial corridors, PPP projects, rural infrastructure, affordable housing and defence. The Union Cabinet decided to amend the Act to provide higher compensation and rehabilitation and resettlement benefits to farmers whose land was being acquired. There is a mandatory condition for the provisioning of jobs for those whose land is getting acquired for industrial corridors.

The government passed the Land Acquisition Amendment Bill in the Lok Sabha on 10 March 2015. But it could not be passed in the Rajya Sabha due to the controversy on compensation and the purpose of the acquisition.

ISSUE OF CONTENTION

There are some controversies regarding the new Act. The compensation for the acquired land is based on the value of the agricultural land; however price increases have been ignored. The land value would increase many times, which the current buyer would not benefit from. The empirical and theoretical studies on displacement through the acquisition of land by the government for development projects have so far focused on the direct and immediate adverse consequences of land acquisition. Most of the analytical as well as descriptive accounts of the immediate consequences of land acquisition for development projects draws heavily from Michael Cernea's (1991) 'impoverishment risk model', which broadly enumerates eight 'risks' or 'dimensions' of development-induced displacement. These eight risks are very much direct and basic in nature and include: (a) landlessness, (b) joblessness, (c) marginalization, (d) loss of access to common property resources, (e) increased morbidity and mortality, (f) food insecurity, (g) homelessness and (h) social disarticulation (Cernea 1991, 2).

The above discussion raises serious questions regarding our developmental policies. Though the nation aspires for development, it needs to be sustainable, equitable and linked with the empowerment of the common people. In the case of land acquisition, the owner needs to be compensated not only financially but also socially and culturally. He needs to be compensated adequately, given alternative jobs and rehabilitated in a dignified manner. Development should not be at the cost of the weaker sections of society. Development has to be inclusive and equitable.

Women in Administration

LEARNING OBJECTIVES

1. To be able to discuss women's participation and role in administration.
2. To understand the theoretical and practical aspects of the gender dilemma and the public–private division perspective.

A gender perspective of administration is an inevitable outcome of heightened gender sensitivity since the 1960s. The feminists have demonstrated how patriarchy has systemically excluded women from the public space and arrested them in the private space by capturing state and public administration. Hence, a feminist perspective is sought to access the role of public administration, especially of bureaucracy, public policy, etc. through a gender lens.

There are innumerable shades and contours to feminism. Only one common thread that distinguishes the feminist position from the rest is its uncompromising stand on gender equity and gender justice. The feminist theory of public administration is in trying to unearth the gender biases embedded in public agencies and administrative practices. Camilla Stivers (2002, 132) writes that 'feminist theories of Public Administration, then use gender as a lens through which to analyze critically women's current status and role in public agencies, bring to light ways in which gender bias inhabits ideas and practices in the field, and formulate new theoretical approaches'.

The feminist discourse in public administration is crystallized into two categories—descriptive and conceptual. While the descriptive theories record the manifestations of the underlying gender inequalities in public institutions on the basis of empirical studies; the conceptual theories on the other hand use gender to rethink the existing philosophy of public administration. At the beginning the feminist scholarship of public administration was mostly confined to descriptive theorization. The conceptual theorization in Public Administration begins only recently (Stivers 2002, 132). Hence, the feminist theory in public administration can be seen as an application of the overall feminist epistemology in the theory and practice of public administration. Feminist theory has shown that women have been subjugated on the pretext of biology, and that gender discrimination is so pervasive because it is socially and culturally embedded. Hence, gender empowerment is recommended in order to break free from the invisible shackles of male domination.

FEMINIST ASSERTION

The feminist assertion in public administration was a mid-1970s development. It was basically the outcome of a symposium on 'Women in Public Administration' in 1976 under the leadership of Nesta M. Gallas, the first female President of the American Society for Public Administration (ASPA). The symposium organized under the auspices of the *Public Administration Review,* a noted journal of the discipline, was mainly concentrated on issues including how and why women had been trapped under the glass ceiling, what kind of affirmative action was needed to ameliorate the status of women, strategies to facilitate women administrators perform better, the idea of women's right as a basis for public policy and the like. Other important examples of the descriptive feminist theory of Public Administration were Lorraine D. Eyde's *The Status of Women in State and Local Government* (1973) and Judith

Mohr's *Why Not More Women City Managers?* (1973). In both these publications, the discrimination against women was questioned.

The conceptual theories were of the view that behind the so-called objectivity of public institutions, there were hidden gender biases. Hence, fundamental theoretical assumptions, approaches and concepts needed to be re-evaluated. The earliest attempt in this regard was the joint article by Robert B. Denhardt and Jan Perkins (1976), entitled 'The Coming Death of Administrative Man'. They argued that organizational theory despite its avowed universal neutral orientation was in 'actuality culturally masculine'.

The feminist perspective of public administration sought to interrogate the structural inequality, embedded in public institutions and values. Hence, it suggested that the core areas of public administration be thoroughly revamped with more sensitivity towards female related issues. The two major arguments of the feminist perspective in public administration include: first, according to the feminist theorists, public administration, like any other branch of social sciences, has been instrumental in systematically excluding women from the purview of public spaces on the pretext of biology. Second, feminist thinkers have argued that in a patriarchal society, public institutions, bureaucracy and so on are nothing but structures of subordination as patriarchal values are entrenched in those institutions. Therefore, to bring about gender equity, attempts need to be made to dislodge patriarchy from the above institutions.

The main thesis of Camilla Stivers 'Gender images in public administration' (2002) is that images of professional expertise, management, leadership, and public virtue that mark justifications of administrative power, contain dilemmas of gender. They not only have features commonly and unthinkingly associated with masculinity but also help to keep in place or bestow political and economic privileges on the bearers of masculine qualities at the expense of those who display culturally feminine ones.

Looking at public administration through the lens of gender, its public dimensions are revealed as gendered rather than neutral. Public administration involves discretionary exercise of public power, and public power is expected to justify itself. Typically, this is accomplished by reference to redeeming features such as the public interest dimensions of administrative decision making, the expertise that is said to serve the public good, the deft management skills that make possible the accomplishment of public purposes and the necessity for administrative leadership in the era of post-industrial complexity. But this publicness is problematic, because it is grounded in a historical understanding of the public sphere as a male preserve, distinct from the domestic realm that has been the primary life space and responsibility of women. Thus, women have been excluded from the public sphere which is dominated by males.

THE PUBLIC–PRIVATE DIVISION

Feminist theorists have criticized the classical liberal state for its marked individualism and for the dependence of its clear boundary between the public and private spheres on the exclusion of women and women's concerns from political life. Classical liberalism according to Camilla Stivers (2002) has always seen boundaries around the public sphere as necessary to prevent tyranny by sheltering individual 'private' concerns from the reach of the state. But paradoxically, the viability of economic and political activities that go on in the liberal public sphere depends on the household: on the provisioning of shelter, food, clothing, and the bearing and nurturing of children. Both pervasively in theory and persistently in practice, the household has been viewed as the realm of women. Women's concerns, when they revolve around their domestic responsibilities, have been seen as private by definition, that is, as not political and not of public interest. Therefore, not only the justice of household arrangements but also the division of human actions into public and private are barred from public discussion.

Throughout history, women have been expected to handle needs related to sustenance and nurturing so that men could have the time and energy for public pursuits. This division of labour persists today despite equal opportunities and affirmative action policies, which have enabled women to shoulder both household and paid work rather than to share them equally with men, and despite recommendations for shared parenting which are honoured more in the breach than in the observance. In recent years, several theorists have suggested that the nature of the boundary between the public and private spheres is itself debatable being political issue. Camilla Stivers (2002) argues that if it is so, the justice of household arrangements can become a matter of public deliberation.

GENDER'S DILEMMA

According to Stivers (2002) like other public sector activities, public administration is structurally masculine despite its apparent neutrality and despite the presence of increasing numbers of women in federal, state, and local governments. It can go on as it does with 'business as usual' because women bear a lopsided share of the burden of domestic functions without which life would simply not be possible. Thus, justifications of public administration take place in a space that (a) depends for its coherence on the subordination of women through their assignment to a set of duties that, no matter how necessary, are generally regarded as less significant and (b) limits both women's opportunities to participate in public life and the time and energy they have to devote to it.

The gender dimensions of this arrangement are paradoxical. The state depends on the household but acknowledges only grudgingly the political relevance of domestic issues. Throughout liberal theory women are treated as 'citizens', but in reality their participation in public life has been restricted, either formally (by law) or practically, by the demands of their household duties. It is this sort of gender paradox which Stivers argues constitutes a dilemma for women in the administrative state.

There has been a tendency to banish norms which are culturally recognized as 'feminine', such as passivity, compliance and vulnerability from public life, thus creating an approach wherein public administrators (both men and women) seek ways to appear as technical experts, tough and heroic, that is, project a more masculine 'competent image'. Stivers (2002) claims that the prevailing ideas about bureaucratic competence and expertise stress a neutral objectivity that depends on a separated self-mastering nature and ideal form of knowledge as hard data, this sort of objectivity supports the individual liberty valued in liberal philosophy by making the state neutral arbiter among competing claims. The feminist perspective, however, reveals this model of knowledge to be anything but neutral, because of the centuries old association between nature and women, the privileging in liberal thought of the public 'male' sphere over the private where the state does not arbitrate, making a firm case that the liberal state depends on the subordination of women.

GENDER IMBALANCE IN PUBLIC ORGANIZATIONS

Gender imbalance in public organizations has been a theme of concern in public administration. It has been observed that women continue to face an uphill struggle to rise to the top rank or higher management in organizations. Many reasons have been found for this including constraints in handling the role of a wife–mother–worker, the perception of women being 'unfit' for management positions, the stereotype that women are more committed to their families than to their work. A research has suggested that marriage and family affect women's ability rather than men for pursuing their career dreams. Female employees' commitment to their jobs is often questioned on the grounds that they go on maternity leave as well sick leave due to family issues or pregnancy. Due to the traditional breadwinner–housewife division of family roles, it leads to the assumption that men are more committed to their work than women. All these factors contribute to a gender imbalance in public organizations and the disempowerment of women.

To sum up, feminist theory is a critic of the existing reality. It views women's historical exclusion from certain human pursuits such as politics and confinement to others such as home-making as, if not always deliberate on the part of individual men, certainly not 'natural'. Feminists argue that such arrangements make women more likely than men to encounter neglected perspectives and to ask submerged questions about the terms and characteristics of their common existence.

Feminists are in general agreement that to be a feminist means to bring up these left out or ignored ideas. According to Stivers (2002), feminist theory sees the barriers between public and private, erected ostensibly to protect the freedom of all, as supportive of the oppression of many. In a space constructed from the exclusion of half the human race, as long as this exclusion remains unexamined no heroism of practice is possible. The most important thing in order to change the present situation is to be conscious of the need to sing different tunes from the ones currently in practice.

Accountability in Administration

LEARNING OBJECTIVES

1. To understand what accountability entails and its importance in administration.
2. To know the provisions of accountability in India and its related challenges.

Accountability is an essential feature of all forms of democratic governments. The concept of accountability refers to the liability of government servants to give a satisfactory account of the use of their official power or discretionary authority to the people. This is considered as an effective safeguard against the misuse of power and abuse of public authority. The substance of accountability, according to Mohit Bhattacharya (2011), places at least four requirements on public administrators:

1. Make laws work as intended with a minimum of waste and delay.
2. Exercise lawful and sensible administrative discretion.
3. Recommend new policies and propose changes in existing policies and programmes as needed.
4. Enhance citizen confidence in administrative institutions.

The notion of accountability carries two basic connotations: answerability, which stands for the obligation of public officials to inform and explain what they are doing, and enforcement, i.e. the capacity of accounting agencies to impose sanctions on power holders who have violated their public duties. S. K. Das (2013) observes that there are three elements that come together in the notion of accountability: answerability, enforcement and responsiveness. Answerability is the need for providing a justification for one's actions. Enforcement consists of sanctions that could be imposed if the justification for action is found to be unsatisfactory. Responsiveness means the ability of those who are held accountable to respond to the demands made on them (Das 2013, 10). On the whole, accountability demands transparency so that actions can be scrutinized and performances can be assessed.

ADMINISTRATIVE ACCOUNTABILITY IN INDIA

In India, administrative accountability is enforced by means of various controls. The purpose of control is to ensure that public servants exercise their power and discretion in accordance with the laws and regulations. Broadly speaking, there are two types of administrative control; namely, internal and external. Internal control operates from within the administrative machinery. The techniques of internal control are: budgetary systems, hierarchical orders, enquiries and investigations, pressure groups, press and annual confidential reports. External accountability over administration in India is maintained through legislative, executive and judicial control.

The administration is responsible towards elected representatives because in a democracy the people are supreme. Thus the legislature has been given certain powers through the Constitution and through Conventions to keep an effective check on the malpractice, and abuse of authority by the administration. The legislature applies a number of methods for controlling the administration namely, asking questions during question hour, Parliamentary discussions, Parliamentary audit, non-confidence motion and complaints to the ombudsman.

Executive control over the administration is another potent instrument in a responsible government. The executive exercises control over the administration through a number of means and techniques like, power of appointment and removal, rule-making power, ordinances etc., civil service code, delegated legislation, budgetary system and making appeals to public opinion. Another important instrument through which administrative accountability is ensured is judicial control and it may take the shape of judicial reviews, statutory appeals to the suits and writs against the government. The primary objective of judicial control over the administration is the protection of the rights and liberties of citizens by ensuring the legality of the Administrative Act (Singh 2002, 216–17).

Thus, the budgetary measures, departmental inquiries, annual confidential reports etc. make the administrative system accountable internally while external accountability over administration is ensured through legislative, executive and judicial controls.

CHALLENGES OF BRINGING ACCOUNTABILITY IN THE PUBLIC SERVICES

It is generally accepted that the administration in India is indifferent, unresponsive and inefficient in providing essential services to the people. Commenting on the poor work culture of government offices, the Fifth Pay Commission (GOI 1997b, 137) observed that government offices were seen as dusty, moth eaten, dingy, paper infested hovel chockfull of babus, which was feudal in its outlook, hierarchical in structure, antediluvian in its procedures and secretive in its dealings with customers. Despite being one of the largest providers of services, there was complete lack of customer orientation in various government departments. Consequently the common man viewed the government functionaries as exploiters rather than facilitators or providers.

The Second Administrative Reforms Commission (GOI 2008b, 1) had a similar perception of the Indian administration. It observed that things had not improved over the years, inefficiency, corruption and delays had become, in public perception, the hall mark of public administration in India. B. P. Mathur (2012) believes that the biggest challenge before policy-makers is to make public services accountable so that they provide efficient, citizen friendly services. He suggests that accountability can be brought by:

1. Linking promotion and career advancement of an officer with his/her actual performance on the job.
2. Bringing competition in the civil services.
3. Prescribing an Ethics Code.
4. Enforcing a strict disciplinary regime.

Accountability is a prerequisite for making the administration responsive to public needs. But it is widely felt that public servants in India are indifferent and unresponsive. The reason for that may be the lack of accountability due to which public servants can shirk work, evade responsibilities and feel like rulers. Thus, there was a pressing need to make the administrative system accountable by creating an effective mechanism to ensure accountability.

Information Technology and Its Impact on Administration

LEARNING OBJECTIVE

1. To explore the impact of information technology on administration in India.

Information technology, popularly known as E-governance, is a mechanism to redress public grievances and thereby bring the people closer to the administration. E-governance is the short form of 'electronic governance'. If service delivery is done with the use of ICT (information and communications technology), it is said to be E-governance. In general E-governance denotes the use of ICT in any organization i.e. governing through the electronics mode. Increasingly E-governance is used to refer to the performance of governmental functions through the application of ICT, the most well-known part of which is the 'Internet'.

Thus E-governance is about a process of reform in the way governments work, share information, and deliver services to internal and external clients. Specifically, an E-government harnesses information and communication technologies, such as the Internet, the web, and mobile phones, to deliver information and services to citizens and businesses. As a first step, information about services is published on a website and citizens can Interact with the site to download application forms for a variety of services. The next stage involves the use of ICT in the actual delivery of services, such as filing a tax return, or renewing a license. More sophisticated applications can process online payments (Bhatnagar 2008, 247).

BRINGING PEOPLE CLOSER TO THE ADMINISTRATION

E-governance provides citizens the ability to obtain government services through electronic means, enabling access to government information and completion of government transactions on an anywhere, anytime basis. In this way it is a tool of bringing people closer to the government and the administration. The idea is simply to create capabilities for providing citizens' access to government departments through electronic networks. The ultimate goal is to bring about better governance which has been termed as simple, moral, accountable, responsive and transparent (SMART; GOI 2002, 187), the aim of which is to create a space for the regular involvement of citizens who, as customers of public services, now have direct access to governmental activities through the ICT. Thus, through E-governance, the aim of SMART governance is achieved which is:

> **Simple:** Because there are no elaborate procedures, no paper work and no need for frequenting government offices,
> **Moral:** The system is cleaned up of corruption and other unethical practices,
> **Accountable:** Since all the information is in the public domain, the government's accountability is enhanced,
> **Responsiveness:** Through the use of ICT, the government can be in regular touch with the masses and get their feedback,
> **Transparency:** The information which was shrouded in secrecy within the dark file chambers will now become available to all at the click of a mouse.

A revolution in ICT has the potential of elevating the governance process to new levels. The ICT facilitates efficient storing and retrieval of data, instantaneous transmission of information, processing information and data faster than the earlier manual systems, speeding up governmental processes, taking decisions expeditiously and judiciously, increasing transparency and enforcing accountability. It also helps in increasing the reach of governments—both geographically and demographically. Recognizing the increasing importance of electronics, the Government of India established the Department of Electronics in 1970. The subsequent establishment of the National Informatics Centre (NIC) in 1977 was the first step towards E-governance in India as it brought 'information' and its communication into focus. Several important initiatives were undertaken by the Union and the state governments in the 1990s. All these culminated in the launch of the National E-governance Programme in 2006.

In the developed countries, governance is a well-established mode in which governmental services are made available to citizens through Internet portals. In India, digital governance has been legalized by the Information Technology Act of 2000. The Act provides:

> legal recognition for transaction carried out by means of electronic data interchange and other means of electronic communication, commonly referred to as 'electronic commerce' which involve use of alternatives to paper-based methods of communication and storage of information, to facilitate electronic filling of documents with the government agencies.

The Act is a watershed in conceptualizing administrative reforms in India. More importantly, governance is certainly an attack on bureaucratic red-tapism, which causes unnecessary delays and corruption. It is a tool for achieving 'good governance especially with regard to improving efficiency, transparency and making interface with government user friendly'. The citizens can not only view online various governmental Acts, they can also provide significant inputs through emails and electronic devices (Chakrabarty and Bhattacharya 2008, 52). ICT is, thus, an important tool for connecting citizens and the government.

The ICT-based E-governance ushered in a new era in government innovations with capacities to, (a) reduce the cost of government, (b) increase citizens' inputs into the government, (c) improve public decision-making, and (d) increase the transparency of government transactions. The object of E-governance is 'to arm the citizens to act as watch dogs to government'. In view of these well-defined functional characteristics, governance is also a very meaningful step towards combating corruption. By reducing discretionary powers, it curbs opportunities for arbitrary action-governance also empowers the citizens by making their intervention in the transactions of governmental business regular through the ICT. The project E-sewa (service) that began in West Godavari district in Andhra Pradesh (India), is a good example here. The project is a tool 'to bridge the digital divide in the rural areas' through extensive use of information technology 'for providing access to various citizen to citizen (C2C) and citizen to government (C2G) services to the people in rural areas'. Managed by a women's self-help group, the project is a class by itself as it enables 'the local women-participants' to emerge as 'information leaders', who remain critical in realizing the goal of E-sewa (Chakrabarty and Bhattacharya 2008, 52).

Thus, E-governance articulates public administration in a refreshing new way. It seeks to forge a link between the citizens and the government in terms of an electronic public service. By doing so, it creates conditions for strong citizen's participation in the government decision-making process. The successful induction of E-governance requires a change of mindsets. This, in turn, requires great political will and determination and a clear-headed and decisive leadership.

Transparency and the Right to Information

LEARNING OBJECTIVES

1. To know the Indian constitutional provisions for the Right to Information.
2. To understand the role played by the RTI Act in Indian administration.

Transparency is an essential pre-condition for good administration. It is the antonym of secrecy, which is the traditional hallmark of public administration. It implies that governmental policies and functioning be known to the larger society. Transparency means that information is freely available and directly accessible to those affected by such decisions and their enforcement. It also means that the information is easily understandable. Transparency enables citizens to keep themselves informed about policies of the government, the rights that they have and what services they should expect from the government. The RTI and the Citizens' Charter are important means of ensuring transparency in administration.

THE RIGHT TO INFORMATION: ENSURING TRANSPARENCY IN ADMINISTRATION

The RTI is the most effective and accessible mechanism of ensuring a transparent administration. It means the freedom of people to have access to government information. It implies that the citizens should have free access to all files and documents pertaining to the governments working processes. The RTI has been seen as the key to strengthening participatory democracy and ushering in people-centred governance since access to information can empower citizens to demand and get information about public policies and actions, thereby leading to their welfare. Transparency in government organizations makes them function more objectively and predictably and also enables citizens to participate in the governance processes effectively. In a fundamental sense, the RTI is a basic necessity of good governance.

In recognition of the need for transparency in public affairs, the Indian Parliament enacted the RTI Act on 11 May 2005. The Act provides for the proactive disclosure of information, the establishment of the Information Commission, the appointment of public information officers, procedures for getting information, etc. It is a path-breaking legislation empowering people and promoting transparency. It provides for the setting up of a practical regime to enable and empower citizens to secure access to information under the control of public authorities. The Act gives citizens the right to request and access information held by the government at different levels, and places a corresponding duty on the government to provide the information proactively and on request.

The Act defines 'information' broadly to include not only information kept in all forms of print and electronic media, but also physical samples of works. In terms of scope, the Act covers the whole of India (except the state of Jammu and Kashmir), and specifically, it gives citizens the right to information held by public authorities established, owned, or substantially financed by the central government, the state governments, and the administration of the union territories. This includes panchayats, municipalities, and other local bodies (Sharma and Devasher 2007, 356).

The RTI Act lays down the time limit for normal applications to 30 days and 40 days where a third party submission is to be called for. In a novel approach, these time limits are reduced to a mere 48 hours where information sought 'concerns the life and liberty of a person'. The application fee is ten rupees per request and no fee is charged from the people below the poverty line. The Act provides for the appointment of Public Information Officers (PIOs) in all administrative units/offices as may be necessary, to provide information to persons requesting it. Assistant IPOs are also to be appointed at each sub-divisional or sub-district level. These provisions are designed to bring access closer to the people by ensuring that applicants can submit requests in their local areas. Every PIO can be penalized ₹250 per day up to a maximum of ₹25,000 for not accepting an application, delaying information without reasonable causes, and providing incomplete, incorrect and misleading information. Information must be in writing, including by e-mails, and the request must be submitted to the PIO. Where no response is received, this will be deemed to be a refusal. But applications must be rejected in writing with appropriate reasons.

The Act also defines ten categories of information that are exempted from disclosure because of their sensitive nature. These are information related to national security, information given in confidence by a foreign government, cabinet papers, trade and commercial secrets. Central Intelligence agencies and security agencies like the IB, RAW, Directorate of Revenue Intelligence, Central Economic Intelligence Bureau, special frontier force, BSF, CRPF, ITBP, CISF, etc., are also excluded from this Act. But information relating to corruption and human right must be given with the approval of the Central or State Information Commissions, as the case may be.

The Act provides for the establishment of an Information Commission at the Centre and in all states comprising a Chief Information Commissioner and ten Information Commissioners. The Commission can make any order required to bring about compliance with the law, including releases of documents, appointments of PIOs and publication of specified information. The Act says that the Central Chief Information Commissioner will be appointed by a committee consisting of the Prime Minister, a leader of the opposition and a union minister nominated by the Prime Minister.

The RTI Act, 2005 is one of the most empowering legislations available to the citizens of India. It facilitates specific actions to solve the existing and emerging problems. The Act should not be taken as a negative measure but rather as a positive approach to improve the machinery of governance at every level. The Act is expected to keep the civil services active through the feedback of the people via the information sought by them. Information asked by the people can also help the civil servants in ascertaining the satisfaction of the people.

However, it is also to be kept in mind that mere conferment of the RTI without changing the prevalent style of governance would make the entire exercise futile. In the context of our present scenario characterized by the lack of political will and reluctant attitude of the bureaucracy to recognize the people's RTI, the role of CSOs will be crucial and significant in ushering in a new era of open, transparent and accountable governance. The more these organizations come forward to enlighten and mobilize the people at the grassroots, the more will be the realization of the immense potential of the RTI.

Liberal Economic Reforms and the Role of the Bureaucracy

LEARNING OBJECTIVES

1. To understand the initial impact of liberal economic reforms on the Indian administration.
2. To know how the bureaucracy and administrative machinery has evolved since the economic reforms.

With the adoption of the New Economic Policy in the early 1990s, there have been attempts at dismantling the centrally directed framework of economic development in India. This was also the beginning of the period when international donor agencies exercised immense influence on the domestic economy by attaching 'conditional ties' while giving aid. These conditionalities were, at the outset, mere prescriptions for the administration of aid but later became modalities for reform in the overall framework of governance itself. Given the rising tide of 'neoliberalism', no country is free from this. The changed empirical context has contributed to a new conceptualism in the form of 'reinventing government' that actually seeks to articulate the transformed role of public administration. Reforms in the administration in India in the 1990s have been basically driven by measures of economic liberalization.

Seeking to articulate the typical Indian response to liberalization, the Industrial Policy Resolution 1991 suggested several steps to 'unshackle the Indian industrial economy from the cobwebs of unnecessary bureaucratic control', though within the overall control of the state. Four specific steps were recommended. First, the government decided to abolish the 'industrial licensing policy' except for a short list of industries related to security and strategic concerns, social concerns, hazardous chemicals and overriding environmental considerations. Second, the government also endorsed 'direct foreign investment up to 51 per cent foreign equity in high priority industries'. To avoid bottlenecks, an amendment to the Foreign Exchange Regulation Act 1973 was suggested. Third, it was also decided to withdraw protection of 'the sick public sector units' and there would be 'a greater thrust on performance improvement' to ensure accountability of those involved in these state-sponsored enterprises. Finally, the 1991 Policy sought to remove 'the threshold limits of assets in respect of those companies functioning under the Monopolies and Restrictive Trade Practices Act' (MRTP). By seeking to amend this act, the 1991 Policy suggested the elimination of 'the requirement of prior approval of the Union Government for establishment of new undertakings, expansion of undertakings, merger, amalgamation and takeover and appointments of Directors under certain circumstances'. Quite clearly, the focus of the policy was on increasing privatization, relicensing and decentralization.

The role of the command and control structure of the government received a new meaning in the regime of economic reforms. Major initiatives towards the restructuring of public sector units (PSUs) were initiated, in view of their low productivity, over staffing, lack of technological up gradation and low rates of return. In order to raise resources and ensure wider public participation in PSUs, it was decided to offer its shareholding stake to mutual funds, financial institutions, general public and workers. Similarly, in order to revive and rehabilitate chronically sick PSUs, it was decided to refer them to the Board for Industrial and Financial Reconstruction (BIFR). The policy also provided for greater managerial autonomy to the Board of PSUs. In order to promote the role of private players, The National Mineral Policy (1993) de-reserved 13 minerals, while the National Telecom Policy (1994) allowed private participation in basic telecom services. The Air Corporation Act, 1994 enabled private air taxi companies to operate regular domestic services. The National Highways Act was amended to enable levy of toll on users of national highways (GOI 1997b, 92). The New Economic Policy (1991) thus envisaged a roll-back of the State and placed a greater reliance on market-friendly policies.

In the post-1990s there were sporadic attempts at disinvestment in the public sector enterprises, but these got embroiled in controversies, culminating finally in the setting up of the Disinvestment Commission in 1996. The Fifth Pay Commission Report (1994) stated that it was increasingly being felt that in capital intensive infrastructural sectors like energy, telecommunications, roads, ports, etc. the shortfalls in investments were so large that a massive infusion of private investment was a must. Many states initiated special measures to attract Foreign Direct Investment for greater industrialization in their regions. Several states introduced single window systems for speedy processing of applications for setting up industrial enterprises and liberal incentives were offered to industrialists for setting up industries in backward areas. The impact of these reforms may be gauged from the fact that total foreign investment in India grew from a minuscule US$132 million in 1991–92 to US$5.3 billion in 1995–96. As part of the economic reforms, the creation of statutory independent regulatory mechanisms has been gaining wider support.

Another significant development in the post-1990s was the decentralization and empowerment of localities for local resources and knowledge-based authentic grassroots governance. The 73rd and 74th Constitutional Amendments (1992) signalled momentous changes in terms of people's empowerment at the grassroots by providing for: (a) regular elections, (b) minimal suppression of Panchayati Raj bodies through an administrative fiat, (c) regular finances through statutory distributions by the Finance Commissions (Chakrabarty and Pandey 2008, 262) and (d) reservation of seats for weaker sections of society including women. The aim, argues Kuldeep Mathur, 'is to reduce the margin of political and administrative discretion and to allow the decentralized institutions to gather strength on the basis of people's involvement' (Mathur 1999, 22). Given the clear legal sanction for decentralization, there was no doubt that decentralization through the panchayats could bring about an enormous change in the way our democracy functioned. This was not only a change in local governance but could also provide a way for deepening political democracy by making it more direct, though it would have all the limitations of 'agency-induced instrumental decentralization' so long as the ideological format in which Panchayati Raj institutions were articulated remained unaltered.

The Indian response to the new circumstances was clearly articulated in the Conference of Chief Secretaries (1996). The focus of the Conference was on having an accountable, open and citizen-friendly government and on improving performance and integrity. It recognized that the public image of the bureaucracy was one of inaccessibility, indifference, procedure orientation, poor quality and sluggishness, corruption and non-accountability for results (GOI 1997b, 1). The follow-up action of the Conference included:

1. Developing grievance redressal machinery.
2. Formulation of citizen's charters by all ministries with public interface.

3. Setting up of an interministerial working group on the RTI and Transparency by H. D. Shourie.
4. Constituting an expert group to look into the computerization in personnel systems and public services headed by N. Vittal.
5. Initiating civil service reforms especially in transfers and promotions in the Centre and the states.

Thus the Conference initiated a national debate on effective and responsive administration which culminated in an Action Plan discussed and adopted in the Conference of Chief Ministers on 24 May 1997. The Action Plan had three components:

1. Accountable and citizen-friendly government.
2. Transparency and right to information.
3. Improving the performance and integrity of the public services.

In order to have an accountable and citizen-friendly government the Action Plan specified that the Central and all state governments would formulate Citizen's Charters for departments and offices, starting with those which had a large public interface, to be operational over the next three months. All central and state departments would facilitate at various levels, the prompt and effective redressal of public grievances from the Secretariat downwards to the village, to be operational over the next three months. The Action Plan also recognized the need for greater decentralization and devolution of administrative powers at all levels. It emphasized the strengthening of people's participation in keeping with the spirit of the 73rd and 74th Amendments of the Constitution, along with the involvement of the people and voluntary agencies in the delivery of services and devolution of administrative powers.

The Conference recognized that secrecy and lack of openness in transactions were largely responsible for corruption in official dealings. Thus steps would need to be taken to ensure easy access of the people to all information relating to government activities and decisions. In this regard, the government would take immediate necessary steps for examining the Report of the Working Group on the RTI and for introducing in the Parliament legislation for the Freedom of Information. The Action Plan also aimed at improving the performance and integrity of the civil services. It was agreed that the elimination of corruption in the public services would require prevention, surveillance and deterrent prosecution. For this investigation agencies and the vigilance machinery would need to be strengthened. It was agreed that institutional arrangements needed to be evolved for enabling objective and transparent decisions in areas such as postings, promotions and transfers of officials, particularly those working in key areas to ensure stability of tenure and depoliticized postings at all levels to sustain the morale.

In view of the above well-directed designs for civil service reforms, the recommendations of the Fifth Pay Commission were another milestone in this direction. True to the spirit, expressed in the Chief Secretaries Conference 1996, the Fifth pay Commission recommended (a) downsizing the government through the corporatization of activities which involved 'malfunctioning of goods or the provision of commercial services'; (b) transparency, openness and economy in government operations through the 'privatization of activities where government does not need to play a direct role' and also the 'contracting out services which can be conveniently outsourced to the private sector' (GOI 1997a, 122–23) and (c) contractual appointments in selected areas of operations 'for the purpose of maintaining a certain flexibility in staffing both the lateral entry of experts, moderating the numbers deployed depending on the exigencies of work and ensuring availability of component and committed personnel for certain sensitive/specialized jobs' (GOI 1997a, 175).

The Central government was advised to go for a 30 per cent reduction in the strength of the civil services, as the Pay Commission felt that it would be unwise to let the government sector continue as 'an island of inefficiency' and 'inertia'. The normal procedure of voluntary retirement after completing 20 years was to be continued. Alongside this, the Commission recommended a special scheme of voluntary retirement in the departments where surplus manpower was identified. In such cases, there would be a provisioning for the selective retirement of persons, the initiative always resting with the government for a golden handshake. The Pay Commission also stated that the role of the government would be more in evolving the policy of governance and less in actual governance. Most government departments would have to function as facilitators rather than as inhibitors of growth. New regulators would have to be evolved and enforced so as to provide a level playing field between the public and private sector enterprises, as also between the domestic and foreign companies. The administered price mechanisms would have to be replaced by mechanisms based on market-determined prices (GOI 1997a, 93).

The Government of India constituted the Sixth Central Pay Commission on 5 October 2006 which submitted its report on 24 March 2008. It is the first Central Pay Commission to be constituted in this century of rapid technological advances and after the coming into force of the RTI and Fiscal responsibility and Budget Management (FRBM) Acts. The government machinery, therefore, needs to gear up for better performance under stricter fiscal discipline and delivery mechanisms. These imperatives were reflected in the 'terms of reference' of the Sixth Central Pay Commission which made it incumbent on the Commission to recommend systematic changes for, (a) transforming Central government organizations into modern, professional and citizen friendly entities dedicated to the service of the people and (b) harmonizing the functioning of Central government organizations with the demands of the emerging global economic scenario.

The Sixth Central Pay Commission, therefore, had to not only evolve a proper pay package for government employees but also make recommendations rationalizing the governmental structure with a view to improving the delivery mechanisms for providing better services to the common man. The main recommendations of the Commission which have a bearing on the role of bureaucracy are as follows: reduction of layers, restoring pride in public services, delegation with accountability, and ensuring the availability of the best possible talent for Government and introducing performance-related incentive schemes.

The Sixth Pay Commission was a watershed in the evolution of India's civil services for a variety of reasons. This was not a Pay Commission in the ordinary sense of the term since it also sought to reshape the bureaucracy in the light of emerging global trends. By suggesting significant changes in the administrative hierarchy, the Commission translated into reality the drive towards 'debureaucratization'.

Thus, the liberal economic reforms initiated by India in the 1990s have had far reaching impacts on its bureaucracy. Today, the focus is on a transparent, accountable and responsive administration. The bureaucracy is supposed to serve the people in a more effective and efficient manner. Professionalism is the buzz word of administration.

REVIEW QUESTIONS

1. What is a disaster? What are the mechanisms to address disasters in India?
2. Write an essay on women's perspective on administration.
3. Accountability is the buzzword in public administration. Discuss.
4. Discuss the impact of liberal economic reforms on the bureaucracy in India.
5. Examine the impact of information technology on public administration.

6. What are the main issues in land acquisition for development in India.
7. Discuss the role of the Right to Information in ensuring transparency.
8. Technology is an aid to transparency in administration. Discuss.
9. The New Economic Policy 1991 is clearly an ideological intervention in administration. Explain.
10. How do you account for the growing importance of civil society in Indian administration? Elaborate your response.

NOTES

1. This is summarized version of the Estimates Committee Report of the 1966 which is available in Maheswari (1995, 155).
2. Fred W. Riggs and Daya Krishna debate on development (1966)—quoted in Arora and Goyal (1995, 559).
3. The first ARC is compared with the Hoover Commission that made a series of recommendation to improve the US administration in the aftermath of the Second World War.
4. The inputs are taken from GOI (2007) unless otherwise stated.
5. This is summarized from GOI (2008a, 223).
6. For details, see Lewis and Kanji (2009, 64–65).
7. (a) Bharat Heavy Electrical Limited (BHEL), (b) Bharat Petroleum Corporation Limited (BPCL), (c) Gas Authority of India Limited (GAIL), (d) Hindustan Petroleum Corporation Limited (HPCL), (e) Indian Oil Corporation Limited (IOC), (f) Indian Petrol Chemicals Limited (IPCL), (g) Mahanagar Telephone Nigam Limited (MTNL), (h) National Thermal Power Corporation Limited (NTPC), (i) Oil and Natural Gas Commission Limited (ONGC), (j) Steel Authority of India Limited (SAIL) and (k) Videsh Sanchar Nigam Limited (VSNL).
8. (a) Coal India Limited, (b) IOC, (c) NTPC, (d) ONGC and (e) SAIL.
9. The discussion is drawn on Chakrabarty and Pandey (2008, 194–203), unless otherwise stated.
10. Yokohama Strategy and Plan of Action for a Safer World: guidelines for natural disaster prevention, preparedness and mitigation. This document is the output of the World Conference on Natural Disaster Reduction, held in Yokohama, Japan, from 23 May to 27 May 1994.

REFERENCES

Arora, Ramesh K., and Rajni Goyal.1995. *Indian Public Administration: Institutions and Issues*. New Delhi: Wishwa Prakashan.

Banks, Nicola, David Hume, and Michael Edwards. 2015. 'NGOs, States and Donors Revisited: Still Too Close for Comfort?' *World Development* 66: 707–18.

Bhatnagar, Subhash C. 2008. 'E-Government: Building a SMART Administration for India's States'. In *The Governance Discourse: A Reader,* edited by Bidyut Chakrabarty and Mohit Bhattacharya, 247. New Delhi: Oxford University Press.

Bhattacharya, Mohit. 2011. *Public Administration: New Issues and Perspectives*. New Delhi: Jawahar Publishers.

Brautigam, Deborah. 1991. 'Governance and Economy: A Review'. Working Paper, Policy and Review Departments, The World Bank, Washington D.C.

Camilla, Stivers. 2002. *Gender Images in Public Administration: Legitimacy and the Administrative State.* London: SAGE Publications.

Centre for Good Governance. 2008. *Citizen's Charter: A handbook*. Centre for Good Governance, New Delhi.

Cernea, M., ed. 1991. *Socio-economic and Cultural Approaches to Involuntary Population Resettlement.* The World Bank, Washington D.C.

Chakrabarty, Bidyut. 2006. 'Voluntary Associations and Development Imperatives: The Indian Experience'. In *Public Administration: A reader,* edited by Bidyut Chakrabarty and Mohit Bhattacharya, 315–16. New Delhi: Oxford University Press.

Chakrabarty, Bidyut, and Mohit Bhattacharya, eds. 2005. *Administrative Change and Innovation: A Reader*. New Delhi: Oxford University Press.

Chakrabarty, Bidyut, and Mohit Bhattacharya. 2008. 'Introduction'. In *The Governance Discourse: A Reader*, edited by Bidyut Chakrabarty and Mohit Bhattacharya, 4. New Delhi: Oxford University Press.

———. eds. 2008. *The Governance Discourse: A Reader*. New Delhi: Oxford University Press.

Chakrabarty, Bidyut, and Rajendra Pandey. 2008. *Indian Government and Politics*. New Delhi: SAGE.

Chakrabarty, Manas, and Ruchita Chakraborty. 2014, July. 'Disaster Management—The Cry of the Day'. *World Focus*: 17.

Dahrendorf, Ralph. 1996. 'Economic Opportunity, Civil Society and Political Liberty'. *Development And Change* 27(2): 231.

Das, S. K. 2013. *The Civil Services in India*. New Delhi: Oxford University Press.

Dror, Yehezkel. 1968, December. *'Specialists vs. Generalists'*. (TSS). Retrieved from www.dtic.tr/fulltext/42/680695.pdf (accessed on 25 April 2015).

Fernandes, Walter. 2008. *Sixty Years of Development-induced Displacement In India: Scale, Impacts and the Search for Alternatives in India*. Social Development Report 2008, Council for Social Development, New Delhi: Oxford University Press.

Fredrich, Carl J. 1989. 'Corruption Concepts in Historical Perspective'. In *Political Corruption: A Handbook*, edited by Arnold J. Heidenheimer, Michael Johnston and Victor T. LeVine, 15. New Brunswick: Transaction Publishers.

GOI. 1966. *Report of the Rural–Urban Relationship Committee*. Ministry of Health, Government of India, New Delhi.

———. 1966–70. *Report of the Administrative Reforms Commission*. Ministry of Home Affairs, Government of India, New Delhi.

———. 1968. *Report on the Machinery of the Government of India and its Procedures of Work*. Administrative Reforms Commission, Government of India, New Delhi.

———. 1997a. *Action Plan for Effective and Responsive Administration*. Statement Adopted at the Conference Of Chief Ministers, New Delhi.

———. 1997b. *Report of the Fifth Central Pay Commission*. Vol. 1. Ministry of Finance. Government of India, New Delhi.

———. 2001. *Handbook of Industrial Policy and Statistics*. Office of Economic Advisor, Ministry of Commerce and Industry, Government of India, New Delhi.

———. 2002. *Tenth Five Year Plan (2002–2007)*. Vol. 1. Planning Commission, Government of India, New Delhi.

———. 2007, January. *Ethics in Governance*. Fourth Report, Second Administrative Reforms Commission, Government of India, New Delhi.

———. 2008a. *Eleventh Five Year Plan*. Vol. 1 (Inclusive Growth). Planning Commission, Government of India, New Delhi: Oxford University Press.

———. 2008b. *Refurbishing the Personnel Administration—Scaling New Heights*. Tenth Report of the Administrative Reforms Commission, Government of India, New Delhi.

———. 2011. *Disaster Management in India*. Ministry of Home Affairs, Government of India, New Delhi.

Jayal, Niraja Gopal. 1997, 22 February. 'The Governance Agenda: Making Democratic Development Dispensable'. *Economic and Political Weekly*: 412.

Kangle, R. P. 1972. *The Kautilya Arthasastra Part II*. Bombay: University of Bombay.

Kothari, Smitu. 1997. 'Whose Independence? The Social Impact of Economic Reforms in India'. *Journal of International Affairs* 51 (1): 85–116.

Lal, Deepak. 1964, 8 August. 'Generalists vs. Specialists in Indian Administration: A Comment'. *The Economic Weekly*: 1355–58

Lalitha, N. V., and Madhu Kohli. 1982. *Status of Voluntary Effort in Social Welfare*. National Institute of Public Cooperation and Child Development, New Delhi.

Leftwich, Adrian, ed. 1996. *Democracy and Development: Theory and Practice*. Cambridge: Polity Press.

Lewis, David, and Nazneen Kanji. 2009. *Non-governmental Organizations and Development*. London: Routledge.

Maheswari, S. R. 1995. *Indian Administration*. 5th ed. New Delhi: Orient Longman.

Malena, Carmen, Reiner Forster, and Janmejay Singh. 2004. 'Social Accountability: An Introduction to the Concept and Emerging Practice'. Social Development Papers: Participation and Civic Engagement, The World Bank, Washington D.C.

Marx, Fritz Morstein. 1949. 'Administrative Ethics and the Rule of Law'. *The American Political Science Review*: 1127–28.

Mathew, P. D. 1994. *Law for the Protection of Human Rights in India*. Legal Literacy Series (38). New Delhi: Indian Social Institute.

Mathur, B. P. 2012. 'Accountability of Civil Services: Creating an Institutional Framework'. *IJPA* LVIII (4, October–December): 680.

Mathur, Kuldeep. 1996. 'Challenge of Good Governance: India in the Post-economic Reform Period'. In *Fiscal Policy, Public Policy and Governance,* edited by Shome Parthasarathi, 315. New Delhi: NIPF & P.

———. 1999. 'Strengthening Bureaucracy: State and Development in India'. *Indian Social Science Review* 1 (January–June): 22.

Mitlin, David, S. Hickey, and A. Bebbington. 2007. 'Reclaiming Development: NGOs and the Challenge of Alternatives'. *World Development* 35 (10): 1699–1720.

MRD (Ministry of Rural Development). 1994. *National Policy for Development-induced Displacement and Rehabilitation of Persons Displaced as a Consequence of Acquisition of Land*. 2nd draft. MRD, Government of India, New Delhi.

Planning Commission. 1951. *First Five Year Plan (1951–56)*. Planning Commission, Government of India, New Delhi.

———. 1961. *Report of the Third Five Year Plan (1961–66)*. Planning Commission, Government of India, New Delhi.

Prasad, Kamala. 2006. *Indian Administration: Politics, Policies and Prospects*. New Delhi: Pearson-Longman.

Roy, Ashok Mohan. 1964, 13 June. 'Generalists vs. Specialists in Indian Administration–1'. *The Economic Weekly*: 1059–64.

Roy, Jaytilak Guha. 2003. 'Human Rights Dimensions of Public Administration in India'. In *Public Administration: A Reader,* edited by Bidyut Chakrabarty and Mohit Bhattacharya, 382–400. New Delhi: Oxford University Press.

Rudolph, S. H. 2000, 30 May. 'Civil Society and the Realm of Freedom'. *Economic and Political Weekly*: 1762.

Shantanam, K. 1964. *Report of the Committee on Prevention of Corruption*. New Delhi: Government of India Press.

Sharma, Pradeep K., and Mandakini Devasher. 2007. 'Right to Information in India: Legislation and Beyond'. In *Decentralisation: Institutions and Politics in Rural India,* edited by Satyajit Singh and Pradeep K. Sharma, 356. New Delhi: Oxford.

Singh, Amita. 2002. *Public Administration: Roots and Wings*. New Delhi: Galgotia Publishing.

Stivers, Camilla. 2000. *Gender Images in Public Administration: Legitimacy and the Administrative State*. 2nd ed. Thousand Oaks: SAGE.

Self, Peter. 1981. *Administrative Theories and Politics*. 1st Indian ed. New Delhi: S. Chand & Company.

Tendulkar, Suresh D., and T. A. Bhavani. 2007. *Understanding Reform: Post 1991 India*. New Delhi: Oxford University Press.

The Industrial Policy Resolution. 1948. Retrieved from http://www.dcmsme.gov.in/policies/iip.htm#Indus1 (accessed on 12 December 2015).

The Report of the Fulton Committee. 1968. Her Majesty's Stationary Office, London.

The World Bank. 1989. *Sub-Saharan Africa: From Crisis to Sustainable Growth: A Long Term Perspective Study*. Washington D. C.: The World Bank.

The World Bank. 1992. *World Development Report*. New York: Oxford University Press.

Transparency International India. 2005, 30 June. 'India Corruption Study 2005: To Improve Governance: Volume I—Key Highlights New Delhi' (Archived from the original [PDF] on 11 August 2013).

UNDP (United Nations Development Programme). 1997. 'Reconceptualising Governance'. Discussion Paper No. 2, UNDP, New York.

Vallabhbhai Patel's address in the Constituent Assembly. 1949. *The Constituent Assembly Debates*, Vol. X, p. 978, 25 November.

Vittal, N. 2002. 'Reform Initiatives in Administration'. Mimeograph, Indian Institute of Public Administration, New Delhi.

Wilson, Woodrow. 1887, 2 June. 'The Study of Administration'. *Political Science Quarterly*: 197–222.

CONCLUSION

I

There are three important ideas that run through this text on Indian administration. First, by focusing on the processes of administration within an institutional set-up, the text reaffirms the argument that a mere structural study is futile unless it is conceptualized as organic to the prevalent socioeconomic milieu. A study of the processes of administration enables us to understand the complex interplay of factors that are at work in actual administration. Second, in a contemporary network society, one needs to be sensitive to the linkages that the administration has with politics or the existent power-relationships shaping the actual functioning of administration in a specific historical context. Administration is therefore not merely responses to any situation, but calibrated responses to demands of the day which remain enigmatic unless understood as integrally linked with politics. Third, in the context of globalization, one needs to be aware of global circumstances which impinge on domestic administration since the issues that the latter deals with have largely become internationalized. Administration is thus an informed response within a perspective which is simultaneously domestic and global along with the fact that most issues which despite being domestic in nature have global significance and vice versa.

What is fundamental here is the fact that administration in the contemporary era has to be comprehended as organically interlinked processes within a historical time frame. This is a conceptual point that needs be highlighted because administration functions within a socially embedded structure which is relative to a specific socio-economic milieu. Given its distinct nature which is drawn on a particular politico-ideological context, it is inconceivable to have a universal model that can indiscriminately be applied anywhere. As administration is relative to circumstances, in other words, it cannot, be universally replicated.

The study of Indian administration is naturally complicated because of its complex evolution since the acceptance of the Westminster form of governance following the consolidation of colonialism in India which created a system of administration that was appropriate to its rule. Along with colonialism, which was ruthless and discriminatory, for obvious reasons, there also emerged a powerful voice of enlightenment which drew on politically progressive forces supportive of self-rule in the colonies. The British state thus confronted a contradiction that was not easy to resolve since both these objectives were strongly justified by equally forceful protagonists of British interests amongst the ruled. The contradiction, however, created circumstances in which liberal nationalism was conceptualized by Indians and those among the rulers who appreciated self-rule for the colonized Indians. This was probably the reason why the Indian administration during the British rule gradually became accommodative of nationalists to address their genuine socio-economic grievances. The administration did not appear to have slackened because colonialism remained the principal ideological force which simply adjusted to the new milieu when the nationalist agitation seemed to have been apparently subversive of the British interests. Indians were accommodated in administration so long as they remained supportive of colonialism. Their training in colonial administration enabled them to understand the complexities of administration in its actual articulation. Even after the British left, the institutions of administration were allowed to remain, more or less in their earlier form. The steel frame of the all India civil services which the British bequeathed was permitted to stay because of the traumatic events following the 1947 partition of India to avoid any further deterioration of the situation. The 1947 transfer of power from the British to the indigenous rulers was smooth and the continuity of the structure of administration never raised any serious debate even when nationalist leaders had a chance to experiment with a different form of administration. A perusal of the debates in the Constituent Assembly on whether independent India should have a centralized and hierarchical civil services shows that despite initial disagreements among the founding fathers, the retention of the steel frame was a *fait accompli* given the circumstance in which India was placed following the outbreak of massive communal riots across the country.

Along with structural continuity, the Indian administration also nurtured the values of British Enlightenment which upheld social virtues such as benevolence, compassion and tolerance. As a result, it was possible for administrators who despite being reared in the colonial tradition were able to actively participate in national reconstruction after the withdrawal of the British from India. For the administrators, administration was a function that needed to be discharged efficiently in accordance with the demands of the day. After independence, they were asked to fulfil a new role in a changed socio-economic environment. An analysis of the role of the civil service immediately after independence confirms that the bureaucracy can hardly be neutral since it is always linked with the prevalent political dispensation: on the one hand, they are neutral in the sense that no bias is shown by them while discharging their assigned roles; they do not seem to be neutral, on the other hand, since their responsibility is to fulfil the ideological commitment of the political regime which they serve. This is a conceptual position that is well articulated by the Indian civil service which, despite being rooted in colonialism, has shown enough resilience to face the challenges that the young nation confronted.

II

Independence brought hope and the Indian administration was the instrument to translate that hope into action by adopting specific steps that were complementary to the hope. Jawaharlal Nehru, India's first Prime Minister, opted for the state-led planned development model for the country which was translated into policy preferences by the civil service. The state was a prime mover in circumstances when the nation was groping for directions for change and advancement. The nationalist leaders were persuaded, so were the bureaucrats, by the Nehruvian model of growth in a context when other options did not appear to be appropriate for India. For Nehru, it was easy to carry forward the same because of the conducive environment that he had created by evolving an ideological milieu in which everybody was drawn. In hindsight one can find fault with Nehru's formula of a state-directed development strategy though it received accolades when it was launched immediately after independence. By being committed to the regime, those involved in administration never felt disconnected presumably because they put their duties as part of the civil service ahead of their personal predilections. During the height of the autarkic phase of Indian development, responses remained very much state-centric; the role of agencies other than the state was relegated to the background.

This phase continued in some form or the other till the mid-1970s when the idea of globalization seemed to have dawned in the arena of governance. Administrators now saw the importance of deregulation as a technique of ascertaining development even when the state-led development paradigm continued to remain dominant. By the early 1980s, there emerged a favourable political climate for globalization since political leadership did not appear to be disinclined to exploring possibilities besides state-driven planned development. The break came in 1991 when the Government of India adopted the New Economic Policy to officially endorse the fundamental ethos of the LPG regime. India became liberalized but with a difference. As detailed in the book, the Industrial Policy Resolution 1991 dispensed with the industrial licensing policy and facilitated foreign investments and technology transfers thereby throwing open the areas hitherto reserved for public sector. The aim was to maintain sustained growth in productivity, enhance gainful employment and achieve optimal utilization of human resources to attain international competitiveness thereby transforming India into a major player in the global economy. In order to carry forward the rate of growth, it was required that the Indian economy be relieved of bureaucratic control that seems to have halted progress to the extent it was expected.

As is evident, India, in different phases of her growth as a nation-state, underwent radical changes from a clearly autarkic state to one where control has almost disappeared. In such a changing context, the Indian administration has addressed newer challenges most effectively by evolving newer techniques and tools of governance. This perhaps confirms that the administration always remains 'instrumental' by being goal-driven which also reinforces the fact that the Indian administration is hardly a stumble block in so far as the fulfilment of political preferences is concerned. Those involved in transforming political decisions into policy options as well as executing them did not find it incongruent with what they preferred to do when asked to discharge their duties as civil servants. There are examples when administration was disrupted because of the tussle between the ministers and the bureaucrats; but they are few. Generally speaking, the relationship remains cordial and friction free. This is usually attributed to the strong roots of democracy in India whereby people's representatives gain an upper hand by virtue of being elected to rule. It is thus accepted that the administrators shall remain an aid to what the political representatives decide to articulate as popular mandates in policy preferences.

III

Public service is widely acknowledged as public trust and if there is anything unique about public service, it derives from this proposition. Upholding public trust means faithfully executing one's duties, as determined through the political process, in support of public interest or the collective good. This has been declining in recent years perhaps due to the deficit of ethics in governance. The importance of ethics in governance has acquired a significant place in contemporary theoretical discussions more so because of the growing decadence in governmental practices largely owing to a decline of ethical values in public administration which has perhaps been singularly responsible for the rise of 'corruption' in a virulent form. The possible reason can be located in the overgrowth of the state in which the bureaucracy has allegedly become a 'rent-seeker', ignoring its Benthamite role of being 'a benevolent guardian' or its foundational Weberian role of a 'neutral' dispenser of administration. In general, corruption in any system is the outcome of three factors: (a) declining individual sense of values, (b) decay of social values and (c) dwindling values in administration. Taken together, these factors direct our attention to a situation where there has been a general decay of values across the board and the administration as an integral part of the social processes cannot remain aloof from the decadence that we witness.

In order to deal with corruption effectively, the government of India appointed the Shantanam Committee that suggested that corruption was not confined to lower ranks of the public service and the number of cases in which higher rank officers were involved was alarming. The Committee thus recommended for the setting up of a Central Vigilance Commission to look into charges of corruption against civil servants. The first ARC report is probably the most exhaustive checklist of steps to streamline the administration in the changed socio-economic environment. Drawing on certain basic considerations, the most significant recommendation has been the appointment of the Lok Pal (at the union level) and Lokayukta (at the state level) apart from the introduction of the concept and technique of performance budgeting.

Based on the need to reform the civil services, the second Administrative Reform Commission was set up by the Government of India in 2005 under the chairmanship of Veerappa Moily to look into issues crippling public administration in India. The Commission attributed the visible decline of ethics to a whole range of factors, including the socio-psychological decline of individuals responsible for redrawing India's path for development. In the light of a general degradation of public administration, the Commission thus observed that 'in our case, at times public office is perceived to be an extension of one's property. That is why sometimes, public offices are a source of huge corruption and a means of extending patronage' (Government of India 2007). What is the way out? Despite having the institutional mechanisms to address issues of corruption in administration, corruption seems to have defied the same, becoming a source of worry for policy-makers. For the Commission, the roots are to be located in the lack of values which are conducive to create an environment of good practices. The inculcation of values facilitating the subordination of the self to a larger, societal good, and engendering a spirit of empathy for those in need of ameliorative state interventions are not skills which can be easily imbibed after joining the civil services. Such attitudes need nurturing over not merely individual life-times, but through successive generations, the 'right' ethos taking a long time to evolve. Nevertheless, it must be accepted that our civil service has a tradition of attitudes and achievements which sets examples to be emulated by current and prospective civil servants. It must also be accepted that the existing framework for maintaining and promoting the norms of 'right conduct' cannot be enforced through the rigid mindless enforcement of laws and rules. It is all a question of striking the right balance. Within the civil services there are formal, enforceable codes setting out norms of expected behaviour with 'sanctions' prescribed for unacceptable departures from such norms. There are also inchoate conventions of propriety and acceptable behaviour without formal sanctions but with non-observance of such practices and conventions attracting social disapproval and stigma.

IV

Indian administration is a witness to dramatic shifts in the political, social, economic and cultural environment. The autarkic state is being replaced in the wake of the consolidation of the LPG regime in India. Progress does not seem to be as fast as is expected presumably because of bureaucratic hassles. Here too, administration is identified as the culprit responsible for the lackadaisical attitude of Indian bureaucracy. This is partly true since a bureaucratic mindset remains integrally linked with the way the Indian administration functions. These are problems associated with the Weberian theoretical bias supporting the hierarchical form of organization that has developed in India since the days of the growing grip of the Haileybury School in Indian bureaucracy. This has created a peculiar situation: while structurally, Indian administration has not changed substantially, nevertheless it is expected to perform a role which does not seem to be compatible with the tasks ahead. An LPG state follows a certain logic of functioning which is contrary to an autarkic state. Indian administration is at a critical juncture where neither the autarkic state has completely withered away nor has its replacement struck deep roots in the Indian soil. This is a peculiar situation in which the Indian administration seems to be seamlessly caught at present. It is true that administration does not change overnight; it is also true that such a situation is not going to last as history revels since uncertainty is an exception rather than a rule.

How to make sense of the peculiar situation in which Indian administration is being torn apart? As is evident now, one can advance the argument that given the global reality and the support that the local political elites extend to the LPG regime, it is safe to suggest that Indian administration is tilted in favour of deregulation, disinvestment and the forces of globalization. There are however dissenting voices supporting the age-old autarkic control of the economy. As a result, Indian administration continues to justify public enterprises in some areas of the economy. For instance, the fact that forces opposing privatization of the railways suggests that the argument for a public sector remains viable even after accepting that globalization cannot be reversed. How this will be resolved is a difficult question to respond to. Nonetheless, it has raised an issue that needs serious probing given the rising importance of globalization in India.

V

Issues arising out of globalization have dramatically changed the nature and scope of Indian administration. No longer confined to domestic circumstances, Indian administration now needs to be sensitive to external stimuli to effectively address newer challenges out of a networked society. It has to respond to challenges of the new economic order that have appeared to have decisively influenced, if not determined, contemporary public administration. In the context of globalization, national economies are becoming more open and subject to, for obvious reasons, supra-national economic influences. As economies lose their discrete, self-contained character and become enmeshed in global networks and processes, they become less amenable to national control and management. In a nutshell, the ideology and practice of globalization privileges voluntarism and the market as the underpinnings of the new economic order.[1] The role of the state as the sole responsible agent for providing welfare services is being challenged. The state, it is now believed, should be more a facilitator than a provider because it is just a part, although crucial, of the processes of decision making in which private players also remain critical.

As an enabler, the state loses its hegemonic role over socio-economic and political processes. There are other major players, including transnational ones who, although are not subject to domestic control, play critical roles in policy making. The scene has become far more complex with the consolidation of several forces and actors, other than the state. An appropriate understanding of Indian administration thus necessitates a careful examination of both domestic and external actors in a specific historical perspective. For instance, the dramatic changes that India witnessed in the early part of 1991 in the wake of massive balance of payment shocks contributed to the articulation of ideas in favour of the LPG regime. It was evident then that India's import-substitution strategy did not appear to be adequately equipped to effectively tackle the crisis that India confronted. As a result, reservations against opening up the economy did not have many takers and India was drawn to an era of globalization. Indian administration adjusted to this new reality which posed new challenges along with new possibilities given the rise of India as a part of the global network.

VI

Indian administration is now faced with newer challenges which need newer responses. With the acceptance of the New Economic Policy in 1991, those in charge of administration got attuned to the new situation which does not mean that it was smooth sailing given the prevalence of the old mindset still supportive of the autarkic state. This was addressed conclusively by various devices. Apart from regular training courses, the civil services were sought to be reframed in the new mould. Several designs were offered by various committees that the Indian state constituted to take care of the task ahead. It was first most powerfully articulated in the Conference of Chief Ministers, 1996 which suggested several corrective steps to gear India's civil services to an already set goal. The primary effort was however to transform an aloof, impersonal and paternalistic bureaucracy into one which is citizen-friendly and sensitive to user-needs. What was suggested in the conference had its roots in the arguments that the former Prime Minister, Rajiv Gandhi made in favour of a responsive administration. In his series of workshops for district magistrates and collectors that spanned almost two years (1987 and 1989), Rajiv Gandhi argued:

> [The] paternalistic model of [our] administration is not suitable for a society where the main thrust of administration is on development. It was agreed that the regulatory functions of administration should not be seen as an end in themselves, as they tended to be in colonial times, but as a means for reinforcing and sustaining the processes of broad based development. [A] more representative and more responsive administration would be better placed to relate the purposes of administration to the larger goals of our national lie—democracy, socialism, secularism and non-alignment.

The other significant point that was made during the course of his speech questioned 'the dependency syndrome' of people which was articulated as the characteristic dependence of people on the government for everything that they needed for their daily survival. The bureaucracy thus continued to remain 'a doer' and not 'an enabler'. The people in general wait for the government 'to do the simplest things which they can do themselves'. The system had become 'so top-heavy' and 'top-oriented' that at every level, people looked to the level above for a solution. What was thus needed was 'to push administration down, not just in the administration but also sometimes out of the administration to the community'. By involving people in both planning and executing developmental programs at the grassroots, the administration would become both 'responsive' and 'representative' in character.[2] The primary concern was to arrest the drift in the management of public services which disturbed everybody regardless of political affiliations. Once the loopholes in the administration were effectively addressed, it was likely to be responsive and citizen-friendly; and unless this was achieved, Indian administration would become a hollow endeavour without much substance.

How to arrest the drift? There are some major mechanisms that have evolved during the last couple of decades: one of them is the Citizen's Charter which allows citizens access to information that has far remained guarded in the name of official secrecy. This is a device which has considerably empowered citizens vis-à-vis public servants who are now bound to release information once it has been asked for to avoid punishment. The second mechanism happens to be the right to seek redressal of public grievances which is potentially a strong means to contribute to citizen's well-being if they are harassed by those holding public responsibility. As the rule demands, all central and state departments need to address public complaints before it is too late, to escape punitive actions by higher authorities. The third step in this direction has been the commitment to review laws, regulations and procedures which are archaic and do not seem to serve the citizens in the twenty-first century. While contributing to the well-being of citizens in general, the Indian state also insists that reforms of the administrative system are necessary to make it friendlier to weaker sections who have historically been most vulnerable. The final step in this is the means to ensure people's participation in administration through the decentralization and devolution of power to make governance at the grassroots people-friendly. Consistent with the spirit of the 73rd and 74th Amendment Acts (1992), the government is expected to undertake steps to articulate the exalted aim of Mahatma Gandhi and the founding fathers who, by their commitment to the principles of democratic decentralization, challenged the Weberian centralized and hierarchical form of administration as most inappropriate for a village-based Indian society.

VII

The Chief Ministers' Conference, 1996 and the intervention of the Prime Minister underlines three important points critical to conceptualizing Indian administration in its contemporary manifestation: *first*, administrative reforms have attracted significant attention from those who matter in decision making; it is now being increasingly felt that administrators are just instruments for public service and citizens remain the prime movers in administration which cannot be ignored. *Second*, bureaucrats should be made to realize that their efficiency will be measured not in terms of what their services purport to offer, but in terms of public satisfaction at the same time. *Third*, one of the reasons for administrative ills is to the deficit of ethics in administration. The civil service needs to have a code of conduct based on a commitment to constitutional principles and values, besides basic integrity and propriety on part of those holding public office. In other words, besides upholding the basic principles of the Constitution, such as secularism, social justice, attention to the needs of the weaker sections and vulnerable groups, equality and rule of law, those involved in making and executing administrative decisions should always set an example by high moral standards and individual integrity.

How does one accomplish the goal in a context when public administration is being rigorously reviewed by proactive citizens who do not appear to be happy being mere recipients of what the decision makers do while purportedly serving them. The following are some suggested measures which are expected to effectively address the administrative-decay that Indian administration has shown in recent years:

1. Citizens' Charter and an accountable administration;
2. Effective and speedy public grievance redressal systems;
3. Empowering elected local bodies in rural and urban areas and the decentralized delivery of services;
4. Review of laws, regulations and procedures to make them relevant in contemporary India;
5. Transparency and the Right to Information;
6. Access to public information from public offices and the creation of facilitation counters in government offices;
7. Code of ethics for public services and zero tolerance of corruption in public offices;
8. Stability of tenure for civil servants and a scheme for the Civil Service Board.

Evidently, the aim is to create circumstances in which the public service will truly become public in content and spirit. Indian administration seemed to have become lackadaisical both because of reasons internal to its functioning and the lack of citizens' initiatives to make it sensitive to their demands. The 1996 Conference was the tipping point for such a realization that in the articulation of administration, public servants are as responsible as the citizens who are to be served by the former. Only with creative interaction between these two complementary components, will Indian administration go beyond its instrumental functions to become responsive and participatory.

VIII

Administration is no longer a closed-door affair in view of the alert citizenry besides the official mechanisms that are in place to ascertain that it does not drift away from the path. What has radically altered the texture of Indian administration is undoubtedly the acceptance of the Right to Information Act, 2005 whereby citizens are now empowered to demand information on any subject from the state. Any failure to provide the required information invites punishments. This is a revolutionary measure which has made administration not only responsive to their clients, but also user-friendly in a significant manner. The campaign launched by the Mazdoor Kisan Sangharsh Samiti in the late 1990s in Rajasthan led to the adoption of the RTI Act 2005 which was based on the idea that a more open and transparent system of administration promotes a more accountable and responsible democracy. Denial of information amounts to the denial of democratic rights. By being empowered to seek information on any subject, citizens seem to have become integrally connected with governance. With their participation in democratic processes, they, in other words, discharge their role as part of an alert citizenry which remains constantly vigilant. In an era when knowledge is power, the RTI Act is not merely a piece legislation, but an instrument for the fulfilment of basic democratic rights. This is most basic to the functioning of Indian democracy since most of citizens, especially in rural areas, remain ignorant of their entitlements as per government stipulations; but now with the right to information, not only do they have access to information at the government's disposal, they also are able to exercise their rights and discharge duties as alert citizens in a vibrant democracy like India. Once the required information is in their possession, they cannot be misguided by bureaucrats who usually take the advantage of their ignorance to guide administration to their advantage. The fact that the citizens are empowered and cannot be taken for a ride is a substantial contribution of this enabling Act that is potentially strong enough to change the well-entrenched archaic mindset supporting the over-bureaucratization of Indian administration. By breaking the barrier between the government and citizens, this Act has truly become an empowering device in an atmosphere when the administration does not seem to be proactive, but merely reactive. In this respect, the Act is a watershed in the processes shaping Indian administration in its different manifestations.

IX

Indian administration is certainly not static, as the text reveals. It has changed in response to stimuli from the socio-economic and political milieu. There are two major inputs that need to be highlighted to comprehend the change that is visible. First, Indian administration is now faced with responsibilities which were not in its purview in the past. This clearly means that it is now dedicated to aims which are part and parcel of the administrative commitments to citizens. Tasks before the government thus have grown immensely in volume and complexity. In order to address them effectively, the available tools do not appear to be adequate. Furthermore, the domain of administration has also considerably expanded and needs to be taken care of in the changed environment. In the new context, the administration has expanded its horizon which means it is drawn to those areas which have so far remained out of its sphere of influence in the old dispensation of authority and power.

The role of politics is very crucial in conceptualizing contemporary Indian administration. In two ways, politics has become a critical variable. First, as in the past, Indian administration is guided by a specific power relationship which impinges on its functioning. There are various political forces which are at work in the decision making processes which are clearly articulated once a particular decision is arrived at. Second, perhaps more important, the growing importance of the public in public administration would have remained inconceivable without the role of politics in linking citizens with governance. Now, citizens, by being proactive, exercise tremendous authority in so far as administration is concerned. As a process, politics is thus integrally linked with the awareness that goes with public assertion in the making of specific decisions. With the constitutional guarantee of democratic decentralization, the scene has further undergone changes in which citizens have not only assumed responsibilities, but have also crafted an independent role in administration at the grassroots. The 73rd Amendment Act can thus be said to have revolutionized rural administration in which politics has played a very critical role.

Indian administration is expansive in comparison with the past when state-led planned development earmarked areas in which it was supposed to reign supreme. The public–private boundary was clearer in the past than it is now in view of the growing importance of agencies other than the government. In other words, it is now difficult to conceptualize public in neat terms because the distinction between public and private hardly makes sense due of their interconnectedness in actual administration. This is more so in the governance era when even private agencies, both domestic and international, remained critical in public administration. In the context of India, the need is increasingly being felt because the government is not always well-equipped to address newer demands due of lack of initiative on its part which automatically creates space for private interests. By being receptive, Indian administration seems to have unfolded new dimensions in governance which were inconceivable in the past when state-driven planned development strategies completely ruled out any role for private entrepreneurs. A unique situation has arises when the conventional approaches to Indian administration are neither tenable nor conceptually helpful in comprehending its complex articulation and evolution.

X

Indian administration is being reinvented in the changed environment when an argument emphasizing less government but more governance is forcefully being made. Consistent with the Governance paradigm, Indian administration, instead of being just reactive, has become proactive and participatory in nature. A developmental state needs to be complemented with a proactive administration; otherwise, the goal for achieving inclusive development will remain unrealized. This is a challenging task which can be accomplished only if Indian administration responds in accordance with what it is expected to do to fulfil the set objectives. There are problem areas which cannot be easily negotiated given the frequent lack of coordination among different layers of administration. Lack of coordination is undoubtedly a source of concern but cannot be avoided in view of the complexities in which administration usually articulates its responses especially in a country like India which is socio-economically and politically so diverse. In other words, it is not an easy task presumably because of the well-entrenched diversity in which administrators function while discharging their responsibilities as part of the bureaucracy. Besides the peculiar socio-economic and political circumstances in which Indian administration is located, one also needs to be sensitive of the exogenous factors that are critical in their response particularly in the context of the growing consolidation of what is so euphemistically characterized as 'the LPG regime'. Transformed because of the increasing grip of globalization, Indian administration cannot thus be conceptualized in the typical Weberian formulation of a boundary conscious bureaucracy that has been linked with a rather simple society in which domestic circumstances continued to remain critical. This was perhaps the reason why Weber conceived bureaucracy as 'an instrument of functioning', the nature of which was contingent on the prevalent socio-economic circumstances, as David Beetham, in his *Max Weber and the theory of modern politics* (1985) has shown. Critical of the argument that Weber did not appear to have shown any concern to the existent socio-economic circumstances, Beetham argues that '[f]ar from embodying the universal and disinterested outlook ascribed to it by conservative mythology, in practice, it was unable to free itself from the outlook of the social classes from which it was recruited and to which it was allied' (Beetham 1985). This is a fundamental theoretical proposition which illuminates the changing nature of Indian administration over a historical period of time. In the context of state-led planned economic development, Indian administration has manifested itself in such a way as to support the ideological preference of policy-makers; India was a state-controlled economy to a significant extent; it was also a socialistic, but not a socialist regime and as a result, private operators remained integrally linked with India's economy. The scene substantially changed from 1991 with the acceptance of the policies of economic liberalization. Structurally the same, Indian administration was expected to transform itself in accordance with the newly found love for globalization which had teething problems at the outset, but was gradually accepted as an unavoidable genie who rose to absorb those opposed to the opening of the economy regardless of its obvious positive outcomes. A witness to these remarkable changes, the Indian administration is therefore not merely a structure performing certain well-defined functions, but an interesting journey through India's complex history.

By locating Indian administration in the constantly changing socio-economic and political circumstances, *Indian Administration: Evolution and Practice* is a unique study that stands apart not because of the depth of its analysis but also because of the effort that it makes to link public administration with the wider socio-economic and political processes. Public administration cannot remain isolated from the milieu in which it is situated because the administrators who run administration do not come from outside, but from within, and hence they reflect the predilections of the society to which they belong. The study is a class by itself because unlike the conventional texts on Indian administration, the book provokes a debate by arguing for the importance of the processes and not merely the structure, while deciphering the unique nature of Indian administration. The key to conceptualizing the complex character of Indian administration lies in comprehending the wider socio-economic and political processes in which it grows. This is the fundamental argument that the book offers on the basis of a thorough study of the dialectical interconnections between the structure and processes of administration in India's unique socio-political and economic context.

NOTES

1. Gerald Caiden has pursued this argument in his 'globalizing the theory and practice of public administration' in Gracia-Zemor and Khatur (1994).
2. These quotes are taken from Rajiv Gandhi's speech in Hyderabad, 13 February, 1988, Government of India Press, New Delhi, 1989, pp. 8–9.

REFERENCES

Beetham, David. 1985. *Max Weber and the Theory of Modern Politics*, 66. Cambridge: Polity Press.

Gandhi, Rajiv. 1988. 'Responsive Administration', speech on 18 June, 1988 at Coimbatore, *The Times of India* (New Delhi).

Government of India. 2007, January. Ethics in Governance, 6. Fourth Report, Government of India, New Delhi.

Gracia-Zemor, Jean-Claude and Renu Khatur, ed. 1994. *Public Administration in the Global Village*, 49–59. West Port, CT: Praeger.

BIBLIOGRAPHY

The purpose of this section is to acquaint the readers with the relevant literature in Indian administration. The field is vast. Hence it is difficult to provide an exhaustive bibliography though an effort is made to identify those texts which are critical in conceptualizing and also comprehending the broad trends in this sub-discipline. While preparing this list of texts, care was taken to locate significant texts in the field. Besides them, this bibliography also contains some critical texts which are useful to grasp those foundational ideas which remain integrally connected with the evolution of Indian administration in the context of rapidly changing socio-economic and political milieu. In this sense, this bibliography is not only a pathfinder for further research it will also equip the readers with an intellectual acumen to unravel the dynamics of Indian administration in its most complex manifestation.

Bardhan, Pranab. 2008. *The Political Economy of Development in India*. New Delhi: Oxford University Press (reprint).

Bagchi, Sanjoy. 2007. *The Changing Face of Bureaucracy: fifty years of the IAS* [Indian Administrative Services]. New Delhi: Rupa & Co.

Bhambri, C. P. 1972. *Administrators in a Changing Society*. Delhi: National Publishing House.

Bhattacharya, Mohit. 2011. *Public Administration: New Issues and Perspectives*. New Delhi: Jawahar Publishers.

Bombwall, K. R. 1978. *Indian Constitution and Administration*. Ambala Cant: Modern Publication.

Braibanti, Ralph. 1985. *Asian Bureaucratic System Emergent from the British Imperial Tradition*. Durham: Duke University Press.

Chakrabarty, Bidyut and Mohit Bhattacharya, ed. 2005. *Administrative Reforms: Innovation and Change*. New Delhi: Oxford University Press.

———, ed. 2003. *Public Administration: A Reader*. New Delhi: Oxford University Press,

———, ed. 2008. *The Governance Discourse: A reader*. New Delhi: Oxford University Press.

Chakrabarty, Bidyut and Prakash Chand. 2012. *Public Administration in a Globalizing World*. New Delhi: SAGE Publications.

Chakrabarty, Bidyut and Rajendra Pandey. 2008. *Indian Government and Politics*. New Delhi: SAGE Publications.

Chakrabarty, Bidyut. 2007. *Reinventing Public Administration: The Indian Experience*. New Delhi: Orient Longman.

Chakravarty, Sukhomoy. 1987. *Development Planning: The Indian experience*. Oxford: Clarendon Press.

Chatterjee, Partha. 1997. "Development Planning and the Indian State." In *State and Politics in India*, edited by Partha Chatterjee. New Delhi: Oxford University Press.

Corbridge, Stuart, John Harriss and Craig Jeffrey. 2014. *India: Economy, Politics and Society*. New Delhi: Oxford University Press.

Heginbotham, Stanley J. 1975. *Cultures in Conflict: The Four Faces of Indian Bureaucracy*. New York: Columbia University Press.

Jalal, Ayesha. 1995. *Democracy and Authoritarianism in South Asia: A Comparative and Historical Perspective*. Cambridge: Cambridge University Press.

Jenkins, Rob, Loraine Kennedy, and Partha Mukhopadhyay. 2014. *Power, Policy and Protest: The Politics of India's Special Economic Zones*. New Delhi: Oxford University Press.

Kohli, Atul. 1992. *Democracy and Discontent: India's Growing Crisis of Governability*. Cambridge: Cambridge University Press.

Maheshwari, S. R. 2003. *Administration of India*. New Delhi: Macmillan.

———. 2000. *Public Administration in India*. New Delhi: Macmillan.

———. 2000. *State Governments in India*. New Delhi: Macmillan.

———. 1968. *Indian Administration*. New Delhi: Orient Longman.

Mathur, Kuldeep. 2013. *Panchayati Raj*. New Delhi: Oxford University Press.
———. 1986. *Development Policy and Administration*. New Delhi: SAGE.
Mishra, B. B. 1986. *Government and Bureaucracy in India*. Delhi: Oxford University Press.
———. 1977. *The Bureaucracy in India*. New Delhi: Oxford University Press.
Mukherji, Rahul. 2014. *Globalization and Deregulation: Ideas, Interests and Institutional Change in India*. New Delhi: Oxford University Press.
———. 2014. *Political Economy of Reforms in India*. New Delhi: Oxford University Press.
O' Malley, L. S. S. 1931. *The Indian Civil Service, 1601–1930*. London: John Murray.
Potter, David. 1986. *India's Political Administrators, 1919-1983*. Oxford: Clarendon Press.
Prasad, Kamla. *Indian Administration. Indian Administration: Politics, Policies and Prospects*. New Delhi: Pearson.
Woodruff, Philip. 1997. *The men Who Ruled India*. New Delhi: Rupa & Co. (reprint).
Vohra, N. N. 1997. "The Rusting Steel Frame." In *India at 50s: Bliss of Hope and Burden of Reality*, edited by V. N. Narayanan and Jyoti Sabharwal, 154–171. New Delhi: Sterling Publishers.

ARTICLES

Bhat, Anil. 1979. "Colonial Bureaucratic Culture and Development Administration: Portrait of an Old-fashioned Indian Bureaucrat." *Journal of Commonwealth and Comparative Politics*, 17, no. 3 (1979).
Breman, Jan. 1985. "I am the Government Labour Officer ... State Protection for Rural Proletariat of South Gujarat." *Economic and Political Weekly* (June 15, 1985)
Jain, R. B. 1991. "Politicization of Bureaucracy: A Framework for Comparative Assessment." *Indian Journal of Public Administration*, 36, no. 4 (1991).
Kaviraj, Sudipta. 1984. "On the Crisis of Political Institutions in India." *Contributions to Indian Sociology*, 18, no. 2 (1984).
Mathur, Kuldeep. 1991. "Bureaucracy in India: Development and Pursuit of Self-interest." *Indian Journal of Public Administration*, 36, no. 4 (1991).
Nandy, Ashish. 1989. "The Political Culture of the Indian State." *Daedalus*, 118, no. 4 (fall 1989).
Rai, Haridwar, and Sukendra Prasad. 1973. "Indian Bureaucracy: The Case for Representativeness." *Indian Journal of Public Administration*, 19, no. 1 (1973).
Subramaniam, V. 1967. "Representative Bureaucracy: A Reassessment." *American Political Science Review*, 67, no. 4 (December, 1967).

INDEX

73rd Amendment Act (1992)
  collectors role of, 102
1853 Northcote-Trevelyan Report, 287
  impact of, 287
1854 Macaulay Report on the Indian Civil Service, 287
1861 Indian Councils Act, 27
  executive council, expansion of, 28
  Indians in administration, introduction of, 28
  power decentralization, 28
1885 Bengal Local Self Government Act, 28
1935 Government of India Act, 30
  divide-and-rule strategy, 36
  parliamentary form of government, 30
  provincial autonomy introduction, 31
  sign of, 31
  strong features, 31
  uncritical look, 31
1955 Avadi session of Congress, 173

Aayog, 196, 197
accountability, 228, 230
  in administration, 324
  in governance, 123
    democracy, deepening, 123
    empowerment, disadvantage, 124
    gender empowerment, 123
Accountant General to the Government of India, 215
Act for the Good Government of India, 1858, 27
  different from, 27
  East India Company rules, end in, 27
  provincial governments, 27
  Queen's proclamation, 27
  revenues transfer and, 27
administration
  problem statement of, 297
agricultural subsidies, 166
Air Corporation Act, 1994, 331
The Air (Prevention and Control of Pollution) Act, 1981, 273
air pollution, 266
  TSP, 266
All India civil services (ICS)
  Fulton Committee, 32
  House of Commons (1922), 32
  Macaulay Committee Report (1854), 32
  position of, 32
  public administration and, 32
  Weberian aspect to, 32
American Political Science Review, 293
American public administration, 286
American Society for Public Administration (ASPA), 321
Amiya Bagchi, 187
Anna Hazare campaign, 293
Appropriation Act, 216
Article, 311
  Vallabhbhai Patel view, 34
Ashok Mehta Committee
  1977, 101
    constitutional recognition for Panchayats, 102
  1978, 115
assistance to disabled persons for purchase/fitting of aids/appliances (ADIP scheme), 254
Atchison Commission of 1887, 133
attached/subordinate offices, 76, 77
  functions, 76
audit
  types of, 217
Auditor General of India in 1860, 215
Avadi Session of Congress (1954), 44
Ayyanger committee (1949), 74

Balwant Rai Mehta Committee (1957)
  collector position, 101, 114
Bengal Village Chowkidari Act, 1870, 113
Beveridge Report (1942), 244
bio-diversity, threat, 271
The Biological Diversity Act, 2002, 274
Board for Industrial and Financial Reconstruction (BIFR), 331
boards and commissions, 77
Bombay Plan, 186
British and American systems of governance, 286
British colonialism, 286
British imperial attitude in India, 171
British liberal education, 287
broad plans of governmental action, 289
budget, 200
  classification in India, 204
  implementation in India, 207
  policy orientations, 201
  process, 206
budget accounting, 208
budgetary process, 202
  in India, 202, 203
budget audit, 208
budget planning, 206, 207
budget scrutiny, 207
budget system in India, 204, 205, 206
  niceties of, 206
budget system reform in India, 211
bureaucracy, 131
  traditional concept of, 291

bygone era
  colonial bureaucratic
    structure of, 302

cabinet resolution
  in India, 193, 194, 195, 196
cabinet secretariat, 72
  administrative head of, 71
  cabinet committee, 74
    categories, 75
    types, 74
  debate on position of, 74
  designated as, 71
  functions, 70, 71, 72
  functions of, 74
  name list since 1950, 73
  organization
    civil wing, 72
    Directorate of Public
      Grievances, 72
    intelligence wing, 72
    military wing, 72
    secretaries, 72
  Prime Minister's Office
    (PMO), 75, 76
    functions, 76
    link between, 75
  responsibilities of, 71
  S.S. Khara, views, 74
  wings of, 72
capital account receipts, 209
capital non-plan expenditure,
  210
central Administration,
  structure
  federal
    levels of, 63
Central Pay Commission, 333
Central Secretariat, 63, 65
  evolution, 64
    Lord Cornwallis, role of, 64
    Regulatory Act of 1773, 64
    Second World War
      contribution in, 64
  functions, 64, 65
    secretariat, think tank as,
      65
  meaning of, 63
  ministry, 65
    deputy secretary, 66
    director, 66
    division, 65
    joint/additional secretary,
      66
    joint/additional secretary,
      functions, 66
    secretary, 65
  role of, 65
Central Secretariat Service
  (CSS), 69
Central Staffing Scheme (1957)
  officers categories, 69
Central Vigilance Commission
  (CVC), 232
  functions and powers, 233
  organizational set-up, 232,
    233
Centre for Media Studies (CMS),
  226
changing economic horizons,
  174
Charter Act, 1833, 26
  enlightenment philosophy,
    26
  James Mill, 26
  Macaulay, 26
  new devices, introduction
    of, 26
    Governor General,
      decisions of, 26
    Governor-General, 26
Charter Act of 1793, 132
Charter Act of 1833, 132
child Labour (prohibition and
  Regulation) Act, 1986, 249
Child Marriage Restraints
  Amendment Act, 1978, 249
chlorofluorocarbons (CFCs),
  274
citizen, 224
  administration, 225
  interactions, 225, 226
  perception about
    administration, 226, 227
citizen-centric administration
  in India, barriers, 227
citizen-friendly administration,
  227
  accessibility, 228
  accountability, 228
  effectiveness and efficiency,
    228
  participatory, 228
  responsiveness, 228
  transparency, 228
citizens and administration
  interaction between, 226
Citizen's Charter, 159, 237, 238
civil servants, 131
  in India, 140
    neutrality, 140
  role of, 291
civil service activism, 140
civil service aptitude test
  (CSAT), 144
civil service examination
  interview, 137
  main examination, 136
  preliminary examination, 135
  review committees, 144, 145
civil service reforms, 141, 142,
  158, 332
Civil services, 131, 133, 146
  British Crown, 132
  in independent India, 133,
    134
    central civil services, 135
    civil service examination,
      pattern, 135
    recruitment and
      placement, 134
  in India, 132, 133
civil society, 125, 219, 240
  articulating citizens' interests
    in a market economy, 240
  in rural development, role
    of, 125
Civil Society Organizations
  (CSOs), 303
  Indian reality, 304, 305
    conclusion, 306
    ninth Five Year Plan (1985-
      90), 305
    seventh Five Year Plan
      (1985-90), 305
  neoliberal approach, 303
  World Bank report, 1994, 303
classical theory
  of bureaucratic neutrality,
    291
Code of Civil Procedure, 1908,
  274
collectors and Panchayati Raj
  institutions
  relation between, 102, 103
colonial budgetary system, 201

Commission of Sati
(prevention) Act, 1987, 249
committed bureaucracy, 288
Communal Award (1932), 32
Comptroller and Auditor
General (CAG), 179, 217, 218
changes during 1990s, 218, 219, 220
of India, 203, 208, 214, 215
history, 214, 215
powers and duties, 216
conceptual and empirical roots
in public administration, 286, 287
conceptual domain
theoretical implications in, 291
concluding observations
in public administration, 287, 288
consolidated fund of India, 215
Constitution, 296
administration, 40
administration–constitution interface, 41
administration,
interconnection between, 40
history, role of, 41
ideology-driven, 40
Indian, 41
administration, 41
salient features surround around, 41
meaning, 40
Constitution of India Bill
(1895)
specifications of, 47
contemporary public administration
complexities of, 285
contingent circumstances and policy making, 176
corruption
in administration, 297, 298, 299
in India, 297
problem statement of, 297
crown administration, 28
crux of democratic governance, 108
Dahsala/Bandobast Arazi/Zabti system
bigha, 20
chachar, 21
polaj, 21
Data from Central Pollution
Control Board (CPCB), 269
debate, 290, 291
decentralization, 110
concepts, 111
significance, 111, 112
decision-making process, 108
deforestation, 271
forest land diversion, 272
National Forest Policy (1952), 271
democracy, 171
democratic decentralization, 112
local governance, 112, 113
post-independence
initiatives, 113, 114
democratic decentralization and the role of collector, 101
Department of Electronics in 1970, 327
dichotomy thesis, 289, 290
Directive Principles of State Policy, 172
disaster management, 315
in India, 314, 316
civil society, role, 318
Disaster Management Act, 2005, 317, 318
institutional arrangement,
emergence, 316, 317
organization and structure of, 317
types of, 314, 315
Disaster Management Act, 2005, 315, 317, 318
Disaster Management Division, 317
disasters in India, 315
disinvestment policy, 309
district administration
British intervention
British East India
Company, 96
district collector, 96
Montagu-Chelmsford
reforms, 96
position of district collector, 96
development imperatives and role of, 100
after independence, 100
collector's duty, 100
district collector, 95
role of, 95
functions, 95
Mauryan period, belongs to, 95
organization, 97
hierarchy, 97
officers, 97
patwari, 97
talukas, 97
tehsildars, 97
post-independent India, 96
Panchayati Raj institutions, 96
rural development
programmes, 96
purpose, 95
district collector, 98
changing roles, 98
IAS cadre, appointed by, 98
independent India, role of, 99
A.K. Dubey indication, 100
change in, 99
factors influences, 99
symbolized as, 100
position
British period, in, 99
Sir William Wilson
Hunter's description on, 98
responsibilities, 98
District Disaster Management
Authorities (DDMAs), 317
Dowry Prohibition Act 1961, 249, 255
drastic overhauling of the machinery, 294
dynamic public policy, 164

economic liberalization, 173, 175
in India, 174
planning in, 190, 191
socio-economic environment of, 288

economic policy, 174
economic services, 205
e-governance, 235, 237, 326, 328
Election Commission, 217
  and Supreme Court, 295
emergency in India, 290
The Employees Provident Fund
  and Miscellaneous provisions
  Act, 1952, 249
Employees' State Insurance Act,
  1948, 249
environmental issues in India,
  265
environmental pollution, 266
environmental protection in
  India
  constitutional and legal
    provisions, 272, 273, 274,
    275
  The Environment
    (Protection) Act, 1986, 273
Equal Remuneration Act 1976,
  249, 255
ethical policies, 166
ethics in governance, 293
  issue, 293, 294
  report, 295

family counselling centres, 256
Federal Public Service
  Commission (FPSC), 137
feminist assertion in Public
  Administration, 321
feminists, 324
Fifth and sixth pay
  commissions, 142, 143
  delegation with accountability,
    143
  government assurance, 143
  layers, reduction, 143
  PRIS, 143, 144
  public services, 143
Fifth pay commission, 158, 332
  1997, 153
Fifth Pay Commission Report
  (1994), 157, 331
finance department, 201
finance expenditure, 210
finance management in India,
  208
finance revenue and
  expenditures, 209
finance system reforms in
  India, 212, 213
financial administration, 200
First Administrative Reforms
  Commission (ARC), 187
  1968, 211
First Central Pay Commission
  (1947), 77
First Five Year Plan and
  Community Development
  Programme in 1952, 287
First Five Year Plan in 1951, 185
Fiscal responsibility and Budget
  Management (FRBM) Act, 333
Five Year Plans, 34
  of India, 100, 101
Foreign Direct Investment, 331
Foreign Exchange Regulation
  Act 1973, 175, 330
Forest Rights Act, 2006, 276
Forty-Second Amendment Act,
  272, 273
Fourth General Election, 292
Fourth State Finance
  Commission on 13th April
  2011, 87
  Panchayati Raj Institutions
  (PRI's), 87
  Urban Local Bodies (ULB's), 87
French public administration,
  286
Funds and government bonds,
  210

Gandhian Civil Disobedience
  Movement (1930-32), 31
Gandhian model of democratic
  decentralization, 184
gender budgeting, 257
Gender equality and women
  empowerment
  in India, 254, 255
    UN Millennium
      Development Goals
      Report, 2011, 254
global –local debate, 126
good governance in India, 229,
  230
  challenges, 301, 302
    concluding observation,
      302, 303
    eighth Five Year Plan, 301
    challenges of, 299, 300
governance, 292, 300
governing council and regional
  councils, 196
government funds in India, 210
Government of India, 333
Government of India Act 1919,
  32, 133
Government of India Act 1935,
  42, 215
government to governance, 108
grievance, 231
grievance redressal
  mechanism in India, 232

Handicapped Finance and
  Development Corporation
  (NHFDC), 254
Hindu Succession Act 1956, 255
House of Commons 1(922), 32
Human rights administration in
  India, 310, 311
  commission
    achievements, 311, 312
    limitations, 312, 313
  conclusion, 313
Human Rights Commission Bill,
  311
Human Rights Courts, 313

Immoral Traffic in women and
  girls Act 1956, 255
imperial services, 133
implications of 73rd and 74th
  Amendment Acts, 122
  administrative powers, 122
  constitutional status, 122
  financial autonomy, 122, 123
Indian administration
  Act for the Good
    Government of India,
    1858, 30
  Akbar, Mughal emperor as, 17
  British administrative, role
    of, 18
  British legacy, 24
    Charter Act, 1833, 26, 27
    Court of Directors, 24
    Court of Proprietors, 24
    East India Company, 24
    Regulating Act of 1773,
      24, 25

bygone eras, 17
colonial administration, 18
colonialism, 36
colonialism, change in, 28
  Indian National Congress
    inauguration, 28
  universities foundation, 28
East India Company, 17
evolution, 17
  administrative thoughts, 18
  Akbar, Mughal emperor
    as, 17
  bygone eras, 17
  character, organic in, 18
  colonial administration, 18
  East India Company, 17
  independent India, 18
  Kautilya, 18
  major landmark decisions,
    18
  pre-British, 17
  transfer of power, 18
  Ziauddin Barani, 19
Government of India Act
  (1935), 30
Mughal era
  British policy, influence
    of, 35
past, 35
philosophical and
  constitutional framework,
  40
  leaders, role in, 59
Pitt's India Act of 1784, 25
pre-British, 17
structure, 17
transfer of power, 18
Indian Administrative Service
  (IAS), 133, 134
Indian Civil Service (ICS), 1861,
  133
Indian Constitution, 41
  1950 Constitution of India
    evidence, uncertain socio-
      political and, 44
    view of, 44
  acceptable-to-all, founding
    fetters, 41
  country partition, 41
  policy-makers, 42
  religion issue, 41
amending procedures, 57
  contemporary times, 59
  introducing an amending
    Bill, 57
  Kesavananda Bharti case,
    judgment on, 58
  limits of, 58
  majority vote of
    Parliament, 58
  two fold procedures by B.
    N. Rau, 57
Central Secretariat
  evolution, 64
  meaning of, 63
colonial constructions,
  retention of, 43
fathers, role of, 41
federalism, 52
  arrival of Indira Gandhi, 53
  functioning, 53
  meaning, 53
  political parties,
    introduction of, 54
  provisions shape on, 52
  The Forest (Conservation)
    Act, 1980, 273
  Westminster model, 52
framers
  Indian citizens, for, 43
  social revolution value,
    appears at, 43
fundamental duties
  42nd amendment (1976),
    49
  insertion of, 49
  oppose of, 49
fundamental rights
  44th Constitutional
    Amendment, 47
  Article 15, 48
  Article 16, 48
  Article 19, 48
  Article 29, 48
  Article 32, 48
  Article 33, 48
  Cabinet Mission Plan's
    suggestions, 47
  Constitution of India Bill
    (1895), 47
  final shape by Advisory
    Committee, 47
  objectives resolution by
    Jawaharlal Nehru, 47
  restrictions, 48
  scope of, 48
indestructibility, as a nation,
  43
longest democratic
  constitution, 41
new look of, 42
  seven decisions by
    Constituent Assembly, 42
parliamentary federalism, 53
parliamentary system, 54, 55
  Austin points, 55, 56
  Jawaharlal Nehru speech, 55
  polity, inconsistent nature,
    56
policy-makers
  other countries
    constitutions,
    comparison with, 42
preamble, 44, 45
  amendments in 1976, 45, 46
  Avadi Session of Congress
    (1954), 44
  Forty-Second Amendment
    on 18th December 1976,
    44
  manifest of, 44
  M. Hidayatullah's pointy
    on, 46
  secularism, 44
  two-nation theory
    of Muslim League,
    opposition of, 45
  word integrity insertion
    of, 45
salient features of surround
  around, 41
seamless web by Austin
  arguments on, 43
seamless web by Austin', 43
shape of, 44
state policy, directive
  principles of, 49
  diversity and scope, 51
  fundamental issues on, 50
  fundamental rights,
    conflicts between, 50
  Golaknath vs. State of
    Punjab, case, 50
  Karachi resolution, 49
  K. C. Markandan
    argument, 50

perspective of government on, 51
vision of Ramrajya
unfettered powers used by, 43
Indian constitution, position in, 215
Indian Councils Act (1892), 28
aim, 28
Morley' statement, 29
Indira Awas Yojana (IAY), 317
indirect tax, 209
Industrial Policy, 1991, 330
Industrial Policy 1997, 307
Industrial Policy Resolution, 175
Industrial Policy Resolution 1956, 309
Information and Communications Technology (ICT)
revolution, 236, 327
information technology
and its impact on administration, 326, 327, 328
Information Technology Act of 2000, 236, 327
institutions of civil society, 301
Integrated Child Development Services (ICDS), 259
Integrated Child Protection Scheme (ICPS), 259
Intellectual Property Right (IPR), 274
International Convention on Biological Diversity (CBD), 274
International Decade for Natural Disaster Reduction (IDNDR), 316
International Monetary Fund (IMF), 190
International Monetary Fund Report, 212

Jan Lokpal bill, 293
Juvenile Justice Act, 1986, 249

Karachi resolution, 49
Kautilya
Mandala theory, 19
circle of state, 19
first circle, 19
four circles, 19
political and administrative system, 18
Saptang theory, 19
Danda, concept of, 19
Dharma, concept of, 19
seven vital organs, focus on, 19
Shadgunyas, 19
theory, aspects, 19
Upayas, 19

land acquisition
for development, 318, 319, 320
Land Acquisition Rehabilitation and Resettlement Act, 2014, 320
contention, issue, 320
land degradation, 269
deforestation, 269
Leninist New Economic Policy, 307
liberal economic reform
and role of bureaucracy, 330, 331, 332, 333
liberalized-privatized-globalized (LPG), 175, 176
licence-quota-permit-raj, 308
line-item method, 204
local governance
new dimensions of, 126
paradigm of, 109
lokayakta in states, 234
Lokpal
and Lokayukta, 233
appointment of, 295
The National Ombudsman, 234
Lokpal and Lokayuktas Act of 2013, 298
lok sabha, 302
long-drawn colonial rule
impact of, 287

Macaulay Committee Report (1854), 32
macroeconomic reforms, 174
Mahalanobis model, 307
Maharatnas, 309
Mahatma Gandhi National Rural Employment Guarantee Act, 302
Mahatma Gandhi National Rural Employment Guarantee Act (MGNREGA) 2005, 177, 259–261
Mahatma Gandhi National Rural Employment Guarantee Scheme and National Rural Health Mission, 297
Mahatma Gandhi Shriman Narayan, 186
Mandal Commission Report 1978, 176
Maoist movement, 173
Marxist formulation, 186
Maternity Benefit Act 1961, 249, 255
Maxwell committee (1937), 68
Mayo resolution
statement, 28
Mazdoor Kishan Sangharsh Samiti movement in Rajasthan, 179
Memorandum of Understanding (MOU), 79
miniratnas, 309
Ministry of Environment and Forests., 77
Ministry of Human Affairs (MHA), 317
Ministry of Social Justice and Empowerment, 252
Ministry of Tribal Affairs, 249
Moily Committee on administrative reforms, 145, 146
Moneylife Foundation in Mumbai, 219
Monopolies and Restrictive Trade Practices (MRTP) Act, 175, 330
Montagu-Chelmsford reforms, 96
Montague-Chelmsford Reform scheme (1919), 29
adoption of diarchy
failure factors, 30
impact of, 30
adoption of dyarchy, 30
four principles, suggestion of, 29, 30
Mont-Ford report (1918), 133
Montreal Protocol, 274
Moot point, 285

Morley-Minto Reforms, 29
failure of, 29
Home Rule League, 31
recognition to muslims, separate community as, 29
swadeshi movement, 31
Mughal administration
Akbar
Todarmal, 21
Mughal era
Abul Fazal administration, 20
administrative structure
Mansab, 21
mansabdari system, 21
mansabdars, 21
personnel administration, 22
Akbar
dastur-ul-amal, 21
municipal wastewater treatment, 267

National commission for safai karamchari, 251
National Commission for Review of the Working of the Constitution, 149
National Commission for women (NCW), 255
National Conference and Dravida Munnetra Kazhagam, (DMK), 54
National Democratic Alliance (NDA) government, 54
National Disaster Management Authority (NDMA), 317
National Disaster Mitigation Fund, 317
National Disaster Response Force (NDRF), 317
National e-Governance Programme in 2006, 327
national environment policy, 275
National Environment Appellate Authority (NEAA), 274
National Environment Appellate Authority (NEAA) Act, 1997, 274
National Environment Tribunal Act 1995, 274
National Green Tribunal Act 2010, 274
National Highways Act, 331
National Human Rights Commission (NHRC), 311
National Institute of Disaster Management (NIDM), 317
National Insurance System, 244
National Mineral Policy (1993), 331
National Mission of Empowerment of Women, 257
national planning
idea of, 186
National Planning Commission, 307
National Police Commission, 1981, 153
National Police Commission (NPC)
report, 153, 154, 155, 156
British imperialism, cause, 153
daroga system, 153
Irish constabulary, 154
Metropolitan model, 154
PAC,154
National Rural Employment Guarantee Act (NREGA), 260
National Rural Health Mission (NRHM), 262
National Safai Karamcharis Finance and Development Corporation, 251
National Telecom Policy (1994), 331
natural disasters, 315
navratnas, 309
navratna status, 309
Nehruvian, 180
era, 180
era of governance, 291
socialist pattern, 175
Nehruvian state led development planning, 196
neoliberal approach, 303
neo-liberal economic reforms in India, 173
New Economic Policy in India, 1991, 197
new localism, 127
noise pollution, 268
air quality standards, 268
Central Pollution Control Board (CPCB) database, 268, 269
WHO guidelines, 268
non-governmental organizations (NGOs), 303, 304
Indian reality, 304, 305
conclusion, 306
ninth Five Year Plan (1985-90), 305
seventh Five Year Plan (1985-90), 305
neoliberal approach, 303
World Bank report, 1994, 303

objectives resolution by Jawaharlal Nehru., 47
official policy-makers, 167
Official Secrets Act of 1923, 298, 301
ombudsman-type institution in India
establishment of, 299
other backward classes (OBCs)
welfare of, 253, 254
Ozone Depleting Substances (Regulations) Rules, 2000, 274

Panchayati Raj Institutions (PRIs), 91, 115, 301
Panchayati Raj System, 34, 117
weakness, 118, 119
Parliamentary Committees, 203
The Payment of Gratuity Act, 1972, 249
people's participation in administrative, 229
performance budgeting method, 204
persons with disabilities
welfare of, 254
Pitt's India Act of 1784, 25
planned development
concept of, 185
planned economic development, 185
planning, 196

Planning Commission, 150, 165, 172, 183, 184, 187, 188, 189, 190, 191, 192, 196, 197
  and encouragement of grassroots planning, 197
  importance, 184
  nature and scope of, 189
  NITI Aayog, 192, 193, 194, 195, 196
  obliteration of, 185
  role of, 187, 188
planning in India
  genesis and development of, 186, 187
planning, programming and budgeting system (PPBS), 201
plan of economic development for India, 186
Police Commission, 1992, 154
policy environment, 166
  socio-economic, 167
political changes, 292
political empowerment of women, 257
  Eleventh Plan (2007–12), 258
  The Ninth Plan (1997–2002), 258
  Twelfth Five Year Plan (2012–17), 258
political executives, 289, 291, 292
  and permanent executives, differences, 291
    conclusion, 292
  in administration, 290
  in public administration, 289
political parties, 168
politics, 179
poor environmental management systems, 267
popular participation, 124
  decentralized planning process, 124
post-bureaucratic notion, 109
post-world war–II, 167
pre and post-liberalization era
  public sector in India, 306, 307
    conclusion, 310
    industrial policy resolution, 307, 308, 309
    neoliberalism, ascendancy, 306, 307
Pre-Natal Diagnostic Techniques (Regulation and Prevention of misuse) Act, 1994, 255
pressure groups, 168
prevalent administrative structure, 150
Prevention of Money Laundering Act of 2002, 298
Protection and welfare of Children, 259
Protection of Human Rights Act, 1993, 311, 313
Provincial Armed Constabulary (PAC), 154
provincial civil service (PCS), 133
Public Accounts Committee and Committees on Pubic Understandings (COPU), 217
public budgeting, 213
Public Distribution System (PDS), 226
public grievances
  redressal of, 231, 232
Public Information Officers (PIOs), 238, 329
Public Interest Litigation (PIL), 178
public policy, 163, 164, 165
  administrative machinery, 169
  define, 164
  importance of, 163
  in India, 178
  politico-ideological and institutional settings, 170, 171
  significance of, 165
  socialistic pattern of society, 172
  subsidies and tax concessions, 166
  Theodore Lowi suggestions, 166
  types of, 166
public–private–NGO interface, 109
public–private partnership (PPP), 126
Public Sector Undertakings (PSUs), 192
Public Service Commission (PSC), 137, 150
Rashtriya Mahila Kosh (RMK), 256
Re-conceptualizing public policy, 175
Regulating Act of 1773, 24
  benefits, Indian administration for reasons, 24, 25
  Edmund Burke, 25
  Warren Hastings, as Governor General, 24
Regulatory Act of 1773, 64
regulatory policies, 166
relief activities
  in disaster management, 316
Report of the Indian Statutory Commission (1930), 99
Research and analysis wing (RAW), 72
responsiveness in accountability, 325
Right to Education Act (RTE), 177
rigid observance of rules and regulations, 226
Ripon Resolution (1882), 28
Rowlatt Satyagraha and the Non Cooperation Movement of 1910-21, 31
Royal Commission, 29
  aim, 29
  factors to follow, 29
    Morley-Minto Reforms, 29
rural local governance
  PRIs, 115
  Seventy Third Constitutional Amendment Act, 1992, 115
Rural–Urban Relationship Committee report 1996, 305
Sampoorn Grameen Rojgar Yojana (SGRY), 317
Saptang theory
  by Kautilya, 19
    Danda concept, 19
    Dharma concept, 19
Sarva Shiksha Abhiyan (SSA), 261
Sati (prevention) Act 1987, 255
Scheduled castes
  national commission, 251
  welfare provisions, 250

welfare schemes, 251
economic empowerment, 252
educational development, 252
Scheduled Tribes and Other Traditional Forest Dwellers (Recognition of Forest Rights) Act, 2006, 275
Scheduled Tribes (STs)
welfare of, 252, 253
Second Administrative Reforms Commission, 79, 104, 295, 296, 326
in India, 298
Second Pay Commission (1957-59), 287
Second United Nations Conference on Human Settlements (Habitat II) in 1996, 109
Secretariat and directorates, relation between
advantages, 86
ARC
recommendation, 86
critics indication, 85
deals with, 85
institutions of, 85
sectoral planning
appreciative of, 192
Seventy-Third Amendment Act (1992), 153, 158
Seventy-Third and Seventy-Fourth Amendment Acts in 1992, 35, 149
adoption of, 302
Seventy-Third and Seventy-Fourth Constitutional Amendment act, 184
Seventy Third Constitutional Amendment Act, 1992, 115
features, 116, 117
Shah Commission report, 290
Shanthanam committee, 298
short stay homes
scheme, 256
Simon Commission (1930), 67
Sixth Central Pay Commission, 333
Sixth central pay commission's (2008), 226
Sixth Pay Commission, 144
Social administration
define, 245
socialistic pattern of society, 172
social welfare, 243, 244
administration, 245, 246
education and training, 246
principles, 247
weaker sections in India, protection of, 247
arguments in, 244
concept, 243, 244
constitutional provisions, 248, 249
define, 244
evolutionary perspective, 244, 245
Indian perspective, 248
legislative measures, 249
Ministry in India, 249, 250
policies in India, 259
Russian Revolution of 1917, 244
socio-psychological decline, 295
solid and hazardous waste
hospital waste, 270
landfills, 270
plastic waste, 270
sovereign bonds, 210
Special Economic Zones (SEZ) Act, 2005, 319
stakeholders, 302
Standing Committees of Voluntary Agencies (SCOVA), 239
state administration
secretariat and directorates, 86
state directorate, 84
state secretariat, 81, 82
chief secretariat, 82, 83, 84
structure, 81
state and local governments
excessive control and conflicts between, 92
division of functions, 92
weaknesses, 92
local government, importance of, 93
state directorate, 84
executive agencies, 84
disparities between, 85
executive agencies, head of, 84
functions, 84
State Disaster Management Authorities (SDMAs), 317
State Finance Commissions, 86
democratic decentralization, 86
local bodies, devolution, 88
principles, 87
recommendations, 88
state revenues, devolution, 89
suggestions for, 88
functions, 87
members, 87
purpose of, 86
set up in states, 87
State Panchayat Act, 124
State secretariat, 81
chief secretary, 82
administrative reforms commission (1968), 83
chosen by, 83
functions, 83
inter-departmental coordinator, as, 82
position in state administration, 83
tenure, 83, 84
concern of, 82
departments, 82
functions, 82
hierarchy, 82
responsibilities, 82
S.R.Maheshwari observation, 82
Structural Adjustment Programmes (SAPs), 190, 212
Support to Training and Employment Programme for Women (STEP), 255
Suppression of Immoral Traffic in women and Girls Act, 1956, 249
Swadhar scheme, 256

temporary executives, 289
total suspended particles (TSP) in air pollution, 266
Tottenham Committee report 1946, 294

Transparency, 328, 329, 330
in governance, 123
Tribal Rights Act, 275
Tribal Sub-Plan (TSP), 253

Union Public Service Commission (UPSC), 144
recruitment body, 137
civil servants, political rights, 140
civil services, 138
code of conduct, civil service, 139, 140
constitutional provisions, 137, 138
in-service training, 138
mid-career training, 139
personnel, management, 139
promotions, 139
union territories, 209
Universalization of Elementary Education (UEE), 261
urban development
civil society, role of, 125
dynamics, 128
urban local governance, 119
74th Amendment Act, 1992, 120, 121
challenges, 121
functions, 120
structure, 119
Uttarakhand State Finance Commission (2010), 89

voluntary agencies
grievance redressal, new players, 239
Vox populi
importance of, 179

waste management systems, 267
water pollution, 267, 268
municipal sewage and industrial waste, 267
Water (Prevention and Control of Pollution) Act, 1974, 273
Weberian logic of neutrality, 290
Weberian role
of 'neutral' dispenser of administration, 293
Welfare
of persons with disabilities, 254
Welfare of Other Backward Classes (OBCs), 253, 254
Welfare schemes for scheduled castes, 251
economic empowerment, 252
educational development, 252
Westminster model of parliamentary democracy, 171
Wheeler committee (1936), 67
Whistle Blowers Protection Act, 298
Wildlife (Protection) Act, 1972, 273
Wilson reviews, 289
women empowerment in India, 255
women in administration, 321
feminist assertion, 321, 322
gender dimensions, 323
public organizations, gender imbalance in, 323
public private division, 322, 323
working women's hostel, 256
World Bank report (2013)
on air pollution, 266
World Development report 1992
dissection of, 300
World Health Organization (WHO), 266
World Trade Organization (WTO), 180
worsening air quality, 266

Zero Based Budgeting (ZBB) in India, 201, 212
Ziauddin Barani
medieval period
Islamic way of administration, 19
medieval period
Shariat, 20
Sultan period, 20
Barani, 20
Fatwa-i-Jahandari, 20
Tarikh-i-Firozeshahi, 20
Zawabit, 20